Running Science

Owen Anderson, PhD

Human Kinetics

Library of Congress Cataloging-in-Publication Data

Anderson, Owen, 1947-
   Running science / Owen Anderson.
      pages cm
   Includes bibliographical references and index.
   1. Running--Training. 2. Sports sciences. I. Title.
   GV1061.5.A63 2013
   796.42--dc23

                                        2013004559
   ISBN-10: 0-7360-7418-X (print)
   ISBN-13: 978-0-7360-7418-6 (print)

This publication is written and published to provide accurate and authoritative information relevant to the subject matter presented. It is published and sold with the understanding that the author and publisher are not engaged in rendering legal, medical, or other professional services by reason of their authorship or publication of this work. If medical or other expert assistance is required, the services of a competent professional person should be sought.

The web addresses cited in this text were current as of January 2013, unless otherwise noted.

Developmental Editors: Tom Hanlon and Heather Healy; **Assistant Editors:** Claire Marty and Sarah Wiseman; **Copyeditor:** Ann Prisland; **Indexer:** Nan N. Badgett; **Permissions Manager:** Martha Gullo; **Graphic Designer:** Joe Buck; **Graphic Artist:** Julie L. Denzer; **Cover Designer:** Keith Blomberg; **Photograph (cover):** © Human Kinetics; **Photographs (interior):** © Human Kinetics unless otherwise noted; **Photo Asset Manager:** Laura Fitch; **Visual Production Assistant:** Joyce Brumfield; **Photo Production Manager:** Jason Allen; **Art Manager:** Kelly Hendren; **Associate Art Manager:** Alan L. Wilborn; **Illustrations:** © Human Kinetics unless otherwise noted; **Printer:** Sheridan Books

We thank Michigan State University in East Lansing, Michigan, and Walt Reynolds of The Trainers Studio in Lansing, Michigan, for assistance in providing the location for the photo shoot for this book.

Human Kinetics books are available at special discounts for bulk purchase. Special editions or book excerpts can also be created to specification. For details, contact the Special Sales Manager at Human Kinetics.

Printed in the United States of America   10 9 8 7 6 5 4 3 2 1

The paper in this book is certified under a sustainable forestry program.

Human Kinetics
Website: www.HumanKinetics.com

United States: Human Kinetics
P.O. Box 5076
Champaign, IL 61825-5076
800-747-4457
e-mail: humank@hkusa.com

Canada: Human Kinetics
475 Devonshire Road Unit 100
Windsor, ON N8Y 2L5
800-465-7301 (in Canada only)
e-mail: info@hkcanada.com

Europe: Human Kinetics
107 Bradford Road
Stanningley
Leeds LS28 6AT, United Kingdom
+44 (0) 113 255 5665
e-mail: hk@hkeurope.com

Australia: Human Kinetics
57A Price Avenue
Lower Mitcham, South Australia 5062
08 8372 0999
e-mail: info@hkaustralia.com

New Zealand: Human Kinetics
P.O. Box 80
Torrens Park, South Australia 5062
0800 222 062
e-mail: info@hknewzealand.com

E4428

To Liz, for your constant, unfailing caring
and support and for keeping me moving forward
even in the most-troubled times with
no thought for yourself

To Chemtai, for teaching me so much about
Kenyan running and never giving up

To my parents, for mentoring me to do
rather than watch

To Cori, for being such a cool, tough,
and loving daughter

To Uncle Bud, for life-long friendship

To all the kids in the Tana River Delta,
for inspiring and trusting me and for
holding on to hope and working
for a better future

To Eunice and Namwezi, for your integrity
and for showing me how to help
the Delta kids

To Lyn, for your great friendship, always
welcoming chair, and incomparable
roast-beef sandwiches

To Le, for introducing me to real friendship
and a positive approach to life

And to pastors Jim and Matt, for your faith,
guidance, and encouragement

Contents

Acknowledgments

I would like to thank my Human Kinetics editors, Claire Marty, Tom Hanlon, Heather Healy, and Sarah Wiseman, for expertly guiding this book to completion.

I would also like to thank Walt Reynolds for our always productive and stimulating discussions of innovative training techniques and for helping me to understand so many valuable concepts and practices concerning running form and running specific strengthening.

I would like to thank Chemtai Rionotukei, Walter Reynolds, and Julia Williams for their patient, wonderful, and skilled work during the photo shoot for this book. Chemtai, Walter, and Julie spent countless hours ensuring that each exercise, drill, and running segment was photographed optimally. I would also like to express my gratitude to Neil Bernstein for his professional and outstanding work taking the photos.

Prologue

The Quest for Knowledge in Running

The science of running is undergoing a revolution that has now entered its fifth decade. In the 1970s, exercise physiologists were sure that endurance running was an oxygen game, with oxygen limitation the key cause of fatigue during exercise and $\dot{V}O_2$max the main physiological variable to be examined.

From a scientific perspective, endurance runners were little more than hearts and leg muscles. The heart was the pump that sent oxygen to the waiting sinews in the lower appendages, and specialized structures in those muscle fibers called mitochondria permitted the muscles to use oxygen to provide the energy necessary for running. Once the limit in that system was reached, anaerobic energy took over, lactic acid built up in the muscles, and the hapless runner was done for the day. A competitor with a better oxygen-delivery and supply system won the race.

In that model, which had its origins in the 1920s at the Harvard Fatigue Laboratory in Cambridge, Massachusetts, where the work of Nobel Prize–winning physiologist A.V. Hill seemed to show that lactic acid could decrease muscular force production, the brain and spinal cord were viewed as just along for the ride, responding meekly to the requests placed by the heart and leg muscles during exercise. If the leg muscles were rollicking along in a steady bath of oxygen, the nervous system sent enough impulses to keep them moving at the requisite rate.

All of this seemed fine until some probing running researchers began to reveal in the 1970s and 1980s that there were other physiological variables that predicted running success. Notably, running economy (i.e., a measure of how stingy runners were with their oxygen) and lactate-threshold velocity (i.e., the velocity above which lactate began to build up in the blood; originally called anaerobic threshold speed) were shown to be relatively reliable predictors of endurance performance.

Limits of $\dot{V}O_2$max and the Role of the Nervous System

Making matters much worse for the traditional model, studies began to appear that revealed that $\dot{V}O_2$max was a decent forecaster of performance if one were comparing elite runners with runners in the middle of the pack— but it was weak at foretelling race times among similarly trained runners (e.g., elites, subelites, medium-level runners, and novices). How could that be? After all, endurance running was and still is a truly aerobic sport, with oxygen usage supplying 99 percent of the energy required to run a 10K and oxygen limitation seemingly crucial in determining what can happen in races. Flying in the face of the conventional model, some studies even had the audacity to determine that 300-meter (.19 mi) sprint time—a primarily anaerobic activity—could predict endurance performance far more effectively than maximal aerobic capacity, or $\dot{V}O_2$max.

Thanks to such findings and to brilliant and innovative research, we learned that endurance runners do have nervous systems after all, and that the nervous system plays a profound role in determining the success or failure of both training and competition. The nervous system can create fatigue and actually regulate running pace during endurance training and racing via what is now termed the anticipatory regulation of exercise performance through effort perception. This is part of the revolution in which exercise science is currently immersed. The understanding of the nervous system's role has not only shaken up exercise physiology but has also had a dramatic impact on the training of endurance runners, as the reader will come to understand by reading this book.

The other part of the revolution concerns fatigue itself. Originally thought to be a simple phenomenon related to intramuscular lactic acid, fatigue is now linked with nervous system functioning along with a whole complex of physiological factors such as velocity at $\dot{V}O_2$max, running economy, lactate-threshold velocity, resistance to fatigue, maximal running speed, intramuscular pH, and even muscular potassium levels. The search for the origins of fatigue during running is an important one: When fatigue is understood, the optimal mode of training to limit that fatigue and thus to optimize performance can be researched and implemented.

Science Sheds Light on Running

As a scientist, I love the fact that an understanding of running performance is approachable via the scientific method and that running science has provided so many valuable clues about optimal training. No longer are we completely bound by tradition and myth: We can look to great research carried out by running scientists around the globe in order to plan our training and prepare for our most important races.

I believe that running is intrinsically tied to science, more so than many other sports. If we attempt to understand why Derek Jeter piled up more than 3,000 hits and why Marv Throneberry struggled so much to hit curve balls and catch soft tosses from his second baseman, we are stymied nearly immediately by the simple process of identifying the key variables that should be examined. In running, the factors important for success have been identified; we simply need to understand how they work together and how they can be optimized by training.

Running science has had a major practical impact on training for improved performance. Thanks to research, runners and coaches now understand how changes in the volume, intensity, and frequency of training impact the key performance variables, including neural drive, $v\dot{V}O_2max$, running economy, lactate-threshold velocity, resistance to fatigue, and maximal running speed. They know which running speeds are best for various types of training and which forms of strength training have the largest positive effect on performance.

Thanks to the establishment of the anticipatory regulation model of fatigue, they also know what to do when extreme tiredness strikes during races: Turn up neural drive instead of turning down speed in response to a perceived crisis in the muscles. With confidence and understanding, runners and coaches can now—thanks to science—properly answer key questions such as: How fast should my work intervals be run today? How many miles should I cover in my long run? How should I set up my overall training program? Answers to these questions and others will be provided in this book.

A Peek Into the Book

I thank Human Kinetics for the opportunity to create this book; I had been wanting to write it for a very, very long time. I am both a scientist and runner. My running career began at the age of 2 when I evaded my mother in a backyard chase and concluded that running was a very joyful and liberating activity. Six decades of running have only enhanced my love of the sport: I run nearly every morning with my Siberian Husky, who defies all hypotheses about fatigue and toys with me during both sprints and long efforts. I am now happily the race director of the Lansing Marathon, the manager of a successful team of elite Kenyan athletes, and the CEO of the nonprofit organization Lansing Moves the World.

Over the past three years, I ran nearly every day during the predawn hours and worked on the organization and content of this book after my workouts. *Running Science* is organized in a unique way. Beginning with a look at the genetics of running performance and the biomechanics of running in parts I and II, it then proceeds to describe the physiological factors that are important for performance (part III). The next unit (part IV) covers different training methods, and part V outlines key variables, such as volume, frequency, and intensity, and offers an overview of recovery techniques, periodization, and strength training. Part VI explores training for optimizing performance variables, and part VII explains the molecular basis of training. Part VIII discusses how to prepare for popular race distances. The closing sections of the volume address a number of key issues, including the prevention of running injuries and the health benefits of running (part IX); nutritional supplements, proper eating for running, and weight control (part X); and psychological strategies linked with top performance and even the addictive aspects of running (part XI). I sincerely hope you enjoy this book!

PART

I

Genetics
and Running

CHAPTER 1

Running's Nature-Versus-Nurture Debate

The years 2011 and 2012 were extremely exciting for middle- and long-distance running: In 2011, Geoffrey Mutai surged to victory in the Boston Marathon in 2:03:02, the fastest marathon time ever recorded, and fellow Kenyan Mary Keitany blazed a new world record of 1:05:50 in the half marathon. In 2012, David Rudisha stormed to a new world record of 1:40.91 for 800 meters at the London Olympic Games. Each time a Kenyan athlete performs in an astonishing manner, the debate seems to begin anew: Is nature or nurture more important for running success?

Runners, coaches, and exercise scientists often wonder whether running performances are determined primarily by genetic factors or by the environment. Fans of distance running speculate whether the current Kenyan dominance of endurance competitions is the result of genetic superiority or an active childhood at higher altitudes in western Kenya. Weekend runners trouble themselves over whether they have the innate capacity (genetic constitution) to break 40 minutes in the 10K. And coaches and exercise scientists may dream of testing athletes genetically to determine potential at different running distances.

Such concerns are much more than curiosities. If performances are indeed primarily shaped by genes, coaches and serious runners will begin using cheek swabs to learn what their DNA determines about their running futures, and deceptive practices such as gene doping could play a prominent role in elite competitions. If the environment rules over genetic composition, runners will optimistically juggle their training programs in hopes of finding the schedules that produce the best possible personal performances, and serious scientific research will begin on exactly *how* East Africans are achieving such amazing levels of running fitness.

Genetic factors include the presence or absence of genes that have an impact on physical performance as well as the interactions between such genes. A runner's environment is composed of training, dietary practices, and social and geographical factors. Training is much more than the faithful following of a workout schedule—it is a complex activity including psychological aspects such as willingness to train and social components such as external motivation and the actual opportunity to exercise consistently. Another important environmental factor is whether the knowledge to create a program that can optimize the physiological and psychological variables important for performance exists.

Genes and Running Performance

Environmental factors and the physiological variables associated with performance are so complex that there is a tendency for many to take the simplistic view that genes are dominant in determining running success.[1] A facile view is that genes can act as magic bullets that propel athletes with the right genetic compositions to inevitable success. As an example, *Scientific American* once predicted that performances at the 2012 Olympic Games would depend on the insertion of key genes into the nuclei of athletes' muscle cells.[2] In a similar vein, a professional rugby team from Australia tested its players for variations in 11 exercise-related genes, believing that training programs specifically suited to each player could then be created.[3] Many exercise scientists have come to believe that athletes can be genetically profiled in order to predict their risk of sustaining specific injuries and their suitability for team positions, roles, and subdisciplines in various sporting activities.[3] There is a belief that an examination of a runner's genes can yield important information about whether he or she should become a sprinter, a middle-distance athlete, or a marathoner. There is also a common perception that East African runners (primarily from Kenya and Ethiopia) have a monopoly on the genes that code for endurance performance.[1]

Proponents of a dominant role for genes, or nature, in determining running performances point to the relatively recent discovery of more than 100 genes that have an impact on physical capacity.[4] Such findings reinforce the idea that an individual's potential for running performance could be largely determined at birth. A runner with the right configuration of this multitude of genes, for example, might have an inborn talent for running that would always elevate him or her above other athletes with less optimal genetic makeup.

At first glance, such thinking does not seem entirely unreasonable. Research has revealed that an individual's genetic makeup has a significant effect on physical characteristics, including body size and shape.[5] Although there are many exceptions to the rule, the best distance runners tend to be relatively short in stature and light in weight with slim calves, factors that probably have some genetic component. Greater height tends to dampen distance-running performance because of added mass: Bone mass increases exponentially as a function of height, instead of linearly, giving the taller runner relatively more dead weight to move around a 10K or marathon course. In general, enhanced body mass, either in the form of fat or non-propulsive muscle mass in the upper body, makes endurance runners less economical and less able to sustain high speeds for continuous periods. Scientific studies also have identified many genes that are linked with greater endurance performance.[6]

Somewhat oddly, the East African dominance of distance running is often cited as further evidence that genes are the strongest determinants of endurance performance.[7] An inescapable fact is that the best middle- and long-distance runners in the world are Africans. Over the last five Olympic Games, from 1996 to 2012, male runners of African origin have captured 11 of the 15 possible gold medals in the 1,500 meters, 5K, and marathon competitions, as well as all 10 gold medals awarded in the 10K and 3K steeplechase events. Males of African origin currently hold 11 of the 12 world records recognized by the International Association of Athletics Federation in events ranging from 800 meters to the marathon, including the 1K, 1.5K, the mile, 2K, 3K, 5K, 10K, 20K, 25K, and the 3K steeplechase.

Such African dominance was not present as recently as 20 years ago when European runners ruled supreme at all competitive distances from 800 meters to the marathon.[8] In 1987, 58 of the 120 runners on the all-time

Stephane Kempinaire/DPPI/Icon SMI

▶ Elite distance running is dominated by runners from East Africa.

top 20 lists of performances in races of 800 meters, 1,500 meters, 5K, 10K, marathon, and steeplechase were European. Just 32 of the 120 best runners of all time were African, and 16 of those 32 were Kenyans. The majority of world-record holders were European.

By 2003 the composition of the lists had changed drastically. There were 67 Kenyans in the top 120 and 102 Africans in all, leaving the entire rest of the world with just 18 slots. The European contribution to the world's-best lists had slipped from 58 runners to only 14.[9] Table 1.1 shows the top 10 male runners for various distances.

Table 1.1 All-Time Top 10 Male Athletes in Various Races

Race distance	Athlete	Time	Country
800 meters	1. David Lekuta Rudisha	1:40.91	Kenya
	2. Wilson Kipketer	1:41.11	Denmark (originally from Kenya)
	3. Sebastian Coe	1:41.73	Great Britain
	3. Nijel Amos	1:41.73	Botswana
	5. Joaquim Cruz	1:41.77	Brazil
	6. Abubaker Kaki	1:42.23	Sudan
	7. Sammy Koskei	1:42.28	Kenya
	8. Wilfred Bungei	1:42.34	Kenya
	9. Yuriy Borzakovskiy	1:42.47	Russia
	10. Timothy Kitum	1:42.53	Kenya
1500 meters	1. Hicham El Guerrouj	3:26.00	Morocco
	2. Bernard Lagat	3:26.34	United States of America (originally from Kenya)
	3. Noureddine Morceli	3:27.37	Algeria
	4. Noah Ngeny	3:28.12	Kenya
	5. Asbel Kiprop	3:28.88	Kenya
	6. Fermin Cacho	3:28.95	Spain
	7. Mehdi Baala	3:28.98	France
	8. Daniel Kipchirchir Komen	3:29.02	Kenya
	9. Rashid Ramzi	3:29.14	Bahrain
	10. Venuste Niyongabo	3:29.18	Burundi
5 kilometers	1. Kenenisa Bekele	12:37.35	Ethiopia
	2. Haile Gebrselassie	12:39.36	Ethiopia
	3. Daniel Komen	12:39.74	Kenya
	4. Eluid Kipchoge	12:46.53	Kenya
	5. Dejen Gebremeskel	12:46.81	Ethiopia
	6. Sileshi Sihine	12:47.04	Ethiopia
	7. Hagos Gebrhiwet	12:47.53	Ethiopia
	8. Isiah Kiplangat Koech	12:48.64	Kenya
	9. Isaac Kiprono Songok	12:48.66	Kenya
	10. Yenew Alamirew	12:48.77	Ethiopia

(continued)

Table 1.1 *(continued)*

Race distance	Athlete	Time	Country
10 kilometers	1. Kenenisa Bekele	26:17.53	Ethiopia
	2. Haile Gebrselassie	26:22.75	Ethiopia
	3. Paul Tergat	26:27.85	Kenya
	4. Nicholas Kemboi	26:30.03	Qatar
	5. Abebe Dinkesa	26:30.74	Ethiopia
	6. Micah Kipkemboi Kogo	26:35.63	Kenya
	7. Paul Koech	26:36.26	Kenya
	8. Zersenay Tadese	26:37.25	Eritrea
	9. Salah Hissou	26:38.08	Morocco
	10. Ahmad Hassan Abdullah	26:38.76	Qatar
Marathon	1. Patrick Makau Musyoki	2:03:38	Kenya
	2. Wilson Kipsang Kiprotich	2:03:42	Kenya
	3. Haile Gebrselassie	2:03:59	Ethiopia
	4. Geoffrey Kiprono Mutai	2:04:51	Kenya
	5. Dennis Kipruto Kimetto	2:04:16	Kenya
	6. Ayele Abshero	2:04:23	Ethiopia
	7. Dunkin Kibet Kirong	2:04:27	Kenya
	7. James Kipsang Kwambai	2:04:27	Kenya
	9. Tsegay Kebede	2:04:38	Ethiopia
	10. Emmanuel Kipchirchir Mutai	2:04:40	Kenya
3000 meter steeplechase	1. Saif Saaeed Shaheen	7:53.63	Qatar
	2. Brimin Kiprop Kipruto	7:53.64	Kenya
	3. Paul Kipsiele Koech	7:54.31	Kenya
	4. Brahim Boulami	7:55.28	Morocco
	5. Bernard Barmasai	7:55.72	Kenya
	6. Ezekiel Kemboi	7:55.76	Kenya
	7. Moses Kiptanui	7:56.16	Kenya
	8. Richard Kipkemboi Mateelong	7:56.81	Kenya
	9. Reuben Kosgei	7:57.29	Kenya
	10. Wilson Boit Kipketer	7:59.08	Kenya

Current as of January 2013.

Source: International Association of Athletics Federations (www.iaaf.org).

The Kenyans and other East Africans were sending shock waves through the endurance-running community with their sizzling performances. The issue was not that the European runners had suddenly begun to run slowly; they were running as fast as they always had. The change occurred because the African runners, particularly the Kenyans, were running extraordinarily fast times.[10] An additional startling fact was that the majority of the Kenyans competing on the world stage were Kalenjins, a rather small tribe of about 3 million people.

Observers of this transformation of the running world have been tempted to conclude that Kenyan runners, and especially Kalenjins, have some inborn capacity for long-distance running. In competitive running, nature seems to be winning out over nurture. Kenyans and other East African runners appear to have the right genes for elite performance. There is indirect evidence this might be true.

The top distance runners emerging from Kenya and Ethiopia, for example, tend to come from distinct regions of those countries (specifically, in Kenya's case, from the areas surrounding Eldoret, Iten, Kapenguria, Kaptagat, and Eldama Ravine in western Kenya), rather than being evenly distributed throughout the countries.[11, 12] In relatively isolated populations, such as in the pockets of endurance-running supremacy in Kenya and Ethiopia, a phenomenon called genetic drift can cause specific genes—including those coding for performance—to increase or decrease in frequency rather dramatically compared with neighboring, less-isolated populations. In areas of Kenya such as Kapenguria, in which a pastoral lifestyle is widely practiced, there might also be a natural selection for genotypes that code for enhanced endurance performance. Such selection would not be likely to occur in Nairobi or Mombasa, parts of Kenya that have produced few international runners, nor would it take place in most urban areas around the world where physical endurance would be a weak predictor of reproductive success.

Analysis of the actions and effects of specific genes has also sometimes suggested that genetic makeup can determine running success. For example, the role played by the angiotensin-converting enzyme (ACE) gene and its variants in determining running performance has received considerable attention in recent years among exercise physiologists, molecular biologists, and sports medicine physicians and researchers.[6] ACE can degrade chemicals that dilate blood vessels and stimulate the production of a vasoconstrictor (a compound that narrows the diameter of blood vessels) called angiotensin II during physical activity.[13] With its strong role in determining blood flow to muscles, ACE might be expected to have an impact on endurance performance, and three studies published in 2005 alone linked certain forms of ACE with greater endurance.[13]

Similarly, research reveals that deactivation of a gene that produces myostatin, a chemical that thwarts muscle growth, results in the appearance of so-called super mice with about twice the normal amount of muscle mass. Another strip of DNA, the PPAR-delta gene, has a profound impact on mitochondrial production inside muscle cells (mitochondria are intracellular sites of energy creation, and research has linked heightened mitochondrial density with increased resistance to fatigue). Manipulation of the PPAR-delta gene in scientific inquiries has resulted in the creation of what are called marathon mice that can run about 70 percent longer and 90 percent farther than unaltered mice. Though the same results may or may not occur in humans, the theory of a gene as a magic bullet is advanced by such investigations.

Testing the Nature-Versus-Nurture Hypotheses

Concluding that genetic differences are the paramount factor underlying endurance-performance success is premature, however. In many cases, further analysis of the actions of specific genes reveals that the effects are not always consistent or that the genes that seem to have the biggest impact on performance are not necessarily monopolized by—or even present in—groups of high-performing endurance runners. Many other possibilities for the determination of performance are apparent. Training, or nurture, is certainly one of those elements; even the biggest advocate of nature over nurture must admit that training plays a large role in determining what the race clock reveals when a runner crosses the finish line. In the East African case, there is considerable evidence that Kenyan training differs dramatically from the training carried out by endurance runners in other parts of the world.[14]

In fact, training is commonly considered to be the most important extrinsic, or environmental, factor affecting performance. Scientists use two techniques in their attempts to disentangle environmental and genetic effects and thus provide answers to the debate over nature versus nurture. One method is to look for evidence of patterns of variation in performance variables (for example, $\dot{V}O_2max$ or responsiveness to training) in a population. As long as there is variation for a given performance-related trait, estimating the relative contributions of environmental and heritable (genetic) factors to this variation is possible.

This kind of work can be carried out with families. For example, maximal aerobic capacity ($\dot{V}O_2max$), a physiological variable linked with exercise capacity, can be studied in large populations containing family groups. If $\dot{V}O_2max$ varies considerably between families but very little among family members, there is evidence that $\dot{V}O_2max$ is strongly determined by genetic factors because individuals in the same family tend to have nearly identical $\dot{V}O_2max$ values and are very similar genetically. If $\dot{V}O_2max$ varies just as much within families as it does between families, then genetic factors would appear to play a small role in determining $\dot{V}O_2max$. The $\dot{V}O_2max$ of one's father, mother, or sibling is not necessarily closer to one's own maximal aerobic capacity than the $\dot{V}O_2max$ of the unrelated stranger living across town.

How to Determine $\dot{V}O_2$max

$\dot{V}O_2$max, or maximal aerobic capacity, is a traditional measure of endurance fitness. Usually expressed in milliliters of oxygen per kilogram of body weight per minute (ml·kg^{-1}·min^{-1} as expressed in scientific terms), $\dot{V}O_2$max reflects the heart's ability to pump oxygen to the muscles and the muscles' capacities to use oxygen to provide the energy required for running. $\dot{V}O_2$max is usually measured on a treadmill in an exercise laboratory, with a subject warming up and then progressing to increasingly quicker treadmill speeds or higher treadmill inclinations until a plateau or near plateau in oxygen consumption rate is reached, reflecting underlying heart, muscle, or neuromuscular limitations. This plateau is then termed $\dot{V}O_2$max. Table 1.2 provides varying fitness levels for aerobic capacity in females and males.

Table 1.2 Fitness Levels for Aerobic Capacity* in Females and Males

Females	AGE					
	20-29	30-39	40-49	50-59	60-69	70-79
Superior	49.6 or higher	47.4 or higher	45.3 or higher	41.0 or higher	37.8 or higher	37.2 or higher
Excellent	43.9-49.5	42.4-47.3	39.6-45.2	36.7-40.9	32.7-37.7	30.6-37.1
Good	39.5-43.8	37.7-42.3	35.9-39.5	32.6-36.6	29.7-32.6	28.1-30.5
Fair	36.1-39.4	34.2-37.6	32.8-35.8	29.9-32.5	27.3-29.6	25.9-28.0
Poor	32.3-36.0	30.9-34.1	29.4-32.7	26.8-29.8	24.6-27.2	23.5-25.8
Very poor	32.2-lower	30.8-lower	29.3-lower	26.7-lower	24.5-lower	23.4-lower
Males	AGE					
	20-29	30-39	40-49	50-59	60-69	70-79
Superior	55.5-higher	54.1 or higher	52.5 or higher	49.0 or higher	45.7 or higher	43.9 or higher
Excellent	51.1-55.4	48.3-54.0	46.4-52.4	43.3-48.9	39.6-45.6	36.7-43.8
Good	45.6-51.0	44.1-48.2	42.4-46.3	39.0-43.2	35.6-39.5	32.4-36.6
Fair	41.7-45.5	40.7-44.0	38.4-42.3	35.5-38.9	32.3-35.5	29.4-32.3
Poor	38.0-41.6	36.7-40.6	34.8-38.3	32.0-35.4	28.7-32.2	25.7-29.3
Very poor	37.9 or lower	36.6 or lower	34.7 or lower	31.9 or lower	28.6 or lower	25.6 or lower

*Aerobic capacity is $\dot{V}O_2$max expressed as milliliters of oxygen per kilogram of body weight per minute (ml·kg^{-1}·min^{-1}).

Data reprinted with permission from The Cooper Institute, Dallas, Texas, from *Physical Fitness Assessments and Norms for Adults and Law Enforcement*. Available online at www.cooperinstitute.org.

Geneticists interested in performance try to establish in their studies what is called heritability of a trait, or H^2. Without delving deeply into the math, it is possible to say that H^2 is nothing more than the ratio of genetic variance to total phenotypic variance for a specific performance variable. Genetic variance refers to the diversity in a variable, such as $\dot{V}O_2$max, that is produced by actual genetic differences, while phenotypic variance is the total measured heterogeneity (maximal amount of the variable possible) in a variable. For math buffs, the equation for heritability follows:

$$H^2 = V_g/V_p$$

with V_g being the variance due to genetic factors and V_p the total phenotypic variance.

If research reveals that H^2 is something small, for example .1, then one can conclude that genes are playing a small role in setting up the variance—the array of characteristics such as aerobic capacity—that one observes in a population. On the other hand, if H^2 is close to 1.0, then genes are playing a huge role.

The rest of the variation above and beyond H^2 (what geneticists call V_e/V_p, which is environmental variance divided by phenotypic variance) can be attributed to environmental factors, including training. Training can be subdivided into willingness to train, ability to train, opportunity to train, and quality of the overall training program. Additional environmental factors can be cultural in nature (e.g., diet, attitude toward running) or geographic (e.g., altitude, temperature, humidity, wind, running surface).

Research using the heritability model has revealed that heritable, or genetic, factors are important but not exclusive determinants of several physiological variables that contribute to success in endurance running. One investigation found that 48 to 74 percent of baseline submaximal aerobic performance—the ability to sustain continuous exercise without previous training—could be attributed to genetic factors. The same inquiry discovered that responsiveness to training—the degree to which aerobic capacity improved as a result of a specific training stimulus—had an H^2 of 23 to 57 percent.[15]

An additional scientific study detected an H^2 of 38 to 87 percent for maximal aerobic capacity, $\dot{V}O_2$max, a traditional measure of running fitness.[16] Another inquiry estimated that the degree to which $\dot{V}O_2$max increases in response to exercise has a heritability of about 47 percent, and that anaerobic, or lactate, threshold has a heritability of 55 to 80 percent.[17]

In an important investigation, the performance of mothers, fathers, daughters, and sons on exercise bikes was measured in 86 nuclear families. $\dot{V}O_2$max turned out to have a heritability of about 51 percent in these individuals. The other 49 percent of the variation might be accounted for by diet, attitude toward exercise, daily activity pattern, or other factors.[18]

Taken together, these wide-ranging values for heritability tell runners and their coaches that genetics *do* play a role in performance; after all, heritability does not drop below 23 percent and can be as high as 87 percent. This is hardly a shocking discovery, however, and it contains no practical information for a runner or coach. It is impossible for an individual to tell to what extent his or her performance is based on genes rather than environment, nor would such knowledge have a significant impact on training, which should always be formulated to be the best, most up-to-date, and most scientifically based regardless of underlying genetic constitution.

Note also that heritability studies have trouble truly differentiating between genetic and environmental factors. Family members share not only their genes but also their environments, which undoubtedly include important dietary and psychological factors. Thus, some unknown portion of the genetic variance H^2 is probably environmental in nature.

Conclusion

The heritability studies referred to in this chapter suggest that an individual's capability for distance running is determined by both genetic and environmental factors, and the exact proportion of influence is unknown. This is certainly logical, because it is unlikely that a runner's performance characteristics would be completely unmarked by either genetic or environmental elements. However, the heritability research has not been carried out with elite athletes, and it does not answer the basic question of whether Kenyan and other African runners enjoy a genetic superiority that causes V_g (i.e., the genetic contribution to performance) to be maximized. To explore these ideas further, chapter 2 discusses a second approach to the genetics of running: an analysis linking specific genes with improvements in performance. Chapter 3 then takes a close look at whether a unique genotype is necessary for achieving elite status as a runner.

CHAPTER 2

Genes That Influence Performance

Most runners and coaches realize that genetic factors affect performance. What is less commonly realized is that heredity can act in two completely different ways. First, specific genes or gene combinations can make certain individuals inherently more fit than others, even in situations in which no training has been carried out. Two sedentary individuals plucked at random from the street would be unlikely to have the same fitness level: One might have a stronger heart, a higher $\dot{V}O_2$max, or reduced perceptions of fatigue during exercise, and these differences could be related to genetic makeup. If the non-trained duo agreed to engage in a 5K run, actual performance would hinge on the inherent physiological variations.

Second, some genes or combinations of genes control the way in which individuals respond to training.[1] Some novice runners adapt dramatically to their training protocols, improving maximal aerobic capacity ($\dot{V}O_2$max) by as much as 80 percent over an 8-week period of serious training. Other, less-fortunate individuals might inch $\dot{V}O_2$max up by just 5 to 10 percent as a result of the same strenuous training. Finally, some individuals do not seem to respond to training at all; their physiological variables related to performance remain stagnant, even after weeks of hard work.[2] Thus, in a group of untrained individuals, variable responses to training can create situations where individuals who are inherently less fit than others can move far ahead of those who were originally more fit.

Both gene-related inherent fitness and gene-related responsiveness to training play roles in determining ultimate performance potential. Of course, quality of training is also important, but it is a nongenetic factor—unless a gene exists that codes for the ability to set up smart training!

Gene-Related Responsiveness

Researchers have identified a gene that influences how runners respond to training; it is a particular variant of the human angiotensin-converting enzyme (ACE) gene. Having the I variant, or I allele (an allele is simply one possible form of a gene), of the ACE gene tends to improve an individual's ability to adapt to endurance training,[3] perhaps by enhancing economy of movement.

Every runner has two ACE genes: Roughly 50 percent of runners have the I allele along with another variant of the ACE gene called the D, or short, allele; 25 percent have two I alleles, and the other 25 percent have two shorts in their ACE chromosomal slots. In one investigation, individuals with two copies of the I allele gained more muscle mass and lost more body fat during 10 weeks of intensive physical training than subjects who had two copies of the short allele or one copy of each.[4]

In a separate study, 58 men underwent an 11-week program that involved interval training on an exercise bike; 35 of these men had two I alleles, while 23 had two short alleles.[5] Prior to and after the training period, the researchers calculated the delta efficiency of exercise for each subject. This variable represents the efficiency with which muscles are working; it is the ratio of the change in work performed per minute to the change in energy expended in the same amount of time expressed as a percentage. Delta efficiency reflects the fact that if a runner can increase rate of work per minute (i.e., muscular power output and thus running velocity) without a large upswing in energy expenditure, the runner is operating efficiently. In contrast, a runner will have a low delta efficiency if energy consumption soars when running speed is increased.

Before the 11 weeks of training began, delta efficiency was the same for both groups of men: about 25 percent, which is average. At the end of the training period, delta efficiency had improved by almost 9 percent for the men with two copies of the I allele but had remained stagnant for the subjects with two short alleles.

Gene-Related Inherent Fitness

One of the key—but often overlooked—adaptations that runners' bodies make to training involves the responsiveness of blood vessels. When a previously sedentary individual runs regularly for a couple of months, many arteries, arterioles, and capillaries relax more easily during exercise, increasing the rate of blood flow—and thus oxygen and fuel—to the muscles. At least some of this arterial expansiveness is mediated by the chemical nitric oxide, which is released by cells lining the arteries. Nitric oxide does not just dilate arteries; it can also prolong vasodilation, helping to ensure that large amounts of blood will flow toward the muscles during extended exertion.

Exercise training increases the production of nitric oxide within arteries, and the presence of two I alleles seems to spike this nitric oxide synthesis even more. In effect, the presence of two I alleles permits the muscles of endurance-trained runners to have more blood. Dr. Hugh Montgomery, the lead scientist in the 11-week study discussed previously, also believes that I alleles may have profound metabolic influences within muscle cells, perhaps improving the efficiency of fuel selection, uptake, and use during exercise.[6]

Scientific studies reveal that runners with two copies of the I allele tend to gravitate toward longer-distance running rather than sprints and middle-distance events. I allele frequency actually increases with the distance run: For example, a genetic survey of Olympic-standard runners detected a higher frequency of the I allele among those athletes competing at 5K or longer compared with runners competing at 3K, 1500 meters, and other shorter distances.[7] Exactly the same situation prevails with competitive swimmers: Long-distance swimmers have higher frequencies of the I allele and short-distance competitors have higher frequencies of the short allele.[7]

Testing the Hypothesis of Kenyans' Superior Adaptation

As a group, Kenyan distance runners are superior to competitors from the rest of the world. One theory attempting to explain this phenomenon has suggested that Kenyan runners have genetic constitutions that make them better responders; that is, they respond to a specific level of training with a greater extent of adaptation compared with runners from other countries. In line with this hypothesis, one study found that physically active adolescent Kenyan boys had maximal oxygen uptakes that were 30 percent higher than others of a similar-age cohort who were inactive, even though the active boys were not carrying out any systematic running training; their activities consisted of farm work, jogging back and forth to school, and walking, among others.[8] A 30 percent response to general activity is considered extremely large. It is assumed that the adaptation would be even greater if serious training were undertaken since it is typical for maximal aerobic capacity to advance by 15 to 25 percent as a normal response to structured training.

To find out if Kenyans are programmed to be better responders, Henrik Larsen and his colleagues from the Copenhagen Muscle Research Centre and the University of Copenhagen traveled to Kenya to work with 24 teenage Kenyan males.[9] All these young men (average age = 16.5 years) belonged to the Nandi subtribe of the Kalenjin tribal group within Kenya; none had been engaged in systematic endurance training prior to beginning the study. The young Kenyans were classified as "town boys" or "village boys" by Larsen and his cohorts. The town runners were recruited from the city of Eldoret in the western part of Kenya. In contrast, the village runners were found at the Kamobo Secondary School located about 50 kilometers southwest of Eldoret; these subjects lived in a highly rural area within a 4-kilometer radius of the school. In total, there were 10 town runners and 14 village runners.

When the research began, the village runners had an average $\dot{V}O_2$max of 56 ml kg^{-1} min^{-1}, which was significantly higher than the 50.3 ml • kg^{-1} • min^{-1} registered by the town runners; this difference was probably due to the higher natural activity levels of the villagers. All 24 young men subsequently completed 12 weeks of endurance training. During the first 5 weeks, training frequency advanced from two to four workouts per week, weekly

Bennett Cohen/Icon SMI

▶ Although Kenyan runners dominate the world of distance running today, they do not have a monopoly on genes linked with high performance.

training distance moved from 8 to 28 kilometers, and actual running intensity increased from 70 to 80 percent of $\dot{V}O_2$max. Over the last 7 weeks, the weekly training consisted of four workouts, 28 kilometers of total running, and a constant intensity of 80 percent of $\dot{V}O_2$max (about 87 to 88 percent of maximal heart rate). Since the village runners were fitter than the town runners, 80 percent of $\dot{V}O_2$max for the villagers corresponded with a faster training pace. Indeed, the village runners trained at an average speed of 13.8 kilometers per hour (about 7 min per mi), compared with 12.4 kilometers per hour (approximately 7:47 min per mi) for the town runners.

Both the town and village runners benefited significantly from the training, and their responses were remarkably similar. For example, after the 12 weeks of training, mean heart rate at a submaximal running speed of 9.9 kilometers per hour declined from 170 to 159 beats per minute in the village runners and from 172 to 160 beats per minute for the town runners. Additionally, blood lactate concentration and plasma ammonia levels (an indicator of protein breakdown during exercise) dropped similarly for both groups, and running economy improved by a similar amount for both the village and town runners.

The only real difference in training response between the two groups concerned $\dot{V}O_2$max, which tended to increase more for the town runners compared with the village runners. For the town runners, the increase in $\dot{V}O_2$max was 10 percent compared with a 5 percent increase for the villagers. This difference was just shy of being statistically significant, but there is nothing particularly notable about it. The gain in $\dot{V}O_2$max that is made during training is related to the magnitude of $\dot{V}O_2$max at the beginning of the training period: Individuals with low $\dot{V}O_2$max values tend to achieve robust expansions of maximal aerobic capacities, while those with higher $\dot{V}O_2$maxs tend to make smaller improvements.[10, 11] Over the 12 weeks, the town runners increased $\dot{V}O_2$max from 50 to 56 ml • kg^{-1} • min^{-1}; the village runners increased $\dot{V}O_2$max from 56 to 59 ml • kg^{-1} • min^{-1}. Although the villagers increased $\dot{V}O_2$max by a smaller amount, they were still aerobically fitter than the Eldoret runners, and so they performed better during a final 5K, achieving an average time of 18:25 minutes (best time was 16:16) versus 20:15 minutes for the town runners (best was 18:40).

The changes observed in $\dot{V}O_2$max, lactate production, ammonia production, and running economy in response to training in these Kenyan runners appear to be routine: Nothing extraordinary stands out. However, to truly compare trainability between Kenyan and non-Kenyan runners, a study needs to involve non-Kenyans of a similar age and fitness level. Such a study does exist: Several years ago, French researchers asked a group of 16- and 17-year-old Caucasian men to participate in an endurance-training program very similar to the Nandis' training regime.[12] Training duration was 3 months for the Caucasians and 12 weeks for the Kalenjins, workout frequency was four sessions per week for both groups, and training intensity focused on 80 to 90 percent of maximal heart rate for both groups.

After their 3-month program, the Caucasians improved $\dot{V}O_2$max by 11.6 percent, a gain similar in magnitude to the 10.2 percent uptick enjoyed by the Nandi town runners and larger than the 5.4 percent increase achieved by the Kenyan villagers. There is no worry that the Caucasians' initial fitness was low, thus leading to an unusually large expansion of maximal aerobic capacity. In fact, the Caucasians began their training with average $\dot{V}O_2$max values of 58.4 ml kg^{-1} min^{-1}, very similar to the pretraining level of the Nandi village runners. In effect, the Caucasians' gain was twice as great as the Nandis' when initial aerobic capacities were similar. In other areas of fitness, the training-related changes in heart rate, blood lactate, and plasma ammonia observed in the Nandi runners were very similar to the changes observed in Caucasians.

This research suggests that Kenyans do not enjoy greater trainability when compared with Caucasians of similar age and initial fitness. There is also no evidence that Kenyans have higher frequencies of the highly touted I allele performance gene. Even if they did, approximately 25 percent of U.S. citizens, or about 75 million people, have two I alleles. This is nearly three times the entire population of Kenya. So, even if all Kenyans had two copies of the I allele, the United States would still have a genetic edge in terms of the total numbers of individuals with heightened delta efficiency.

Other Genes Affecting Running Performance

Another gene that has an effect on running performance codes for insulin-like growth factor I (IGF-I), a protein that stimulates muscle growth and repair. This coding (or creation) is indirect, involving chemical intermediates, such as transfer RNA (tRNA) and messenger RNA (mRNA). To date, the IGF-I research has been carried out only with rodents, but it is reasonable to assume that the results could apply to human runners. In 1998 H. Lee Sweeney and his colleagues at the University of Pennsylvania, working together with Nadia Rosenthal and her co-workers at Harvard University, infected mice with adeno-associated viruses (AAVs), which carried the gene coding for IGF-I.[13] When these AAVs were injected into young mice, their muscular growth rates became 15 to 30 percent greater than normal; as the mice matured, their muscles became super-sized even though the animals were totally sedentary. When the AAVs were injected into middle-aged mice, their muscles resisted the expected losses in strength and function as the mice grew older.

In follow-up work, Sweeney's group and a team led by Roger P. Farrar of the University of Texas at Austin injected AAVs carrying the gene coding for IGF-I into one leg of each laboratory rat and then made the rodents complete an 8-week program of strength training.[14] The rats carried out their training several times a week, climbing up wire ladders with weights attached to their bodies. After 8 weeks, the muscles treated with the AAV were roughly twice as strong as the muscles in the noninfected legs in the same animal. When training stopped, the muscles treated with AAV lost their strength much more slowly compared with muscles in the other legs that had engaged in strength training but had not benefited from the gene-laced viral infection.

Other genes are likely to play a role in determining running performance. Eero Mantyranta, a Finnish cross-country skier who won two world championships plus seven medals over the course of four different Olympic games, had a genetic condition called primary familial and congenital polycythemia (PFCP) caused by a mutation in the erythropoietin receptor (EPOR) gene. This condition produces dramatic increases in blood hemoglobin, red blood cell mass, and the oxygen-carrying capacity of the blood, which are potentially great advantages in endurance sports. Many of Mantyranta's relatives who carry the same mutated gene have also been champion Finnish endurance athletes.[15]

Australian researchers have discovered a gene known as $ACTN_3$ that seems to play an important role in optimizing the function of fast-twitch muscle fibers. An unusually high percentage of elite sprinters have a copy of this gene, and top-level female sprinters tend to have two copies of $ACTN_3$.[16]

Gene Doping

Serious athletes, coaches, and managers are becoming increasingly aware that so-called super-performance genes exist, and some are beginning to look into the possibility of gene doping: having desirable genes added to individuals' genetic constitutions. The technology for doing so is available. While there are different ways to supplement a human's natural DNA constitution with outside genetic material, viruses have become a favored transporter mechanism for coveted genes because they are so adept at eluding the defenses put up by an individual's immune system.

The way in which gene doping is accomplished is straightforward. First, researchers select a type of virus that has a low probability of producing a serious infection. The researchers then strip down the viruses' genetic material, leaving only the genes that code for the viruses' outer coats, the protein wrappers that surround the inner core of genetic material. To these coat genes researchers add the genetic material of interest, for example the gene coding for IGF-I. The resulting, highly unusual viruses can then be injected into muscle tissue where they enter muscle cells and may insert the added gene into the muscle fibers' genetic packages within the cell nuclei. The muscles may then go on an IGF-I production spree, and muscular growth can be dramatically enhanced.

IGF-I

The gene for IGF-I is perhaps one of the most likely to be used for doping. If the chemical IGF-I were injected by itself, instead of the gene for IGF-I, it would be broken down easily by various processes and would have little effect on muscle growth.[17] However, the gene for IGF-I can be easily vectored into human muscles, via the viral mechanism mentioned earlier, where it can create a massive overproduction of IGF-I. Once the IGF-I genes take up shop within muscle cells, the results can be dramatic. IGF-I's key action appears to be on satellite cells, essentially muscle stem cells that normally reside between muscle fibers in an intact muscle. When the stem cells are hit with concentrations of IGF-I that are higher than normal, they undergo a flurry of activity, dividing and eventually fusing with muscle cells to create stronger, larger fibers capable of greater force production. As a result, IGF-I's actions might improve maximal running speed in endurance runners. However, it is important to note that IGF-I stimulates tumors as well as satellite cells to increase their activity.

Myostatin

A key physiological process always has a counterpoint mechanism to keep it from going out of control. While IGF-I stimulates satellite-cell activity and muscle growth and repair, these same activities are dampened by the action of a chemical called myostatin. It is the interplay between IGF-I and myostatin that ultimately creates a runner's characteristic physique. If a runner undertakes vigorous strength training with heavy weights, for example, IGF-I production is amplified and myostatin creation is toned down producing muscle enlargement, or hypertrophy. If a runner sits in a rocket ship on a long ride to the moon, on the other hand, myostatin will take over, leaving him or her with wasted, weaker muscles by the end of the journey.

Myostatin control is another potential avenue for gene doping by using either a gene that creates a protein product that blocks normal myostatin action or—perhaps better yet—a gene that creates a nonfunctional form of myostatin. Pharmaceutical and biotech companies are already working on various forms of myostatin inhibitors, stimulated by work previously carried out in the cattle industry. Certain cattle, notably the Belgian Blue and Piedmontese breeds, have a genetic variation that creates an ineffective form of myostatin. The result is not a defective cow but rather a ripped, astonishingly muscle-bound specimen. The so-called good news for athletes interested in gene doping is that the absence of normal myostatin in these cattle also obstructs the creation of fatty tissue, which in the end gives the animals incredible body compositions. The same effects would likely occur in human runners, although the risks are unknown.

EPO

While endurance athletes might not necessarily be interested in IGF-I promoters or myostatin blockers because of worries about excessive muscle growth, some will certainly be attracted to the gene that stimulates increased production of erythropoietin (EPO), the compound that boosts red blood cell production by the bone marrow. A synthetic form of EPO, a drug called Epoietin that was originally developed to treat anemia, has been widely used by Tour de France cyclists in order to expand $\dot{V}O_2$max and thus endurance. An entire team of cyclists has been excluded from the famous race because of EPO use, but its use in sports continues.[17]

The gene for EPO is readily available, and science has already looked at what happens to monkeys, baboons, and macaques when they are supplied with the gene. The results have been predictable: Macaques, for example, dramatically increase their red blood cell production when they are given the EPO gene. However, the resulting physiological processes make many observers believe that gene doping with EPO material is much like opening a pernicious Pandora's box. The macaques that received the EPO genes, for example, produced so many red blood cells that their blood became like sludge, increasing the risk of heart failure. As a result, macaques with EPO genes must have blood removed on a regular basis to reduce the risks of clotting and heart failure.[18]

Paradoxically, some of the macaques with EPO genes eventually developed severe anemia. As it turned out, the excess EPO created by the macaques was slightly different from their normal version of EPO, perhaps because it was being created in unusual locations in the macaques' bodies, not just in its usual production site in the kidneys. As a result, the animals' immune systems began clearing the excess EPO and in the process also attacked normal EPO, leading to a massive falloff in EPO levels and thus a plummeting rate of red blood cell creation. This kind of immune system overreaction is a key danger associated with gene therapy and gene doping.

PPAR-Delta

Based on initial studies with rodents, there are a number of genes in addition to $ACTN_3$ and the genes for IGF-I and EPO activity that could have major upsides for athletes. Researchers at the Salk Institute in San Diego, California, have inserted genes that code for a fat-burning protein called PPAR-delta into mice. The idea was to help prevent obesity in these mice, which did stay slender even when ingesting a high-fat diet. An extremely interesting aspect of this research, however, was that the mice also developed an extraordinarily large number of slow-twitch muscle cells, the kinds of fibers that are so valuable for extended endurance performance. As Ronald Evans, one of the Salk investigators put it, "This change produced the 'marathon mouse,' able to run twice the distance of its normal littermates."[19]

AMPK

Scientists at Dartmouth college have worked with mice bearing a gene that codes for a highly activated form of an enzyme called AMP-activated protein kinase (AMPK).[20] The activities and functions of this enzyme are complex, but one of its key effects appears to be the activation of glycogen synthase, the enzyme that boosts glycogen storage within muscles. As a result, mice carrying the special gene for activated AMPK have unusually large glycogen depots in their leg muscles and can exercise for unusually long periods of time. "Our genetically altered mouse appears to have already been on an exercise program," notes Dr. Lee Witters, a professor of medicine and biochemistry at Dartmouth Medical School.[21]

Conclusion

An important point for runners and coaches to understand is that while specific genes seem to promote higher performance, having such genes is not *mandatory* in order for runners to improve dramatically or even achieve elite status as long-distance competitors. If we examined the 20 fastest 10K runners from Kenya or Ethiopia, for example, not all would have two copies of the I allele for the ACE gene; in fact, their ACE-allele frequency would be no different from the frequency observed in the general population.[22] Currently no reason exists for any runner to think he or she lacks the genetic credentials to achieve dramatic improvement in performance.

In addition, although gene doping may seem to be an attractive option for runners focused on achieving unusually large gains in performance, the practice is neither predictable nor safe. Unusual—and sometimes lethal—side effects can occur when a runner's natural genetic makeup is artificially manipulated.

CHAPTER 3

Genetic Differences Between Elite and Nonelite Runners

Specific genes can have a positive impact on running ability (as described in chapter 2), and thus geneticists and exercise scientists have wondered whether top-level runners have an optimal genetic profile, that is, the right combination of performance-related genes. The fundamental questions include the following: Is the DNA of an elite runner quite different from the genetic material of those who perform in the middle of the pack? Is a certain DNA dossier required to achieve elite running status? Do elite runners who climb to the highest level of endurance performance—the world champions and Olympic medalists—have unique genes that other elites lack?

Research Examining Genetic Differences

Researchers from the Karolinska Institutet in Stockholm, Sweden, investigated these possibilities by comparing the genetic makeup of 46 elite Spanish Caucasian athletes with the genetic composition of 123 Spanish Caucasian sedentary control individuals.[1] The Karolinska investigators examined the frequency of seven genes known to have an effect on endurance performance and computed what they called a "genotype score" for each individual based on the presence or absence of the seven favorable genes, with 100 being the maximal possible rating.

The 46 elites had an average score of 70.2, significantly higher than the 62.4 mark for the controls, implying that top athletes have superior genetic profiles. However, not a single elite athlete had the best possible score for the seven genes, and only 3 of the 46 top performers had the right makeup for six of the performance genes. Such findings suggest that it is not necessary to have all the best genes to be an elite athlete. Expressed another way, elite athletes may be slightly different genetically from nonelites, but having a superb genetic makeup is not mandatory in order to become a top-level athlete.

Along similar lines, investigations carried out with elite Polish rowers have revealed that these high-level performers have a higher frequency of the I allele of the angiotensin-converting enzyme (ACE) gene (see chapter 2) by a margin of 56 to 44 percent.[2] Such a finding suggests that the I allele is an important ticket for admission to the elite-athlete club, yet almost 20 percent of the elite Polish rowers carried no I allele at all in the ACE position, while another 51 percent had just one copy of the I allele instead of the possible two copies.

Other studies have found a higher frequency of $ACTN_3$, another performance-related gene, in elite endurance athletes in Finland[3] and also in power athletes (sprinters and throwers) in Greece.[4] In the latter study, 48 percent of elite power-oriented athletes in Greece had the RR genotype for the $ACTN_3$ gene (the R allele of the ACTN gene is linked with greater muscle size and power), compared with just 26 percent of the overall nonelite population in Greece, a significant difference. This finding suggests that elite, power (sprint) athletes are indeed genetically different from nonelite athletes and sedentary control individuals. However, the data also reveal that having a certain genotype is not necessary to become an elite athlete: In the study from Greece, 52 percent of the power athletes did not have the RR genotype and yet were elite. Individuals without the optimal genetic makeup can still become elite.

In addition, some research has failed to find any connection at all between the $ACTN_3$ genotype and athletic status. In an inquiry carried out with Caucasian individuals of European ancestry, 50 top-level male professional cyclists and 52 Olympic-class male professional runners were found to have essentially the same $ACTN_3$ compositions as 123 healthy but sedentary control subjects.[5]

Numerous studies have failed to find any genetic discrepancy at all between elite and nonelite athletes. In one investigation, scientists from Israel, Portugal, Spain, and Sweden compared the frequency of the T allele of the GNB3 C825T gene, believed to have a positive impact on maximal aerobic capacity, in 174 elite endurance athletes and 340 nonathletic control individuals.[6] In this research, which included participants from two different ethnic and geographic backgrounds (Israel and Spain), the likelihood of having the key T allele was no greater in elites than in controls.

Because of its established links with endurance-performance capacity,[2] the ACE gene is certainly the most widely studied strip of genetic material in elite runners and other high-level athletes. One might expect the I allele of this gene to be considered prize DNA, the right genetic stuff for elite runners, but research does not support this idea.

In a study carried out with 76 elite Ethiopian endurance runners whose competitive distances ranged from 5K to the marathon, the distribution of

Dave Thompson/PA Archive/Press Association Images

▶ Scientists have not been able to pinpoint a genetic difference in elite endurance runners that predicts success.

ACE genotypes (II, ID, and DD) was not significantly different from that found in 410 nonelite Ethiopian endurance athletes, 38 sprint and power athletes from Ethiopian national teams, and 317 sedentary Ethiopian controls.[7] From the standpoint of the performance-promoting ACE gene, the Ethiopian elites were just like everyone else (see following discussion of ACE gene frequencies in elite Kenyan runners).

Myth of the Genetic Edge in East Africans

In spite of the tenuous connection between genetic makeup and elite-athlete status, there is a widespread perception that elite East African endurance runners enjoy a kind of genetic advantage over sedentary individuals around the world and also over non–East African elites. This conception has been put forth on scientifically based websites and in the popular press.[8]

According to this thinking, elite Kenyan and Ethiopian runners have specific genes or optimal combinations of genetic material that promote superior running performances and are a fundamental cause of these runners' success. These high-performance genes and genetic complexes are supposedly absent in non-African runners or perhaps are present in much lower frequencies. The hypothesis is that Kenyan and Ethiopian endurance-running supremacy can be explained primarily by genetic differences between African and Caucasian runners as opposed to training disparities or dissimilar cultural factors.

As noted in chapter 1, a finding that appears to support this genetic hypothesis is that the world's best runners do not come from all parts of Kenya and Ethiopia but rather seem to emerge from discrete geographic regions and specific, somewhat small subpopulations within those two countries.[9, 10] In Kenya a disproportionate number of international elite runners have grown up in the rural areas and are members of the Kalenjin tribe; as many as 70 percent of Kenyan elites are Kalenjin, even though Kalenjins make up just 4 percent of the total Kenyan population. In western Kenya, Kalenjins do not marry freely with members of other tribes, and as noted in chapter 1, the existence of small, somewhat isolated populations of people can lead to genetic drift, which may cause certain variants of genes, including those related to performance, to increase dramatically in frequency.[11] If such genetic variants, or alleles, have a major impact on endurance-running capacity, the subpopulations may produce unusually high numbers of outstanding endurance runners.

This line of thinking is not without its perils. Research reveals, for example, that the top runners within the East African subpopulations that have produced an unusual number of world-class athletes are those individuals who have simply run the farthest to school.[9, 10] When running is the form of basic transportation, baseline maximal aerobic capacity ($\dot{V}O_2max$) is about 30 percent higher than when little running is done when going from place to place.[12] The endurance platform from which these runners begin their careers may be loftier from the outset in East African athletes. What appears to be a genetically based phenomenon might rather be, at least partially, the outcome of an extremely high level of childhood activity.

Contentions about the genetic superiority of Africans when it comes to athletic endeavors are not confined to distance running. The stars of the 2008 Beijing Olympics were clearly Usain Bolt, a black Jamaican sprinter, and Michael Phelps, a white swimmer from the United States. Post-Olympic discussions of Bolt's amazing success were focused primarily on his presumed genetic advantage, even though very little is known about the genes and gene combinations that are linked with top-level sprinting.[13] In contrast, the commentary about Phelps centered on his diet and incredible training habits; genetic hypothesizing was completely absent.[14] Scientific support for the idea that elite runners of African descent have an exceptional genetic profile is minimal. Propositions about genetic advantages for these runners as compared to Caucasians thus appear to have little or no scientific basis.

Research on the ACE Gene

As described in chapter 2, one of the best-known performance genes is the strip of genetic material that codes for the angiotensin-converting enzyme, or ACE; this gene is found on chromosome 17 in the human genome and has been linked with improved running economy and heightened endurance.[15] The I allele of this gene, when present on both members of the chromosome 17 pair, leads to lower circulating concentrations of ACE, decreased ACE tissue activity, increased endurance performance.[16-21] and superior average running speed during an intense 30-minute effort.[16] Possession of the D allele has been linked with higher maximal running velocity[16] and the attainment of elite-level sprint and anaerobic performances.[22, 23] Thus, one might expect elite endurance runners to have an unusually high frequency of the I allele.

To determine whether superior endurance runners are more likely than others to have the I allele on chromosome 17, researchers from the International Centre for East African Running Science (ICEARS) at the University of Glasgow took DNA samples from 221 national-level Kenyan runners, 70 international Kenyan competitors, and 85 individuals drawn at random from the Kenyan population.[24] The Glasgow investigators also assessed genetic composition at a site known as A22982GD that has been closely linked with ACE levels in subjects of African descent as compared with Caucasians.

The ICEARS scientists found absolutely no association between running performance and I allele frequency or A22982GD status among the Kenyan subjects. Contradicting the idea that elite runners enjoy a genetic edge, the findings indicated that elite and national-level Kenyan runners were not more likely to carry the I allele or A22982GD when compared with the Kenyan population at large. A separate study also found no association between I allele frequency and being an elite endurance athlete.[25] Finally, there is also no evidence that Kenyan runners have a higher frequency of the I allele compared with Caucasian competitors.

Research on mtDNA and Haplogroups

Mitochondrial DNA (mtDNA) analysis has been used with elite Ethiopian distance runners to determine whether they are genetically distinct from the general population.[26] Variations in mtDNA could have a significant effect on endurance performance because mtDNA codes for the creation of the enzymes necessary for oxidative phosphorylation (the use of oxygen to create the energy needed for muscular work) within muscle cells. MtDNA is inherited directly and entirely from mother to child and will change only if mutations in the mtDNA occur. An extremely interesting consequence is that linked complexes of mutations may occur in different branches of descent from a single female ancestor (the so-called mitochondrial Eve). Each branch of this tree is referred to as a haplogroup.

If superior mtDNA is a reason for the success of elite Ethiopian runners, such individuals should be confined to one specific branch of the tree. However, the mtDNA analysis revealed that the elite Ethiopians were scattered throughout the tree; they had a wide distribution of haplogroups that was similar to the general Ethiopian population.[26] Surprisingly, some of the elite Ethiopian runners shared a recent, common mtDNA variant with many Europeans. The similarity of mtDNA between elite Ethiopians and Europeans negates the ideas that elite Ethiopians are a genetically distinct, isolated population and that unusual patterns of mtDNA could be responsible for their success.

The notion that elite African runners are not a genetically distinct group is further supported by research on Y chromosome haplogroups. The Y chromosome, present only in males, contains a small amount of genetic material that may have relevance for physical performance. Y chromosomes are passed from fathers to sons, with no maternal contribution, and thus haplogroups may arise that are the branches created from one so-called ancestral Adam. As is the case with mtDNA, mutations in Y chromosomes cause entirely different branches to sprout from the overall genetic tree. However, the research with Y chromosome haplogroups in Ethiopian runners has revealed that the elites have the same distribution of Y haplogroups found in the general population.[27]

An interesting aspect of this study of Ethiopian Y chromosome haplogroups is that some of the Y chromosome haplogroups were present in significantly different frequencies in the elite runners compared with the population at large. As this book goes to press, frequencies of Y chromosome haplogroups in elite Kenyan runners are being studied. If the same specific Y chromosome haplogroups are found to be over- or underrepresented in elite Kenyan and elite Ethiopian runners, the obvious conclusion would be that the Y chromosome has a major impact on endurance-running performance in males, and that males who find themselves on the correct branch, or haplogroup, of the genetic tree have an inherent advantage over the endurance-running males on another branch. It should be noted, however, that there is currently no evidence that specific Y haplogroups are more common in elite African runners compared with relatively underachieving elite American or European runners.

Conclusion

The existing research indicates that elite African runners are not a genetically distinct group. It is highly unlikely that East Africa produces performance-optimizing genotypes that cannot be matched in other regions of the world. Overall, the hypothesis that the world's best runners are genetically distinct from average athletes and even sedentary controls remains a very shaky and unproven proposition. In addition, elite athletes from non–East African countries have genetic constitutions that are very similar to the genetic makeups of nonelite athletes and sedentary individuals in those countries.

PART

II

Biomechanics of Running

CHAPTER 4

The Body While Running

Emil Zatopek ran with the worst upper-body form imaginable: His head rolled from side to side, his torso tilted unpredictably, and he let out an earsplitting wheezing that earned him the nickname the "Czech Locomotive." In spite of his seemingly dysfunctional form, the indomitable man from Koprivnice checkmated his opponents in four different Olympic competitions, bringing home a quartet of gold medals, including three from the 1952 Games alone.

When Tirunesh Dibaba runs, she appears to fly over the ground like a well-tuned jet plane, with silky-smooth movements of her appendages and an upper body always balanced and under control. Dibaba has two world records in her dossier, not to mention four world championships, three Olympic gold medals, and five world cross-country championships.

It would be impossible for the body movements of Zatopek and Dibaba during running to be any more different (see figure 4.1, *a-b*), and yet each athlete achieved a similar level of international success. Such a contradiction forces exercise scientists to examine how the body actually moves during running—and to investigate whether optimal motions can be identified.

Sport biomechanics—a discipline in which the laws of mechanics are employed in order to gain a greater understanding of athletic movement and performance—can help resolve such issues. The biomechanics of running is usually divided into two key components: kinetics and kinematics. Human kinetics, also called kinesiology or dynamics, is the study of the actions of external and internal forces on an individual's body during movement, especially with regard to muscles, tendons, ligaments, and skeletal system. For running, kinetics can be described as the study of the forces and motions characteristic of the running gait. Human kinetics employs the sciences of biomechanics, anatomy, physiology, psychology, and neuroscience to understand how runners and other athletes move. For example, a kinesiologist might study the way in which the nervous system alters its control of the leg muscles in response to training or how force production by the hamstrings is changed after a program of hill work. The word *kinetics* comes from the Greek words *kinesis* (movement) and *kinein* (to move).

PA Archive/Press Association Images

Rogan Thomson/Actionplus/Icon SMI

▶ **Figure 4.1** Kinematic analysis of successful runners like (a) Emil Zatopek and (b) Tirunesh Dibaba reveals significant disparities in form.

Kinematics is the branch of biomechanics that analyzes the body's motion during running without taking into account the body's mass or the various forces acting on it. This discipline includes the study of the movements and positions of muscles, joints, and various parts of the body such as the feet, legs, pelvic area (core), and torso. For example, kinematics is employed to study the timing and extent of pronation (inward rolling of the foot) and supination (outward rolling of the foot) during the stance phase of gait and also the magnitudes of hip, knee, and ankle flexion and extension during running.

Both approaches are extremely valuable. Kinematic analysis can be very useful for studying a runner's form and ultimately improving it. Kinetics helps coaches and runners understand a broad range of important running phenomena including muscle actions in response to fatigue, the relative activities of various muscle groups as maximal running speed is improved, and the ways in which foot-strike pattern shapes work output by various muscles of the legs.

Kinematic View of Running Form

A kinematic approach reveals that running is a highly repetitive movement. About 85 to 95 times per minute, each leg passes through a stance phase, during which the foot is in contact with the ground, and a swing phase, during which the foot is free from the ground and the leg swings forward from the hip preparing for subsequent foot strike and initiation of another stance period. One gait cycle (figure 4.2, a-d) begins at the moment when a foot strikes the ground, continues through stance, progresses through swing, and ends when the foot hits the ground again.

Since running movements are so repeatable, they would appear to be well suited for optimization, the establishment of specific patterns of motion that would be relatively uniform among runners with similar training backgrounds and that would improve both performance and injury prevention.[1] Many runners and coaches believe that there is a right way to run from a kinematic perspective—and a variety of wrong ways associated with poorer performances and an increased risk of injury.

Scientific research has struggled in its attempt to identify biomechanical optima, however, and endurance and middle-distance runners with similar training backgrounds and performances often display wide variation in

▶ **Figure 4.2** A gait cycle begins when the foot (*a*) strikes the ground, (*b*) continues through stance, (*c*) swings, and (*d*) makes contact with the ground again.

kinematic variables. One study found that support time, the duration of time a foot spends on the ground during the stance phase of the gait cycle, averaged 179.9 milliseconds in a group of 54 elite female runners but varied considerably between runners: up to 6 percent quicker than average for some competitors and 7 percent longer than usual for others.[1] This is a substantial difference: A runner with a support time of 170 milliseconds would spend 4 fewer seconds anchored to the ground for each 200 steps than would a runner with a support time of 190 milliseconds, a time that would produce a considerably higher velocity for the 170-millisecond athlete if stride length were relatively equal. Support time is a biomechanical variable intimately connected with stride rate—the briefer the support time, the faster the stride rate—and thus maximum running velocity; there is an expectation that support time would be quite uniform across runners of high competitive ability. Research rejects this hypothesis but does reveal that support time is quite malleable, with explosive training providing an important way of upgrading, or shortening, the stance phase of running gait and boosting maximal speed.

Similarly, the extent of knee flexion during the swing phase of gait should be a factor linked with running performance. Reduced flexion straightens the legs during the swing phase and thus expands the length of the leg lever (see figure 4.3). A lever is simply a rigid object that moves about a fixed point, or fulcrum. In the case of a human runner involved in the swing phase of gait, the leg is the rigid object and the hip is the fulcrum.

The beauty and advantage of levers is that a heavy object, such as the leg and its attached foot, can be moved relatively easily by applying a relatively small force near the fulcrum. However, the force required to move the leg increases as the leg straightens and lengthens and thus a highly flexed knee should be most economical during swing. It saves energy because less force is required to pull the leg forward.

Somewhat surprisingly, though, maximal knee flexion varies considerably among elite runners of comparable ability: The average maximal flexion is 127.9 degrees, but the observed range in maximal flexion is from approximately 109 to 140 degrees.[1] Knee-flexion angle is measured between the shin and an imaginary straight line that runs

▶ **Figure 4.3** Knee flexion during the swing phase of the gait cycle is linked with economical movement and superior performance.

straight down the thigh and through the knee. When the leg is fully extended and perfectly straight at the knee, knee-flexion angle is 0 degrees.

These studies reveal that there is wide variation in kinematic variables among runners, even in well-trained elite competitors. One purpose of carrying out such research is to determine how kinematic variables influence performance. If a kinematic study determines that a decrease in duration of stance is linked with improved running economy and faster 5K performances, for example, researchers can then explore the factors and training modes that reduce stance time. Kinematic variables respond to training, and thus to the development of muscular strength and neural coordination, although they are also dependent on individual characteristics such as skeletal structure, flexibility, joint stiffness, and muscle length.

There can be significant differences in kinematic variables even between similarly trained runners, but *general* movement sequences and force-application patterns are similar among runners. When the gait cycle is divided into stance (the period between first contact with the ground and toe-off) and swing (the period between toe-off and the next foot strike), certain patterns of movement, muscle action, and joint angle are uniform among runners. This can be illustrated by examining what happens to the thigh, knee, and ankle during stance and swing and linking the movements of these parts of the leg with muscular activity and force production (i.e., connecting kinematics with kinetics).[1]

Thigh

The key functions of the thigh during running are to stabilize the knee; cushion the impact of the foot colliding with the ground on each step, accomplished in part by changing the angle between the thigh and lower part of the leg; and produce forward propulsive force during knee and thigh extension, which occurs during every stance phase of gait.

At the precise moment of foot strike at the beginning of stance for a heel-striking runner (an athlete who makes first contact with the ground with the heel rather than the mid- or forefoot), the thigh is ordinarily at about a 25-degree forward angle from an imaginary vertical line drawn straight down through the center of the body (figure 4.4). In other words, the thigh is not directly under the torso but is inclined forward by 25 degrees with respect to the imaginary line. For the heel-striker, the thigh reaches an angle of 0 degrees (positioned directly under the upper body) about half-way through stance and reaches about 35 degrees of extension (inclined behind the upper body with a 35-degree angle between thigh and midline) at toe-off (figure 4.5).

These kinematics tend to change significantly in the runner who is a midfoot striker (one who makes first contact with the ground with the midfoot area rather than the heel or forefoot). At first contact with the ground, the angle of hip flexion tends to be significantly less than 25 degrees while the

▶ **Figure 4.4** The thigh of a heel-striking runner reaches about a 25-degree angle in front of the body as the foot strikes the ground.

▶ **Figure 4.5** At toe-off the thigh usually reaches about 35 degrees of extension behind the body.

▶ **Figure 4.6** Midfoot-landing runners have a reduced thigh angle during initial impact with the ground, lessening the braking forces and duration of stance.

knee is flexed to a greater degree and the thigh reaches an angle of 0 degrees more quickly during stance (figure 4.6). Logic suggests that midfoot striking therefore produces less braking action with each step since the foot is not as far ahead of the body and the leg is less straight and thus should be more economical. Research also indicates that a reduced thigh angle helps minimize the duration of stance. About 95 percent of nonelite distance runners are heel strikers, but the prevalence is much lower among elite competitors. Taken together, these findings suggest that midfoot striking is superior to heel striking and that heel strikers can improve economy and performance by progressively shifting to midfoot landings. This idea will be discussed further in chapter 5.

The muscles that control the thigh during stance include the gluteus maximus, rectus femoris, hamstrings, vastus lateralis, and vastus medialis (figure 4.7). The activities of these muscles during stance are complex, and understanding these activities is necessary to create an optimal strength-training program for the thigh muscles. After toe-off, when the thigh begins moving forward so that contact with the ground can be made again, gluteus maximus activity is maximized (as determined by electromyographic analysis) compared with all other segments of the overall gait cycle. Human anatomy textbooks commonly state that the most important function of the gluteus maximus is to produce thigh extension, and yet during running the glutes are most active and forceful during thigh flexion when the thigh

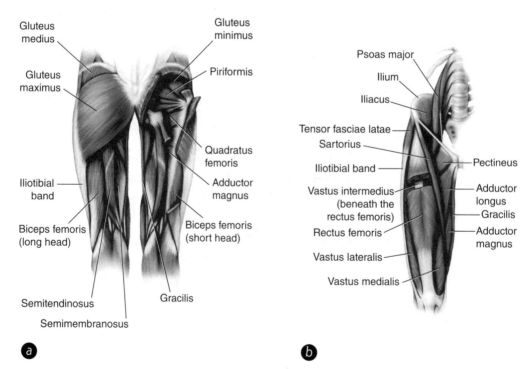

a   b

▶ **Figure 4.7** The muscles of the hip and upper leg: (*a*) posterior view and (*b*) anterior view.

is in a forward angle from the hip. Clearly, the most important role of the glutes during running is to control thigh flexion, and exercises designed to strengthen the glutes for running should mimic this phase of the gait cycle. (See chapter 14 for more information.)

Carrying out hip extensions on a machine in the gym does not strengthen the glutes very effectively for running because doing so produces concentric actions of the glute during hip extension. (In concentric actions, muscles produce force while shortening.) The key actions of the glutes during running are eccentric actions during hip flexion. (In eccentric actions, muscles lengthen as they exert force.) Eccentric, running-specific drills for the glutes and hamstrings are provided in chapter 14.

The rectus femoris muscle, which is the middle of the quadriceps muscles, becomes moderately active just before foot strike and remains moderately active throughout the first two-thirds of stance: Its purported action, according to basic human anatomy texts, is to produce thigh flexion; however, since the thigh is gradually moving into extension over the course of stance, the key role of the rectus femoris during running stance is to act eccentrically to prevent the knee joint from collapsing. In other words, the rectus femoris stops the knee joint from flexing too much during stance. Running-specific exercises for the quadriceps are outlined in chapter 14.

The vastus lateralis and vastus medialis muscles, which are the outer and inner parts of the quads, respectively, are activated shortly before foot strike and are extremely active over the first 67 percent of stance.[2] This seems odd from a traditional perspective because the vastus lateralis and vastus medialis are supposed to assist with thigh flexion; in fact, these two muscles act most strenuously and in an eccentric way to control excessive rotational movements of the thigh as thigh extension develops during stance. The vastus lateralis and vastus medialis muscles also assist the rectus femoris with the job of preventing too much flexion at the knee during stance.

The hamstrings, which are also thigh controllers, maximize their activity just before foot strike, toward the end of the swing phase of gait. They are eccentrically controlling forward motion of the thigh and preloading themselves to have increased stiffness at the moment of touch-down, when the foot first hits the ground. This enhanced stiffness allows the hamstrings to recoil effectively throughout stance and provide a great deal of propulsive force. A traditional view is that the hamstrings provide direct concentric force for hip extension shortly before and during toe-off, which would drive the body forward, but in actuality the hamstrings are completely inactive during the last third of stance. This doesn't mean that the hamstrings aren't doing any work; it's just that the work can't be measured by electromyography (EMG) since it is all based on the recoil of the hamstrings, which were stretched out during swing.

During swing, the thigh gradually moves out of extension, reaches an angle of 0 degrees with no extension or flexion halfway through swing, and then maximizes its forward angle (flexion) about 70 percent of the way through swing, retreating just slightly before foot strike. The gluteus maximus waits until the very end of swing, just before foot strike, to become really active, which helps to stop flexion of the thigh. The rectus femoris is extremely forceful during the first 50 percent of swing because it is boosting the forward acceleration of the leg so that stride length can be maintained and the foot can find an appropriate landing point. The vastus lateralis and vastus medialis stay out of swing until the very end, when they preload the thigh, stiffening the knee joint for touch-down. The hamstrings wait until approximately the last 30 percent of swing, when they become active in order to control forward movement of the thigh and to stiffen the leg properly.[2]

For coaches and runners, information about how the thigh muscles function during running is not esoteric or a late-night antidote for insomnia. Rather, understanding thigh operations leads to the creation of an optimal strength-training program that maximizes thigh-muscle function during quality training and competitive running. Traditional strengthening exercises for runners, including movements carried out on machines, non-gait-related drills for specific muscles, and even two-leg activities can no longer be considered productive. These should be replaced by the running-specific movements described in chapter 14.

Knee

The functions of the knee during running are to minimize the shock forces associated with impact with the ground by increasing knee flexion at the initial moment of foot strike and to produce propulsive force by undergoing extension during stance. To understand how the knee works during running, it is important to examine the various angles adopted by the knee during gait. The angle of the knee during running is defined as the angle between the actual position of the shin and an imaginary line drawn to indicate the position the shin would occupy if the leg were perfectly straight. Thus, the knee angle is always positive during running because the knee cannot hyperextend during normal running gait, and the leg is never perfectly straight at the knee.

At the moment of foot strike, the knee angle is somewhere between 0 and 25 degrees in the heel-striking runner and usually significantly greater in the midfoot striker. An increase in knee angle helps the heel striker position his or her foot more closely under the center of gravity of the body and is probably why impact forces tend to be smaller in midfoot-striking runners compared with heel strikers. With greater flexion, the knee can function more like a spring-like device instead of being part of a stiff pole extending from foot to hip.

The knee angle increases for roughly the first third of stance as the knee flexes to absorb the shock of impact with the ground. At the end of this first third, the knee joint is maximally flexed for the stance phase of gait, and the knee gradually goes through extension as the rest of stance unfolds in preparation for a nearly straight-legged toe-off, with an angle of almost 0 degrees at the knee. The greater initial knee flexion associated with midfoot striking helps explain why the stance phase is shorter in duration for the runner who strikes midfoot; maximal knee flexion can be reached more quickly from the preflexed state, followed closely by knee extension.

The muscles that govern the knee joint track these actions during stance. The rectus femoris muscle is active during the first part of stance to control the knee and prevent excessive flexion. The vastus lateralis and vastus medialis become extremely active about one-third of the way through stance as the knee joint begins to extend, presumably to control rotational movements of the knee that would block optimal force production at toe-off but also to straighten the knee as stance proceeds in preparation for toe-off. The hamstrings are active during the first two-thirds of stance, which would ordinarily be expected to increase knee angle throughout this part of stance. However, the hamstrings tend to be overruled by the rectus femoris and vastus muscles so that knee extension can proceed. In reality, the hamstrings are more occupied with the thigh and hip because they are engaged in the process of hip extension.

The knee angle increases through the first 50 percent of swing, moving above 90 degrees (see figure 4.8) before retreating back to an angle of near 0 degrees again just before foot strike in the heel striker. The vastus lateralis, vastus medialis, and hamstring muscles are all relatively quiet as the knee angle increases; they don't reach full activity until the final 30 to 40 percent of swing. It is only the rectus femoris that is truly active during the first half of swing, and it is obviously acting to increase forward swing of the thigh rather than to block knee flexion. The knee flexes during the first half of swing because there is nothing to stop it from doing so; it begins to extend during the second half of swing as the hamstrings and glutes kick into gear to slow down forward movement of the thigh, giving the lower part of the leg a chance to catch up.

▶ **Figure 4.8** During the first half of the swing phase, the knee angle increases, optimally moving above 90 degrees.

Ankle

The functions of the ankle during running are to produce propulsive force during stance via plantar flexion of the ankle and to stabilize the leg and upper body by resisting excessive pronation, inward rolling of the ankle, and supination, the ankle's outward movement. To understand how the ankle works during running, it is important to comprehend what is meant by ankle angle, which is defined as the angle between the bottom of the foot and an imaginary line that begins at the knee, runs down the shin and through the heel, and extends past the bottom of the foot at the heel. (A 0-degree angle would have the foot pointing directly down from the shin.) When the foot is flat on the ground as a runner stands in place, the knee is locked, and the leg is straight, and this angle is 90 degrees. Angles greater than 90 degrees signal ankle dorsiflexion with toes moving toward shin (figure 4.9a) while angles less than 90 degrees indicate ankle plantarflexion, with the toes moving away from the shin (figure 4.9b).

Ankle angle at foot strike depends on whether a runner is a forefoot, midfoot or heel striker (see figure 4.4). For the heel striker, ankle angle tends to be greater than 90 degrees at first impact with the ground (figure 4.10a), while ankle angle is close to 90 degrees for the midfoot striker (figure 4.10b) and less than 90 degrees for the forefoot athlete. Ankle angle quickly increases as the foot passes through dorsiflexion during the first 60 percent of stance but then decreases steadily as the ankle moves toward toe-off. At toe-off, the ankle is plantar flexed, with the angle typically at 67 degrees. Over the course of swing, the ankle angle gradually increases, reaching close to 90 degrees again for the following foot strike.

Two key muscles work in opposition to each other to control ankle angle (figure 4.11). The gastrocnemius muscle plantar-flexes the ankle and controls the rate and range of dorsiflexion, and the tibialis anterior muscle dorsiflexes the ankle and controls the rate and range of plantar flexion.

▶ **Figure 4.9** The ankle angle increases with *(a)* dorsiflexion and decreases with *(b)* plantar flexion.

▶ **Figure 4.10** At foot strike, the ankle is *(a)* at an angle greater than 90 degrees for a heel striker and *(b)* at about 90 degrees for a midfoot striker.

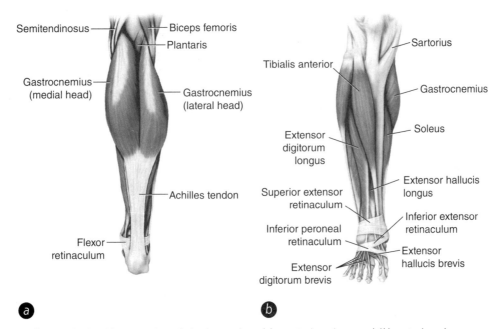

▶ **Figure 4.11** The muscles of the lower leg: *(a)* posterior view and *(b)* anterior view.

During the first part of stance, as the ankle dorsiflexes, the gastrocnemius muscle is active in its role as a dorsiflexion controller. As the ankle unwinds over the second part of stance and moves into plantar flexion, the gastrocnemius becomes inactive from an EMG standpoint. This doesn't mean that the gastrocnemius is not working and producing force. In fact, this muscle is highly stretched during dorsiflexion, and its snapback motion provides much of the force for the plantar flexion that can produce a powerful toe-off. No nervous system stimulation is required for this snapback; it happens as naturally as the recoil of a stretched-out rubber band, without any need for additional energy input. Thus, the EMG recording for the gastrocnemius toward the end of stance shows no activity despite the considerable force being produced.

Surprisingly, the tibialis anterior muscle mimics the gastrocnemius during the first third of stance as dorsiflexion is occurring. This is perhaps because one of the functions of the tibialis anterior muscle is to prevent rotational actions of the ankle, which could become a problem during the first part of stance. The tibialis anterior muscle becomes totally inactive during the plantar flexion phase of stance. It is as though it is saying, "Let it happen: Nothing should be blocking the strong forces that can be produced by the gastrocnemius to achieve toe-off and get the body flying forward."

During swing, the tibialis anterior is very active, especially during the middle stages. Apparently, the muscle is producing the forces required to get the ankle into neutral position for foot strike because the ankle is significantly plantar flexed at toe-off. The gastrocnemius stays out of swing until near the end when it becomes active in order to prevent too much dorsiflexion at the initial moment of foot strike—and when it stiffens itself properly for the inevitable dorsiflexion that follows the beginning of foot strike. If the gastrocnemius were not active at the end of swing, the ankle would flop into dorsiflexion like a limp noodle at the beginning of stance, and there would be less energy returned in order to move the ankle into plantar flexion and provide a powerful toe-off.

Upper Body

The actions of the upper body during running involve the pelvic area, core muscles, and arms. The functions of the upper body during running are to provide an anchor point against which the legs can work with strength and economy, maintain proper posture in order to avoid a negative impact on stride length and rate, and balance forward actions of the legs so that the body does not move excessively in rotational directions.

Upper body actions are coordinated with leg movements during running. When the left leg moves forward during swing, there is a natural tendency for the torso to rotate in a clockwise fashion. This tendency is counteracted during running by actions of the abdominal muscles and a forward swing of the right arm: These actions create forces directed in a counterclockwise motion that stabilize the body, conserve energy, and prevent excessive, washtub-like torso movements. As the right leg moves forward during swing, it initiates a counterclockwise upper body movement that is then counteracted by a simultaneous forward movement of the left arm and appropriate abdominal muscle actions.

A strong, stabilizing abdominal core and appropriate arm actions that are synchronous with the opposite leg during swing should enhance running economy and improve running performances because oxygen-consuming muscular actions would not be needed to correct unproductive and energy-wasting movements. No study has ever directly linked upper-body mechanics and running performance, however. Some research has suggested that the effects of seemingly inappropriate upper-body movements on running-relevant physiological factors are small. In one study, running while holding the arms directly overhead instead of coordinating them with the legs (a major change in upper-body kinematics) harmed running economy by only 1 percent.[2] This may be why Zatopek succeeded with ungraceful form. However, most athletes and coaches are aware that a 1 percent difference can be highly significant during competition; for example, it represents the difference between a 2:07 and a 2:05:44 marathon.

Stretch-Shortening Cycle

Runners may be surprised by the biomechanical information presented in this chapter so far because it seems to defy conventional wisdom about how the muscles produce the forces necessary to sustain running. The hamstrings, for example, are supposed to contract and provide the force necessary for hip extension while the foot is on the ground, yet biomechanical analysis reveals that the hamstrings are actually most active during swing when the leg is moving forward and the thigh is flexed.

One basic problem is that runners are routinely taught that there are three basic types of muscle activity:

- Isometric actions—a muscle exerts force without lengthening or shortening
- Concentric contractions—a muscle produces force, shortens, and moves a body part
- Eccentric actions—a muscle creates force but elongates instead of shortening[3]

It is natural to expect that the leg muscles use these actions to produce the propulsive and braking forces required to run on firm ground. However, as the Finnish exercise physiologist Paavo Komi has pointed out, the fundamental aspect of muscle activity during running is quite different.[4] Movement and propulsion during running are produced by what is called the stretch-shortening cycle (SSC), in which a leg muscle is first stretched (preactivated) and then recoils, producing with each snapback the propulsive force that moves the body forward. This has extremely important consequences for strength training for running and for pure running training.

A close inspection of hamstring actions during running illustrates the operation of the SSC. As mentioned, a popular conception among runners and coaches is that the hamstrings move a runner's body ahead by contracting while the foot is on the ground, thereby extending the hip and pushing the upper body forward.

EMG measures the electrical activity of muscles, the degree to which the muscles are using energy to generate force. In the case of the hamstrings, EMG recordings show that these key muscles are actually only moderately active during the first two-thirds of stance, the portion of the overall gait cycle when a foot is on the ground, when they are supposedly working to create propulsive forces. Surprisingly, the hamstrings are totally inactive during the last third of stance, when they are supposedly driving the body forward.[1] The hamstrings produce the propulsive force required to move the body forward by being stretched, or preactivated, during swing and then recoiling elastically and snapping back like a rubber band during stance; this recoil extends the hip and pushes the body forward. Thus, it is the operation of the SSC in the hamstrings, not active concentric contractions, that produces propulsion.

From an EMG standpoint, the hamstrings are actually most active toward the end of swing, just before their associated foot hits the ground. This is because the hamstrings are producing braking force for the swinging leg, helping to keep the leg under control and preparing for the impending collision with the ground. The hamstrings are also preactivating themselves, becoming stiffer so that the resulting recoil after ground impact will be a forceful, economical action. If the hamstrings are too loose, they will act like limp pieces of spaghetti when the foot hits the ground, producing sloppy, slow, and low-power recoil.

An understanding of the SSC is essential for designing optimal strength training for runners. A key goal of such strength training is to optimize the amount of propulsive force generated by the leg muscles during running. However, gains in strength are always specific to the movements used during strength training. Working the hamstrings in a manner that does not replicate the SSC will not maximize gains in running-specific strength; in fact, it might not lead to any increases at all.[5]

For example, many runners rely on traditional fundamental exercises such as hamstring or thigh curls in their attempts to boost hamstring strength,[6,7] even though such exertions have little resemblance to the stretch-shortening cycle. During hamstring curls, the hamstrings are stimulated by the nervous system and expend energy to contract as they are exerting force, the exact opposite of what happens during running when the hamstrings shorten and generate force by recoiling elastically. When hamstring curls are performed, the essential swing phase of hamstring action is totally missing, and thus the hamstrings' key running-related action—exerting braking force and stiffening at the very end of swing—is not replicated or strengthened. There is no moment of high activation at the end of swing when hamstring curls are conducted. A much better hamstring-strengthening exercise for runners, one that includes hamstring activation at the end of swing and elastic recoil, would be bicycle leg swings. This exercise and other drills that emphasize the SSC of muscle activity are presented in chapter 14.

During running, the hamstrings are not alone in their preference for SSC activity, as opposed to isolated concentric, eccentric, or isometric actions. The all-important gastrocnemius muscle in the calf is automatically stretched during running whenever the foot hits the ground. This ground impact forces the ankle joint into dorsiflexion, a joint-angle change that stretches the gastrocnemius significantly.

A traditional view is that the gastrocnemius is fully active during stance, creating the force necessary to plantar-flex the ankle, lift the heel, and move the foot into toe-off position so that the body can soar forward through the air before landing on the opposite foot. EMG analysis reveals that the gastrocnemius is actually barely active during the last half of the stance phase and not active at all over the final 25 percent of stance. Like the hamstrings, the gastrocnemius uses elastic recoil energy to provide propulsive force rather than an energy-consuming concentric contraction. Also like the hamstrings, the gastrocnemius becomes preactivated just before the foot makes contact with the ground in order to control impending dorsiflexion and provide a stiffer, stronger spring that increases force production during subsequent gastrocnemius snapback.[1]

Conventional exercises employed by runners to enhance gastrocnemius strength fail to simulate the SSC. One popular exercise, heel raises, uses concentric contractions of the gastrocnemius throughout the full range of plantar flexion, quite different from the pattern established by the gastrocnemius during the stance phase of running. Heel raises help to build general strength in the gastrocnemius, but fail to properly preload the muscle in a manner specific to running. A far better and much more specific—but seldom-used—gastrocnemius strengthener would be an exercise called falls to earth with forward hops. This exercise—and others like it that rely on the SSC—is described fully in chapter 14.

Conclusion

For the runner and coach, the study of biomechanics is extremely important. It leads to a comprehension of how the human body actually works during running and thus a firm grasp of how to strengthen running-relevant movements. The specificity of training principle, developed after years of research, reveals that motions are strengthened optimally through the use of training movements that effectively mimic those motions. Thus, drills and exercises bearing a small to moderate resemblance to the actual movements of running gait will have a much smaller impact on running capacity than those routines that are highly running specific and in line with our understanding of running biomechanics.

CHAPTER 5

Refinement in Running Form

The science of running form is still in its infancy, but there are a number of studies that have linked adjustments in running form with positive changes in running economy (the oxygen-consumption rate associated with a specific running velocity), competitive performances, or the risks of various running-related injuries. Endurance runners should nonetheless be wary about running-form transformations advocated by so-called running-form experts, prescribed by coaches, or proposed in magazine articles; often there are very little or no scientific data available to support these recommendations in these forums. Runners interested in changing form should rely on the results of well-controlled scientific research rather than on fad or unsupported speculation.

Research on Running Form

In an investigation of form carried out at Wake Forest University, researchers Stephen Messier and K.J. Cirillo worked with 11 runners over a 5-week period.[1] Three times per week, the Wake Forest scientists discussed their conceptions of proper running form with the runners and displayed videotapes of athletes with allegedly excellent form as the subjects ran on laboratory treadmills. As a result of the instruction, the 11 runners gradually transformed their gait characteristics in the following ways:

1. They increased stride length slightly so that more ground was covered with each step during running.
2. They decreased the amount of time spent in the support phase of running so that the feet didn't rest lazily on the ground.
3. They lifted the heel more forcefully at the end of the contact phase of stance in order to provide a more vigorous push-off.
4. They flexed the knee to a greater extent during leg swing to increase the speed of swing.

5. They flexed the knee to a greater degree at impact in order to facilitate shock absorption.

6. They kept the trunk slightly flexed forward as they ran.

7. They held their forearms at 90-degree angles to the upper portions of their arms as the arms moved back and forth.

8. They landed on the heel and rolled forward to the front of the foot with each step.

Note that some of these advocated changes are controversial. For example, it is not clear that an expansion of stride length (1) would be advantageous for all runners; it might actually create greater braking force per step because the foot would be farther in front of the center of mass and thus harm running economy. It is also not certain that the trunk should be flexed during running (6); while the entire body should probably be inclined forward, trunk flexion per se could prestretch the lower back and gluteus muscles and decrease stride length. Heel striking (8) is the recommendation that arouses the most suspicion: Compared with midfoot striking, heel striking has been linked with longer ground-contact times and higher impact forces that are undesirable running gait features.

Messier and Cirillo suspected that the changes in form would improve running economy in the 11 runners after the 5 weeks of training. Many coaches of endurance runners would agree that most of the preceding changes are desirable. However, the 11 athletes were not even slightly more economical with oxygen at the end of the study. Even though the runners looked more graceful as they ran, their average rate of oxygen consumption for any chosen speed was the same as it had been prior to the form makeovers. Assessment of economy is a very logical way to determine whether form makeovers are actually valuable. Running economy is a valid predictor of endurance performance. It is the oxygen cost of running and is expressed as milliliters of oxygen used per kilogram of body weight per minute.

One goal of form transformations is to make runners more economical, another is to decrease the risk of injury, and a third is to enhance performance. The recommended enhancements in form also failed to make running *feel* any easier for the 11 runners in the Wake Forest study. When the subjects ran at a typical training intensity, they looked better than before, but to them the workout felt as tough as it had always been.[2]

The study can be criticized for its use of controversial transformations and also for its brevity: There is no specific reason to believe that a 5-week period is long enough for running economy to improve in response to a change in running form; economy enhancement might take longer. Running economy probably depends to some extent on muscle length, dynamic mobility of joints, muscle and tendon flexibility and stiffness, and other factors that could respond to training over longer periods of time.

Messier and Cirillo's research also raises the possibility that each runner may adopt a style of running that, although it might look awkward or unconventional, actually produces the best economy for that individual and his or her unique anatomical and neuromuscular characteristics; in such cases, a shift to a smoother or more acceptable style could actually harm running capacity. Supporting this notion, research reveals that economy deteriorates and oxygen cost increases for *most* runners when they increase or decrease their stride rate even slightly.[3] Runners tend to be most economical when they run with their freely chosen stride lengths, even when they appear to observers to be overstriding or understriding.

In their laboratory at Penn State University, biomechanics researchers Peter Cavanagh and Keith Williams studied stride length and economy in 10 fit runners as they moved along at a 7-minute-per-mile pace.[4] Cavanagh and Williams found that most of the runners naturally moved along with very close to their most economical stride lengths. On average, the 10 runners were merely an inch away from their optimal stride lengths, the ones that produced the lowest oxygen cost during running, and that small deviation away from the optimum boosted oxygen-consumption rate by a paltry 0.4 percent.

Athletes in other sports also appear to use their most economical stride lengths. Research carried out with race walkers reveals that the oxygen cost of race walking increases when the athletes increase or decrease their stride lengths by just 5 percent of leg length.[5] However, it is important to note that the conclusion that runners naturally adopt the best stride length is not without a troubling caveat: The initial, immediate downturns in economy associated with stride-length change might be due simply to the nervous system's unfamiliarity with the new stride length, thus resulting in a diminishment of control by the nervous system and a greater degree of uncoordinated, uneconomical movement. With gradual nervous system adaptation, however, the new stride length might actually become effective over time—even better than the freely chosen original style.

In addition, it is undoubtedly true that some runners use suboptimal stride lengths and should undergo a stride transformation. One athlete in Cavanagh and Williams' investigation tended to overstride by about 2.5 inches per stride, an expansion that would have tacked an extra 3 minutes to his marathon time and forced him to use an extra 10 liters of oxygen over the course of the race compared with the oxygen use associated with his most economical stride length.[2] Despite what experts may say, it can be difficult to detect such form problems and oxygen issues merely by *watching* an athlete run; laboratory testing with oxygen-measuring equipment is required for definitive diagnosis.

Kinematics of Improved Form

Research concerning the kinematics of running has provided strong clues about ways in which endurance runners might improve form. Nancy Hamilton at the University of Northern Iowa has approached the form problem from a unique angle by linking changes in running form to the process of aging.[6] The impetus for her research came from her observation that running performances and running form change significantly and simultaneously as runners get older. Traditionally, most investigators have linked age-related performance falloffs with declines in cardiac power and losses in muscle mass and strength, but Hamilton wondered whether alterations in form might also account for an important part of the performance downturn (note that drop-offs in muscular strength would probably alter form, so the factors may be linked). Hamilton set out to identify those aspects of form that must be preserved in order to sustain fast velocities and run economically at quality speeds.

At the 1989 World Veterans' Games in Eugene and the National Championships in San Diego, California, Hamilton spent many hours filming 162 competitive runners (83 males and 79 females) as they engaged in competition. She then digitized the performances into a computer and devoted hundreds of hours to analyzing the runners' kinematics. Fast runners were compared with slow ones, and senior runners were compared with younger individuals. Hamilton was unable to measure running economy, but she did identify three aspects of running form that were linked to higher maximal running speeds and superior performances: (1) greater hip extension at push-off, (2) increased knee flexion during forward swing, and (3) avoidance of excessive knee flexion during stance. These as well as some factors based on other research are discussed in detail in the sections that follow.

Hip Extension at Push-Off

Hamilton demonstrated that maximal running speed declined by about 40 percent between the ages of 35 and 90, and range of motion at the hip fell by 38 percent. This decrease in range of motion at the hip was tightly connected to the direct cause of the falloff in maximal running velocity: a drop in stride length. While stride *rate* during top-speed running for runners in their eighties was only 4 to 5 percent lower than that of runners in their thirties, stride *length* declined by nearly 40 percent for older runners.

The fundamental factor associated with the decline in stride length was a loss of range of motion at the hip during running. Hamilton found that the key to optimal range of motion at the hip during high-speed running was the conservation of hip mobility in the kick or drive phase of running: When the foot becomes a lever for toe-off, the gluteal and hamstring muscles recoil to propel the leg backward, and the quads also activate themselves to straighten the leg for the backward push. The basic motion during the drive phase is hip extension—the backward movement of the leg at the hip. A decline in hip extension means that less force is applied to the ground with each step, and thus stride length must shorten (with less force exerted, the body flies a shorter distance forward per step). What was lost with aging was hip extension and thus stride length and speed, not hip flexion.

Hamilton argued that significant hip extension is a key element of good form and suggested that a runner should deliberately alter the way in which he or she runs, focusing on the muscles around the buttocks so that they push backward with significant amounts of force with each step. "Rather than reaching out with the leg in an effort to get maximal forward distance, a runner should think about pushing back as forcefully as possible with each step," said Hamilton. "Runners should use the buttocks and hamstrings to do so, very much the way a sprinter pushes out hard from a set of starting blocks."[7]

It is possible that greater hip extension during the end stage of stance can be developed in response to specific training strategies, including high-speed running, hill training, speed bounding, and the deliberate mental focus on hip extension Hamilton recommends. This possibility has yet to be demonstrated in scientific research, however, primarily because no one has studied it. It is clear that enhanced dynamic flexibility of the quadriceps muscles would be required in order to permit augmented hip extension since overly tight quads would resist backward movements of the legs. Systematic stretching of the quads and drills that increase the quadriceps' dynamic flexibility (for example, the explosive one-leg squats with lateral hops described in the speed progression section of chapter 28) could be very productive from a hip-extension standpoint.

Knee Flexion During the Swing Phase

Hamilton found that increased knee flexion during the swing phase of gait was another form factor that correlated with higher maximal speed. (This was also one of the eight aspects of gait recommended by Messier and Cirillo in the Wake Forest study discussed earlier.) With her video analysis, Hamilton demonstrated that the fastest runners had their knees highly flexed during the swing phase of gait so that their feet were significantly angled toward their buttocks (see figure 5.1). The slowest runners held their knees less flexed during swing so that the lower part of the leg was essentially at a right angle with the thigh.

Keeping the knee less flexed and the foot down at the level of the knee during swing—rather than having the foot perched near the buttocks—as the leg is brought forward to prepare for the next contact with the ground converts the leg into an extra-long lever with a heavy foot dangling at its

▶ **Figure 5.1** Runner with highly flexed knee and foot angled toward buttocks during the swing phase.

end. When the knee is highly flexed, the lever is no longer than the distance from the hip to the knee; when the knee is less flexed, the lever length extends to the foot. Less flexion of the knee is a negative during the swing phase of running because longer levers are harder to move compared with short levers. Longer levers require more force and thus more oxygen to move. In addition, the foot represents a significant weight, and having a large weight at the end of a long lever makes it very difficult to accelerate forward. This is why the heavier person on a teeter-totter tends to remain planted on the ground unless he or she moves toward the middle.

In running, as the leg moves forward during swing, it is best to have the knee highly flexed and the foot tucked up by the buttocks, in effect cutting the leg lever almost in half by making the knee—rather than the foot—the endpoint of the limb. It is unclear whether runners can increase knee flexion during swing simply by practicing this form adjustment. Once again, upgrades in the quadriceps' dynamic flexibility should have the positive effect of making the knee joint more permissive during swing and allow a greater range of flexion.

Excessive Knee Flexion During Stance

Hamilton discovered that while knee flexion was very good during swing, excessive knee flexion was a negative factor during stance when the foot was on the ground. The problem with too much knee flexion during stance is that extra time must then be taken to straighten the knee out again just before push-off. "The greater the flexion of the knee during stance, the greater the amount of time spent in stance," Hamilton noted.[7] This makes it more difficult for a runner to reach his or her true speed potential since too great a time is being spent with the feet attached to fixed points on terra firma.

Decreases in knee flexion during stance that lead to reductions in contact time can have significant effects on performance. An experienced female road racer who requires 32 minutes to complete a 10K and takes 190 steps per minute during the race will need $32 \times 190 = 6{,}080$ steps to get from the starting line to the finish. If she lands with stiffer legs (i.e., with less flexion at the knees) and thus saves just 5 milliseconds per step—and there is no loss in stride length associated with the stiffer landings—her race time will improve by $6{,}080 \times .005 = 30.4$ seconds, an excellent performance upswing.

Research has shown that increased leg stiffness is also associated with enhanced running economy (see chapter 8 for more on running economy). In one study in which knee stiffness decreased and knee flexion increased during the stance phase of running, the oxygen cost of movement increased by almost 50 percent.[8] Scientific research has revealed that explosive strength training increases leg stiffness, probably to some extent by limiting knee flexion during stance. Endurance runners are wise to use explosive strength training (see chapter 28) since it appears to optimize various aspects of form, including shortening the stance phase of gait, increasing leg stiffness, upgrading dynamic flexibility of the quads, and promoting hip-extension range and power.

Vertical Oscillation

Additional components of good form have been substantiated in other inquiries. Research has shown that elite runners have less vertical change in their centers of mass during running; that is, the center of mass moves *upward* to a smaller extent during the jumps from one foot to the other for elite runners than for middle-of-the-pack competitors. The investigations have also revealed that a reduction in vertical movement during running tends to enhance economy.[9] A focus on pushing or bouncing *forward* with each step during running, instead of pushing or bouncing upward, should be helpful in reducing vertical oscillation of the center of mass. Leaning forward from the ankles slightly during stance instead of adopting a completely upright posture during gait should also help decrease vertical oscillation (see figure 5.2).

Straight Leg at Toe-Off

Having an almost straight leg at toe-off (similar to Hamilton's hip-extension conclusion) has been linked with upgraded running economy when compared with maintaining greater flexion at the knee at the end of stance[9] (see figure 5.3). It appears to be important to eliminate knee flexion almost totally at the moment of toe-off but then rapidly flex the knee for the subsequent swing stage of the gait cycle.

Research carried out by Williams and Cavanagh has demonstrated that heightened plantar flexion of the ankle at toe-off and increased *rapidity* of plantar flexion are also associated with enhanced running economy.[10] The optimal anatomical position, or form, for toe-off seems to be a straight leg

▶ **Figure 5.2** Runners can enhance economy by focusing on moving forward instead of upward and decreasing the vertical movement of the center of mass.

▶ **Figure 5.3** Runner using a nearly straight leg during toe-off.

with fully pointed toes. No scientific research has explored the question of how to train to advance the rapidity and extent of plantar flexion at toe-off, but logic suggests that high-speed running and explosive drills would have the greatest effect on these variables.

Economical Arm Swing

Many runners, believing that arm movements help propel them forward, use rather expansive arm swings while running. Scientific research convincingly shows that this is not a good strategy. Faster, more economical runners actually tend to have less arm movement than slower, less-economical competitors.[11] Quick, *little* arm movements carried out in synchrony with the swings of the legs (i.e., right arm swings forward as left leg moves ahead, and vice-versa) appear to be the ones that produce the most economical running.[12] This is one form change runners should be able to make consciously without much effort. Swinging the arms across the front of the body is energy consuming and unlikely to be linked with optimal economy. The arms should swing forward and backward.

Excessive movements of the upper body have been linked with poor economy. As both the speed and amount of rotation of the shoulders and hips around the center axis of the body increase during running, economy is harmed.[12] Such washtub motions are controlled by the body's core muscles, the muscles of the torso that attach to the pelvic girdle and spine, bringing into focus the potential importance of acquiring great, running-specific core strength. Optimal routines for increasing core strength are described in chapter 13.

Foot-Strike Pattern

Another form factor—foot-strike pattern—may have a very strong impact on running economy, performance, and the incidence of injury. Although foot-strike pattern is an essential element of form, it is often ignored by runners or simply assumed to be okay. Foot-strike technique has a strong impact on the duration of stance phase of gait, stride rate, and the work performed by various muscles of the feet, ankles, and legs during running. Although research in this area is still rudimentary, foot-strike pattern is likely to have an effect on running economy, competitive performance, and the likelihood of overuse injuries.

The two most commonly used foot-strike techniques are the rear-foot strike or striking pattern (RFS), in which the heel of the running shoe (or foot for the unshod runner) is the first structure to make impact with the ground during gait, and the midfoot strike or striking pattern (MFS), in which the middle portion of the running shoe's sole (or sole of the foot) makes initial contact or at least makes contact simultaneously with the heel. RFS is more popular than MFS: In a recent, elite-level half marathon, about 75 percent of participants were using the RFS pattern at the 15K point of the race, 24 percent were using MFS, and 1 percent were using the forefoot strike or striking pattern (FFS), in which the front portion of the foot hits the ground first.[13]

Fast Runners and MFS

While experienced runners tend to favor RFS over MFS by at least a three-to-one margin, motion analysis of Olympic Games competitors has suggested that Olympic medalists are more likely to employ MFS. In addition, video analysis of world-champion and world-record-holding runners, including Paul Tergat, Haile Gebrselassie, and Paula Radcliffe, has indicated that such competitors employ MFS and occasionally FFS, but not RFS, while training and competing.

Research has also shown that the frequency of the MFS pattern increases with competitive ability; in a study carried out with elite and near-elite runners, 36 percent of the male, top-50 finishers employed MFS in a race as contrasted with just 20 percent of runners finishing in places 51 through 200 in the same competition.[13] In this investigation, MFS was used by 3 of the first 7 female finishers (43 percent) but by only 4 of the other 28 (14 percent) slower women in the race.

Compared with RFS, performance may be enhanced with MFS because ground-contact time is shorter by about 17 milliseconds at a running velocity of approximately 5 to 5.5 meters (16-18 ft) per second and by approximately 10 milliseconds at slower speeds. As a consequence of the more abridged contact time, stride rate is also higher for MFS at any specific speed. Decreases in ground-contact time and increases in stride rate have been linked with enhanced running economy and faster 5K performances.[14] In addition, a key difference between the top competitors and the slower performers in an elite road race is the shorter average ground-contact time of the faster finishers. Such findings suggest that MFS may be the superior foot-strike pattern from a competitive standpoint.

Comparing MFS and RFS

Although the world's best endurance runners prefer MFS over RFS, the effects of either on running economy have yet to be completely determined. One study has detected enhanced economy with RFS compared with MFS. Research has also revealed that runners tend to adopt the most economical running style possible for their individual anatomical and physiological characteristics. At least 75 percent of experienced runners favor RFS over MFS, suggesting that rear-foot striking may be the most economical pattern. However, another strong possibility is that highly cushioned, big-heeled modern running shoes tend to push runners toward an RFS pattern even though it is suboptimal; this will be discussed further in chapter 6.

Although RFS is the most popular way to hit the ground during running, it is important to note that it is highly likely the world's best endurance runners have optimized most aspects of their running mechanics, and that such optimization has elevated them to their superelite status. Given that running economy is such a strong predictor of performance, the ubiquity of MFS among superelite runners suggests that MFS may produce highly economical running. Compared with MFS, it is also clear that RFS leads to a more extended leg at foot strike and a longer time of maximal knee flexion during the support phase of gait. This suggests that RFS produces a longer period of muscle activation per running step, which might increase the oxygen cost of running and lead to poorer economy with the RFS pattern.

Interestingly, runners who have trained barefooted for their entire running careers almost always employ MFS rather than RFS, and runners who shift from shod to unshod running tend to change from RFS to MFS as part of this changeover. Compared with shod locomotion, barefoot running is more economical, is linked with a higher stride rate, and limits impact forces traveling up the legs. These positive aspects of barefoot running may be strongly tied to the nearly universal use of the MFS pattern. (See chapter 6 for more about barefoot running.)

There is very little scientific information available to assess whether the MFS and RFS patterns have different effects on the likelihood of running injury. Ground-reaction force (GRF) is thought to be an important predictor of running injury: Runners with higher vertical maximal forces tend to experience greater lower-extremity pain, and elite runners with elevated GRFs tend to have an increased risk of stress fracture. The extent of motion around the ankle and knee joints during gait is also believed to be a predictive factor for injury.

It is clear that MFS and RFS produce different GRF patterns. Runners who employ RFS generally demonstrate a pronounced, initial spike in GRF during the first few moments of stance, which is usually absent when MFS is the ground-contact strategy. In contrast, average peak-to-peak amplitude for *mediolateral* GRF can often be three times greater in MFS runners than in RFS competitors.

Research reveals that MFS and RFS are associated with different patterns of muscular work, force production, and power absorption in various parts of the leg during running. Compared with RFS, MFS has been linked with higher peak power absorption and eccentric work at the ankle during gait. It is possible that these effects may lead to overworking the lower-leg muscle groups and increase the risk of Achilles tendon injury for MFS runners. An alternative possibility is that the use of MFS will progressively lead to dramatic improvements in ankle strength compared with using the RFS pattern. Anecdotal evidence suggests that runners who attempt to convert from RFS to MFS experience significant muscle fatigue and sometimes severe delayed-onset muscle soreness in their calves, although these factors may merely be the result of a change in running style and thus motor-recruitment patterns rather than a reflection of the negative characteristics of MFS. Runners changing from RFS to MFS should do so gradually to permit the neuromuscular system to adjust optimally to the new gait pattern.

Although RFS may reduce the forces placed on the ankle during running, research suggests that it tends to increase the power absorption and total work performed at the knee as compared with MFS. Thus, it is possible that RFS could be connected with a higher rate of knee injury.

Accelerometers attached to the skin or embedded in the tibia have been used to gauge loads placed on the lower extremities during running. Accelerometer studies demonstrate that peak acceleration measures are greater at slower stride rates, and thus longer stride lengths, for any specific running speed. Such data suggest that the loading rate for impact forces would be lessened by a shift from RFS to MFS since the latter is strongly linked with higher stride rates and shorter strides.

It is clear that the differing effects of MFS and RFS on ground-reaction forces, rotational forces, and muscle and tendon strain in various parts of the leg during running are not yet completely understood. However, future research will probably find that MFS

- enhances economy because it is not associated with the braking effect present with RFS,

- promotes performance because of shorter foot-strike times and thus higher stride rates, and

- lessens the likelihood of injury because of its lower level of strain placed on the knee as compared with RFS.

Shin Angle

A critically important—but almost completely ignored—element of running form is shin angle at impact with the ground. Shin angle can be defined as the angle the shin makes with the ground as the foot makes first contact and initiates the stance phase of gait (see figure 5.4). By definition, if the shin is perfectly perpendicular to the ground, the shin angle is 0 or neutral. If the shin is inclined forward from an imaginary line drawn perpendicular to the ground at the impact point, then the shin angle is positive. If the shin is inclined backward from the imaginary line, then the shin angle is negative.

Shin angle is tremendously consequential during endurance running because horizontal *braking* force increases as shin angle becomes more positive.[15] A runner whose shin angle advances in a positive direction must use more force, energy, and oxygen per step to overcome the braking force that is automatically created compared with another runner traveling at the same speed whose shin angle is less positive.

The problems associated with a large positive shin angle can be discerned from table 5.1, which examines shin angle in the momentous 2011 Boston Marathon. (In this particular race, two men completed the competition in

▶ **Figure 5.4** *(a)* Positive and *(b)* negative shin angles.

Table 5.1 Shin Angles of Elite Runners in the 2011 Boston Marathon

Runner	Race placement	Shin angle at contact
SMALLER SHIN ANGLE		
Maasai boy	For comparison with the marathon runners	Vertical –4 degrees (shortly after contact and, yes, that is a minus sign)
Geoffrey Mutai	Men's champion in world-record time (unofficial)	Vertical +3 degrees
Moses Mosop	2nd place, men's division	Vertical +4 degrees
Gebre Gebremariam	3rd place, men's division	Vertical +5 degrees
Caroline Kilel	Women's champion	Vertical +7 degrees
LARGER SHIN ANGLE		
Ryan Hill	4th place in American record time (unofficial)	Vertical +12 degrees
Sharon Cherop	3rd place, women's division	Vertical +12 degrees
Kara Goucher	5th place, women's division in personal best time	Vertical +16 degrees
Desiree Davila	2nd place, women's division in personal best time	Vertical +20 degrees

Unpublished data used courtesy of Walter Reynolds, III.

times faster than the world record, and American runner Desiree Davila made a strong bid to win the race outright.)

The reader will note that the first-, second-, and third-place male finishers all come from the group with smaller positive shin angles while Ryan Hall, the American entrant, had a large shin angle and finished fourth. On the women's side, the winner, Caroline Kilel, ran with a relatively small shin angle, 65 percent smaller than that of Desiree Davila, the second-place American finisher. It is tempting to speculate that Davila could have beaten Kilel had she not had to overcome greater braking forces with each step. It is also reasonable to assume that Hall would have been much closer to Geoffrey Mutai and Moses Mosop had he employed a smaller shin angle.

Stride Rate

Having a relatively high stride rate is an element of form associated with higher performance and enhanced economy. Studies reveal that elite runners almost always use stride rates of 180 steps per minute *or greater* during competitive situations, while less accomplished runners often move along at about 170 steps per minute. It is interesting to note that increasing stride rate—not elongating stride length—is also the primary way in which most runners upgrade their maximal running velocity. Runners can work on increasing stride rate by running with a watch or metronome that beeps at the appropriate rate (3 times per second or 90 times per minute if one foot is being monitored). Alternatively, contacts with the right or left foot can be counted over a 1-minute period, and stride rate can consciously be adjusted upward if it is found to be slow. Using a midfoot strike and conducting explosive training also tend to heighten stride rate.

Pose Method

A so-called revolutionary new way of running was introduced by running-form researcher Nicholas Romanov. Called the pose running method, the technique involves striking the ground with the midfoot and maintaining a flexed knee during the stance phase of the gait cycle. The characteristic pose geometry is achieved with a simultaneous vertical alignment of the ipsilateral shoulder, hip, and heel of the supporting foot (see figure 5.5). From this posture, a runner is supposed to lean forward; in fact, movement is initiated with the forward fall of the upper body. As motion of the upper body is initiated, the supporting foot is lifted by flexing the knee; actual pushing away from the supporting surface (i.e., the ground) is avoided. Note how different this is from usual running. In each successive stance, contact is made with the ground by the midfoot (i.e., the ball of the foot), not the toes or the heel, and flexed knees are maintained throughout the entire gait cycle.

The pose method seems to be an attempt to let gravity provide a significant fraction of the energy required to move forward. Essentially, one is falling forward and then catching oneself with the forward-swinging foot instead of producing high-energy-cost, propulsive forces against the ground with the various leg muscles. There is an intuitive appeal to this approach: A similar pattern of gait has been observed in scientific studies of Kenyan women who manage to carry increasingly heavy loads without significantly expanding their energy expenditure.[16]

▶ **Figure 5.5** Vertical alignment of the ipsilateral shoulder, hip, and heel of the supporting foot as prescribed by the pose method.

In research carried out by Romanov and Tim Noakes of the University of Cape Town, the biomechanics of pose running were compared with heel-toe running and the midfoot-landing style.[17] Twenty male and female runners who normally ran with a heel-toe style were recruited from running clubs in the Cape Town area and were given instructions on how to run using the midfoot style and also using the pose method. It took them about 15 minutes to learn how to run with the midfoot-landing style and 7.5 hours to assimilate the pose technique. All of the runners then ran 10 different trials at self-selected speeds with each of the three styles of running (heel-toe, midfoot, and pose), and data related to running speed and biomechanical factors were collected as they ran.

As it turned out, the average speed selected by the subjects for midfoot running was about 6 percent faster than that used for pose running. Pose running was associated with shorter stride lengths and smaller vertical oscillations of the pelvic girdle compared with both heel-toe and midfoot running. With pose, the feet are kept closer to the ground and stride lengths are shorter, making a smaller arc of the center of mass as the body moves forward from one foot to the other. Naturally, since the pose method involves falling forward rather than launching oneself upward and forward with a strong push on the ground, stride lengths and vertical oscillations tend to be diminished.

Horizontal propulsive forces were lower with the pose method than with midfoot and heel-toe running. Although peak knee flexion during the swing phase of the gait cycle was the same in all three running styles, the knee flexed to a greater extent in preparation for initial foot contact with pose than with the other two styles. Finally, the eccentric work done at the knee during stance was less with pose than with heel-toe and midfoot running. Since the pose knee is already highly flexed when the foot hits the ground, the quads have very little eccentric work to do to control knee flexion during the stance phase. With both midfoot and heel-toe running, the knee is straighter when the foot strikes pay dirt, so the quads have a much bigger job controlling the resulting knee flexion that occurs, and thus eccentric work is greater. (The quads stretch as they work while the foot is on the ground, and so their task is termed eccentric.)

This might suggest that pose running would be more economical than the other styles since those large muscles, the quads, are doing less work, but the eccentric work carried out at the ankle during stance was actually *greater* with pose than with heel-toe and midfoot running. Perplexingly, the researchers did not publish any data related to running economy in relationship to the three styles, nor did they make any attempt to determine the effects of pose running on performance.

The lower eccentric work carried out at the knee during pose running might suggest that pose is kinder to the knees—or at least to the quads—during running and thus might be recommended for runners with knee problems. However, GRFs were equivalent between pose and midfoot running, even though midfoot running was carried out at a faster pace because GRFs usually increase as running speed goes up. No scientific research has explored the relationship between pose running and injury rates. Anecdotal reports indicate that most of the pose trainees in the study previously described became injured during the two-week period after the adoption of the technique. However, this sharp rise in injury rate might have resulted from the quick transition to pose running and the *changes* in work output required for various muscles in the pose-trained legs—particularly the muscles around the ankle areas, which have to work harder—rather than a fundamental deficiency in pose running per se. The lesson to be learned is probably not that pose produces many injuries but rather that any shift in running form must be adopted gradually, giving muscles, connective tissues, and nerves a chance to adapt.

A supporting, follow-up investigation completed by a team of researchers from the Exercise Science Department at Colorado State University at Pueblo revealed that 12 weeks of instruction in the pose method for a group of experienced triathletes actually led to a significant *deterioration* in running economy along with a reduction in stride length.[18] In these pose-trained athletes, the oxygen cost of running at a specific speed actually increased by about 8 percent over the course of the study.

Conclusion

The results of scientific research suggest that good running form is linked with the following:

- greater hip extension during the drive phase of gait,
- enhanced knee flexion during swing,
- augmented plantar flexion and a straighter leg during toe-off,
- smaller arm movements,
- limited upper-body motions,
- higher stride rates,
- midfoot striking,
- slight forward inclination of the body from the ankles during stance,
- flexion of the leg at the knee at initial moment of foot strike, with the foot relatively close to being under the center of mass (leg is not straight), and
- shin angle at 0 degrees or just slightly positive.

Coaches and runners can use this information in a very practical way. For example, a runner's metronome, sold online and at running-specialty stores, can be used to adjust stride rate. The use of a metronome can often help straighten out other form problems in addition to a slow stepping rate: When an athlete who has been running at 170 steps per minute suddenly begins to keep pace with a metronome set at 180, the stride rate obviously improves, the leg tends to be less straight at impact with the ground, the knee is more flexed at impact, the ground-contact pattern is more likely to be midfoot striking, and the foot will be more nearly under center of mass at impact, thus improving the previously described shin angle. Running unshod or with minimal shoes will also help a runner adjust form properly: Barefoot running makes it difficult to be a heel striker and thus increases stride rate and discourages landings where the leg is straight out in front of the body.

Drills can be used to improve body-forward inclination: The best one is to stand in a running-ready position, lean forward slightly from the ankles, and then run quickly while preserving the forward lean. Runners can consciously work on using smaller arm movements, and upgraded core strength should keep the torso under control. Explosive training should improve hip extension and increase control of the knee during stance.

Video analysis is critical for monitoring all form adjustments. Before-and-after video examination of foot-strike pattern, stride rate, body inclination, foot position at landing relative to center of mass, knee flexion at landing, arm movement, upper-body stability, and leg dynamics is critical for determining the extent of progress which is being made. Fortunately, great video cameras are now available for less than $100, and the modern cell phone with video capability can also be used to monitor form progressions.

CHAPTER 6

Running Surfaces, Shoes, and Orthotics

During running, a force greater than two times body weight passes up the leg each time the foot hits the ground.[1] Over time, these repetitive impact forces can produce injuries in the muscles, bones, cartilage, tendons, and ligaments of the legs.[2]

Runners have two general ways to limit the potentially destructive effects of these impact stresses. First, running shoes contain midsoles that deform, or compress, each time the foot collides with the ground, absorbing and temporarily storing some of the impact force as elastic energy. This absorbed force is prevented from passing upward into the structures of the foot, ankle, shin, calf, knee, thigh, hip, and upper body; instead, it is returned to the running surface to produce some of the propulsive force required for toe-off.

In addition, a runner's internal structures (e.g., muscles, tendons, ligaments, bones, joints) compress and change position at impact, muffling the upward transference of force through the leg. With each footfall, the arch of the foot flattens, the ankle joint torques and flexes, the knee undergoes rotation and flexion, and the hip flexes. All these actions soak up impact forces and can reduce direct trauma to muscles, connective tissues, and joints.

Impact of Running Surfaces

Many runners believe that the surfaces on which they run also play a role in determining the magnitude of impact forces and thus the risk of injury. Early scientific research seemed to support this idea. In one investigation, subjects who trained on hard concrete floors developed abnormal changes in knee joint cartilage after 2.5 years of training.[3] This study helped spawn the notions that running on hard surfaces promotes injury and that endurance running is generally bad for athletes' knees.

The so-called athletes in this study were actually sheep, however, and the loading forces and neuromuscular responses to force applications associated with foot-ground impacts are likely to be quite different in humans. No study with human runners has ever detected differences in knee cartilage wear and tear associated with differing running surfaces. In addition, a little-known aspect of the sheep research was that the bones around the sheep's knees remodeled themselves and were unusually strong after 30 months of walking on concrete.

Follow-up research with human runners in this area defied conventional wisdom and found that the ground-reaction forces (GRFs) at the foot and the shock transmitted up the leg and through the body after impact with the ground varied little as runners moved from extremely compliant to extremely hard running surfaces.[4] As a result, researchers gradually began to believe that runners are subconsciously able to adjust leg stiffness prior to foot strike based on their perceptions of the hardness or stiffness of the surface on which they are running. This view suggests that runners create soft legs that soak up impact forces when they are running on very hard surfaces and stiff legs when they are moving along on yielding terrain. As a result, impact forces passing through the legs are strikingly similar over a wide range of running surface types. Contrary to popular belief, running on concrete is not more damaging to the legs than running on soft sand.

In one study, researchers at the University of California at Berkeley hypothesized that runners coordinate the actions of the muscles, tendons, and ligaments in their legs so that the lower limbs behave like mechanical springs during ground contact.[5] The data obtained in this investigation suggested that the stiffness of a leg spring is highly dependent on the running surface. If this were not true, peak GRF and ground-contact time would change dramatically as athletes ran on different surfaces; in reality, these measures stay relatively constant. The Berkeley researchers found that runners tripled their leg-spring stiffness as they moved across a compliant, soft surface compared with running over hard ground.[6] Ground-contact time and center of mass vertical displacement remained constant in spite of a thousand-fold change in running surface stiffness. The inquiry indicated that the sum of leg stiffness and surface stiffness does not change when humans run, even when surface stiffness is altered dramatically. As surface stiffness increases, leg stiffness decreases, and vice-versa.

Regulation of leg stiffness can occur before runners even take their first steps on a surface of altered resiliency, indicating that a runner's nervous system creates an expectation of surface hardness before it is actually physically encountered. In a fascinating study, six runners trained at a velocity of 3 meters per second on a track with two types of rubber surface: a compliant, soft surface (surface stiffness = 21.3 kN per meter) and a noncompliant, hard surface (surface stiffness = 533 kN per meter). (A kN is a kiloNewton, or 1,000 Newtons; a Newton is the force required to accelerate a mass of 1 kilogram at a rate of 1 meter per second squared, that is one meter per second per second.) As they ran along the track, the runners completely adjusted leg stiffness for their first steps on the different surface: They decreased leg stiffness by 29 percent between the last step on the soft track and the first step on the hard surface.[7] As a result, stride rate and the vertical displacement of the center of mass during stance did not change as the transition was made despite a reduction in running-surface compression (deformation of the running surface in response to being struck by a runner's foot) from 6 centimeters to less than .25 centimeters per footfall.[7]

Sizing Up Running Shoes

Scientific research on running shoes has often yielded surprising results and has shattered many of the most popular beliefs about running footwear. For example, brand loyalty may be a bad idea from an injury-prevention standpoint, motion-control shoes might actually enhance motion, more expensive shoes could increase the risk of injury, and the life expectancy of running shoes might be much longer than expected.

Running-shoe midsoles are also surfaces on which endurance runners must run. The research on running surfaces suggests that midsole stiffness would have little effect on the forces transmitted up the leg during ground contact, despite certain manufacturers' contentions that their running shoes provide better cushioning and thus protection from impact forces than models produced by different companies. Science suggests that runners simply change the stiffness of their legs in response to changes in midsole stiffness, which would mean that all running shoes provide similar levels of cushioning.

Midsole Stiffness Affects Proprioception

The story is complicated, however, by the fact that midsoles of modern running shoes also change proprioception, or the way a runner's foot feels and experiences the running surface. The running-shoe midsole is a kind of mattress on which the foot lands with each foot strike and therefore can be viewed as an information limiter, robbing a runner's nervous system of key information about the actual running surface. Wearing running shoes may change a runner's interaction with the ground in the same way that wearing thick gloves alters an individual's ability to play the piano or determine the texture, density, and stiffness of any object.

Putting on a pair of running shoes with soft, compressible midsoles might fool a runner's nervous system and create the illusion that impact forces are slight. This could curb nervous system responsiveness and might prevent a softening, or decrease in stiffness, of the leg itself. It does not seem surprising, then, that scientific evidence suggests that soft, compliant, cushiony midsoles might actually permit the highest impact forces to travel through the legs during running.

This evidence comes in part from research in which well-trained athletes stepped off a platform 27 inches high and landed either on a compliant mat or on a hard surface. In each case, the impact force transmitted into the leg associated with the hard landing was lower than the force associated with the soft touch-down.[8] It appears that athletes make careful musculoskeletal adjustments to minimize shock forces when they know they are going to land on a hard surface and are less careful when they realize that each landing will take place on a soft material. While such findings seem to contradict the research on running surfaces, which indicates that forces are the same across all surfaces, these findings do reinforce the idea that runners automatically adjust leg stiffness in response to the kind of surface on which they are landing.

In the platform research, the athletes perceived that the impact forces were greatest on the hard surface even though they were actually of the highest magnitude on the soft surface. The yielding surface was creating a feeling of comfort, an illusion of lower GRF, and as a result, a higher actual impact force was transmitted through the leg.

Soft and Thick Midsoles May Increase Impact Forces

Such findings have suggested to some sports medicine experts that modern running shoes are being created on the basis of an incorrect paradigm: the notion that relatively thick, softer, more deformable midsoles provide better cushioning and therefore less stiff midsoles are optimal for a large number of runners. An extension of this thinking is the conception that runners' feet and legs are fragile objects that must be protected by extensive cushioning from the hard impacts of running. However, this cushioning might produce a feeling of comfort that knocks out a runner's intrinsic neuromuscular defense mechanisms against impact forces, providing an explanation for why athletes landing on soft surfaces permitted higher forces to shock their legs. Expanded midsole cushioning might spike force transmission and perhaps augment the risk of running injury.[9]

Research in this area has yielded interesting results. One study found that when runners used both hard and soft shoes and maximal vertical forces were similar, the runners had slower rise times to peak vertical force during foot strike when they wore the softer, more cushiony shoes.[10] The phrase "rise time to peak vertical force" refers to the period after the foot hits the ground during running and acknowledges the fact that the GRF actually increases for the first 20 to 50 milliseconds of stance. One hypothesis is that the rate at which the force increases is linked with a higher risk of injury. In other words, slower rise times to peak vertical force would be connected with a reduced likelihood of injury, presumably because the slower rise times give a runner's nervous system more time to react and change leg stiffness.

A separate study found that harder shoes were linked with a slower rise time to peak vertical force and reduced peak vertical impact forces, supporting the idea that less stiff midsoles thwart neuromuscular responsiveness.[11] However, a third inquiry found no relationship at all between shoe midsole hardness and force-loading magnitudes.[12]

Taken together, these studies suggest that running-shoe midsole hardness appears to have an unpredictable effect on the impact forces experienced by the legs during running. The true take-home lesson is that endurance runners should not believe that soft, cushiony shoes—or running shoes advertised as having greater cushioning—will actually reduce the impact forces passing through their legs. Runners' legs are not inert objects of fixed stiffness but rather are complicated, responsive structures that can change configuration and overall stiffness very quickly—even immediately before they encounter a particular running surface.

Running Shoe Design and Injury Prevention

A popular belief among endurance runners is that certain running shoes, usually the more expensive models, provide greater protection against injury. When surveying the running shoe market, runners find models with air cushioning, honeycombed midsoles, foam springs, microchips, microspheres, and specialized gels—and accept the notion that such advances must be linked with greater injury protection. Scientific research indicates that this is not the case. As running shoes have incorporated more so-called injury-preventing features since the 1970s, injury rates have not decreased at all. Injury investigations indicate that currently from 50 to 91 (!) percent of endurance runners are injured over the course of a training year when injury is defined as a physical problem severe enough to limit normal training.[13]

Misconceptions About Shoe Price

The available scientific evidence indicates that higher-cost, seemingly more protective running shoes are actually linked with a greater risk of injury. In one study, a Swiss physician analyzed the training habits and shoe preferences of 5,038 runners as they prepared to compete in a 16K road race in Bern, Switzerland.[14] The physician found that during the 16-month training period, 14 percent of the runners who spent less than $40 for their shoes were injured as were 17 percent of the runners investing $40 to $60 and 21 percent of the athletes who shelled out $60 to $95. In contrast, 32 percent of the runners who paid more than $95 for their shoes were injured—that's more than double the injury rate of the runners with the cheapest shoes.

Training mileage and history of injury were equivalent in these four groups, which meant that the reduced risk of injury for those who bought the lower-cost shoes was not the result of a more modest training regime or a higher frequency of prior injuries among the those who purchased the more expensive shoes. The physician concluded that the amount of money spent per pair of running shoes was a predictor of the income of the purchaser and an inverse indicator of the quality and injury prevention characteristics of the shoes.

Recent research has shown that more expensive shoes do not provide better cushioning than cheaper models. Researchers from the University of Dundee in the United Kingdom provided runners with low- (US$80-$90), medium- (US$120-$130), and high-cost (US$140-$150) running shoes and then measured plantar pressure as the individuals walked and ran on a treadmill. The assumption was that better cushioning should decrease the pressure placed on the plantar surface of the foot during running.[15] Plantar-pressure measurements were recorded under the heel, across the forefoot, and under the great toe. Results indicated that the low- and medium-cost running shoes provided the same—if not better—protection from plantar pressure compared with the most expensive shoes. There was also no difference in comfort between the three types of shoes.

The mechanism underlying the Swiss physician's discovery of the link between injury and more expensive running shoes described previously has not been fully explained by scientific research. It is clear that more costly running shoes often have more features than their cheaper peers, including thicker midsoles and more developed motion-control features such as heel counters that are supposed to prevent overpronation of the ankle during the stance phase of gait. Unfortunately, thicker midsoles actually tend to increase medial and lateral rocking of the ankle during the stance phase of gait, effects that could put more stress on the ankle and knee during each impact with the ground. In addition, antipronation devices in the heels of running shoes have actually been linked with faster and more extensive amounts of pronation, which might increase the risks of ankle and knee injury.[16]

The explanation for this latter, surprising finding may be that the hard heel structures, or counters, promoted as pronation preventers may actually serve as stiff levers that accelerate medially, that is, toward an imaginary midline running down the middle of the body, during stance more quickly than do softer-sided heels. If this seems paradoxical, bear in mind that lever speed is a direct function of lever length: As a lever increases in length, the speed at which the end of the lever moves must also increase. Having a hard structure against the side of the heel of a running shoe creates a lever on the inside of the heel, and the top of this lever must accelerate rapidly once natural pronation of the ankle is initiated during stance. Without the counter, there would be no such effect.

As mentioned, it is also possible that wearing more expensive shoes fools runners into thinking that their lower limbs are better protected during running. Scientific research indicates that this idea is not as implausible as it might appear to be at first glance. In one study, researchers asked subjects to step down, barefoot, on separate force-measuring platforms.[17] Each platform was covered with exactly the same shoe sole material, but the materials were made to look different because of cloth coverings of varying colors. The subjects were told that the material on one platform provided superior impact absorption and protection (a deceptive message) and that the material on a second platform offered poor impact absorption and was linked with a high risk of injury (a warning message).

The results revealed that the subjects landed with the highest impact forces on the surface associated with the deceptive message; apparently believing it to be safer, they made fewer adjustments in their lower limbs to absorb shock. The subjects landed with the lowest impacts on the surface associated with the warning. The authors concluded that injury rates are highest in wearers of the most expensive running shoes because advertising has seduced them into believing that the more costly shoes provide a higher level of safety. Such misperceptions may attenuate impact-moderating changes in lower-limb action during landing and thus heighten impact forces and increase the risk of injury.

Rethinking Duration of Shoe Life

To prevent injury, endurance runners are frequently advised to throw away running shoes that have been used for more than 200 to 300 miles (322-483 km), or at least to use them for gardening rather than running. Research does show that the midsoles of such shoes have lost a significant amount of compression-set resistance, or the ability to deform and then spring back into original configuration with each footfall. Such a loss would apparently require the foot, ankle, and perhaps higher regions of the leg to soak up more force with each ground contact since less impact force would be used to deform the midsole.

However, research has shown that as running shoe midsoles lose their compression-set resistance over time, individuals wearing the shoes actually improve the control of their feet during running, an effect that should decrease injury risk.[18] The presumed mechanism is that cushiony midsoles that have not lost their compression-set resistance prevent a runner's feet from truly feeling the surface upon which he or she is running and therefore prevent the nervous system from reacting effectively and with enhanced coordination. As shoe researchers S.E. Robbins and G.J. Gouw have stated, cushiony midsoles may create a kind of "pseudo-neuropathy" in runners.[19] Research does reveal that modern running shoes tend to create a perceptual illusion causing runners to consistently underestimate impact forces.[19] A surprising conclusion that can be drawn from such research is that running shoes may actually get better—not worse—with age from the standpoints of motion control and injury prevention.

Potential Improvements for Midsoles

The solution to the problem of loss of impact-force detection might be straightforward. Research has indicated that the mere addition of surface irregularities on running shoe insoles on the sides of the insoles in contact with the soles of the feet significantly improves runners' estimates of impact forces,[19] presumably because such irregularities provide runners with a heightened sense of the pressures exerted during ground contact on various parts of the bottom of the foot, and also because the bumps, or irregularities on the midsole, provide runners with a better estimate of horizontal shear forces during ground contact. Unfortunately, no such commercial insoles exist.

Making running-shoe midsoles thinner should also improve coordination and balance during running. In one study, male subjects walked along a beam while wearing shoes with soles of different hardness and thickness. The thinner, harder soles were linked with significantly better balance.[20] Many endurance runners and coaches might worry that thinner soles would increase impact forces experienced by the legs and thus increase injury risk, but research does not support the idea that thicker midsoles provide truly better cushioning. As noted previously, running shoe midsole thickness has burgeoned since the 1970s, and there has been no decrease in running injury rates. Runners' legs appear to be quite capable of learning to absorb increased forces—assuming they are passed up the legs as a result of the use of thinner midsoles—in a safe and effective way provided that the transition from thick to slim midsoles is made carefully over time.

Brand Loyalty's Perils

Swiss physician B. Marti's research on training habits and shoe preferences described in this chapter also showed that runners with no preference for running shoe brand had a 25 percent lower risk of injury over a 16-month period of training as compared with runners who favored one particular shoe model. One hypothesis emerging from this finding is that each model of running shoes produces unique stresses on the musculoskeletal system; if the shoes are worn long enough, these stresses can lead to injury. If the shoes are changed, the stresses change, and the risk of injury is reduced because the previously stressed tissues get a break while other structures begin to take a pounding.

Marti also found that runners who chose their shoes based on style or color had a 20 percent reduction in injury rate compared with competitors who attempted to choose running shoes with orthopedically correct design and construction(!). This suggests that either runners are unaware of the true nature of orthopedically correct running shoes or else that orthopedic optimality in running shoe design does not currently exist.

Facts About Motion Control

Running shoe companies market motion-control running shoes that are alleged to reduce excessive pronation and thus limit the risk of knee and other injuries. This view is proclaimed to be a mainstream development in running shoe technology.[21] Such shoes usually have an assortment of unique features, including greater stiffness on the medial side of the midsole, greater support in the vertical wall of the medial side of the heel, and valgus (laterally inclined) heel wedges. It is certainly true that such shoes can change the kinematics of the ankle joint during running. There is no scientific evidence, however, to support the claim that the use of motion-control shoes reduces the risk of knee problems—or any other kind of injury—in endurance runners.[22]

Why is this so? It is very possible that motion-control shoes have an impact on the movement of the feet and ankles during running, but the changes in movement that are produced are not optimal. It is also possible that motion-control shoes produce changes in kinetics that are often outweighed from an injury-prevention perspective by other factors, including training volume, nutrition, and recovery. It seems highly probable that strengthening the foot and ankle joint with running-specific exercises would have a greater impact on foot, ankle, and knee injuries than wearing a motion-control shoe. Research supports the idea that strength training limits the risk of running injury but has never reinforced the notion that motion-control shoes reduce injury rates.

Scientific evidence suggests that the primary function of running shoes may be to protect the bottom of the foot from harsh, potentially damaging surfaces. All other proposed functions (e.g., stability, motion control, increased cushioning, advanced energy return) may lie within the domain of marketing rather than exercise science and foot and ankle biomechanics. Science also suggests that the purchase of expensive running shoes may represent a symbolic act rather than the actual acquisition of higher-quality shoes.

Barefoot Running

Since modern running shoes get failing marks from the standpoints of injury prevention, motion control, energy return, stability, and cushioning, it is not surprising that barefoot running is becoming increasingly popular among endurance runners. The popular press and a large number of runners and coaches have proposed that unshod running strengthens the feet more than shod running, helps relieve current injuries, and also lowers the risk of future injury. Proponents of barefoot running also suggest that the technique diminishes impact forces with the ground and the rate at which such forces are transmitted up the legs during running and that barefoot running can even improve performances. From the performance standpoint,

Courtesy of Owen Anderson

▶ Barefoot running is linked with lower impact forces and enhanced running economy.

research reveals that donning a pair of running shoes instantly harms running economy by about 1 percent compared with barefoot running, an effect that should slow distance-running performances to a similar extent.[13]

The strong interest in barefoot running is partly the result of the publication of Christopher McDougall's bestselling book *Born to Run*, in which the author claims that barefoot running dramatically enhances endurance and is the panacea for nearly all running-related injuries. McDougall also proposes that modern running shoes are a principal cause of injury in endurance runners.[23]

Research on Barefoot Running

Research carried out by Daniel Lieberman and colleagues at Harvard University has bolstered the movement toward barefoot running.[24] These researchers looked at the kinematics and kinetics of running in five different groups: (1) habitually shod athletes from the United States, (2) currently shod runners from the Rift Valley in Kenya who had grown up running barefoot, (3) U.S. runners who began running using shoes but have now adopted a barefoot-running style, (4) adolescent Kenyan runners who have never worn shoes, and (5) adolescent Kenyan runners who have run shod for most of their lives. The study led to the following findings:

• Habitually shod runners (groups 1 and 5) who grew up wearing shoes are usually rear-foot strikers (RFS), meaning that their heels make the first impacts with the ground during running at the beginning of the stance phase of gait. The strong link between running in shoes and heel striking has been detected in other research.[25]

• Runners who grew up running barefooted or who switched to running barefooted (groups 2, 3, and 4) are generally forefoot strikers (FFS); they tend to land initially on the balls of their feet while running, after which their heels drop down to make contact with the ground.

• Impact forces transmitted through the foot, ankle, and leg immediately after impact with the ground are *about three times greater* in shod runners using RFS than in barefoot runners using FFS. Some—but not all—previous studies have shown this same relationship, with RFS producing greater impact force during the first portion of stance compared with midfoot strikers (MFS) and FFS. The sudden rise in force with RFS immediately after ground contact is known as the *impact transient*. The disparity in impact transient between barefoot and shod running represents a foundation for the belief that barefoot running is safer and less injury producing.

• During the early stance phase of barefoot FFS running, there is greater knee flexion, greater dorsiflexion at the ankle, and a 74 percent greater drop in the center of mass than with shod RFS running. Vertical compliance is the drop in the runner's center of mass relative to the vertical force during the impact period of stance, and it is greater in barefoot FFS running than with shod RFS running. Vertical compliance varies as a function of running-surface hardness, and this is why force-loading rates are similar for barefoot FFS runners over a wide array of running surfaces as the runners adjust compliance according to surface.

• During barefoot FFS running, the ground-reaction force torques the foot around the ankle, increasing the amount of work carried out by the ankle compared with what occurs in shod RFS running. With shod RFS running, the ankle converts little impact energy into rotational energy. Potentially, this difference could actually spike the rate of ankle-area injuries in the Achilles tendon and calf, for example, for barefoot runners, especially if a runner plunges into barefoot running without adequate preparation.

Deciding to Shift and Doing So Safely

What does all of this mean to endurance runners? Although a shift from shod to barefoot running is attractive for a number of reasons (e.g., improved economy, reduced impact transient), such a change, if carried out over a relatively short period of time, might actually increase the risk of getting hurt.

As mentioned previously, barefoot running increases the work carried out by the ankle joint during gait compared with shod running. A sudden upswing in strain at the ankle induced by a change from shod to barefoot running could actually heighten injury rates in the calf and Achilles tendon. The increase in work carried out at the ankle, reduction in impact forces, and diminishment of work carried out at the knee associated with barefoot running are exactly the same effects observed in runners who adopt the pose running method (see chapter 5). Research suggests that up to 95 percent of pose newcomers are injured during the first 2 weeks after adopting the technique![25]

It is important to remember that most injuries in running are caused by an imbalance between the strain and microdamage experienced by a muscle or connective tissue during training and the tissue's ability to recover from such stress. This imbalance can occur when training is conducted shod or barefoot. A weak or overly tight hamstring muscle that has been undone by excessive running won't care if its owner was running barefooted or wearing shoes—it will still feel painful to the owner.

It is certainly true that barefoot and shod running are different from kinematic and kinetic standpoints, and this may have a bearing on injury rates. Shod running, at least shod running in big-heeled modern running shoes, almost automatically means RFS. With RFS, the ankle plantar-flexes immediately after impact as the bottom surface of the foot moves downward to make contact with the pavement. This places the shin muscles under strain immediately after heel impact since they have to control this significant plantar flexion. In contrast, during barefoot (FFS or MFS) running, the ankle immediately dorsiflexes after impact, placing eccentric strain on the Achilles tendon and calf muscles as they attempt to control the dorsiflexion. Thus, it's possible that shod RFS might be linked with a higher risk of shin injuries, while barefoot FFS and MFS could be connected with a greater rate of Achilles and calf problems. These hypotheses have not been tested, however.

A runner who decides to abandon running shoes and carry out all training barefoot will almost automatically be shifting from RFS to MFS. This will mean that the Achilles tendon and calf muscles will encounter unprecedented pressures that they had not encountered before during the athlete's running career. So, caution is advised.

Instead of tossing one's shoes away and immediately running unshod, it seems prudent at first to employ very comfortable, relatively minimal running shoes that permit actual proprioception, protect the bottoms of the feet from rough surfaces, and are conducive to MFS. From a performance standpoint, this overall strategy should eliminate the braking action commonly associated with thick-heeled shoes and RFS, in which the foot tends to land out in front of the center of mass, creating a slowing effect, and thus should upgrade speed and enhance economy. A shift from RFS to MFS will also eliminate the impact transient that might be a cause of running injury; it will heighten the compliance of the leg, fostering the ability to run on surfaces of increased hardness without amplifying the impact forces experienced by the legs. MFS also tends to lead to an increased cadence while running (> 180 steps per minute), which has been associated with faster performances. As a runner becomes used to wearing minimal shoes, he or she can gradually increase the amount of running done barefoot.

A shift from RFS to MFS should be accomplished gradually. Abruptly changing from 40 miles (64 km) per week of RFS to the same volume with MFS is a nearly certain way for a runner to find the Achilles heel in his or her running program.

Orthotics

Orthotics (also called orthoses) are frequently recommended by sports medicine physicians, podiatrists, physical therapists, and even running-shoe clerks for runners with assorted lower-limb pains and injuries. The popular belief is that such devices can correct misalignments and improper movements in productive and functional ways that can decrease the risk of injury.

Scientific research has not been particularly kind to such practices and beliefs. Research reveals that injury rates among endurance runners have not declined over the past 30 years, even though the use of orthotics has increased. While it is true that some clinical studies have linked orthotic use with pain relief and the successful management of running injuries,[26, 27] in most investigations that favor orthotics, it is difficult to disentangle the effects produced by the orthotics from those associated with natural recovery from injury over time (i.e., the body's own healing mechanisms).

Up to 40 percent of runners do not get better after they are fitted with orthotics.[28] Orthotics are of little use in runners with high-arched (cavoid) feet,[29, 30] and orthotic usage has also been linked with the appearance of new injuries,[31] suggesting that using orthotics might simply replace one kind of stress on the musculoskeletal system with another. Such findings intimate that the underlying injury-inducing problem for many runners may be a general lack of functional strength, a deficiency that orthotics would not correct.

An additional problem is that static measurements of the feet are often used to create custom orthotics, which are thought to take into account an individual runner's unique anatomical and functional characteristics. These static measurements may do a poor job predicting the dynamic behavior of the feet and ankles during running,[32, 33] creating a situation in which orthotics might work well when a runner is standing around, but not when that runner is surging toward the finish line of a 5K race. Researchers have also questioned the ability of orthotic makers to properly define normal feet and normal foot function during running; [34, 35] seemingly misaligned feet might be fully functional and not promote injury in certain runners with unique anatomical characteristics. No optimal pattern of motion of the foot and ankle during gait has ever been defined.

The use of orthotics can also have unexpected effects. Identical orthotics can have widely varying effects on movement patterns in different runners, indicating that there can be potentially strong interactions between orthotics and the neuromuscular and anatomical characteristics of specific individuals.[36] Orthotics can also produce unanticipated results: In one study, podiatrists fitted 12 runners who had histories of Achilles tendon problems with orthotics that were intended to reduce ankle pronation. Kinematic analysis revealed that the orthotics did change ankle movements during running, but the devices actually tended to increase eversion, or outward rotation, of the ankles, an effect that magnified pronation.[37]

It would appear from the scientific evidence that orthotics might work most effectively in runners with unchangeable anatomical misalignments (e.g., leg-length discrepancies), problems that cannot be corrected via therapy or vigorous, running-specific strength training. When injuries occur as the result of functional weakness, rather than anatomical defects, it is logical to assume that running-specific strength training would provide a better resolution than the use of orthotics, which might weaken neuromuscular function even further by taking over supportive functions and the control of joint movements, processes that should be regulated by nerves, muscles, and tendons.

Conclusion

The scientific research on running shoes and orthotics shatters many myths and is very liberating to runners. It is important for runners to know that specific running shoes don't really provide superior cushioning, stability, motion control, or protection from injury compared with using other types of running shoes, and especially compared with running barefoot. Soft shoes don't cushion the feet and legs better than hard shoes, nor do more expensive shoes ensure greater defense against injury and higher performance—in fact, perhaps the opposite. The life expectancy of a pair of running shoes is probably longer than commonly believed, and no brand of running shoes is better than any other. As a result, runners can buy their shoes based on fit and moderate purchase price instead of feeling that they must go for pricey, high-tech, high-end footwear. In addition, runners can take a close look at doing at least some of their running barefoot, a practice that enhances economy, stride rate, and foot-strike pattern and seems to reduce the impact forces running up the legs.

PART

III

Physiological Factors in Running Performance

CHAPTER 7

Maximal Aerobic Capacity ($\dot{V}O_2$max)

Without oxygen use, there would be no such thing as endurance running. The leg muscles provide the propulsive force required for sustained running, and they depend on oxygen to create the continuous supply of energy needed to complete any distance-running event.

A popular belief is that oxygen provides energy by burning carbohydrates and fats in the leg muscles during running. In reality, oxygen latches onto electrons at the end of a key metabolic pathway inside muscle cells called the electron transport chain. If an adequate supply of oxygen is not available to catch the electrons, the pathway grinds to a halt, energy production slows to a trickle, and running must stop.

Turning Oxygen Into Energy

The electron transport chain creates large quantities of a chemical called ATP (adenosine triphosphate), which provides the direct energy muscles must have to produce force. If oxygen is in abundant supply within the muscles, the reactions in the electron transport pathway can proceed at a high rate, ATP creation can be maximized, and high-quality running can be undertaken and sustained for a significant period of time. If oxygen is in short supply, the reactions in the pathway proceed at a slow rate, ATP generation decreases, and running speed must be reduced. In one sense, setting a personal record in an endurance race is dependent on having an adequate supply of oxygen at the ends of the electron transport chains in the leg muscles.

Oxygen takes a circuitous route to those muscles, passing from the atmosphere through the small air sacs (alveoli) of the lungs into the blood and then through the pulmonary veins to the left side of the heart, where the oxygen-rich blood is pumped through the arteries to the muscles (see figure 7.1). The muscles can then utilize this oxygen to create the energy required for running. Inside muscle cells, half of an oxygen molecule accepts two electrons coming down the electron transport chain and also connects with two hydrogen ions to form a molecule of water; the other half of the oxygen

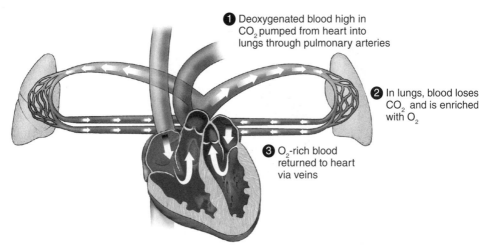

❶ Deoxygenated blood high in CO_2 pumped from heart into lungs through pulmonary arteries

❷ In lungs, blood loses CO_2 and is enriched with O_2

❸ O_2-rich blood returned to heart via veins

▶ **Figure 7.1** The heart sends oxygen-poor blood to the lungs and receives oxygen-rich blood before pumping it out to the body.

molecule does the same thing. Thus, a runner's muscles use the oxygen that comes from the atmosphere to create energy and make water. The water is produced by combining hydrogen and oxygen, and it can be used throughout the body to preserve blood volume, intracellular water content, and interstitial fluid.

Oxygen usage is a function of running velocity: As running speed increases, more muscle cells in the legs become active; muscles need more energy to provide greater propulsive forces, so the muscles consume oxygen at higher rates. In fact, the rate of oxygen consumption advances as a nearly *linear* function of running velocity[1] (see figure 7.2). A typical runner cruising along at a speed of 15 kilometers per hour (about 6:27 per mi) is likely to be consuming oxygen at a rate of about 50 milliliters per kilogram of body weight per minute. At 17.5 kilometers per hour (approximately 5:30 per mi), the consumption rate is often close to 60 milliliters of oxygen per kilogram per minute. If the runner can make it to 20 kilometers per hour (4:50 per mi), oxygen consumption would be close to 70 ml • kg^{-1} • min^{-1}.

Defining $\dot{V}O_2$max

Obviously, there must be some upper limit on oxygen use; oxygen cannot be transported by the heart and used by the muscles at an infinite rate. The topmost rate of oxygen consumption in an individual runner is called the maximal rate of oxygen consumption, or $\dot{V}O_2$max.

In humans, the variation in $\dot{V}O_2$max is exceptionally large. Because of difficulties getting oxygen through the alveoli in the lungs, an individual with a significant pulmonary disease might have a $\dot{V}O_2$max of just 13 ml • kg^{-1} • min^{-1}. Due to a lack of cardiac muscle strength, and thus a reduced capacity to send blood to the muscles, a post–heart attack patient might check in

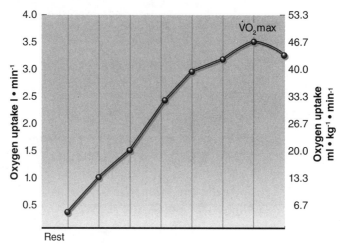

Exercise on the treadmill

Speed km/h	4.8	8.0	11.2	11.2	11.2	11.2	11.2
Treadmill grade, %	0	5.5	7.5	9.5	11.5	13.5	15.5
Time, min	0-2	2-4	4-6	6-8	8-10	10-12	12-14

▶ **Figure 7.2** The oxygen-consumption rate increases in an almost linear function as the intensity increases, but it eventually levels off as it reaches $\dot{V}O_2$max.

Adapted, by permission, from W.D. McArdle, F.I. Katch, and V.L. Katch, 1991, Exercise physiology: Energy, nutrition and human performance, 3rd ed. (Philadelphia: Lea & Febiger), 213.

with a $\dot{V}O_2$max of 22. A sedentary adult plucked at random from a U.S. street could be at 35, and a relatively sedentary young person would probably be close to 45 ml • kg^{-1} • min^{-1}. In contrast, a runner with a 5K personal record of 18 minutes might reach a $\dot{V}O_2$max of about 60, an elite endurance runner could easily have a $\dot{V}O_2$max of 75 to 80, and an international-level cross-country skier might attain 85 ml • kg^{-1} • min^{-1}.[2-4] The highest $\dot{V}O_2$max ever recorded for an endurance athlete is 93 ml • kg^{-1} • min^{-1} in a Scandinavian cross-country skier, which is seven times higher than the maximal aerobic capacity of the pulmonary disease patient and almost three times greater than the $\dot{V}O_2$max of an average adult.[5]

The figures cited above are examples of *relative* $\dot{V}O_2$max, which is always expressed in milliliters of oxygen per kilogram of body weight per minute (ml • kg^{-1} • min^{-1}). *Absolute* $\dot{V}O_2$max is expressed in milliliters of oxygen consumed per minute without the body mass factor in the denominator. Compared with relative $\dot{V}O_2$max, absolute $\dot{V}O_2$max is a better indicator of whole-body oxygen consumption and thus energy expenditure, but relative $\dot{V}O_2$max provides more information about potential running ability. A 400-pound (181 kg) man, for example, would have a high absolute $\dot{V}O_2$max because of the massive size of his oxygen-using organs and muscles, but one would not expect him to storm through a 10K race at high speed; his relative $\dot{V}O_2$max would not be high, with that 400-pound (181 kg) number lurking in the denominator of the $\dot{V}O_2$max formula.

Possible Factors Limiting Aerobic Capacity

Since oxygen transport and use depend on many different way stations within the body (e.g., lungs, blood, heart, muscles), exercise scientists have asked which portion of the oxygen-transportation and usage system is most limiting. That is, which part creates the upper cap on oxygen utilization and thus sets up a $\dot{V}O_2$max that can't be exceeded.

Pulmonary ventilation, the moving of air in and out of the lungs, does *not* appear to be a factor that limits $\dot{V}O_2$max in runners. Even when they are at rest, healthy athletes can move more air into their lungs than they require during extremely intense running. The maximal ventilation rate for a distance runner is about 200 liters (53 gal) of air per minute, but elite athletes, even during highly strenuous running, generally do not require more than 180 liters (47 gal) of air per minute to satisfy their oxygen needs.[6]

So what factors might limit aerobic capacity? These might be the passage rate of oxygen through the lungs into the blood; the ability of the muscles to use blood-borne, incoming oxygen at high rates; the cardiovascular system's ability to distribute blood to the muscles; or the nervous system's capacity to recruit muscle cells during intense exercise. A limitation on neural recruitment would cap the oxygen-usage rate by limiting the number of muscle fibers using oxygen.

Scientific studies reveal that the oxygen content of arterial blood emerging from the heart can fall during high-intensity running, suggesting that the diffusion rate of oxygen across the alveolar walls of the lungs into nearby blood capillaries may be limiting in some cases. This seems to occur only in elite runners who are capable of sustaining high intensities for a significant period. However, it is probably not a relevant limiter for the vast majority of endurance runners.[7]

Ingenious investigations in which athletes exercise one leg intensely while the other leg remains dormant suggest that, in this unique situation, the capacity of the leg muscles to use oxygen does not limit $\dot{V}O_2$max. In this research, the $\dot{V}O_2$max associated with one-leg exercise is more than half the $\dot{V}O_2$max for a two-leg exertion, which means that the leg muscles can increase their rate of oxygen consumption if given the opportunity to do so. A greater supply of oxygenated blood from the cardiovascular system presents such an opportunity. This opportunity is possible in one-leg exercise because the cardiovascular system diverts blood from the nonworking to the working leg.

However, during a two-leg exertion such as running, the cardiovascular system is not able to supply both legs with enough blood and oxygen to reach each limb's highest-possible level of oxygen usage. This is probably a protective mechanism. If the cardiovascular system opened the flood gates and permitted more blood to flow into the legs, cerebral blood pressure could drop significantly, leading to a potential collapse.

The ability of the leg muscles to raise the oxygen-consumption rate when supplied with a greater inflow of blood during one-leg exercise suggests that the cardiovascular system might limit $\dot{V}O_2$max during demanding running. However, as Dr. Tim Noakes and colleagues at the University of Cape Town have pointed out, stroke volume (the amount of blood ejected from the heart per beat) and cardiac output (the amount of blood pushed out of the heart per minute) often do not reach plateaus (i.e., do not attain topmost values) during laboratory tests that are used to determine $\dot{V}O_2$max values in runners.[8] If stroke volume and the total outflow of blood from the heart have not peaked, yet $\dot{V}O_2$max is reached, it is possible that the cardiovascular system is not capping $\dot{V}O_2$max.

As T.D. Noakes and A. St. Clair Gibson have noted, overall muscular performance and thus the oxygen-consumption rate during running are determined by the nervous system's recruitment of motor units (collections of muscle cells) inside the leg muscles.[9, 10] If this seems confusing, remember that the muscles cannot act alone during running; they must wait for commands from the brain and spinal cord in order to engage themselves in the act of running.

A sustained, high level of muscle engagement by the nervous system would inevitably lead to a high $\dot{V}O_2$max in an individual runner. In contrast, a more limited level of recruitment would produce a lower $\dot{V}O_2$max, even in a case in which a runner had ample reserves for oxygen shipment and use in the heart and leg muscles. As Noakes has observed, runners with higher values of $\dot{V}O_2$max appear to have nervous systems that not only recruit a greater number of muscle cells during intense running but also sustain this recruitment for greater than average time periods.[8] This observation has important implications for training that will be discussed throughout this book.

Basically, the research on neural output means that in order to maximize $\dot{V}O_2$max and performance, endurance runners must train their nervous systems in ways that optimize motor-unit recruitment. This can hardly be accomplished by high-volume, submaximal training, the traditional way to train for $\dot{V}O_2$max enhancement, since motor recruitment during such work is modest. Rather, it can only result from highly intense, Kenyan-style training that relentlessly provokes greater neural outputs and motor-unit activations. For an individual runner, the key to developing the highest-possible $\dot{V}O_2$max appears to involve optimizing motor-unit recruitment, with supporting roles played by expanded heart and leg muscles that can sate an intense thirst for oxygen by the neurally fired-up muscles.

Impact of Training on $\dot{V}O_2$max

$\dot{V}O_2$max usually responds readily to training, but the response depends on a variety of different factors and can be quite unpredictable. When a relatively untrained group of individuals embarks on a 3-month program of endurance-running training, the average increase in $\dot{V}O_2$max after 12 weeks will be about 15 to 20 percent, but some subjects may boost $\dot{V}O_2$max by just 2 to 3 percent—or not at all.[11] A small number of individuals will increase $\dot{V}O_2$max to a considerable degree, that is by as much as 30 to 50 percent.[12-14] If the training program is uniform across all individuals, genetic factors will be responsible for some portion of this variation in response. (Refer to chapter 2 for a discussion of the interaction between genetics and endurance-running performance.)

Intrinsic $\dot{V}O_2$max also plays a role: Individuals with naturally high values of $\dot{V}O_2$max at the beginning of training will tend to increase maximal aerobic capacity less than individuals with lower values. Intrinsic $\dot{V}O_2$max, or the maximal aerobic capacity present in a person who is not engaged in regular endurance training, may to some extent also be under genetic control.

$\dot{V}O_2$max can be expressed by the following equation:

$$\dot{V}O_2\text{max} = HR\text{max} \times SV\text{max} \times (\text{a-v } O_2 \text{ difference})\text{max}$$

HRmax is maximal heart rate, SVmax is maximal stroke volume (the greatest amount of blood the heart can pump out of its left side per beat), and (a-v O_2 difference)max is maximal arteriovenous oxygen difference, which reflects the disparity in oxygen content of the arterial blood coming into the muscles from the oxygen content of the venous blood flowing away from the muscles. An increase in the (a-v O_2 difference)max means that the muscles are extracting more oxygen from incoming blood.

Clearly, $\dot{V}O_2$max can be increased in endurance runners only by working the right side of this equation, that is, by enhancing HR max, SVmax, or the arteriovenous difference. Scientific studies reveal little difference in maximal heart rate between sedentary individuals and well-trained endurance runners, so upgrades in stroke volume or the (a-v O_2 difference)max or both must account for gains in $\dot{V}O_2$max associated with training. Although considerable variation can exist among runners, research suggests that about 50 percent of the increase in $\dot{V}O_2$max that results from endurance training is often produced by an upswing in maximal stroke volume with the other 50 percent coming from upticks in the arteriovenous difference.[12-14]

Increases in Stroke Volume

Endurance training enhances stroke volume in a variety of ways. First, the heart's key pumping chamber, the left ventricle, expands in size in response to endurance work. In addition, plasma volume, or the volume of the liquid portion of blood without the red and white cells, also increases so that the left ventricle can fill with more blood between beats. This allows more blood to be ejected per beat, thus fostering a greater rate of movement of oxygen toward the muscles.

In intriguing research, exercise scientists have mimicked this endurance-training effect by infusing about 200 to 300 milliliters (7-10 oz) of fluid into runners' bloodstreams; when this occurs, $\dot{V}O_2$max automatically increases by about 4 percent. When runners don't train for a couple of weeks, the resulting drop in $\dot{V}O_2$max is caused primarily by a loss in plasma volume, which is a key aspect of detraining.[15, 16] In effect, fitness is urinated out of the body.

Increases in Arteriovenous Difference

Advances in the arteriovenous difference occur for two key reasons. First, endurance-running training stimulates an increase in capillary density around muscle fibers in the legs. The capillaries are tiny blood vessels with thin walls across which oxygen can easily diffuse.[17, 18] This upswing in capillary density increases blood flow to the muscles during running, decreases the distance across which oxygen must move to get to the mitochondria where the electron transport chain is located, and slows the velocity of blood flow through the sinews. While this latter effect might seem like a bad thing, it actually provides more time for oxygen in the capillaries to diffuse through capillary and muscle cell walls and travel into the mitochondria. An increase in capillary density enhances leg-muscle blood flow and whole-body $\dot{V}O_2$max during endurance training.[13]

Secondly, the arteriovenous difference is advanced by the upswing in motor-unit recruitment described earlier as a key limiting factor for $\dot{V}O_2$max. As more motor units are activated within a muscle during running, the muscle becomes a heavier consumer of oxygen and thus permits less oxygen to end up in the veins, draining the muscle.

$\dot{V}O_2$max as an Indicator of Performance

An individual runner's endurance performances will usually improve as $\dot{V}O_2$max increases. A runner who trains diligently and pushes $\dot{V}O_2$max from 50 to 60 ml • kg^{-1} • min^{-1} over a period of several months will often upgrade 5K time from 22 to about 18 minutes, for example.[19] Research also tells us that $\dot{V}O_2$max is generally a quite good predictor of endurance-performance capability *when athletes of widely varying abilities are compared.* The runners finishing in the top 20 percent of a 10K race will almost always have higher maximal aerobic capacities than individuals finishing in the last 20 percent.[20-28]

Paradoxically, there is little relationship between $\dot{V}O_2$max and performance when runners with fairly similar training backgrounds and performance capacities are compared. For example, two famous U.S. runners, Frank Shorter and Steve Prefontaine, had personal records for 3-mile (4.8 km) races that differed by only .2 seconds and yet their $\dot{V}O_2$max values varied by 16 percent. Prefontaine's $\dot{V}O_2$max registered 84 ml • kg^{-1} • min^{-1} while Shorter was able to push his oxygen meter up to a mere 71 ml • kg^{-1} • min^{-1}.[5]

Exercise scientists have also noted that elite athletes with nearly identical $\dot{V}O_2$max values can have vastly different race times. Three elite marathon runners, Alberto Salazar, Cavin Woodward, and Grete Waitz, had $\dot{V}O_2$max readings of about 74 to 75 ml • kg^{-1} • min^{-1}, and yet their best performance times in the marathon were 2:08:13, 2:19:50, and 2:25:29, respectively.[5]

Baumann/Imago/Icon SMI

Karl-Heinz Stana/Imago/Icon SMI

▶ Steve Prefontaine (lead runner, top) and Frank Shorter (lead runner, bottom) had very similar three-mile performances even though Shorter's $\dot{V}O_2$max was about 16 percent below Prefontaine's.

In a similar vein, Joan Benoit-Samuelson had the highest $\dot{V}O_2$max ever recorded in a female runner, 78 ml • kg^{-1} • min^{-1}, and her maximal aerobic capacity was 13 percent higher than the $\dot{V}O_2$max of former world-record holder Derek Clayton (69 m ml • kg^{-1} • min^{-1}); however, Benoit-Samuelson actually ran the marathon about 10 percent *slower* than Clayton (2:21 for Benoit-Samuelson versus 2:08:33 for Clayton).

For the past 85 years, it has been assumed that differences in endurance-running capability result primarily from differences in the maximal ability to transport and use oxygen.[5] For the past 50 years, the most popular laboratory test for assessing endurance-running ability has been the $\dot{V}O_2$max exam,[5] and many coaches and runners consider a high $\dot{V}O_2$max to be the sine qua non of endurance performance. However, the $\dot{V}O_2$max performance comparisons mentioned above reveal that these basic assumptions are incorrect.

The truth is that there is a very poor association between $\dot{V}O_2$max and race times among competitive distance runners. A startling paradox is that a single individual who improves $\dot{V}O_2$max from 60 to 66 can usually be assured of an approximate 10 percent improvement in performance, but a runner with a $\dot{V}O_2$max of 66 has no assurance that he or she is 10 percent better than a competitor with a $\dot{V}O_2$max of 60. Such observations make it certain that physiological and biomechanical factors other than $\dot{V}O_2$max are required to explain observed differences among runners in their endurance-running performances. These key elements will be discussed in upcoming chapters. The traditional view that $\dot{V}O_2$max is the primary predictor of performance has been destroyed.

WEREK/Imago/Icon SMI

▶ In her prime, Joan Benoit-Samuelson had a $\dot{V}O_2$max similar to an elite male endurance runner.

$\dot{V}O_2$max and the Faulty Muscle Fatigue Theory

$\dot{V}O_2$max is also at the very core of a key theory that attempts to explain why performance-thwarting muscular fatigue occurs during endurance running. Careful scientific research has led to the rejection of this theory, but it continues to be used as the linchpin of many popular endurance-running training programs.

According to the theory, fatigue during intense endurance running occurs in the following way: A runner moving along at a high-quality pace reaches a plateau in oxygen consumption, that is, the runner's $\dot{V}O_2$max. Further increases in speed cause the leg muscles to begin working anaerobically, which leads to the release of high amounts of lactic acid. The lactic acid then interferes with muscle contraction, producing fatigue and necessitating a slower pace or leading to complete exhaustion.

This model of fatigue has reinforced the idea that increasing $\dot{V}O_2$max should be the key goal of endurance training. In theory, such an increase would keep endurance athletes away from the dangerous realm of anaerobic muscle contractions and consequent fatigue by permitting increasingly higher training and race speeds to be handled aerobically, without the need for anaerobic energy production.

For example, the traditional Lydiard system of training endurance runners, created by legendary New Zealand coach Arthur Lydiard, has as its primary goal the aggrandizement of maximal aerobic capacity accomplished via the completion of huge amounts of running and the relative minimization of high-speed, anaerobic training. As Noakes has pointed out, this represents "brainless" training and exercise physiology since it ignores the need for an endurance-athlete's nervous system to develop the capacity to sustain high levels of motor-unit recruitment.[29]

The traditional theory of fatigue has not held up well under close scrutiny. As Noakes and other exercise scientists have determined, some endurance runners become exhausted and are unable to continue during their laboratory $\dot{V}O_2$max tests without ever hitting a plateau in oxygen consumption (i.e., without ever reaching an actual $\dot{V}O_2$max).[29] Thus, they are never falling into anaerobic peril, and still they are becoming completely fatigued.

The explanation based on reaching an oxygen plateau followed by anaerobiosis cannot adequately account for fatigue during endurance running. The research has also revealed that among runners who do reach a plateau, and thus exhibit a $\dot{V}O_2$max, the *top speed* attained during the test is a far better predictor of performance than $\dot{V}O_2$max itself.[30, 31] Additional research has demonstrated that lactic acid does not hamper muscle contractility; in fact, it is a key fuel for leg muscles and can advance rather than retard endurance.[32, 33]

Nonetheless, the traditional conception of the origin of fatigue continues to be used to justify the creation of high-mileage training programs to increase $\dot{V}O_2$max.

Improving $\dot{V}O_2$max

Although $\dot{V}O_2$max is a weak predictor of endurance performance unless runners of widely varying ability levels are compared, it is nonetheless true that *individual* endurance runners who increase their personal $\dot{V}O_2$max will often improve their individual performances. As a result, exercise scientists have attempted to identify training strategies that have the greatest possible positive impact on $\dot{V}O_2$max. Many runners believe that the best way to optimize $\dot{V}O_2$max is to conduct high-mileage training. However, the scientific study that detected one of the largest improvements ever recorded in $\dot{V}O_2$max in well-trained runners actually linked an upswing in intense training *and a decrease in mileage* with the big jump in $\dot{V}O_2$max.[34]

In this investigation, experienced runners were using a variety of different training techniques prior to the onset of the research, including long, slow distance work; speed sessions; tempo training; overspeed efforts; and weight training. Over a 4-week period, the athletes conducted two high-intensity interval sessions per week. Each workout consisted of six intervals performed at the intense pace of $v\dot{V}O_2$max, or the minimal running velocity that elicits $\dot{V}O_2$max. (Chapter 9 provides a method for estimating $v\dot{V}O_2$max.) These work intervals lasted from 3 to 4.5 minutes. The rest of the weekly training was composed of light recovery runs.

After just 4 weeks, the runners upgraded their 3K performance times by about 3 percent, and $\dot{V}O_2$max jumped by 5 percent from 61 to 64 ml • kg^{-1} • min^{-1}. This kind of aggressive increase in aerobic capacity is totally unexpected and almost unprecedented in highly trained distance runners, who often have a difficult time getting $\dot{V}O_2$max to budge at all. As mentioned, this is one of the largest increases in aerobic capacity ever recorded in a published scientific study carried out with experienced runners.[35]

Separate research also supports the idea that intense training has the strongest impact on $\dot{V}O_2$max By definition, *intense training* means work carried out at a high percentage of $\dot{V}O_2$max—that is, at high speed. It is far different from *high-volume training*, which means heavy mileage running carried out at moderate intensity. In a study completed with relatively inexperienced athletes, 12 individuals exercised at an intensity of 100 percent of $\dot{V}O_2$max over a 7-week period, while 12 other subjects worked at an intensity of 60 percent of $\dot{V}O_2$max. For a 20-minute 5K runner, 100 percent of $\dot{V}O_2$max would be a pace of about 90 seconds per 400 meters (~6 minutes per mi), while 60 percent would correspond with 150 seconds per 400 meters (10 minutes per mi).

The latter group actually trained for longer periods of time so that the total amount of work per training session was equivalent between groups. After 7 weeks, the group working at 100 percent of $\dot{V}O_2$max achieved a 38 percent greater increase in $\dot{V}O_2$max compared with the lower-intensity, greater duration of training group, prompting the researchers to conclude that high-intensity exercise at around 100 percent of $\dot{V}O_2$max is the key factor for the promotion of optimal $\dot{V}O_2$max improvements.[36, 37]

A follow-up review that looked at 78 published scientific studies exploring the relationship between intensity, training volume, workout duration, and $\dot{V}O_2$max found that optimal gains in $\dot{V}O_2$max could be achieved by training as often as possible at an intensity of 90 to 100 percent of $\dot{V}O_2$max.[38] Ninety percent of $\dot{V}O_2$max roughly corresponds with 10K race speed, while 100 percent of $\dot{V}O_2$max is often close to competitive speed for a mile.

Traditionally, high-volume training carried out at moderate intensities has been categorized as aerobic running, while low-volume training conducted at high intensities has been termed anaerobic running (and has been presumed to have a smaller impact on maximal aerobic capacity), but research indicates that these concepts are misleading. In an inquiry carried out at the August Krogh Institute at the University of Copenhagen, one group of experienced endurance runners ran about 100 kilometers (62 mi) per week at an average intensity of 60 to 80 percent of $\dot{V}O_2$max (so-called aerobic running), while a second group of experienced runners ran just 50 kilometers (31 mi) per week while emphasizing fast-paced interval sessions (so-called anaerobic running); work-interval length varied from 60 to 1,000 meters (.03-.6 mi). After 14 weeks, the lower-mileage, higher-intensity runners had improved the main marker of aerobic metabolism, $\dot{V}O_2$max, by 7 percent, while the higher-mileage, lower-intensity runners had failed to upgrade $\dot{V}O_2$max at all. The 1K performance times also improved for the lower-mileage, higher-intensity group (from 2:41 to 2:37) but failed to increase for the higher-mileage, lower-intensity runners.[39, 40]

Conclusion

$\dot{V}O_2$max is a terrible predictor of performance among experienced runners with similar training backgrounds and has been linked with an inadequate theory of fatigue during running. However, individuals who improve their maximal aerobic capacities often enjoy significant gains in performance. A limitation on neural output seems to be the key factor which caps $\dot{V}O_2$max. Overall, scientific research strongly supports the idea that high-intensity training, rather than high-volume work, produces the greatest improvement in $\dot{V}O_2$max. Specific training techniques for optimizing $\dot{V}O_2$max are outlined in chapter 24.

CHAPTER 8

Running Economy

Unlike $\dot{V}O_2$max, running economy is a very strong predictor of distance-running capacity.[1] Scientific research reveals that running economy can sometimes account for almost two-thirds of the variation in 10K performances in a group of well-trained runners.[2] Each 1 percent improvement in economy achieved during training is linked with about a 0.4 to 0.7 percent upgrade in competitive-performance time.[3] Improvements in economy of almost 7 percent have been reported after as little as 6 weeks of training in highly fit distance runners, which could lead to a greater than 4 percent enhancement of performance.[3]

Defining Running Economy

Running economy is the oxygen cost of running at a specific speed; it is usually expressed in milliliters of oxygen consumed per kilogram of body weight per minute (ml • kg⁻¹ • min⁻¹). Runners with good running economy use less oxygen to run at a specific velocity compared with runners with less optimal economy. When runners with similar $\dot{V}O_2$max values are compared, runners with better economy will move along at a lower percentage of $\dot{V}O_2$max at any given submaximal speed. Economy is usually assessed in a laboratory setting with an athlete running on a treadmill while attached to a device that carefully monitors the oxygen content of the air coming out of the runner's lungs. The difference between the oxygen content of incoming and outgoing air over the course of 1 minute is the runner's economy.

Why does economy have such a strong impact on performance? The percentage of $\dot{V}O_2$max associated with a specific running speed is one way of expressing a runner's economy: A runner with great economy will tend to work at lower percentages of $\dot{V}O_2$max for various speeds than a runner who requires lots of oxygen and therefore has poor economy.

The percentage of $\dot{V}O_2$max associated with a particular velocity has a strong effect on how long that speed can be sustained. When well-trained ultra-runners move along at an intensity of about 67 percent of $\dot{V}O_2$max, for example, they can often sustain the speed for up to 85 kilometers (53 mi) before fatigue induces a drop in pace or complete exhaustion. When fit runners cruise along at approximately 82 percent of $\dot{V}O_2$max, they can complete a marathon before slowing the pace or stopping. At 94 percent of $\dot{V}O_2$max, most highly fit runners can run no farther than 5K before slowing the pace.[4] Therefore, if two runners competed against each other, starting at the same pace, but one runner's oxygen-consumption rate was 82 percent of $\dot{V}O_2$max while the second runner's oxygen-consumption rate was 94 percent of $\dot{V}O_2$max, the first runner could continue on for more than 26 miles, but the second runner would have to stop after just 3 miles.

Therefore, being able to run in a quality way at a lower percentage of $\dot{V}O_2$max prolongs endurance, which is why good economy is advantageous for endurance runners.

Factors Affecting Running Economy

The factors that affect running economy can be divided primarily into two categories: extrinsic and intrinsic.[5] Knowledge of these factors can be extremely beneficial to coaches and runners. Manipulation of extrinsic factors can enhance running economy during workouts and therefore improve training quality by enhancing the speed and length of a session. Understanding the intrinsic factors leads to the creation of the best running and strengthening workouts for enhancing economy—the sessions that can optimize intrinsic economy variables. For example, ground-contact time is an intrinsic economy factor: shorter ground-contact times are linked with better running economy. Thus, coaches and runners can carry out specific drills and running routines that abbreviate ground contact and thereby promote superior economy.

Extrinsic Factors

Extrinsic factors that act on running economy include the effects of the environment; running surfaces; and running equipment, primarily shoes and orthotics. Increases in ambient temperature tend to enhance economy initially by moderately raising core body temperature, which increases the mechanical efficiency of the muscles. As running in the heat continues, however, further advances in core temperature spike sweat-gland activity and induce hyperventilation, which can increase the oxygen cost of running and hurt economy.[6] Running into a headwind thwarts economy, while running with the wind improves it.[7] Running on an incline hampers economy compared with running at the same speed on level ground,[7] while downslope running upgrades economy and leads to a lower rate of oxygen consumption.[8, 9] Running in shoes that contain orthotics worsens economy; running barefoot enhances economy when compared with running in shoes, even in runners who have not practiced running barefoot.[10] Running on springy surfaces tends to increase economy, but running on hard, stiff surfaces can increase oxygen cost and thus may have a negative impact on economy.[11]

Intrinsic Factors

When extrinsic factors are constant, intrinsic factors—including genetic, anthropometric, kinetic, and kinematic factors—can produce considerable variation in running economy: Exercise scientists have discovered a 20 to 30 percent range in the rate of oxygen consumption associated with a particular velocity in trained endurance runners.[12, 13] Some of this variation is associated with genetic factors (see discussion in chapter 2). The often-researched angiotensin-converting enzyme (ACE) gene appears to play a role. Anthropometric variables account for a significant portion of the variance, too. Research suggests that whole-body leanness, small calf circumference, and unusually long shank length (i.e., the part of the leg between the knee and foot) are associated with increased running economy.[14] In contrast, having relatively large feet tends to hurt running economy,[4] although some researchers contend that having feet slightly larger than normal actually promotes better stability during foot contact with the ground and thus enhances economy.

Other Factors

The costs of supporting body weight, exerting stabilizing force, and producing propulsive force, all done while a foot is on the ground, determine the energy and thus oxygen costs of running, and these costs can vary widely among runners.[15] Scientific research reveals that runners who exhibit greater-than-usual vertical motion (i.e., more up-and-down movement of the body) during running tend to have poor economy, suggesting that directing propulsive forces vertically rather than horizontally leads to excessive rates of oxygen consumption.[16]

Shorter Ground-Contact Times

Shorter ground-contact times have also been linked with enhanced economy.[17, 18] A reduction in contact time implies better control of the foot, ankle, leg, and entire body whenever a foot is on the ground during gait; time is not being wasted on the correction of nonproductive motions, so contact time decreases. Better control implies a lower need for muscular action to correct suboptimal movements and thus a reduced oxygen cost associated with ground contact.

Shorter contact time also implies that propulsive force is being supplied by the elastic springback of stretched muscles and connective tissues rather than by active work of the muscles. Elastic springback is very economical—it requires no oxygen! It is also explosive, thus fostering quick ground contacts.

Training methods designed to abbreviate ground-contact time are described in chapters 16, 25, and 28.

Leg Stiffness

Scientific studies reveal that economy and ground-contact time are both functions of the springiness of the legs.[19] As the leg springs become slightly stiffer, economy tends to improve because more propulsive force can be created as a result of elastic recoil of the springs, not because of active, oxygen-consuming muscle contractions. As the leg springs stiffen, the leg becomes less sloppy and less collapsible during contact, permitting shorter, more explosive contact with the ground. Thus, runners with enhanced leg stiffness will tend to have good economy and short ground-contact times, too. Runners with suboptimal stiffness will tend to have poor economy and longer ground-contact times. When running is viewed through this springiness prism, the oxygen cost of running will always be linked to contact time: As ground-contact time expands, oxygen cost increases; as ground-contact time falls, oxygen cost goes down, too.

Although leg stiffness is often viewed in a negative light, research strongly supports the idea that reasonably increased stiffness is linked with good economy. One study looked at 11 measures of trunk and lower-limb flexibility in 100 subjects and found that the tightest (i.e., those with greatest leg stiffness) third of the runners had superior economy compared with the loosest third.[20] Another inquiry carried out with 19 well-trained, subelite, male distance runners discovered that inflexibility in the hip and calf regions of the legs was associated with enhanced running economy.[21] The mechanism underlying these somewhat surprising findings may simply be that tighter leg springs compared with looser, limper springs do a better job of storing and releasing energy, decreasing the need for active muscular contractions and thereby lowering oxygen cost.

Step Length

Other aspects of running form can influence economy, with research suggesting that a more acute (i.e., closed) knee angle during the swing phase of the gait cycle and a smaller amplitude (i.e., range) of arm motion are associated with enhanced economy.[22] Step *length* during running can have a significant impact on economy, with research suggesting that steps that are too long can hurt economy more than steps that are too short.[23] This is possibly because longer steps can produce a braking effect that increases ground-contact time and necessitates extra muscular-force production, and thus oxygen usage, to counter the braking action.

Some research suggests that the step lengths naturally adopted by runners optimize economy,[23] but it is difficult to interpret such inquiries. The basic problem is that runners may indeed select step lengths associated with the lowest oxygen costs of running, but it is also possible that they gradually become more coordinated and therefore more economical at the step lengths that are freely chosen—and less coordinated and economical at the step lengths that are not selected. Had a different step length been chosen during the early stages of a runner's training, it might have become even more economical than the favored one.

Certainly, there is no assurance that one's freely chosen step length (FCSL) is automatically best for economy. In one investigation carried out with nine distance runners, researchers noted that FCSL was about 10 percent longer than the step length associated with optimal economy.[24] This study provided hope for coaches and runners who believe that tinkering with running form and mechanics can lead to enhanced economy. Three weeks of training using optimal step length supported by combined audio and visual feedback gradually reduced step length and brought the oxygen cost of running under control. However, it would be risky for the average runner to change step length based on the recommendation of a coach or running peer without actual oxygen-cost measurements showing that the new stride length is indeed more economical.

High $\dot{V}O_2$max

Somewhat surprisingly, having a high $\dot{V}O_2$max increases the likelihood that a runner will have subpar economy; excellent economy is rarely linked with a high $\dot{V}O_2$max.[25] The mechanisms underlying this disconnect are not entirely clear, but a highly fit runner with large calves and big feet would tend to have a high $\dot{V}O_2$max because of the extra oxygen expenditure associated with placing massive weights at the ends of the leg pendulums; that runner would also have poor running economy. A well-trained runner with small calves and feet might have more difficulty driving $\dot{V}O_2$max up to a lofty plateau yet could enjoy good running economy. Anthropometric characteristics may make it difficult for optimal $\dot{V}O_2$max and economy to occur together.

Impact of Training on Running Economy

In individual runners, running economy can improve or worsen over time. The following five forms of training seem to have the strongest, most positive impact on this crucial variable:

- **Tapering.** Reducing the quantity and quality of training over a period of 4 to 21 days can have a major impact on running economy. One study found that a 7-day taper that contained a core of high-intensity training improved 5K performances by 3 percent and running economy by 6 percent in a group of well-trained endurance runners.[26]
- **Hill training.** Research indicates that hill training can have a very strong effect on running economy. In a classic study carried out at the

Karolinska Institutet in Stockholm, Sweden, the addition of twice-a-week hill workouts to a 12-week training regimen boosted running economy by about 3 percent. Chapter 15 outlines hill-training techniques that promote economy.[27]

▶ Hill training is a proven way to enhance economy.

- **Strength training.** There is convincing evidence that strength training can enhance economy in endurance runners. In a study carried out at the University of New Hampshire, six experienced female distance runners added upper- and lower-body strength workouts to their regular running programs during a 10-week training period, while six other female runners avoided resistance training and continued their usual running patterns for 10 weeks.[28] The strength training led to a 4 percent improvement in economy that was not matched by the control subjects. Different types of strength training promote economy in different ways and with varying magnitudes of response (see chapters 13, 14, and 23).

- **Explosive work.** Explosive training (i.e., combining reps of fast running with high-speed strengthening movements, including hops, jumps, and bounding drills) is also great for economy. Research carried out by Leena Paavolainen, Heikki Rusko, and their colleagues at the Finnish Research Institute for Olympic Sports has linked 9 weeks of explosive training with an 8 percent gain in economy at a 5K running pace, the largest gain ever described in published research.[29] A separate investigation carried out by Rob Spurrs and his colleagues from the Human Movement Department at the University of Technology in Sydney, Australia, found that 6 weeks of explosive drills with 15 total explosive workouts enhanced running economy by 4 to 7 percent and upgraded 3K performance time by almost 3 percent.[3] (See chapters 25 and 28 for more details about explosive training as an economy enhancer.)

- **Pace-specific training.** Running carried out at a specified tempo is believed to enhance running economy at the chosen training speed.

Indeed, research suggests that runners who bias their training toward running long miles at moderate tempos tend to become economical at moderate speeds, while runners who train at very quick paces tend to enhance their economy at faster speeds.[30] Critics of this research have suggested that it is not the training per se that elicits greater economy. They contend it is possible that runners who are already economical at high speeds tend to gravitate to high-speed events like the middle distances, while competitors who are naturally economical at slower speeds tend to take up the longer competitive distances.

However, research tells us that training tends to improve economy the most at the specific speed(s) that are actually used during training.[31] This has important implications for the overall construction of a training plan. For example, 5K runners should include a significant amount of training at the goal 5K pace in order to optimize economy at their desired intensity, and marathoners should insert segments paced at their marathon goal speeds into their long runs. More details about speed-specific training for economy enhancement is provided in chapter 25.

Conclusion

Running economy is a critically important performance variable; both experienced and inexperienced runners can enhance running economy in a relatively short period using extrinsic and intrinsic factors. With regard to extrinsic factors, runners can improve economy instantly by shifting to barefoot running, or at least by running in truly minimal shoes. Knowledge of the importance of extrinsic factors can upgrade performance. For example, runners who are aware that downhill running lowers oxygen cost (i.e., improves economy) can speed up significantly during downhill portions of their race courses without augmenting their oxygen consumption rate and overall sense of effort, thus gaining an advantage over competitors who are less aware of this fact.

Using the five key training techniques that enhance running economy—tapering, explosive work, hill training, strength training, and pace-specific effort—initiates significant upgrades in intrinsic running economy factors. Proper methods for using the five techniques are outlined fully in chapter 25.

CHAPTER 9

Minimum Velocity for Maximal Aerobic Capacity ($v\dot{V}O_2$max)

$\mathbf{A}$s mentioned in chapter 7, $\dot{V}O_2$max is a surprisingly poor predictor of performance. Although a runner who improves his or her $\dot{V}O_2$max from 60 ml • kg^{-1} • min^{-1} to 66 ml • kg^{-1} • min^{-1} can anticipate a 10 percent improvement in performance, a runner with a $\dot{V}O_2$max of 66 ml • kg^{-1} • min^{-1} is not necessarily 10 percent faster than an athlete with a $\dot{V}O_2$max of 60 ml • kg^{-1} • min^{-1}, nor is there any assurance that the runner with the higher $\dot{V}O_2$max would out-compete the runner with the lower aerobic capacity in a 5K, 10K, or marathon. There is a significant chance that the competitor with the lower $\dot{V}O_2$max would win.

However, $v\dot{V}O_2$max, a related physiological variable, *is* a strong predictor of endurance performance.[1] Unlike $\dot{V}O_2$max, which is a rate of oxygen consumption, $v\dot{V}O_2$max is a running velocity. Specifically, it is the *minimum* running velocity that elicits a runner's maximal rate of oxygen consumption or $\dot{V}O_2$max. As explained in the next sections, there are many intense running speeds that cause an individual runner to attain $\dot{V}O_2$max; $v\dot{V}O_2$max, although fast, is the slowest of these speeds.

Defining $v\dot{V}O_2$max

To understand $v\dot{V}O_2$max more completely, consider a hypothetical runner named Liz who can run quite easily at a pace of 8 minutes per mile. As she runs at that rate, her exercise intensity is 70 percent of $\dot{V}O_2$max. Expressed another way, the 8-minute pace requires an oxygen-consumption rate of just 70 percent of maximum to provide the necessary rate of energy production to keep her body moving forward at 3.35 meters per second, the tempo needed to run 8-minute miles.

As Liz gradually speeds up, her rate of oxygen consumption also increases in order to provide the higher rates of energy production required for faster running. When she moves up to a 7-minute tempo per mile, she might increase oxygen consumption to 85 percent of $\dot{V}O_2max$, for example, and a 6:30 pace could get her to 92 percent of her $\dot{V}O_2max$. Even faster speeds would move her closer and closer to $\dot{V}O_2max$.

In Liz's case, she might reach $\dot{V}O_2max$ for the first time when she accelerates to a 6-minute tempo per mile. Running at a 6:10 pace would not cause her to hit $\dot{V}O_2max$; that would be slightly too slow. Since 6:00 per mile is the first tempo that elicits $\dot{V}O_2max$, it corresponds with $v\dot{V}O_2max$. In Liz's case, $v\dot{V}O_2max$ would be 1,609 meters divided by 360 seconds (because there are 1,609 meters in a mile and 360 seconds in 6 minutes), or 4.47 meters per second. By convention, $v\dot{V}O_2max$ is almost always defined in meters per second.

If Liz warms up on a subsequent day and begins running at a 5:30 per mile pace, she would also reach $\dot{V}O_2max$, probably after just 2 minutes or so of running. Thus, a 5:30 tempo is also associated with the attainment of $\dot{V}O_2max$, but—importantly—it is not the *minimum* velocity that elicits $\dot{V}O_2max$; that distinction falls to the 6:00 tempo in Liz's case. The 5:30 tempo cannot be $v\dot{V}O_2max$, even though $\dot{V}O_2max$ is reached when Liz runs at this pace.

In fact, there is a range of tempos —in Liz's case, most likely from 6:00 to about 4:45 per mile (her maximal velocity)—that she could handle for short periods of time and that could cause her to attain $\dot{V}O_2max$. Although this range of speeds can be used in training to reach $\dot{V}O_2max$, only one tempo—in Liz's case, 6:00 per mile—corresponds with $v\dot{V}O_2max$, the minimum velocity that produces the maximal rate of oxygen consumption. All the other relevant tempos are faster than $v\dot{V}O_2max$.

It is also true that Liz could probably run at faster than a 4:45 pace, perhaps even as quickly as 4:16 per mile (a pace of about 64 seconds per 400 m). However, her ability to sustain this tempo would be quite limited; she might be able to sustain this pace for just 100 meters (16 seconds). This would be too short a time for her heart to attain maximal cardiac output and for her leg muscles to respond with the highest-possible rate of oxygen consumption; thus, she would not reach $\dot{V}O_2max$ while running at this higher speed because of its short duration.

Importance of $v\dot{V}O_2max$

For endurance runners, knowing $v\dot{V}O_2max$ is highly important. This is because training at $v\dot{V}O_2max$ is one of the most potent ways to enhance the physiological variables critical for endurance performance, including $v\dot{V}O_2max$ itself, plus running economy and velocity at lactate threshold (see chapter 10).[1]

Endurance runners, coaches, and exercise physiologists have pondered *why* $\dot{V}O_2max$ is so poor at predicting endurance performance, while $v\dot{V}O_2max$ is so good. The answer is simple: $\dot{V}O_2max$ contains no information about an athlete's running economy. A runner might have a high $\dot{V}O_2max$ and yet quite miserable running economy, in which case his or her performances would be disappointingly slow despite the high aerobic capacity. In fact, exercise physiologists have noted that a higher aerobic capacity is to some extent a predictor of *subpar* running economy, or at least that high aerobic capacities and superb running economies do not often go together in the same runner.

Like $\dot{V}O_2$max, v$\dot{V}O_2$max reflects maximal rate of oxygen consumption, but it also incorporates running economy, how well a runner can translate rates of oxygen consumption into various running speeds. A runner with a high v$\dot{V}O_2$max must be doing that translating very well; otherwise, he or she would not be able to reach a high speed (v$\dot{V}O_2$max) when maximal oxygen consumption is attained. Poor running economy would mean that $\dot{V}O_2$max would be attained rather quickly at relatively low speeds (see figure 9.1 for an accompanying plot of oxygen consumption as a function of running speed).

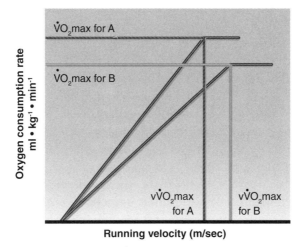

▶ **Figure 9.1** Runner A has a higher $\dot{V}O_2$max compared with runner B, but runner B has a superior economy and greater v$\dot{V}O_2$max.

Predictive Power of v$\dot{V}O_2$max

To begin to comprehend the lack of predictive power of $\dot{V}O_2$max in contrast to that of v$\dot{V}O_2$max, consider an extremely well-trained runner who happens to have large, clunky feet. Such a runner will tend to have a high $\dot{V}O_2$max because of the demanding training he or she has been undertaking, and the clunky feet will add to $\dot{V}O_2$max, driving it higher compared with a similarly trained runner with small feet. Having to move those large feet down the road at high rates of speed will call for extremely high rates of oxygen production. However, large feet will not make the runner competitive; in fact, they will cause this runner to reach $\dot{V}O_2$max at a rather modest speed since so much oxygen is being used to move the big feet along. Thus, this runner will have a high $\dot{V}O_2$max but relatively poor running economy, and thus a moderate v$\dot{V}O_2$max and moderate performances. As usual, v$\dot{V}O_2$max will be more reflective of performance potential than $\dot{V}O_2$max.

This big-foot scenario is an extreme example of why $v\dot{V}O_2max$ predicts performance quite well. It is important to bear in mind that the same situation prevails for runners in general who have modest to poor running economy for reasons other than big feet. Such athletes might have high levels of $\dot{V}O_2max$. If running economy is subpar, however, any particular running speed will elicit an unusually high rate of oxygen consumption, and $\dot{V}O_2max$ will be reached at relatively mediocre running speeds. Thus, performance potential will be below what might be expected from the determination of $\dot{V}O_2max$ alone.

The power of $v\dot{V}O_2max$ to predict performance is illustrated in a study carried out at Lynchburg College in Virginia in which 17 well-trained distance runners (10 males and 7 females) underwent physiological testing and then competed in a 16K race.[2] Laboratory tests determined $\dot{V}O_2max$, $v\dot{V}O_2max$, running economy, percentage of maximal oxygen uptake at lactate threshold (%$\dot{V}O_2max$ at lactate threshold), running velocity at lactate threshold, and peak treadmill velocity. The Lynchburg researchers found that among all the measured physiological variables, $v\dot{V}O_2max$ had the highest correlation ($r = -.972$) with 16K performance, while %$\dot{V}O_2max$ at lactate threshold had the lowest correlation ($r = .136$). Overall, $v\dot{V}O_2max$ was found to be the best predictor of 16K running time, explaining all but just 5.6 percent of the variance. The Virginia scientists concluded that $v\dot{V}O_2max$ is the best predictor of endurance-running performance because it integrates maximal aerobic power with running economy.

In a separate study carried out at Fitchburg State College in Massachusetts,[3] 24 female runners from four different high school teams competing at the Massachusetts 5K State Championship Meet were tested in the laboratory. These tests revealed a high correlation between $v\dot{V}O_2max$ and 5K performance ($r = .77$). In contrast, the correlation between $\dot{V}O_2max$ and 5K speed was lower, and running economy at a slow velocity (215 m per minute) was poorly correlated with 5K outcome. Note that economy at race-like speeds is predictive of race competitiveness, while economy at slow velocities is not necessarily linked with racing capacity (another argument against conducting a lot of training at medium to low speeds).

In a classic study carried out at Arizona State University in Tempe, $v\dot{V}O_2max$ was found to be a primary determinant of 10K performance in well-trained male distance runners.[4] Among these runners, the variation in 10K running time attributable to $v\dot{V}O_2max$ exceeded that due to either $\dot{V}O_2max$ or running economy.

Impact of Training on $v\dot{V}O_2max$ and Running Economy

French researchers Veronique Billat and Jean-Pierre Koralsztein have concluded that $v\dot{V}O_2max$ predicts running performances very well at distances ranging from 1,500 meters to the marathon. They also noted that $v\dot{V}O_2max$

has similar predictive power in cycling, swimming, and kayaking; of course, v$\dot{V}O_2$max would have to be determined for each sport since running v$\dot{V}O_2$max does not carry over to other activities.[5] Billat and Koralsztein also discovered that training that emphasizes intervals conducted at v$\dot{V}O_2$max can be extremely productive for distance runners.

In one study, Billat and Koralsztein asked eight experienced runners to take part in 4 weeks of training that included one interval session per week at v$\dot{V}O_2$max.[6] The athletes specialized in middle- and long-distance running (1,500 m up to the half marathon), and their average $\dot{V}O_2$max was a fairly lofty 71.2 ml • kg^{-1} • min^{-1}. This program included six workouts per week, including four easy efforts, one session with work intervals at v$\dot{V}O_2$max, and one session at lactate-threshold speed with longer intervals. Total distance covered per week was about 50 miles (~ 80 km). Over the 4-week period, the runners' weekly training schedules were formatted in the following way:

- Monday: One hour of easy running at an intensity of just 60 percent of $\dot{V}O_2$max.
- Tuesday: A 4K warm-up and then v$\dot{V}O_2$max interval training consisting of 5 × 3 minutes at exactly v$\dot{V}O_2$max. During the 3-minute work intervals, the runners covered an average of 1,000 meters (.62 mi; their v$\dot{V}O_2$max tempo was 72 seconds per 400 meters). Recovery intervals were equal in duration (3 minutes), and the cool-down consisted of 2K of easy running. Overall, the workout was a 4K warm-up, 5 × 3 minutes at v$\dot{V}O_2$max, with 3-minute easy jog recoveries, and a 2K cool-down.
- Wednesday: 45 minutes of easy running at an intensity of 70 percent of $\dot{V}O_2$max.
- Thursday: 60 minutes of easy running at 70 percent of $\dot{V}O_2$max.
- Friday: A session designed to enhance lactate threshold composed of a warm-up and then two 20-minute intervals at 85 percent of v$\dot{V}O_2$max; for example, if v$\dot{V}O_2$max happened to be 20 kilometers per hour (5.55 m per second), the speed for these intervals would be .85 × 20 or 17 kilometers per hour (4.72 m per second). A 5-minute, easy jog recovery was imposed between the 20-minute work intervals, and a cool-down followed the second work interval.
- Saturday: Rest day with no training at all.
- Sunday: 60 minutes of easy running at an intensity of 70 percent of $\dot{V}O_2$max.

After 4 weeks, the results were amazing, to say the least. Although maximal aerobic capacity ($\dot{V}O_2$max) failed to make any upward move at all, v$\dot{V}O_2$max rose by 3 percent from 20.5 kilometers per hour to 21.1 kilometers per hour. In addition, running economy improved by a startling 6 percent. This enhancement of economy was probably behind most of the uptick in v$\dot{V}O_2$max since it lowered the economy line on the graph of oxygen consumption as a function of running speed and thus pushed v$\dot{V}O_2$max out to the right for the French runners (see figure 9.1).

After the 4 weeks of training, lactate threshold remained locked at 84 percent of $v\dot{V}O_2$max. However, since $v\dot{V}O_2$max was 3 percent higher at the end of the training period, running velocity at lactate threshold had also increased by a similar amount. Most of the key variables associated with endurance performance—$v\dot{V}O_2$max, economy, and lactate-threshold speed—had advanced in just 4 weeks.

The 6 percent gain in economy associated with $v\dot{V}O_2$max training was particularly impressive. A handful of training manipulations have been linked with upgraded economy, and the gains in economy have usually been far below the one documented by Billat and Koralsztein's research. A classic Scandinavian hill-running study (see chapter 25) detected only a 3 percent increase in running economy, even though the hill training was conducted for three times as long (12 weeks versus the 4 weeks needed by the French runners in Billat and Koralsztein's study). Similarly, improvements in economy associated with strength training have usually been in the 3 percent range, also after fairly long periods of training. It appears that $v\dot{V}O_2$max training can work economy magic in as little as 4 weeks, especially for those runners who have not carried out $v\dot{V}O_2$max work previously.

Advantages of Training at $v\dot{V}O_2$max

Runners, coaches, and exercise physiologists have speculated why training at $v\dot{V}O_2$max simultaneously improves $v\dot{V}O_2$max, running economy, and lactate-threshold speed. It appears that running at $v\dot{V}O_2$max increases leg-muscle strength and power to a considerably greater extent compared with running at slower speeds. Enhanced muscle strength tends to upgrade running economy automatically: Since individual muscle cells are stronger, fewer muscle fibers need to be recruited to run at a specific velocity, and thus the oxygen cost of running is reduced. Or put another way, there are fewer muscle cells grabbing oxygen molecules at high rates and using them to supply the energy needed for running. It is also probable that running at $v\dot{V}O_2$max boosts neuromuscular responsiveness and coordination to a greater degree than does easier pacing. Advances in coordination should also drive down the energy cost of running and thus promote better economy because less energy would be needed to correct suboptimal movements of the lower limbs.

The results obtained by Billat and Koralsztein have some interesting consequences, as is apparent in the chapters in parts IV and V. A traditional belief in endurance running is that a runner works on a single variable at a time during training: For example, the runner might carry out intervals at a 5K pace to increase $\dot{V}O_2$max and conduct reps at faster than 5K tempo in order to enhance economy. It is clear that Billat's $v\dot{V}O_2$max sessions do not work on a single variable but rather improve several key physiological variables in concert: $v\dot{V}O_2$max, running economy, and lactate-threshold speed were all upgraded through the use of a single running pace.

Expressed another way, it is clearly possible for endurance runners to work on all the key performance variables at once with the use of a high-quality training pace such as v$\dot{V}O_2$max. The traditional formulation of the periodization of training—working on a single variable during an isolated block of training—is out of date since the key variables can move concurrently in response to strong workouts. As outlined in chapters 22 and 23 on building a training program, periodization is thus not the division of the training year into separate blocks of single-variable training but rather is a method of increasing the difficulty and specificity of training over time in a manner that optimizes total running fitness.

The v$\dot{V}O_2$max variable has a sister measurement—time limit at v$\dot{V}O_2$max (t_{lim}v$\dot{V}O_2$max) —that is also important for distance-running performance. Time limit at v$\dot{V}O_2$max is simply the amount of time a runner can sustain his or her v$\dot{V}O_2$max without slowing the pace or stopping. There is fairly wide variation in time limit at v$\dot{V}O_2$max among endurance runners, with 4 minutes being the approximate lower limit and 10 minutes the top end.[7] Time limit at v$\dot{V}O_2$max can be a decent predictor of performance in its own right, especially among runners with similar values of v$\dot{V}O_2$max. It is quickly apparent that two runners with similar running velocities at $\dot{V}O_2$max would have quite different results in a 9-minute race (like a 3K), for example, if one of the runners had a t_{lim}v$\dot{V}O_2$max of 4 minutes while the other could maintain v$\dot{V}O_2$max for 10 minutes. The latter runner could sustain v$\dot{V}O_2$max for the entirety of the race while the former would have to back off v$\dot{V}O_2$max after just 4 minutes.

Training to improve time limit at v$\dot{V}O_2$max is discussed in chapter 10, which focuses on improving velocity at lactate threshold. As it turns out, upgrading lactate-threshold velocity is a key way to increase time limit at v$\dot{V}O_2$max. For now, the most important fact to know is that the average time limit at v$\dot{V}O_2$max in endurance runners is 6 minutes.[7] This knowledge permits any runner to estimate v$\dot{V}O_2$max properly and then carry out v$\dot{V}O_2$max interval training. This v$\dot{V}O_2$max training (outlined in chapter 26) produces an array of benefits, including sizable improvements in running economy and lactate-threshold velocity plus improvements in v$\dot{V}O_2$max itself.

Conclusion

Research on v$\dot{V}O_2$max has changed the way coaches and scientists think about setting up and periodizing training plans. It's important for coaches and runners to realize that v$\dot{V}O_2$max is a key indicator of performance potential; thus, they should relentlessly pursue ways to optimize v$\dot{V}O_2$max during training. There is no evidence that high-mileage training improves v$\dot{V}O_2$max; rather, high-quality running at v$\dot{V}O_2$max and faster speeds is necessary to keep v$\dot{V}O_2$max moving upward. Conducting intervals at v$\dot{V}O_2$max has positive impacts on v$\dot{V}O_2$max, running economy, and lactate-threshold velocity. Thus, it has remarkable effects on performance enhancements. The challenge, as discussed in chapter 26, is to arrange v$\dot{V}O_2$max workouts properly throughout the overall training program.

CHAPTER 10

Velocity at Lactate Threshold

Running velocity at lactate threshold is simply the velocity *above which* lactate begins to accumulate in the blood. At lactate-threshold and lower velocities, blood lactate tends to be stable. Like running economy and $v\dot{V}O_2max$, running velocity at the lactate threshold is a strong physiological predictor of endurance performance.[1] In individual runners, running velocity at lactate threshold responds readily to training, and lactate-threshold upgrades lead to major improvements in race times.

Glycolysis and the Krebs Cycle

To grasp why running velocity at lactate threshold has such a tight grip on endurance performances, it is first important to understand a basic metabolic process called glycolysis. Glycolysis is so critical metabolically that its loss would mean that a runner would never be able to run another 5K or marathon. In fact, without glycolysis an athlete would not be able to ride around the block on a bike or even walk to the corner store in a reasonable amount of time. Glycolysis is actually a series of 10 different chemical reactions that break down glucose, the simple six-carbon sugar that is the body's most-important source of carbohydrate fuel, into something called pyruvic acid (see figure 10.1). This glycolytic conversion of glucose to pyruvic acid can quickly provide some of the energy a runner's muscles need for running.

For endurance athletes, the most important aspect of glycolysis is actually what happens after the glycolytic reactions take place. The pyruvic acid created during glycolysis can be funneled into a complex series of energy-creating reactions called the Krebs cycle. In addition to breaking down the pyruvic acid produced from glucose, the Krebs cycle also metabolizes fats; overall, it furnishes more than 90 percent of the energy required to run in a sustained manner. Since glycolysis provides muscles with quick energy and also jump-starts the Krebs cycle, it is a paramount player in muscular energy production. In fact, without glycolysis the muscles would grind to a halt after only 10 to 15 seconds of intense activity.

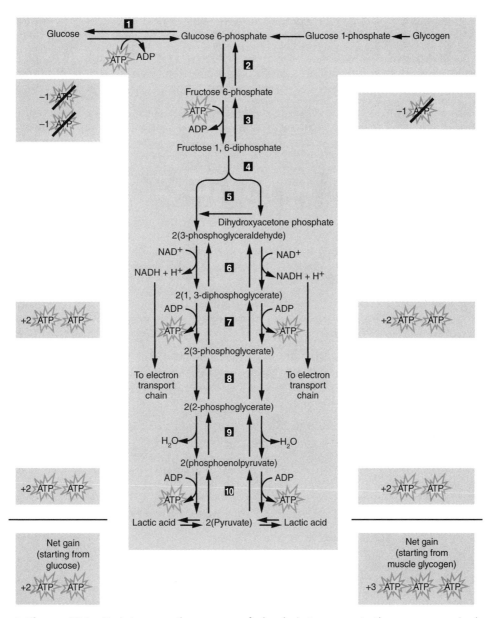

▶ **Figure 10.1** Sprinters use the process of glycolysis to generate the energy required for top performance.

Fortunately, glycolysis usually proceeds normally inside muscle cells, and it also keeps pace with a runner's level of activity: the faster the athlete runs, the hotter the glycolysis fires burn. This has a very interesting consequence: When an athlete is running at a quick pace, pyruvic acid is produced via glycolysis at high rates, but not all of the pyruvic acid that is produced can be instantaneously shuttled into the Krebs cycle. As pyruvic acid waits to be admitted to the Krebs cycle process, an enzyme called lactate dehydrogenase converts some of the pyruvic acid to lactic acid. When an athlete is at rest or running at slow to moderate intensity, modest amounts of pyruvic acid will be formed; almost all of it will go into the Krebs cycle, and there will consequently be relatively little lactic acid lingering in the muscles. When an athlete runs strenuously, however, everything changes: To supply the energy required for the fast running, glycolysis proceeds at a high rate, and thus lots of pyruvic acid ends up waiting in the Krebs cycle queue. Unusually large amounts of lactic acid can then be created in the muscles, and some of this lactic acid surfeit can be dumped into the blood.

Lactic Acid's Real Role

Two popular myths in running are that the burn felt in the leg muscles during fast running is caused by this buildup of lactic acid and that the soreness experienced the day after an especially tough workout is produced by the same troublesome compound. Two other widespread misconceptions are that lactic acid is a waste product formed in muscles during vigorous exercise and that lactic acid shows up in the muscles when athletes run out of oxygen or enter a mysterious process called oxygen debt. A final untruth is that lactic acid causes fatigue during intense running; unfortunately, this unfounded principle is still accepted as gospel by many coaches and runners.

Science tells us that all five of these assertions about lactic acid are untrue: Lactic acid doesn't produce burning sensations, it doesn't induce soreness, and it's not a form of metabolic garbage that must be eliminated from muscle cells as quickly as possible. The burn experienced during high-speed running is probably a protective mechanism created by the nervous system in order to stop runners from damaging their muscles with too much high-speed effort. The soreness experienced 24 to 48 hours after a tough workout is most likely the result of an inflammatory process occurring in muscle cells that have been partially damaged by very strenuous running; lactic acid is not involved.[2-5]

In addition, oxygen shortfalls are not required in order to make lactic acid appear in the muscles and blood, and lactic acid does not induce fatigue. The truth is that lactic acid is produced in the body all the time, even when athletes are at rest, because it's a natural byproduct of the key energy-producing process of glycolysis. Furthermore, running velocity at lactate threshold occurs at 60 to 88 percent of $\dot{V}O_2$max, that is, at an exercise intensity at which oxygen is not yet limiting since $\dot{V}O_2$max has not been reached.

The concentration of lactic acid in the muscles and blood can rise significantly whenever a carbohydrate-containing meal is consumed; many of the ingested carbs are broken down glycolytically to pyruvic acid, which is then converted to lactic acid. If lactic acid really caused muscle soreness and fatigue, runners would experience muscle pain and tiredness every time they wolfed down their favorite carbohydrate-rich meals!

Instead of being a dangerous compound that wreaks havoc inside muscle cells, lactic acid (or, more accurately, lactate, which is just lactic acid without a hydrogen ion) plays a paramount role in carbohydrate processing throughout a runner's body. Lactate can move out of the muscles and travel through the bloodstream to the liver; the liver can then use lactate to produce glucose, a runner's most important source of carbohydrate fuel. This is an incredibly significant role for lactate because the liver relies on glucose to maintain normal blood sugar levels.

In addition, up to 50 percent of the lactate produced during a very tough workout or race may be used eventually to synthesize glycogen in the muscles. Glycogen is the key *storage* form of carbohydrate in the body. This is important because the muscles use carbohydrates as *the major energy source* during high-quality workouts and competitive endurance performances. Far from damaging tissues or inducing soreness, the glycogen that comes from lactate provides the energy needed to carry out subsequent, high-quality workouts; the glycogen can be broken down into countless molecules of glucose, which then undergo glycolysis.

During exercise, lactate is also an irreplaceable source of immediate energy for muscles and other tissues because lactate can be converted back to pyruvate, which can then quickly enter the energy-producing Krebs cycle. Enhancing the ability to use lactate can improve a runner's race times rather dramatically. Thus, lactate can go two ways in muscles: (1) into glycogen formation, or energy storage, or (2) into energy creation via pyruvate's entry into the Krebs cycle. Developing the ability to process lactate effectively helps athletes run faster and longer. You'll learn how to do this in chapter 27.

Lactate's Movement Through the Body

Lactate moves through a runner's body in important ways after meals. Most of the carbohydrate from ingested food enters the bloodstream as glucose and moves directly to the liver. The liver picks up a large quantity of this glucose from the blood and converts a significant fraction of it via glycolysis to lactate. This lactate is then released from the liver into the bloodstream, destined for all points around the body.

Why does the liver like to ship out carbohydrate as lactate? Why doesn't it simply keep the carbohydrate packaged as pure glucose? Glucose tends to enter body tissues, including muscles, rather sluggishly; it must be guided by an important hormone called insulin, and the overall process can be rather lethargic. That's why your blood sugar levels can remain elevated for a couple of hours after a carbohydrate-rich meal.

Lactate, on the other hand, does not depend on insulin and can enter muscle and other cells very quickly. In other words, lactate represents quick energy for your muscles and other organs. This is why the heart is a huge sink for lactate: It picks lactate right out of the bloodstream to support its beating around the clock and uses it to supply its vast energy demands during strenuous exertion. It's a good thing that lactate doesn't really cause fatigue. Otherwise, your heart would have to take a break now and then, which would not be good. Lactate can be viewed as a kind of shortcut mechanism for getting energy into the muscles, heart, and other tissues.

This overall process means that blood levels of glucose and lactate rise after a high-carbohydrate meal. However, lactate levels don't appear to rise as fast as glucose concentrations, primarily because lactate is rapidly removed from the blood once it appears, while glucose is taken away more slowly. By changing some of the absorbed glucose to lactate, the liver quickens the disposal of blood carbohydrate. A key benefit of this glucose-lactate conversion is that the amount of insulin that pours into the blood from the pancreas after meals decreases. This limiting of insulin production may help to enhance body composition, since one feature of insulin is that it coaxes glucose into adipose cells, where it can be converted readily to fat.

Lactate Shuttle

Overall, lactate is the primary player in an extremely important process called the "lactate shuttle." Described in detail by the noted George Brooks and his colleagues at the University of California at Berkeley,[6] the lactate shuttle involves the following chain of events:

1. Lactate is formed in ample amounts in tissues in which glycogen and glucose are being broken down at high rates via glycolysis. This happens in the leg muscles during vigorous running; as mentioned previously, pyruvate is actually formed first, but pyruvate can be readily converted to lactate.

2. The lactate formed from pyruvate can slip quickly out of muscle cells and into surrounding tissues and the blood. This lactate escape from the cells enables glycolysis, the conversion of glucose to pyruvate and lactate, to keep going at high rates. If pyruvate could not be transformed into highly dispersible lactate, pyruvate might build up to overly generous levels within muscle cells; this would shut down glycolysis via a feedback mechanism and thwart energy production. The muscles would have to reduce their rate of force production because of the lack of energy, and a runner would have to slow down. As lactate is released from hard-working muscle cells, it can be picked up by nearby muscle cells that are not so overflowing with lactate, or it can enter the bloodstream and be transported to other muscles and tissues throughout the body, including cardiac muscle fibers in the heart.

3. The muscle cells and tissues receiving the lactate have a couple of options: They can use lactate as an energy-rich fuel by converting it back to pyruvate and sending it into the Krebs cycle, or they can use it as a building block for glycogen storage to satisfy future energy needs.

The lactate shuttle demonstrates that lactate is very far from being a soreness-inducing toxin, a metabolic waste product, or a key inducer of fatigue, as some have described it. Lactate's easy diffusibility prevents glycolysis from shutting down, and its high-octane fuel status helps the muscles, heart, and other cells meet their immediate energy requirements or else store significant amounts of energy for later use.

Physiology of the Lactate Threshold

These descriptions of lactate's activities and roles make it easier to understand the often-misunderstood phenomenon called running velocity at lactate threshold. At the beginning of a moderate to difficult workout, lactate levels in the blood initially rise because glycolysis is working to provide the energy required to initiate running. If there were plenty of oxygen around, the pyruvate formed from glycolysis would enter the Krebs cycle and would be broken down all the way to carbon dioxide and water, releasing a lot of important energy in the process.

However, the workout has just begun, so heart rate is just beginning to increase, and the capillaries leading into the muscles are not yet in their fully open position. Therefore, blood and oxygen flow to the muscles is still somewhat limited. As a result, a fair amount of pyruvate will be converted to lactate, and lactate will begin piling up inside leg-muscle cells and spilling out into the blood. If blood lactate level is measured at this early stage of a workout, it can be surprisingly high, even when an athlete is moving along at a moderate pace.

If running is continued at a moderate intensity, blood lactate concentration will quickly drop. As heart rate increases and capillaries dilate, oxygen will pour into muscle cells, pyruvate will be oxidized for energy, and the lactate spillover process will abate. Blood lactate concentration will decrease and then hold steady, which means the entry and exit rates of lactate into and out of the blood are equal. Some lactate may continue to move into the blood from muscle cells, but other muscles, the heart, and various tissues around the body will remove it approximately as fast as it appears.

Lactate levels might continue to hold steady even as the intensity of the workout is gradually increased. As long as an athlete is not going too fast, that is, as long as oxygen is moving into muscle cells at an adequate rate, and the muscle cells are doing a good job of taking care of the pyruvate produced by glycolysis and thus limiting lactate spillover, blood lactate concentration will remain steady.

However, as running velocity increases, a speed is eventually reached at which glycolysis tears along so fast that the leg muscles begin to have difficulty breaking down most of the pyruvate into carbon dioxide and water via the Krebs cycle. Once this speed is attained or surpassed, lactate begins building up inside the muscle cells, and the lactate-spilling process may accelerate so much that lactate levels in the blood may increase significantly.

This happens when the rate of lactate spilling into the blood is greater than the rate of lactate uptake from the blood.

This point may be reached because not enough oxygen is getting into muscle cells to handle all of the pyruvate being produced. Causes vary: The heart may be unable to pump oxygen-carrying blood at the needed rate; the capillary density around muscle fibers may be too limited; there may not be enough enzymes available to guide pyruvate through the Krebs cycle at very high rates; or muscle cells may be somewhat lacking in mitochondria, the tiny structures inside muscle cells in which the key reactions of the Krebs cycle take place.

This threshold velocity at which blood lactate levels begin to increase dramatically may also be reached if the muscles and tissues are not very good at clearing large amounts of lactate from the blood once they appear, a fact that has important implications for training. Whatever the underlying mechanism, the rate of lactate appearance in the blood suddenly outstrips the rate of lactate disappearance, and so blood lactate levels begin to climb somewhat precipitously. The running speed above which this lactate increase begins to occur is the running velocity at lactate threshold (see figure 10.2). Any higher speed produces a significant buildup in blood lactate. Any lower speed is associated with relatively low, stable blood lactate levels.

Every endurance runner has a running velocity at lactate threshold; even the fittest elite runner eventually reaches a velocity at which lactate begins to build up in the blood. The actual value of running velocity at lactate threshold, usually expressed in meters per second, reveals a lot about the overall fitness and performance capability of a runner. If running velocity at lactate threshold is reached at a relatively slow speed, for example, it often

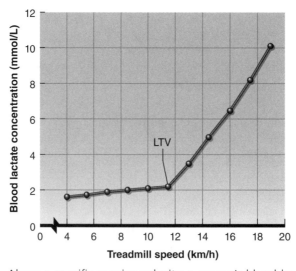

▶ **Figure 10.2** Above a specific running velocity, a runner's blood-lactate level begins to increase dramatically. This specific speed is termed the lactate threshold velocity (LTV).

means that the oxidative energy systems in the muscles are not working very well based on one of the causes described previously. If the oxidative energy systems were operating at a high level, they would easily break down the modest amounts of pyruvate and lactate produced at the relatively slow speed, and lactate would not pour out into the blood.

If running velocity at lactate threshold is attained at a modest speed, it might also mean that the heart is not capable of sending oxygenated blood to the muscles at an adequate rate; this could thwart the breakdown of pyruvate and increase lactate production. Since blood lactate depends not only on lactate formation and spillage but also on how well the muscles and other tissues can remove lactate from the blood once it appears, a low running velocity at lactate threshold can also mean that the muscles, heart, and other tissues are not very good at extracting lactate from the blood.

Impact of Training on Running Velocity at Lactate Threshold

In practical terms, a key goal of training should be to move the running velocity at lactate threshold to progressively faster speeds; doing so will mean that cardiac output and the oxidative energy systems are improving and that the muscles are getting better at pulling lactate out of the blood and using it for energy. Having a high running velocity at lactate threshold means that an athlete can process pyruvate at greater rates and thus has the energy needed to run fast and long during endurance competitions.

A strong link exists between running velocity at lactate threshold and how difficult running feels, or the perceived exertion. In general terms, any running speed above running velocity at lactate threshold tends to feel difficult, while exertions completed below that velocity are comparatively comfortable. As an athlete moves up the velocity scale, perceived exertion increases dramatically. Thus, as running velocity at lactate threshold increases over time in response to appropriate training, previously uncomfortable paces suddenly begin to feel more comfortable and sustainable because they are now below the velocity at lactate threshold, and athletes complete their races at much faster paces than before. For many endurance athletes, improving running speed at lactate threshold can be *the* key to unlocking better performances. A variety of different scientific studies have suggested that running velocity at lactate threshold can sometimes be the single best predictor of endurance performance.[7, 8]

Runners and coaches sometimes wonder why running velocity at lactate threshold is such a great fitness indicator and race predictor. The reason for this predictive power is that this measurement includes information about lactate dynamics, and thus indirectly about oxygen use and running economy. Runners cannot have poor running economy and great velocity at lactate threshold. Poor economy means that lots of energy must be used to maintain a particular pace, and high rates of energy consumption generally mean heavy-duty carbohydrate (glycogen and glucose) breakdown rates. Ramped-up glucose metabolism means ample glycolysis, resulting in high rates of lactate production. It's difficult to have a great running velocity at lactate threshold if lactate is flooding the blood at moderate speeds because of poor economy.

In contrast, great running economy means minimal energy expenditure, lower rates of carbohydrate metabolism, calmer rates of glycolysis, and therefore reduced lactate production, which goes hand in hand with an advanced running velocity at lactate threshold. Overall, a runner with a fine running velocity at lactate threshold is usually also one with excellent running economy, and that is why running velocity at threshold can be such a great performance predictor. Running velocity at lactate threshold actually includes information about three important factors for running success: lactate-breakdown capacity via oxidative metabolism, the ability to clear lactate from the blood, and running economy.

Responsiveness to Training

Scientific research reveals that running velocity at lactate threshold is *very* responsive to training. In fact, it is much more reactive than $\dot{V}O_2$max in most male experienced runners.[9] If an athlete has been running consistently for several years, $\dot{V}O_2$max may not move upward at all over the course of a single training year, but running velocity at lactate threshold might increase by 3 to 10 percent depending on the training program followed.

Why is running velocity at lactate threshold so dynamic? "The skeletal muscles can adapt rather suddenly and strikingly to training, producing major gains in running velocity at lactate threshold," says Marc Rogers, exercise physiologist at the University of Maryland. $\dot{V}O_2$max depends to a great degree on the size of the heart's left ventricle, which pumps oxygenated blood into the body, and that structure doesn't change much in volume after runners have been training for some years. So $\dot{V}O_2$max may not increase at all or only by a few percentage points even with increased training.[10]

Scientific research strongly supports Rogers' contention that $\dot{V}O_2$max can be a rather stubborn, static variable, while running velocity at lactate threshold is extremely responsive to training. When scientists at Georgia State University and the Emory University School of Medicine followed nine elite distance runners over a 30-month period during which the athletes prepared for the 1984 Summer Olympic Games in Los Angeles, they found that $\dot{V}O_2$max remained unchanged over the entire period, while running velocity at lactate threshold rose by an average of 6 percent. The upswing corresponded with either improved personal records or higher competitive rankings for the runners involved in the study.[9]

Older Runners

Another exciting aspect of running velocity at lactate threshold improvement is that it is much less limited by the aging process compared with upswings in $\dot{V}O_2$max and enhancements of running economy.[11, 12] Research shows that as male runners get older, one of their best opportunities for improving performance is through upgrading the running velocity at lactate threshold. While research with women has yet to be conducted, there are no indications that the results would be different. As a runner ages, maximal heart rate tends to decline by an average of one beat per year; the strength and flexibility of the left ventricle, the heart's primary pumping chamber, also tend to diminish. These factors downgrade maximal cardiac output, a key component of $\dot{V}O_2$max.

In contrast, the muscle mitochondria that play such a large role in improving running velocity at lactate threshold and the aerobic enzymes that give running velocity at lactate threshold a boost are not necessarily reduced by the aging process. In fact, they may increase almost as much in 60-year-old athletes in response to training as they would in competitors who are 30 years younger![13]

The ability of older runners to make significant advances in running velocity at lactate threshold helps explain a fascinating piece of research carried out several years ago by researchers at Washington University in St. Louis. In that investigation, eight runners with an average age of 56 were compared with eight other runners with an average age of 25. Both groups ran 41 miles (66 km) per week and demonstrated the same 10K performance ability: average finishing time was around 41:30. As it turned out, $\dot{V}O_2$max in the older competitors was almost 10 percent lower than that of the younger runners, again illustrating the poor predictive power of maximal aerobic capacity, and running economy was fairly similar in the two groups.[14] So why were the older runners able to keep up with the younger competitors?

A difference in running velocity at lactate threshold proved to be the answer. Both the older and young runners reached running velocity at lactate threshold at a velocity of approximately 230 meters per minute (about 7 minutes per mi), so it was no surprise that both groups ran their 10Ks at a pace of around 6:45 per mile (10K pace tends to be about 2.5 percent faster than running velocity at lactate threshold). The higher $\dot{V}O_2$max values of the younger runners were irrelevant for predicting relative performances because the lactate-threshold speeds of the older runners occurred at a higher percentage of $\dot{V}O_2$max. In fact, running velocity at lactate threshold for the older competitors settled in at 85 percent of $\dot{V}O_2$max but at only 79 percent of $\dot{V}O_2$max for the younger runners. As a result, the older runners were able to complete their 10Ks at about 88 to 90 percent of $\dot{V}O_2$max, while the younger competitors could only handle 81 percent. If the younger runners had attempted to run their 10Ks more quickly, they would have exceeded the intensity of velocity at lactate threshold (as a percentage of $\dot{V}O_2$max), and their perceived exertion would have been too great. Thus, the older runners were able to entirely compensate for the higher maximal aerobic capacities of the younger competitors.

There's another important lesson here. An older athlete who is serious about maintaining or raising his or her level of performance should place a strong emphasis on training that improves running velocity at lactate threshold. That's because after the age of 40 or so, $\dot{V}O_2$max begins a relentless decline that trims about 0.3 to 0.5 percent from aerobic capacity each year, even when vigorous training is sustained. The drop-off in $\dot{V}O_2$max is related to the fact that the heart becomes a stiffer, less-potent pump as middle age progresses. Thus, the muscles are supplied with less oxygen-rich blood during strenuous exercise, and $\dot{V}O_2$max edges downward. There's little that can be done about this decline in oxygen availability in the blood stream, but it is possible to compensate for the loss of aerobic capacity by continuing to improve running velocity at lactate threshold. It is possible to improve or maintain race times after the age of 40 by optimizing this key variable.

Training to increase running velocity at lactate threshold is not reserved for older runners, however. Improving running velocity at lactate threshold upgrades race times and allows competitive endurance athletes to keep pace with—and often beat—other runners who have higher maximal aerobic capacities. Appropriate, scientifically validated training techniques for increasing running velocity at lactate threshold are described in detail in chapter 27.

Conclusion

Conducting training that increases running velocity at lactate threshold is extremely important for the competitive runner and the athlete who wants to maximize overall fitness. This training is productive, leading to large increases in performance without corresponding changes in aerobic capacity, especially in the older runner. Important for all runners, the intense training once thought to harm muscles by producing large quantities of lactic acid is in fact exactly the kind of work necessary to optimize lactate threshold and thus promote the muscles' ability to operate at high levels in a sustained fashion.

CHAPTER 11

Maximal Running Speed

Maximal running speed—the highest speed that can be sustained for a 50-meter sprint carried out from a running start—is an outstanding predictor of endurance performance. It is such a powerful forecaster that if 100 endurance runners lined up according to their 10K finishing times, from fastest to slowest, and then rearranged themselves according to 50-meter sprint times, again from fastest to slowest, the two lines would look similar.

As explained in chapter 7, this tight linkage would not occur if the runners organized themselves according to 10K performance and that highly vaunted physiological variable $\dot{V}O_2$max. Runners with the highest aerobic capacities would not necessarily be fastest over the 10K, nor would those with the lowest $\dot{V}O_2$max be the slowest.

In other words, 50-meter sprint time is superior to aerobic capacity when it comes to predicting 10K and other competitive endurance performances. Many endurance runners are unaware of this close relationship between maximal speed and endurance success. For others, it is difficult to accept the idea that maximal velocity and the stamina required to run a 10K or marathon successfully can be so closely related. This is unfortunate because it means that the objective of advancing maximal speed is not incorporated into many runners' training programs.

Maximal Speed and Endurance

One of the difficulties many runners have in understanding the significance of maximal speed is that 5K, 10K, half marathon, marathon, and ultramarathon running have always been viewed as aerobic events, with almost all the required energy needed to complete these distances coming from aerobic metabolism, the use of oxygen to break down carbohydrates and fats for energy. In contrast, running 50 meters as fast as possible is thought to be anaerobic, that is, depending on the breakdown of glucose to lactate without any oxygen involvement at all. From the standpoint of energy systems, it is very difficult for runners to understand why anaerobic prowess (i.e., running very fast 50-meter sprints) would lead to success in almost entirely aerobic distance-running events.

In addition, many popular training programs place a high value on building up mileage at moderate intensities, the kind of training believed—although incorrectly—to optimize $\dot{V}O_2$max. Running fast during training and thus developing raw speed is traditionally viewed as kind of a dangerous thing to do, something that might even damage muscles or lead to a kind of muscular schizophrenia in which anaerobic development increases at the expense of much needed aerobic changes. New Zealand coach Arthur Lydiard was a proponent of such thinking, and his views on endurance training continue to have a large following around the world.

Nonetheless, scientific research strongly supports the ideas that maximal running speed is a very reliable predictor of endurance-running success and that improving one's maximal speed over short distances will almost automatically lead to upgraded race performances in endurance events.

The first real intimation that maximal speed is a strong determinant of endurance performance emerged from a groundbreaking study carried out in 1990 by Noakes and his colleagues at the University of Cape Town in South Africa.[1] They tested 20 experienced marathon runners and 23 well-trained ultramarathon competitors and found that *peak treadmill running velocity* was the best predictor of performance among the ultramarathoners and was just as good a predictor as running velocity at lactate threshold (see chapter 10) for the marathoners. Compared with peak treadmill velocity, $\dot{V}O_2$max was an inferior predictor, a rather remarkable finding given that the two races under study—the marathon and ultramarathon—seem to be the kinds of events that stress aerobic capacity and endurance rather than raw running speed.

Noakes and his fellow researchers concluded that the "factors that determine the peak treadmill running velocity . . . are not likely to be related to maximal rates of muscle oxygen utilization."[1] In other words, the best foretellers of endurance performance did not seem to be a function of aerobic capacity at all.

Noakes' surprising findings did not exactly take the running community by storm, but other researchers began to obtain the same sorts of results as they attempted to come to an understanding of the various factors that produce endurance success. For example, investigators from the University of Technology in Sydney, Australia, found that maximal running speed was the best predictor of competitive ability in endurance events like the 3K.[2] And when Kris Berg and his colleagues at the University of Nebraska at Omaha tested 36 trained runners (20 men and 16 women), they learned that just two variables—*300-meter sprint time and plyometric leaping ability*—could explain nearly 78 percent of the variance in 10K performances.[3] Berg and colleagues developed a mathematical equation that could predict 10K time fairly accurately using these variables alone:

$$10K \text{ time} = 57.22 - (5.15 \times \text{plyometric-leap distance in meters}) + (.27 \times 300\text{-m time in seconds})$$

Note that this best-fit, predictive equation includes near-maximal running capacity (300-m time) and plyometric leaping ability but does not incorporate any variable related to aerobic fitness such as $\dot{V}O_2$max. Despite the lack of aerobic variables, the equation is able to explain most of the variation in 10K performances. The importance of optimizing maximal running velocity and neuromuscular power during 10K and 5K preparations cannot be overemphasized. It is likely that such optimization will also be beneficial for the marathon and half marathon. The researchers cautiously concluded that "it may be beneficial for distance runners to supplement aerobic training with some power and speed development."[3]

Finnish researchers Paavolainen and Rusko have also been able to document a tight bond between maximal speed and endurance performance. They divided 18 competitive endurance runners into two teams: one group trained in a conventional manner and a second group carried out explosive strength training for about one-third of the available training time.[4] The two groups were monitored by Paavolainen, Rusko, and colleagues over a 9-week period. The control group athletes conducted typical endurance training, devoting just 3 percent of their training time to the explosive work.

Meanwhile, the athletes in the explosive-training group participated in explosive strength sessions lasting from 15 to 90 minutes each and consisting of sprints (e.g., 5 to 10 reps of 20-100 m) and jumping exercises (e.g., alternative jumps, bilateral countermovement jumps, drop-and-hurdle jumps, and one-leg, five-jump drills). Sometimes the jumps were done without any additional weight; at other times, each runner held a barbell across the shoulders. The explosive-trained athletes also performed leg presses, knee extensions, and knee flexions with low resistance and close-to-maximal movement velocities (i.e., 5-20 reps per set, 30-200 reps per session, with resistance set at less than 40 percent of the 1-rep maximum).

The use of this experimental scheme meant that during the 9-week investigation, the explosive-trained group did much less endurance-type training compared to the control athletes. The explosive-trained athletes devoted about 3 hours per week to high-speed sprints and jumps and 6 hours to traditional running workouts, while the control group spent almost every minute of their 9 training hours locked into their usual running habits. Naturally, the total volume of run training was significantly less in the explosive-trained group. In fact, the runners in this group ran about 20 to 25 fewer miles (32-40 km) per week, or about 200 fewer miles (322 km) during the 9-week period compared with the control runners. Control-group runners covered about 70 miles (121 km) of running per week, versus 45 miles (72 km) per week for the explosive-trained athletes.

At the beginning and end of the 9-week training period, all 18 athletes ran an all-out 20-meter sprint and a 5,000-meter race as fast as possible on an indoor track. After 9 weeks, the explosive athletes had upgraded their 20-meter, maximal-effort sprint times from a running start by nearly 4 percent, while the traditionally trained athletes were no faster at all after their 630 total miles (1,014 km) of running. In the 5K event, the explosive-trained runners were 30 seconds faster than they had been initially for about a 3 percent improvement. The story was depressing on the other side: The traditional, high-mileage trainees had stagnant race times even though they had improved their average $\dot{V}O_2$max values. This study provides strong evidence that explosive training advances maximal running velocity and that upgrades in maximal speed are closely coupled with improvements in endurance performances.

False Dichotomy of Aerobic and Anaerobic

How can advances in maximal running velocity and maximal speed improve endurance performance given that high-speed running is anaerobic and endurance running is aerobic? When runners look at endurance running solely through the traditional anaerobic-aerobic lens, it is very difficult to understand what is really happening. The trouble is that successful running involves much more than the mere presence of anaerobic and aerobic enzymes in the muscles.

Even if it were possible to micropipette a huge quantity of anaerobic enzymes into a runner's leg-muscle cells, it would be unlikely the runner would be able to run any faster. The reason for this is that the nervous system is required to coordinate and direct the leg muscles in a more powerful way in order for faster running to occur. Such coordination and direction must be developed over time with the use of high-speed running and explosive drills. The nervous system's role as director of speed development is independent of the energy-producing systems inside the muscle fibers.

When runners change the lens through which they view endurance training and begin to examine endurance running as a function of neuromuscular characteristics, they begin to understand why maximal speed and endurance performances are tightly linked. Maximal speed improves as the nervous system learns to coordinate the muscles in ways that promote faster stride rates, shorter contact times with the ground per step, and quicker generation of substantial propulsive forces. These factors are extremely important for competitive endurance running. Shorter contact time was another key factor underlying the improvements achieved by the endurance runners in the Paavolainen and Rusko study discussed earlier. Endurance runners who develop rapid stride rates, short contact times, and ample strides will tend to do very well in their distance events, and they will outrun individuals who are significantly less explosive.

A key goal for endurance runners is to develop the ability to run more quickly while simultaneously expanding the capacity to *sustain* higher speeds over extended periods. When runners do this, they will be highly successful in distance events. Since they are able to run fast, they will fare well in sprint tests, too. This explains why researchers keep finding maximal speed and distance performance to be tightly knotted together.

This does not mean that world-class sprinters could automatically become elite distance runners. Compared with an endurance runner, the world-class sprinter is different, with a fast-twitch muscle-fiber composition that makes it very difficult to run at quality speeds for prolonged periods. The announcement that maximal speed is a critically important component of endurance success is aimed at distance runners, not elite sprint athletes.

Breaking Down Maximal Speed at the Subatomic Level

To gain a better understanding of maximal speed and its importance for distance running, it is possible to break it down to the subatomic level, taking the components of maximal speed apart one by one. The formula for running velocity is a simple one:

$$speed = stride\ rate \times stride\ length$$

Maximal running velocity involves the optimization of these two variables, stride rate and stride length. It's as basic as that! If a runner wants to get faster—and thereby improve race times—he or she must increase either stride rate or stride length without dampening the other variable. For example, if a runner increases stride rate, he or she must make certain that stride length does not shorten. If a runner increases stride rate and stride length at the same time, the upswing in speed will be even greater compared with improving one variable at a time.

To understand the options for increasing maximal speed, the subatomic equation should be examined closely. The example of an 18-minute 5K runner will work for this purpose, but the arguments work for racers at other distances and times as well. An 18-minute 5K runner typically takes about 92 strides (184 steps) per minute. A stride is two steps, one with the right and one with the left; 92 strides per minute is a normal stride rate for an experienced runner. Since this runner's 5Ks last for 18 minutes, by definition, the runner is taking 1,656 strides (18 minutes × 92 strides = 1,656 strides), or 3,312 steps, during each race. So, the runner's stride length is 3.02 meters per stride (5,000 meters / 1,656 strides = 3.02 meters per stride).

The runner's 5K speed could then be expressed as follows:

$$stride\ rate \times stride\ length = 5k\ speed$$

92 strides per minute × 3.02 meters per stride = 277.8 meters per minute for 5K speed

The rate of 277.8 meters per minute doesn't exactly roll facilely off the tongue and is a bit cumbersome to use during training, so it should be converted to meters per second and to a tempo per 400 meters. First, 277.8 meters per minute is the same as 277.8 meters per 60 seconds, resulting in the following calculations:

$$277.8 / 60 = 4.63 \text{ meters per second}$$

$$400 / 4.63 = 86.4 \text{ seconds per 400 meters}$$

In checking the numbers, the calculated pace is 4.63 meters per second, and there are 1,080 seconds (18 minutes) in the race. Thus, 1,080 seconds × 4.63 meters per second = 5,000 meters. The math is correct, and based on that, it is possible to begin to understand how changes in stride rate and length will determine 5K performance.

Let's assume the 18-minute 5K runner embarks on a program that includes high-speed sprints and explosive drills and thus improves stride rate by 1 percent. Of course, the easiest way for the runner to do this would be to simply decrease stride length a little—that way the feet would hit the ground more often and stride rate would go up. But, as mentioned previously, decreasing stride length could decrease speed, so that is not optimal. Instead, the runner should increase stride rate by decreasing foot-strike time. In other words, the stance phase of the gait cycle will be shorter: The runner will produce the same amount of propulsive force he or she always did, thereby keeping stride length the same, but over a briefer amount of time. Since less time will be spent in stance as a result of this change, the runner's feet will hit the ground more often each minute, and stride rate will go up!

When this runner improves stride frequency by 1 percent, the new *rate* will be 92.92 strides per minute. The runner's 5K racing will also change as shown:

$$92.92 \text{ strides per minute} \times 3.02 \text{ meters per stride} = 280.6 \text{ meters per minute}$$

The old pace was 277.8 meters per minute, so the runner has advanced 5K speed by 2.8 meters per minute, or 1 percent. The new 5K time would be 17.82 minutes (5,000 / 280.6 = 17.82), or about 17:49. This simple, easy way to produce a 1 percent uptick in stride rate led to a 1 percent (11 / 1,080 = .01) improvement in overall 5K time.

Of course, the same kind of thing happens if a runner upgrades stride *length* rather than rate. For that same hypothetical 5K runner, if stride length goes up by 1 percent, from 3.02 to 3.05 meters per stride, without a change in stride rate, the new equation is this:

$$92 \text{ strides per minute} \times 3.05 \text{ meters per stride} = 280.6 \text{ meters per minute}$$

This is the same velocity obtained when stride rate is increased by 1 percent. If stride rate *and* stride length are each increased by 1 percent, the resulting equation is this:

$$92.92 \times 3.05 = 283.4 \text{ meters per minute}$$

This is a 2 percent jump in 5K velocity, which would bring 5 K time down to about 17:38 or so. That would not be a hard thing to swallow for most 5 K competitors. In general, each 1 percent improvement in stride rate or stride length leads to a 1 percent improvement in race performance. A 5 percent uptick in stride rate and a corresponding increase in stride length would do nice things for 5K clocking—and even more for marathon times. The total 10 percent improvement would knock 1:48 off an 18-minute 5K time and would reduce a 3:19 marathon down to approximately 2:59!

Improving Maximal Speed

The way to improve *maximal* speed, then, is to know *how* to increase stride rate and stride length in ways which optimize the velocity equation. Some runners believe that sprint training is the answer, but sprint training by itself simply will not do the job. Speed work on the track may also appear to be the right medicine, but speed work is only a small part of the story. When most runners carry out speed training, they are usually working at velocities with which they are already all too familiar, making the effects of the training on maximal running speed quite small because the neuromuscular system is not being adequately challenged.

Fortunately, the things an endurance runner needs to do to improve stride rate and stride length are quite straightforward. In fact, there are just three simple steps a runner should take to increase stride rate, and three additional steps to expand stride length.

Before examining these factors in depth, it is important to know whether alterations in stride rate and stride length are really feasible. Are these components of gait locked in to each runner's basic running form and mechanics, or are they quite plastic and responsive to training? This question has not yet been extensively studied because of the traditional thirst for information about $\dot{V}O_2$max; as a result, the subatomic side of running has been relatively ignored. However, the work of scientists such as Paavolainen and Rusko reveals that foot-contact time and thus stride rate are quite responsive to training. The research by Paavolainen and Rusko described earlier showed that 5K runners were able to narrow their average foot-strike time from 210 to 195 milliseconds (a 7 percent improvement) without shortening stride length after just 9 weeks of training.[4] As you might expect from the subatomic equation, the research team found that contact time was highly correlated with 5K success: the shorter the contact time, the faster the 5K performance.

Some runners might think that a 15-millisecond improvement in contact time is quite small. But improvements measured in milliseconds can lead to large improvements, even in races timed in minutes and seconds. A runner completing a 10K in about 36 minutes takes about 6,624 steps, or 36 minutes × (92 strides × 2 steps), during the race. If each contact is shortened by 15 milliseconds without hurting stride length, the improvement in performance would be about 99 seconds (6,624 steps × .015 second = 99.36). Along similar lines, a marathon runner completing the race in 3:08 would take approximately 34,592 steps (188 minutes × 184 steps) in the race; a 15-millisecond improvement in contact time could lead to a 519-second improvement (34,592 steps × .015 second), enough to slip below the 3-hour mark.

It is clear from the available research that contact time and thus stride rate are quite plastic, varying significantly from one runner to another and responding aggressively to training. Studies carried out with elite runners cruising along at tempos between 4:45 and 5:00 minutes per mile reveal that average contact time is around 179 milliseconds—with wide variations ranging from around 160 to 190 milliseconds.

Instead of increasing stride length, shrinking ground-contact time is *the* method that most runners use to attain top speeds. In general, runners pick up the pace by lengthening their strides when they are running at modest speeds. When they are already going very fast, however, stride lengthening doesn't cut it, and further upswings in velocity are accomplished by shortening contact time and thus upgrading stride rate.[5]

Z Sports Images/zuma/Icon SMI

▶ Highest possible speeds are obtained by minimizing contact time and heightening stride rate.

As mentioned, contact time and stride rate are very responsive to training. It seems likely that stride length is also trainable, but the way in which it responds to various kinds of training has not been carefully examined. It is clear that contact time can change significantly in as little as 6 to 8 weeks in response to explosive training. The possible magnitude of improvements in ground-contact time is not well known, but it's clear that 10- to 15-millisecond increases are feasible and lead to major gains in performance. It would not be surprising to learn that some runners could improve contact time by 20 milliseconds or more, which would carve huge chunks of time from their performances.

Methods for Increasing Stride Rate

But what must a runner actually do in training to shorten contact time and increase stride rate without hurting stride length and thereby advance maximal speed? Fortunately, the methods are straightforward (see chapter 28 for in-depth, practical details concerning this kind of training). Following are the basic steps a runner must take to increase stride rate.

- Emphasize high-speed running. This does not mean going to the track and knocking off intervals at current or even goal 5K speed since these are paces with which a runner is already familiar and which the runner's neuromuscular system can already handle effectively. Rather, allot time in training for running at maximal speed for 300, 150, 100, and 50 meters. These efforts force the nervous system to learn how to minimize contact time.

- Carry out explosive drills. These drills should supplement the diet of high-quality running. They require the feet to get on and off the ground as quickly as possible; at the same time, the legs are producing as much propulsive force as they can in the shortest possible time. While these drills do not usually involve actual running, they should be as specific to the gait cycle of running as possible, replicating key aspects of running biomechanics.

- Emphasize agility and coordination training. This training reduces the requirement to stabilize the leg and body when the foot makes contact with the ground. Since fewer milliseconds are required for stabilization during each interaction with the ground, contact time is abbreviated and stride rate is heightened.

Methods for Increasing Stride Length

To increase stride length, a runner must increase the ability to apply propulsive force to the ground. More propulsive force means longer stride lengths. There are three key ways to create more propulsion:

- Carry out running-specific strengthening movements. These movements should mimic the mechanics of running but be performed with increased resistance. Heavy weights can be used because the idea is not to get the foot on and off the ground quickly; rather, the goal is to maximize propulsive strength. Full resistance should be supported by one leg at a time, not by both legs simultaneously, since running does not involve jumping forward on two feet.

- Conduct ample amounts of hill training. This is the most specific form of strength training for running. More work is done per step and propulsive force that is greater than usual is required to move a runner's body uphill compared with flat-ground running; thus, propulsive strength is advanced dramatically, leading to longer strides.

- Develop agility and coordination. As is the case with contact-time subatomic training, agility and coordination should be developed so that an optimal amount of the leg-muscle force, which is developed during ground contact, can be used for propulsion rather than mere stabilization and correction of nonproductive, uncoordinated movements.

Incorporating the Methods for Faster Running

The subatomic approach is the key to upgrading maximal velocity and running faster, but it is also just one component of the overall training picture. Subatomic workouts must be blended with high-quality running training to ensure that $v\dot{V}O_2max$, lactate-threshold speed, running economy, and resistance to fatigue are all optimized. This will make certain that outstanding speed and stamina at quality speeds exist side by side, happy in their personal record–producing marriage. The union of *high-quality* running training and subatomic work is a blissful one. However, joining *high-volume* and subatomic work together does not work as well because high-volume effort does not optimize $v\dot{V}O_2max$, lactate-threshold speed, and running economy. Although a runner might think that high-volume exertion would optimize resistance to fatigue, it is important to remember that endurance capacity and fatigue resistance are always speed specific. Running tons of miles at moderate paces enhances endurance at modest speeds—but not at more sizzling levels of effort.

Subatomic training by itself not only makes a runner faster; it also makes it easier for a runner to *sustain* the higher speeds that previously were unthinkable. The reason is that subatomic training invariably leads to improvements in running economy and reduces the oxygen cost of running at a specific speed (see chapter 8).

In Paavolainen and Rusko's research, the subatomic drills produced an enormous running economy enhancement of 8.1 percent. One mechanism underlying this dramatic gain is probably that subatomic training improves the springiness and energy-return properties of the legs. This development saves energy because more propulsive force is created as a result of cost-free elastic recoil of muscles and tendons; thus, less force has to be created from energy-expensive muscle contractions. Subatomic training also upgrades coordination during gait, an effect that would decrease the amount of energy required for stabilizing the body, thus enhancing running economy. As a result of running economy enhancements, high-end speeds can be run at a lower fraction of $\dot{V}O_2$max, and thus it is considerably easier to *sustain* such higher velocities. Runners can move to higher speeds in races without incurring a higher cost—and without greater perceived effort—once subatomic training has been undertaken.

Another important consideration is that competitive races are ordinarily run at fixed percentages of maximal speed. For example, a runner whose personal record for the mile is about 5 minutes is typically running the mile at about 80 percent of maximal speed and 5Ks at around 74 percent. When maximal velocity increases, mile and 5K speeds also must increase since they are tightly linked with maximal velocity; 10K, half-marathon, and marathon velocities would also advance.

Conclusion

An apparent paradox of running is that extremely high-speed training with short-duration sprints and drills leads to dramatic improvements in prolonged endurance running. However, this marriage of fast with slow, of speed with endurance, is not really paradoxical: The benefits gained from explosive training—shorter ground-contact times, higher stride rates, and longer strides—are great for both short sprints and longer distances, including the marathon. The distance runner who can move very quickly over 42 meters can use the same skills of short contacts, quicker stride rate, and longer stride length to run powerfully for 42K, too. The endurance runner who has optimized maximal running velocity has a huge edge over competitors who have not developed this key performance variable.

12

Resistance to Fatigue

Resistance to fatigue is the ability to sustain a high-quality velocity, a specific fraction of $\dot{V}O_2$max, or a specified percentage of maximal running speed for an extended time without a falloff in pace or intensity. It is an important predictor of performance. However, science has not yet determined exactly what factors determine a runner's resistance to fatigue. The top theories have focused on glycogen concentrations, the ability to dissipate heat while running, stretch-shortening cycle function, and the operations of the neural governor.

Differences in Factors Determining Resistance to Fatigue and $\dot{V}O_2$max

Exercise scientists first became interested in resistance to fatigue when it was noticed that black South African runners could maintain a specific percent of $\dot{V}O_2$max for a longer time period compared with their Caucasian peers. In a study carried out at the University of Cape Town, researchers compared the performances of the nine best Caucasian runners with the 11 best black competitors in the country.[1] In this investigation, the runners had similar performance times at distances ranging up to about 3,000 meters. Beyond 3K, however, the performances of the black runners were considerably better, even though the $\dot{V}O_2$max values of the two groups were identical.

As the South African investigators searched for the mechanism(s) underlying the performance differences between the two groups, they discovered that the black runners could sustain an intensity of 89 percent of $\dot{V}O_2$max for a half marathon, while the Caucasian runners could handle just 82 percent of $\dot{V}O_2$max over the same distance. In fact, the Caucasian runners could maintain the intensity of 89 percent of $\dot{V}O_2$max for only about 5 miles. The researchers noted that the black runners could also sustain 92 percent of $\dot{V}O_2$max for a full 10K race, while their competitors were forced to drop down to 86 percent of $\dot{V}O_2$max for this distance. The black runners had superior resistance to fatigue: They could run much longer than the Caucasians at any fraction of $\dot{V}O_2$max.

In a separate study, also carried out at the University of Cape Town, nine black runners and eight Caucasian distance runners with similar 10K race times, $\dot{V}O_2$max values, and peak treadmill velocities were compared. Peak treadmill velocity is the maximal speed reached on the treadmill during a $\dot{V}O_2$max test; it has actually been found to be a better predictor of performance than $\dot{V}O_2$max.[2] Despite the close similarities between the groups in $\dot{V}O_2$max, 10K performance, and peak treadmill velocity, the black runners had superior resistance to fatigue: They could run for 21 percent longer at an intensity of 92 percent of peak treadmill velocity compared with the Caucasians.[3]

Such inquiries suggest that the physiological factors that determine $\dot{V}O_2$max and the factors that determine resistance to fatigue—the percent of $\dot{V}O_2$max that can be sustained over an extended period—might be quite different. After all, the runners in these two key studies had quite similar $\dot{V}O_2$max values but very different characteristics with respect to resistance to fatigue. Exercise scientists have struggled to explain the mechanisms responsible for these kinds of variations.

Glycogen Concentrations

One theory that might explain differences in resistance to fatigue has to do with glycogen concentrations. Runners with superior resistance to fatigue might have a higher capacity to store glycogen in their muscles and liver. If this were the case, they would run low on essential fuel less quickly during endurance competitions and thus would be able to sustain faster paces for longer periods of time.

This glycogen hypothesis has a logical basis: Research shows that the appearance of fatigue during distance running often coincides with the development of low glycogen levels in the liver and muscles.[4, 5] Ingesting easy-to-absorb carbohydrates to counteract glycogen depletion during prolonged runs of 60 minutes or more improves performance, most likely by giving muscles something to turn to for fuel when internal supplies of glycogen begin to run short.[6] Carbohydrate availability is certainly important for performance.

Overall, the greater resistance to fatigue displayed by certain distance runners might be a consequence of their above-normal ability to store liver and muscle glycogen before competitions. It could also be the result of an enhanced capacity of their livers to produce glucose during long-distance running or a slowdown in the rate at which glycogen is used while running at a specific speed.

Scientific research has been unable to verify this glycogen-depletion model of resistance to fatigue, however. The energy-depletion hypothesis suggests that individuals with different degrees of resistance to fatigue would begin their races at similar percentages of $\dot{V}O_2$max, with those who were less fatigue resistant gradually falling off the pace as glycogen depletion develops. There is no scientific or anecdotal evidence to suggest that this is the case. Rather, runners with greater resistance to fatigue seem to adopt faster paces at early stages in their races before glycogen depletion becomes a factor, compared with runners with diminished resistance to fatigue.

Heat Dissipation

A competing theory suggests that resistance to fatigue is closely related to an athlete's ability to dissipate heat while running. A high rate of heat accumulation during running is directly related to fatigue: Race times during the marathon[7] and also during 10K competitions and the 3K steeplechase worsen as the environmental heat load increases.[8] Runners whose internal temperatures rise slowly during running tend to experience less fatigue compared with individuals who heat up quickly.[9] Small runners tend to dissipate heat more quickly and experience slower increases in body temperature during running compared with larger runners. This is thanks in part to the larger surface-to-mass ratio in the smaller individuals.[10]

The black runners in the South African fatigue-resistance study discussed previously were considerably smaller than their Caucasian competitors. The black runners weighed an average of 56 kilograms (123 lbs) compared with 68 kilograms (150 lbs) for the white runners, and the blacks were only 169

▶ Fatigue tends to increase as the environmental temperature rises, and some research suggests that the ability to dissipate heat promotes fatigue resistance.

centimeters (5.6 ft) in height compared with 181 centimeters (5.9 ft) for the Caucasians.[1] Presumably, this would have allowed the black runners to get rid of heat more easily during longer-distance running and thus have cooler body temperatures. During shorter events of 1.5K to 3K, heat dissipation is not such an important factor because shorter duration of effort makes it more difficult to attain a critically high core body temperature. The performances of both groups of runners were equivalent for distances of 1.5K to 3K.

It is unlikely that heat-dissipation capacity can completely account for differences in resistance to fatigue, however. For one thing, black runners from Kenya with similar degrees of resistance to fatigue can vary tremendously in height and weight.[11] Their wide variations in body size should produce great differences in heat-loss capacity and thus broad disparities in resistance to fatigue, but they don't.

Stretch-Shortening Cycle

A stronger theory may be that resistance to fatigue is related to the way in which runners' leg muscles function as reverse springs during running. The leg muscles are often referred to as springs but in reality function quite differently. To understand how the leg muscles work, consider what happens when an automobile hits a bump in the road: its springs first compress to soak up the energy of impact and then expand, releasing that energy. The spring-like activity of the leg muscles is quite different: When a runner's foot hits the ground, key leg muscles actually lengthen at impact instead of compressing and then shorten, the reverse of what happens with a mechanical spring. The quads, for example, are stretched out as the knee flexes after ground impact and only then shorten and straighten the leg to drive the body forward (see figure 12.1). The leg muscles are thus reverse springs during running, and the process they undergo, in which they stretch and then shorten, is often referred to as the stretch-shortening cycle.

This stretch-shortening cycle in the leg muscles is essential for economical running. The rubber-band-like snapback of the muscles after they have been lengthened provides much of the propulsive force required to move forward. Furthermore, the process is extremely sparing of energy and thus oxygen use: Once the muscles have been stretched during impact with the ground, the resulting shortening occurs without the need to expend additional energy. In effect, the energy stored in the leg muscles at impact is simply released to provide propulsive force. This is an extremely economical process, especially when compared with the alternative, which would require active, energy-consuming muscle contractions to move the body forward.

This stretch-shortening cycle, as economical as it is, is not without its problems and perils. Research suggests that muscles become more resistant to being stretched and less willing to transfer energy in the stretched-to-shortened phase of the cycle during an extended running effort. This

▶**Figure 12.1** The quadriceps undergo the stretch-shortening cycle during each stance phase of the gait cycle. They are at (a) midlength when the foot hits the ground, (b) stretched as the knee flexes, and (c) shortened as the leg straightens and drives the body forward.

breakdown in muscle functioning during running has been called stretch-shortening muscle fatigue.[12]

The resistance to stretching may decrease subsequent force production because less energy is stored in the reverse spring with each impact with the ground; the result will be to diminish stride length. The slowdown in energy transfer may create a situation in which the push-off phase of stance is elongated, leading to a decrease in stride rate and thus running speed. Such changes do not occur to different degrees in various runners because of differences in oxygen use or disparities in heat accumulation; rather, these variations are probably related to the quality of the muscles, the ability of the nervous system to optimally control the muscles to facilitate stretching and energy transfer, and the overall capacity of the neuromuscular system to stand up to the stresses of the stretch-shortening process. Runners with a more effective neuromuscular system should sustain optimal stretch-shortening function longer during competitions and thus should have greater resistance to fatigue.

Why might some runners experience less loss of stretch-shortening function during running? Stretch-shortening expert Paavo Komi of Finland has determined that the stretch-shortening cycle creates real damage to muscle cells during prolonged running.[12] Much of the breakdown probably occurs when muscles are stretched out at impact, and the damage has a significant effect on muscle mechanics, including the ability to "snap back" after stretching, and muscle and joint stiffness. Runners with the greatest resistance to fatigue might then be the ones with the least stretch-shortening muscle damage during running.

Optimizing running form and using running-specific strength training may limit stretch-shortening damage. From a form standpoint, research suggests that the use of a midfoot landing pattern reduces impact forces experienced by the legs compared with the more typical heel-strike technique.[13] The result may be less wear and tear on the muscles during running. (See chapter 5 for a discussion of appropriate running form.) Strength training for running decreases the risk of running injury, probably in part by fortifying the muscles to such an extent that stretch-shortening damage is minimized.[14] Running-specific strengthening techniques are provided in chapter 14.

One potential problem with the stretch-shorten theory is that it predicts that runners with similar physiological characteristics (e.g., $\dot{V}O_2$max and maximal treadmill speed) would start their races at a very similar pace, with the runners who experience greater damage subsequently falling off the pace as the race proceeds. However, the existing research indicates that runners with greater resistance to fatigue actually run more quickly than their more fatigue-prone peers, right from the opening gun.[15] It's possible that runners who have less resistance to fatigue carry more muscle damage accrued during prerace training into their races and thus are able to run with their more fatigue-resistant peers for only short periods of time.

Neural Governor

Although the muscle-damage hypothesis is appealing, a considerably more powerful and better-tested theory suggests that resistance to fatigue is actually a function of neural output, the extent to which the nervous system is willing to stimulate the leg muscles. Runners with the greatest fatigue resistance would be the ones whose nervous systems pour out and maintain a greater flow of stimulatory messages to the leg muscles. Under this theory, the functioning of the nervous system explains fatigue during long-distance running, a far cry from traditional conceptions that limitations in oxygen usage and the extent of leg-muscle damage are the foundations of fatigue.

Neural output during running would necessarily be controlled by a neural governor, a region of the brain's motor cortex that determines appropriate exercise intensity. Scientific support is strong for the presence of an active neural governor that tightly controls neural output. For example, research reveals that individuals undergoing a $\dot{V}O_2$max test in an exercise physiology laboratory often become exhausted and stop exercising prior to attaining a maximal rate of oxygen consumption, a maximal heart rate, or even a high level of blood lactate.[16] Fatigue in such cases cannot be well explained by oxygen limitation, cardiac fatigue, or excessive lactic acid in the muscles; rather, it would appear to be caused by a neural-output setting in the neural governor that does not permit exercise of high intensity to continue beyond a fixed duration.

If the neural governor theory of fatigue is correct, there should be studies showing that the nervous system gradually reduces its stimulation of muscles during fatiguing exercise and that this reduction parallels the actual increases in fatigue. In fact, such investigations do exist. In one inquiry, cyclists completed a 100K ride that included a series of 1K sprints at maximal speed.[17] Over the duration of the 100K effort, the quality of the sprints declined. Paralleling this drop-off in sprint power, integrated electromyography (IEMG) activity also fell, which indicated that the athletes' central nervous systems were recruiting fewer and fewer motor units as the ride progressed (an IEMG is a recording of the electrical activity produced by muscles in response to stimulation by the nervous system). This was true even though less than 20 percent of the available motor units in the cyclists' leg muscles were being recruited at any one time. There was an opportunity for the athletes' nervous systems to bring more motor units into play, but that opportunity was not taken, apparently because of the tight control exerted by the athletes' neural governors.

In a separate study, experienced cyclists completed a 60-minute time trial that included six sprints at maximal speed.[18] Over the course of the trial, there was a reduction in power output and IEMG activity from the second through fifth sprint. However, both power and IEMG activity almost magically revived—and even increased significantly—during the sixth sprint, which took place during the last minute of the overall ride. In this study, it is impossible to explain the fatigue that occurred during the second through fifth sprints as being the result of either cardiac or muscular shortcomings. If there were true problems in the cardiac or muscle tissue, the sixth sprint could not have been carried out at such a fast pace. A more reasonable explanation is that the nervous system tightly controlled cycling intensity during the second through fifth sprints, maintaining a built-in reserve of neural output and preserving a capacity to recruit that reserve during the sixth sprint. In other words, fatigue and overall performance during the 60-minute time trial were controlled by the nervous system, not by the muscles.

Some runners may believe that the neural governor theory cannot possibly explain the crippling fatigue, and thus lack of fatigue resistance, that occurs toward the end of a marathon. During a marathon, runners simply run out of carbohydrate fuel, muscle glycogen is depleted, and no amount of increased neural activity seems able to restore running pace to its usual level over the last stage of the race. Although this argument is compelling, it overlooks the simple fact that fewer than 20 percent of motor units are recruited in a marathoner's legs at any time during the competition. Figuring out a way to recruit at least some of the 80 percent of missing motor units might indeed fight fatigue and even increase running velocity over the last 6 miles of the big race. When fatigue strikes severely at the 20-mile point of a marathon, it might be time to begin recruiting more muscle fibers instead of ramping down running speed.

Two conclusions emerge from these kinds of investigations. First, there is strong evidence that a type of neural governor creates fatigue during intense or prolonged running and attempts to limit performances. Studies reveal that runners who sustain a higher level of IEMG activity during races perform significantly better in those races compared with runners with lower levels of IEMG activity.[19] Second, there is also evidence that the neural governor is trainable. After all, experienced athletes stop their exertion at higher fractions of maximal heart rate and $\dot{V}O_2$max compared with untrained individuals. Training that makes the neural governor more permissive should improve performances.

Endurance athletes hoping to achieve optimal levels of performance can no longer simply worry about their hearts and muscles; rather, they must also advance neural output to its highest level. Research on optimizing neural output is limited, but it is known that high-intensity, explosive strength training upgrades neural output compared with other forms of strengthening.[20] This is not surprising since explosive training calls for high levels of neural output; thus, the specific, desired result is being rehearsed in training, perhaps teaching the nervous system that high levels of output are safe and manageable.

In the running arena, it would certainly appear that intense, high-quality running would enhance neural output to a greater extent compared with prolonged submaximal running with its lower required level of neural stimulation. An important finding is that East African runners tend to conduct more training at high intensity (>80 percent of $\dot{V}O_2$max) compared with American and European elites, which should set the East-African governors at higher running velocities.[1] Techniques of explosive and high-speed training are outlined in chapter 28 and 29.

Neural governor activity is the best explainer of fatigue resistance, but the setting on the neural governor would not be the only factor that determines performances. In addition to having a high neural governor set point, a runner would also require a high metabolic capacity in the muscles, a strong $v\dot{V}O_2$max, a high lactate-threshold speed, an enhanced running economy, and an elevated maximal running velocity in order to reach his or her true potential. An overly restrictive neural governor, however, could potentially stop such superb physiological attributes from being expressed. An important point for runners to remember is that fatigue during running is to a significant extent a mental construct that may not accurately reflect what is really happening in the heart and muscles. In races and challenging workouts, it makes sense to treat fatigue as a sensory message rather than as a crippling crisis in the muscles, and not as a dictator of how the remainder of the competition or training session will proceed.

Conclusion

Scientific research on fatigue resistance is still developing, but that should not stop runners and coaches from conducting workouts that have the best chance of optimizing this important performance predictor. Workouts that involve high levels of neural drive, including sessions in which high neural output must be sustained over an extended period, should have the greatest effect on fatigue resistance. This means that explosive strength sessions and high-speed running workouts with short intervals conducted at close to maximal speed will be helpful, as will longer runs at very high quality tempos. Continuous 2.5K runs at 5K race pace, 4K runs at 8K race speed, and 5K runs at 10K pace should also lead to increases in neural drive, relaxation of the neural governor, and improvements in resistance to fatigue.

Training Modes
and Methods
for Runners

CHAPTER **13**

General Strength Training

General strength training workouts consist of movements that increase the strength of a runner's entire body. The term *general* implies that the activities involved in the training are not specific to the precise neuromuscular patterns associated with running, although this is not always the case. The rationale for general strength training is that it improves body control during gait and thus enhances running economy since less energy needs to be devoted to the correction of destabilizing kinematics. General strength training should also upgrade resistance to fatigue in all parts of the body and thus promote improved running performances.

It is common, for example, for runners' shoulders to slump forward during late stages of intense or prolonged competitions, an action that decreases stride length and thus running velocity. Upgraded upper-body strength—achieved through general strength training—should help prevent this problem. General strength training should also pave the way for the running-specific strength training that follows in a progressive, properly periodized training program. General work creates the strength and coordination necessary to carry out the more technical movements associated with running-specific training sessions.

The challenge for the runner is to create workouts that do an outstanding job of improving general strength. Such sessions should activate every part of a runner's body, shoring up weaknesses and promoting excellent whole-body coordination and movement skills. General strength workouts thus need to include a variety of different drills and exercises that challenge and fortify a runner's neuromuscular system.

Circuit Training

Circuit training— the completion of a series of exercises, drills, and even running segments with little recovery between activities—can be effectively used to enhance general strength. Circuit training began to be examined scientifically in the 1970s when researchers at the National Athletic Health Institute (NAHI) in Inglewood, California, asked 20 men and 20 women to complete workouts that contained three circuits of 10 different exercises.[1]

The exercises included bench presses, inclined sit-ups, leg presses, lat pulls, back arches, shoulder presses, leg extensions, arm curls, leg flexions, and upright rows. All 40 subjects in this study performed 15 to 18 repetitions of each exercise in 30 seconds, using a resistance equal to about 40 percent of their individual 1-repetition maximum (1RM), that is, 40 percent of the greatest weight that could be handled for one repetition.

The participants in this NAHI study took 15-second breaks as they moved from one exercise to another, making the work-rest ratio 30:15, or 2:1. The nearly continuous nature of the workout kept heart rate and oxygen consumption high and thereby created aerobic benefits, or upgrades in $\dot{V}O_2max$, for the session in addition to the obvious strength gains. Male subjects averaged more than 75 percent of maximal heart rate during their training, while the female participants were above 80 percent of maximum. The energy requirement for the circuit training was also ample, soaring as high as 800 calories per hour, equivalent to running more than 7 miles (11 km) in the same amount of time.

In a follow-up study carried out by the NAHI group, individuals completed the same circuit session described earlier three times a week for 10 weeks, but they increased the resistance from 40 to 55 percent of 1RM for many of the exercises.[2] The circuit training had strong effects both on lean body mass and on running endurance. On average, male and female participants gained about 3 pounds (1 kg) of muscle and lost about 2 pounds (.9 kg) of fat. Both men and women achieved reductions in skin-fold thickness, another indicator of fat loss, and significant gains in muscle strength.

Although none of the participants in this follow-up work carried out any running training at all during the 10-week period, both males and females improved running endurance by about 5 to 6 percent at the end of 10 weeks. In addition, female subjects improved $\dot{V}O_2max$ by 11 percent—about the same average gain that would be achieved by women undertaking a 10-week program of running for the first time!

This result was a bit shocking since the circuit workout consisted of no traditional aerobic activities (e.g., continuous submaximal jogging, cycling, swimming) and was composed of only anaerobic strength drills. However, the continuous nature of the session kept oxygen-consumption rates high, fostering at least some of the gains in aerobic capacity. In addition, improved muscular strength and resistance to fatigue would allow circuit-trained individuals to run for a longer time during a treadmill $\dot{V}O_2max$ test, thus producing greater rates of oxygen consumption and higher $\dot{V}O_2max$ that previously might have been hidden because of relatively poor resistance to fatigue.

Such findings were reproduced by other research groups. In one study, 20 weeks of circuit training promoted a 9 percent increase in treadmill endurance, and two other studies linked circuit training with increases in $\dot{V}O_2$max.[3]

In the early 1980s, researchers at the Institute for Aerobics Research in Dallas, Texas, carried out circuit-training research with 36 females and 41 males over a 12-week period. One group of participants carried out a circuit session similar to the one in the NAHI study: three sessions a week with three circuits of 10 exercises per workout. A second group served as the control, and a third group combined the circuit exercises with actual running.[3] This study was the first to look at the effects of combining running with strength work during circuit training.

While the first group (the conventional circuit trainers) rested for approximately 15 seconds between exercises to allow time to move from one exercise station to another, the third (running) group's members ran for about 30 seconds on an indoor track in between their exercises. The circuits, completed by both the strength-only (SO) and strength-plus-running (SPR) groups, consisted of two-leg squats (also called body-weight squats), shoulder presses, knee flexions, bench presses, leg presses, elbow flexions, back hyperextensions, elbow extensions, sit-ups, and vertical flies, with each exercise conducted for 30 seconds (12-15 reps) per circuit at 40 percent of 1RM. The running segments (for the third group) were fairly relaxed and were conducted at a velocity of 189 meters per minute (8:30 per mi tempo).

During the 12-week study, not a single injury was reported; an outstanding feature of circuit training is its relatively low injury rate, especially compared with running long distances. The SO and SPR groups lost the same amount of weight, trimmed away a similar quantity of body fat, and added equal levels of muscle tissue. The two groups also improved bench press and leg press strength to the same degree.

After 12 weeks, SO athletes increased running endurance by 12 percent compared with 19 percent for SPR athletes and increased $\dot{V}O_2$max by 12.5 percent compared with 17 percent for SPR subjects. This disparity would probably have been greater if the SPR group had used higher running intensities during their circuits. The study suggests that the inclusion of running intervals within circuits is advantageous to running capacity, as one would expect, without harming gains in general strength.

The use of relatively light resistance levels (40-55 percent of 1RM) may be advantageous during circuit training. Research suggests that during strength training, oxygen flow through muscles is greatest when an athlete is using resistance ranging from 30 to 60 percent of 1RM. Below 30 percent, activity is so light that heart rate does not increase appreciably; therefore, the flow rate through muscles barely changes. Above 60 percent of 1RM, muscle contractions may be strong enough to actually constrict blood vessels within muscles, decreasing overall flow and temporarily altering the oxygen-consumption rate.

It is clear that circuit workouts can be quite beneficial for improving strength and upgrading running capacity. Circuit-training sessions can also be quite variable and thus endlessly interesting: The number of general strength exercises that can be included in a circuit session is nearly limitless. An important key for any circuit workout is to attempt to work all regions of the body; the basic circuit session presented in the following section does just that.

Basic Circuit Training

After a thorough warm-up consisting of about 2.5K (1.5 mi) of light running and a variety of dynamic mobility drills, the activities in the list that follows should be performed in order. The exercises themselves are described in detail in this section as well. The circuit looks fairly easy on paper but can be quite demanding to complete. Runners should move steadily from exercise to exercise to keep heart and oxygen-consumption rates high. They should maintain good form at all times and avoid the temptation to rush; recovery between drills should last for no more than a few seconds, just long enough to get into position for the next exercise. The overall philosophy is to perform each exercise methodically and carefully—and then almost immediately start on the next one. This enhances the oxygen-consumption rate.

1. Run 400 meters at current 5K pace.
2. Do 5 chin-ups. If a chin-up bar is not available, perform 12 biceps curls with dumbbells while standing on the right leg and then the left leg.
3. Complete 36 abdominal crunches.
4. Perform 15 squat thrusts with jumps (burpees).
5. Do 15 push-ups.
6. Complete 30 two-leg squats (body-weight squats).
7. Run another 400 meters at 5K tempo.
8. Do 12 squat and dumbbell presses.
9. Complete 10 feet-elevated push-ups.
10. Perform 36 low-back extensions.
11. Do 15 bench dips.
12. Complete 15 lunge squats with each leg.
13. Run another 400 meters at 5K pace.
14. Repeat steps 2 through 13 to complete two circuits in all; then cool down with about 2 miles (3.2 km) of light jogging, followed by thorough stretching and exercises to build core strength.

Some preworkout planning will be required to accomplish this routine. For example, dumbbells should be positioned near the track or beside the treadmill so that the dumbbell-assisted activities can be conducted without great delay, and a chair or bench will be needed for the feet-elevated push-ups and bench dips. If certain equipment is unavailable, substitute exercises can replace the recommended ones. For example, if there is no chinning bar to use for chin-ups, a runner can perform pull-downs with a stretch cord, biceps curls with dumbbells (see step 2), or any exercise that calls for using the arms and shoulders to lift the body.

Skeptics may contend that exercises such as push-ups are hardly whole-body strengthening exercises since they seem primarily to activate the arms and shoulders. However, exertions such as push-ups are actually whole-body in nature: They force the core muscles in the hips, abdomen, and lower back to support and stabilize the body while the trunk is held horizontally and moves up and down. The same is true of the other apparently isolating exercises within the circuit, including chin-ups, low-back extensions, and bench dips.

The circuit exercises as a group, with running segments included, contribute an essential component to a runner's foundation of fitness. They enhance resistance to fatigue and thus permit quality activities, both running and strengthening, to be conducted at higher intensities during the period following the general strengthening phase of training. The circuit exercises also promote general strength and stability, an effect which permits the technical, high-skill running-specific strength movements in the follow-up phase of training to be carried out with greater proficiency and better running form.

The research also reveals that circuit training can advance aerobic capacity and overall running performance, which demonstrates that circuits provide a very productive form of training from a purely running standpoint. They are more than simply a preamble to other methods of training.

Following are descriptions of key circuit exercises.

Chin-Up Stand below the bar, jump up and grasp the bar with hands, and then pull the body upward until the chin moves above the bar (figure 13.1). Lower the body fully to a vertical position while hanging from the bar to complete one rep.

▶ **Figure 13.1** Chin-up.

Abdominal Crunch Lie on the back with knees bent and feet flat on the ground. Cross the arms over the chest, and then use the abdominal muscles to lift the torso up and forward as far as possible (figure 13.2). Slowly return the shoulders to the ground to complete one rep.

▶ **Figure 13.2** Abdominal crunch.

Six-Count Squat Thrust (Burpee) Do six movements for each rep. Stand erect and then perform a squat (figure 13.3a), straighten the legs and torso out behind the upper body to move into a plank or push-up position with the body nearly parallel to the ground (figure 13.3b), complete a quick push-up, return to the squatting position, do a maximal vertical jump (figure 13.3c), and return to the standing, erect position.

▶ **Figure 13.3** (a) Initial squat, (b) push-up position, and (c) maximal vertical jump.

Push-Up Assume a plank position on the floor or the ground, supported by the palms and the toes (figure 13.4a). The arms should be straight and directly below the shoulders. Slowly lower the body until the chest touches the floor or ground (figure 13.4b), and then gradually raise the torso to the starting position.

▶ **Figure 13.4** Push-up (a) start position and (b) down position.

Two-Leg (Body-Weight) Squat Stand with erect posture and feet directly below the shoulders. Then, move into a squatting position so that thighs are parallel with the floor (figure 13.5). It is fine for the upper body to incline forward slightly as this happens. Return to the starting, erect position to complete one rep.

▶ **Figure 13.5** Two-leg squat movement.

Squat and Dumbbell Press   Perform a two-leg squat while holding dumbbells directly in front of the shoulders. The palms of the hands face forward. Perform a squat (figure 13.6a) and return to the standing position; then press the dumbbells directly overhead (figure 13.6b). Return the dumbbells to the front-of-shoulder position to complete one rep.

▶ **Figure 13.6**   (a) Squat and (b) dumbbell press.

Feet-Elevated Push-Up   Feet-elevated push-ups are normal push-ups except that the feet are positioned on a bench, chair, or wall and thus are higher than the shoulders (figure 13.7).

▶ **Figure 13.7**   Feet-elevated push-up.

Low-Back Extension   Lie on the stomach with arms by the sides, hands extended toward feet, and palms touching the floor. Contract the muscles at the back of the neck to lift the head so the gaze is forward and upward. For each rep, contract the lower-back muscles so that the trunk is lifted well off the ground (figure 13.8); then slowly ease the torso back to the floor. Do not use the hand or arms to lift the torso. All movement is achieved through lower-back muscle activation.

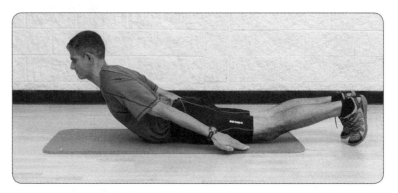

▶ **Figure 13.8**   Low-back extension.

Bench Dip   Sit on a bench or chair with hands at the sides, gripping the front edge of the seat. While keeping hands in position, slide forward off the chair and put feet as far forward as possible so that all body weight is supported only by the hands and heels of the extended feet (figure 13.9a). Lower the buttocks smoothly to the floor (or almost to the floor; figure 13.9b) and then come back up to seat level to complete one rep.

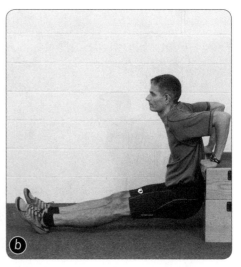

▶ **Figure 13.9**   (a) Starting position and (b) movement.

▶ **Figure 13.10** Lunge squat.

Lunge Squat Lunge squats are similar to exaggerated steps. Start with erect posture and feet directly under the shoulders; step forward with one foot. After the forward foot makes contact with the ground, move into a squat position so that the thigh of the forward leg becomes almost parallel with the ground (figure 13.10). The upper body may incline forward slightly as this happens. Emphasize actions of the gluteal muscles and hamstrings to reverse the squat and return the forward leg back under the trunk. Return to the starting position to complete one rep.

Progressing the Basic Circuit

Progressions with the basic circuit workout are straightforward. As strength and overall fitness improve, the athlete can increase the number of repetitions of the exercises, use dumbbells or a barbell while performing the exercises, expand the number of circuits from two to three or even four, increase the distance of the running intervals within the circuits, ramp up the velocities of the running segments, or substitute more difficult exercises for those listed in the circuit list provided.

Experienced runners who have been training for at least a year often begin general strength training with two circuits per workout and with 400-meter intervals as the running components; novice runners usually start with one circuit. Such a session (i.e., two circuits with 400-meter running intervals) would be conducted approximately twice a week in order to optimally boost whole-body strength.

Runners with some degree of fitness frequently begin general strength training with 400-meter intervals included in the circuits for two or three workouts, move up to 600-meter intervals for at least a couple of sessions, advance to 800-meter intervals, and may even reach intervals of 1,200 or 1,600 meters as the interval duration of choice. The chosen intensity for the running intervals is often v$\dot{V}O_2$max or 5K speed for the shorter intervals (i.e., 400s and 600s); 5K speed for the 800s; and 10K, half-marathon, or even marathon pace for the 1,200- and 1,600-meter intervals. This sort of advancement in running-interval difficulty often takes place over a 6-week period, or phase, of general strengthening, with two circuit workouts conducted each week.

During such a 6-week phase of training, whole-body strength will steadily advance, and lactate-threshold speed and $\dot{V}O_2$max will also improve. The lactate-threshold uplift is partially due to the high blood-lactate levels attained during circuit training. Thus, general strengthening represents an ideal beginning-of-the-season type of training, especially since it prepares runners for the more difficult running-specific training that will follow.

Over the course of the 6-week period, the number of repetitions of the various exercises can increase by about 5 to 10 percent from week to week. Alternatively, or simultaneously, the resistance employed with each drill can advance. For example, dumbbells or a barbell can be used with two-leg squats and lunge squats, a medicine ball can be incorporated with abdominal crunches, and the dumbbell weight can be increased for squats with presses.

An important feature of general strength training is that the circuit sessions within this phase function as tests of overall fitness. If a runner does well with the running segments but struggles with the exercises, for example, he or she knows that strength is an area of weakness that needs to be upgraded. If the various drills are relatively straightforward and easy but running leads to wheezing and hands-on-the-knees syndrome, then it is clear that running fitness is subpar.

Circuit workouts are also especially effective during tapering periods before important competitions because they tend to push whole-body strength and running capacity upward at a crucial time. Psychologically, circuit training has an incredibly positive effect: Many runners feel much stronger when they are engaged in circuit training, and this positive feeling often carries over into great racing. Circuits are especially good for marathon runners, particularly when the workouts include long intervals at marathon pace: These workouts give marathoners confidence that they can run at goal tempo even in the face of great fatigue.

Advanced Circuit Training

All forms of training must be progressive or a runner's body simply adapts to the constant level of training and fitness does not increase. When a runner returns to general strength training after the major competition of the year or after completing a cycle of running-specific strength training, hill work, and explosive training, more advanced circuit training can be employed. An advantage of the advanced general strength session compared with the basic circuit workout is that the advanced format includes exercises that are excellent for general strength but are also more difficult to perform and more specific to running. The exercises for this type of circuit training are detailed in this section.

To carry out this advanced circuit training session, warm up with 2.5K to 3.2K (1.5-2 mi) of easy running and a series of dynamic-mobility drills. Then, perform the exercises in order.

1. Run 800 meters at 5K race pace.
2. Complete 8 high-bench step-ups with jumps on each leg (use dumbbells).
3. Do 6 plyometric (clapping) push-ups.
4. Perform 3 series of the six-way lunge with arm drop.
5. Run another 800 meters at 5K race pace.
6. Complete 2 sets of 8 reps of the hanging scissors plus double-knee raise.
7. Do 12 one-leg squats with hops on each leg.
8. Perform 16 prone trunk extensions with arm raises.
9. Run another 800 meters at 5K race intensity.
10. Repeat steps 2 through 9 one more time to complete two circuits in all; then cool down with about 2.5K (1.5 mi) of light running, plus stretching and core work.

As is the case with the basic circuit training, advanced circuit work can be made more difficult over time by adding dumbbells to the six-way lunge and one-leg squat with hops, increasing the weight of the dumbbells, and by increasing the number of repetitions of the exercises, the lengths of the running intervals, the actual running speed, and the number of circuits per workout.

HIGH-BENCH STEP-UP WITH JUMP

PURPOSE

This exercise develops muscular power, especially in the hips, quadriceps, and hamstrings. These muscles are mainly responsible for the propulsive force required for fast running, especially over hilly terrain.

EXECUTION

Stand on top of an approximately knee-high sturdy bench with full body weight on one foot and weight shifted slightly toward the heel of that foot. The other foot is free and held slightly behind the body (figure 13.11a). Hold the hands at the sides and maintain upright body posture. Lower the body in a controlled manner until the toes of the free foot touch the ground (figure 13.11b). Keep all body mass on the supporting leg; the toes of the free leg should not support weight at any time. Return to the starting position by pushing down with the heel and foot of the supporting leg and straightening the leg as quickly as possible, resulting in a vertical jump from the bench (figure 13.11c). The landing of the jump should be in the same spot as the take-off. Repeat for the desired number of repetitions on one leg and then the other. Caution: Failure to perform this exercise on a stable surface could easily result in injury.

▶ **Figure 13.11** (a) Starting position, (b) lowering, and (c) jump.

PLYOMETRIC (CLAPPING) PUSH-UP

PURPOSE

This exercise develops upper-body power to match the development of leg power and also improves stability in the core muscles (i.e., abdominal, oblique, and lower-back muscles). All of these muscles work together to stabilize the upper body during running, so strengthening them should have a strongly positive impact on running economy.

EXECUTION

First, establish the standard push-up position on the floor. Support the upper body with the hands on the floor, shoulder-width apart. Fully extend the arms and support the legs and feet on the toes. Lower the chest toward the floor by bending the elbows while keeping the trunk and hips extended and rigid. When the chest is about 1 inch (3 cm) from the floor, rapidly straighten the arms and push the body upward as fast as possible. As the arms reach full extension, remove the hands from the floor and clap them together as rapidly as possible (figure 13.12) before returning the hands to the floor in the same position they were in before the clap. Repeat these actions for the prescribed number of reps.

▶ **Figure 13.12** Plyometric push-up and clap.

SIX-WAY LUNGE WITH ARM DROP

PURPOSE

This exercise strengthens and stretches the hamstrings and gluteal muscles in all three key planes of motion: sagittal, frontal, and transverse. Strong, flexible hamstrings and glutes stabilize the knee during stance, control the leg during forward swing, and help provide the propulsive force needed for powerful strides.

EXECUTION

Stand with feet pointing straight ahead, hip-width apart. Bend the arms at the elbows, with hands in front of the shoulders. Step forward with one foot into a long-lunge position (figure 13.13a). As the forward foot makes contact with the ground, drop the hands on either side of the forward knee. Quickly extend that knee to bring the hamstrings and gluteal muscles into action to return the leg and body to the original, standing position. Repeat this exercise on the other leg.

To continue from the standing position, step directly to one side into a lateral-lunge position (figure 13.13b). The upper body should face that side and lean forward over the lateral-lunge leg at about a 30-degree angle. Drop the hands on either side of the lunging knee as that foot makes contact with the ground; keep the other foot pointed straight ahead. Extend the lunging knee to activate the gluteal muscles and hamstrings and bring the lunging leg and the body back to beginning position. Repeat the action on the other leg.

Then, from the original standing position, step diagonally *and to the rear* with one leg into a backward lateral-lunge position (figure 13.13c). The upper body should face to the rear and lean over the backward lateral-lunge leg at about a 30-degree angle from vertical. Drop the hands alongside the lunging knee as that foot makes ground contact; keep the other foot pointing straight ahead. Extend the lunging knee to activate the hamstring and gluteal muscles to help bring the body back to the starting point. Repeat the pattern using the other leg for the prescribed number of times.

▶ **Figure 13.13** *(a)* Forward, *(b)* lateral, and *(c)* backward lateral lunges.

HANGING SCISSORS PLUS DOUBLE-KNEE RAISE

PURPOSE

This exercise strengthens the hip flexor, abdominal, and oblique muscles. All of these muscles stabilize the upper body during running.

EXECUTION

Begin by hanging by the hands from a bar or overhead support. The height of the bar should allow the body to hang fully extended without the feet touching the ground. Raise one knee vertically with the knee bent as in a running stride as high as possible; simultaneously, push the other leg and foot downward and backward (figure 13.14a). Keep the backward leg nearly straight. Quickly reverse this action: Swing the knee of the backward leg forward and upward with that knee bent; move the other leg downward and backward (figure 13.14b) keeping the backward leg nearly straight. Repeat this scissoring action for the required number of reps before beginning the second part of the exercise, the double-knee raise.

To perform a double-knee raise, return to the straight, hanging position. Quickly lift both legs as high as possible toward the chest, keeping both knees bent (figure 13.14c). Slowly lower both legs to the starting position. Complete this raising and lowering movement for the prescribed number of reps.

▶ **Figure 13.14** Scissor movement on (a) one side and (b) then the other (c) followed by a double-knee raise.

ONE-LEG SQUAT WITH HOP

PURPOSE

This exercise develops coordination and power in a running-specific way.

EXECUTION

Stand with one foot forward and one foot back with feet about one shin-length apart from front to back and hip-width apart from side to side. Place the toes of the back foot on a step or block that is about 6 to 8 inches (15-20 cm) high. Support all body weight on the forward foot. From this position, bend the forward leg at the knee and lower the body until that knee reaches an angle of about 90 degrees between the thigh and calf (figure 13.15a).

Immediately hop upward off the forward foot while maintaining contact with the step or block with the back foot. After landing from this hop, immediately go into another squat and hop upward again while still maintaining contact with the step or block with the back foot (figure 13.15b). Maintain upright posture with the upper body and keep the hands at the sides throughout this hopping action. Complete the required number of reps on one leg before moving to the other leg. Throughout the exercise, make sure the supporting foot isn't too far out (like overstriding) or too far in (like understriding). At the deepest point of the squat, the rear, or nonsupporting, knee should be about 0 to 4 inches (0-10 cm) behind an imaginary line drawn perpendicular to the support foot at the heel. Make sure the bench is not too tall: If using it pushes your body forward, it can be uncomfortable for the quads of the nonsupporting leg. Make sure the toes of the back foot stay on the step at all times.

▶ **Figure 13.15** *(a)* One-leg squat and *(b)* hop.

PRONE TRUNK EXTENSION WITH OVERHEAD ARM RAISE

PURPOSE

Prone trunk extensions strengthen the muscles of the upper and lower back. These muscles coordinate with the abdominals and obliques to stabilize the trunk during running.

EXECUTION

Lie face down on the floor or ground with legs straight and arms extended forward (they would be overhead if you were in a standing position). Use your back muscles to raise your chest, shoulders, and arms toward the sky or ceiling as high as possible (figure 13.16); then slowly and smoothly return to the floor or ground. Never let the trunk rest on the floor—retain some muscle tension in the back for the entire exercise. Repeat this up-and-down action for the required number of reps.

▶ **Figure 13.16** Trunk extension.

Conclusion

For runners of all ability and experience levels, circuit training provides an outstanding way to upgrade running fitness and whole-body strength. When conducted twice a week, circuit sessions improve lactate-threshold velocity; $\dot{V}O_2$max; and overall coordination, strength, and fatigue-resistance. Circuits are exciting additions to a training program because the sessions can be constantly tweaked with changes in running-interval length, running speeds, and strengthening movements; rote, drudge-like training is avoided.

Circuit training is an ideal precursor to the more advanced running-specific strength training (chapter 14) and thus should be included early in an overall training program. It can also be employed effectively in the late stages of training, just before a critical competition. It forms an important part of base training and is more effective than submaximal running, which is the usual foundation of traditional base training, for improving running capacity and strength.

CHAPTER 14

Running-Specific Strength Training

After a runner has improved general strength significantly, he or she is ready to move on to more technical movements. The coordination, strength, and balance gained from general strengthening enhance the ability to perform running-specific strengthening activities, or gait-mimicking maneuvers performed on one leg at a time. Many of these movements are challenging and require a runner to use the stability and body control acquired during the general-strengthening phase in order to perform the movements correctly.

The tandem of general strength training followed by running-specific strength training provides a powerful progression within a runner's training program. Both types of training improve running economy and resistance to fatigue, but running-specific strength training heightens propulsive force during the stance phase of gait, thus expanding stride length. Running-specific strengthening also protects runners from injury.

Benefits of a Running-Specific Program

What is the underlying rationale for running-specific strength training? When a runner repeatedly performs a strengthening activity, with proper progressions, the runner advances his or her strength during the specific movements of that activity. However, the strength associated with other actions may not improve at all, even when the same muscle groups are involved. This reality is part of what is often called the *specificity-of-training* principle.[1]

The specificity-of-training principle states that one must perform a specific action in order to upgrade one's strength during that action. Performing large numbers of seated leg extensions, for example, can dramatically increase quadriceps strength but won't improve quadriceps strength during running. Isolating the quadriceps muscles during leg-extension activity is not specific to the complex neuromuscular patterns of running.

Runners wanting to optimize strength for running must use a program containing exercises that mimic the biomechanics of running, including first contact with the ground, stance, toe-off, and swing. The workout presented in the next section contains a series of exercises that are specific to the gait cycle and promote greater running-specific strength. Improvements in running-specific strength enhance running economy and promote higher maximal speed by helping runners apply more propulsive force to the ground with each step and by minimizing ground-contact time.[2]

Running-Specific Strength Session

For exercises primarily carried out in a one-footed stance, assume an optimal kinetic-chain alignment: Stand on one foot, lift the arch of that foot, and point that knee straight ahead. Contract the quads and glutes lightly on that side of the body. Pull in the abs by contracting them and make sure the lower back is in neutral position (i.e., the spine has a natural curve inward but not an exaggerated one). Keep the ribs in neutral position—not rotated up, which would cause the upper back to lean backward, nor rotated down, which would produce a hunched-over position. Retract the shoulder blades by pulling the shoulder blades together and slightly down, which pulls the head of each humerus into its shoulder socket. Pull the head back slightly so that it is in alignment with the body and is held in a neutral position.

Warm up with about 15 minutes of light running; then perform the following strengthening exercises in this order:

1. One-leg squat
2. Runner's pose
3. One-leg heel raise: 12 reps per heel
4. Toe walking with opposite-ankle dorsiflexion
5. Balance and eccentric reach with toes
6. Wall shin raise with pulse
7. High-bench step-up
8. Running-specific arm swing
9. One-leg, straight-leg dead lift
10. Bicycle leg swing
11. Reverse bicycle leg swing with resistance
12. Sprints
13. Partial squat
14. Falls to earth with forward hops

Finish this workout by running and stretching. Jog easily for 800 meters, run at 5K race intensity for 5 minutes, and then cool down with 1,600 meters (~ 1 mi) of light, relaxed running. Then stretch the legs and lower back thoroughly for about 15 minutes. The easy running relaxes the leg muscles; the 5K run allows $\dot{V}O_2$max to be reached, lifts blood lactate concentrations, and enhances economy at 5K race speed. Stretching prepares the legs for moderate activities that follow. Runners can make this section of the workout more challenging by moving along more quickly than 5K pace.

ONE-LEG SQUAT

PURPOSE

This exercise improves strength and control during the stance phase of gait and thus enhances economy, promotes propulsive force, and protects the legs from injury.

EXECUTION

Stand relaxed with correct kinetic-chain body posture and feet placed on either side of an imaginary midline running through the center of the body. Place full body weight on one leg, which is directly under the shoulder, with the knee and hip barely flexed. Balance the toes of the other foot on a bench or step behind the body (figure 14.1a). The bench or step should be about 6 to 8 inches (15-20 cm) high. When in position, the feet are about shin-length apart from front to back and shoulder-width apart from side to side.

Strongly flex the knee and hip of the supporting leg so that the torso descends and the thigh becomes roughly parallel with the ground. At the bottom of the squat, the knee of the nonsupporting leg should be close to an imaginary line drawn perpendicular to the heel of the supporting leg (figure 14.1b). The torso inclines forward slightly during the squat, and full body weight remains on the supporting foot; the toes of the other foot are on the step or bench just to provide balance. Once the supporting thigh is parallel with the ground, extend the hip and knee of the supporting leg and push the torso upward to return to the original, standing-tall position, thus completing one rep on that leg. Do two sets of 10 reps on each leg. Complete the first set with one leg and then switch to the other leg. Then complete the second set.

PROGRESSION

Progress over time by adding dumbbells held in the hands. As strength advances considerably, use a weighted bar on the shoulders instead of dumbbells. Gradually increase squatting speed while preserving form.

▶ **Figure 14.1** (a) Starting position for the squat and (b) bottom of the squat.

RUNNER'S POSE

PURPOSE

This exercise improves leg stability during stance and also enhances the power of the swing phase of gait.

EXECUTION

Assume the correct kinetic-chain alignment with body weight on one supporting leg. Flex the other leg at the knee so that the foot is not touching the ground. The thigh should be slightly extended behind the hip (figure 14.2a). Move the thigh forward and upward until it is just above parallel with the floor, flexing that knee so that the lower part of the leg is pointing backward behind the center of mass (figure 14.2b). As the thigh moves forward and up, swing the opposite arm forward as would be the case during a normal running stride. Keep the hip, knee, and ankle of the supporting leg slightly flexed at all times. Hold this position for 5 seconds while maintaining relaxed stability and balance; then bring the leg back to its starting position and return the opposite arm to a relaxed position at the side to complete one rep. Do two sets of 12 poses with each leg, completing the reps for one leg and then switching to the other side. Then complete the second set.

PROGRESSION

Attach a stretch cord around the thigh of the upward-moving leg. Stand on the other end of the stretch cord with the supporting leg so that there is considerable resistance to the upward swing of the thigh. As strength and coordination improve, increase the resistance and tension of the stretch cord.

▶ **Figure 14.2** (a) Starting position and (b) striding pose.

ONE-LEG HEEL RAISE

PURPOSE

These heel raises improve the strength of the calf muscles and Achilles tendon, thereby improving control of the foot during the stance phase of gait.

EXECUTION

Stand with one leg on a 6-inch-high (15 cm) box in relaxed, kinetic-chain posture with all body weight supported on one leg and with that knee barely flexed. (This exercise can also be performed standing on the floor.) Flex the other knee so that the other foot is off the ground and the shin is roughly parallel with the floor (figure 14.3a). Contract the calf muscles of the supporting leg as strongly as possible so that the heel of the supporting leg rises vertically off the box. Rock forward on the supporting foot, keeping full body weight on the toes and extreme forefoot (figure 14.3b). Use a wall, chair, or other structure for balance, if necessary.

Then lower the heel toward the ground smoothly, evenly, and swiftly. During this movement, keep the ankle straight, keep the foot from wobbling, and keep the upper body still and coordinated. As the heel moves downward, shift body-weight support from the toes and forefoot to the midfoot region. Then dorsiflex the ankle naturally and simultaneously increase knee flexion, maintaining the hip in a slightly flexed position (figure 14.3c). Then, slightly increase the flexion of the ankle and knee compared with the stance phase. Immediately after flexing the ankle and knee, rock back up onto the toes, plantar-flex the ankle, and straighten the knee (figure 14.3d). Hold this position on tiptoes for 2 seconds to complete the rep. Do two sets of 12 reps per heel; complete the reps for one foot and then switch to the other foot. Then complete the second set.

As the exercise is performed, move in a relaxed, rhythmic manner with no hesitation in the overall movement except for the hold on the tiptoes at the end. Maintain good balance, posture, and stability at all times, use a running-specific posture, and sustain a feeling of relaxed running while carrying out the back-and-forth rocking. Do not tighten up the upper body; avoid looking at your legs and feet as the movements are completed.

PROGRESSION

Hold dumbbells in the hands or put a weighted bar on the shoulders to provide added resistance, increasing the weight gradually over time. Turn the weight-bearing foot outward to improve inside-ankle strength; turn the weight-bearing foot inward to improve outside-ankle strength.

▶ **Figure 14.3** (a) Starting position, (b) heel raise, (c) heel lowering, and (d) knee and ankle flexing.

TOE WALKING WITH OPPOSITE-ANKLE DORSIFLEXION

PURPOSE

This exercise improves the strength of the arches of the feet, promoting energy return during the stance phase of gait. It also upgrades the dynamic flexibility of the ankle joint, Achilles tendon, and calf muscles, thus preventing injury to those key parts of the leg.

EXECUTION

Assume a standing-tall posture as high up on the toes of both feet as possible. Balance for a moment on the toes, and then walk forward on the toes with slow, small steps, taking one step every 1 to 2 seconds (figure 14.4a). On each step, dorsiflex the ankle of the stepping foot as much as possible after it leaves contact with the ground (figure 14.4b); then plantar-flex the foot again just before making contact with the ground at the end of the step (figure 14.4c). Maintain balance on the toes and ball of the support foot during forward movement. Move so that each step is about 10 to 12 inches (25-30 cm) in length; keep your posture tall and balanced at all times. Complete 2 sets of 20 meters (65 ft) with a short break between sets.

PROGRESSION

Increase the speed of overall movement and the amount of dorsiflexion after the foot leaves the ground. Hold dumbbells in your hands during toe-walking, gradually increasing weight over time.

▶ **Figure 14.4** *(a)* First step, *(b)* dorsiflexion during the step, and *(c)* plantar flexion on the landing.

BALANCE AND ECCENTRIC REACH WITH TOES

PURPOSE

This exercise strengthens the Achilles tendon and calf muscles in all planes of motion during the stance phase of gait, thereby promoting stability of the foot and ankle during stance, shortening ground-contact time, improving toe-off power, and reducing the risk of injury to the Achilles and calf muscles. Each reach is eccentric because the calf muscles must work actively to control the ankle of the supporting leg even while they are being stretched.

EXECUTION

Begin in the correct kinetic-chain position by standing on one foot while facing a wall or other structure with the toes of the supporting foot about 30 inches (76 cm) or so from the wall. This distance may need to be adjusted slightly as the exercise is performed. Flex the hip of the nonsupporting leg slightly to hold the other foot off the ground and position the nonsupporting leg toward the front of the body, keeping that leg relatively straight (figure 14.5a). Bend the supporting leg at the knee and dorsiflex the support ankle, going into a relatively shallow one-leg squat while maintaining the upper body in a nearly vertical position, almost directly over the supporting foot. As the supporting leg flexes at the knee, move the nonsupporting foot toward the wall until the toes touch the wall (figure 14.5b). Keep the nonsupporting leg relatively straight during this movement and do not let the upper body lean backward. Return to the starting position.

Next, conduct the same motion but move the nonsupporting foot forward and laterally, to the outside (figure 14.5c). During this action, the supporting foot tends to roll to the inside, the ankle tends to pronate, and most of the body weight tends to be supported by the inside half of the supporting foot. Control the ankle to prevent this inward movement and maintain good balance. Do not let the ankle collapse to the inside. The nonsupporting foot may not quite reach the wall since the movement is now in the frontal plane (side to side) in addition to the sagittal plane (straight ahead). Return to the starting position.

Finally, move the nonsupporting foot medially, to the inside, crossing in front of the body, and attempt to touch the wall (figure 14.5d). As this is done, the supporting ankle naturally supinates and the foot rolls to the outside so that most of the body weight is supported by the outside half of the foot. Control supination actively to prevent this rolling movement; keep the inside half of the foot on the ground. After touching the wall with the nonsupporting foot, return to the starting position to complete one rep. Complete 10 reps, with three reaches (straight ahead, lateral, and medial) per rep, with each foot, and then repeat for another set.

When this exercise is done correctly, rotational stress should be felt in the Achilles tendon of the supporting leg during the lateral and medial movements of the wall-touching foot. Keep the torso in a vertical position throughout all

(continued)

BALANCE AND ECCENTRIC REACH WITH TOES *(continued)*

reps; avoid the two most common form faults with this exercise: rocking the torso backward in order to facilitate touching the wall or leaning forward from the hips as the reaches are made. Do not let the trunk rotate.

PROGRESSION

Hold dumbbells in your hands while performing the eccentric reaches, gradually increasing the weight over time.

▶ **Figure 14.5** *(a)* Starting position, *(b)* toe reach, *(c)* outside movement, and *(d)* inside movement.

WALL SHIN RAISE WITH PULSE

PURPOSE

These upgrade the strength of the shin muscles, improving control of the foot and ankle during the stance phase of gait and lowering the risk of shin injuries.

EXECUTION

Stand with the back toward a wall with the heels about the length of the feet from the wall. Maintain a relaxed, standing-tall running posture. Lean back until the buttocks and shoulders rest against the wall (figure 14.6a). Dorsiflex both ankles simultaneously, keeping the heels in contact with the ground (figure 14.6b). Bring the toes as far toward the shins as possible and then lower the toes back toward the ground until the forefeet are just lightly touching the surface, completing one rep. Carry out two sets of 40 reps.

After completing the 40 reps, dorsiflex the ankles to their fullest extent. Then, instead of lowering the feet the whole way, lower them about half way to the ground and then quickly plantarflex and dorsiflex the ankles 40 times using a small range of motion, smaller than the full range used for the basic shin raises. These short, quick ankle movements are called *pulses*, and they usually produce a burning sensation in the shins. Carry out the pulses in a middle zone of motion about half-way between full dorsiflexion and a feet-on-the-ground position. Do two sets of 40 shin raises, plus two sets of 40 pulses.

PROGRESSION

Carry out the shin raises on one leg at a time.

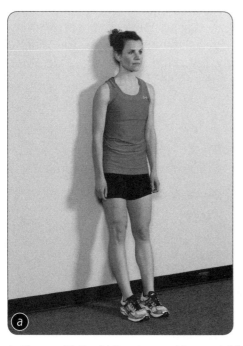 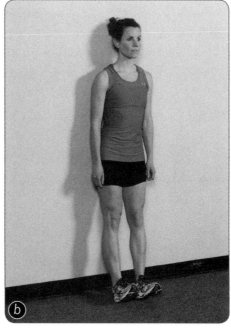

▶ **Figure 14.6** *(a)* Starting position and *(b)* dorsiflexion.

HIGH-BENCH STEP-UP

PURPOSE

This exercise improves leg strength in a running-specific way and has a uniquely positive effect on the glutes and hamstrings. Carrying out high-bench step-ups is sometimes called hill training on a bench because the body is lifted vertically with each repetition, similar to what happens with each step during hill running.

EXECUTION

Stand in kinetic-chain position on a 6- to 24-inch-high (15 to 60 cm) bench or step while holding a 5-pound (2.3 kg) dumbbell in each hand. Place all body weight on one foot (figure 14.7a). Hold the other foot free and slightly behind the body. Lower the body in a controlled manner while performing a one-leg squat on the supporting leg until the toes of the nonsupporting foot lightly touch the ground (figure 14.7b). Keep the torso in an upright position at all times. Maintain body weight on the supporting foot. Do not support any weight, even at the bottom of the squat, with the nonsupporting, moving foot.

Then, push downward on the bench with the supporting foot and straighten that leg (figure 14.7c). As this is done, swing the nonsupporting leg upward and forward until that hip is flexed and the thigh is parallel with the surface of the bench or step. As the thigh swings upward, keep the nonsupporting leg bent at the knee. Swing the opposite arm forward naturally as the nonsupporting leg moves upward. Hold that leg in a thigh-up position for a moment before starting the next rep. Do two sets of 12 reps on each leg with a short break between sets.

PROGRESSION

Gradually increase speed of movement while staying under control at all times; don't increase velocity if support leg is still shaking and moving from side to side. Increase dumbbell weight. Ultimately, perform exercise with a weighted bar across the shoulders. Gradually raise the height of the bench.

▶ **Figure 14.7** *(a)* Starting position, *(b)* squat, and *(c)* step-up.

RUNNING-SPECIFIC ARM SWING

PURPOSE

These arm swings improve stability during the stance phase of gait, upgrade core strength during stance, and increase shoulder strength during running movements. These effects should enhance running economy and fortify resistance to fatigue.

EXECUTION

Attach a medium-strength stretch cord to a post or other sturdy structure in front of the body. Stand on one foot only with the body in correct kinetic-chain position, and hold the other end of the stretch cord in the hand opposite the support leg, near the hip. Keep the cord at maximal tension—if the cord has slack, increase distance from the post. Keep the arm bent at the elbow throughout the exercise to mimic the correct running position. Move the hand holding the cord straight forward in a steady, controlled way (figure 14.8a). Resist the forward acceleration provided by the cord, keeping the hand and arm movement as smooth as possible. Continue until the elbow moves past the hip, and then pull the cord backward until the hand returns to the hip (figure 14.8b). During the pulls, maintain correct kinetic-chain arrangement of body, avoiding rotational trunk action; always move the hand and arm straight forward, not across the body. Complete two sets of 40 reps per side.

PROGRESSION

Use stretch cords of increasingly greater resistance. Speed up arm movement without losing any control.

▶ **Figure 14.8** *(a)* Forward arm movement and *(b)* pull back.

ONE-LEG, STRAIGHT-LEG DEAD LIFT

PURPOSE

This exercise improves the strength of the glutes, hamstrings, and lower-back muscles in a running-specific way. These muscles are critically important for stability and forward propulsion during running.

EXECUTION

Stand on one foot only using optimal kinetic-chain body position with arms hanging naturally at the sides and weighted bar in your hands (figure 14.9a). Keep the lower back and ribs neutral (i.e., the spine has a natural curve inward; the upper back is not leaning backward or hunched over), pull the shoulder blades together and slightly down so that the humerus heads are pulled into the shoulder sockets, and pull the head back slightly as though balancing a book on top of the head.

Bend forward at the hips in a smooth, coordinated way by shifting the buttocks back while keeping the natural alignment of the spine, retracting the shoulder blades, and letting the bar slide down the front of the leg, which should be kept straight (figure 14.9b). Bend forward as much as possible but don't push forward into a painful position. Return to the starting position by actively contracting the supporting leg's glutes and hamstrings. As the full dead-lift movement is carried out, be careful not to let the shoulder blades move to the outside and don't round the back; keep the shoulders retracted at all times, with the back flat. If the hamstrings or glutes are tight, the range of motion may be small, but that is acceptable at first. Complete 12 reps on one foot and then 12 on the other. Repeat with one more set on each leg.

PROGRESSION

Gradually use a heavier bar.

▶ **Figure 14.9** *(a)* Starting position and *(b)* execution.

BICYCLE LEG SWING

PURPOSE

This exercise promotes hamstring and glute strength during the swing phase of gait, thus improving control of the leg during swing and reducing the risk of hamstring cramping and breakdown during prolonged running.

EXECUTION

Stand in proper kinetic-chain position with body weight fully supported on one leg. Attach one end of a stretch cord to a firm post or other solid structure at about knee height and the other end around the ankle of the nonsupporting leg. Stand facing the post at a distance so that the stretch cord significantly accelerates the leg forward during the forward-swing phase of the exercise. This enhanced forward acceleration puts the hamstrings under additional eccentric stress and ultimately strengthens the hamstrings in a running-specific way. Initially, place the opposite hand on a wall or other support to maintain balance. Flex the hip and knee on the nonsupporting side, raising the knee waist high and creating close to 90-degree angles at the hip and knee (figure 14.10a) with the thigh parallel with the ground. Then, swing the lower part of the nonsupporting leg forward until the knee is almost fully extended (figure 14.10b), keeping the thigh parallel to the ground.

Next, drop the thigh downward and backward until the entire thigh and leg are extended behind the body as though following through on a running stride. Paw the ground with the nonsupporting foot as it passes under the body, scraping the ground with the midfoot area (figure 14.10c). Keep the knee at close to full extension through the backswing. At the end of the hip extension, bend the knee and move the heel close to the buttocks (figure 14.10d). Finally, move the knee quickly forward, returning to the starting position with the thigh parallel to the ground. Complete this entire sequence in a smooth manner so that the hip and leg move through a continuous arc without stopping or pausing. When the movement is well coordinated, perform the swings at a cadence of about 12 to 15 swings every 10 seconds. Carry out 50 reps on each leg, and then repeat.

PROGRESSION

Gradually increase velocity without loss of control and balance. When the basic bicycle leg swing can be performed with control, balance, and excellent movement speed, use a cord that provides greater resistance.

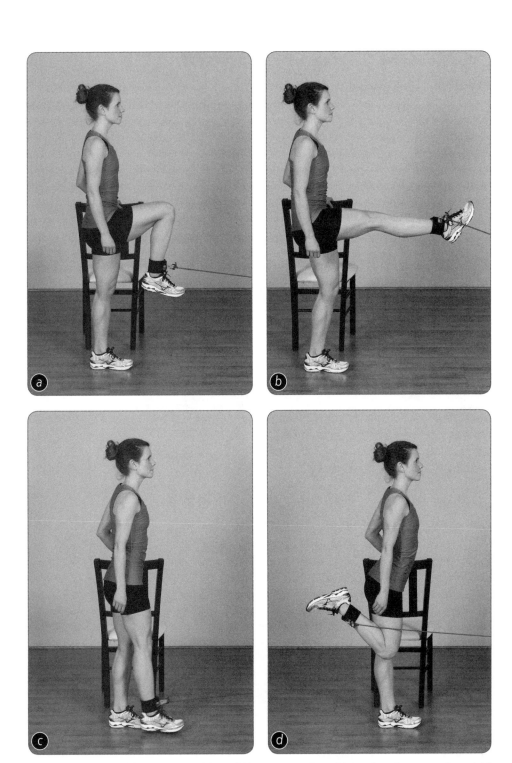

▶ **Figure 14.10** *(a)* Starting position, *(b)* knee extension, *(c)* pawing the ground, and *(d)* end of hip extension.

REVERSE BICYCLE LEG SWING WITH RESISTANCE

PURPOSE

This version improves the strength of the hip flexors, promoting increased resistance to fatigue in these muscles during running.

EXECUTION

The movements employ an intermediate-strength stretch cord and are the same as the regular bicycle leg swing except you face away from the stretch cord's attachment point, which is also at knee height for this exercise. The cord then resists forward leg swing (figure 14.11) instead of enhancing it, and the overall effect is to strengthen the hip flexors. Do two sets of 50 reps with each leg.

PROGRESSION

Increase the resistance of the stretch cord and speed up movement without losing coordination.

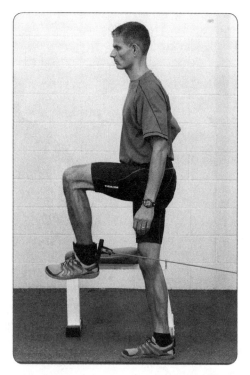

▶ **Figure 14.11** Starting position.

SPRINTS

PURPOSE

Carrying out running-specific strengthening movements fires up the nervous system and enhances the ability to run fast. Thus, when sprints are carried out following running-specific drills, faster running velocities are reached. The higher-speed running steadily advances maximal running speed, a key predictor of endurance performance.

EXECUTION

Run at close to maximal speed for 8 × 100 meters. Accelerate for the first 20 meters of each sprint, and then maintain close-to-maximal velocity for the final 80 meters (figure 14.12). Take short, 20-second walking breaks between the sprints. Stay relaxed at all times during the powerful sprints; avoid the tendency to tighten up. Maintain fluidity of motion. Complete eight 100-meter reps in all.

PROGRESSION

Run faster! Additionally, run on a surface with a slight declination.

▶ **Figure 14.12** Sprinting at close-to-maximal velocity.

PARTIAL SQUAT

PURPOSE

Of all the running-specific exertions, these are the most specific. Partial squats improve the strength of the entire leg in a running-specific way and thereby augment propulsive force, stability, resistance to fatigue, and running economy.

EXECUTION

Stand in the kinetic-chain position with one foot directly under the shoulder, keeping that knee just slightly flexed and maintaining relaxed, upright posture. Flex the other, nonsupporting leg at the knee so that foot does not touch the ground. Hold a barbell on the top of the shoulders just behind the neck and incline the upper body slightly forward for balance (figure 14.13a). Direct your body weight through the middle of the supporting foot.

For a traditional one-leg squat, one would ordinarily move from this basic position by bending the supporting leg at the knee and lowering the body until that knee almost reaches a 90-degree angle and the thigh is parallel with the ground. For the partial squat, bend the supporting leg at the knee and lower the body approximately half the regular distance so that the angle between the back of the thigh and lower leg is about 135 degrees (figure 14.13b). Initially, spot-touching the floor with the nonsupporting leg occasionally for balance is acceptable. To complete one rep, return to the starting position, maintaining upright posture with the trunk.

Complete 10 normal reps and then without any recovery initiate another partial squat and hold in the down position for 10 seconds. Continuing without rest, complete a second set of 10 partial squats, another static hold in the down position for 10 seconds, a third set of partial squats, and a third 10-second hold in the down position. Then, repeat this sequence on the other leg. Finally, complete one more round on each leg. Do two sets on each leg.

PROGRESSION

As soon as it is possible to complete two full sets on each leg without having to stop, add additional weight to the barbell using 5- to 10-pound (2-5 kg) increments. Continue to add weight for subsequent workouts each time two sets can be completed on each leg without major problems.

▶ **Figure 14.13** *(a)* Starting position and *(b)* the squat.

FALLS TO EARTH WITH FORWARD HOPS

PURPOSE

This exercise imrpoves the strength and explosiveness of the ankles and upgrades stability during landing and stance.

EXECUTION

The runner stands on a step or box that is 6 to 12 inches in height. Ankles, knees, and hips should be slightly flexed, and abdominal muscles and buttocks should be tightened (figure 14.14a). Step forward off the box with the left foot and release the right foot from the box to lean forward into a free fall (figure 14.14b). Do not reach down and touch the ground with the left foot while the right foot is still on the box. Let the lean turn into a fall so that the whole body is accelerating toward the ground. When the left foot hits the ground, explosively hop forward, spending as little time as possible on the ground (figure 14.14c). Land with great stability on the left foot and preserve the landing position for three seconds with an upright torso and as little quavering in the leg and upper body as possible (figure 14.14d). Repeat seven times on the right and seven times on the left.

PROGRESSION

Over time, increase to two sets of 12 repetitions per leg, focusing on maintaining solid coordination and explosiveness. Then, increase the height of the box, working up to a little more than knee height.

▶ **Figure 14.14** (a) Starting position, (b) lean, (c) hop, and (d) landing.

Tips for Implementing Running-Specific Strength Training

When carrying out the running-specific exertions, maintain a feeling of actual running as much as possible. Do not tense the upper body and gaze downward at the legs during movement because this would not happen during normal running. Perform the exercises rhythmically and smoothly, not with choppy timing and movements. Do the workout on days when you are well rested; fatigue blocks the attainment of good form during the exercises. If time is a limiting factor, complete half the session on one day and the other half on the following day.

Conduct this running-specific strength session about twice a week during the running-specific-strength phase of overall training. The running-specific phase should last from 4 to 8 weeks, follow a thorough general-strengthening program, and precede hill and explosive work in a runner's overall training plan. Carry out the running-specific workout occasionally within the subsequent hill and explosive phases of training to preserve running-specific strength.

Conclusion

Running-specific strength training is the perfect follow-up to general strengthening and paves the way for outstanding hill work and explosive workouts. It augments pure running training (i.e., workouts with no strengthening components) by increasing running economy, resistance to fatigue, and maximal running velocity. Running-specific strength training gives its devoted followers a decided edge in competitive situations: Most competitors will not be adhering to a running-specific strength program and will thus not have optimized the performance-related variables that are so responsive to this type of training.

CHAPTER 15

Hill Training

Most coaches and runners realize that hill training is highly beneficial, and science backs them up by confirming that hill training offers many advantages. In fact, few other training modalities are as productive from a fitness-enhancing standpoint. For example, hill training can

- enhance running economy,
- lift lactate-threshold velocity,
- improve resistance to fatigue,
- increase maximal running speed,
- increase $\dot{V}O_2$max and $v\dot{V}O_2$max,
- protect against soreness and injury, and
- prepare runners to compete on hilly race courses.

Though coaches and runners are aware of the benefits of hill training, what occasionally stumps them is not the question of why but rather how to do it. Fortunately, science provides answers to many of these questions, and this chapter explores them by explaining which hills—long and gradual or short and steep—provide the most benefits, the optimal incline of training hills, how often hill training should be conducted, and when to include hill training in an overall program.

Effects on Muscle Groups

Compared with flat-ground running, hill running places considerably different demands on the leg muscles. The calf muscles in particular are placed under greater strain and must perform significantly more work per minute of running during hill training compared with running on even surfaces. The reason for this is simply that greater ankle dorsiflexion occurs during the stance phase of gait during uphill running compared with running on pancake-flat ground. The increased dorsiflexion during stance increases eccentric strain on the calf muscles, particularly the gastrocnemius and soleus, enhancing their eccentric strength over the long term. An upswing in calf-muscle eccentric strength improves stability of the ankle and foot during the stance phase of gait, which should enhance running economy and also improve ankle springiness during running.

In addition, for a specific stride rate, the velocity of calf-muscle contraction must increase during hill running compared with running on the flat; the calf muscles are more stretched out because of the increased dorsiflexion during stance, so they must snap back into place more quickly than they would on flat surfaces in order to create toe-off and propel the body forward. In a study carried out with turkeys at Oregon State University, velocity of calf-muscle contraction during uphill running increased by 21 percent compared with flat-ground running at the same speed.[1] Mechanically, turkey muscles work very similarly to human sinews, with the same stretch-shortening cycle, eccentric strains, and increased velocity of calf muscle contraction following augmented dorsiflexion. Ultimately, uphill running should promote greater power development in the calf muscles, which are key sources of propulsive force during running. With this additional propulsive force, runners can go farther between steps and increase speed significantly.

The quadriceps muscles in the front of the thigh also benefit greatly from hill training, although it is the *downhill* component of hill work that optimizes quad functioning. During downhill running, each impact with the ground creates an unusual level of eccentric strain on the quads, which must create significant force to control knee flexion and keep the leg from collapsing. As the quads generate this force, they are stretched considerably by the natural, postimpact flexion of the knee. This combination of force production and simultaneous stretching dramatically enhances quad eccentric strength and makes the quads less prone to soreness during subsequent training. This increased eccentric strength also makes the leg more stable and springier during the stance phase of gait, enhancing economy and speed.

Hill Training Considerations

Unless a runner lives in the flattest of areas on the globe, he or she has a variety of hills from which to choose for training. These hills will differ in length and incline, two variables that have an impact on the physiological responses to a hill session and therefore must be considered when a hill workout is planned. Treadmills can also be used to simulate hill workouts if the surrounding terrain cannot accommodate a runner's needs. Of course, a hill workout includes both up and down running: The up portion is usually viewed as the productive part of the session, but downhill running—when performed correctly—also provides several benefits.

Longer Versus Shorter Hills

Coaches and runners frequently have a range of different hills from which to choose for hill training but are uncertain about optimal hill length. An advantage of relatively short inclines is that higher average running velocities can often be sustained because the more abbreviated durations of the uphill surges keep fatigue at manageable levels and thus facilitate faster running. Faster running speeds teach the neuromuscular system to operate with greater motor-unit activation and power outputs that can generate higher heart rates and larger percentages of $\dot{V}O_2max$, as well as higher levels of blood lactate compared with running more slowly on longer slopes. However, it is possible that longer hills could actually create greater physiological demands, for example higher heart and oxygen-consumption rates, because of the more sustained nature of the effort.

The relative merits of long versus shorts hills were examined in a study carried out at Pennsylvania State University, where exercise scientists asked 10 participants (5 men and 5 women) to complete two separate workouts each of which included 960 seconds of simulated hill climbing on laboratory treadmills.[2] Both training sessions used inclines of 6, 12, 18, and 24 percent, but in one instance the subjects completed 5 treadmill climbs of 192 seconds each that simulated long hills; in another situation, the participants finished

▶ Hill work is the most running-specific type of strength training.

Jochen Tack/imagebroker/age fotostock

20 hill intervals of 48 seconds each that simulated shorter hills. Recovery intervals lasted for 60 seconds each during the long-hill workouts and 12 seconds for each shorter climb. Each workout lasted a total of 20 minutes.

The metabolic cost of the workout was actually about 10 percent greater when the 192-second intervals were employed compared with the short intervals, indicating that average oxygen-consumption and heart rates were higher with the longer climbs. This is advantageous since increased demand on the oxygen-delivery and use system (i.e., the heart, blood vessels, and leg muscles) should promote superior adaptation and thus higher levels of fitness.

Interestingly, top exercise physiologists often recommend a duration of about 3 minutes (180 seconds) for hill-climb repetitions,[3] very close to the 192-second intervals used in the Penn State inquiry. A potential weakness of the Penn State study, however, is that treadmill speed was held constant. If athletes could sustain higher average speeds during shorter climbs compared with longer efforts, which is likely, the total metabolic cost might actually be greater with the shorter hills, and the power-advancing effect on the neuromuscular system would increase. This possibility has not been carefully studied in controlled scientific research.

What is the take-home lesson? At any specific running speed (for example, 15 kilometers per hour, or about 6:26 per mile), longer hills are better than short hills for training because they maximize the probability that extremely high heart and oxygen-consumption rates, plus high blood lactate levels, will be reached during each climb. In general, a short hill can be defined as an incline that requires a minute or less to climb; a long hill takes more than a minute to climb.

The more abbreviated inclines can be superior, however, if an athlete runs faster on shorter hills than on longer hills, which is likely because runners tend to run more quickly when they know that the duration of each intense effort is minimized. Shorter hills are linked with higher neural outputs, greater motor-unit recruitment, and advanced power outputs by the leg muscles. The brief recoveries (e.g., the time taken to run quickly back down the hills) associated with short hills should also keep heart and oxygen-consumption rates from falling too far between climbs, allowing both rates to climb progressively over the course of a workout.

Shorter hills are great because they allow runners to take off like rockets and thus optimize their neuromuscular power, but the potential disadvantage of shorter hills is that the duration of each climb is shorter. Thus, short hills may not be as good for optimizing resistance to fatigue—the capacity of the brain to tolerate and then promote continuous, hard exertion for *longer and longer periods of time.* (For discussions of fatigue resistance and how to improve it, see chapters 12 and 29).

Taking these factors into account, a runner should balance short and long hills in training; each kind of incline has its place in the overall program:

Short hills are great for advancing power and running speed, and long hills should be excellent for promoting fatigue resistance.

Hill Incline

The optimal incline for hill training has not been identified. It is clear that steeper inclines (for example, 8-10 percent) force runners to perform more work per step during uphill climbing, provided step length is not drastically compromised on those steeper slopes, than do inclines of 2 to 3 percent because the body must be lifted a greater distance vertically with each step. Greater work output per step should be more strengthening compared to the lower outputs associated with gentler hills assuming total climbing distance is comparable in the two situations. A potential disadvantage of steeper inclines, however, is that they often reduce stride length and running speed compared with workouts on easier slopes.[4]

Although science provides no definitive evidence on the matter, it is reasonable to believe that the use of different hill types—from relatively gentle to steep surfaces—would be an optimal way to conduct hill training. Research carried out with baseball pitchers has revealed that employing both a heavy ball and a light ball during training improves fastball velocity to a greater extent than the use of a regular baseball alone.[5] Using the heavy ball improves the maximal strength of the throwing motion; bringing the light ball into play fosters faster arm speed and, in combination with the uptick in strength produced through use of the heavy ball, optimizes power, the creation of more force in a shorter period of time. This translates into greater fastball velocity.

Comparably, running up steep hills might slow a runner's pace but would have a major impact on running-specific strength because of the increased amount of work per step; running up more gentle hills could then promote power because of the higher running velocities. Together, the fast speeds used on the relatively short, gentle hills and the greater work outputs employed on the steep grades could dramatically increase running power and maximal speed.

Downhill Running

Runners frequently are most focused on the uphill portions of their hill-training sessions, yet downhill training also provides several advantages. One major effect of downhill running is to promote greater resistance to delayed-onset muscle soreness, especially in the quadriceps. In an investigation completed at the University of Massachusetts at Amherst, a single instance of downhill running (~ 15 minutes in duration) promoted greater resistance to muscle pain during training for up to 6 weeks (the pain was simply the runners' perceived discomfort in their quadriceps muscles following challenging workouts).[6] Improved resistance to muscle soreness can prevent delays in the conduct of high-quality training and thus lead to greater gains in running fitness over specific periods of time.

Downhill running should not be approached cavalierly. In a study carried out at California State Polytechnic University with nine well-trained distance runners, a single workout including 30 minutes of downhill running on a 10 percent slope altered normal stride mechanics for at least 2 days and harmed running economy by 3.2 percent over the same duration.[7] This suggests that workouts with extended periods of downhill running should not be followed closely by high-quality workouts unless a runner has already had considerable experience with downhill training.

Hill Drills

Many serious runners create hill-training workouts that consist of little more than running uphill and then jogging back down for recovery, but scientific evidence suggests that it may be advantageous to carry out special drills (e.g., bounding, hopping, backward running) on hills as well. Such drills can amplify force production by the leg muscles during uphill movement and thus promote greater gains in strength compared with just running. The drills can also enhance coordination during uphill effort, which should improve competitive ability during hilly competitions and greater stability during flat-ground running.

In a relevant study completed at the Karolinska Institutet in Stockholm, Sweden, 11 Swedish marathon runners added hill workouts to their normal training programs over a 12-week period.[8] An interesting feature of this research was that the Swedish runners included a drill called bounce running during their uphill climbs, which ranged in intensity from relaxed to maximal efforts. Bounce running varies from normal hill running, which generally involves leaning forward slightly and moving up a hill as quickly as possible. In bounce running, a runner springs up more vertically onto his or her toes with each step, attempting to achieve greater loft, or vertical elevation, with every stride.

Bounce-running technique is as follows: On a hill, as a runner springs up onto the toes of one foot, the runner lifts the other knee as high as possible as he or she becomes airborne (see figure 15.1). The runner then lands on the mid- to front part of the other foot, letting the heel plunge quickly below the level of the toes, before springing up onto the toes of that foot while lifting the nonsupporting knee as high as possible. A runner bounce-runs by moving up a hill with a series of exaggerated yet quick leaps.

After 12 weeks of hill workouts that emphasized bounce running, running economy improved in the Swedish runners by approximately 3 percent at a running velocity of 4 minutes per kilometer, enough to trim about 6 minutes from marathon finishing time for a 3-hour marathoner. Although research

▶ **Figure 15.1**   Runner at the airborne moment in bounce-running technique.

in this area is limited, it is logical to assume that the inclusion of a variety of different hill drills, including one-leg hopping, bounding, backward uphill running, and downhill heel walking, would be beneficial. These exercises can be performed as part of the warm-up for a normal hill session.

Quick bursts of downhill running should also be included in hill sessions because fast downhill running on a gentle slope helps improve maximal running speed. During downhill running, each foot falls farther with each step compared with flat-ground running. Thus, each foot hits the ground with higher velocity compared with running on the flat, and the nervous system learns to control the foot, ankle, and leg more effectively during high-speed efforts.

Downhill running also improves confidence and balance during downward effort, enhancing competitive ability and upgrading economy during downslope movement. Proper form is absolutely essential: When running downhill, runners should lean forward slightly and use midfoot landings, avoiding the common tendencies to lean back and land on the heels. Leaning forward and landing midfoot will feel uncomfortable at first, giving a runner the feeling that he or she is close to losing control. Slow speeds on more gentle slopes should be used initially to avoid tripping, with downhill velocity gradually increasing over time as downward-running skill and coordination improve.

Hill Training by Elite Kenyans

As a group, Kenyan runners dominate the world of elite distance running.[9] Elite Kenyans are also well known for their rather relentless use of hill training as a fitness enhancer.[10]

When Moses Kiptanui was setting world records in the 3,000-meter steeplechase, 3K, and 5K his program centered on hill training in a rugged area near Nyahururu, Kenya. When Sammy Lelei ran the first-ever sub-60-minute half marathon, he had been training extensively on a challenging slope called Sergoit hill on the outskirts of Eldoret, Kenya.

Elite Kenyans appear to take two basic approaches in their hill training: (1) using an extremely long hill, or mountain, that permits sustained climbing for an extended duration and (2) using a shorter but steep hill to do as many repetitions as quickly as they can. Well-known examples of the first strategy include the Fluorspar climb employed by many elite Kenyans, as well as the Menengei crater ascent. The Fluorspar workout begins in a small village at the western edge of the Rift Valley near Iten and involves climbing steadily on mountain roads with an average uphill slope of 5 percent for 21 kilometers (13 mi). As Sammy Lelei himself has pointed out, it is usually necessary to complete only one repetition per workout on this incline. Countless elite Kenyans have used the Fluorspar session to improve running economy, lactate-threshold speed, $\dot{V}O_2max$, $v\dot{V}O_2max$, and fatigue resistance.

The Menengei crater ascent, carried out on the slope of a volcano near Nakuru, Kenya, is shorter but similar in nature, providing 12 kilometers (8 mi) of steady climbing at an approximate 5 to 7 percent incline. Four-time world-record holder Tegla Loroupe used this challenging ascent on numerous occasions prior to her victories at the New York Marathon and four world records for the 1-hour run as well as 20K, 25K, and 30K competitions.

When a shorter hill—often about 200 meters (656 ft) in length with an incline of 8 to 10 percent—is used during training, elite Kenyans will simply charge up the hill at a speed greater than 5K race intensity and quickly run back down to keep recovery periods minimal. They maintain this quick up-and-down pattern for about 45 minutes rather than for a fixed number of repetitions. Such training ensures that oxygen-consumption rate, blood lactate, resistance to fatigue, neural output, and motor-unit recruitment are all maximized, creating a situation in which $\dot{V}O_2max$, $v\dot{V}O_2max$, running economy, lactate-threshold speed, maximal running speed, and fatigue resistance are all simultaneously enhanced.

Incorporating Hill Work Into a Training Program

No scientific inquiry has examined the question of *when* hill work should be emphasized within an overall training program, so this point must be addressed logically. It is clear that hill training places great demands on a runner from the standpoints of general whole-body strength, running-specific strength, and coordination. Excellent whole-body strength is needed for training on hills because it preserves form during hill running, preventing undesirable outcomes such as excessive arm drive and the loss of upper-body control. Great general strength should also promote resistance to fatigue so that runners can climb farther and conduct greater numbers of hill repetitions per workout, thus increasing the number of adaptations associated with hill training.

Greater running-specific strength, which is the ability to produce greater force during the specific movements involved in gait, should also be extremely beneficial to hill training. As running-specific strength improves, more force can be applied to the ground per step during hill running, thus enhancing both work output per step and hill-running speed. Upgraded running-specific strength should also promote greater coordination during uphill climbing, promoting the intensity and quality of hill work.

For these reasons, it appears to be optimal to place hill training *after* periods of general and running-specific strength training in an overall program. A productive training program would feature general strengthening first, followed by running-specific strengthening and then hill training. Chapters 22 and 23 provide full details concerning this kind of periodization of training.

Conclusion

Hill training provides runners with many powerful benefits. Runners should use a variety of different hill types in their training; short hills on which high speeds can be maintained and longer hills that necessitate sustained efforts at submaximal but high-quality speeds. When structured to follow general and running-specific strength training, hill work is so strengthening that it sets the stage perfectly for subsequent weeks of explosive running and high-speed drills. Hill drills and downhill running are valuable adjuncts to regular hill training and should never be overlooked.

CHAPTER 16

Speed Training

Speed training can be defined in various ways, but in this book it means running that is carried out at faster than lactate-threshold velocity but not quicker than 800-meter race pace. Since lactate-threshold velocity corresponds roughly with a 15K race pace, workouts conducted at 10K, 5K, 3K, 1,500-meter, and 800-meter speeds would all qualify as speed-training sessions. Speed training is not the same as maximal-speed training, which is conducted at velocities faster than 800-meter race pace and is superior for improving maximal running velocity. (See chapter 28.) Readers who never race the 800-meter distance should not worry: 800-meter race tempo can be calculated easily from performances at 5K and 10K.

Speed training plays a powerful role in the development of a distance runner. Speed work represents the most productive and time-efficient way to improve almost all the key performance variables: $\dot{V}O_2max$, $v\dot{V}O_2max$, lactate-threshold velocity, running economy, and resistance to fatigue. Speed training is also highly effective at promoting specific race performances; for example, conducting speed sessions at 10K speed fosters confidence, resistance to fatigue, and economy at a 10K pace and thus leads to an improvement in 10K race time.

Dozens of different speed workouts are valuable for the endurance runner. This chapter describes the basic speed sessions that can be used by distance runners of all ability levels. These sessions are organized by pace, and each includes a unique type of speed training. Among other topics, this chapter will focus on race-specific speed training, fartlek training, Kenyan-style fartlek sessions, VP speed workouts, and $v\dot{V}O_2max$ training.

Speed Training Using Race Paces

Frank Horwill, founder of the British Milers' Club, strongly advocated using specific race paces to create speed workouts.[1] This is an extremely valuable approach: Workouts conducted at 10K, 5K, 3K, 1,500-meter, and 800-meter race paces use speeds that are faster than lactate-threshold velocity and thus promote improvements in that and the other key performance variables.

The following sessions also provide specific preparations for popular races and form bridges that can be employed to improve performances.

For example, a runner who carries out speed workouts at 10K and 5K paces eventually becomes much more comfortable at 10K speed and much more fatigue resistant at a 5K pace, increasing the likelihood that he or she will eventually be able to run 10Ks at close to current 5K speed. As Horwill recommended, the speed workouts described in this chapter will focus on 10K, 5K, 3K, 1,500-meter, and 800-meter race paces.

Speed Training at 10K Pace

In speed training, a general rule is that work-interval length expands at the slower end of the speed spectrum, that is, toward 10K and away from 800-meter speed. A 10K pace can hardly be considered lethargic, yet it is the slowest velocity used in speed training, and therefore the work intervals are the longest. A commonly used, practical, and productive work-interval length for 10K-paced speed training is 2,000 meters (1.2 mi). Thus, a speed-training session at 10K pace would include a thorough warm-up, a specified number of 2,000-meter work intervals at 10K pace, jog recoveries after each work interval, a cool-down, and then stretching at the very end.

The special warm-up (SWU) is effective prior to 10K-paced speed training since it prepares both the neuromuscular and cardiovascular systems for dynamic activity. The SWU is described in chapter 23.

The 2,000-meter intervals are easy to set up. For example, let's say that a runner is completing 10K races in about 40 minutes. Since there are 25 400-meter segments within a 10K, that's a 400-meter tempo of 40/25 = 1.6 minutes, or 96 seconds. There are five 400-meter components in a 2,000-meter work interval, so the goal time for each 2,000-meter interval would be 5 × 96 = 480 seconds, or 8 minutes flat.

10K-paced intervals are demanding and facilitate a runner's capacity to move along at 10K tempo in continuous fashion for an extended period of time. Average work-interval intensity will automatically be about 90 percent of $\dot{V}O_2$max, and blood lactate will be elevated during the intervals, so $\dot{V}O_2$max and lactate-threshold velocity will improve. Anecdotal evidence also suggests that running at 10K speed enhances economy at this pace, an effect that should lead to upgrades in $v\dot{V}O_2$max. Thus, a platform is created that makes current 10K speed easier to handle in race situations—and the physiological advancements prepare a runner to move up to faster velocities in future 10Ks.

If a runner has no experience with 10K racing, 10K pace can be calculated easily from other race tempos. For most runners, 10K speed is about 4 seconds per 400 meters *slower* than 5K pace, 4 seconds per 400 meters *faster* than half-marathon pace, and 8 seconds per 400 meters *quicker* than marathon tempo (all of these correspondences are from Frank Horwill's famous "Law of Running").[1] In elite runners, the same trends are apparent, but the gap in 400-meter pace between races is usually 2.5 to 3 seconds per 400 meters rather than 4 seconds. For example, an elite runner might slow down by just

2.5 to 3 seconds per 400 when moving from a 10K to a half marathon and by only 5 to 6 seconds per 400 when jumping from a 10K to a marathon.

Another rule of speed training is that relative recovery interval duration shortens as training speed moves toward the 10K end of the overall spectrum. There is little science behind this dictum; it is simply a logical concept based on the decreased intensity of work intervals at the 10K end, which thus permits a faster recovery. Training velocity has decreased to the greatest extent with 10K-paced speed training, and therefore recovery length as a fraction of work-interval length can be small. A good beginning with the 10K-based speed training sets recovery length at 25 percent of work-interval duration. Recoveries for the session described previously, with 8-minute work intervals, would consist of 2 minutes of easy running. The workout difficulty can be increased over time by gradually trimming the recovery time, with just 1 minute of recovery being the ultimate goal.

Science can't guide us as to whether the recoveries should involve running or walking because there are no relevant data, but running is certainly more specific to race situations and will also tend to keep the overall quality of the workout higher than walking by keeping average oxygen-consumption rate more elevated. A caution is that the recovery running should not be so intense that the subsequent work interval is impaired. A normally easy pace should be used for recovery, although it may not feel particularly easy due to lingering fatigue from the preceding work interval.

The *number* of work intervals to be performed per session can be approached progressively. Runners carrying out 10K-paced speed workouts for the first time might simply complete two 2,000-meter intervals during the initial session and then—depending on the challenge of the session and recovery during the 48 hours afterward—progress to three and ultimately four intervals per workout. Jack Daniels' quality rule is also a good guide for this situation.[2] Daniels suggests that the amount of quality running (i.e., running at faster than lactate-threshold velocity) per week should generally not exceed 25 percent of weekly volume. Thus, a runner completing 30 miles (48 km) of training per week would be allowed .25 × 30 = 7.5 miles (12 km) of weekly quality training. If the runner completes two quality workouts per week, it would make sense to include three 2,000-meter work intervals in the 10K-paced speed session, which would total 6,000 meters (3.75 mi) of quality running. The other 3.75 miles could be incorporated into the second quality workout of the week.

Speed Training at 5K Pace

While adhering to the speed-training rules regarding work-interval length and recovery duration, an excellent speed-training session at 5K pace would incorporate 1,200-meter (.75 mi) work intervals at 5K speed with recoveries lasting for about 75 to 80 percent of the work-interval time duration.

The 5K-paced workout creation is straightforward. Take the case of a runner who is completing 5K races in about 19 minutes. Since there are 12.5 400-meter segments within a 5K, this runner's average time per 400 meters is 19/12.5 = 1.52 minutes, or 91 seconds. There are three 400-meter segments in a 1,200-meter work interval, so goal time for each 1,200-meter interval would be $3 \times 91 = 273$ seconds, or 4:33.

In the case of 5K-paced speed training with recovery-interval duration initially set at about 75 to 80 percent of work-interval length, recovery would be about 3:30. The workout can be toughened by gradually paring time from each recovery—first to 3:00, then to 2:30, and so on—with about 90 seconds being the ultimate goal duration for recovery.

Like 10K pace, 5K tempo can be easily estimated from other race distances. For mortal runners, 5K pace is about 4 seconds per 400 faster than 10K speed, 8 seconds per 400 faster than half-marathon speed, and 12 seconds per 400 quicker than marathon speed.[1] This time correspondence is closer to 2.5 to 3 seconds per 400 for elite runners.

The 5K-paced speed workout is thus easy to implement. For the hypothetical 19-minute 5K runner described earlier, the workout would consist of the SWU, three to four 1,200-meter work intervals in about 4:33, with easy-paced recoveries of about 3:30 after each 1,200 meters, a cool-down at the end, and then stretching. This kind of session improves running economy and performance variables at current 5K speed, and thus represents a solid platform for moving up to faster 5Ks.

Speed Training at 3K Pace

Although the 3K distance is less commonly raced, training at 3K pace offers a number of advantages for distance runners. Compared with training at a 10K or 5K pace, 3K work heightens workout intensity and thus provokes greater positive physiological adaptations. For the runner accustomed to working at 5K and 10K intensities, 3K training is also a powerful prelude to maximal-speed training.

The 3K pace is easy to estimate from 5K race times since 3K speed will be about 3 seconds per 400 meters faster than 5K speed for most athletes. If a runner is averaging 18 minutes for his or her 5Ks, the 400-meter tempo for the 5K is 18/12.5 = 1.44 minutes, or 86 seconds. The resulting 3K pace would then be 86 − 3 = 83 seconds per 400 meters.

Continuing to employ the speed-training principles of work-interval length and recovery duration leads to a 3K-based session incorporating 800-meter work intervals with recoveries of equal duration. For our hypothetical runner with 18-minute 5Ks, this means that each 800-meter interval would be completed in about $2 \times 83 = 166$ seconds, or 2:46.

The 3K-paced workout could be constructed as follows: SWU, about four 800s in 2:46 each, 2:46 easy-paced recoveries, a cool-down, and then stretching. The workout can be increased in difficulty over time by adding additional 800-meter work intervals or decreasing the durations of the recovery periods.

Speed Training at 1,500-Meter Pace

Because of its high intensity, speed training at a 1,500-meter pace is a great bridge to maximal-speed training. Thus, endurance runners should avoid the common tendency to ignore training at a 1,500-meter pace in favor of intervals at a 5K pace. A great plan is to employ 400-meter work intervals with recovery intervals as long in duration as the work intervals or slightly longer. Intervals at a 1,500-meter pace are about 7 seconds per 400 meters faster than 5K-paced work intervals and competitions.

Take the case of a runner completing 5Ks in about 21 minutes, which is a tempo of 21/12.5 = 1.68 minutes, or 100 seconds per 400 meters. The 1,500-meter pace would be 7 seconds faster, or 93 seconds per 400.

The basic workout at a 1,500-meter pace would then be SWU, eight 400s in 93 seconds each, 93- to 120-second jog recoveries, cool-down, and stretching. The session can be upgraded in difficulty by adding more 400s or shortening the recovery durations.

Speed Training at 800-Meter Pace

Endurance runners should include highly intense intervals at an 800-meter pace in their training programs even if they simply want to run marathons. The high quality of this training means that it is a powerful producer of overall fitness, creating marked improvements in running economy and $v\dot{V}O_2max$. Compared with the other speed workouts, 800-meter sessions represent the best door opener to maximal-speed training. Heightened maximal speed improves paces at all race distances, including the marathon.

As is the case with the other types of speed training, the actual workouts are easy to create. An 800-meter pace is about 10 to 11 seconds faster per 400 than a 5K pace. If a runner completes 5Ks in about 17 minutes, that is a tempo of 17/12.5 = 1.36 minutes, or 82 seconds per 400. The resulting 800-meter pace would thus be around 72 seconds per 400.

By following the speed-training principles of work-interval length and recovery duration, the workout would be SWU, 12 × 200-meter intervals in 36 seconds (half of 72) each, about 1-minute recoveries, cool-down, and stretching. As always, the session can be toughened by increasing the number of work intervals or shortening the recovery periods.

Putting It All Together

Tables 16.1 to 16.3 summarize speed training based on race paces for runners of three ability levels. Table 16.1 is for the 50-minute 10K runner (~24:10 for 5K), table 16.2 is for the 40-minute 10K runner (~ 19:10 for 5K), and table 16.3 is for the 30-minute 10K competitor (~14:10 for 5K).

Table 16.1   Speed Workouts Based on Race Pace for the 50-Minute 10K Runner

	10K race pace	5K race pace	3K race pace	1,500 m race pace	800 m race pace
No. of intervals	3-4	3-4	4	8	12
Interval length	2,000 m (1.2 mi)	1,200 m (.75 mi)	800 m (.5 mi)	400 m (.25 mi)	200 m (.12 mi)
400 m pace for intervals	120 sec	116 sec	113 sec	109 sec	105 sec
Total time per interval	600 sec (10:00)	348 sec (5:48)	226 sec (3:46)	109 sec (1:49)	52.5 sec
Recovery time	120 sec (2:00)	4:30	3:46	109 sec (1:49)	~60-90 sec

Table 16.2   Speed Workouts Based on Race Pace for the 40-Minute 10K Runner

	10K race pace	5K race pace	3K race pace	1,500 m race pace	800 m race pace
No. of intervals	3-4	3-4	4	8	12
Interval length	2,000 m (1.2 mi)	1,200 m (.75 mi)	800 m (.5 mi)	400 m (.25 mi)	200 m (.12 mi)
400 m pace for intervals	96 sec	92 sec	89 sec	85 sec	81 sec
Total time per interval	480 sec (8:00)	276 sec (4:36)	178 sec (2:58)	85 sec	40.5 sec
Recovery time	2:00	3:30	2:58	85 sec	60-75 sec

Table 16.3   Speed Workouts Based on Race Pace for the 30-Minute 10K Runner

	10K race pace	5K race pace	3K race pace	1,500 m race pace	800 m race pace
No. of intervals	3-4	3-5	4-6	8-12	12-16
Interval length	2,000 m (1.2 mi)	1,200 m (.75 mi)	800 m (.5 mi)	400 m (.25 mi)	200 m (.12 mi)
400 m pace for intervals	72 sec	68 sec	65 sec	61 sec	57 sec
Total time per interval	360 sec (6:00)	204 sec (3:24)	130 sec (2:10)	61 sec	28.5 sec
Recovery time	2:00	2:30	2:10	61 sec	40-50 sec

Fartlek Training

Fartlek means speed play in Swedish, and fartlek training was developed by Swedish coach Gosta Holmer in the 1930s in an attempt to wrestle world cross-country running supremacy away from Finland, Sweden's chief rival. Holmer was well aware that Swedish distance runners needed greater speed to succeed in endurance competition, and his fartlek workouts featured running at speeds faster than race pace.

Classic fartlek sessions have four key features. First, they last about 45 minutes, not counting warm-up and cool-down. The number 45 is interesting because many elite Kenyans structure their quality workouts to take exactly this amount of time, not including warm-up and cool-down.

Second, during the approximately 45 minutes of fartlek, quick yet relaxed running is spontaneously alternated with easy recoveries. There is no set duration for the quality segments; an athlete adjusts the durations of quality running according to how he or she feels. Practically, the quality components usually last from 1 to 5 minutes but vary within the workout; an athlete usually does not know how long a quality segment will last and simply continues until a break is needed. Easy-running recoveries are often 1 to 2 minutes in duration, continuing only until a runner is ready to run powerfully again.[3]

Third, the quick segments of a fartlek session are often completed at faster than race pace in order to enhance speed development. No specific speed is targeted—after all, the workout involves speed *play*. The intense segments should simply *feel* faster than race tempo. Fourth, within the quality sections, there are spontaneously created superfast runs at close to maximal speed. Often, these spiked bursts last for 10 to 100 meters or so, after which the fast-pace effort is resumed. This spiking enhances the development of speed and increases the capacity to surge within competitions.

Fartlek training has not been rigorously studied in scientific research, but it's easy to see that the fartlek scheme is beneficial psychologically for the mentally stale endurance runner who has been locked into a rigid program of timed intervals and strictly specified running paces. Fartlek work involves top velocities, high rates of oxygen consumption, high lactate levels—and improved coordination because the sessions are often completed over somewhat uneven terrain. Thus, fartlek training should advance $\dot{V}O_2max$, $v\dot{V}O_2max$, lactate-threshold velocity, running economy, and maximal speed.

Holmer's fartlek training has been credited with the development of two great Swedish runners who dominated international 1,500-meter and mile racing in the early 1940s: Arne Andersson and Gunder Häagg. Each athlete set three world records in the mile, and Hägg's excellent 4:01.4 remained the world mark from 1945 until 1954.

Kenyan-Style Fartlek Training

The type of fartlek training commonly carried out by elite Kenyan runners has several things in common with traditional fartlek work: a 45- to 50-minute duration, the frequent use of fast training speeds, and variation in pace within a session. However, work- and recovery-interval lengths in Kenyan fartlek workouts are highly structured. Although called fartlek training by elite runners throughout western Kenya, the workout is more like a classic interval session with well-defined work intervals and recoveries. However, physiological and performance gains associated with Kenyan fartlek training should be similar to those achieved through traditional fartlek work.

Kenyan fartlek training is usually carried out by a group of runners working together, and it operates as follows: After a warm-up, group members run fast for 1 minute, after which there is 1 minute of easier-paced running. This pattern is often continued until 25 challenging 1-minute work intervals and 25 recoveries have been completed, followed by a brief cool-down plus stretching and drills. Occasionally, elite Kenyans will use a 2:1 pattern, with two minutes at a faster pace and one minute at a slower pace. In this case there are 15 to 16 two-minute work intervals per session instead of 25.

The pace for the one-minute work intervals can vary dramatically between sessions depending on desired goals and prior training. Sometimes, a 10K-like pace is emphasized, but on other occasions considerably higher speeds may be used. For recovery fartlek sessions, which may be held after a couple of days of hard training, the pace may even be as slow as half-marathon tempo. Pace also varies *within* workouts: In fartlek fashion, individual members of the group may suddenly and unexpectedly surge ahead during a work interval and then be closely followed by the other runners. The 1-minute work and recovery intervals are usually monitored by a coach or helper on a motorcycle or in an accompanying car—with the sound of the horn blowing every 60 seconds calling for the change from fast to slow, or vice-versa.

Variable-Pace Speed Training

Variable-pace (VP) speed training involves the use of *two* important quality speeds within a training session's work intervals, not the usual one speed per interval, with no break or recovery between the different tempos. VP workouts can take many forms. A marathon runner, for example, might use 800-meter work intervals, with the first 400 at 5K pace and the second 400—launched with no recovery from the 5K running—at marathon tempo. A goal of this kind of VP session would be to enhance the ability to run at marathon intensity after within-race surges and in spite of mounting fatigue.

A 5K runner can set up a VP workout to include 800s: the first 400 at 3K pace and the second 400 at 5K tempo with no break between 400s. This not only spikes the overall intensity of the workout but also augments a runner's capacity to sustain 5K velocity and hit short blasts of high-speed running within 5K races.

Longer VP intervals can be very productive. For example, a 10K runner might employ 1,600-meter (1 mi) work intervals, with the first 400 to 600 meters (.25-.37 mi) at 5K pace and the subsequent 1,000 to 1,200 meters (.63-.75 mi) at 10K intensity. A marathon runner could productively use 2,400-meter (1.5 mi) VP intervals, with the first 800 at 10K race pace and the following 1,600 meters at marathon tempo.

Recovery periods between the VP work intervals are usually kept relatively short—never greater than the duration of the VP interval—as part of the overall effort to heighten fatigue resistance. For example, if a 10K runner set up a VP workout with 800-meter intervals, with the first 400 of the 800 at 5K pace (assume 80 seconds) and the second 400 of the 800 at 10K tempo (assume 84 seconds), the recovery running between the VP work intervals would never last longer than 80 + 84 = 164 seconds (2:44).

VP speed training tends to be intense: Up to half of each work interval may be at faster than race speed. Thus, VP training promotes strong fatigue resistance at race pace and improves $\dot{V}O_2max$, $v\dot{V}O_2max$, lactate-threshold velocity, and running economy.

$v\dot{V}O_2max$ Speed Training

$v\dot{V}O_2max$ work is specifically designed to produce significant improvements in $v\dot{V}O_2max$, a key predictor of running performance. It also has a strong impact on lactate-threshold velocity and running economy. See chapter 26 for a complete discussion of $v\dot{V}O_2max$ training.

Incorporating Speed Work Into a Training Program

Science does not provide applicable studies regarding the arrangement of speed workouts over time. Horwill suggests simply moving through the list, starting with the 10K-pace session, proceeding on to the 5K-pace session on the next quality-training day, then on to 3K-pace work, and so on.[1] Once the five different speed-workout types are completed, the runner then goes back to the beginning session and repeats the sequence once more. This is the five-tiered system of training developed by Horwill and used by such great athletes as Sebastian Coe, Säid Aouita, and Noah Ngeny.

A problem with Horwill's system is that it leaves out other valuable forms of speed training, including fartlek sessions, VP efforts, and v$\dot{V}O_2$max training. However, Horwill's training system can be inserted into an overall program at any appropriate point; it is not necessary to relentlessly follow the 10K through 800-meter scheme. A key goal in any training program is variation. With variation as a guiding factor, a great balance for a 10K-paced session with 2K work intervals would be intervals at 800-meter race pace, traditional fartlek running, Kenyan fartlek training, or v$\dot{V}O_2$max work on a subsequent quality training day.

Naturally, the specifics of each workout type would change as running capacity improves. For example, achieving a personal record in the 5K would produce upswings in tempo for all other speed sessions since all of the velocities are related. One would not have to wait for a 10K personal record to adjust 10K-tempo training; the 10K workout pace would be adjusted based on the 5K personal record to 4 seconds per 400 slower, even if that is faster than current 10K time. Using the principle of variation is quite logical and attractive. For example, conducting workouts at 800-meter pace, either in an 800-meter workout or a fartlek session, fosters faster running and heightened physiological adaptations per minute of quality training; completing sessions at 10K speed focuses on a slower pace but nonetheless enhances the runner's ability to *sustain* quality running, not to mention the capacity to compete well in 10Ks. The in-between sessions (i.e., paced for 1,500-meters, 3K, and 5K) provide valuable benefits that are intermediate between these two ends of the spectrum with less speed but longer durations of work intervals as the runner moves up the scale.

Conclusion

Speed training is an essential component of a runner's overall training program. Speed work produces advances in $\dot{V}O_2$max, v$\dot{V}O_2$max, running economy, lactate-threshold velocity, and fatigue resistance. It provides an excellent platform from which a runner can progress to large gains in maximal running velocity. When carrying out speed training, variation is extremely important; a runner should not carry out speed sessions at one velocity, week after week. Rather, an array of intensities, covering the range of velocities from 800-meter to 10-K race pace, will produce the greatest advancements in fitness and performance.

CHAPTER **17**

Cross-Training

Anecdotal evidence and logic suggest that cross-training is not beneficial for endurance runners. The movements involved in cross-training are seldom specific to the kinematics of running and thus should have little impact on the production of propulsive force during gait. Nonetheless, cross-training remains a popular practice among endurance runners. Should runners engage in regular cross training, or do they gain the most by focusing solely on running?

Scientific research suggests that certain forms of cross-training *can* be highly beneficial to runners. Strength training, cycling, and playing soccer appear to be particularly advantageous, with aqua running and stair climbing also offering some benefits. Other forms of cardio workouts can also benefit runners. This chapter examines all these ways to cross-train.

Intense cross-training sessions produce extremely high rates of oxygen consumption and high lactate levels in the blood, physiological responses that can ultimately lead to improvements in maximal aerobic capacity ($\dot{V}O_2$max) and lactate-threshold velocity. Cross-training may decrease the risk of running-related injury by strengthening the leg muscles and core and by diverting a runner away from a relentless diet of daily leg pounding on the roads.

Cross-training could also improve leanness by expanding the number of calories burned during exercise per week and heightening average workout intensity because fitting a demanding bicycle workout into an already-full running program is easier than adding another tough running session. A running session produces more muscle damage and thus creates a greater need for recovery. Furthermore, the strengthening that results from running-specific resistance work with movements that mimic the mechanics of running should enhance running economy and promote resistance to fatigue.

Cycling

Several studies support the use of cycling as a cross-training activity for runners. In an investigation carried out at California State University at Northridge, 16 lean, fairly fit runners were divided into two equal groups. For 9 weeks, 8 of the runners engaged only in running workouts, while a second group of 8 worked out only on exercise cycles.[1] Each group trained four times per week for 40 to 45 minutes per session, and exercise intensities were equivalent between groups. Two days a week, the athletes simply trained continuously at between 80 and 85 percent of maximal heart rate. On the other two days, the exercisers conducted interval training, with heart rates rising to 90 to 95 percent of maximum during 1- to 2-minute work intervals.

During a typical interval session, six 2-minute and four 1-minute intervals were completed, with 1-minute recoveries after each work interval. The rest of the interval workout consisted of steady exercise at 80 to 85 percent of maximal heart rate, with the entire session lasting for at least 40 minutes.

Before and after the 9 weeks of training, all athletes were measured for both $\dot{V}O_2max$ and ventilatory threshold (VT), both while running and while cycling. VT is very similar to lactate threshold, the exercise intensity above which lactate begins to accumulate in the blood. Scientific studies have confirmed that VT can be a reasonably strong predictor of endurance performance.

The runners who engaged in just the cycling training improved markers of running fitness rather dramatically. Even though these individuals had not run a single step during the 9-week period, they increased their running $\dot{V}O_2max$ by 15 percent and running VT by 13 percent; in addition, they increased their cycling $\dot{V}O_2max$ by 15 percent and cycling VT by 31 percent. The athletes also increased their running $\dot{V}O_2max$ from 55 to 63 ml • kg^{-1} • min^{-1} and their cycling $\dot{V}O_2max$ from 50.5 to 58 ml • kg^{-1} • min^{-1}. For an athlete who both runs and cycles, running $\dot{V}O_2max$ is often higher than cycling $\dot{V}O_2max$, presumably because in running the oxygen-using muscles are required not only to push the body forward but also to support body weight, while in cycling the bike holds the athlete upright; the additional work required for running pushes oxygen-consumption rate upward.

Surprisingly, the runners who carried out only running training did not improve running fitness *to a greater extent* than the bike-using trainees. These runners increased running $\dot{V}O_2max$ by 18 percent and running VT by 17 percent, about the same gains achieved by the cyclists.

This investigation indicates that cycling can promote large gains in aerobic fitness in fairly experienced runners. Even when cycling training is carried out by itself, without complementary running training, it can produce major gains in running aerobic capacity over a 9-week period. However, this would probably not be the case in highly trained elite runners who have already come close to maximizing their running aerobic capacity. This does not mean that elite runners should avoid high-quality biking, however; for such athletes, powerful bike sessions might produce other advantages, including upgraded leg strength and superior blood lactate removal.

Implications for Triathletes' Training

Triathletes may be particularly interested in the study reviewed in the previous section since the results revealed that 9 weeks of running training boosted cycling $\dot{V}O_2max$ by only 9 percent and failed to lift cycling VT at all. Since 9 weeks of cycling increased cycling $\dot{V}O_2$max and VT and running $\dot{V}O_2$max and VT to a considerably greater degree, it seems evident that the cycling workouts in a triathlete's program may have a broader impact on overall fitness than running sessions. If cycling and running capacity have been equally advanced by prior training, a triathlete might reasonably select cycling over running on an open training day when the greatest overall advance in fitness is desired.

Gaining Fitness With Less Risk of Injury

In a separate study carried out at the University of Toledo, 10 well-trained runners who were averaging 30 to 35 miles (48-61 km) of running per week added three weekly bicycle workouts to their existing schedules over a 6-week training period.[2] The supplemental cycling sessions were quite simple: On Mondays, the runners carried out five 5-minute work intervals on exercise cycles with heart rates at 95 to 100 percent of maximum during the intervals, which were always followed by 5-minute recoveries. On Wednesdays, the runners pedaled continuously for 50 minutes, with heart rates at around 80 percent of maximum. Each Friday, the runners added three 150-second cycling intervals and six 75-second cycling intervals at close to maximal intensity with rest intervals equal in duration to the work intervals.

The added cycling training did not have any adverse effects on the runners' endocrine, immune, or muscular systems; there was little sign of overtraining. Most important, the supplemental cycling produced physiological and performance bonuses. After six weeks, perceived effort during highly intense running was lower: The runners felt that difficult running speeds were easier to sustain. In addition, the runners' 5K times improved by almost 30 seconds, from 18:16 to 17:48. This study suggests that the addition of cycling training to a running program can produce gains in fitness and competitive performance.

The gains achieved by the runners who added cycling to their training were the same as those attained by another group of runners who added a trio of running workouts to their weekly schedules. In other words, from the standpoints of physiological and competitive improvements, adding extra running to the programs of experienced runners was not more effective than adding cycling sessions. Over the long run, the addition of cycling might be more effective than extra running since the cycling would be less likely to produce damage from eccentric strains or from impact with the ground in the tendons and muscles of the legs during training; thus, postworkout recovery would be quicker.[3]

An inescapable conclusion from the Toledo research is that many runners would probably be able to improve their performances and decrease perceived effort during intense running by adding cycling workouts to their training programs. Cycling seems to allow runners to add more high-quality work to their schedules without heightening the risk of leg-muscle strain. Many runners who ordinarily can handle just two quality workouts per week can step up to three high-intensity weekly efforts, provided the third exertion is on the bike rather than on the feet. There is also evidence that runners can complete supplemental bike sessions at higher intensities (i.e., higher percentages of $\dot{V}O_2$max) compared with supplemental running workouts.[3]

Runners including cross-training for the first time in their overall programs can do well by adding one cycling workout per week to their existing schedules. The number of weekly cycling sessions can gradually increase to two, one hot and one cool. The hot cycling session can incorporate high-intensity intervals ranging in duration from 30 seconds to 5 minutes, along with hill climbing and even difficult tempo rides lasting for an hour or so. Cool cycling would consist of 45 to 60 minutes of easy pedaling; this permits more recovery on a day following a hard running workout compared with running for the same amount of time.

Improving 10K Times With a Stand-Up Routine

It's no joke; there is also evidence that cycling training can improve 10K running performance. In a study carried out with year-round runners between the ages of 18 and 65 who had been competing for at least 3 years, nine individuals (five males and four females) supplemented their running workouts with interval training on exercise bikes.[4] The key investigator in this study, Tom Miller, had been influenced by statements made by Olympic gold medalist Frank Shorter and six-time Ironman champion Dave Scott that standing up on bicycles while pedaling intensely uphill had positively influenced their running performances, and thus Miller required his bike-interval trainees to conduct their bike intervals standing on the pedals as they rode. Work-interval cadence was set at 75 to 90 revolutions per minute, and pedal resistance was heavy, so that the overall effort was comparable with running up a steep hill at maximal possible speed.

Toe clips were removed from the bikes to ensure that the runners' main muscular work was an active pushing down on the pedals. The interval sessions, conducted once a week over a 6-week period, always began or ended with 10 minutes of warm-up or cool-down.

All bike workouts used a pyramid work-interval scheme with this sequence of work intervals: two at 30 seconds each, two at 45 seconds, two at 60 seconds, two at 45 seconds, and two at 30 seconds. Each 30-second work interval was followed by 15 seconds of spinning (i.e., pedaling at 90 rpm against light resistance), while 45- and 60-second intervals were followed by 30 seconds of spinning. The spin segments were designed to simulate downhill running after an intense uphill climb. Sixty seconds of recovery while pedaling at only 60 rpm against comfortable resistance followed each work-spin combination. Overall, spin pedal resistance was about one-half of work-interval resistance, and recovery resistance was approximately one-third as great.

Each biking interval workout proceeded as follows: 10 minutes of warm-up, a 30-second work interval, 15 seconds of spinning, 60 seconds of recovery, another 30-second work interval, 15 seconds of spinning, a 60-second recovery, a 45-second work interval, 30 seconds of spinning, 60 seconds of recovery, and so on. Pedal resistance was increased whenever the athletes found it fairly easy to complete their work intervals and was lessened if pedaling rate dropped below 75 rpm during work efforts. The runners were always encouraged to replicate their running motion as much as possible during work intervals. Spins and recoveries were completed while seated.

After 6 weeks of the supplemental biking interval training, six of the nine subjects achieved personal best 10K times, and average 10K time for the group improved significantly by 8.6 percent from 47:09 to 43:07. All the athletes reported that after the bike training, they felt stronger while running on hills and also during the closing mile of the 10K than they had at the beginning of the research.

Preserving Running Fitness During Off Times

Science suggests that cycling can preserve running fitness during a complete furlough from running, which might occur following a running injury, even when all of the cycling training is moderate in intensity.[5] In a study carried out at the University of Waterloo in Ontario with 12 female runners, one group of 6 runners continued their usual running training program, running about 30 minutes per day, 4 days per week, at an intensity of 80 to 85 percent of maximal heart rate (i.e., a level of effort corresponding with about 70-76 percent of $\dot{V}O_2$max). A second group of 6 runners did not run at all during the 4-week period but instead used exercise bicycles to train with a similar frequency and intensity: 4 days per week, 70 to 76 percent of $\dot{V}O_2$max. Individuals in the two groups were identical in training background, height, weight, and percent of body fat.

Running capability was assessed by asking the participants to warm up and then run as long as possible on a treadmill at an intensity of 90 percent of $\dot{V}O_2$max, or about 95 percent of maximal heart rate. Prior to the 4-week study, the runners who participated only in cycling during the research could run for an average of 16 minutes during this key test. After the 4 weeks of cycling with no running, these individuals could still run for 16 minutes at 90 percent of $\dot{V}O_2$max, indicating that there was no drop-off in performance. Running $\dot{V}O_2$max was also maintained during the 4 weeks of cycling, resting steady at about 50 ml • kg^{-1} • min^{-1}. $\dot{V}O_2$max can ordinarily decline by as much as 7 percent in as little as 3 weeks when little relevant training is performed. It is clear that biking constitutes appropriate training from the standpoint of preserving running fitness.

Stair Climbing

Science indicates that the use of a stair-climbing machine can also have a beneficial impact on running $\dot{V}O_2$max and performance.[6] In another study carried out at California State University at Northridge, 11 active college women carried out solely stair-climbing workouts for 9 weeks using an automated stair machine that is quite similar to a downward moving escalator, while 12 other women participated solely in running workouts on an outdoor track. Each group worked at the same intensity—70 to 80 percent of maximal heart rate—for 30 minutes per workout, 4 days per week, over the first 2 weeks of the study. During weeks 3 through 9, all athletes trained at 85 to 90 percent of maximal heart rate, 4 days per week, for about 40 minutes per workout. Before and after the 9-week training period, all the women ran a 1.5 mile (2.4 km) race and had their aerobic capacities measured.

At the end of the 9-week period, it was virtually impossible to distinguish the stair-machine users from the runners during running, even though the stair-machine users had carried out no pure running training at all. Race times improved by 1 minute for the stair-machine users and by 1.4 minutes for the runners, but the difference was not statistically significant. $\dot{V}O_2$max—measured while running—rocketed upward by 12 percent for the stair climbers and by 16 percent for the runners, a difference that was not significant. Each group improved by a similar amount during submaximal running. Prior to the 9 weeks of training, the chosen submaximal tempo had forced the women's heart rates to reach 90 percent of maximum; following the stair climbing and running training, heart rate for both groups had settled at a calmer 84 percent of maximum at the chosen pace.

Although running performances were similar between the groups, the stair climbers did enjoy an advantage over the runners: *They didn't get injured.* Two runners had to drop out of the research due to serious injuries, and two other runners missed valuable training time because they were hurt. Due to its low-impact characteristics, stair climbing appears to carry a significantly lower risk of overuse injury compared with running.

After 9 weeks, when running at a very moderate intensity of 66 to 72 percent of $\dot{V}O_2$max, the running group relied less on carbohydrates and more on fat to fuel their efforts; the stair-climbing group relied more heavily on carbohydrates. The mechanism underlying this finding may be that the muscular power required to lift one's body against gravity during stair climbing may increase the recruitment of fast-twitch muscle fibers, which are notoriously weak at fat burning. It will be interesting to see whether stair climbing has positive effects on hill-running ability and sprint speed (to date, no research has been conducted in these areas).

This study suggests that stair climbing has a positive effect on running performance and running aerobic capacity. Note, however, that the women in the study were relatively untrained at the beginning of the research; the positive effects associated with stair climbing might have been the result of training rather than the outcome of a unique transfer of fitness from stair climbing to running. It should be noted also that unlike the situation with cycling, no research has examined whether the *addition* of stair-climbing workouts to an experienced runner's training regime can heighten running performance.

Nonetheless, it is quite likely that stair climbing can be beneficial for runners: When climbing stairs, the work output per step is significantly greater compared with flat-ground walking, an effect that should strengthen the muscles. Also, stair climbing without holding onto the bars of the stair machine should advance coordination and stability during gait. Finally, there is little doubt that high rates of oxygen consumption and lactate production can be attained during stair-machine exertion, effects that could easily spur gains in $\dot{V}O_2$max and lactate-threshold velocity.

Aqua Running

Although its popularity appears to be decreasing in recent years, aqua running has been an attractive cross-training activity to runners for a number of reasons:

- Mimics running form. Normal running form can be almost completely replicated during aqua-running movements even though there is no impact with the ground and no stance phase of gait, so there is a reasonable hope that running-specific neuromuscular patterns will be preserved and running-specific strength will be maintained, perhaps to a greater extent than would be the case with cycling.

- Aids in recovery. Unlike regular running, aqua running features has no impact with the ground. Thus, recovery from intense or prolonged aqua-running sessions is probably quicker than from running on firm surfaces because there is less strain on muscles and connective tissues.

- Promotes flexibility. Compared with normal ground running, greater range of motion is often attained in the water, perhaps promoting flexibility and dynamic mobility, two areas of weakness for many runners.

- Offers high-intensity exercise. High levels of exercise intensity are possible during aqua running; high heart rates, rates of oxygen consumption, and lactate levels can be achieved readily along with possible corresponding gains in $\dot{V}O_2$max and lactate-threshold velocity.

Scientific research has generally supported the idea that aqua running can have a positive impact on running fitness and performance. In a study carried out at Brigham Young University in Provo, Utah, 32 runners who

Lucenet Patrice/Phototeque Oredia/age fotostock

▶ Aqua running can be a valuable way to maintain fitness when an injury makes running on firm ground impractical or painful.

could complete a 1.5-mile (2.4 km) run in less than 10:45 (i.e., at faster than 7:10 pace) were divided into three groups with equal levels of fitness: (1) 10 trained exclusively by running in deep water while wearing life jackets; (2) 11 trained only on exercise bicycles; and (3) the remaining 11 continued their usual running training. All 32 athletes trained five times a week, 30 minutes per day, at an intensity of approximately 80 percent of maximal heart rate.[7]

After 6 weeks of such training, $\dot{V}O_2$max (measured while running on a treadmill) remained equivalent between the three groups, even though the cyclists and aqua runners had not carried out a single running workout. Somewhat surprisingly, all three groups improved 2-mile (3.2 km) race times by 1 percent perhaps because the subjects were training a little more than they usually did. This study suggests that aqua running can preserve aerobic capacity and upgrade performance in medium-level runners even when it is carried out to the exclusion of firm-ground running workouts. However, the training load used in this study—five 30-minute workouts per week—might have been greater than the load preceding the study, and thus the upgrade in 2-mile (3.2 k) race performance could have been the result of an increase in the amount of training rather than a specific aqua running effect. Even if that were the case, the gain in competitive fitness was as large for aqua running as it was for regular running.

In research carried out at the University of Toledo in Toledo, Ohio, that explored the effects of aqua running on 5K performance, 11 well-trained competitive runners (10 males and 1 female) trained exclusively in deep water for a period of 4 weeks, averaging five to six workouts each week. These athletes preserved their average treadmill 5K performance time of about 19 minutes flat, $\dot{V}O_2$max, and running economy, even though they completed no treadmill or regular running at all during the 4-week study.[8]

Maximal heart rate during deep-water running is about 8 to 10 percent lower than it would be during firm-ground running.[9] Otherwise, the physiology of aqua running is similar to that of dry-ground running. A study carried out at the University of Montana tracked eight college-age male cross-country runners as they ran on the treadmill and in deep water at heart rates corresponding to 60 and 80 percent of the heart rate associated with $\dot{V}O_2$max; oxygen consumption, ventilation, and energy expenditure were comparable in the two situations. A key physiological difference was that the athletes burned more carbohydrate and used less fat for energy when they exercised in the water.[10] This is certainly not a negative factor since well-trained runners who compete at distances ranging from 800 meters to the marathon use carbohydrates as their primarily fuel.

Another disparity is that training at a specific fraction of $\dot{V}O_2$max tends to feel about 20 percent harder during aqua running than in regular, dry-land running.[10] This is one reason why some exercise scientists recommend working more intensely in the pool than would be done on firm ground. Higher intensity may be required to increase the oxygen-consumption rate; if a runner trains in the pool with his or her usual perceived effort, oxygen consumption may be considerably lower compared with the same perceived effort while running on land.

A potential bonus associated with running in the pool is that it might have a unique effect on lactate threshold. In one investigation, lactate levels in well-trained runners reached a modest 2 millimoles per liter during dry-land running but increased to 6 to 8 millimoles per liter at the same intensity in the water.[10] This effect should stimulate leg muscles to improve lactate clearance, an effect that would heighten lactate-threshold velocity.

Soccer

Participation in soccer practices and competitions may be quite advantageous for runners. During a typical soccer game, athletes cover from 9,000 to 11,000 meters (5.6-6.2 mi), a total that normally includes about 4,000 meters (2.5 mi) of jogging, 2,000 meters (1.4 mi) of running at high but not maximal speed, 800 to 1,000 meters (.5-.6 mi) of maximal-speed running, 2,500 meters (1.6 mi) of walking, and 600 meters (.4 mi) of running or walking backward.[11] Soccer players' heart rates are above 150 beats per minute for most of a game, and blood lactate levels often rise as high as 6 to 10 millimoles per liter

(108-180 mg/dL), comparable to the concentrations observed during 5K and 10K running competitions.

For runners, participating in a soccer competition is like conducting a prolonged, intense interval workout. The changes in direction required for soccer play may also be beneficial for leg strength, muscle balance, agility, coordination, and injury prevention. It is hardly surprising that many elite Kenyan runners began their athletic careers on the soccer pitch; Paul Tergat (five-time world cross-country champion and former world-record holder for 10,000 meters, half marathon, and marathon) is a notable example of this phenomenon.

Strength Training

Explosive and running-specific strength training are especially productive forms of cross-training for runners. As explained fully in chapters 14 and 28, both types of strength training can enhance running economy, a key predictor of performance. In addition, explosive strength training heightens maximal running speed, another great performance predictor, and has been tightly linked with improvements in performance times. Furthermore, running-specific strength training promotes resistance to fatigue and decreases the risk of injury, leading to greater training consistency. Running-specific strength training also enhances running economy and can improve lactate-threshold velocity, fatigue resistance, maximal running speed, and $v\dot{V}O_2max$. As a result, running-specific training forms part of the backbone for periodized running programs, along with explosive training

Treadmill Workouts

Many runners rely on treadmill training to complete their required workouts and sometimes wonder whether treadmill running is close enough to running on firm ground to produce comparable benefits. The biomechanical differences between treadmill and land running have not been examined in a controlled scientific setting, so science provides little guidance on this issue. No one knows whether a steady regimen of treadmill running might impair running form and running economy when running on firm ground.

Runners can be reassured, however, by the fact that treadmill running can produce the same high rates of oxygen consumption and blood lactate levels observed during ground running. Thus, high-quality treadmill training can undoubtedly have positive impacts on maximal aerobic capacity, lactate-threshold velocity, and fatigue resistance.

When conducting treadmill workouts, runners should keep one factor in mind: The lack of air resistance, and perhaps subtle biomechanical alterations, associated with treadmill running make treadmill efforts less costly from an oxygen-consumption standpoint than training on firm ground. At a specific velocity of 10 miles (16 km) per hour, for example, a runner will ordinarily use less oxygen per minute and thus operate at a lower fraction of $\dot{V}O_2max$

on a treadmill than when running on the ground, street, or track. This means that higher speeds can generally be attained and maintained during treadmill training at a similar percentage of $\dot{V}O_2$max. This is a good thing from a neuromuscular standpoint because it teaches the neuromuscular system to operate at a slightly higher level. It also means that a treadmill adjustment must be made if an athlete wants to train at the same intensity on the treadmill as would be achieved over regular ground. Specifically, tweaking the treadmill to a 1 percent incline will match intensities for a given speed between treadmill and ground. Running on a treadmill at 10 miles (16 km) per hour with a 1 percent incline produces about the same oxygen cost and percent of $\dot{V}O_2$max as running at the same speed on perfectly flat ground.

Other Cardio Workouts

Although scientific research is scant, it is likely that sustained, intense exercise using various forms of cardio equipment can be beneficial for runners. Specifically, training on an elliptical machine, swimming, rowing, and sculling can provide challenges for a runner's general strength and fatigue resistance and also heighten oxygen-consumption rates and blood lactate levels. These physiological challenges should produce adaptations and thus higher levels of fitness for runners without the higher risk of injury associated with carrying out similar-intensity sessions while running. While the effects might be small, even a 1 percent improvement in resistance to fatigue or lactate-threshold velocity could be important for a competitive runner.

A similar argument can be made for cardio sports such as cross-country skiing and even sports played with flying disks. In fact, any activity that involves rapid movement, sudden changes of direction, abrupt stopping, and high levels of coordination should produce higher oxygen-consumption rates and blood lactate levels and demand a great degree of general strength and neuromuscular control, all factors that are beneficial for runners.

Conclusion

Running-specific strength training, including explosive strength training, and cycling are the two most productive forms of cross-training for runners. Cycling training transfers gains in fitness directly to running and can be used to boost fatigue resistance, lactate-threshold velocity, and $\dot{V}O_2$max. Running-specific strength training and cycling are also tools runners can use to increase their average weekly training intensity with small risk of overuse injury. This is extremely important since intensity, rather than amount or frequency of training, is the most potent producer of fitness. Furthermore, stair climbing, aqua running, treadmill workouts, soccer participation, and other cardio workouts can preserve fitness during periods when running volume is reduced.

CHAPTER 18

Altitude Training

A ltitude training consists of conducting workouts at an elevation of approximately 1,527 meters (5,000 ft) or greater. Many coaches and runners believe that altitude training is highly beneficial, and elite athletes often structure their overall training programs to include periods of high-altitude work. Many coaches believe that altitude training provides a natural blood-doping effect, heightening red blood cell concentrations and thus upgrading aerobic capacity. Another popular belief is that altitude training increases lactate-threshold velocity and improves muscle buffering capacity, or the ability to compensate for increases in acidity, thus heightening resistance to fatigue; one theory of fatigue is that it is caused by acidic conditions in muscles. Many elite runners believe that altitude training expands respiratory system capacity so that more oxygenated air can be brought into the lungs during intense running.

The fact that the majority of elite Kenyan and Ethiopian runners carry out their training at altitude when they are in their home countries provides anecdotal support for the practice. Reflecting the popularity of altitude training, high-altitude training centers have appeared in such places as Kaptagat and Iten, Kenya; Flagstaff, Arizona; Colorado Springs, Colorado; and Mammoth Lakes, California.

Perceived Benefits of Altitude Training

For the past 40 years, exercise scientists have been curious about the effects of living or training at high altitude on endurance performance. Their research has explored the ways in which altitude shapes cardiovascular function, red blood cell production, lactate dynamics, and respiratory function in the endurance athlete.

Connection Between EPO, Red Blood Cells, and $\dot{V}O_2max$

It is certainly true that altitude training can have an impact on the aerobic system. Unless an endurance runner owns a personal helicopter, training at altitude also generally means that he or she is living at altitude, and altitude residency naturally boosts a runner's blood concentration of erythropoietin

▶ Altitude training boosts hemoglobin concentrations and thus $\dot{V}O_2$max. The problem with altitude training is that it reduces training speeds and thus has a negative impact on neuromuscular development and the attainment of an improved maximal velocity.

(EPO), a powerful hormone synthesized in the kidneys that stimulates bone marrow to increase red blood cell production (see chapter 2). As red blood cell density increases, the blood is naturally able to carry more oxygen per unit volume. This means that the heart sends out more oxygen per beat, and that additional oxygen is delivered to the muscles in any unit of time, changes that tend to augment the aerobic system and thus $\dot{V}O_2$max. A runner who manages to increase his/her $\dot{V}O_2$max is often able to achieve higher levels of performance. This relationship between EPO, red blood cells, and $\dot{V}O_2$max is often used as a justification for altitude training.

Although this model of altitude training and its benefits is widely accepted, it has very shaky scientific support. For one thing, $\dot{V}O_2$max is *not* a good predictor of performance among similarly trained endurance runners. Altitude training thus appears to involve the pursuit of a variable that does not have a large impact on competitive ability. In addition, if the altitude model is valid, one would expect elite, altitude-trained Kenyan runners to have heightened hemoglobin levels compared with elite athletes who trained at sea level (hemoglobin is the oxygen-carrying molecule found inside red blood cells). Scientific research carried out at the University of Bayreuth in Germany reveals that hemoglobin mass in elite, altitude-trained Kenyans is actually no different from the hemoglobin of elite German runners trained at sea level.[1] In the Bayreuth study, relative $\dot{V}O_2$max was also the same in the two groups. Importantly, the Kenyans ran the 10K in about 28:29 compared with 30:39 for the Germans. Clearly, something other than altitude-enhanced red blood cells (i.e., oxygen-transport capacity of the blood) and $\dot{V}O_2$max was behind the difference in performance!

Lactate-Threshold Blood Concentrations

Undeterred, proponents of altitude training point out that there is another physiological bonus associated with altitude training: When running at altitude at any velocity, blood lactate levels are higher compared with running at the same velocity at sea level. Since heightened blood lactate concentrations during workouts have been linked with greater increases in lactate-threshold velocity, a decent predictor of performance, it has been assumed that training at altitude would enhance lactate-threshold velocity. Scientific support for this hypothesis is scant, however. In fact, it is much more difficult to sustain speeds greater than sea-level lactate-threshold velocity at altitude, and thus total time spent above lactate-threshold velocity during training can actually decrease at altitude.

Running Economy

Some research has suggested that training or living at altitude might enhance running economy, another predictor of endurance performance. In research carried out at the Australian Institute of Sport that looked at the impact of altitude *residency* on economy, nine elite athletes spent about 400 hours at a simulated altitude of 2,860 meters (9,367 ft) but carried out all their training at sea level. A control group of runners did not spend any time at simulated altitude; they trained and lived at sea level. After about 7 weeks, including sleeping at simulated altitude for 46 nights, the athletes at simulated altitude had upgraded running economy by about 3 percent; the control subjects had failed to improve at all.[2]

In a related study conducted at the University of Tokyo, runners who slept at a simulated altitude of 3,000 meters (9,843 ft) for 29 nights enhanced economy by approximately 5 percent, while runners who trained at the same simulated altitude but slept at sea level did not upgrade running economy at all.[3] It appears that altitude or simulated-altitude residency but not training improves running economy in runners who have previously lived at sea level. The mechanism underlying this effect is unknown.

Nonhematological Effects

It is likely that altitude residency or training has other nonhematological effects that could have an impact on endurance performance. For example, it is believed that altitude residency can increase capillary growth around muscle cells (angiogenesis), improve intramuscular pH regulation, and upgrade respiratory system capacity. All of these outcomes might improve endurance-running performance, but research in these areas needs to be more fully developed.

Intermittent Hypoxic Training

The belief in the benefits of altitude training has led some exercise scientists to hypothesize that intermittent hypoxic training (IHT)—carrying out intense training at simulated altitude while living at sea level—is desirable. In IHT workouts, runners usually conduct high-speed intervals while wearing masks attached to devices that supply reduced-oxygen air. Research has failed to find a consistently positive effect of IHT on sea-level running performance, although IHT is probably beneficial for altitude exercise capacity.[3, 4] In other words, IHT might prepare an athlete living at sea level for the rigors of altitude training but has little impact on running ability at sea level.

Intermittent Hypoxic Exposure

Altitude's attractiveness has also led to the hypothesis that intermittent hypoxic exposure (IHE) while at rest—breathing in hypoxic air for 5 to 6 minutes at a time alternated with breathing normal room air for 4- to 5-minute intervals during sessions lasting a total of 60 to 90 minutes—can produce gains in athletic performance. In other words, an endurance runner might be able to sit around at home and magically breathe in fitness. Although hypoxic equipment suppliers widely tout IHE as a potent performance enhancer, there is no scientific evidence that it actually produces significant physiological changes or upswings in performances at sea level.[5]

Slower Training Paces at Altitude

It is often forgotten that living or training at altitude, despite its potentially positive impacts on $\dot{V}O_2$max and nonhematological performance factors, almost inevitably leads to *slower* training compared with training at sea level. Take the case of an 18:36 5K runner, for example, who normally conducts his or her 800-meter interval training sessions at sea level in 3:00 each, right at 5K tempo. 5K speed ordinarily corresponds with an intensity of about 95 percent of $\dot{V}O_2$max.

Now, put this runner in Kaptagat, Kenya, at an altitude of 2,438 meters (8,000 ft) to attempt the same workout. At this altitude, $\dot{V}O_2$max will be reduced by about 8 percent or so compared with running at sea level. The runner's 5K speed will remain linked with 95 percent of $\dot{V}O_2$max, but now $\dot{V}O_2$max has decreased by 8 percent, so 5K speed will drop by a similar amount. Although the runner will certainly try his or her best, the 800-meter intervals at Kaptagat will automatically slow from 3:00 per 800 meters to approximately 3:15 or so.

So what? Remember that a key development in endurance running is the discovery that an endurance runner is more than just a heart and a set of leg muscles: The runner has a nervous system, too. That is very important. If a runner's neuromuscular system learns to handle and coordinate 3:15 per

800-meter tempo but fails to develop the capacity to function well at 3:00 per 800, that runner cannot optimize his or her ability to run an 18:36 5K. It will be easier to progress from 18:36 to even faster 5Ks if one is training at 3:00 per 800-meter tempo at sea level rather than a 3:15 pacing at altitude.

Altitude Training Lacks Scientific Support

Exercise scientists have been hard pressed to demonstrate the specific benefits associated with altitude training. In fact, one of the earliest investigations of the practice revealed that altitude training could be quite detrimental to performance. In this research, well-trained collegiate runners completed 9 weeks of altitude training and residency at an elevation of about 4,000 meters (~ 13,000 ft) and returned to sea level in a *detrained* state.[6] During postaltitude time trials at sea level at distances of 880 yards (805 m), 1 mile, and 2 miles, the athletes ran 3 to 8 percent slower compared with their performances before altitude training. Follow-up studies at more moderate elevations have usually struggled to link altitude training with specific performance advantages.[7]

The esteem with which altitude training is nonetheless regarded depends entirely on an outdated model of the determinants of endurance-running success. In this obsolete schema, running performance hinges primarily on the functioning of the heart and leg muscles, with the nervous system just along for the ride. The heart is supposed to be a big oxygen pump, and the muscles are understood to be acceptors of massive amounts of the oxygen sent their way by the mass of cardiac tissue. When this so-called aerobic system is optimized, endurance running potential is also maximized.[8] Unfortunately this ignores the important role played by the nervous system.

In a study carried out in France,[9] nine international swimmers who ordinarily trained at sea level conducted 13 days of training at an elevation of 1,850 meters (~ 6,000 ft). This relatively short period of altitude training had no effect at all on $\dot{V}O_2$max or 2,000-meter (6,562 ft) swimming performance.

In another study, elite distance runners trained for 4 weeks at a high-altitude training camp (1,500-2,000 m, or 4,921-6,562 ft); a group of runners of similar ability trained at sea level.[10] When the altitude-trained athletes returned to sea level, they exhibited no improvements at all in lactate-threshold speed and running economy; in fact, high-speed performance *declined* by 2 percent. This downturn in high-velocity running capacity is exactly what one would predict because training at altitude slows down speed. At altitude, the nervous system spends less time controlling speeds of sea-level $v\dot{V}O_2$max because it is more difficult to attain and sustain such velocities at altitude; therefore, high-speed running capability can be harmed.

Summing up, it is fair to say that scientific research does not support the idea that carrying out a period of training at altitude will improve endurance performance at sea level.[11]

Live High, Train Low

Over the past 10 years, a scientific consensus has gradually developed that suggests it is optimal for endurance athletes to *live* at altitude but *train* at sea level. Living at higher altitudes is supposed to improve blood characteristics (e.g., higher red blood cell concentration and therefore augmented $\dot{V}O_2$max) and nonhematological factors, while sea-level training is believed to upgrade overall training quality (e.g., attaining higher speeds during workouts, sustaining those speeds for longer periods).

This combination of living at altitude and training at sea level appears to be a potent producer of fitness, and research supports this strategy of living high and training low. In studies carried out by James Stray-Gundersen and B.D. Levine of the Cooper Clinic in Dallas, Texas, runners who live for about 4 weeks at an altitude of approximately 2,500 meters (8,203 ft) and carry out their intense training sessions at close to sea level are able to upgrade $\dot{V}O_2$max by around 5 percent and improve their running performances in events lasting from 7 to 20 minutes by an average of about 1.5 percent.[12]

By following this approach, some runners actually augment their performances by up to 6 percent after 4 weeks of live high, train low, while others do not improve at all, accounting for the overall 1.5 percent average gain. Although it might seem odd that some athletes do not respond to higher-altitude living, research has revealed that there is considerable variation among people in altitude responsiveness and adaptation; the sources of this variation are poorly understood.[12] The improvements—when present—ordinarily last for about 3 weeks after returning to sea level. For a runner with a normal standard of 18:36 for the 5K, a 1.5 percent improvement would trim approximately 17 seconds from his or her finishing time.

Like Stray-Gundersen and Levine, other researchers have shown that improvements in performance after a regime of living high and training low can be extremely variable, with some runners improving greatly and others showing no improvement.[13] Factors unrelated to altitude including unfamiliar living situations, changes in daily schedule, disturbances in sleep patterns, and motivation issues may play significant roles that tend to override the specific impact of living at altitude.

For marathon running capability, logical thinking suggests that altitude training would probably not be useful. The proposed, most positive effect of altitude training is the enhancement of aerobic capacity, an outcome that should improve performance in high-speed endurance events in which runners top out or reach $\dot{V}O_2$max. In such events, oxygen usage is limiting performance because $\dot{V}O_2$max is a maximum; no further oxygen is available to spur faster running. Therefore, it would be better to have a higher $\dot{V}O_2$max. Elite marathoners run the event at just 85 to 88 percent of $\dot{V}O_2$max, however, indicating that oxygen supply to the muscles is not a limiting factor in the event and thus $\dot{V}O_2$max expansion is not critical.

Simulated Altitude

While living at 2,000 to 2,500 meters (6,562-8,203 ft) and training simultaneously at sea level will enhance performance for most runners, from a practical standpoint it is out of reach for most endurance athletes, elite and nonelite. As a result, considerable interest has developed in sleeping high: sleeping in an enclosure, usually a tent-like structure, within which the air has oxygen pressure similar to what prevails at altitude. This approach can be costly. A sturdy hypoxic tent with low-oxygen generator can sell for about US$5,000. Paula Radcliffe, who holds the world marathon record, is said to employ such a system, and the World Anti-Doping Agency (WADA) has considered artificially induced hypoxic conditions to be so performance productive that it has considered outlawing them and placing so-called hypoxic tents and similar structures on its list of prohibited substances and methods.

Scientific research supports the idea that sleeping or living at simulated altitude can enhance endurance performance.[14] The minimal amount of simulated altitude sleeping or living for increasing red blood cell production may be 11 to 12 hours per day, and the amount of total time required at simulated altitude to induce performance benefits may be 320 to 400 hours.[14] There is a suggestion in the scientific literature that simulated altitudes of 2,200 to 2,500 meters (6,562-8,203 ft) may be best for upgrading hematological factors, while about 3,000 meters (9,843 ft) may be optimal for producing nonhematological changes (e.g., alterations in running economy, muscle buffering capacity, and ventilatory function).

Despite the lack of scientific support for the usefulness of altitude *training*, many elite runners and their coaches continue to spend significant periods of time each year engaged in the practice. This is particularly true for elite marathon runners and their coaches who seem to believe that altitude training is essential for optimal marathon preparation. This strong attraction toward altitude training is the natural consequence of a belief in the outdated paradigm that running success depends entirely on the heart, muscles, and aerobic capacity.

Conclusion

When an endurance runner embarks on a period of high-altitude training, $\dot{V}O_2max$ may improve as a result of living at higher altitudes, but the effect on performance will be uncertain. A key problem is that altitude training harms average training speed. Altitude residency is good for running capacity, and a strategy of living high and training low can improve performance. Exposure to simulated altitude can also upgrade endurance capacity.

Training Variables and Systems in Running

CHAPTER 19

Frequency and Volume

Volume and frequency are two basic training variables fundamental to all programs. "How much should I run?" (volume) and "How often should I run?" (frequency) are two questions runners face every week of training. Volume is simply the number of miles or kilometers completed in a specified period (usually a week), and frequency refers to the number of running workouts conducted per week. As runners explore different permutations of volume and frequency, they are constantly attempting to find the sweet area of training between too much and too little; many runners try to push their bodies and expand their limits by advancing volume and frequency without pushing so hard that injury occurs. Decisions about volume and frequency are often made without much scientific backing, even though science has much to say about the issues.

Training Frequency

Scientific studies suggest that training frequency—the number of workouts conducted per week—can have a positive impact on $\dot{V}O_2$max and performance. Research indicates that the improvement in $\dot{V}O_2$max that occurs during a training program is directly proportional to the frequency of training.[1] In one study in which male subjects ran for 30 to 45 minutes per workout over a 20-week period, upgrades in $\dot{V}O_2$max were significantly greater for individuals who trained four times per week than for runners who worked out just two or three times weekly.[2]

For beginning runners, frequency usually has a profound impact on aerobic-capacity improvement. Research indicates that a training frequency of five to six times per week can increase $\dot{V}O_2$max by up to 43 percent for initially unfit runners with a low $\dot{V}O_2$max. With a frequency of two to four times per week, $\dot{V}O_2$max increases average just 20 to 25 percent.[3] It usually takes 6 to 9 weeks for such changes in $\dot{V}O_2$max to appear.

Noncontrolled cross-sectional studies also support the idea that training frequency is related to performance. In an analysis carried out with 50 male runners whose marathon times ranged from 2:19 to 4:58, the total number of workout days during the 9 weeks prior to the race was inversely related to marathon performance: the higher the number of workouts, the lower, or faster, the marathon finishing time.[4] In this study, a workout was defined as any kind of run: fast, medium paced, or slow. In a separate survey of 35 female runners whose average marathon time was 3:47, the total number of workouts completed over a 12-week period was negatively correlated with marathon performance: again, the greater the number of workouts, the faster the overall time for the race.[5] A Swiss study conducted with 4,000 joggers showed that a higher training frequency was linked with better performance times in a 16K (~10 mi) race, the Berne Grand Prix.[6] Individuals who trained five to six times per week completed the 16K significantly more quickly compared with runners who completed three workouts weekly.

However, it is necessary to use care when interpreting such analyses. Good runners tend to train more frequently than slower runners and also tend to achieve superior performance times. Thus, it is sometimes the quality of the runner and not training frequency that is the fundamental underlying basis for the connection between frequency and both performance and $\dot{V}O_2$max.

Training Volume

An additional problem is that training frequency is confounded with another important variable: training volume, the number of miles or kilometers run per week or the number of minutes of running training completed each week. Increases in training frequency tend to be linked with upswings in volume unless workouts are shortened as frequency rises, and thus it is possible that volume—not frequency—of running training is the primary cause of increases in $\dot{V}O_2$max and performance improvements. Research into the true effects of frequency on fitness would have to hold volume constant while varying frequency. This research could answer questions such as these: Are six 5-mile (8 km) workouts per week actually better than three 10-mile (16 km) sessions for $\dot{V}O_2$max improvement or competitive success? Do advances in frequency hold some fitness magic of their own?

Fortunately, several studies have been completed in which volume was held constant while training frequency varied. In one study, 18 middle-aged men ran for 30 minutes per day over an 8-week period, while 18 other male subjects completed three 10-minute periods of running each day with at least 4 hours separating the 10-minute workouts. Running intensity was the same in the groups (65 to 75 percent of maximal heart rate), and thus training volume was equivalent. After 8 weeks, overall endurance and the decrease in heart rate associated with submaximal running were the same in the two groups of runners, but $\dot{V}O_2$max increased to a significantly greater extent in those who ran for 30 minutes per workout.[7] This implies that training frequency may actually be inversely related to the gain in aerobic capacity when volume is held constant; in addition, there might be something important about longer-duration workouts for achieving gains in $\dot{V}O_2$max, at least when running intensity is moderate. The mechanism underlying this relationship between workout volume and $\dot{V}O_2$max is uncertain although it is known that longer workouts deplete leg-muscle glycogen to a greater extent than do shorter sessions; glycogen depletion in muscles stimulates the production of aerobic enzymes and structures that can lead to an increase of $\dot{V}O_2$max.

In a similar study carried out with middle-aged women, 12 subjects took three 10-minute walks per day, five times per week, over a 10-week period, while 12 other females completed one 30-minute walking workout 5 days each week during the same period.[8] The intensity of the walking was 70 to 80 percent of maximal heart rate in both groups, and thus training volume was equal. Both training plans produced gains in $\dot{V}O_2$max and enhancements of blood lactate profiles, but there were no significant differences between the groups. This research seems to refute the previous study that showed that one longer workout was better than three shorter ones, but it does support the idea that training responses are relatively independent of training frequency as long as intensity and volume are held constant.

The Swiss study mentioned earlier, in which higher training frequency was linked with superior 16K (10 mi) performance time, actually supports the idea that training frequency is not a major player in fitness improvement *when training volume is similar.*[6] In a subanalysis, 414 of the Swiss joggers who used the same training volume (20-25 km or 12-16 mi per week) were further divided into groups that had trained either two, three, or four times per week to achieve this volume. Although training frequency and thus workout duration were dramatically different in these three groups, finishing time in the 16K did not vary significantly between the runners.

In some research, training *volume* has been found to have a fairly strong effect on performance-related physiological variables and competitive race times. In general, runners who increase their training volume from a low level of about 5 to 10 miles (8-16 km) per week to 35 to 40 miles (56-64 km) per week can expect upgrades in $\dot{V}O_2$max of about 15 to 20 percent or more.[9] Studies carried out with marathon runners have revealed that the total volume of training during the year preceding a marathon and also during the two months prior to the race are significantly correlated with marathon finishing time.[10] Another study conducted with 18 male Swedish marathoners found that marathon running performance was directly related to lactate-threshold speed and the ability to run at a velocity close to that speed during the race. In turn, these two variables were significantly related to training volume.[11]

Ability

Research does not always show that more volume means higher performance. When S.Y.J. Grant and colleagues at the University of Glasgow in Scotland analyzed the training and performance of 88 male and female runners who competed in the Glasgow Marathon, they found there was only a limited relationship between weekly training volume and marathon finishing time.[12] In this study, the best predictor of marathon running pace was the average speed used during competitors' 6- to 10-mile (10-16 km) training runs. Grant and colleagues concluded that the intensity of marathon training was the key factor that determined marathon success.

The applicability of such studies, including the ones that link higher volume with better performance and those that find little connection between volume and finishing time, is weakened, however, by the consideration mentioned previously: Excellent runners tend to adopt greater training volumes and also perform at a higher level in races than average competitors. It may be the quality of the runner and not the volume of training that truly underlies the contrasting connections between volume and performance.

Some better-controlled studies that monitored runners as they increased their mileage suggest that volume can be important. In one such study, experienced marathon runners who boosted their training volume by about 20 percent, from 76 to 91 kilometers (47-56 mi) per week, managed to improve marathon time significantly from 3:20:42 to 3:10:48.[13]

However, a study carried out at the University of Northern Iowa with first-time marathoners found that a significant uptick in mileage had no effect on marathon performance.[14] High-mileage runners in the study increased their weekly training volume from 23 to nearly 50 miles (37-81 km) over the course of an 18-week training period, while low-mileage marathoners increased their volume from 18 to almost 40 weekly miles (29-64 km) during the same period. Despite the 25 percent volume advantage, high-mileage marathoners did not finish the race faster than their lower-mileage counterparts. Average finishing time was 4:17 for both higher- and lower-mileage males and 4:51 for the corresponding two groups of females. Surprisingly, improvements in $\dot{V}O_2$max, running economy, lactate-threshold speed, and body composition were also equivalent between the groups, defying the notion that increases in mileage are especially important for fitness enhancement in relatively inexperienced runners who start from low-mileage bases. It is likely that changes in volume have a strong impact on performance at low mileage levels and a much weaker influence as volume increases. For many runners, 40 miles (64 km) per week may represent a volume cutoff point beyond which improvements are difficult to measure.

Knowing When Enough Is Enough

There is an upper limit of weekly training distance beyond which increases in volume do not enhance $\dot{V}O_2$max or performance. The Swiss research on 16K (10 mi) runners suggested that performance time does not improve as training mileage expands above about 80 to 100 kilometers (50-62 mi) per week.[6] In a study carried out at Ball State University, Dave Costill monitored two runners who gradually increased weekly mileage after a layoff period.[15] In these two individuals, $\dot{V}O_2$max continued to increase until a weekly volume of 75 miles (121 km) was attained. Above that level, there were no further improvements in aerobic capacity, even when volume soared to 225 miles (362 km) per week! The upper volume limit of 50 to 75 miles (81-121 km) per week probably applies to other variables. For example, a survey conducted by Swedish researchers Bertil Sjodin and Jan Svedenhag found that improvements in the fractional usage of $\dot{V}O_2$max at marathon pace were capped at a specific number of kilometers completed per week.[16]

Research carried out with swimmers strongly supports the idea that the benefits of training volume are kept to a relatively modest volume level. In another of Costill's studies, swimmers who trained for 1.5 hours per day performed just as well as swimming competitors who worked out for 3 hours daily.[17] The athletes who trained for 3 hours per day did not do as well during various tests of swimming fitness as those who trained for 1.5-hours a day.

No scientific study has ever linked advances in running-training volume beyond 91 kilometers (57 mi) per week with increases in running performance or performance-related physiological variables, yet elite and serious runners routinely climb the so-called volume ladder beyond this mileage point instead of focusing on tweaking the intensity of their training and developing an outstanding running-specific strength program. Intensity of training can often be the most potent producer of running fitness, trumping both volume and frequency. The importance of training intensity is discussed in chapter 20.

Conclusion

Runners often ask, "How many times should I train per week?" hoping there is a magic number of weekly workouts that will have the greatest impact on fitness. Science reveals that there is no optimal number of weekly workouts and that volume usually has a stronger impact on running fitness than does frequency. Volume has its limits, however: The gain in fitness decreases as volume expands, approaching zero as training volume rises beyond about 40 miles (64 km) per week for many runners, and perhaps beyond 50 to 70 miles (81-113 km) per week for more experienced and highly competitive athletes.

20

Intensity

The training of endurance runners characteristically emphasizes the completion of long-duration, low- to moderate-intensity efforts, especially during the base or preparation phase of training, but research reveals that such running has a rather weak effect on performance-related variables and running performance compared with higher-intensity exertions.

Intensity can be defined as a percent of maximal heart rate or an actual running speed, but it is usually defined as a percentage of $\dot{V}O_2$max. When an athlete is said to be running at an intensity of 90 percent of $\dot{V}O_2$max, it simply means that the runner's speed is producing an oxygen consumption rate that is 90 percent of maximum.

Studying the Effects of Intensity

One of the first published scientific investigations examining the effects of intensity on fitness asked three groups of subjects to train three times a week at intensities of either 65, 75, or 85 percent of maximal heart rate.[1] All three groups expended the same number of calories per session, which meant that the lower-intensity groups had to exercise longer per workout. Workout duration was 14.5 minutes for the 85 percent group, 22.5 minutes for the 75 percent group, and 35 minutes for the 65 percent group. Over a 10-week training period, the 85 and 75 percent groups raised $\dot{V}O_2$max by about 20 percent, while the 65 percent group failed to improve $\dot{V}O_2$max at all! This study was one of the first to reveal that intensity is a considerably stronger force than workout duration (i.e., total time spent training) from the standpoint of improving fitness. Note that the 75 percent group trained 50 percent longer than the 85 percent group and yet failed to gain a fitness advantage over the 85 percent group. The 65 percent group trained more than twice as long and didn't improve $\dot{V}O_2$max at all.

In a subsequent study, university students trained five times per week for 2 weeks at a heart rate of either 140 or 172 beats per minute.[2] At the end of two weeks, $\dot{V}O_2$max increased by 16 percent for the high-intensity group but failed to move upward at all for the lower-intensity group.

Since then, many studies have revealed that training at relatively higher intensities produces superior physiological adaptations compared with training at lower levels of effort. In one study, 40 runners were randomly assigned to one of four training groups:

1. Long, slow distance training at 70 percent of $\dot{V}O_2$max
2. Lactate-threshold training at 85 percent of maximum heart rate (probably corresponding to about 76 percent of $\dot{V}O_2$max)
3. High-intensity 15/15 interval running (i.e., 15 seconds of running at 90 to 95 percent of maximal heart rate alternating with 15 seconds of recovery at 70 percent of maximal heart rate)
4. High-quality 4 × 4 interval training (i.e., four work intervals, each consisting of 4 minutes of running at 90 to 95 percent of maximal heart rate with 3 minutes of recovery at 70 percent of maximal heart rate after each work interval)

All four plans resulted in similar total oxygen consumption during training so that total work performed would be roughly equivalent between groups; the workouts were conducted three times a week for 8 weeks.[3] At the end of the 8-week period, $\dot{V}O_2$max had increased by 5.5 percent in the 15/15 group and by 7.2 percent in the 4 × 4 group but had failed to improve at all in the long, slow distance group and the lactate-threshold group. Stroke volume, or the amount of blood pumped by the heart per beat, increased by approximately 10 percent in both interval groups (i.e., 15/15 and 4 × 4) after 8 weeks but failed to budge in the slow-distance and lactate-threshold groups. This study is one of many that reveal that higher training intensities produce greater training responses compared with lower intensities of effort.

Greater Intensity Equals Greater Improvement

In research conducted by three-time Olympic gold medal winner Peter Snell and his colleagues at the University of Texas Southwestern Human Performance Center, well-trained runners with average $\dot{V}O_2$max values of 61.7 ml • kg^{-1} • min^{-1} participated in a 16-week study that initially involved running 50 miles (81 km) a week for 6 weeks.[4] For the next 10 weeks, half of the runners substituted tempo training twice a week for their usual daily runs; these tempo sessions involved 29 minutes of continuous running at intensities of about 70 to 80 percent of $\dot{V}O_2$max. The other half substituted two interval sessions per week for their usual workouts. Each interval session involved about 3 miles (5 km) of work intervals, with the intensity of each interval at 90 to 100 percent of $\dot{V}O_2$max, or about 10K to 3K race pace.

After the 16 weeks, the runners who followed the interval plan improved their 800-meter times by 11.2 seconds and their 10K times by a full 2.1

minutes. In contrast, the group that used tempo training boosted 800-meter performances by just 6.6 seconds and 10K efforts by 1.1 minute. $\dot{V}O_2$max increased by 12 percent for the higher-intensity interval group but by only 4 percent for the group using tempo training. Overall, the higher-intensity interval training produced greater improvements in performance and aerobic capacity than did a greater volume of lower-intensity work.

Since intense training is such a potent producer of running fitness, it follows that the careful and progressive replacement of moderate-intensity running with higher-speed effort in an overall training program should produce upswings in fitness and performance. In one study, experienced 5K runners replaced about 32 percent of their usual moderate-intensity aerobic running with explosive efforts involving high-speed sprints, bounds, and hopping drills; they subsequently upgraded their 5K performance by about 3 percent.[5] In the process, these 5K runners also enhanced running economy, a key indicator of endurance-running capability.

In a separate investigation, experienced, competitive 10K runners added 3 days a week of high-intensity interval training at 90 to 95 percent of $\dot{V}O_2$max, or 10K to 5K race pace, to their programs. As a result, they upgraded 10K performances, bolstered endurance during high-speed running, and decreased plasma lactate concentrations at intensities of 85 and 90 percent of $\dot{V}O_2$max, which indicates an underlying improvement in lactate-threshold speed.[6]

In a study that examined the merits of high-volume versus high-intensity training, a group of experienced runners replaced 82 kilometers (51 mi)

Anthony Stanley /Action Plus/Icon SMI

▶ Upgrading training intensity is the most potent producer of higher fitness.

per week of moderate-intensity running with high-intensity running and cycling.[7] Running volume was reduced to about 30 weekly miles (48 km) of hard effort, and three tough cycling sessions were inserted into the program each week. The cycling workouts were 5 × 5: five 5-minute work intervals at an intensity that produced $\dot{V}O_2$max with 5-minute recoveries. Despite the significant decrease in running volume, the emphasis on intense running and cycling training led to significantly faster 10K race times: Average 10K clocking improved by 81 seconds.

Searching for the Training Threshold

Many runners believe that there is an exercise intensity that must be exceeded during a workout in order for the session to produce physiological adaptations. The theoretical training intensity above which adaptation occurs and below which no response in fitness is observed has sometimes been called the *training threshold*. Identification of this threshold is of more than esoteric interest since many runners would like to know whether there is a danger of dipping too low on the intensity scale during their relatively easy workouts.

Unfortunately, scientific research has had a difficult time locating a training threshold with any degree of precision or unanimity. Various studies have suggested that the threshold might occur at about 50 percent of $\dot{V}O_2$max;[8] 75 percent of maximal heart rate, which would correspond with approximately 62 percent of $\dot{V}O_2$max;[1] slightly above 60 percent of the difference between maximal heart rate and resting heart rate;[9] or simply at a heart rate of about 140 to 150 beats per minute.[2, 10] This range of results is substantial enough to call the training threshold concept into question. In addition, a heart rate of 140 to 150 would correspond with the highest-possible level of exertion for a runner with a maximal heart rate of 145 or so and yet would represent easy effort for a runner with a maximal heart rate of 220.

Casting more than a little suspicion on the threshold concept, one study found that adaptation to training occurred at the extremely light intensity of 36 percent of $\dot{V}O_2$max, or about 55 percent of maximal heart rate.[11] Other studies have noted that adaptation can occur when training intensity is maintained at just 45 percent of $\dot{V}O_2$max.[12, 13] Adaptation has also been documented when exercise intensity is set at a relatively low heart rate of 110 to 120 beats per minute.[14] It would seem that just moving around—jogging at a very slow pace—would produce physiological change in relatively untrained runners.

Nonetheless, it appears that a threshold exists for some runners, particularly those with a significant training background. In one study, moderately trained individuals who ordinarily trained 45 minutes per day, three times a week, embarked on a program involving exercise durations as great as 5.5 hours per day (!) carried out six times per week over an 8-week period.[15] The average exercise intensity was an extremely moderate 45 percent of $\dot{V}O_2$max, or about 63 percent of maximal heart rate. Since no training effect (i.e., adaptation) was observed at all after the 8 weeks, it can be assumed that these athletes were below some sort of training threshold—or else that they were not recovering enough for the adaptations to become apparent.

Such studies have an inherent weakness in the sense that all of the training was conducted at a specific intensity, after which the involved athletes were checked for adaptation. In the real world, runners train at a variety of intensities over the course of a week or month. A more-interesting question would focus on whether lighter days of training really provide enough stimulus for adaptation to complement the higher-quality work conducted during the same period. For example, if a runner is covering 40 miles (64 km) total per week during training, with 10 quality miles (16 km) above lactate-threshold speed, is it necessary for the other 30 miles (48 km) to be completed above a certain intensity in order for increased fitness to accrue? No study has provided an answer to this basic question.

The solution to the training threshold paradox may also be that the actual training response depends to a large extent on the underlying fitness of the individual. Specifically, very fit runners require a high intensity of training to move performance capacity upward, while less fit individuals may benefit from running that is much more moderate in intensity.[16, 17] Beginning runners can benefit a lot from running at an intensity of 70 percent of $\dot{V}O_2$max, for example, but it is unlikely that such an intensity would produce major physiological movements in an experienced runner. Unfortunately, many elite runners fail to take this training truism into account and adjust their training to include higher and higher volumes of moderate-intensity work instead of shifting toward gradually increasing amounts of *high-intensity* effort.

Determining the Ideal Intensity

Runners have a wide range of intensities from which to choose for their high-quality workouts. Can a specific intensity be identified as the most potent producer of running fitness? Is there one training intensity that produces the greatest combined improvements in the key predictors of endurance-running performance—$v\dot{V}O_2$max, running economy, lactate-threshold speed, and maximal running velocity—as well as in performance itself?

These are tough questions to answer. One could survey the published scientific work in this area and attempt to draw conclusions, but it would be very difficult to compare different research investigations. Studies use runners with different backgrounds and ability levels and subject the runners involved to training regimens that vary in frequency, workout duration, volume, and intensity. Nonetheless, a consensus is gradually emerging that the most productive intensities may be in the range of 95 to 100 percent of $\dot{V}O_2$max.[18]

This suggests that $v\dot{V}O_2$max, the minimal running speed that elicits $\dot{V}O_2$max, may be an extremely beneficial training intensity. In research carried out by French physiologist Veronique Billat, 8 experienced runners with high aerobic capacities of 71.2 ml • kg^{-1} • min^{-1} carried out one v$\dot{V}O_2$max workout each week over a 4-week period in addition to their usual training. The actual v$\dot{V}O_2$max session was 5 × 1,000 meters (.6 mi) at v$\dot{V}O_2$max, with 3-minute jog recoveries. After just the 4 weeks, v$\dot{V}O_2$max improved by 3 percent, running economy was enhanced by an extremely impressive 6 percent, and lactate-threshold speed rose by 4 percent![19] In addition, one of the greatest gains in maximal aerobic capacity ever documented in a study carried out with experienced, competitive runners resulted from using v$\dot{V}O_2$max as the key training intensity.[20]

Such findings do bring coaches and runners back to the threshold questions: If quality training is conducted at 95 to 100 percent of $\dot{V}O_2$max or at 90 to 100 percent of $\dot{V}O_2$max, which would be from a 10K pace up to v$\dot{V}O_2$max, what is the minimal intensity for *complementary*, easy workouts? How fast must one run on light days to nudge key performance variables in the right direction?

The answer is that on easy days, a runner is simply playing the volume game, using miles or kilometers rather than intensity to advance fitness. Thus, it probably does not matter how fast the runner is moving—just covering the miles will produce the desired positive effect, with most of the gains in running capacity coming from the quality efforts on other days of training. Note, though, that the volume game can be overplayed. If a runner is already covering 50 to 70 miles (81-113 km) per week or more, additional easy miles are unlikely to have any effect on fitness at all.

Conclusion

Runners, running coaches, and especially proponents of high-volume training models often suggest that a relatively high volume of moderate-intensity training can produce an adaptive response similar to the one associated with a lower volume of high-intensity work. In relatively inexperienced and untrained runners, this can sometimes be true.[21] However, it is unlikely to be the case in experienced and elite runners, who *require* a steady diet of high intensities to make the indicators of physiological variables move upward.[4, 5, 7, 16, 17]

A reasonable idea is to keep track of intense volume (i.e., number of miles or kilometers run at 10K pace or faster) as a percentage of the total volume, or the number of miles or kilometers completed per week. If this percentage is consistently below about 25 percent, a runner should certainly begin replacing less intense miles with more intense exertions until the 25 percent figure is attained. After 25 percent is reached successfully, without injury or overtraining, the relative amount of intense training can cautiously and progressively be increased over a training year.

CHAPTER 21

Recovery

Recovery involves the restoration of neuromuscular, cardiovascular, and endocrine function following a training session. Recovery also includes *adaptation*, a process by which various physiological systems transform themselves and improve their ability to function during exercise. For runners, the recovery period spans the time between running workouts; it includes immediate recovery (i.e., what a runner does during the critical hour after a running session ends) and between-session recovery (i.e., what a runner does between running workouts, including nonrunning activities carried out on off days).

When endurance runners do not recover properly during training, their overall fitness is not optimized and competitive performances are subpar. Reaching an optimal state of fitness is always the result of high-quality training combined with outstanding recovery from that training. Beneficial, long-term adaptations to strenuous exercise only occur during recovery periods, not during exertion itself, and some recovery strategies increase adaptation while others slow down or even retard positive physiological changes. Furthermore, inadequate recovery can increase the risk of injury.[1]

Cool-Downs

Historically, runners and coaches have believed that a postworkout cool-down (i.e., jogging easily for 1 or 2 miles), is an important element in *immediate* recovery from training. According to conventional thinking, cooling down properly after a heated effort clears lactate from the blood most effectively, smoothes out the decline in body temperature associated with the cessation of training, and mellows nervous system activity so that it will be possible to rest more completely during the remainder of the day and sleep more soundly at night. Some exercise researchers have also suggested that cool-downs can enhance immune system functioning, leaving runners less vulnerable to respiratory system infections during periods of tough training.

It is certainly correct that a cool-down produces a more gradual decline in body temperature after a strenuous exertion than does resting.[2] However, no research has ever demonstrated that more temperate reductions in body heat optimize recovery processes or lead to better performances. Similarly, the link between cool-downs and stronger immune system activity is quite tenuous. There *is* an indication in the scientific literature that good cool-downs can lead to improved sleep.[3] (See the section on sleep later in this chapter for more information.)

The key question, however, is whether cool-downs can actually modulate recovery in a way that is performance enhancing. To find out, Thomas Reilly and M. Rigby took a look at various postexercise strategies used by two groups of university athletes.[4] One group conducted an active cool-down after a soccer match and then used the same strategy during training over the course of the week leading up to a second match. No cool-down was conducted after this second match or during the following week. The second group, which had not used cool-downs after the first match or during the week following, cooled down after the second match and then used cool-downs as a recovery technique during a second week of practice.

The cool-down contained three phases:

1. Five minutes of easy jogging
2. Five minutes of stretching
3. Two minutes of lying in a prone position while the legs were shaken down by another player. Shaking down a leg involves gripping it by the ankle and moving it quickly in a variety of directions while the athlete relaxes and provides little resistance to movement; the goal is to reduce tightness and improve the leg's dynamic flexibility.

During the weeks without active cool-downs, the players simply rested in seated positions for 12 minutes after the match or following workouts.

Immediately after competitions, performance during vertical and standing long jump tests was down for both groups compared with pregame results, presumably because of the muscle stress and lingering fatigue associated with the matches. However, the drops in jumping ability were smaller in the group that had cooled down. Athletes who didn't cool down after a game were still unable to jump normally 48 hours afterward, while players who had cooled down returned to normal functioning during that time.

Similarly, the deterioration in 30-meter (98 ft) sprint performance following a match was almost 50 percent greater for the group that had no cool-down compared with the group that used cool-downs. Forty-eight hours after the game, performance during a sprint-fatigue test, which included seven 30-meter (98 ft) sprints with 20 seconds of jog recovery in between, was fine for the athletes who had cooled-down but still subpar for the individuals who had only rested. *Muscle soreness* had almost completely disappeared in those who had cooled down within 48 hours after the match, but muscle pain increased on successive days following competition for those who had just rested after the match.

Unfortunately, the exact mechanisms involved in producing the superior recoveries for those who had cooled down are unknown. In this study, three different cool-down techniques (jogging, stretching, and shaking) were used, and the specific role played by each of these recovery strategies is unclear.

Myths About Cool-Downs and Lactic Acid

A traditional view is that cool-downs are beneficial because they remove lactic acid from the blood and muscles at a more rapid rate than does rest. This supposition is based in part on research carried out by lactate researcher Arend Bonen and his colleague Angelo Belcastro who monitored blood lactate levels in well-conditioned runners after fast, 1-mile runs.[5] When the athletes cooled down by jogging continuously, blood lactate concentrations returned to nearly normal levels within 20 minutes. In contrast, intermittent exercise, consisting of light calisthenics and jogging, or complete rest had much more modest impacts on lactate levels over a 20-minute postexercise period. Full rest cleared just half of the excess lactic acid in the blood in 20 minutes; intermittent exercise fared only slightly better.

Similar results were obtained in a separate study in which athletes either jogged lightly or rested after an intense workout.[6] Athletes who rested after a strenuous workout needed 25 minutes to clear half of the above-normal lactic acid from their bloodstreams, while the easy joggers need just 11 minutes to eliminate a similar quantity of lactic acid.

Such data inspired some exercise experts to recommend rather prolonged, active cool-downs. For example, physiologist Edward L. Fox concluded that intense workouts should be followed by *a minimum* of 30 minutes of what he called "exercise recovery" (e. g., slow, continuous jogging).[7] Fox believed that active, 30-minute recoveries could remove at least 80 percent of the excess lactic acid appearing in the blood in response to challenging running.

Such recovery recommendations hinge on a very shaky proposition: that elevated postworkout blood lactic acid is a bad thing and thus that its rapid removal is beneficial. The truth is that unusually high blood levels of lactic acid are not deleterious in any way (refer to chapter 10 for more on the role of lactic acid during running). Lactate is a great fuel for skeletal and cardiac muscles, and thus an increased blood lactate concentration can be viewed as a good thing—an indication that fuel will be distributed widely throughout the body, to the heart, muscles, and liver, for example. Postexercise blood lactate is increased simply because the net release of lactate by the muscles during exercise has been greater than the net uptake of lactate by the sinews. This is a natural consequence of exercise conducted at an intense level (i.e., above the lactate-threshold velocity). It is not a sign that muscles are in a perilous physiological position or that lactic acid will suddenly begin attacking muscles and preventing good recovery.

Thus, it is not logical to suggest that cool-downs are good because they reduce blood levels of lactic acid. In the two studies mentioned earlier, active cool-downs drove lactate downward because the cool-downs were carried out at an intensity below lactate threshold, leading to a situation in which lactate uptake by the muscles was greater than lactate output. In effect, the muscles were using the blood lactate as a source of energy to sustain jogging as the centerpiece of the cool-down. There is nothing about this process that would optimize recovery.

Cool-Downs and Potential Harm to Recovery

Exercise physiologist Dave Costill of Ball State University argued that in many cases active cool-downs can hurt the recovery process and decrease performance potential in subsequent workouts or competitions.[8] Costill's hard-to-refute reasoning is as follows:

1. Runners cannot complete high-quality workouts in the best possible way unless their leg-muscle glycogen concentrations are ample.

2. Many runners have trouble keeping their leg-muscle glycogen depots full on a day-to-day basis during periods of challenging training.

3. A thorough, active cool-down following a quality or prolonged workout will significantly expand total glycogen breakdown in the leg muscles, making it more difficult to return glycogen to top levels for subsequent training sessions.

4. In contrast, *inactivity* (i.e., rest) following a strenuous workout accentuates glycogen storage and thus increases the likelihood that future training sessions will proceed in an optimal way.

In fact, Costill and his Swedish research colleague Bengt Saltin discovered that up to 75 percent of the glycogen burned during a difficult workout could be restored fairly quickly to leg muscles when runners rested rather than jogged after such a workout.[9] Since adequate levels of muscle glycogen are required for high-quality training and top running performances, Costill concluded that extended cool-downs should be avoided during repeated days of demanding training, meaning either intense or prolonged work.

How is it possible to square such findings with Reilly's research showing that cool-downs seem to boost recovery? Reilly's cool-downs involved just 5 minutes of active effort, not enough time to put a significant dent in muscle glycogen stores. Costill's concern was that the more extended cool-downs, such as Fox's 30-minute sessions, could deplete large stores of carbohydrate. The take-home message for runners and coaches is that Reilly's 5-minute cool-downs are optimal during periods of strenuous training; they produce beneficial effects with little risk of glycogen depletion. In addition, it is quite likely that an expansion of the stretching phase of Reilly's cool-downs would be advantageous. Stretching prepares muscles for the postworkout state without using up precious glycogen fuel; in fact, some research has suggested that stretching boosts intramuscular glycogen synthesis.

Cool-Downs and Cardiac Arrhythmia

Some runners are concerned that the lack of an appropriate cool-down can increase the likelihood of a potentially dangerous condition called *cardiac arrhythmia*. However, research has shown that from a health standpoint it is perfectly acceptable to exercise lightly after an intense workout—or lie on one's back! The real problem can occur if a runner elects to simply stand around after training ends. During strenuous exercise, blood concentrations of the key hormone noradrenaline can increase significantly. Noradrenaline is an important regulator of blood pressure; it tends to increase pressure by stimulating the heart. Noradrenaline levels can peak dramatically once intense exercise ends as a way of preventing blood pressure from falling rapidly. Unfortunately, high levels of noradrenaline have been linked with an increased risk of irregular heartbeats. Standing still after a tough workout is a bad idea because it decreases blood pressure (i.e., the leg muscles stop pushing blood upward toward the heart). More noradrenaline is released to raise blood pressure, and thus the chances of arrhythmia increase.

In contrast, jogging, walking, or lying on one's back during cool-down helps maintain blood pressure: Jogging and walking keep the heart rate up naturally and allow the leg-muscle pumps to do their job, while lying down makes it easier for blood to slip back to the heart since it doesn't have to travel uphill. As a result, less noradrenaline is released following intense work, and the risk of arrhythmia is reduced.[10]

Thus, brief cool-downs do not seem to increase the chances of heart problems as long as runners avoid standing around in one position following intense exercise. The available evidence suggests that abbreviated cool-downs, with 5 minutes of jogging, 5 minutes *or more* of stretching, and perhaps even 2 minutes of leg shake-downs, are beneficial for recovery.

Deep-Water Running

A nonimmediate, between-session recovery technique that has been linked with improved restoration of muscular function after intense training is deep-water running. The logical support for deep-water running as a recovery strategy is as follows: Many runners recover from demanding workouts by jogging easily on their rest days. However, this jogging, as easy as it may be, places an additional burden on already stressed muscles because sinews must still deal with the impact forces associated with jogging. Muscle membranes and filaments, already frayed from a prior, intense workout, may undergo further fraying or may be blocked from repairing damage even though the chosen running pace is quite easy.

In contrast, there are no impact forces during deep-water running (unless the unlucky deep-water runner smacks into a pool wall during an exuberant water-sprint). The normal eccentric strains associated with running are quite mild since water resists and thus controls leg movements, preventing muscles from being stretched out explosively as they are trying to shorten. Perhaps this protection from strain allows muscles to devote more of their energies to adapting positively instead of repairing additional traumas incurred by land-based training.

In one study carried out with 30 individuals, deep-water running was better at reducing muscle soreness and restoring muscle strength following plyometric exercise than were a variety of other recovery-enhancing strategies.[11] The plyometric workout used to induce muscle soreness and dysfunction involved a series of drop-jumps from a platform 50 centimeters (20 in) high, performed once every 7 seconds until exhausted. Five different 3-day recovery strategies were used following the plyometric sessions:

- Three days of complete rest
- Complete rest on day 1 followed by 2 days of deep-water running
- Complete rest on day 1 followed by 2 days of treadmill running
- Treadmill running on all 3 days
- Deep-water running on all 3 days

For the treadmill and deep-water recovery exercise periods, intensity was set at about 75 percent of maximum heart rate. As it turned out, the most effective way to recover exercise capacity occurred when *deep-water running was undertaken on all 3 days following the plyometric workout.* Deep-water running for 3 days was more effective than pure rest and also better than 1 day of rest and 2 days of deep-water running.

Deep-water running did not prevent the delayed-onset muscle soreness that is almost certain to occur after an exhaustive plyometric session, especially when little plyometric training has been previously conducted. However, 3 days of deep-water running did lead to a quicker disappearance of overall soreness, and it produced a faster restoration of muscle strength compared with the other four strategies. Creatine kinase is a muscle cell enzyme, the appearance of which in the blood often signals muscle damage; concentrations of this enzyme peaked earlier—and at a lower value—when deep-water running was carried out for 3 days compared with the other four strategies.

The subjects in this study reported that muscle soreness disappeared completely while they were actually running in deep water. Some soreness returned after they climbed out of the pool, but these results suggest that on the days following a very rugged workout, it might be possible to sustain higher-quality exercise while running in deep water than by running more stiffly and with more pain on a treadmill or on regular ground. The researchers reported that deep-water running allowed study participants to maintain better range of motion at the hip while working out within the time frame during which muscle soreness was present.

The fact that muscle pain disappeared during deep-water running only to return when subjects ventured back onto dry land suggests that soreness is to at least some extent a neural phenomenon without a muscle base, that is, an array of sensations created by the nervous system primarily to curb an athlete's appetite for and tolerance of strenuous exercise and thus prevent significant muscle damage from occurring. When the nervous system senses that no damage related to impact force will occur during an exertion, it may then turn off the pain and stiffness sensations and thus allow an athlete to exercise more strenuously.

This study found that easy treadmill running was a poor recovery technique because it probably added additional injury to leg muscles on top of the stresses that were already present as a result of the plyometric exertions. In contrast, deep-water running, with its lack of impact forces, allowed the muscles to begin the adaptive process after the plyometric challenge.

It is not clear why deep-water running was superior to rest, however. The subjects in the study were relatively untrained, so it is possible that the deep-water running simply constituted above-normal training, which could have increased muscular strength. This is somewhat unlikely, however, given the short duration of the study. In addition, it is not clear why deep-water running led to lower creatine kinase levels compared with rest, unless deep-water exertion upgraded creatine kinase clearance from the blood, or why deep-water running produced a reduction in overall pain levels during routine, daily activities undertaken outside of the pool.

Nonetheless, it appears that deep-water running can be useful in many runners' training programs. On the day(s) following a high-quality or prolonged workout, for example, a period of regular running, even at an easy pace, might augment muscle damage and block basic recovery processes. Regular running could also be psychologically taxing since it would be completed with sore, throbbing muscles and a fair amount of mental worry. On the other hand, relatively pain-free deep-water running might not interfere with recovery because it should produce no further damage. Since the deep-water running could be carried out at a fairly high intensity without interference from perceived pain, it might also lead to larger long-term gains in fitness. This possibility needs further checking by exercise scientists. It will also be interesting to see whether deep-water running has a positive effect on joint mobility during regular running.

Rehydration

Unless training is very light or water losses via sweating are negligible, a third restoration technique—*rehydration*—is also an essential part of the recovery process. Runners can lose up to 2 liters of body water per hour during strenuous effort, and losses in body fluids can amount to over 3 percent of body mass in certain situations; performance can suffer when depletion exceeds just 1 percent of mass. Ingestion of fluids during workouts and races generally cannot keep pace with the amount of fluid lost via sweating. Research suggests that it is advantageous to reverse fluid deficits as quickly as possible following workouts and competitions.

Bottled water has become very popular with runners, but pure water is not the drink of choice for such reversals unless it is combined with electrolyte-rich foods. The problem is simply that pure water, when taken by itself during the immediate recovery from strenuous exertion, lowers blood plasma osmolality and plasma sodium concentrations. As a result, thirst is reduced, and urine output increases—the exact opposites of the effects desired for optimal rehydration.[12]

Instead, fruit juices and sports drinks with electrolytes are preferred for quick rehydration. Bear in mind that satiation of thirst is a poor indicator of the restoration of body water, and thus it is important to continue drinking electrolyte-containing drinks in a reasonable way even after the sensation of thirst disappears. If travel is undertaken during the period between workouts or just before an important competition, remember that the dry air in airplanes increases respiratory evaporative water loss; athletes have been found to have reduced urine volumes after long flights, a sign of dehydration.[13] During air travel carried out before competitions or during periods of strenuous training, drinking electrolyte-rich beverages during the flight(s) would appear to be optimal.

When workouts or competitions are carried out in a dehydrated state, running capacity is impaired. Cardiac output is depressed because of the decrease in blood volume, and thus $\dot{V}O_2$max falls. If significant dehydration is present, body temperature may rise too quickly during running, and studies suggest that dehydration may lead to a loss of motor control, which would harm running economy.[14] Runners should drink electrolyte-rich beverages after workouts and then consume enough fluids of all types between training sessions so that urinary output is light yellow in appearance; dark urine suggests dehydration, while colorless urine can be an indicator of overhydration.

Downhill Running

In addition to a cool-down, deep-water running, and rehydrating properly, carrying out a session of *downhill running* on a regular basis can also boost recovery. This is indeed surprising since downhill running has often been linked with muscle damage and soreness. The link between downslope exertion and gradually improved recovery is an example of the repeated-sessions effect in which an activity that initially produces pain tends to produce increasingly less discomfort and trouble when repeated over time. This phenomenon was described by M.J. Cleak and R.G. Eston of the

Wolverhampton School of Physiotherapy and the University of Liverpool in 1992.[15] Cleak and Eston noted that strenuous or unfamiliar training often produces delayed-onset muscle soreness (DOMS) and that the appearance of DOMS is associated with prolonged recovery times. Therefore, they reasoned, anything that thwarts DOMS should speed recovery time and lead to more consistent and more productive training.

Cleak and Eston also noticed that DOMS is most likely to occur as a result of repeated *eccentric* contractions during which muscles are stretched out while they are simultaneously exerting force and attempting to contract.[16] In contrast, isometric and concentric contractions, even when completed with high force loads, seem to produce significantly less DOMS.[17] Most runners know this already. Any runner who has carried out a training session that involved a significantly unusual amount of downhill running can testify to the pain eccentric contractions can leave behind.

Downhill running can put the quadriceps muscles and hip adductor sinews under enormous eccentric strain. The quads attempt to control flexion of the knee under high-impact loads as the body falls farther with each step downhill. The adductors try to restrain abduction of the femur under intense accelerative forces created by the extra downward falling. The DOMS that results in the quads and adductors can amplify the need for recovery and force the postponement of high-quality workouts.

▶ Downhill running provides significant protection against muscle soreness, especially in the quadriceps muscles.

However, actions that involve high eccentric loads, while they may initially produce significant DOMS and a recovery time that is significantly longer than usual, also have a protective effect that makes it much harder for muscle soreness to develop after subsequent challenging training sessions: the repeated-session effect.

This effect was noticed in a study completed by J.A. Schwane and R.B. Armstrong in 1983 that found downhill running caused muscle damage *but then prevented muscle injury* during subsequent sessions of downhill exertion; *uphill running did not have a similar, protective effect* because uphill work could not block the damage correlated with downhill effort.[18] The protection provided by downhill running against soreness induced by subsequent downhill, level, *or* uphill training has been documented in a number of follow-up investigations. Protection from soreness and underlying muscle damage gained via an occasional session of downhill running is an important recovery-enhancing technique: It reduces the recovery time required between quality workouts and thus promotes more frequent and higher-quality training.

Unfortunately, the amount of downhill running required to produce an effective DOMS shield and thus faster recovery is not known. In the laboratory, as few as 12 strong eccentric contractions have been linked with a protective effect against DOMS, a barrier to soreness that lasts for about 2 weeks.[19] However, it is very doubtful that 12 downhill running steps would produce a similarly tough barrier against running-linked DOMS. An intriguing study found that two 12-minute sessions of downhill running on a 10 percent gradient provided protection against DOMS in a subsequent downhill run completed 3 days later.[20] Unfortunately, this investigation was not continued over a longer period.

There is even debate about how long the protection lasts, with some experts indicating 2 weeks and others suggesting that the obstruction of significant DOMS may persist for 10 weeks or more after a major eccentric challenge. It is reasonable to think that a hill session that involves at least 15 total minutes of downhill running conducted *every 3 weeks or so* will provide good protection against DOMS and thus decrease the amount of time required for recovery after high-quality or prolonged workouts.

Naturally, it makes little sense to bound downhill for a total of 15 minutes if one's training has featured very little downhill work in the past. If this is the case, an athlete might profitably start with just 3 minutes of downhill running and progress in 3-minute increments every week or so until the 15-minute goal is reached. Of course, unless a runner lives at the top of a mountain or canyon, completing 15 minutes of downhill running means that he or she will have to be able to finish off *more than* 15 minutes of uphill running prior to the downhill surge. It is nice to note that such upslope training will be great for running-specific strength, running economy, lactate-threshold speed, and $v\dot{V}O_2max$.

> ## Doubts About Some Recovery Techniques
>
> Little evidence exists that several putative recovery techniques actually enhance recovery. *Pharmacological recovery techniques*, with the use of nonsteroidal antiinflammatory drugs, have generally been found to be ineffective.[21] The same can be said for ice massage[22] and contrast bathing (i.e., alternating cold and warm water around the legs).[23]
>
> Endorsed by marathon world-record holder Paula Radcliffe, cold-water immersion (i.e., placing the legs in a tub of ice water) is a popular recovery technique among competitive endurance runners and is widely believe to minimize inflammation and soreness. However, cold-water immersion, also called cold therapy, ice bathing, and cryotherapy, has not fared well in scientific research.[24] One study carried out by Australian researchers suggested that cold-water immersion could actually "do more harm than good."[25] In this inquiry, ice-bath therapy actually increased soreness on the day after an intense workout and had no positive impact on swelling, strength, performance, or blood concentrations of chemicals that are linked with muscle damage. Other research suggested that ice baths should not be used during training because they tend to retard the "growth and strengthening of muscle fibers."[26]

Sleep

There is one recovery technique that is unquestionably beneficial, however, even though it is probably the restorative strategy that is most often overlooked. Good-quality, adequate sleep can speed recovery and boost running performances while poor sleep can lead to subpar times. In a study carried out at the Centre for Sport and Exercise Sciences at John Moores University in Liverpool, eight physically fit males who normally slept about 8 hours per night were abruptly restricted to 3 hours of sleep for 3 consecutive nights.[27] Workouts were conducted between 17:00 and 19:00 in the evening.

Before and during the sleep-deprivation period, the subjects conducted training sessions that included four weight-lifting movements: biceps curls, bench presses, leg presses, and dead lifts. For each of the exercises, the subjects began with 20 reps at about 40 percent of the one-repetition maximum, followed by a maximal lift. For the maximal effort, the load handled on the baseline day before sleep deprivation was used to begin the test. This load was then increased or decreased in a progressive fashion to determine the heaviest weight that could be lifted.

The results indicated that sleep loss hurt both submaximal and maximal performances. One night of restricted sleep had a minor impact on both kinds of performance; 2 nights of bad sleep were required before submaximal *and* maximal strength were truly impaired. Such findings suggest that runners should not worry about a night of bad sleep. Significant downturns in performance do not appear to occur until 2 nights of limited sleep have been experienced, with things getting even worse after 3 nights of insomnia.

Since sleep can have a major impact on performance, a sleep schedule should be planned as carefully as the workout. It is important to set a regular time to go to sleep—and stick to it—and to avoid disruptions of sleep, avoid taking the problems of the day to bed, and enjoy each night of sleep. The best endurance runners in the world—the elite Kenyans—are usually in bed and fast asleep each night by 9:30 p.m. and ordinarily sleep until at least 6:00 a.m.[28]

Nutrition

Proper nutrition also enhances recovery. For runners, high-carbohydrate diets optimize muscle glycogen levels, and higher muscle glycogen concentrations improve endurance-exercise performance.[29] Achieving high glycogen levels is not just a matter of eating plenty of carbs, however; the timing of carbohydrate intake is important. For example, consumption of carbohydrate *immediately after either endurance or resistance exercise* may enhance total daily muscle glycogen resynthesis compared with consuming the same amount of carbs earlier in the day or postponing carb consumption until a few hours after exercise.[30, 31] Chapter 44 discusses nutrition for endurance and speed in greater depth.

Taking in carbohydrate right after an exertion does more than boost muscle glycogen creation: It also seems to have a pronounced effect on *protein* metabolism. Proteins are the building blocks of muscles, and certain proteins can also serve as energy-releasing enzymes within muscle cells. For example, postworkout carb consumption can decrease the rate of protein degradation in muscles[32] and increase whole-body protein synthesis.[33] These twin effects are highly desirable for endurance athletes, whose performances will generally fall if significant quantities of protein are lost.

When day-to-day training is strenuous, or when training increases in volume or intensity, considerations related to total carbohydrate intake, the timing of that intake, and the impacts of diet and training load on protein metabolism become particularly crucial aspects of recovery. Upswings in training can deplete muscle glycogen stores and throw runners into a state of negative nitrogen balance, in which they are losing more protein than they are making.

Research strongly suggests that endurance runners should ingest 4 grams of carbohydrate per pound of body weight per day during periods of strenuous training, including 1 gram of carbohydrate per pound of body weight immediately after a workout ends. This postworkout carbohydrate intake should be accompanied by 10 to 20 grams of protein (see chapter 44 for more details).

Conclusion

Overall, the importance of recovery should not be underestimated; runners should never forget that the benefits of great training can be canceled quite easily by poor recovery practices. After strenuous workouts, it is good to cool down with about 5 minutes of easy running and 5 or more minutes of stretching. Remember that *prolonged* cool-downs may hurt muscle glycogen levels during periods of challenging training. Rehydration is a key component of recovery; runners should try to ensure that their urine retains its ideal pale-straw coloration during periods of challenging training. Carbohydrate and protein intakes should be optimized between training sessions.

Deep-water running is also an excellent recovery strategy on the first day or so following a rugged running session. During deep-water running, it is even possible to crank up the intensity without inducing additional muscle soreness or stiffness—and probably without setting back the ability to conduct subsequent, high-quality running sessions on land. Downhill workouts minimize the risk of recovery-retarding DOMS, and occasional blips in the quality of sleep should be followed by solid nights of slumber.

The elite Kenyan runners may be the absolute best in the world at recovering between workouts, with their reliance on minimal cool-downs, substantial sleep, rehydration (with colossal cups of Kenyan tea), postworkout carb and protein intakes, and repeated sessions of downhill running (sadly, no deep-water running is involved . . . the crocodiles, you know). Runners can use these same strategies to optimize their own recoveries and thus move their training intensity and overall fitness up several notches. The end result should be improved performances in key competitions.

CHAPTER 22

Periodization and Block Systems

Runners who want to improve their performances cannot train in the same way all the time. Training that remains fixed at a specific volume and intensity produces adaptations that cannot advance above a certain level. For example, running 35 miles (56 km) per week throughout the year, or over the course of many years, with a speed session each Tuesday, a tempo run each Thursday, and a long run during the weekend, can push $\dot{V}O_2$max and v$\dot{V}O_2$max up to specific heights beyond which no further improvements are possible without a productive change in the overall training plan.

Figuring out how to modify training in order to keep improving key physiological variables is thus a primary goal of serious runners. The human body's strong tendency to merely maintain physiological status quo in association with a certain level of training, even when that training is challenging and is continued indefinitely, is an inescapable fact. Nonetheless, many runners train in the same fashion nearly year round, year after year. In spite of their inability or unwillingness to change training in a productive way, such runners expect dramatically improved competitive results over time.

An individual runner's ability to improve his or her performances will depend on success in upgrading the seven key performance variables:

- v$\dot{V}O_2$max
- t_{lim}v$\dot{V}O_2$max (i.e., the length of time a runner can actually sustain v$\dot{V}O_2$max; t_{lim}v$\dot{V}O_2$max varies from 4 minutes to a maximum of about 10 minutes, and performance capacity improves as a runner moves up this scale over time)
- Running economy
- Lactate-threshold velocity
- Resistance to fatigue (i.e., the ability to sustain desired goal speed over the full distance of one's competitive event)
- Running-specific strength
- Maximal running speed (i.e., power)

When each of these variables is pushed during training to its maximal limit, a runner's training has been optimized, and the best possible performances will be achieved.

Exercise scientists believe that no single workout can simultaneously improve all seven variables. A long run, for example, might be good for upgrading resistance to fatigue at the pace chosen for the long run, but it would have no positive impact on maximal running speed because of the submaximal pace, and it would have little effect on lactate-threshold velocity because the training tempo is below threshold speed. Similarly, a hill workout might thrust oxygen-consumption rate and blood lactate upward, thus possibly benefiting $\dot{V}O_2max$, $v\dot{V}O_2max$, and lactate-threshold velocity, and the hills would definitely enhance running-specific strength and therefore running economy, but the slower pace used on hills compared with intense running on the flat would be unlikely to provide a major boost for maximal running speed.

No single workout can serve as a fitness magic bullet; therefore, workouts must progress in difficulty over time to continue challenging the body, and workouts need to be *changed* over time in order to optimize all seven variables. Finding the most productive workouts—and scheduling them in an optimal way—is one of the key challenges of endurance training.

Improving Through Progression

The strategy of changing training in order to make it more physiologically and competitively productive is called *progression* or *progressing*. The most guileless and popular pattern of progressing with training is to increase weekly mileage; two other popular techniques are increasing the intensity and the frequency of training. The problem with these techniques is that they are strategies that merely hope for the best: A runner may move from 30 to 40 miles (48-64 km) per week and hope for good results, for example, without knowing exactly how he or she will change physiologically in response to the increase in volume.

A more sophisticated approach involves identifying the key variables associated with endurance-running performance and then figuring out a way to simultaneously optimize these variables over the course of a training period, which is usually the amount of time available to prepare for a specific competition. To perform at their highest levels, endurance runners should optimize the seven key characteristics provided previously.

It is impossible to optimize all these variables at once with a fixed, unchanging mode of training; progression is needed. For example, it is clearly suboptimal to engage in power training without first building a broad platform of running-specific strength. The upgraded strength protects against injury during high-quality, power-promoting workouts. Science also suggests that maximal gains in power can't be achieved unless muscles first develop the ability to generate greater force. The lesson is that improvements must be accomplished in a step-by-step, progressive manner during training.

A complicating factor is that gradual development of proficiency in one aspect of endurance running may change the way the body adapts to training. For example, research has shown that novice shot-putters make major advances in performance primarily by improving the strength of their arm muscles, while experienced shot-putters increase the lengths of their throws mainly by increasing the strength and power of their legs.[1] Investigations also reveal that pole vaulters initially make large increases in performance by improving the strength of their abdominal muscles but can only continue to progress by achieving major improvements in shoulder and arm strength.[2]

A similar phenomenon happens with running. Beginning runners or runners coming back from layoffs can make rather large gains in performance simply by boosting the distance they run, while highly experienced runners must tweak the intensity of their training and perform special strength- and power-building drills in order to continue to make further progress.[3] Endurance runners must optimize $\dot{V}O_2$max and running economy before they can maximize $v\dot{V}O_2$max, and lactate-threshold velocity must ordinarily be lifted to its highest level before resistance to fatigue can be heightened maximally. For all these reasons, the *periodization* of training is critically important.

Progressing Through Periodization

Complicated definitions of periodization exist, but the term simply means the division of an overall training program into periods that accomplish specific goals. Since everything cannot be accomplished at once, training must be periodized into discretely different units of time.

More than 2,500 years ago, the ancient Greeks were the first to use the principles of progression and periodization in their training. Milos, a Greek wrestler who won wrestling events at five different Olympic Games, according to legend progressed his training by carrying around a calf each day; as the calf grew in size and mass, Milos' training became more challenging.[4] This is the first recorded example of what is often called *progressive-overload training*, which is advancing the training load over time by using increasingly heavy weights. For runners, an example of this would be a gradual increase in workout length and thus total weekly distance run.

After the Greeks, periodization theory entered a 2,000-year lull, only to be revived early in the twentieth century during the Russian Revolution.[5] Over the following 70 years, the Russians led the world in the development of periodization theory. Prior to the fall of the Soviet Union in 1989, the Russians also enjoyed one key advantage over other countries: They were able to test different periodization schemes with large numbers of their international athletes and accumulated an extensive amount of practical information about periodizing training properly.

The first periodization schemes developed by the Russians in the 1920s and 1930s were basic; their exercise scientists theorized that training programs should be divided into what they called general, preparatory, and specific phases. The general stage of training, often lasting for about 2 months, was supposed to develop the heart and lungs. The preparatory training, also lasting about 2 months, sought to boost muscle strength and endurance; the specific period of about 8 months prepared an athlete for a specific event by emphasizing extensive practice of the precise movements and speeds required for success.

Finnish and English scientists gradually entered the periodization arena, but the majority of their work provided lots of theories about periodization with a smattering of real results. One difficulty has been that meaningful research concerning periodization needs to cover rather broad time frames. When the training differences between successful and nonsuccessful athletes are examined, it is important to study how the runners train over several years, not just over a few months. Proper periodization means coordinating training correctly over extended periods of time—long enough to make large gains in fitness and prepare optimally for major competitions.

That makes the understanding of periodization very challenging for exercise scientists, many of whom need to limit investigations to 8 to 12 weeks in duration as part of the publish-or-perish nature of academia. There are also major difficulties associated with getting a group of athletes to adhere to a specific training program for a year or more at a time: Many athletes will drop out, others will not follow the prescribed training very closely, and some will become injured. For an exercise researcher, embarking on a long-term periodization project is a somewhat risky thing to do.

As a result, periodization *theorists*—rather than experimenters—have held sway, and they have achieved major success in one area: They have given runners a large amount of training-related jargon.

Periodization Cycles

The jargon of periodization includes the terms macrocycles, mesocycles, and microcycles. While these words may seem foreign at first to endurance runners, their meanings are actually quite simple. A microcycle is simply a number of training sessions that form a recurrent unit of training. If a training program consists of a hard day, an easy day, and then a rest day, followed by the same pattern again, the 3-day pattern represents the basic training unit, or microcycle. If a typical training week consists of a hill workout, an interval session on the track, a long run, three easy runs, and a rest day, this repetitive weekly pattern is the microcycle.

A mesocycle is a block, or discrete period, of training consisting of a number of microcycles A mesocycle is focused on the attainment of a particular goal. A macrocycle is a long stretch of training intended to accomplish an important overall goal such as the preparation for and completion of a key marathon or 10K. A macrocycle is made up of a number of different mesocycles and usually covers a period of many months.

Typically, a microcycle lasts 5 to 10 days—for many runners, a microcycle is simply one week of training in a predictable way—a mesocycle usually covers 3 to 8 weeks, and a macrocycle lasts for 6 to 12 months. Many runners who periodize their training do not alter their macrocycles very much; one year is structured very much like the next, and thus the year is the largest unit of periodization. Some athletes like to plan in more extended terms and may use what are called large macrocycles consisting of two to four regular macrocycles and lasting for up to 4 years or more. These subunit macrocycles may be considerably different from each other.

Knowledge of these different cycles does not ensure proper periodization, and it is important to note that there is probably not one best periodization plan for endurance runners: What works for one athlete may actually be counterproductive for another. One reason for this is the inherent variability in genetic makeup between runners. Another is that individual athletes can have dramatically different strengths and weaknesses and thus unique training needs.

A runner with relatively poor muscular strength might need to spend several mesocycles of training within a year focusing on developing general and running-specific strength by carrying out a variety of progressively more difficult resistance routines in addition to running training. Such a runner would also need to devote a large amount of time to hill training, which increases the force-development capacities of the leg muscles. In contrast, a strong runner could spend considerably less time on such activities and might more profitably mark off large periods of time to work on upgrading another weakness—perhaps a low lactate threshold or $v\dot{V}O_2max$.

Types of Periodization

It is clear that each runner needs his or her own unique periodization plan. Periodizing an individual's program requires skill in figuring out what the runner really needs—and knowledge of the various periodization possibilities. The existing overall programs include wave-like periodization, step periodization, skill-strength periodization, emphasis periodization, and the Lydiard system of periodization, all discussed in the following sections. Choosing which type of periodization is not easy because there are many models and considerable debate about which scheme works most effectively.

Wave-Like Periodization

Many runners use the most basic of all periodization strategies: the wave-like periodization pattern. With this scheme, runners first build up their training volume, or mileage, to a rather lofty level (creating a big wave of miles) while intensity, or speed, remains modest. This initial period of training is supposed to establish strength and endurance. The wave of increased mileage is then gradually deemphasized, replaced by a comparatively short but steadily increasing wave of intensity: Mileage is reduced, but the average running speed rises as the quality of workouts increases. According to convention and tradition, the runner is ready for major competitions once the intensity wave has peaked. After the competitive season is over or the major competition has been completed, the athlete rests for a defined period of time before catching another big wave of mileage at the beginning of the next season or macrocycle.

This basic wave-like pattern of periodization is used, year after year, by millions of runners all over the world. It has a certain appealing logic because it seems to gradually build muscular and connective-tissue strength before subjecting a runner's body to the harsh reality of high-intensity training; it is important to remember, however, that most running injuries are *overuse* injuries that occur during high-mileage training, that is, at or near the top of the volume wave.

The fundamental wave-like pattern also parallels the classic dyad of aerobic and anaerobic training that countless numbers of coaches and runners still use to plan training programs. The idea is to build up aerobic endurance gradually by logging lots of moderately paced runs during the mileage wave and then to sharpen runners with intense anaerobic conditioning, which is supposed to improve speed and heighten surging and kicking abilities in races. When viewed from a muscle-fiber paradigm, the notion is to work on slow-twitch muscle fibers first and then shift attention to the fast-twitch fibers in time for competition.

Such views of training are misguided and far too simple. For one thing, the strength gained in the volume wave is strength that is specific to slow running and not to the higher speeds required for competition. Improvements in strength are always tied to the *speed* with which strengthening movements are conducted; advances in strength at slower running speeds do not foretell upgraded strength at the higher speeds included within the subsequent intensity wave. In this sense, a volume wave is not optimal preparation for the intensity wave.

It is also highly misleading to categorize an endurance runner's high-quality training as anaerobic since the high-speed training carried out by endurance runners is usually conducted at $v\dot{V}O_2max$ and above, speeds that elicit $\dot{V}O_2max$, *the highest rate of oxygen consumption*. For example, when Haile Gebrselassie burned 55-second 400s during workouts, most of the energy created to run those fast 400s was produced aerobically, not anaerobically. The truth is that the two systems—aerobic and anaerobic—work together closely, even during the most intense mesocycle of training. This is true no matter how fast workouts become, unless they consist solely of 100-meter sprints, separated by long recoveries.

Finally, wave-like periodization fails to address the key task faced by runners who are serious about fitness and performance: the optimization of the performance-related physiological variables. The two waves fail to maximize $v\dot{V}O_2max$, enhance running economy to its greatest extent, lift lactate-threshold speed, increase running-specific strength, or optimize resistance to fatigue. The waves lack the specific mechanisms required to do so. For these reasons, coaches and runners can safely avoid or abandon wave-like periodization, despite its popularity.

Step Periodization

As an alternative to the wave-like periodization pattern, Russian exercise scientist A.N. Vorobyev proposed what is now known as step periodization, in which training loads and intensities are changed abruptly rather than smoothly and progressively from workout to workout or in weekly and monthly cycles.[6] In this bumpy periodization plan, series of light to moderate workouts are alternated with intense efforts with little break between the difficult sessions. Different studies have shown this approach to be a fairly effective way to develop muscular strength.[6] For runners, step periodization involves several successive days of high-quality training, down periods of easy work, and then step-ups to another series of challenging exertions carried out consecutively over several days. For example, a runner using step periodization might carry out an intense interval session on Monday, conduct hill training on Tuesday, complete a long run with an inner core of difficult continuous running on Wednesday, and then run lightly from Thursday through Sunday. The following week would then include a similar format, except with a progressive toughening of the workouts on Monday through Wednesday, and so on.

While step periodization is intriguing, a key weakness is the lack of recovery between high-quality running sessions, which can lead to injury. An additional problem, common to many periodization plans, is the lack of attention paid to the improvement of specific physiological variables. A runner using step periodization follows the plan and simply hopes that the tough workouts will magically produce optimal gains in fitness.

Skill-Strength Periodization

An advancement over step periodization, skill-strength periodization was used repeatedly by highly successful track and field teams from the former Soviet Union to prepare for Olympic competitions. Skill-strength represents an advance in periodization because one cycle of training logically follows the previous cycle, building on the preparatory strengths already gained. With skill-strength periodization, athletes spend an extensive amount of time perfecting their technical skills during the preparatory phase of training prior to developing strength and endurance. For runners, this would mean spending a considerable amount of time on learning appropriate form before advancing to other kinds of training. This is highly recommended for distance runners, yet very few endurance runners perfect their form prior to embarking on the main phases of their training. As a result, endurance runners often end up with bad form habits (e.g., heel striking, slow cadence, grossly positive shank ankle at contact with the ground, erect posture) that prevent them from optimizing key performance variables during their overall training. (Optimal running form is discussed in chapter 5.)

The basic idea underlying skill-strength periodization is that once athletes are skilled (e.g., once they are technically proficient jumpers or economical runners with optimal form), they can then carry out the most productive training possible because their training uses the most effective patterns of motion. Skill-strength periodization is in one sense the opposite of many traditional schemes that build strength at slow speeds first and worry about technique later. In an important way, it is the reverse of the classic, wave-like periodization pattern, which emphasizes a large initial wave of strength building at slow to moderate speeds, followed by the gaining of technical proficiency (e.g., running economy, coordination) while running fast. No carefully controlled research has ever contrasted skill-strength periodization with basic wave-like periodization, but the Russians reported excellent results with the former, and their teams did exceedingly well in Olympic competitions.

Emphasis Periodization

Another plan for organizing training is called emphasis periodization (EP), or concentration of loading, in which training is divided into 4- to 10-week blocks, with each block having a special concentration. Each emphasis period is supposed to act as a foundation for the following one; for runners, this would mean the development of running-specific strength before the creation of running power, or attaining enhanced economy in advance of optimizing $v\dot{V}O_2max$. A runner would not be considered to be fully prepared for competition until all the emphasis periods have been completed. This kind of periodization goes far beyond mere fiddling with volume and intensity of training and actually addresses a runner's specific goals: the physiological targets that must be reached before maximal fitness can be attained.

The Lydiard System

Developed by New Zealand coach Arthur Lydiard, this system gained world-wide popularity partly because of the successes of athletes coached by Lydiard, including Peter Snell, Barry Magee, and Murray Halberg. The Lydiard system is still used by a large number of competitive runners today.

The Lydiard system begins with an extensive period of base training, during which running volume steadily expands, followed by a strengthening phase consisting of an ample amount of hill climbing and drills carried out on hills. The subsequent training constitutes Lydiard's misnamed anaerobic phase with its emphasis on intense sessions and the development of speed; this phase is deliberately kept short—no more than 4 to 6 weeks—because of Lydiard's mistaken belief that the high lactate levels associated with intense training can harm muscle cells. The final phase within the Lydiard system is a tapering phase, during which volume and intensity of training are reduced and preparatory, fine-tuning races are conducted.[7]

Few can argue with Lydiard's success as a coach, but his system has not stood up to the steady forward march of running science. The notions that fast training is anaerobic and that lactic acid can injure muscle tissue are now outdated. Furthermore, the Lydiard system does not address the specific goals of optimization of $v\dot{V}O_2max$ and maximal running speed, which are key predictors of endurance-running performance. British coach Frank Horwill has criticized the Lydiard approach, noting that approximately 110 kilometers (68 mi) of weekly running are all that are necessary to optimize aerobic capacity; Lydiard recommended approximately 160 kilometers (99 mi) per week, including a Sunday run of 35 kilometers (22 mi) completed over mountainous terrain, if possible. Horwill has also contended that the Lydiard approach increases the risks of injury because of accumulated distance and psychological burnout.[8]

Training Blocks

Historically, endurance runners and their coaches have approached this organizational challenge by arranging training into blocks, or mesocycles. A block of training is simply the period during which a specific mode of training is emphasized and thus a specific outcome is sought. For example, a traditional speed block might last 4 to 6 weeks and contain many workouts conducted at high speeds, with the goal being to lift maximal running velocity and establish a powerful kick for the final moments of competitions.

A traditional base block, or period, might also last 4 to 6 weeks and would include gradually increasing amounts of submaximal running with the goals being the establishment of running-specific strength and an increase in aerobic capacity. If a base block is placed before a speed block or some other block in a runner's program, then one can say that training has been periodized. Periodization is nothing more than the arrangement of training blocks in a specific way with the ultimate goal to optimize the key endurance-performance variables.

That makes periodization sound simple enough, but in fact the process of periodizing training is far from simple. Important, difficult questions need to be answered correctly in order to produce the best periodization plan: How many different blocks should be included in the overall program? What are the proper goals for each block? How long should blocks last? How should the workouts be arranged within the blocks, and which training sessions should be included? How much time is needed to peak prior to the most important competition? Should blocks be repeated after they have all been completed, and if so, how should they be upgraded for the next major training cycle? These are among the fundamental questions of training and periodization theory.

Basic One-Block Systems

In the simplest training program, there is actually just one block that lasts all year long. For example, many individuals simply run several times a week throughout the year, usually at steady, submaximal paces, with an aim of completing a certain weekly volume of running, often 30 to 50 kilometers (18-30 mi) or so. The overriding goals might simply be to expand aerobic capacity ($\dot{V}O_2max$) and to run an occasional 5K, as well as to lose weight and improve overall health. There is no periodization because the training contains just one block. This kind of program will bring fitness up to a certain level and then preserve that fitness, but it is not ideal for the competitive runner.

Complex One-Block Systems

A slightly more complicated one-block system is used by many endurance runners. In this plan, there is also an emphasis on attaining a certain threshold training volume; a typical week is constructed so that a speed workout is conducted on Tuesday, usually with intervals at approximately 5K race pace; some type of hill work or tempo training is carried out on Thursday, with tempo training understood as running continuously at a relatively hard intensity for 20 minutes or more; and a long run is reserved for the weekend. The specific goals for this system are often unspoken, but one can see that the arrangement might initially have an impact on most of the seven key performance variables.

The problem is that with the single block, there is often very little progression. Progression is defined as a gradual forward movement to different forms of training that vary significantly from initial training formats and are also more challenging and productive in skill, intensity, or duration. Without new training stimuli (i.e., without progression), a runner's rate of physiological improvement slows and then falls to zero. Surprisingly, many runners expect a single-block kind of system to provide continued benefits and fitness upgrades and become very frustrated and even disillusioned when performances stagnate. Without progression and periodization, training cannot move past a physiological dead end.

Two-Block Systems

Many runners employ a two-block system, with one period emphasizing the development of endurance and the other focused on developing greater speed. The contents of each block vary greatly from runner to runner, but the endurance block ordinarily contains substantial amounts of running below maximal and race-pace velocities, while the speed block emphasizes a higher frequency of workouts conducted at race paces or faster.

As described previously, this approach is sometimes called the wave periodization training pattern because runners initially build their volume to a rather high level, creating an extended distance wave, and then let the distance wave at least partially collapse while setting up a greater frequency of high-quality workouts in an intensity wave. According to conventional wisdom, a runner is ready to accomplish a personal record or perform extremely well in competition once the intensity wave has peaked. After the competitive season is over, the runner rests for awhile and then catches another wave to begin a new season of training.

Although attractive and simple, the two-block wave pattern is far from optimal for the competitive distance runner. For one thing, the stamina and resistance to fatigue acquired during the first block is specific to the submaximal paces used during training. Rather than developing the ability to run fast for a longer period of time, the runner is developing the capacity to run slowly for extended periods.

An additional difficulty is that many endurance runners find increasing maximal running velocity, a key predictor of performance, to be a difficult undertaking; in the two-block pattern, improvement in maximal running velocity is ignored in the first block and treated lightly in the second.

Tracking the Elusive Best Plan

So what is the best periodization plan? Exercise scientists have had a great deal to say about periodization theory but have provided very little data concerning the merits of various periodization programs. One reason for the lack of solid facts about periodization is that meaningful research on the topic needs to cover broad time frames. To understand which periodization plan is best, it's necessary to understand how an endurance athlete should arrange his or her training each week, each month, and over the course of an entire year or longer. It is difficult to imagine that any 2- to 3-month periodization plan would provide the magic bullet that hits the fitness bull's eye and produces optimal performance.

To periodize training, many runners and coaches rely on a system developed by Jack Daniels, a highly respected coach and exercise scientist. Daniels has developed a popular emphasis-periodization training plan with a strong scientific basis.[9] In Daniels' system, there are four different blocks, also known as emphasis periods or mesocycles:

1. A base period, often lasting 4 to 6 weeks. In this phase, a runner simply expands training volume gradually while running, for the most part, at moderate, submaximal speeds. The basic goals are to increase strength and endurance.

2. A $\dot{V}O_2$max block, also lasting 4 to 6 weeks. In this block, a runner emphasizes interval workouts conducted at 5K intensity, with work-interval lengths often set at 800 to 1,200 meters (0.5-0.75 mi) with recoveries equal in duration to the work intervals. Since 5K intensity is ordinarily about 95 percent of $\dot{V}O_2$max, such intervals should push $\dot{V}O_2$max upward, as Daniels has proposed. As the block's name suggests, the basic goal is to augment $\dot{V}O_2$max, a predictor of performance for an individual runner but not a predictor of performance among runners with similar training backgrounds.

3. A lactate-threshold block, lasting 4 to 6 weeks. The goal is to increase lactate-threshold velocity, and the key workouts include longer intervals of 1,600 to 2,000 meters (1 to 1.2 mi) at 10K race speed and tempo runs, or continuous efforts lasting 20 minutes or longer conducted at lactate-threshold velocity, which for Daniels is about a 15K (9 mi) race pace. For those runners who never race the 15K (9 mi) distance, 15K tempo is usually about 8 seconds per mile slower than a 10K pace.

4. An economy block, again with a typical duration of 4 to 6 weeks. The key economy workouts are reps carried out on the track at a pace that is 4 seconds per 400 meters faster than 5K tempo. Often the reps are 400 meters in length; recoveries are longer in duration than the reps. The goal of this block is to enhance economy (how did you guess that?).

After the four blocks are completed, a runner is believed to be ready for competition. The value of the Daniels system is immediately clear: It emphasizes the improvement of three variables—$\dot{V}O_2$max, lactate-threshold speed, and running economy—that can have an impact on an individual runner's endurance performance. Another plus is that volume and intensity of training can easily be adjusted in each of the four blocks.

The Daniels plan is also quite sophisticated: In a 6-week economy block, for example, a runner might emphasize the development of better economy by completing seven total economy reps or hill sessions but at the same time address continuous improvement of lactate threshold and $\dot{V}O_2$max. The runner might also conduct five workouts that advance lactate threshold and three that improve $\dot{V}O_2$max during the economy block, preserving or advancing the gains that have already been made in those variables and thus averaging 2.5 quality workouts per week, in effect completing two difficult sessions the first week and three the next.

The potential weaknesses of the Daniels system lie in what it leaves out and also in its logical inconsistency. For example, there is no block for v$\dot{V}O_2$max, even though this is a key predictor of performance; in fairness, though, Daniels' blocks of $\dot{V}O_2$max and economy, taken together, should have a positive effect on v$\dot{V}O_2$max. There is also no emphasis on running-specific strength: The strength acquired in the base period is specific to the submaximal paces used during that phase of training, and the stimuli for increasing maximal running speed are rather weak.

The logical inconsistency quickly becomes apparent when one examines specific workouts within the blocks. Take the intervals at 5K paced in the $\dot{V}O_2$max block, for example. At the desired intensity of 5K speed, these intervals should produce improvements in the heart's pumping ability and the capacity of the leg muscles to use oxygen. As a result, $\dot{V}O_2$max increase is a near certainty unless a runner has already topped out because of prior training. However, note that 95 percent of $\dot{V}O_2$max is well above lactate-threshold speed, and thus the workout will produce generous amounts of blood lactate, nicely enhancing lactate-threshold velocity. Running fast at 5K speed should also improve running economy in general and specifically running economy at a 5K pace. The workout is simultaneously having effects on $\dot{V}O_2$max, lactate threshold, and running economy, and yet it is called a $\dot{V}O_2$max session. In truth, the workout could be a lactate-threshold effort in the lactate block or an economy driver in the economy segment of the overall plan.

Hill workouts present a similar dilemma. Although they undoubtedly improve running-specific leg strength and thus economy, they also elicit high rates of oxygen consumption and produce high levels of blood lactate. Thus, a hill session is an economy workout while being great for $\dot{V}O_2$max and lactate-threshold speed, too.

Four-Phase Emphasis Periodization

A scientifically-based and more logically consistent periodization plan has been developed slowly by coaches and exercise scientists over the last decade. Ironically, this program depends on strength training for its backbone of blocks, even though strength training has historically been considered to be rather unsuitable for endurance runners, partly based on concerns about building excess muscle mass and partly because strength training is thought to be anaerobic while endurance running is aerobic. These concerns have proven to be unfounded.

   The new system has four phases; each generally lasts 3 to 6 weeks. The phases do not have to be equal in length. For example, if a runner has great general strength but poor maximal speed, the first phase can be shortened and the last block lengthened.

   1. An initial skill and general-strength phase, during which running skill, especially form and cadence, are emphasized, and whole-body strength is developed fully. The goals of this phase are to eliminate bad running habits (e.g., poor foot-strike pattern, slow cadence, improper form) and to promote a vast upgrade in overall strength, not just leg strength. Establishing optimal form improves running capacity immediately and heightens the quality of all workouts because average running velocity increases; therefore, each training session becomes a more potent producer of fitness. Optimal form also permits subsequent gains in running-specific strength to be channeled directly into powerful running instead of being wasted on suboptimal movements. Gains in whole-body strength promote resistance to fatigue and lead to more economical running, and the workouts that enhance whole-body strength (e.g., circuit sessions) also lift lactate threshold.

   2. A running-specific strength phase, during which strength is optimized for all components of running gait: initial ground contact, midstance, toe-off, and swing. The obvious goal for this phase is to optimize running-specific strength, which enhances running economy dramatically and heightens resistance to fatigue. Augmenting running-specific strength is also a foundation for improving maximal running speed because the latter depends so heavily on applying more force to the ground with each step. Finally, the running-specific strength phase heightens preparation for the next stage of training—hill work.

   3. A hill-training phase, during which running-specific strength is advanced to an ultimate degree—after all, surging up hills is the most specific form of running-specific strengthening—and $\dot{V}O_2max$, $v\dot{V}O_2max$, economy, lactate-threshold speed, and resistance to fatigue are also augmented.

4. An explosive-training phase, in which high-speed drills and exercises are used relentlessly; overall training quality, or average running speed, soars. The combination of explosive training and the prior work on general strength, running-specific strength, and hill-running capacity creates an unbeatable upswing in fitness.

From a biomechanical standpoint, a runner is now able to put more force on the ground with each step—thanks to phases two and three—and also apply that force more quickly, that is, spend less time on the ground per step, thanks to the explosive work. The result is a dramatic increase in maximal running velocity along with corresponding advancements in $v\dot{V}O_2$max, running economy, lactate-threshold speed, and resistance to fatigue, all of which are spiked because of the intensity of the training. After the completion of phase four, a runner has improved all seven components of running fitness and is prepared for his or her best possible performances.

Within the framework of these four phases, high-quality running workouts progress over time and continuously promote improvements in the key performance variables. There is a gradual progression in volume of training and a steady advance in quality training, the percent of total work carried out above lactate-threshold velocity. The quality workouts vary significantly over time to increase motivation for training and to prevent the fitness stagnation that can result from repetitive training.

Conclusion

Of the periodization systems outlined in this chapter, the most attractive option for distance coaches and runners is certainly four-phase emphasis periodization (EP). This system identifies the factors that endurance runners need to optimize; it incorporates the enhancement of these factors into discrete training cycles so that a runner can be fully prepared for competition at the end of an EP macrocycle. Surprisingly, optimal EP includes phases of training that are not part of many endurance runners' preparations for competition.

Coaches and runners are often perplexed about how to set up their training blocks and periodize training properly, but they shouldn't be. The process is relatively simple using the four-phase system. This plan puts heavy positive pressure on all seven performance variables and is so varied that it also keeps runners mentally sharp. With its emphasis on strength training, the system also reduces the risk of injury and thus makes consistent training possible. The result is a high likelihood of reaching lofty goals and setting exciting personal records.

CHAPTER 23

Integrated Strength and Endurance Training Programs

Traditional training for endurance runners has been relatively simple in composition. It includes a standard array of workouts—interval sessions, tempo runs, hill workouts, an occasional session of fartlek running, and long runs—and tends to avoid strength training since it is assumed that kind of training has a negative impact. Conventional endurance-running training is also rather simple in its progressions and periodization, with a buildup in volume followed by an increase in intensity, including an abbreviated period devoted to increasing maximal running velocity, even though this is a key predictor of running performance and many endurance runners have poorly developed speed.

These facile conceptions of training pay little attention to optimizing the seven key performance variables (see chapter 22 for discussions of training systems that address some or all of these variables and individual chapters on the key variables), the factors identified by exercise scientists as being predictors of performance. Fortunately, exercise science has marched forward steadily over the last 25 years, and at least a partial understanding of the training techniques required to optimize the seven variables has been attained. This chapter outlines a new and productive way of carrying out strength training for running with key progressions that enhance performance variables. It also describes an optimal way to warm up before workouts and demonstrates how to incorporate strength training and running sessions in an extended half-marathon training program. Many of the exercises used in the programs discussed in this chapter are those that have been presented in detail in chapters 13 and 14. The special warm-up and half-marathon training programs also contain additional exercises; these are presented in this chapter after descriptions of the programs.

Strength Training: A Fresh Look

One of the most exciting developments in the science of endurance-running training has been the recent discovery that a complex, progressive strength-training program can have a dramatic effect on endurance performance.[1, 2] This breakthrough has come as a shock to many distance runners and their coaches because strength training has seldom been viewed in a very favorable light. Criticisms of strength training include the contentions that it adds surplus, economy-hindering muscle mass and that it cannot possibly aid aerobic exertions such as endurance running because resistance work is intrinsically anaerobic.

Those critiques, although long-standing and popular, have little merit. Strength training does not automatically build muscle mass. It is possible to conduct an effective program that builds strength without any increase in overall muscle mass; improvements in strength can come from coordination upgrades rather than from brute muscle expansion. Optimal resistance training for running would enhance skill and strength without causing muscles to pop.

In addition, some strength workouts are actually highly aerobic, not anaerobic. Circuit-training sessions that incorporate a series of challenging exercises and drills carried out one after the other, without a significant break, can often push oxygen-consumption rates up to 90 to 100 percent of $\dot{V}O_2$max and heart rates above 90 percent of the maximum.

Even if resistance sessions couldn't push oxygen consumption so high, the anaerobic tag placed on strength workouts would not really be a problem. Over the past 10 years, it has become increasingly understood that endurance runners do have nervous systems after all—they are not simply leg muscles hooked up to a big pump, the heart. New research indicates that the nervous system is not just along for the ride during quality endurance workouts and high-speed endurance races. Rather, the nervous system regulates everything that happens in a runner's body, including the degree to which the leg muscles are stimulated; changes in heart rate and cardiac output, which match the demands placed on them by the neuromuscular system; and the extent to which a runner experiences fatigue.

Thus, an endurance runner's nervous system is an appropriate target for overall improvement during training. When an endurance runner's nervous system is functioning optimally, it is controlling gait in a way that maximally enhances running economy. The brain and spinal cord are able to stimulate and coordinate leg muscles in ways that push running velocity to its upper limit by optimizing stride rate and stride length, which the muscles and cardiovascular system cannot do. The nervous system is capable of sustained, high-level neural output—the ability to continuously provoke muscles to work at high levels of intensity without fatigue. In response to proper training, the neural governor residing within the nervous system is set at 10 rather than 5 or 6; that is, it enables high intensities of running to occur for unusually long periods. All of these desired outcomes for the nervous system are influenced by strength training.

Forms of Strength Training

What forms of strength training are best for endurance runners? There are four key types:

- Circuit training, which improves maximal aerobic capacity, v$\dot{V}O_2$max, general strength, lactate threshold, and performance by including a series of whole-body strengthening activities in a continuous manner. Its ability to upgrade v$\dot{V}O_2$max is critically important because this variable is a predictor of running performance.[3] Circuit work can also augment maximal aerobic capacity ($\dot{V}O_2$max) in nonelite runners.[4] When circuit sessions are composed of high-intensity strengthening activities, agility while sprinting and stamina during high levels of effort are enhanced.[5] Circuit training has also been linked with an increase in lactate threshold.[6] When carried out immediately before a 4K (2.5 mi) time trial, circuit training can improve performance by 8.6 percent.[7]

- Running-specific strength training fortifies resistance to fatigue, running economy, maximal running speed, and v$\dot{V}O_2$max. Two weekly sessions of running-specific strength training using exercises that closely mimic the mechanics of gait carried out over an 8-week period have been demonstrated to minimize the loss in stride length that occurs during fast, fatiguing running in well-trained runners.[8] In other words, running-specific strengthening helps preserve running speed during challenging efforts because it promotes resistance to fatigue during quality running. It is logical to believe that running-specific strength training would have a positive effect on running economy and therefore on v$\dot{V}O_2$max. Running-specific strength training should also augment maximal running speed because it increases the amount of force applied to the ground per step, thereby extending stride length. Maximal running velocity is simply the optimal combination of stride length and stride rate.

- Hill training focuses on running economy and maximal running velocity. Hill training is the most specific form of running-specific strength training since an athlete is actually running while carrying it out. Hill work has been linked with enhancement of running economy[9] and increases in maximal running velocity.[10]

- Explosive training optimizes running cadence, maximal running velocity, running economy, v$\dot{V}O_2$max, lactate-threshold speed, and performance. Explosive strength training involves conducting running-specific, high-speed drills and exercises that use minimal ground-contact times. It enhances running economy in well-trained endurance runners.[11] Explosive training also upgrades stride rate during intense running and improves 5K running performance by about 3 percent in well-conditioned runners.[1] A combination of explosive one-leg jumps and maximal sprints carried out over a period of approximately 6 weeks can improve maximal running speed by about 2 percent, lactate-threshold velocity by 3.5 percent, 800- and 1,500-meter speeds by approximately 3.6 percent, and 5K velocity by 1.2 percent.[12] Finally, explosive training can upgrade 3K (1.9 mi) performances by about 3 percent and alter muscle stiffness in a way that significantly enhances running economy.[2]

Chapter 22 outlined the four-phase system that provides the optimal periodization plan for these four critically important forms of strength training. An actual training program that includes periodization of strength training and simultaneous, proper progressions of pure running workouts is provided later in this chapter for the half marathon, one of the most popular race distances. Appropriate formats and advances in difficulty for circuit training, running-specific strength training, hill work, explosive training, and quality running sessions are included.

Special Warm-Up

Many runners simply jog easily, stretch, and carry out some fairly non-specific drills to warm up, but the value of a warm-up can be enhanced if it does more than just elevate your heart rate and loosen up your muscles a little. It's good to turn the warm-up into a small-scale strength workout, too, so that you are improving your strength while you are getting ready to run. It's also good to wake up your nervous system, not just your heart, during a warm-up. The special warm-up (SWU), developed by Walt Reynolds, accomplishes that, too. After a couple of times, the SWU will become routine—and even fun to carry out.

Here are some key SWU pointers:

- Stay relaxed as you do the exercises.
- Don't look at your feet as you perform the various drills. Look ahead, as you would do when running. Always try to maintain good running posture with your torso and head relaxed and well balanced.
- Once you have completed the last component of the SWU, move immediately into the workout. If you rest for more than a minute or so between the SWU and the main body of your training session, some of the benefits of the SWU will be lost.
- When you first begin carrying out the SWU, make sure that all your bouncing, hopping, and skipping is completed on a forgiving surface such as grass, soft dirt, carpet, or resilient gym floor. Avoid concrete and tarmac, at least for the first few weeks.

- In your schedule, the SWU counts for 2.3 miles (3.7 km) of running with .25 quality miles (400 m).
- In general, you will complete the SWU, or something like it, before all quality running workouts and before your competitions.

The SWU program outline follows; after that, a selection of the exercises used in the SWU is provided with detailed explanations and photos. The entire SWU takes about 20 to 25 minutes to complete.

1. Jog easily for about 10 minutes to loosen up.
2. Toe walk.
    a. Toe walk with toes pointed straight ahead for 20 meters (66 ft).
    b. Toe walk with toes pointed outward for 20 meters.
    c. Toe walk with toes pointed inward for 20 meters.
    d. Repeat each toe walk for another 20 meters.
3. Heel walk.
    a. Heel walk with toes pointed straight ahead for 20 meters.
    b. Heel walk with toes pointed outward for 20 meters.
    c. Heel walk with toes pointed inward for 20 meters.
    d. Repeat each heel walk for another 20 meters.
4. Skip.
    a. Skip for 20 meters with toes pointed straight ahead, landing on midfoot.
    b. Skip for 20 meters with toes pointed outward, landing on midfoot.
    c. Skip for 20 meters with toes pointed inward, landing on midfoot.
    d. Skip, landing on toes, all three ways.
5. Spring jog.
    a. Spring jog for 1 minute followed by 10 seconds of regular jogging.
    b. Spring jog, alternating three consecutive contacts by one foot with three ground contacts by the other foot for 20 meters followed by 10 seconds of regular jogging. Repeat two more times.
    c. Spring jog on one foot for 20 meters, then on the other foot for 20 meters. Rest and then repeat.
6. Dorsiflexion bounce.
    a. Complete 12 bounces and then rest for 10 seconds.
    b. Complete 12 more bounces.
    c. After 6 to 8 weeks, do this exercise on one foot at a time.
7. Rhythm bounce.
    a. Complete 10 jumps at moderately fast speed and with medium height; then rest for a few seconds.

   b. Complete 20 jumps with a 1-inch (3 cm) height as quickly as possible.

   c. Complete this exercise on one foot after 6 to 8 weeks.

 8. Jog easily for 1 minute or so.

 9. Speed bound 4 × 50 meters at a pace that feels nearly as intense as 1,500-meter race speed; jog easily for about 20 seconds between the reps.

10. Run 2 × 100 meters at what feels like 5K pace or faster with a short jog recovery between the intervals.

11. Jog easily for 1 minute to end the SWU and then begin the workout.

Used courtesy of Walter Reynolds III.

Toe Walk   Walk with toes pointed straight ahead, getting as high up as possible on the toes (figure 23.1*a*). Keep the legs relatively straight and take fairly small steps. Then, walk as high as possible on the toes with toes pointed outward about 45 degrees. Rotate the legs outward *from the hips* during this movement (figure 23.1*b*). Don't merely turn each foot at the ankle; involve the whole leg in the rotation. Finally, walk high on the toes with toes pointed inward. As you do, rotate the legs inward at the hips (figure 23.1*c*) not just at the ankles. For each step, when the non-weight-bearing foot swings forward, make sure the foot dorsiflexes as much as possible with the toes coming as close to the shins as possible while the foot is in the air.

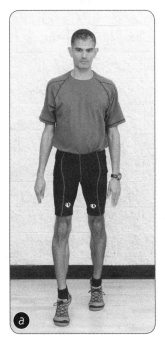  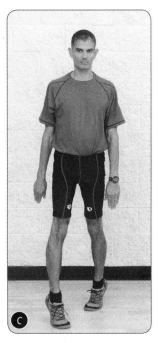

▶ **Figure 23.1**   Toes *(a)* straight ahead, *(b)* turned outward, and *(c)* turned inward.

Heel Walk   Walk on your heels with toes pointed straight, getting as high up as possible on your heels. Keep the legs relatively straight and take fairly small steps (figure 23.2). Use a coordinated movement and erect posture while keeping the ankles dorsiflexed as much as possible. Then, walk on your heels with toes pointed outward and then with toes pointed inward.

▶ **Figure 23.2**   Heel walk with toes straight.

Spring Jog   Jog with short, springy steps, landing on the midfoot with each contact and springing upward after impact (figure 23.3a-c). Your ankles act like coiled springs, compressing slightly with each midfoot landing and then recoiling quickly, causing you to bound upward and forward. Move with quick, small, spring-like strides, alternating feet as if running.

Additional versions of the spring jog include alternating the feet in various patterns. One variation is to spring jog for the desired distance, alternating three consecutive spring-like ground contacts, or hops, with one foot and then three contacts with the other. Another variation is to hop for the desired distance on one foot and then switch to the other for the same distance.

For all variations, be sure to land on the midfoot with each ground contact. As you become stronger and more skilled with spring jogging, increase the length, amplitude (i.e., vertical height), and quickness of each hop.

▶ **Figure 23.3** The spring jog *(a)* preparation, *(b)* explosive take-off, and *(c)* landing, quickly followed by an explosive take-off on the opposite foot.

Dorsiflexion Bounce Begin jumping vertically to a moderate height, landing on the midfoot with both feet; then spring upward quickly after each ground contact (figure 23.4). Keep the legs relatively straight; barely flex the knees. Dorsiflex the ankles, pulling the toes toward the shins on each jump up; plantar-flex the ankles slightly by pointing the toes just before ground contact. After 6 to 8 weeks, do this exercise on one foot at a time.

▶ **Figure 23.4** Ankles are dorsiflexed on each ascent.

Rhythm Bounce Start by jumping in place at a moderately fast speed, with medium height. Don't try for maximal verticality as if dunking a basketball. Keep the legs relatively straight on the jumps (figure 23.5). Use maximal ankle motion and action with little flexion or extension at the knees and hips.

Another version is to change the amplitude, or height, of the jumps to less than an inch (3 cm) and complete the jumps as fast as possible as if your feet were hitting a hot stove and you want to minimize ground-contact time. Use maximal ankle motion and action with little flexion or extension at the knees and hips.

▶ **Figure 23.5** Relatively straight legs and maximal ankle action.

Speed Bound Run fast and focus on pushing against the ground with more force than usual (figure 23.6). Keep the foot-strike time short and take longer strides than normal. Be certain to utilize mid-foot landings.

▶ **Figure 23.6** Bound with extra force.

Half-Marathon Training Program

The 26-week half-marathon training program that follows includes a properly progressing strength-training regimen that incorporates all four phases.

For the circuit workouts included in the program, perform the exercises in the order presented. Move quickly from exercise to exercise but don't perform the drills themselves overly hastily. In other words, don't sacrifice good form to get them done in a hurry. The idea is to do each exercise methodically and efficiently—and then almost immediately start on the next exercise. Complete the SWU when indicated; no SWU is needed for the easy workouts.

The heel and toe walks noted in the half-marathon training program tables are described in the SWU section earlier in this chapter; many of the exercises listed in the program tables are presented in detail and with photos in chapters 13 and 14. Descriptions and photos for exercises not yet covered in the text are presented after the half-marathon training program tables.

Half-Marathon Training Program Week 1

Monday	**Circuit workout I**
	Warm-up: 1.5 mi (2.4 km) of easy jogging
	  1. 400-m (.25 mi on treadmill) run at what feels like 10K pace*
	  2. 3 chin-ups**
	  3. 40 sit-ups
	  4. 15 six-count squat thrusts (burpees)
	  5. 15 bench dips
	  6. 400-m run at 10K intensity
	  7. 6 feet-elevated push-ups
	  8. 12 squat and dumbbell presses using 10-lb (4.5 kg) dumbbells
	  9. 40 low-back extensions
	  10. 10 lunges with each leg
	  11. 400-m run at 10K effort
	  12. Repeat steps 2-11 for two circuits total
	Cool-down: 1.5 mi (2.5 km) of easy running
	Totals: 4.25 mi (6.84 km) of running with 1.25 quality mi (2.01 km)

Tuesday	4 mi (6 km) of easy running

Wednesday	**Circuit workout II**
	Progressions occur in steps 3, 8, 9, and 11.
	Warm-up: SWU
	  1. 400-m run at what feels like 10K pace*
	  2. 30 wall shin raises and 30 pulses
	  3. 45 sit-ups
	  4. 15 six-count squat thrusts (burpees)
	  5. 12 bench dips
	  6. 400-m run at 10K intensity
	  7. 6 feet-elevated push-ups
	  8. 20 two-leg squats (body-weight squats)
	  9. 45 low-back extensions
	  10. 10 lunges with each leg
	  11. .3-mi (.5 km) run at 10K effort
	  12. Repeat steps 2-11 for two circuits total
	Cool-down: 1.5 mi (2.4 km) of easy running
	Totals: 5.15 mi (8.29 km) of running with 1.6 quality mi (2.6 km)

Thursday	6 mi (9.7 km) of easy running
Friday	Rest
Saturday	One hour of moderate-intensity cross-training (e.g., elliptical machine, swimming, cycling, rowing)

Sunday	**v$\dot{V}O_2$max test**
	This is a no-pressure test to obtain a baseline reading for v$\dot{V}O_2$max. Relax and do as well as you can.
	Warm-up: SWU
	  1. Run as far as you can for 6 minutes and record your distance.
	  2. Recover with 800 m of easy jogging.
	  3. Run 2 × 3 minutes each time covering about half the distance of the 6-minute test and jog easily for 3 minutes to recover between the intervals.
	Cool-down: 2 mi (3.2 km) of easy running
	Totals: ~7.1 mi (11.4 km) of running with ~2.2 quality mi (3.5 km)

	Weekly totals: 26.5 mi (42.7 km) of running with 5.05 quality mi (8.13 km) (19% of total)

*Don't worry about the actual time. Relax and run fluidly and powerfully with the kind of intensity you would use in a 10K race. This can also be completed on a treadmill.

**If no chin bar is available, substitute 2 sets of biceps curls with 10-lb (4.5 kg) dumbbells, alternating arm action, about 10 reps on each arm; the first time, stand on one foot; the second time, stand on the other foot while doing the curls.

Half-Marathon Training Program Week 2

Monday	Rest
Tuesday	**Circuit workout III** Progressions occur in steps 4, 10, and 11. Warm-up: SWU 1. 400-m run at what feels like 10K pace 2. 10 one-leg biceps curls with each arm; alternate arm action with 10-lb (4.5 kg) dumbbells for 2 sets.* 3. 45 sit-ups 4. 18 six-count squat thrusts (burpees) 5. 15 bench dips 6. 400 m run at 10K intensity 7. 7 feet-elevated push-ups 8. 12 squat and dumbbell presses on two legs with 10-lb dumbbells 9. 45 low-back extensions 10. 10 one-leg squats with each leg 11. 800-m run at 10K effort 12. Repeat steps 2-11 for two circuits total Cool-down: 2 mi (3.2 km) of easy running Total: 6.05 mi (9.74 km) of running with 2 quality mi (3.2 km)
Wednesday	6 mi (9.7 km) of easy running (no SWU for easy workouts)
Thursday	**v$\dot{V}O_2$max session** Warm-up: SWU Run 12 × 200 m at v$\dot{V}O_2$max time established in previous Sunday's test with jog recoveries that are equal in duration to the work-interval periods. Cool-down: 2 mi of easy running Total: ~6.55 mi (10.54 km) of running with 1.75 quality mi (2.82 km)
Friday	Rest
Saturday	**Circuit workout IV** Progressions occur in steps 10 and 11. Warm-up: SWU 1. 400-m run at what feels like 10K pace 2. 10 one-leg biceps curls with each arm; alternate arm action with 10-lb dumbbells* 3. 45 sit-ups 4. 18 six-count squat thrusts (burpees) 5. 15 bench dips 6. 400-m run at 10K intensity 7. 7 feet-elevated push-ups 8. 12 squat and dumbbell presses on two legs with 10-lb dumbbells 9. 45 low-back extensions 10. 10 one-leg squats with each leg with 5-pound (2.3 kg) dumbbells in hands) 11. 1,000-m (.62 mi) run at 10K effort 12. Repeat steps 2-11 for two circuits total Cool-down: 2 mi of easy running Total: 6.3 mi (10.1 km) of running with 2.25 quality mi (3.62 km)
Sunday	6 mi of easy running (no SWU)
	Weekly totals: 30.9 mi (49.7 km) of running with 6 quality mi (9.7 km) (19% of total)

*The first time, stand on one foot; the second time, stand on the other foot while doing the curls.

Half-Marathon Training Program Week 3

Monday	**Sustained tempo run** Warm-up: 2 mi (3.2 km) of light, relaxed running In an area where you enjoy running, run a couple of 100-m intervals at what feels like 5K pace with a short jog break after each; then run 3 mi (4.8 km) continuously, pushing the pace throughout to feel like 10K effort. Cool-down: 2 mi of easy running Total: 7.25 mi (11.67 km), with 3.1 quality mi (4.9 km)
Tuesday	3 mi (4.8 km) of easy running (no SWU)
Wednesday	Progressions occur in steps 1-5. Warm-up: 2 mi of light running (no SWU) 1. 15 one-leg biceps curls with 10-lb (4.5 kg) dumbbells with each arm; alternate arm action* 2. 10 one-leg heel raises on a block or step on one leg and then on the other 3. 20-m (66 ft) heel walk straight forward and then 20-m heel walk straight backward (!) with smooth, coordinated movement and erect posture; keep ankles dorsiflexed and move toes as far toward shins as possible** 4. 20-m toe walk forward and backward; stay high up on toes; keep posture relaxed 5. 10 one-leg balance and reach with toes, 10 reps on one foot and then 10 on the other; maintain relaxed, fairly upright posture at all times 6. Repeat steps 1-5 one more time Cool-down: 3 mi (4.8 km) of easy running
Thursday	5 mi (8 km) of easy running
Friday	Rest
Saturday	Progressions occur in steps 1-3. Warm-up: 2 mi of light running (no SWU) 1. 10 one-leg biceps curls with 10-lb dumbbells with each arm; alternate arm action* 2. 10 one-leg overhead dumbbell presses with 10-lb dumbbells* 3. 12 one-leg heel raises on a block or step, first on one leg and then on the other*** 4. 20-m heel walk straight forward and then 20-m heel walk straight backward (!) 5. 20-m toe walk forward and backward with opposite-ankle dorsiflexion; stay high up on toes and keep posture relaxed 6. 10 one-leg balance and reach with toes: 10 reps on one foot and then 10 on the other; maintain relaxed, fairly upright posture at all times 7. Repeat steps 1-6 one more time Cool-down: 3 mi of easy running
Sunday	**v$\dot{V}O_2$max session** Warm-up: SWU Run 8 × 400 m at v$\dot{V}O_2$max, with jog recoveries that are equal in duration to the work-interval periods. Cool-down: 2 mi of easy running Total: ~7.3 mi (11.8 km) of running with 2.25 quality mi (3.62 km)
	Weekly totals: 32.55 mi (52.38 km) of running with 5.35 quality mi (8.61 km) (16% of total)

*Stand on one foot only with running-specific posture: Don't let other hip droop down; keep other hip slightly flexed as though that leg was beginning to swing forward. Perform 2 sets with each arm while standing on each foot.

**Yep—that means actually walking backward; don't just turn around and go the other way.

***Continue in a smooth, rhythmic manner until you have completed 12 reps on one foot; rest for a few seconds and then complete 12 on the other foot.

Half-Marathon Training Program Week 4: Recovery Week

Monday	5 mi (8 km) of easy running
Tuesday	**Circuit workout V** Progression occurs in step 6. Warm-up: SWU 1. 400-m run at what feels like 10K pace 2. 10 one-leg biceps curls with 10-lb (4.5 kg) dumbbells with each arm; alternate arm action* 3. 45 sit-ups 4. 18 six-count squat thrusts (burpees) 5. 15 bench dips 6. 800-m (.5 mi) run at 10K intensity 7. 7 feet-elevated push-ups 8. 12 squat and dumbbell presses on two legs with 10-lb dumbbells 9. 45 low-back extensions 10. 10 one-leg squats with each leg with 5-lb (2.3 kg) dumbbells 11. 800-m run at 10K effort 12. Repeat steps 2-11 for two circuits in all Cool-down: 2 mi (3.2 km) of easy running Total: 7.55 mi (12.15 km) of running with 2.5 quality mi (4.02 km)
Wednesday	3 mi (4.8 km) of easy running
Thursday	Rest
Friday	Progressions occur in steps 2 and 4-9. Warm-up: 2 mi of light running (no SWU); then perform the following: 1. 20 one-leg biceps curls with each arm; alternating arm action* 2. 20 one-leg overhead presses (light dumbbells today); move the arms quickly without losing control 3. 15 one-leg heel raises on a block or step first on one leg and then on the other 4. 20-m (66 ft) heel walk straight forward; keep toes pointed outward by rotating the legs outward at the hips; use smooth, coordinated movement and keep posture erect and ankles dorsiflexed 5. 20-m heel walk; keep toes pointed inward by rotating the legs inward at the hips; maintain smooth, coordinated movement and erect posture; keep ankles dorsiflexed 6. 20-m toe walk forward with opposite-ankle dorsiflexion; rotate hips out and keep toes pointed out 7. 20-m toe walk forward with opposite-ankle dorsiflexion; keep toes pointed in by rotating the legs inward at the hips 8. 12 one-leg balance and reach with toes: 12 reps on one foot and then 12 on the other; maintain relaxed, fairly upright posture at all times 9. 10 one-leg, straight-leg dead lifts with weighted bar 10. Repeat steps 1-9 one more time Cool-down: 5 mi of easy running
Saturday	Rest
Sunday	**Fartlek session** Warm-up: ~1.5 mi (2.4 km) of light loping Then alternate 2- to 3-minute relaxed but explosive bursts at what feels like 5K tempo with 1- to 2-minute floats at an easy tempo until you have been running for a total of 4 mi Cool-down: 1.5 mi (2.4 km) of easy running Total: ~7 mi (11.3 km) of running with ~3 quality mi (4.8 km)
	Weekly totals: 27.55 mi (44.34 km) of running with 5.5 quality mi (8.9 km) (20% of total)

*For the first time, stand on one foot; the second time, stand on the other foot while performing the curls (no dumbbells today); speed up the pace of your arm movements without losing control.

Half-Marathon Training Program Week 5

Monday	6 mi (9.7 km) of easy running
Tuesday	**Circuit workout VI** Progression occurs in step 11. Warm-up: SWU 1. 400-m run at what feels like 10K pace 2. 10 one-leg biceps curls with 10-lb (4.5 kg) dumbbells for 2 sets; alternate arm action* 3. 45 sit-ups 4. 18 six-count squat thrusts (burpees) 5. 15 bench dips 6. 800-m (.5 mi) run at 10K intensity 7. 7 feet-elevated push-ups 8. 12 squat and dumbbell presses on two legs with 10-lb dumbbells 9. 45 low-back extensions 10. 10 one-leg squats with each leg with 5-lb (2.3 kg) dumbbells 11. 800-m (.5 mi) run with 5K effort 12. Repeat steps 2-11 for two circuits total Cool-down: 2 mi (3.2 km) of easy running Total: 7.55 mi (12.15 km) of running with 2.5 quality mi (4.02 km)
Wednesday	6 mi of easy running
Thursday	Progression occurs in step 8 with new exercise. Warm-up: 2 mi (3.2 km) of light running (no SWU); then perform the following: 1. 10 one-leg biceps curls with alternating arm action: 10 reps on one foot, short break, and then 10 reps on the other foot 2. 10 one-leg alternating overhead dumbbell presses first on one foot and then on the other foot with a short break in between 3. 15 one-leg heel raises on a block, step, or platform first on one leg and then on the other 4. 12 one-leg balance and reach with toes: 12 reps on one foot and then 12 on the other; maintain relaxed, fairly upright posture at all times 5. 8 one-leg, straight-leg dead lifts: 8 reps on one foot and then 8 reps on the other 6. 15 one-leg squats with 10-lb dumbbells in hands: 15 reps on one leg and then 15 reps on the other leg 7. 15 bench dips 8. 15 runner's poses with each leg 9. Repeat steps 1-8 one more time Cool-down: 4 mi (6.4 km) of easy running
Friday	Rest
Saturday	**5K-type intervals** Warm-up: SWU Run 5 × 800 m at 5K pace (i.e., about 12 seconds slower per 800 m compared with v$\dot{V}O_2$max) with 3-minute jog recoveries after the first four intervals. Cool-down: 1 mi of easy running Total: 7.3 mi (11.7 km) with 2.75 quality mi (4.43 km)
Sunday	5 mi (8 km) of easy running
	Weekly totals: 37.85 mi (60.56 km) of running with 5.25 quality mi (8.45 km) (14% of total)

*The first time, stand on one foot; the second time, stand on the other foot while performing the curls.

Half-Marathon Training Program Week 6

Monday	**Tempo session** Warm-up: SWU Run 3 mi (4.8 km) with 10K feel (i.e., pace should be about 40 seconds per mile slower than $v\dot{V}O_2$. Cool-down: 2 mi (3.2 km) easy running Total: ~7.3 mi (11.8 km) with 3.25 quality mi (5.23 km)
Tuesday	Progression occurs in step 8 with a new exercise. Warm-up: 2 mi (3.2 km) of light running 1. 10 one-leg biceps curls with alternating arm action: 10 reps on one foot, short break, and then 10 reps on the other foot 2. 10 one-leg alternating overhead dumbbell presses first on one foot and then on the other foot with a short break in between 3. 15 one-leg heel raises on a block, step, or platform first on one leg and then on the other leg 4. 12 one-leg balance and reach with toes: 12 reps on one foot and then 12 on the other foot; maintain relaxed, fairly upright posture at all times 5. 8 one-leg, straight-leg dead lifts: 8 reps on one foot and then 8 reps on the other 6. 15 one-leg squats with 10-lb (4.5 km) dumbbells in hands: 15 reps on one leg, and then 15 reps on the other leg 7. 15 bench dips 8. Medicine ball drills* 9. Repeat steps 1-8 Cool-down: 4 mi (6.4 km) of easy running.
Wednesday	5 mi (8 km) of easy running
Thursday	7 mi (11.3 km) of easy running
Friday	Rest
Saturday	**$v\dot{V}O_2$max session** Warm-up: SWU Run 9 × 400 m at $v\dot{V}O_2$max with jog recoveries equal in duration to the work-interval periods. Cool-down: 2 mi (3.2 km) of easy running Total: 7.7 mi (12.39 km) with 2.5 quality mi (4.02 km)
Sunday	6 mi (9.7 km) of relaxed running in an area where you really like to run
	Weekly totals: 39 mi (63 km) of running with 5.75 quality mi (9.25 km) (15% of total)

*New exercise

Half-Marathon Training Program Week 7

Monday	Progressions occur in steps 5 and 7 and the cool-down. Warm-up: 2 mi (3.2 km) of light running (no SWU) 1. 10 one-leg biceps curls with a 10-lb (4.5 kg) dumbbell alternating arm action: 10 reps on one foot, short break, and then 10 reps on the other foot 2. 10 one-leg overhead presses with 10-lb (4.5 kg) dumbbells alternating arm action; first on one foot and then on the other foot with short break in between 3. 15 one-leg heel raises on a block, step, or platform first on one leg and then on the other leg 4. 12 one-leg balance and reach with toes: 12 reps on one foot and then 12 on the other foot; maintain relaxed, fairly upright posture at all times 5. 10 one-leg, straight-leg dead lifts with 5-lb (2.3 kg) dumbbells in each hand: 10 reps on one foot and then 10 reps on the other foot 6. 15 one-leg squats with 10-lb (4.5 kg) dumbbells in hands: 15 reps on one leg and then 15 reps on the other leg) 7. 18 bench dips 8. Medicine ball drills 9. Don't repeat steps 1-8 Cool-down: 3 mi (4.8 km) of easy running
Tuesday	**Quality paces** Warm-up: SWU Run 1 mile about 16 seconds per mile slower than 10K pace followed by a 4-minute jog recovery; then run 1 mile at 10K pace with a 4-minute jog recovery; and then run 1 mile at 5K pace (i.e., 16 seconds faster than 10K mile). Cool-down: 2 mi (3.2 km) of easy running Total: 8.3 mi (13.4 km) with 3.25 quality mi (5.23 km)
Wednesday	6 mi (9.7 km) of easy running
Thursday	Warm-up: SWU 1. Medicine ball drills 2. 30 bicycle leg swings: 30 swings with one leg and then 30 with the other leg 3. 15 one-leg squats with 10-lb (4.5 kg) dumbbells in hands: 15 reps on each leg 4. 18 bench dips 5. 10 one-leg dead lifts with 10-lb (4.5 kg) dumbbells in hands: 10 reps on one foot and then 10 reps on the other 6. 20 runner's poses per leg 7. 10 pistol squats: 10 reps on one leg and then 10 reps on the other 8. Repeat steps 1-7 Cool-down: 4 mi (6.4 km) of easy running. Total: 6.3 mi (10.1 km) of running with .25 quality mi (.40 km)
Friday	Rest
Saturday	**5K repeats** Warm-up: SWU 3 × 1 mile at 5K pace with 4-minute jog recoveries after the first 2 miles Cool-down: 2 mi (3.2 km) of easy running after the third mile Total: 8.3 mi (13.4 km) of running with 3.25 quality mi (5.23 km)
Sunday	7 mi (11.3 km) of easy running
	Weekly totals: 40.9 mi (65.8 km) of running with 6.75 quality mi (12.47 km) (17% of total)

Half-Marathon Training Program Week 8: Recovery Week

Monday	**Strength session** Repeat Thursday session from week 7. Total: 6.3 mi (10.1 km) of running with .25 quality mi (.04 km)
Tuesday	3 mi (4.8 km) of easy running
Wednesday	**Specific half-marathon prep** Warm-up: SWU 4 mi (6.4 km) at half-marathon intensity (i.e., about 56 seconds per mile slower than v$\dot{V}O_2$max) Cool-down: 1 mi of easy running Total: 7.3 mi (11.8 km) of running with 4.25 quality mi (6.84 km)
Thursday	4 mi (6.4 km) of easy running
Friday	Rest
Saturday	Progressions occur in steps 2, 8, and 9. Warm-up: SWU 1. Medicine ball drills 2. 40 bicycle leg swings: 40 swings with one leg and 40 swings with the other leg 3. 15 one-leg squats with 10-lb (4.5 kg) dumbbells in hands; 15 reps on each leg 4. 18 bench dips 5. 10 one-leg dead lifts with 10-lb dumbbells in hands: 10 reps on one foot and then 10 reps on the other foot 6. 20 runner's poses per leg 7. 10 pistol squats: 10 reps on one leg and then 10 reps on the other leg 8. 8 one-leg push-ups: 8 push-ups with only one foot in contact with ground and 8 with only the other foot in contact with ground* 9. 8 alternating walking lunges with each leg with 5-lb (2.3 kg) dumbbells 10. Repeat steps 1-9 Cool-down: 3 mi (4.8 km) of easy running Total: 5.3 mi (8.5 km) of running with .25 quality mi (.4 km)
Sunday	Warm-up: 2 mi (3.2 km) of easy running 3 mi of fartlek running; change pace often, surge when you feel ready, jog effortlessly when you need to, and stay relaxed at all times. Cool-down: 1 mi of easy running Total: 6 mi (9.7 km) of running with ~2 quality mi (3.2 km)
	Weekly totals: 31.9 mi (51.3 km) of running with 6.5 quality mi (10.5 km) (20% of total)

*Performed on floor or with hands on bench if necessary.

Half-Marathon Training Program Week 9

Monday	Rest
Tuesday	**Mini-tempo session** Warm-up: SWU 2 mi (3.2 km) at 10K pace Cool-down: 3 mi (4.8 km) of easy running Total: 7.3 mi (11.8 km) of running with 2.25 quality mi (3.62 km)
Wednesday	**Strength session** Repeat Saturday from week 8 Total: 6.3 mi (10.1 km) of running with .25 quality mi (.4 km)
Thursday	7 mi (11.3 km) of relaxed, light, easy running
Friday	**Lactate stackers** Warm-up: SWU Run 8 × 1 minute intervals at faster than v$\dot{V}O_2$max with 2-minute easy jog recoveries Cool-down: 2 mi (3.2 km) of easy running Total: ~7.7 mi (12.30 km) of running with ~1.7 quality mi (2.7 km)

Saturday	Progressions occur in steps 3, 6, and 9.
	Warm-up: 2 mi (3.2 km) of light running to get loose
	  1. Medicine ball drills
	  2. 40 bicycle leg swings: 40 swings with one leg and 40 swings with the
	     other leg
	  3. 12 strong one-leg fatigue-fighting rows
	  4. 15 one-leg squats with 10-lb (4.5 kg) dumbbells in hands: 15 reps on each leg
	  5. 18 bench dips
	  6. Side walking with strength band for 20 m (20 yd) in each direction
	  7. 10 one-leg dead lifts with 10-lb dumbbells in hands: 10 reps on one foot
	     and then 10 reps on the other foot
	  8. 8 one-leg push-ups: 8 push-ups on one foot and then 8 on the other foot
	     with a short break in between
	  9. 10 alternating walking lunges with each leg with 5-lb (2.3 kg) dumbbells
	  10. Repeat steps 1-9
	Cool-down: 4 mi (6.4 km) of easy running

Sunday	Rest
	Weekly totals: 34.3 mi (55.2 km) of running with 4.2 quality mi (6.8 km) (12% of total)

Half-Marathon Training Program Week 10

Monday	7 mi (11.3 km) of relaxed, easy running
Tuesday	**Mega-tempo session** Warm-up: SWU 4 mi (6.4 km) with 10K feel Cool-down: 2 mi (3.2 km) of easy running Total: 8.3 mi (13.4 km) of running with 4.25 quality mi (6.84 km)
Wednesday	5 mi (8 km) of easy running
Thursday	**Strength session** Repeat Saturday from week 9
Friday	Rest
Saturday	**v$\dot{V}O_2$max session** Warm-up: SWU 10 × 400 m at v$\dot{V}O_2$max with jog recoveries equal in duration to the work-interval periods Cool-down: 1 mi of easy running Total: ~7.7 mi (12.39 km) of running with 2.75 quality mi (4.43 km)
Sunday	**Strength session** Similar to Thursday session but with reasonable progressions in resistance and reps if possible
	Weekly totals: 40 mi (64.4 km) of running with 7 quality mi (11.3 km) (18% of total)

Half-Marathon Training Program Week 11

Monday	60 minutes of easy cross-training (e.g., cycling, swimming, rowing, elliptical machine)
Tuesday	6 mi (9.7 km) of easy running

Wednesday	A progression occurs in step 5.
	Warm-up: 2 mi (3.2 km) of light running
	  1. Medicine ball drills
	  2. 40 bicycle leg swings: 40 swings with one leg and 40 swings with the other
	  3. 15 one-leg fatigue-fighting rows per leg
	  4. 15 one-leg squats with 10-lb (4.5 kg) dumbbells in hands: 15 reps per leg
	  5. 20 bench dips
	  6. 10 m (33 ft) of side walking with strength band in one direction and then in the other direction for the same distance
	  7. 10 one-leg dead lifts per leg with 10-lb (4.5 kg) dumbbells in hands
	  8. 8 one-leg push-ups: 8 push-ups on only one foot and then 8 on only the other foot with a short break in between
	  9. 10 alternating walking lunges with each leg with 5-lb (2.3 kg) dumbbells
	 10. Repeat steps 1-9
	Cool-down: 4 mi (6.4 km) of easy running

Thursday	**v$\dot{V}O_2$max plus** Warm-up: SWU Run 10 × 1 minute at a pace a little faster than v$\dot{V}O_2$max; complete 2-minutes of easy jogging between reps for recovery. Cool-down: 1 mi of easy running Total: ~7 mi (11.3 km) of running with ~2 quality mi (3.2 km)
Friday	Rest

Saturday	Progressions occur in steps 4, 6, and 8.
	Warm-up: 2 mi (3.2 km) of light running
	  1. Medicine ball drills
	  2. 20 bench dips
	  3. 10 one-leg dead lifts per leg with 10-lb (4.5 kg) dumbbells in hands
	  4. 8 one-leg lunge squats with jumps
	  5. One-leg push-ups: 8 push-ups on one foot and then 8 on the other foot with a short break between
	  6. 15 high-knee explosions
	  7. 10 m (33 ft) of side walking with strength band in one direction and then in the other direction for the same distance
	  8. 2 × 20 seconds of Shane's in-place accelerations (SIPAs) with a short break in between
	  9. Repeat steps 1-8 one time
	Cool-down: 4 mi (6.4 km) of easy running

Sunday	**Half-marathon prep** Warm-up: 2 mi (3.2. km) of easy running 5 mi (8 km) at half-marathon intensity (i.e., about 56 seconds per mile slower than v$\dot{V}O_2$max) Cool-down: 2-mi of easy running Total: 9 mi (14.5 km) of running with 5 quality mi (8.0 km)
	Weekly totals: 34 mi (54.7 km) of running with 7 quality mi (11.3 km) (21% of total)

Half-Marathon Training Program Week 12

Monday	60 minutes of easy cross-training (e.g., cycling, swimming, rowing, elliptical machine)
Tuesday	7 mi (11.3 km) of easy running
Wednesday	**v$\dot{V}O_2$max session** Warm-up: SWU 5 × 800 at v$\dot{V}O_2$max with jog recoveries equal in duration to the work-interval periods after the first four work intervals Cool-down: 2 mi (3.2 km) of easy running Total: ~8.3 mi (13.4 km) of running with 2.75 quality mi (4.43 km)
Thursday	Progressions occur in steps 2, 4-6, 8, and 9. Warm-up: 2 mi (3.2 km) of light running 1. Medicine ball drills 2. 10 single-leg lunge squats with jumps and 5-lb (2.3 kg) dumbbells in hands: 10 reps per leg 3. 20 bench dips 4. 12 snap-'n'-taps: perform 12 taps while hopping at least 36 times; rest for a moment and then reverse the hopping and tapping feet 5. 10 alternating walking lunges with each leg with 10-lb (4.5 kg) dumbbells* 6. 12 one-leg hand walk to triceps push-ups 7. 15 high-knee explosions 8. 15 m (49 ft) of side walking with strength band in one direction and then in the other direction for the same distance 9. 2 × 25 seconds of Shane's in-place accelerations (SIPAs) with a short break in between. 10. Repeat steps 1-9 one time Cool-down: 4 mi (6.4 km) of easy running
Friday	Rest
Saturday	**5K mile repeats** Warm-up: SWU 3 × 1 mi at 5K pace with 3-minute jog recoveries after the first two intervals Cool-down: 2 mi (3.2 km) of easy running Total: 8.3 mi (13.4 km) of running with 3.25 quality mi (5.23 km)
Sunday	**Explosive strength session** Repeat of Thursday session
	Weekly totals: 35.6 mi (57.3 km) of running with 6 quality mi (9.7 km) (17% of total)

*Move forward continuously as you do this exercise.

Half-Marathon Training Program Week 13

Monday	6 mi (9.7 km) of easy running
Tuesday	**Lactate stackers** Warm-up: SWU Run 10 × 1 minute at a pace at faster than v$\dot{V}O_2$max; complete 2 minutes of easy jogging between reps for recovery. Cool-down: 1 mi of easy running Total: 7 mi (11.3 km) of running with 2 quality mi (3.2 km)
Wednesday	6 mi of easy running

Thursday	Progressions occur in steps 2, 6, 7, and 9.
	Warm-up: 2 mi of light running
	  1. Medicine ball drills
	  2. 10 single-leg lunge (on each side) squats with jumps with 10-lb (4.5 kg) dumbbells in hands: 10 reps on one leg, 12 reps on the other leg
	  3. 20 bench dips
	  4. 15 snap-'n'-taps: 15 taps while hopping at least 45 times on the opposite leg; rest for a moment and reverse legs.
	  5. 10 alternating walking lunges with each leg with 10-lb dumbbells*
	  6. 8 one-leg hand walk to triceps push-ups on each leg; alternate between legs
	  7. 18 high-knee explosions
	  8. 15 m (49 ft) of side walking with strength band in one direction and then in the other direction for the same distance
	  9. 2 × 30 seconds of Shane's in-place accelerations (SIPAs) with a short break in between
	 10. Repeat steps 1-9 one time
	Cool-down: 4 mi (6.4 km) of easy running
	Total: 6 mi (9.7 km) of running with .4 quality mi (.6 km)**

Friday	Rest
Saturday	6 mi of easy running
Sunday	**Tempo session** Warm-up: SWU 3 mi (4.8 km) with 10K effort Cool-down: 3 mi of easy running Total: 8.3 mi (13.4 k) of running with 3.25 quality mi (5.23 km)
	Weekly totals: 39.3 mi (63.3. km) of running with 5.65 quality mi (9.10 km) (14% of total)

*Move forward continuously as you do this exercise.

**Start counting SIPAs in the quality total.

Half-Marathon Training Program Week 14: Recovery Week

Monday	45 minutes of easy cross training (your choice of modes)
Tuesday	Warm-up: 2 mi (3.2 km) of easy running 1. 10 one-leg biceps curls on each leg with 10-lb (4.5 kg) dumbbells 2. 10 one-leg overhead dumbbell presses on each leg with 10-lb dumbbells 3. 10 one-leg heel raises on each leg 4. 3 chin-ups* 5. 10 one-leg reaches with toes with each leg 6. 30 sit-ups 7. 30 low-back extensions 8. 18 bench dips 9. 8 one-leg hand walk to triceps push-ups: 8 reps on each leg 10. 10 m (33 ft) of side walking with strength band in one direction and then in the other direction for the same distance 11. Repeat steps 1-10 one time Cool-down: 3 mi (4.8 km) of easy running
Wednesday	**Cross-training** Warm-up: 2 mi of light running On a stair machine, climb easily for 5 minutes. Then, gradually pick up the intensity of climbing: Tweak the machine speed and the resistance, if possible, until you feel as though you're working at 5K race effort. Hit 4 × 3 minutes at this 5K intensity—it should feel like a 9 on a scale from 1-10, with 10 being maximal effort. Follow each interval with 3-minute easy-climb recoveries. Cool-down: 8 minutes of light climbing Total: ~6 mi (9.7 km) of running with ~2 quality mi
Thursday	6 mi (9.7 km) of easy running
Friday	**Cross-training** Warm-up: 12 minutes of light cycling on a stationary bike; add a couple of 30-second sprints to fire up your nervous system 1. One-leg cycling: 4 sets of 1 minute of intense cycling followed by 1 minute of recovery; repeat with the other leg 2. Cycling acceleration: 1 minute at 90 rpm then 1 minute at 100 rpm for 10 minutes 3. Cycling big gears: 1 minute easy followed by 1 minute on the highest gear; 5 times total 4. Ride 3 mi as fast as possible, pedal easily for 4 minutes, and then ride 3 mi as fast as possible Cool-down: 12 minutes of light cycling
Saturday	Rest
Sunday	7 mi (11.3 km) of easy running
	Weekly totals: 24 mi (38.6 km) of running with 2 quality mi (8% of total)

*If no chin bar is available, skip this exercise.

Half-Marathon Training Program Week 15 With 10K Race

Monday	**Hill session** Warm-up: SWU On challenging quarter-mile (.4 km) hill, carry out four climbs at 5K intensity; jog back down each time to recover. Cool-down: 2 mi (3.2 km) of easy running after the fourth recovery Total: 6.3 mi (10.1 km) of running with 1.25 quality mi (2.01 km)
Tuesday	6 mi (9.7 km) of easy running

Wednesday	Warm-up: 1.5 mi (2.4 km) of light running
	1. Medicine ball drills
	2. 12 single-leg lunge squats with jumps with 10-lb (4.5 kg) dumbbells in hands;
	   12 reps per leg
	3. 20 bench dips
	4. 15 snap-'n'-taps: 15 lightning-quick taps with one foot while hopping 45 times
	   on the other foot; after a moment of rest, change feet and repeat the exercise
	5. 12 alternating walking lunges with each leg with 10-lb dumbbells*
	6. 8 one-leg hand walk to triceps push-ups; alternate between legs
	7. 18 high-knee explosions
	8. 15 m (49 ft) of side walking with strength band in one direction and then
	   in the other direction for the same distance
	9. 5 × 30 seconds of Shane's in-place accelerations (SIPAs) with a short break
	   in between
	10. Repeat steps 1-9 one time
	Cool-down: 4 mi (6.4 km) of easy running
	Total: 6 mi (9.7 km) of running with .4 quality mi (.6 km)

Thursday	**5K Repeats** Warm-up: SWU 3 × .75 mi (1.21 km) at 5K pace with 3-minute easy jog recoveries after the first two intervals Cool-down: 1 mi of easy running Total: 6.3 mi (10.1 km) of running with 2.5 quality mi (4 km)
Friday	5 mi (8 km) of easy running
Saturday	Rest
Sunday	**10K race or simulated 10K race** Warm-up: SWU 10K of hard running Cool-down: 1 mi of easy running Total: 9.5 mi (15.3 km) of running with 6.45 quality mi (10.38 km)
	Weekly totals: 39.1 mi (62.9) of running with 10.2 quality mi (16.4 km) (26% of total)

*Move forward continuously as you do this exercise.

Half-Marathon Training Program Week 16

Monday	60 minutes of easy cycling
Tuesday	6 mi (9.7 km) of light running
Wednesday	**Hill session** Warm-up: SWU On challenging quarter-mile (.4 km) hill, carry out five climbs at 5K intensity; jog back down each time to recover Cool-down: 2 mi (3.2 km) of easy running after the fifth recovery Total: 6.8 mi (10.9 km) of running with 1.5 quality mi (2.4 km)
Thursday	6 mi (9.7 km) of easy running
Friday	Rest

Saturday	**v$\dot{V}O_2$max retest**
	Warm-up: SWU
	Run as far as you can in 6 minutes. Record your distance; jog easily for 800 m
	    to recover, and then run 2 × 3 minutes, each time covering about half the
	    distance you covered in the 6-minute test. Jog easily for 3 minutes to recover
	    between these two intervals.*
	Cool-down: 2 mi of easy running
	Total: ~7.2 mi (1.6 km) of running with ~2.3 quality mi (3.7 km)

Sunday	Warm-up: 1.5 mi (2.4 km) of light running
	  1. Medicine ball drills
	  2. 12 single-leg lunge squats with jumps with 10-lb (4.5 kg) dumbbells in hands:
	     12 reps on one leg, 12 reps on the other leg
	  3. 20 bench dips
	  4. 15 snap-'n'-taps: 15 lightning-quick taps with one foot while hopping 45 times
	     on the other foot; after a moment of rest, change feet and repeat the exercise
	  5. 12 alternating walking lunges with each leg with 10-lb dumbbells**
	  6. 8 one-leg hand walk to triceps push-ups: 8 reps on each leg alternating
	     between legs
	  7. 18 high-knee explosions
	  8. 15 m (49 ft) of side walking with strength band in one direction and then
	     in the other direction for the same distance
	  9. 5 × 30 seconds of Shane's in-place accelerations (SIPAs) with a short break
	     in between.
	 10. Repeat steps 1-9 one time
	Cool-down: 3 mi (4.8 km) of easy running
	Total: 4.9 mi (7.9 km) of running with .4 quality mi (.6 km)

	Weekly totals: 30.9 mi (49.7 km) of running with 4.2 quality mi (6.8 km) (14% of total)

*This is a no-pressure test; simply relax and do as well as you can.

**Move forward continuously as you do this exercise.

Half-Marathon Training Program Week 17: 5K Race Week

Monday	60 minutes of easy cycling
Tuesday	**New v$\dot{V}O_2$max workout** Warm-up: SWU Hit 8 × 400 m at new v$\dot{V}O_2$max with jog recoveries equal in duration to the work-interval periods. Cool-down: 2 mi (3.2 km) of easy running after the eighth recovery Total: ~7.8 mi (12.6 km) of running with 2.25 quality mi (3.62 km)
Wednesday	6 mi (9.7 km) of easy running
Thursday	**5K workout** Warm-up: SWU Run 4 × 400 m at 5K pace (6 seconds per 400 m slower than v$\dot{V}O_2$max), with jog recoveries equal in duration to the work-interval periods. Cool-down: 1 mi of easy running after the fourth recovery Total: ~5 mi (8 km) of running with 1.25 quality mi (2.01 km)
Friday	Rest
Saturday	Warm-up: SWU 5K race Cool-down: 1 mi of easy running Total: 6.4 mi (10.3 km) of running with 3.35 quality mi (5.39)
Sunday	10 mi (16.1 km) of easy running
	Weekly totals: 35.2 mi (56.7 km) of running with 6.85 quality mi (11.02 km) (19% of total)

Half-Marathon Training Program Week 18

Monday	60 minutes of light biking
Tuesday	6 mi (9.7 km) of easy running
Wednesday	**Hill session** Warm-up: SWU On challenging quarter-mile (.4 km) hill, carry out six climbs at 5K intensity; jog back down each time to recover. Cool-down: 2 mi (3.2 km) of easy running after the sixth recovery Total: 7.3 mi (11.8 km) of running with 1.75 quality mi (2.82 km)
Thursday	7 mi (11.3 km) of easy running
Friday	Rest
Saturday	**Half-marathon prep** Warm-up: SWU 6 mi at half-marathon intensity (i.e., about 56 seconds per mile slower than new v$\dot{V}O_2$max; or 16 seconds slower per mile than 10k pace) Cool-down: 2 mi (3.2. km) of easy running Total: 10.3 mi (16.6 km) of running with 6.25 quality mi (10.06 km)
Sunday	**Strength session** Repeat session from Sunday week 16 Total: 4.9 mi (7.9 km) of running with .4 quality mi (.6 km)
	Weekly totals: 35.5 mi (67.1 km) of running with 8.4 quality mi (13.5 km) (24% of total)

Half-Marathon Training Program Week 19

Monday	6 mi (9.7 km) of easy running
Tuesday	**New v$\dot{V}O_2$max workout** Warm-up: SWU Run 9 × 400 m at the new v$\dot{V}O_2$max with jog recoveries equal in duration to the work-interval periods. Cool-down: 2 mi (3.2 km) of easy running after the ninth recovery Total: ~8.1 mi (13 km) of running with 2.5 quality mi (4.02 km)
Wednesday	7 mi (11.3 km) of light running
Thursday	**Hill session** Warm-up: SWU On challenging quarter-mile (.4 km) hill, carry out seven climbs at 5K intensity; jog back down each time to recover. Cool-down: 2 mi of easy running after the seventh recovery Total: 7.8 mi (12.6 km) of total running with 2 quality mi
Friday	Rest
Saturday	**Strength session** Repeat session from Sunday week 16 Total: 4.9 mi (7.9 km) of running with .4 quality mi (.6 km)
Sunday	**Tempo session** Warm-up: 2 mi (3.2 km) of easy running 3 mi (4.8 km) at 10K tempo Cool-down: 2 mi of easy running Total: 7 mi (11.3 km) of running with 3 quality mi (4.8 km)
	Weekly totals: 40.8 mi (65.7 km) of running with 7.9 quality mi (12.7 km) (19% of total)

Half-Marathon Training Program Week 20: Another 5K Race

Monday	Rest
Tuesday	5 mi (8 km) of easy running
Wednesday	**v$\dot{V}O_2$max workout** Warm-up: SWU Hit 5 × 800 m at the new v$\dot{V}O_2$max with jog recoveries equal in duration to the work-interval periods. Cool-down: 1 mi of easy running after the fifth recovery Total: ~7.7 mi (12.39 km) of running with 2.75 quality mi (4.43 km)
Thursday	6 mi (9.7 km) of easy running
Friday	Rest
Saturday	Warm-up: SWU 5K Race Cool-down: 1 mile of easy running Total: 6.4 mi (10.3 km) of running with 3.35 quality mi (5.39 km)
Sunday	8 mi (12.9 km) of easy running
	Weekly totals: 33.1 mi (53.3 km) of running with 6.1 quality mi (9.8 km) (18% of total)

Half-Marathon Training Program Week 21

Monday	**Cross-training** Warm-up: 12 minutes of easy pedaling on an exercise bike ; include a couple of 30-second sprints to fire up your neuromuscular system Hit 4 × 5 minutes at what feels like 5K intensity with 3-minute, easy-pedal recoveries after the first three intervals Cool-down: 12 minutes of easy pedaling
Tuesday	**Hill session** Warm-up: SWU On challenging half-mile (.8 km) hill, carry out four climbs at 5K intensity; jog back down each time to recover. Cool-down: 1 mi of easy running after the fourth recovery Total: 7.3 mi (11.8 km) of running with 2.25 quality mi (3.62 km)
Wednesday	6 mi (9.7 km) of easy running
Thursday	Warm-up: 1.5 mi (2.4 km) of light running 1. Medicine ball drills 2. 12 single-leg lunge squats with jumps: 12 reps per leg with 10-lb (4.5 kg) dumbbells in hands 3. 20 bench dips 4. 15 snap-'n'-taps: 15 lightning-quick taps with one foot while hopping 45 times on the other foot; after a moment of rest, change feet and repeat the exercise 5. 12 alternating walking lunges with each leg with 10-lb dumbbells* 6. 8 one-leg hand walk to triceps push-ups: 8 reps on each leg alternating between legs 7. 18 high-knee explosions 8. 15 m (49 ft) of side walking with strength band in one direction and then in the other direction for the same distance 9. 5 × 30 seconds of Shane's in-place accelerations (SIPAs) with a short break in between 10. Repeat steps 1-9 one time; then run 1 mile at 10K intensity Cool-down: 2 mi (3.2 km) of easy running Total: 4.9 mi (7.9 km) of running with 1.4 quality mi (2.3 km)
Friday	Rest
Saturday	**Half-marathon prep** Warm-up: SWU 7 mi (11.3 km) at half-marathon intensity Cool-down: 2 mi of easy running Total: 11.3 mi (18.1 km) of running with 7.25 quality mi (11.67 km)
Sunday	6 mi (9.7 km) of easy running
	Weekly totals: 35.5 mi (57.1 km) of running with 10.9 quality mi (17.5 km) (31% of total)

*Move forward continuously as you do this exercise.

Half-Marathon Training Program Week 22

Monday	60 minutes of light biking
Tuesday	**Circuit workout VII** Warm-up: SWU 　1. .25 mi (.4 km) run at 5K intensity 　2. 10 one-leg biceps curls with 10-lb (4.5 kg) dumbbells for 2 sets: 10 reps on each arm with alternating arm action* 　3. 45 sit-ups 　4. 18 six-count squat thrusts (burpees) 　5. 15 bench dips 　6. .25 mi (.4 km) run at 5K intensity 　7. 7 feet-elevated push-ups 　8. 12 squat and dumbbell presses on two legs with 10-lb dumbbells 　9. 45 low-back extensions 　10. 10 one-leg squats with each leg, 10-lb dumbbells in hands 　11. .5 mi (.8 km) run at 5K intensity 　12. Repeat steps 2-11 for two circuits total Cool-down: 2 mi (3.2. km) of easy running Total: 6.05 mi (9.74 km) of running with 2 quality mi
Wednesday	6 mi (9.7 km) of easy running
Thursday	**Hill session** Warm-up: SWU On challenging .5-mile (.8 km) hill, carry out five climbs at 5K intensity; jog back down each time to recover. Cool-down: 1 mi of easy running after the fifth recovery Total: 8.3 mi (13.4 km) of running with 2.75 quality mi (4.43 km)
Friday	Rest
Saturday	6 m (9.7 km) of easy running
Sunday	**vVO$_2$max workout** Warm-up: SWU Run 5 × 800 m at the new VO$_2$max with jog recoveries equal in duration to the work-interval periods. Cool-down: 1 mi of easy running after the fifth recovery Total: ~7.7 mi (12.39 km) of running with 2.75 quality mi
	Weekly totals: 34.05 mi (54.80 km) of running with 7.5 quality mi (12.1 km) (22 percent of total)

*During the first set of curls, stand on one foot. Then during the second set, stand on the other foot.

Half-Marathon Training Program Week 23

Monday	5 mi (8 km) of easy running
Tuesday	**Explosive routine** Warm-up: 1.5 mi (2.4 km) of easy jogging 1. Run intensely for 1 minute while counting the number of times one foot hits the ground; don't count both feet. If the number is less than 90, rest for a moment and repeat two more times, attempting to increase stride rate to *at least* 90 on each occasion. If the number is greater than or equal to 90, move on to step 3. 2. Skip on the balls of your feet for 30 seconds, using quick leg action, keeping your feet on the ground for a minimal amount of time; rest for a moment, and then repeat 3. 5 sets of two-leg hurdle hops of eight hurdles 4. 2 sets (40 seconds each) of one-leg hops in place on each leg 5. Diagonal hop for 45 seconds, rest for 15 seconds, and then diagonal hop for 45 more seconds 6. 8 greyhound runs 7. 2 × 12 one-leg squats with lateral hops on each leg; 1-minute break between sets 8. 15 high-knee explosions; rest for a few seconds and repeat 9. 3 × 20 seconds of Shane's in-place accelerations (SIPAs) 10. 4 × 800 m at a pace faster than $v\dot{V}O_2max$—stay relaxed and run rhythmically; insert 2- to 3-minute jog recoveries after each interval Cool-down: about 2 mi (3.2 km) of easy running Total: 7.5 mi (12.1 km) of running with 3 quality mi (4.8 km)*
Wednesday	60 minutes of easy cycling
Thursday	**Tempo run** Warm-up: SWU 2 mi at 10K intensity (i.e., about 40 seconds per mile slower than $v\dot{V}O_2max$) Cool-down: 3 mi of easy running Total: 7.3 mi (11.8 km) of running with 2.25 quality mi (3.62 km)
Friday	Rest
Saturday	6 mi (9.7 km) of easy running
Sunday	**Half-marathon prep** Warm-up: SWU 1 mi of easy running; 7 mi (11.3 km) at half-marathon intensity Cool-down: 2 mi of easy running Total: 12.3 mi (19.8 km) of running with 7.25 quality mi (11.67 km)
	Weekly totals: 38.1 mi (61.3 km) of running with 12.5 quality mi (20.1 km) (33% of total)

*This workout involves approximately 7.5 mi (12.1 km) of total running, with almost 3 high-quality miles (4.8 km), including the step-counting, skipping, and SIPAs. Make sure all activities that enhance stride rate are completed on a forgiving surface (e.g., soft dirt, grass, cushioned artificial turf, compliant track, wooden gym floor).

Half-Marathon Training Program Week 24

Monday	3 mi (4.8 km) of easy running
Tuesday	**v$\dot{V}O_2$max workout** Warm-up: SWU Hit 5 × 800 m at the new v$\dot{V}O_2$max, with jog recoveries equal in duration to the work-interval periods. Cool-down: 1 mi of easy running after the fifth recovery Total: ~ 7.7 mi (12.39 km) of running with 2.75 quality mi (4.43 km)
Wednesday	4 mi (6.4 km) of easy running

Thursday	**Explosive strength routine**
	Repeat routine from Tuesday Week 23 but substitute one-leg hurdle hops
	  for two-leg hurdle hops in step 3; hop explosively over the hurdles five times
	  on one leg and five times on the other leg.
	Total: 7.5 mi (12.1 km) of running with 3 quality mi

Friday	Rest
Saturday	5 mi (8 km) of easy running
Sunday	**Tempo run** Warm-up: SWU 3 mi at 10K intensity Cool-down: 2 mi (3.2 km) of easy running Total: 7.3 mi (11.8 km) of running with 3.25 quality mi (5.23 km)
	Weekly totals: 35.5 mi (57.1 km) of running with 9 quality mi (14.5 km) (25% of total)

Half-Marathon Training Program Week 25

Monday	4 mi (6.4 km) of easy running
Tuesday	**Explosive strength routine** Repeat workout from Thursday Week 24 Total: 7.5 mi (12.1 km) of running with 3 quality mi (4.8 km)
Wednesday	4 mi of easy running
Thursday	**5K-paced mile repeats** Warm-up: SWU Run 3 × 1 mi at 5K intensity (i.e., about 24 seconds per mile slower than v$\dot{V}O_2$max) with 3-minute jog recoveries after all three intervals. Cool-down: 1 mi of easy running after the third recovery Total: 7.3 mi (11.8 km) of running with 3.25 quality mi (5.23 km)
Friday	Rest
Saturday	5 mi (8 km) of easy running
Sunday	**Explosive strength routine** Repeat workout from Tuesday Total: 7.5 mi (12.1 km) of running with 3 quality mi
	Weekly totals: 30.3 mi (48.8 km) of running with 9.25 quality mi (14.89 km) (31% of total)

Half-Marathon Training Program Week 26: Half-Marathon Race Week

Monday	4 mi (6.4 km) of easy running
Tuesday	Warm-up: SWU Run 5 × 400 m at 5K pace with 200-m jog recoveries after the first four 400s Cool-down: 1 mi of easy running Totals: 5.05 mi (8.13 km) of running with 1.5 quality mi (2.4 km)
Wednesday	4 mi (6.4 km) of easy running
Thursday	SWU 2 mi (3.2 km) at half-marathon intensity Cool-down: 1 mi of easy running Totals: 5.3 mi (8.5 km) of running with 2.25 quality mi (3.62 km)
Friday	Rest
Saturday	Warm-up: SWU Half-marathon race Cool-down: .5 mi (.8 km) of easy running Totals: 15.9 mi (25.6 km) of running with 13.35 quality mi (21.48 km)
Sunday	One hour of easy biking
	Weekly totals: 34.25 mi (55.12 km) of running with 17.1 quality mi (27.5 km) (50% of total); total distance prior to race is 18.35 mi (29.53 km)

BICEPS CURL

PURPOSE

The purpose of this exercise is to strengthen the arms, shoulders, and core.

EXECUTION

Stand with arms at the sides and a dumbbell in each hand. Complete a biceps curl on alternating arms (figure 23.7) for the desired number of reps.

▶ **Figure 23.7** Alternating biceps curls.

BICEPS CURL ON ONE LEG

PURPOSE

The purpose of this exercise is to strengthen the arms, shoulders, upper body, and core while simultaneously strengthening the legs in a running-specific manner.

EXECUTION

Stand on one foot in a running-specific posture with the nonsupporting knee flexed so that the shin is parallel with the ground; hold a dumbbell in each hand. Don't let the nonsupporting hip droop down; keep it slightly flexed as though that leg was beginning to swing forward. Alternately curl the dumbbells by flexing the elbows and bringing the weights to the shoulder (figure 23.8). Maintain upright posture with the upper body; don't let the upper body rotate or move in any direction. Perform the required number of reps; then shift and repeat while standing on the other foot.

▶ **Figure 23.8** Biceps curl on one leg.

SIT-UP

PURPOSE

The purpose of this exercise it to strengthen the core.

EXECUTION

Lie on the back with legs bent at the knees so that the heels of feet are on the floor. Place hands beneath chin and use abdominal muscles to pull torso off the floor and into a vertical position (figure 23.9). Gradually let torso return to ground to complete one rep.

▶ **Figure 23.9** Sit-up.

ONE-LEG SQUAT WITH LATERAL HOPS

PURPOSE

The purpose of this exercise is to upgrade strength and explosiveness.

EXECUTION

Begin as if doing a regular one-leg squat. Stand with one foot forward and one foot back with feet about one shin-length apart from front to back and hip-width apart from side to side. Place the toes of your back foot on a block or step 6 to 8 inches (15-20 cm) high. Keep most of your weight on the midfoot of the supporting foot. Bend the supporting leg and lower your body until that knee reaches an angle of approximately 90 degrees between the back of the thigh and the calf.

At that point, hop laterally on the supporting foot about 6 to 10 inches (15-25 cm) (figure 23.10a), hop back to center (figure 23.10b), hop medially to the opposite side 6 to 10 inches (figure 23.10c), and then hop back to center and return to the initial standing position to complete one rep. Throughout the exercise, maintain upright posture with the trunk. For lateral and medial hops, keep the toes of the supporting foot pointed straight ahead. Keep the other foot on the block or step during the hops. Perform a squat that is close to 90 degrees in each position: medial, lateral, and center.

▶ **Figure 23.10** (a) Lateral hop, (b) center hop, and (c) medial hop.

ONE-LEG HEEL RAISE

PURPOSE

The purpose of this exercise is to strengthen the calf muscles for running.

EXECUTION

Stand with the ball of one foot toward the edge of a step so that the heel can sink down directly behind the step; the foot is perpendicular to the front edge of the step with the heel hovering in midair. Use a wall or banister for balance if needed. Adopt a running-specific posture with the hip and knee of the supporting leg just slightly flexed; flex the other leg at the hip as though that thigh was swinging forward during running. Let the heel of the supporting leg sink down as far as it will go (figure 23.11); then use the calf muscles of that leg to lift the heel up as high as possible and rock forward onto the toes. Complete 10 smooth, rhythmic reps on that leg; rest for a few seconds and then repeat the sequence on the other leg.

▶ **Figure 23.11** One-leg heel raise.

BACKWARD HEEL WALKING

PURPOSE

The purpose of this exercise is to improve balance and shin strength.

EXECUTION

Walk backward on your heels with toes pointed straight. Keep the legs relatively straight and take fairly small steps (figure 23.12). Maintain coordinated movement and erect posture; keep the ankles dorsiflexed as much as possible.

▶ **Figure 23.12**   Backward heel walking.

ONE-LEG OVERHEAD DUMBBELL PRESS

PURPOSE

The purpose of this exercise is to improve core and upper-body strength and to upgrade leg strength in a running-specific way.

EXECUTION

Stand on one foot in a running-specific posture. Flex the nonsupporting knee so that the shin is parallel with the ground; flex that hip slightly so that the thigh is slightly in front of the body. Hold the dumbbells in front of the shoulders with palms facing forward and dumbbells facing straight ahead, and then press both arms straight overhead simultaneously (figure 23.13). Perform 10 presses. Rest for a moment; switch feet and perform 10 presses while standing on the other foot.

▶ **Figure 23.13** One-leg dumbbell press.

ONE-LEG ALTERNATING OVERHEAD DUMBBELL PRESS

PURPOSE

The purpose of this exercise is to improve upper-body and core strength while also upgrading leg strength in a running-specific way.

EXECUTION

Stand on one foot in a running-specific posture. Flex the nonsupporting knee so that the shin is parallel with the ground; flex that hip slightly so that the thigh is slightly in front of the body. Hold the dumbbells in front of the shoulders with palms facing forward and dumbbells facing straight ahead. Use alternating arm action (figure 23.14) to perform 10 presses with each arm. Rest for a moment; switch feet and perform 10 presses with each arm while standing on the other foot.

▶ **Figure 23.14** One-leg alternating dumbbell press.

ONE-LEG MEDICINE BALL DRILLS

PURPOSE

The purpose of this exercise is to strengthen the feet, ankles, legs, core, and upper body for running.

EXECUTION

Stand in a natural running position on one foot about 4 to 5 feet (1.2 to 1.5 m) from a smooth wall; hold a medicine ball in front of you. The nonsupport foot is held just off the ground. Throw 10 chest passes at the wall, catching the ball on the return before it hits the ground. Throw the ball hard and a little high so that it bounces right back at about chest level. Maintain balance on the supporting foot through each throw and catch. Put the toes of the nonsupporting leg on the ground behind you for support if you need extra balance.

Next, throw 10 overhead passes and catch each return in front of your chest. Then, throw 10 underhand passes (figure 23.15a) and catch each return. Use an action a bit like the one-leg squat: squat and lean forward slightly with your upper body before the throw. Next, turn sideways so that your supporting side is closer to the wall and hurl the ball 10 times across your body to the wall (figure 23.15b); catch it on the return before it hits the ground. This movement is great for the trunk rotator muscles. Finally, turn so that the nonsupporting leg is closer to the wall; throw the ball across your body and against the wall 10 times, catching it as before. For the sideways throws, use a natural swing action by swinging the ball away from the wall before accelerating it across your body and releasing it; the upper body rotates away from the wall and then toward it for each throw. Switch feet, stand on the other foot, and repeat each variation.

▶ **Figure 23.15** (a) Underhand and (b) across-the-body throws.

PISTOL SQUAT

PURPOSE

The purpose of this exercise is to strengthen the leg muscles in a running-specific manner, with strong effects on the hamstrings and gluteal muscles.

EXECUTION

Stand on one leg directly in front of a chair, weight bench, or platform; face away from the chair or bench. Keep the nonsupport leg straight and extended out in front of your body. Slowly descend with your buttocks moving downward to the chair by squatting on the supporting leg; continue to hold the nonsupporting leg out straight (figure 23.16). Keep the upper body relatively vertical and relaxed at all times. When your buttocks reach the chair or bench, gradually rise by straightening the supporting leg. Move in a smooth, controlled manner at all times. Don't let the buttocks slam onto the chair and move upward after reaching the chair in a smooth and coordinated manner.

▶ **Figure 23.16** Pistol squatting onto a platform.

ONE-LEG PUSH-UP

PURPOSE

The purpose of this exercise is to strengthen the upper body and core.

EXECUTION

This exercise is just like a regular push-up except it is done with the body weight supported by the toes of one foot and the hands. The ankle of the other foot is draped over the ankle of the supporting leg or held in the air (figure 23.17).

▶ **Figure 23.17** One-leg push-up.

WALKING LUNGE

PURPOSE

The walking lunge upgrades the strength and dynamic flexibility of the legs.

EXECUTION

Stand tall, take a big step forward with one foot, and land on the midfoot with the knee in line vertically with the foot. Immediately drop down into a lunge squat (figure 23.18a), contract the glutes to power back up into erect body position, bring the rear foot forward to be next to the front foot, and stand tall and balanced to complete one rep. Then reverse the feet, taking a big step forward with the other foot, and follow the same procedure (figure 23.18b) to complete one rep on both legs. Continue moving forward, alternating legs, until each leg has lunged 8 times. Make sure the torso doesn't fall forward during the lunges; upper-body posture should be straight and tall, and there are no lateral movements of the legs or trunk during the lunge and squat.

▶ **Figure 23.18** Lunge *(a)* with one leg and *(b)* then the other.

ONE-LEG FATIGUE-FIGHTING ROW

PURPOSE

This exercise strengthens the upper body and core for running.

EXECUTION

Loop a stretch cord over a post or support structure and stand far enough back from the support so that the cord is taut. Stand on one leg with the other knee bent just enough to keep the nonsupporting foot off the ground. Hold the cord handles in the hand opposite the supporting leg straight forward with good tension on the stretch band (figure 23.19a). Point the supporting foot, knee, and hips straight ahead toward the post or structure. Keep the head up, retract the shoulders (i.e., shoulder blades are squeezed together and pulled down), and hold the arm close to the side during pulling. Pull the cord so that the elbow moves past the body and backwards so that your hand is brought to your side (figure 23.19b). Stand tall at all times with no forward or backward leaning. Keep the shoulders down as you perform the movement. This exercise will help stabilize your shoulders as you run, maintain your standing-tall alignment when fatigued, keep your arms close to your sides, augment your basic leg strength, upgrade your balance, increase core strength, and improve your running economy. Repeat the exercise with the opposite arm and leg.

▶ **Figure 23.19** Row movement (a) start and (b) pull.

SIDE-WALKING WITH STRENGTH BAND

PURPOSE

The purpose of this exercise is to strengthen the iliotibial bands.

EXECUTION

Stand tall, keep feet parallel, stand on the strength band with the arches of both feet, and cross the band in front of body making an X with the band in front of the legs. Hold the band at your sides with arms hanging straight down, thumbs pointed out, and shoulders back and down. Don't let the legs turn out. Move laterally to one side for about 10 meters (33 ft) and then back the same distance to the starting location (figure 23.20). Move along with small sideways steps with the torso upright, the shoulders back and down, and the head looking forward. This exercise strengthens your iliotibial bands; prevents iliotibial band syndrome; lowers the risk of knee pain; improves hip stability and control of the thigh during stance; prevents medial collapse of the thigh during stance, especially in a fatigued state; and enhances running economy.

▶ **Figure 23.20** Side steps using the strength band.

HIGH-KNEE EXPLOSION

PURPOSE

The purpose of this exercise is to enhance explosiveness.

EXECUTION

Stand with erect but relaxed posture with feet directly below the shoulders. Jump lightly in place; then suddenly make an explosive, nearly maximal vertical jump and swing both knees up toward your chest while maintaining fairly erect posture (figure 23.21). Land on your feet in a relaxed and resilient manner, jump lightly for a few moments, jump maximally again with appropriate knee action, and then repeat the sequence 13 more times. Make sure to keep the upper body fairly erect without hunching forward to meet your knees. The key action is the dramatic upward acceleration of the knees toward the chest. A key progression is to eventually carry out the high-knee explosions on one leg at a time.

▶ **Figure 23.21** High-knee explosion.

SHANE'S IN-PLACE ACCELERATION (SIPA)

PURPOSE

The purpose of this exercise is to enhance explosiveness.

EXECUTION

Stand with erect but relaxed posture with feet directly below the shoulders. Begin by jogging in place; when ready, dramatically increase the in-place stride rate, building up fairly quickly to as rapid a stride rate as you can sustain (figure 23.22) without moving forward to any significant degree. Keep feet close to the ground as you do this; you are not shooting for high knee lifts but rather for dramatically minimized foot-contact times. Maintain erect but relaxed posture. When learning this exercise, it may help to turn the legs slightly outward at the hips as you build up toward top speed. One goal is to achieve at least 230 steps per minute as you carry out these accelerations.

▶ **Figure 23.22** In-place acceleration.

SNAP-'N'-TAP

PURPOSE

The purpose of this exercise is to promote explosiveness and coordination.

EXECUTION

Begin hopping quickly in place on one foot. Hold the nonhopping leg so that the knee is flexed and the shin is parallel with the ground. On every third contact with the ground, quickly tap the other foot on the ground in synchrony with the hopping foot (figure 23.23). The tap by the nonsupporting foot should be so light that if someone stuck a hand under the tapping foot, there would barely be any pressure at all. Perform 12 taps while hopping at least 36 times on the supporting foot. Rest for just a moment; then reverse the hopping and tapping feet. Tap on every third hop until 12 taps have been completed. Make the hops lightning quick with little vertical amplitude.

▶ **Figure 23.23** Hopping on one foot and tapping with the other foot.

ONE-LEG HAND WALK TO TRICEPS PUSH-UP

PURPOSE

The purpose of this exercise is to advance upper-body and core strength.

EXECUTION

Raise one foot off the ground so that the knee is flexed and the shin is parallel with the ground and stand on the other leg. Perform a one-leg squat on the supporting leg; then bend forward at the hips and touch the floor with straight arms. Walk forward with the hands (figure 23.24a) to a straight-arm plank position while keeping just the supporting foot and hands in contact with the ground. Keep arms and elbows close to the ribs and bend the elbows to perform a triceps push-up (figure 23.24b). Continue to balance on the supporting leg, walk the hands back to the initial hand-to-ground contact point, and use the glutes and lower-back muscles to return to standing, erect posture. This completes one rep.

Switch legs for the next rep. Do 8 reps on each leg by alternating between them. Use appropriate squat and hip flexion to avoid throwing the upper body forward onto the ground. Keep the back flat and the head aligned with the rest of the body on the push-ups. Maintain good balance at the end of each rep.

▶ **Figure 23.24** *(a)* Walk out with the hands and *(b)* the push-up.

ONE-LEG CYCLING

PURPOSE

The purpose of this exercise is to augment leg strength.

EXECUTION

On the bike, with straps in place on the pedals, pedal with one foot for 1 minute at an easy intensity. Keep the other foot on the bike housing. Then, increase the resistance or gear so that the effort is hard (i.e., about 9.5 on a scale from 1 to 10). Once this very difficult minute is completed, lower the resistance and pedal easily with the same leg for one minute. Continue this pattern until six one-minute intervals (three easy and three hard) have been completed. Then switch legs and repeat the six-minute pedaling sequence with the other leg.

Throughout this one-leg cycling, concentrate on forcefully pushing the pedals downward and pulling them back up. Think of the pedal stroke as a four-sided rectangle. For the first corner (the top one nearest you), think of driving the knee forward. For the second, forcefully drive the foot down from 12 o'clock to 6 o'clock. For the third, think of scraping the mud off the bottom of your shoe by pulling it across the bottom of the rectangle. For the fourth, pull up very hard, driving your knee to the ceiling. Keep the torso relaxed and fairly upright—do all the work with the legs. Don't stand up on the pedals.

CYCLING ACCELERATION

PURPOSE

The purpose of this exercise is to enhance explosiveness.

EXECUTION

Ride a stationary or regular bicycle, pedaling with both legs at about 90 rpm at a moderately hard intensity for 60 seconds; then increase the cadence as quickly as possible to 110 to 120 rpm. Stay relaxed and hold this higher cadence for 60 seconds; then cycle moderately at 90 rpm for another 60 seconds. Continue this pattern until you have completed three 60-second intervals at 110 to 120 rpm. There should be enough resistance during the 110- to 120-rpm intervals so that they feel quite difficult.

CYCLING BIG GEARS

PURPOSE

The purpose of this exercise is to augment leg strength.

EXECUTION

Pedal with both legs on a stationary or regular bicycle alternating 1 minute of riding at easy intensity with light resistance and 30 seconds of riding against very heavy resistance so that it feels as though you are going up a steep hill. Continue alternating until you have completed five tough 30-second intervals. Try to stand up on the pedals for the 30-second intervals. Complete the 30-second intervals at 90 rpm.

TWO-LEG HURDLE HOP

PURPOSE

The purpose of this drill is to improve explosiveness.

EXECUTION

Position eight hurdles in a row, 45 inches (1.1 m) apart, with the height of each hurdle set at 23 inches (58 cm). Starting from one end, jump over each hurdle (figure 23.25), landing and taking off on two legs until all eight hurdles have been cleared. Maintain continuous movement. Minimize ground-contact time with each landing and try to be as explosive as possible. Once you have cleared the eighth hurdle, jog back to the beginning point and repeat 4 more times for 5 reps in all. Avoid taking little hops between hurdles and making more than one contact between hurdles. This exercise may also be performed on one leg at a time as a progression.

▶ **Figure 23.25** Single contact with explosive take off.

ONE-LEG HOP IN PLACE

PURPOSE

The purpose of this exercise is to promote explosiveness in a running-specific manner.

EXECUTION

Stand with one foot forward and one foot back with feet about one shin-length apart front to back and hip-width apart from side to side. Place the toes of back foot on a block or step 6 to 8 inches (15 to 20 cm) high. Direct your weight through the middle to the ball of the supporting foot. Hop rapidly on the supporting foot at a cadence of 2.5 to 3 hops per second, or 25 to 30 foot contacts per 10 seconds for the prescribed time (figure 23.26). Lift the knee of the hopping leg about 4 to 6 inches (10 to 15 cm) with each upward hop; keep the other leg and foot stationary on the block. Keep the hopping foot striking the ground and springing upward rapidly as if in contact with a hot stove. Keep the hips fairly level and virtually motionless throughout the exercise with little vertical displacement. After completing the first set, rest for a moment, and then repeat the one-leg hops on the other leg. Rest again and perform one more set on each leg. A set is 60 seconds of continuous hopping on one foot.

▶ **Figure 23.26** One-leg hop.

DIAGONAL HOP

PURPOSE

The purpose of this exercise is to improve explosiveness, coordination, and ankle strength.

EXECUTION

Jog a few strides and then move diagonally to one side (figure 23.27a). When the foot that moved to the side makes contact with the ground, hop once quickly in place. Then, explosively jump diagonally forward, landing on the other foot (figure 23.27b). When this foot makes contact with the ground, hop once quickly in place and then explode diagonally in the opposite direction. Repeat the cycle for about 40 meters. Stay relaxed at all times and move in a rhythmic, coordinated manner. Look straight ahead, not at your feet.

▶ **Figure 23.27** Diagonal hop (a) take-off and (b) landing on opposite foot.

GREYHOUND RUN

PURPOSE

The purpose of this exercise is to improve maximal running velocity.

EXECUTION

Use an area with 100 meters of unobstructed surface. Accelerate for 20 meters (66 ft), maintain a nearly maximal pace for 60 meters (196 ft), decelerate for 20 meters, rest for several seconds while walking, and repeat in the opposite direction. Complete 8 of these 100-meter greyhound runs, 4 in each direction.

Conclusion

Although strength training is excluded from many runners' training programs or treated as occasional cross-training to be carried out on nonrunning days, it is the backbone of great endurance running training. When overall training is periodized to include phases of general strengthening, running-specific strengthening, hill training, and explosive work, running fitness can be maximized; each form of strengthening builds on the previously completed modalities. Within each phase, proper progressions are included to gradually expand resistance and overall exertion difficulty. High-quality running training wraps around the strength-training backbone and ensures that the seven key performance variables will be optimized: $v\dot{V}O_2max$, $t_{lim}v\dot{V}O_2max$, running economy, lactate-threshold velocity, resistance to fatigue, running-specific strength, and maximal running velocity.

Optimal Training for Specific Conditioning

Increasing $\dot{V}O_2max$

Most runners and running coaches believe that it is essential to build a base of strength, aerobic capacity, and fitness prior to embarking on a rigorous training program. A popular conception is that this base should include gradually increasing distance, most of which is conducted at easy to moderate tempos. It is generally believed that a runner's body is not yet ready for high-quality work during an early, base portion of the training year and thus must be gradually acclimated to higher volume and intensity. The easy running is thought to provide a foundation of strength and serve as an upgrade of aerobic fitness that helps smooth the transition into higher-quality effort.[1] However, evidence shows that this traditional approach and its alleged benefits may not be optimal for improving $\dot{V}O_2max$ and running-specific strength.

Weaknesses of Traditional Approaches to Base Training

In their book *Better Training for Distance Runners*, David Martin and Peter Coe suggest that base periods should contain "sizable volumes of continuous, longer-distance running at below race pace for any of the middle- and long-distance running events."[2] Martin and Coe indicate that base running should be "conversational" in nature—slow enough to permit easy talking during a workout. They recommend a base training intensity of between 55 and 75 percent of $\dot{V}O_2max$, which would be well below marathon pace for most runners, and they even provide a method for runners to use to determine whether their training speeds fall within this range of intensities. Martin and Coe caution against running faster than 75 percent of $\dot{V}O_2max$ during a base period because such effort "causes the beginning of anaerobic glycolytic activity, which may mark the beginning of lactic-acid accumulation that is not appropriate for training emphasis in this zone."[2] No evidence is provided to demonstrate that lactic-acid accumulation is counterproductive during base periods, however.

In his book *Daniels' Running Formula*, coach and exercise physiologist Jack Daniels indicates that base training, which he calls "phase-one" work, should consist of easy running plus a few strides (i.e., brief intervals of accelerated running) regardless of whether one is a middle- or long-distance runner.[3] For Daniels, an optimal duration for a base period is about 6 weeks, and the easy running performed during such a period is believed to foster "cell adaptation and injury prevention."[3] Unfortunately, Daniels cites no research that documents optimal cellular adaptation and enhanced injury prevention with this approach compared with other forms of base training that include higher-quality running or strength training.

Coach Arthur Lydiard was also a proponent of base periods that keep intensity at a moderate level while gradually increasing mileage.[4] Lydiard's theory was that such running improves runners' aerobic capacities dramatically by enhancing cardiac output, increasing aerobic enzyme concentrations inside muscle cells, and expanding the number of capillaries around individual muscle cells. Capillaries are the tiniest blood vessels in a runner's body; they are the components of the cardiovascular system that actually deliver oxygen to working muscle fibers. Lydiard eschewed fast running during base periods, believing that such efforts promoted the production of lactic acid—his favorite muscle nemesis—with consequent damage to muscle cells. As discussed in chapter 7, scientific research reveals that lactic acid does not actually harm muscle fibers.

Cell adaptation, prevention of future injuries, increased cardiac output, advanced aerobic enzyme concentrations, and greater capillarization appear to be appropriate—if limited—goals to aim for during base periods. Scientific research indicates that such changes would at least improve $\dot{V}O_2$max and thus place subsequent running training on a higher plain of fitness.

There are two basic problems with these approaches, however. First, running science has not been kind to the traditional idea that easy training intensities are optimal for $\dot{V}O_2$max improvement during base periods. Second, these approaches represent old-school thinking with the focus of training centered almost entirely on cardiovascular and oxygen-usage development and almost no emphasis placed on neuromuscular progress, that is, the ability of the nervous system to recruit the leg muscles in ways that enhance coordination and quickness and thus boost maximal running speed. It is difficult to comprehend why this critically important, latter process should be ignored.

Aerobic Development Through Capillary Growth

To fully understand the impact of different types of base training on $\dot{V}O_2$max improvement, it is important to examine research that pertains to aerobic development during base periods. In 1934 exercise scientists were first able to show that endurance training increases capillary densities within animal muscles; the same effect was finally observed in human subjects in the 1970s.[5] This important capillary adaptation was apparent when scientists measured either the number of capillaries per muscle fiber or the density of capillaries per square millimeter of muscle tissue, and investigators estimated that the additional capillaries that sprung up around muscle cells as a result of training could spike intramuscular blood flow by 50 to 200 percent.[6] While this study was completed with rodents, the changes are likely similar in humans. This would have a profound impact on $\dot{V}O_2$max by increasing the rate of delivery of oxygen to muscles.

Although new capillary growth is often considered to be one of the slower adaptive processes associated with endurance training, an interesting finding was that capillaries began to proliferate *around* muscles even before the sinews exhibited increased concentrations of *intracellular* aerobic enzymes in response to training.[7] The discovery that new capillary growth is a relatively quick process carried with it the implication that many weeks of steady, moderate running were not required to boost capillary densities.

Advanced capillary density is usually tightly connected with a burgeoning $\dot{V}O_2$max, and a higher aerobic capacity permits training to be conducted for more prolonged periods and at higher intensities. Both of these outcomes are ideal developments for base training periods that are supposed to prepare runners for tougher times ahead. Since these early studies were conducted, exercise scientists have searched for the best ways to promote optimal capillary growth and produce the greatest upswings in $\dot{V}O_2$max.

Impact of Volume, Frequency, and Intensity

Many scientific studies have attempted to sort out the effects of volume, frequency, and intensity of training on $\dot{V}O_2$max. In an important inquiry, Dr. T. Jurimae and his Finnish colleagues asked two groups of university students to engage in 8 weeks of base running training.[8] The total volume of training was identical for the two groups, but the intensities were significantly different. One group of runners carried out their base training at an easy intensity of 140 to 150 heart beats per minute while the second group used a higher intensity of 165 to 175 beats per minute. Average maximum heart rate for both groups was about 200, so the easy-running group worked at approximately 70 to 75 percent of maximum heart rate while the harder-running group trained at 82 to 88 percent.

Base periods should improve a runner's physiological status; they should not simply preserve the status quo. The underlying idea in base training is to move forward and prepare for the more strenuous impending training by upgrading basic fitness. As this Finnish study showed, 8 weeks of training at the lower, traditional base intensity (i.e., 70 to 75 percent of maximum heart rate) failed to improve $\dot{V}O_2$max at all; working more intensely (i.e., at 82 to 88 percent of $\dot{V}O_2$max) enhanced $\dot{V}O_2$max significantly. There was no increased risk of injury at the higher intensity. This study suggested that the lower intensities commonly chosen for base training periods are actually poor choices since they had no positive impact on $\dot{V}O_2$max and presumably capillarization, too. This would be especially true for experienced runners who already have relatively high aerobic capacity.

Advocates of easy running during base periods might argue that the lower-intensity group in this Finnish study could have achieved the same $\dot{V}O_2$max spike as the high-quality runners by boosting their volume (i.e., distance run) during the base period. However, the best predictor of injury in endurance runners is the total time spent training.[1] Thus, major increases in distance run during base periods, undertaken in hopes of raising aerobic capacity, might produce a result that is the exact opposite of one of the fundamental goals of base training: Instead of lowering the risk of subsequent injury, such base training might increase the risk of injury.

In a separate study, Glenn Gaesser and Robert Rich of the University of California at Los Angeles asked two groups of healthy young men to initiate base training.[9] All the subjects worked out three times a week for 18 weeks, but a high-intensity group trained for 25 minutes per workout at an intensity of 80 to 85 percent of $\dot{V}O_2$max, while a low-intensity group trained for double the amount of time—50 minutes per session—at an easy intensity of 45 percent of $\dot{V}O_2$max.

In this study, the use of light intensity and the doubling of total training time were not advantageous. After 18 weeks and 1,350 total minutes of training, the high-intensity group had improved $\dot{V}O_2$max by almost 20 percent, while the low-intensity group had upgraded $\dot{V}O_2$max by 17 percent with 2,700 minutes of workouts. In other words, the slow-paced, traditional base training tended to produce less improvement in aerobic capacity than the higher-quality base training even when the low-intensity trainees increased total workout time by 100 percent. This study suggested that traditional base-training plans are inefficient ways to bolster running fitness.

Key information about the type of training necessary for $\dot{V}O_2$max expansion during base training periods is also available from studies that have looked at training-related changes in muscle cells' aerobic enzyme concentrations. An important discovery through this work is the so-called saturation response, which indicates that there is a specific workout duration beyond which little further stimulus for aerobic enzyme improvement can be created. The research has been carried out with rodents, not humans, but it suggests that about 60 minutes of training per workout represents the saturation point beyond which the postworkout adaptive process will produce no further increases in aerobic enzymes.[10] Shifting from 60 to 90 minutes per session does not increase aerobic enzyme concentrations by 50 percent, nor does changing from 60 to 120 minutes double enzyme levels.

The saturation response strongly implies that such workout expansions will have little effect on aerobic enzyme concentrations.

If a similar effect is present in human runners, the benefits of expanding workout durations beyond 60 minutes during base training periods would be questionable. It is possible that setting the workout duration at about 60 minutes during a base period and then attempting to increase the intensity of effort within that hour might work much more effectively in improving aerobic enzyme concentration, capillary density, and $\dot{V}O_2$max compared with moving to a 75- to 120-minute workout at a lower intensity.

Improving $\dot{V}O_2$max Through Intensity

Research suggests that manipulations of intensity—not volume—represent the most powerful ways to upgrade $\dot{V}O_2$max and capillarization during base periods. In a rigorous investigation,[10] Gary Dudley and his colleagues at the State University of New York at Syracuse made laboratory rats use a variety of different workout durations—from 5 to 90 minutes per day—and a range of training intensities from 40 to 100 percent of $\dot{V}O_2$max. Dudley and colleagues examined the effects of duration and intensity on $\dot{V}O_2$max and specifically analyzed how different training modalities influenced fast-, intermediate-, and slow-twitch muscle fibers.

As mentioned, these researchers were able to demonstrate that training for more than 60 minutes per day was without benefit in terms of increasing aerobic enzyme concentrations for all three muscle-cell types. The researchers also concluded that 10 minutes of running per day at an intensity of 100 percent of $\dot{V}O_2$max were enough to roughly triple aerobic enzyme concentrations in fast-twitch muscle fibers over an 8-week period. In contrast, running for 27 minutes at 85 percent of $\dot{V}O_2$max increased aerobic enzymes by only 80 percent, while 60 to 90 minutes of daily running at the traditionally preferred base intensity of 70 to 75 percent of $\dot{V}O_2$max moved enzyme levels up by just 74 percent in fast-twitch cells.

In intermediate muscle cells, which are from a physiological standpoint roughly half-way between fast-twitch and slow-twitch fibers, training intensity also had the most powerful effect on aerobic enzyme improvement. Just 10 minutes of running daily at 100 percent of $\dot{V}O_2$max increased aerobic enzyme concentrations just as much as running 27 minutes daily at 85 percent of $\dot{V}O_2$max or 60 to 90 minutes at 70 to 75 percent of $\dot{V}O_2$max. Presumably, using a workout containing 10 minutes of running at 100 percent of $\dot{V}O_2$max broken into intervals plus approximately 20 minutes at 70 percent of $\dot{V}O_2$max would have a far-greater impact on aerobic capacity than the conventional 60 to 90 minutes at 70 to 75 percent of $\dot{V}O_2$max.

For slow-twitch fibers, running a total of 2,400 minutes (40 hours) at an intensity of 70 to 75 percent of $\dot{V}O_2$max increased aerobic enzyme concentrations by approximately 40 percent. That change works out to be an improvement of .017 percent per minute of training. Running for a total of 1,080 minutes (18 hours) at 85 percent of $\dot{V}O_2$max created a 28-percent upturn in aerobic enzyme levels, a change of .026 percent per minute of training. Finally, running fast for 400 minutes (6.67 hours) at close to 100 percent of $\dot{V}O_2$max expanded aerobic enzymes in slow-twitch cells by 10 percent, a .025-percent per minute rate of improvement. When the change was expressed per minute of training, the two higher intensities were better at upgrading aerobic enzymes, even in the slow-twitch muscle cells, than the lower, traditional base intensity.

Note from this study that 38 minutes of running at 85 percent of $\dot{V}O_2$max would produce a $\dot{V}O_2$max upswing of 1 percent. To produce a similar change in maximal aerobic capacity, almost one hour of running at 70 to 75 percent of $\dot{V}O_2$max would be required. If an athlete ran for just 20 minutes at 85 percent of $\dot{V}O_2$max and for 40 minutes at 70 percent of $\dot{V}O_2$max for a 1-hour workout, the upward movement on $\dot{V}O_2$max would be 20 percent greater than running the whole hour at the slower intensity. It's clear from such research that traditional base training is an inefficient way to build an aerobic base, that is, to expand $\dot{V}O_2$max.

Comparing High-Intensity and Traditional Base Training

It might be argued that conventional base training is nonetheless an effective way to boost running strength and thus decrease the risk of subsequent injury during more intense phases of training, but this contention ignores the fact that the strength gained in training is always velocity specific.[11] Strength acquired at slow speeds does not automatically transfer to faster muscle contraction (e. g., faster running velocities). In this sense, running at easy base speeds provides poor preparation for higher-speed running. There is also no proof that traditional base training periods lower the rate of injury during follow-up training. With their emphasis on increased volume, traditional base periods may actually increase injury rates.

Recent research carried out by Mark Tarnopolsky, Martin Gibala, and their colleagues in the department of kinesiology and the department of medicine at McMaster University in Hamilton, Ontario, Canada, suggests that base periods containing significant amounts of high-intensity training are superior to conventional base periods.[12] These researchers became interested in the possibility of relying on high-quality—and even sprint—training during base periods after they examined several scientific studies showing that high-intensity sprint-interval training increases the maximal activity of mitochondrial enzymes.[13-15] Mitochondrial enzymes are the key chemicals that allow muscle cells to use oxygen at higher rates, thus heightening aerobic capacity, or $\dot{V}O_2$max.

The research team also noted that high-intensity sprint training tends to produce two key adaptations that are beneficial for endurance runners: a reduced rate of glycogen usage during exercise and a smaller buildup of lactate during strenuous effort. A decrease in the rate at which glycogen is burned during running promotes stamina because more glycogen fuel remains in the tank to be used after any specific duration of effort. A diminished buildup in lactate can indicate that lactate, a key fuel for running, is being used more effectively for energy: It is being broken down quickly instead of accumulating in the muscles and blood.

As if all that were not enough, many studies have shown that high-intensity sprint training upgrades performance during exertions that rely primarily on aerobic metabolism.[16, 17] Finally, sprint intervals improve the buffering capacity of muscles (i.e., the ability to control advances in acidity),[18, 19] an effect that usually promotes better tolerance of high-intensity running and thus greater endurance at intense paces.

Such findings suggest that reasonable amounts of high-intensity work might be optimal during a base-building phase of training, promoting many adaptations that would be tremendously useful during subsequent periods of strenuous training. To put high-intensity base-building to the test, Tarnopolsky, Gibala, and colleagues recruited 16 fairly fit male McMaster University students who normally worked out two to three times a week by running, cycling, or swimming. The average age of the students was 22, mean mass was 172 pounds (78 kg), body mass index was 23 (i.e., they were not overweight or obese), and average $\dot{V}O_2$max was 52.6 ml • kg^{-1} • min^{-1}.

At random, eight of the subjects were assigned to the sprint-training group, and the other eight were placed in an endurance-training group that used the old-fashioned base with moderately paced distance work. All training was carried out on a cycle ergometer. The base training period lasted 2 weeks, and the six total workouts were performed on Monday, Wednesday, and Friday of each week with 1 to 2 recovery days between sessions.

The sprint- and endurance-training bases were incredibly different. For the sprint group, training consisted of 30-second, maximal, all-out intervals, with power outputs soaring as high as 700 Watts and 4 minutes of recovery between intervals; the recovery consisted of either rest or light cycling at an intensity of about 30 Watts. This was done progressively: The subjects completed four maximal intervals during the first and second workouts, five all-out reps during workouts three and four, and six scalding intervals for workouts five and six. Meanwhile, the endurance group started with 90 minutes of work during sessions one and two at the modest intensity of 65 percent of $\dot{V}O_2$max, moved up to 105 minutes of cycling for sessions three and four, and peaked to 120 minutes of exertion during workouts five and six—all the while remaining at the workload of 65 percent of $\dot{V}O_2$max, a traditional base intensity.

Before and after the base periods, all subjects completed a 30K (18.6 mi) and a 2K (1.2 mi) time trial. After the 2 weeks of base training, the time required to finish the 30K (18.6 mi) trial dropped by 10.1 percent for the sprint group and by 7.5 percent for the endurance group; this difference was not statistically significant. After the base, average power output during the 30K (18.6 mi) trial rose by 10 percent for the sprint-training group and by 6.5 percent for the endurance-training group; again, this disparity was not statistically relevant. Finishing time in the 2K (1.2 mi) test improved by 4.1 percent for the sprint group and by 3.5 percent for the endurance group; the difference was not statistically significant. Similarly, mitochondrial enzyme activity increased in both groups by essentially the same amount after the base period, and so did muscle glycogen content.

The high-intensity sprint group spent just 2 to 3 minutes per workout exercising at high intensity—and trained for just 18 to 27 minutes total per session with recovery time included. Meanwhile, the endurance-training group logged from 90 to 120 minutes per workout. Overall, for the whole 2-week period, those in the sprint group completed 15 minutes of quality intervals and spent only 135 minutes training, with recovery time included, in contrast to the 630 minutes of work put in by the endurance-training subjects. In effect, each minute of sprint-interval training produced the same benefits as 42 minutes of endurance training at 65 percent of $\dot{V}O_2$max.

Since the resulting adaptations were the same, this means that sprint training was a far more efficient way to build a base. There is also a strong implication that if a few more intervals had been included in the spring training or if additional moderate-intensity work had been added to the challenging intervals, the sprint-focused base efforts would have far outstripped the endurance-based exertions in terms of the magnitudes of the resulting adaptations.

High-Intensity Training Does Not Increase Injury

No evidence exists to suggest that higher-quality training heightens the risk of injury during base periods. Since total time spent training (e.g., volume) is usually the best predictor of running injury,[1] a traditional, endurance-oriented base, in which distance is steadily ramped up, might be much harder on muscles and tendons than a high-intensity base.

Indeed, the fact that sprint training is carried out in a base period does not automatically mean that the sprint work should be undertaken unwisely or excessively. The high-quality work would be modest in volume and would only gradually progress in difficulty and extent. A focus on higher-quality training would also invite neuromuscular development on board during base periods. Thus, both the neuromuscular and cardiovascular systems would be prepared for the rigors of subsequent stages of training.

Conclusion

A base period is a time to get started on upgrading $\dot{V}O_2$max and the seven key physiological variables that determine performance: $t_{lim}v\dot{V}O_2$max, $v\dot{V}O_2$max, running economy, lactate-threshold speed, maximal running speed, resistance to fatigue, and running-specific strength. Base periods work best when they make runners fitter. When runners have higher capacities, they are able to train at higher intensities during subsequent periods of training and thus make more substantial improvements in their performance characteristics. Traditional base periods do a modest job of making runners fitter. It makes sense to replace traditional bases with foundation periods that initiate the forward progress of critical physiological variables. Base periods do not need to feature the volume included in later phases of training, but they do require an essential core of quality to optimize the training process.

Circuit training (see chapter 13) should be a particularly effective training modality during base periods. Circuit training advances aerobic capacity, lactate threshold, running economy, and $v\dot{V}O_2$max. Its high-quality running elements enhance neuromuscular development. Circuit work also builds whole-body strength, which should promote resistance to fatigue and heightened running economy. The completion of two circuit sessions per week, along with the inclusion of some additional high-quality running on a third day, would help create an extremely productive base period that would make runners fully prepared for the demands of subsequent, challenging running-specific strength training and intense running workouts.

CHAPTER 25

Enhancing Economy

As outlined in chapter 8, running economy—the rate of oxygen consumption associated with a specific running speed—is an important determiner of performance.[1] At competitive running velocities, individuals who have lower oxygen costs associated with such speeds generally fare better in the competitions than do runners with higher costs, although other factors such as neural output, lactate-threshold speed, and resistance to fatigue may be more important than running economy in certain situations. So how do runners enhance economy? There are a number of factors to consider, including some that have a greater impact than others.

Changes in Running Form

Exercise scientists have been curious about whether changes in running form can enhance economy. In a study carried out at Wake Forest University in the United States, researchers asked a group of runners to incorporate a number of new form elements into their running, including greater flexion of the knee during the stance phase of gait, more upright posture, and better control of the arms and upper body.[2] Somewhat surprisingly, these popular changes in form did not improve running economy to any significant degree. It is possible that the study duration was not long enough (10 weeks) for improvements in economy to occur; the time needed for economy enhancement in response to form alteration has not been well established. It is also possible that the form adjustments advocated in this research were not the correct ones.

The Wake Forest scientists had their subjects adopt longer strides and a heel-strike landing pattern during running, for example. While heel striking is a very popular form of running, and studies suggest that at least 75 to 90 percent of endurance runners use this technique instead of midfoot or forefoot striking,[3] recent research reveals that heel striking is linked with higher impact forces and a longer stance phase of gait,[4] factors that could actually increase the cost of running and thus harm economy. Using relatively longer strides while running is also risky from an economy standpoint because longer steps can increase braking forces during impact with the ground and thus increase the work and oxygen cost required to run at a specific speed.

Despite the inability of the Wake Forest study to link form changes with better running, exercise scientists have continued to speculate that certain changes in running form would have a positive impact on running economy. Specifically, scientists have been intrigued by the idea that form adjustments leading to less energy wasted on braking forces and reduced vertical oscillations of the center of mass can enhance running economy.[5] Running form intended to reduce braking forces and vertical oscillations would incorporate a slight forward lean of the body from the ankles (figure 25.1a) during gait so that the body would tend to bounce *forward* rather than straight up with each step, midfoot striking (figure 25.1b; heel striking is linked with greater braking forces), a high cadence, and a relatively neutral shin angle at foot strike.

A relatively fast cadence (i.e., greater than or equal to 180 steps per minute) should upgrade economy because it favors midfoot striking over heel striking; heel striking increases the amount of time on the ground per step, and therefore it is more difficult to use a heel-strike pattern in conjunction with a rapid step rate. Runners can work on cadence, and thus economy, by using a metronome (no, not the kind that sits atop pianos—the small electronic models are preferable) and following its 180- to 190-beeps per minute frequency as they run. Just this simple adjustment will change form in a positive way for the majority of runners who—when metronome guided—will suddenly begin to get their feet under their centers of mass at impact with the ground and start landing with a midfoot pattern.

Shin angle (see figure 25.2), defined as the angle between the shin and an imaginary line perpendicular to the ground and running through the

▶ **Figure 25.1** A *(a)* slight forward lean of the body and a *(b)* midfoot strike are thought to reduce braking forces.

▶ **Figure 25.2** *(a)* Positive, *(b)* negative, and *(c)* nearly neutral shin angles.

knee at the exact moment the foot first touches the ground during impact, should be linked with economy, too. A highly positive shin angle of more than a few degrees means that the shin and foot are well forward of the body's center of mass and thus will accentuate the braking forces. A negative shin angle of any degree generally means that a runner is about to fall forward on his or her face. A neutral shin angle, with the shin more or less perpendicular with the ground, indicates an absence of braking force and perhaps optimal economy.

Overly positive shin angles can be transformed to slightly positive or neutral shin angles over time by increasing cadence and using the metronome at first, wearing minimal shoes with zero heel drop, or by running unshod. The resulting suite of changes—slight forward lean of the body from the ankles, a fast cadence, slightly positive to neutral shin angle at impact with the ground, and midfoot striking— should be associated with the best possible running economy. Coaches and runners can track changes in shin angle, body lean, and foot-strike pattern over time with inexpensive video cameras or with apps such as Coaches Eyes.

Differences Between Economy and Efficiency

Classic exercise research carried out about 30 years ago noted that marathon runners tend to have superior running economy compared with competitors at shorter distances (e.g., 5K and 10K) and middle-distance runners. At the time, this result was viewed as being logical and predictable since it was thought that marathon runners would have to be highly economical and efficient to compete well over a long distance like 42K (26.1 mi).

Economy and efficiency have entirely different meanings, however. While economy is the oxygen cost of running at a fixed speed, efficiency is the ratio of work performed to energy expended. No study has ever documented an improvement in efficiency in response to training in endurance runners, and there is little evidence that efficiency varies widely among runners. Economy, on the other hand, is responsive to training and varies widely.

When scientists took a closer look at the hypothesis that marathoners are more economical, they discovered that the runners being studied were usually having economy measured at relatively slow running velocities. When speeds quicker than marathon pace were used in economy research, middle-distance runners (i.e., competitors at 800 and 1,500 meters) were actually the most economical—more so than 5- and 10K runners and marathoners.[6] This suggests that either middle-distance runners are inherently more economical than longer-distance competitors, or the use of high running speeds and explosive drills during training is an economy enhancer.

Jacob De Golish/Icon SMI

▶ While studies have not been able to pinpoint practices that enhance efficiency, marathon runners can improve their economy by including training typically used by middle distance runners such as high running speeds and explosive drills.

Explosive Drills and High-Speed Training

One of the best promoters of enhanced economy is the use of explosive drills, exercises in which there is a great emphasis on getting the feet on and off the ground quickly. In a study carried out in Australia by Rob Spurrs and his colleagues, well-trained endurance runners who incorporated explosive drills (e.g., jumps, hops, leaps, hurdle clearing) into their overall training program over a 9-week period benefited from a 3 percent improvement in economy; athletes who avoided the explosive exercises failed to enhance economy at all.[7]

In another study supporting the idea that explosive training spurs economy enhancements, researcher Heikki Rusko and his colleague Neena Paavolainen asked a group of well-trained 5K runners to add explosive work (e.g., sprints, jumps, hops, squats) to their training program while a second group of similar runners added volume (i.e., distance) without the explosive exercises.[8] Rusko and Paavolainen set up the study so that the added distance and additional explosive routines took similar amounts of *time* so that neither group could benefit from an increase in training time.

After 9 weeks, the group that added explosive work enhanced economy by 3 percent and also ran a simulated 5K race 3 percent faster than previously; the group that had added distance to their training failed to upgrade economy or race performance. The mechanism for this difference appears to be that explosive training converts runners' legs into slightly stiffer springs that provide more propulsive force with each step; in contrast, less-stiff springs tend to collapse too much during stance and lack adequate recoil power.

Veronique Billat's classic work also supports the idea that higher-speed training is highly beneficial to running economy. In one of Billat's studies, experienced endurance runners added weekly training sessions conducted at $v\dot{V}O_2max$ (i.e., about 2K [1.2 mi] race speed) to their training programs and moved running economy in the right direction by about 4 percent over a 9-week period.[9]

Strength Training

Along with high-speed running and explosive work, one of the best enhancers of running economy is strength training. In a study carried out with female collegiate runners who incorporated strength training into their overall programs, including adding a variety of running-relevant movements such as squatting, the participants upgraded running economy by about 3 percent over a 12-week period, while runners without the strength training failed to enhance economy at all.[10] Several other investigations have linked the adoption of strength training with enhancement of running economy.[11-13]

One mechanism involved in this linkage is probably that strength training improves coordination while running, thus lowering the cost of movement because lower energy and oxygen expenditures are required to correct movements that are not optimal. Strength training may also improve force production while the feet are on the ground, in part by strengthening individual muscle cells in relevant muscles. As muscle cells become stronger, perhaps fewer cells and motor units are needed to run at a specific velocity, thus reducing the oxygen cost of that speed.

An important area of future strength-training and running-economy research will undoubtedly be whether running-specific strength training (i.e., strength training focusing on movements that mimic the mechanics of running) is superior to more general strength training. Research has shown that the gains in strength associated with strength training are specific to the movements involved in the training as well as to the velocity of those movements.[14, 15] For example, the strength of the quadriceps muscles during squatting movements is undoubtedly enhanced more by actual squat training than by leg-extension exercises using similar resistance, even though the latter focuses intently on the quads. In a similar vein, running-specific strength training—with an emphasis on one-leg squats, partial squats, bench step-ups, runner's poses, bicycle leg swings, eccentric reaches with toes, among others—should be better than general movements (e.g., two-leg squats and exercises on machines) from the standpoints of propulsive force production and injury protection during running.

Other Factors

Carrying out explosive work and conducting appropriate strength training can enhance economy, but so can a variety of other training techniques and strategies. Running unshod, upgrading psychological skills, tapering, drafting, carrying out hill training, using $v\dot{V}O_2$max training, and losing weight have all been linked with improved economy.

Running Barefoot

As noted in chapter 8, one of the easiest steps a runner can take to improve his or her economy is simply to take off those shoes. A change from shod to barefoot running generally upgrades running economy by 1 to 3 percent.[16] There is debate about whether this improvement is entirely a consequence of the mass of running shoes—moving 11-ounce running shoes or even the lightest racing flats through space costs energy and therefore oxygen—or is also a result of changes in form associated with barefoot running.[16]

When moving from shod to barefoot gait, runners commonly shift from heel to midfoot striking, strike the ground with greater plantar flexion at the ankle, and adopt a higher stride rate, factors that might be linked with better economy.[17] Runners should not adopt barefoot running quickly and cavalierly, however, as the work performed by various regions of the legs may dramatically increase with a shift from shod to shoeless running; specifically, the calf muscles are much more active during barefoot running and susceptible to injury during the transition.

Psychological Skills

The adoption of specific psychological skills may also improve economy. Research suggests that runners who employ an associative strategy—focusing on relaxing and coordinating breathing and body-segment movements during running—tend to have superior economy compared with runners who use a disassociative technique in which mental focus is on ideas and events removed from the actual act of running.[18]

Overall mood also plays a significant role in determining running economy. Runners who are depressed and anxious tend to have poorer economy than runners who are optimistic and relaxed.[19] In addition, runners who adopt an empowerment strategy, in which they feel more in control of their training and are less weighed down by bad workouts and unrealistic expectations, tend to have significantly better economy compared with runners who appear to be less empowered.[18] Positive self-talk strategies also seem to be effective at enhancing economy.[19]

Tapering

Tapering is another training technique that can enhance running economy. In a study carried out with 5K runners, individuals who cut training volume by about 60 percent over a 1-week period improved economy significantly. Note that these runners also focused heavily on fast 400-meter training during the tapering week, which might have accounted for at least some of the economy upgrade.[20] Other inquiries have supported the idea that reductions in training volume can promote better running economy.[21]

Hill Training

As described in chapter 15, hill training is another strategy that enhances economy. In classic Scandinavian research, runners who added hill running and hill bouncing to their training over a 12-week period upgraded economy by 3 percent.[22] It is important to note that although such improvements in economy seem small, they are linked with important changes in performance. Each 1 percent gain in economy can lead to a 1 percent faster race time, and thus a 3 percent economy enhancement could bring a marathon runner from a time of 3:05 down to the much more desired 2:59:30.

v$\dot{V}O_2$max

Running economy is a variable that is built in to v$\dot{V}O_2$max. Inherently, v$\dot{V}O_2$max is an expression of a runner's ability to increase running velocity as much as possible, given the constraints of his or her oxygen-consumption system. A high v$\dot{V}O_2$max automatically means solid economy because a runner could not extract high speeds from his or her oxygen-delivery system unless economy was quite good. Thus, training methods that increase v$\dot{V}O_2$max also tend to enhance running economy.

One of the best ways to optimize $v\dot{V}O_2$max—and thus running economy—is to carry out training that contains quality segments conducted at very close to $v\dot{V}O_2$max itself.[23] These quality portions of workouts are usually intervals lasting from 30 to 180 seconds, with recoveries equal to the work-interval times. Each work interval is performed at $v\dot{V}O_2$max, which is commonly estimated from an all-out 6-minute test on the track. (See chapter 26 for more on $v\dot{V}O_2$max.)

Drafting and Losing Weight

Nontraining strategies can also enhance economy. Drafting behind another athlete, for example, reduces the oxygen cost of moving at a specific speed during cycling and swimming and is probably also slightly effective at lowering oxygen consumption during running.[24] Losing weight also tends to upgrade economy since there is a lower oxygen expense associated with moving a smaller mass through space. The lost weight should be non-productive weight, however. Losses in leg-muscle mass might curb propulsive force and could actually disturb coordination during running and increase foot-strike time, thus hurting economy. Losses of abdominal fat, on the other hand, usually push economy toward a lower oxygen requirement.

Tyler Kaufman/Icon SMI

▶ Drafting during a race may reduce oxygen consumption, which could enhance running economy.

Anatomical Factors

Anatomical factors certainly have an effect on running economy. Runners with large, heavy feet, for example, are unlikely to have superior economy since those large feet must be swung through space with each step, a process that consumes considerable oxygen compared with swinging small feet. There is a countertheory, however, suggesting that larger feet are better for economy because they provide more stability during stance. The optimal strategy would be to have large feet during stance and tiny feet during the swing phase of gait, but unfortunately this is impossible. Informal surveys carried out with elite Kenyan runners suggest that these runners have medium-sized feet for their body size (e.g., many elite Kenyan men fall into the range of shoe sizes from 8B to 9C in U.S. sizing).[25] Having medium-sized feet may produce a compromise between stability during stance and lightness during swing.

One hypothesis concerning the superiority of elite Kenyan runners is that their upgraded economy, compared with runners from the rest of the world, is a result of their very slim calves, which allow calf muscles to exert force on the Achilles tendon more vertically and directly, perhaps saving oxygen and making toe-off more explosive. This is a difficult hypothesis to test, however: It would be hard to make the calves of Kenyan runners fatter experimentally or to trim muscle fibers from the lateral edges of U.S. runners' calves. It is also important to note that some research has found the running economy of elite Kenyans is not significantly different from that of elite Americans and top-level Europeans.[26, 27]

Intriguing recent research has revealed that runners with relatively long Achilles tendons tend to have poorer running economy compared to athletes with short Achilles tendons.[28] There is also evidence that the possession of a relatively longer heel bone (i.e., calcaneus) hurts economy and that having short calcaneal tubers, the posterior projections of the heel bones, was advantageous for early members of the species *Homo sapiens* in running down prey.[28] Surprisingly, about 80 percent of the variation in economy among nonelite individuals can be explained by the length of the calcaneal tuber.[28]

Impact of Increasing Mileage

One of the most popular strategies for enhancing running economy is actually quite a weak stimulus for upgrading economy especially when economy is measured at competitive speeds. Many runners believe that the strategy of increasing the weekly distance run, or volume, is a powerful way to become more economical, but scientific research fails to support this contention. In classic work conducted by Finnish exercise scientists, one group of runners increased weekly running volume from 45 to 70 miles (72-113 km) while a second group remained at 45 miles (72 km) per week and added explosive training to their program. The group that added volume failed to enhance economy at all, while the explosive group improved economy significantly by approximately 3 percent.[8]

This Finnish research is quite revealing, giving researchers and runners a clear picture of a key mechanism by which running economy can be improved. In the study, the runners who added explosive training shortened foot-strike time as a result of the high-speed training; the change in foot-strike time was tightly correlated with the gain in economy. In effect, after explosive training, the runners' feet needed to be on the ground for less time per step to maintain a specific velocity.

This reduction in contact time apparently reduces the oxygen cost per step and thus enhances economy. It is difficult to see why increasing the overall distance run would produce a similar effect. When distance is increased significantly, a large portion of the additional volume is conducted at sub-maximal intensities, the kinds of speeds that do not require a shortening of foot-strike time. Thus, the nervous system does not learn to regulate a quicker foot-strike; on the contrary, a pattern of slower running and more lethargic reaction of the feet with the ground may be locked in to the neuromuscular system, hurting economy at competitive velocities.

Training That Hampers Economy

Certain forms of training actually harm economy. For example, the use of a weight vest during running over a several-week period can hurt economy by 3 to 6 percent.[29] It is not clear why this is true, although it is possible that using the vest changes coordination patterns of the motor units in the legs, in effect teaching the muscles to run while supporting greater weight, and thus negatively affects economy without the vest. The new pattern involving running with weight is not as economical as the vest-free mode of running—and this effect is maintained for awhile even after a runner abandons the vest.

Overtraining, or conducting training that exceeds the body's capacity to recover and adapt, can also disturb running economy. There are two likely mechanisms for this. One possibility is that muscles are physically damaged in the overtrained state and thus less able to use oxygen economically. When damaged, muscle cells produce less propulsive force and thus require the assistance of other muscle cells, an extra recruitment of muscle fibers that increases oxygen cost. Another likely scenario is that the nervous system becomes less responsive than usual in the overtrained state and thus does a poorer job of regulating gait. This would be a protective mechanism, of course, the nervous system's way of telling an overtrained runner to back off for awhile.

Conclusion

It is clear from scientific research that runners have many tools in their training programs for enhancing running economy. It is extremely important for runners to use all of their economy-enhancing strategies since running economy is such a strong predictor of performance. Although runners may be daunted by the array of training techniques that have an impact on economy, they should be reassured by the knowledge that training that incorporates high-quality running, explosive drills, hill training, and strength training will be extremely economy enhancing. The pursuit of better economy should be a year-long process, not an undertaking confined to a few weeks at a time.

26

Gaining v$\dot{V}O_2$max

Optimizing v$\dot{V}O_2$max produces major gains in endurance performance. As outlined in Chapter 9, v$\dot{V}O_2$max is simply the minimal running velocity that elicits maximal aerobic capacity, or $\dot{V}O_2$max. While $\dot{V}O_2$max is a relatively poor predictor of performance among runners of fairly similar ability, v$\dot{V}O_2$max has excellent predictive power. The mechanism underlying this apparent paradox is simply that a runner might have an extremely high $\dot{V}O_2$max but still perform relatively poorly if somewhat-mediocre running speeds caused that runner to use nearly all of that prodigious oxygen-processing capability. In other words, a voluminous $\dot{V}O_2$max is of modest benefit if running economy is subpar.

In contrast, a runner with a high v$\dot{V}O_2$max is always in great shape, literally and figuratively. Such a runner can run very quickly at $\dot{V}O_2$max and thus must have good running economy. Since v$\dot{V}O_2$max includes an economy factor, it contains more physiological information than $\dot{V}O_2$max alone and can explain differences in performance for which $\dot{V}O_2$max cannot be held accountable. For example, runner A has a higher $\dot{V}O_2$max than runner B, but runner B has a higher v$\dot{V}O_2$max than runner A because of better running economy, which creates a lower cost of oxygen for a given velocity. Runner B will be better than runner A at $\dot{V}O_2$max, v$\dot{V}O_2$max, and all percentages of these variables because runner B will operate at a higher speed than runner A.

Research carried out by French exercise physiologist Veronique Billat has revealed that one of the best ways to boost v$\dot{V}O_2$max is actually to run *at* v$\dot{V}O_2$max during training.[1] By working at v$\dot{V}O_2$max, a runner improves neuromuscular control and thus economy while running at a rapid velocity. By attaining $\dot{V}O_2$max during the session—an inevitable outcome of the training since by definition v$\dot{V}O_2$max is fast enough to elicit $\dot{V}O_2$max—a runner provides the optimal stimulus for expanding $\dot{V}O_2$max to the greatest extent possible. The consequent changes in economy and $\dot{V}O_2$max drive v$\dot{V}O_2$max upward to a significant degree because v$\dot{V}O_2$max depends on both economy and $\dot{V}O_2$max.

Determining v$\dot{V}O_2$max

To determine v$\dot{V}O_2$max, a runner could visit an exercise physiology laboratory and pay a substantial amount of money to carry out an incremental treadmill test. Although the expensive laboratory equipment involved in such a test might seem to make it authoritative, a weakness is that such an exam is carried out on the treadmill, where running economy is likely to vary, compared with running on terra firma. Thus, lab v$\dot{V}O_2$max is unlikely to be the same as that derived from running on a track or ground. Unless a runner plans to do all training on a treadmill, the latter variable would appear to be more useful.

The alternative to the laboratory test is for a runner to go to the track, warm up, and then—when he or she is feeling loose, energized, and ready—run as far as possible on the track for 6 minutes. The distance covered in 6 minutes can then be divided by 360 seconds to yield a very good estimate of v$\dot{V}O_2$max.[1] If a runner covers 1,600 meters (1 mi) in 6 minutes, the estimated v$\dot{V}O_2$max would be 1,600/360 = 4.44 meters per second.

Of course, the distance covered might not be a nice round number like 1,600. Odd distances on the track can be measured with the use of a measuring wheel purchased at a home-supply store or online from a track and field website. Naturally, a GPS device can be used as well, freeing a runner to carry out the 6-minute test on any adequate stretch of flat terrain. Coaches and runners who lack a wheel or GPS setup will have to eyeball and estimate the distance covered on the track.

To create practical and productive v$\dot{V}O_2$max workouts, it is convenient to convert the v$\dot{V}O_2$max from the 6-minute test into a pace per 400 meters (see table 26.1). This calculation can be made in two ways. One way is to determine the number of 400-meter segments in the distance covered and divide 360 seconds by that number. For example, running 2,000 meters in 6 minutes would correspond with a v$\dot{V}O_2$max tempo of 72 seconds, which is calculated by dividing 360 seconds by 5 (the number of 400-meter segments in 2,000 meters). Covering 1,800 meters in 6 minutes would produce a v$\dot{V}O_2$max tempo of 80 seconds per 400 meters, which is calculated by dividing 360 seconds by 4.5 (there being 4.5 400-meter segments in 1,800 meters).

The second method, which works well for odd track distances, uses the v$\dot{V}O_2$max estimate in the calculation. For example, if a runner completes 1,728 meters during the 6-minute test, the first step is to compute v$\dot{V}O_2$max. In this case, 1,728 meters divided by 360 seconds equals 4.8 meters per second. This is the estimate of v$\dot{V}O_2$max. The second step is to calculate the 400-meter tempo:

400 meters / 4.8 meters per second = 83 seconds per 400 meters

This tempo can be immediately put to use in training, for example by running 400-meter intervals in 83 seconds.

Table 26.1 Calculating vV̇O₂max 400-Meter Paces

6-minute distance (m)	vV̇O₂max (m/sec)*	400-m pace (sec)**
2,000	5.56	72
1,800	5.00	80
1,728	4.80	83

*Calculated by dividing total meters completed in 6 minutes by 360 seconds.

**Calculated by dividing 360 seconds by the number of 400-meter segments covered in the test or by dividing 400 by the vV̇O₂max.

Improving vV̇O₂max and Running Economy

Once vV̇O₂max tempo is determined, appropriate workouts that advance vV̇O₂max can be created. As discussed in chapter 9, Billat and her colleagues at the University of Lille, the Center of Sport Medicine, and the National Center of Health in France made a head start on this process when they asked eight experienced runners to take part in 4 weeks of training that included one interval session based on vV̇O₂max per week.[2] The vV̇O₂max tempo for these athletes was 72 seconds per 400 meters, and the interval workout created by Billat was simply 5 × 1,000 meters in 3 minutes each, with 3-minute, easy jog recoveries. (In vV̇O₂max sessions, recovery durations are always equal to work-interval periods.) Covering 1,000 meters in 3 minutes involves running at exactly 72 seconds per 400-meter tempo.

vV̇O₂max training cannot exist in a vacuum; it is always blended with easy sessions and other quality workouts. In Billat's research there was one other quality workout during each week of training: a session that included two long 20-minute intervals at 85 percent of vV̇O₂max. If vV̇O₂max happened to be 20 kilometers per hour (5.55 m/sec), the speed for this long-interval sessions was 85 percent of that, or 17 kilometers per hour (4.72 m/sec, or about 5:40 per mile). There was a 5-minute, easy jog recovery between the two 20-minute intervals. All other sessions were conducted at an easy pace.

Although V̇O₂max did not budge at all over the 4-week training period, vV̇O₂max rose by 3 percent from 20.5 kilometers per hour to 21.1 kilometers per hour. This indicates that the economy factor in vV̇O₂max was the key mechanism by which vV̇O₂max improved, not the aerobic capacity factor. In other words, after the vV̇O₂max training period, the runners were able to run faster while using the same internal oxygen-delivery system as before.

Indeed, running economy improved by an astounding 6 percent in Billat's research. This 6 percent gain in economy is particularly impressive. In scientific research carried out to explore the effects of different kinds of training on economy, the observed gains in economy have usually been far less than the one induced by Billat and her colleagues with the vV̇O₂max-based training. For example, enhancements of economy associated with hill work or strength training are usually in the 3 percent range.

To see if more would be better, Billat and co-workers put their eight athletes through 4 additional weeks of training, but this time the runners carried out *three* interval sessions at vV̇O₂max each week, again using the 5 × 3 minute protocol but at the new vV̇O₂max established after the initial 4 weeks. The workout at 85 percent of vV̇O₂max and easy runs were blended with these torrid sessions.

The next 4-week follow-up revealed that more vV̇O₂max training is not always better. This major increase in vV̇O₂max work served primarily to increase muscle soreness and blood levels of norepinephrine, a stress hormone, and decrease the runners' quality of sleep. In addition, vV̇O₂max, running economy, and lactate-threshold speed all refused to improve in the face of the trio of weekly vV̇O₂max sessions. A logical conclusion is that about one vV̇O₂max session per week may be optimal for upgrading vV̇O₂max in experienced runners, while three such sessions represent overkill.

30-30 Workouts

Working under the reasonable assumption that the completion of more vV̇O₂max running *per workout* could be productive, rather than more vV̇O₂max workouts per week, Billat began experimenting with different work-interval lengths. In a follow-up study, Billat and her co-researchers asked the runners to complete vV̇O₂max sessions that consisted of 30-second intervals at vV̇O₂max instead of the classic 3-minute durations.[3] The runners warmed up with 15 minutes of easy jogging and then alternated 30-second work intervals at vV̇O₂max with 30-second recoveries at 50 percent of vV̇O₂max, sustaining this pattern for as long as possible. A runner with a vV̇O₂max tempo of 78 seconds per 400 meters would have been covering 154 meters in each 30-second interval. (Calculate this distance by dividing 30 by 78 and then multiplying by 400.)

The runners also employed a second kind of quality workout in this follow-up investigation: a continuous run, sustained for as long as possible, at a velocity of about 91 percent of vV̇O₂max. During the 30-second interval workout, the athletes were running at an average tempo of 78 seconds per 400 meters, broken up into 30-second chunks with 30-second breaks; in the continuous session the runners moved along at a pace of 85 seconds per 400 meters, without stopping, until fatigue brought the effort to a halt. The athletes conducted both sessions on a synthetic track while breathing through portable, telemetric, metabolic analyzers that allowed Billat to determine their actual rates of oxygen consumption.

Although short intervals are sometimes criticized by coaches as nonspecific, that is, too far removed from competitive situations, the 30-30 workout appeared to offer some unique advantages. The average number of work intervals completed prior to the onset of exhaustion was 19, which meant that 9.5 minutes of quality running were completed. Out of this 9.5-minute total, 7 minutes and 51 seconds (83 percent of the total quality time) were actually spent at $\dot{V}O_2$max. If this seems confusing, remember there is a lag time in oxygen-consumption rate. Even if one begins running at $v\dot{V}O_2$max (a velocity), it takes a while for the oxygen-consumption mechanisms to kick into gear and begin operating at the highest-possible level; as a result, the attainment of the maximal rate of oxygen consumption is delayed.

In contrast, the continuous run at 91 percent of $v\dot{V}O_2$max lasted for an average of only 8 minutes and 20 seconds and featured a total time of less than 3 minutes at the maximal rate of oxygen consumption. Overall, 309 more seconds were spent at $\dot{V}O_2$max during the 30-30 effort compared with the sustained running.

Readers should not worry too much about why a continuous run at only 91 percent of $v\dot{V}O_2$max was nonetheless able to produce the maximal rate of oxygen consumption, which one might expect to be reached only at speeds of 100 percent of $v\dot{V}O_2$max and above. This attainment of $\dot{V}O_2$max at velocities less than $v\dot{V}O_2$max is due to the slow component of oxygen usage during sustained running and should not be concerning here.

A remarkable feature of the follow-up investigation was that three of the eight runners were able to continue with the 30-30 intervals for a long period of time, completing as many as 27 of the 30-second work intervals at $v\dot{V}O_2$max. The completion of 27 work intervals was linked with spending 18.5 minutes at the maximal rate of oxygen consumption, or $\dot{V}O_2$max. This may appear to be a paradox, since only 13.5 minutes (27×30 seconds) were spent at $v\dot{V}O_2$max, but it is important to note that the runners often sustained maximal aerobic capacity during the 30-second recovery intervals, too, even though they were running at an intensity of only 50 percent of $v\dot{V}O_2$max! The reason for this is that there is another physiological lag occurring: the runners' bodies take longer than 30 seconds to downshift oxygen usage after their running paces slowed. This is important because many exercise physiologists believe that the total time spent at the maximal rate of oxygen consumption is an important indicator of workout value.

The 30-30 workout can thus be a powerhouse, and—anecdotally—it is tolerated very well by runners, even by rather inexperienced runners who tend to struggle with the classic 5×3 minutes session. In another piece of research carried out with modestly fit physical education students, Billat revealed that using 30-30 workouts twice a week can boost $\dot{V}O_2$max by 10 percent in just 8 to 10 weeks.[4] Billat recommended using the 30-30 session early in the season as an excellent, easily tolerated way to kick-start improvements in $\dot{V}O_2$max, $v\dot{V}O_2$max, running speed, and lactate-threshold speed.[4]

After about 4 weeks of 30-30 training, a runner could progress to 60-60 workouts, with 60 seconds at $v\dot{V}O_2$max and 60 seconds of easy jog recovery. After another 4 weeks or so of 60-60, the runner could make the jump to 5 $\times 3$ minutes, which is often considered the ultimate $v\dot{V}O_2$max session. The average amount of time spent at maximal aerobic capacity during the 5×3 is around 10 minutes, about 25 percent more high-octane time compared with the average 30-30 session.[4] Thus, moving from 30-30 up to 5 × 3 appears to be an excellent training progression.

Note that some runners may run uniquely well with the 30-30, however. As mentioned, some of those in Billat's research were able to complete 27 intervals during a 30-30 session, resulting in 18.5 minutes at a maximal rate of oxygen consumption. Even if such a runner spent all 5 × 3 work intervals at a maximal rate of oxygen consumption, it is unlikely that the runner would be able to amass as much time at $\dot{V}O_2$max.

T$_{lim}$v$\dot{V}O_2$max Approach

Although the Billat v$\dot{V}O_2$max formula—30-, 60-, and 180-second intervals at v$\dot{V}O_2$max, with recoveries equal in duration to the intervals—is often considered to be the gold standard for v$\dot{V}O_2$max-boosting training, there are cases when runners may profitably diverge from this path. Work carried out by Tim Smith and colleagues at the School of Human Life Sciences at the University of Tasmania in Australia suggests that modest *expansion* of v$\dot{V}O_2$max work-interval length may produce striking gains in fitness.[5]

To enhance understanding of this Australian research, it is important to focus on the variable t_{lim}v$\dot{V}O_2$max, which is the amount of time a runner can sustain v$\dot{V}O_2$max. The average t_{lim}v$\dot{V}O_2$max for all of the human runners on planet earth is 6 minutes; that's why Billat recommends the use of the 6-minute v$\dot{V}O_2$max test. For the majority of runners, the pace established in the 6-minute test will be very close to v$\dot{V}O_2$max and thus is quite usable for v$\dot{V}O_2$max training. However, *individual* runners may have readings of t_{lim}v$\dot{V}O_2$max that stray considerably from the 6-minute average. In fact, there is good reason to believe that the shortest t_{lim}v$\dot{V}O_2$max in the world is around 4 minutes and the longest is about 10 minutes. As you might expect, t_{lim}v$\dot{V}O_{22}$max is not a bad predictor of performance in its own right: Runners with longer values of t_{lim}v$\dot{V}O_2$max tend to fare better in competition than runners with similar v$\dot{V}O_2$max values but shorter t_{lim}v$\dot{V}O_2$max values. Thus, t_{lim}v$\dot{V}O_2$max is an indicator of one's ability *to sustain* a scalding running pace like v$\dot{V}O_2$max.

Note, however, that the t_{lim}v$\dot{V}O_2$max situation has the *potential* to create troubles for some runners who can't measure their v$\dot{V}O_2$max values precisely in the laboratory—in other words, almost everyone. The trouble can come this way: Let's say that your t_{lim}v$\dot{V}O_2$max is actually 4 minutes, but you take the 6-minute test. Since by definition you can only handle v$\dot{V}O_2$max for 4 minutes, the pace established in your 6-minute test will be slower than your true v$\dot{V}O_2$max; your subsequent training, revolving around the results of the 6-minute test, will actually focus on a sub-v$\dot{V}O_2$max intensity instead of on the real result. The good news is that your training will still be high in quality, and eventually your t_{lim}v$\dot{V}O_2$max should climb toward at least the 6-minute mark, especially if you use longer work intervals of about 180 seconds rather than 30 seconds, for example. The reasoning here is that these longer intervals can compensate a bit for the lower intensity by allowing oxygen-consumption rate to climb. Thus, on subsequent $v\dot{V}O_2$max re-tests, the pace you establish for 6 minutes should be closer to your real $v\dot{V}O_2$max.

Alternately, if your $t_{lim}v\dot{V}O_2$max is really 10 minutes and you take a 6-minute test, you will probably run faster than your $v\dot{V}O_2$max during the 6-minute effort, and your subsequent training will be above your real $v\dot{V}O_2$max. The good news here is that these sessions might be better at augmenting your maximal running speed, which is also a good predictor of performance compared with $v\dot{V}O_2$max exertions, and the sessions will also augment $v\dot{V}O_2$max, lactate-threshold speed, and running economy.

In the Australian research, nine runners were asked to complete their weekly $v\dot{V}O_2$max interval workouts with a work-interval duration of *60 percent* of $t_{lim}v\dot{V}O_2$max instead of the usual 50 percent (the Billat formula centers on a 6-minute test ultimately followed by 3-minute work intervals with 3 minutes being *50 percent* of the 6-minute $t_{lim}v\dot{V}O_2$max). Nine other runners were required to be even more courageous with work-interval lengths of *70 percent* of $t_{lim}v\dot{V}O_2$max. The nine control competitors completed no work at $v\dot{V}O_2$max and focused on moderate-intensity, long-duration running. All the runners were monitored over a 4-week period, and those running at 60 percent and 70 percent $t_{lim}v\dot{V}O_2$max completed two interval sessions at $v\dot{V}O_2$max each week. The hitch was that the 60-percent athletes performed six work intervals at $v\dot{V}O_2$max per session while the 70-percent runners conducted only five intervals per workout; the idea was that the 70-percenters were compensating for their reduced number of intervals by running longer per interval. In a departure from the classic Billat method, recovery intervals were twice as long in duration as the work intervals.

After 4 weeks and eight total interval workouts with the intensity set at $v\dot{V}O_2$max and work-interval length at either 60 percent or 70 percent of $t_{lim}v\dot{V}O_2$max, only the 60-percent group had improved 3K (1.9 mi) race times significantly, enjoying a nice 18-second upgrade compared with just 6 seconds of improvement in the 70-percent group (not statistically significant) and a half-second improvement for the controls. In addition, $t_{lim}v\dot{V}O_2$max was significantly higher than before in the 60-percent group after 4 weeks of training—23 percent (50 seconds) higher—but had not improved for the other two groups of runners.

Why did the group running at 60 percent of $t_{lim}v\dot{V}O_2$max fare better than the 70-percent group? A key problem for the runners at 70 percent of $t_{lim}v\dot{V}O_2$max was that they were more likely to be unable to fully complete their work intervals compared with the group at 60 percent of $t_{lim}v\dot{V}O_2$max. In fact, the 70-percent group completed just 86 percent of its required interval time compared with the 96 percent completed by the 60 percent group; this meant that the 60-percent group spent about 768 seconds running at $v\dot{V}O_2$max per v$\dot{V}O_2$max workout, compared with just 655 seconds per workout for the 70-percent group. To put it simply, it is very difficult to rack up five complete intervals at v$\dot{V}O_2$max within an interval workout when the work-interval duration is set at the rather-expansive 70 percent of t_{lim}v$\dot{V}O_2$max.

This Australian research reveals that 4 weeks of *twice-a-week* v$\dot{V}O_2$max training can raise t_{lim}v$\dot{V}O_2$max and improve 3K (1.9 mi) performances to a substantial degree in already well-trained runners and does not elevate the risk of overtraining. The runners were monitored closely for fatigue, sleep quality, stress, and muscle soreness to determine whether the high-intensity v$\dot{V}O_2$max training was pushing them toward the overtrained state. Secondly, 60 percent of t_{lim}v$\dot{V}O_2$max is a viable work-interval length for v$\dot{V}O_2$max training. With 60 percent of t_{lim}v$\dot{V}O_2$max, the runners were able to complete 96 percent of their prescribed work-interval running. If t_{lim}v$\dot{V}O_2$max is assumed to be 6 minutes, this would mean pushing v$\dot{V}O_2$max work-interval length to 3:36 instead of Billat's standard of 3 minutes.

Conclusion

The bottom line? Runners should be progressive with their v$\dot{V}O_2$max workouts, gradually working their way from 30-30 sessions up to Billat's standard of 5 × 3 minutes and then to the Australian goal of 6 × 3:36. As long as runners are progressing with their v$\dot{V}O_2$max sessions (i.e., from shorter to longer work intervals, from fewer to more work intervals per session, from an occasional v$\dot{V}O_2$max session to one or two such efforts per week), the gains in fitness that accrue from v$\dot{V}O_2$max training will be sizable. And v$\dot{V}O_2$max training can be conducted year-round: It is so potent, and works so effectively for runners of all ability levels, that it would be absurd to confine it to short 4- to 6-week blocks, or mesocycles, of training.

CHAPTER 27

Upgrading Lactate Threshold

As outlined in chapter 10, running velocity at lactate threshold is an important predictor of performance at distances ranging from 800 meters to 100K (62.14 mi). This variable is simply the running speed above which lactate begins to accumulate in the blood. Running velocity at lactate threshold predicts performance so well because lactate—far from being a runner's nemesis—is actually a key fuel that provides the energy needed to run far and fast. When running velocity at lactate threshold is high (i.e., at a good speed), the runner has an outstanding ability to break down lactate for energy inside muscle cells and also a powerful capacity to remove lactate from the blood and use it to create propulsive force.

Approaches for Optimizing Running Velocity at Lactate Threshold

As described in chapter 10, scientific research indicates that there are two somewhat different ways to approach optimizing running velocity at lactate threshold. First, it is reasonable to train in ways that enhance muscle cells' oxidative energy systems, including their ability to take oxygen from the blood and use it to break down lactate at high rates. Of course, if lactate is broken down extremely rapidly, lots of energy will be produced, relatively modest amounts of lactate will be spilled into the blood, and the runner with such characteristics will be a highly fit, fast competitor with a high running velocity at lactate threshold. Enhancing the oxidative energy systems involves boosting the concentrations of aerobic enzymes inside muscle fibers and augmenting the number of mitochondria within muscle cells.

The second approach to optimizing running velocity at lactate threshold, however, is quite different: It focuses on expanding the abilities of the heart and muscles *to clear* lactate from the blood. Lactate levels in the blood, and thus the running velocity at lactate threshold, are the result not only of the *appearance* of blood lactate (i.e., the rate at which lactate spills out of muscles into the bloodstream) but also the *disappearance* of lactate from the blood (i.e., the rate at which the muscles and the heart pull lactate out of the blood plasma). For many years, exercise scientists were not certain that it would actually be possible to improve the ability of muscles to seize large quantities of lactate from the blood and then break down the lactate for energy. However, in 1993 a study carried out by lactate expert Arend Bonen and his research group at the University of Waterloo in Ontario, Canada, showed that muscle fibers could indeed develop the capacity to clear lactate from the blood at advanced rates if the training stimulus was appropriate.[1] At that time, however, no one knew *how* the muscles were actually transporting the lactate inward.

In 1996 Bonen and his research team discovered a unique muscle protein called MCT1 (for monocarboxylate transporter 1). Bonen and colleagues were able to show that MCT1 is indeed a lactate transporter, moving lactate directly into muscle cells where it can be metabolized for energy.[2] MCT1 is found on the outer edges of muscle membranes where it can come into direct contact with lactate. As MCT1 concentrations advance, lactate-disappearance rates increase correspondingly, and running velocity at lactate threshold also improves.[3] Thus, MCT1 optimization should be a key goal of lactate-threshold training. MCT1 levels are so important that MCT1 concentration in the muscles can actually be an excellent predictor of resistance to fatigue and endurance performance.[4] (Don't worry, though. We won't add it to our already rather extensive list of seven key performance enhancers.)

Poor Ways to Boost Running Velocity at Lactate Threshold

Endurance runners and their coaches have been interested in running velocity at lactate threshold since about 1980 when the lactate-threshold concept was first developed by exercise scientists. Over the last 33 years, two popular training techniques have been favored by the majority of runners to advance running velocity at lactate threshold: prolonged moderate exercise and tempo training. Prolonged moderate exercise involves doing a lot of running at submaximal speeds that are actually slower than running velocity at lactate threshold. Tempo training, on the other hand, consists of running steadily for 20 to 30 minutes at a pace that is as close to running velocity at lactate threshold as possible. Both of these techniques have proved to be poor ways to boost this variable.

Prolonged Moderate Exercise

Runners and other endurance athletes have traditionally believed that prolonged moderate exercise represents the ultimate way to increase running velocity at lactate threshold. From one perspective, that is somewhat logical thinking. After all, extended, medium-intensity exertions tend to increase the muscles' abilities to metabolize fat during exercise. If muscle fibers rely more heavily on fat and therefore less heavily on carbohydrate for fuel, less lactate will be produced because lactate is generated primarily from carbohydrate breakdown, not from fat degradation. Thus, at least in theory, less lactate spilling should take place, and running velocity at lactate threshold should not be reached until a relatively high speed is attained.

There are many problems with this approach, however. As a practical point, moderate training speeds are dissimilar from actual racing speeds from the standpoint of neuromuscular control of gait; therefore, it is difficult for the moderate-intensity runner to develop good economy at race velocities since those higher speeds are deemphasized during training. Moderately paced training is not very *specific* to racing, and the medium-intensity runner faces a difficult task in developing optimal neuromuscular coordination patterns for high-speed racing.

In addition, even when an athlete develops a great fat-burning capacity, that capability is seldom used in high-intensity racing situations. One problem is that fat becomes an increasingly minor source of energy at intensities above running velocity at lactate threshold.[5] Since most runners reach running velocity at lactate threshold at about 10-mile (16 km) race speed, all shorter distances will be raced at intensities above that threshold.[6] This means that fat metabolism is fairly unimportant at race distances of 10 miles (16 km) or less, even in those athletes who have built up prodigious fat-burning furnaces. Thus, the huge training investment in long, moderately paced miles rarely attenuates lactate production above running velocity at lactate threshold since fat can't replace carbohydrate at those intensities. In fact, high-volume, medium-intensity training may actually increase lactate levels above running velocity at lactate threshold because the muscles of athletes who train in that way are unschooled at clearing and processing lactate and tend to work uneconomically at tempos beyond this threshold.

If you are a marathon runner, is the situation different? If you simply jog your marathons, moving along easily without stocking up on leg-muscle glycogen before the race and without consuming sports drinks during the event, then fat oxidation will be important, and the high-volume, moderate-intensity training will help raise your fat-oxidation capacity. But, if you are trying to run as fast as you can in the marathon, loading glycogen before the competition and quaffing sports drinks during the event, the marathon itself becomes a carb race; research suggests that up to 80 to 90 percent of the energy needed to run the 26.2 miles (42.2 km) comes from carbohydrate.[7] Thus, the high-volume, moderate-intensity training designed to optimize fat oxidation becomes much less useful.

Tempo Training

Swedish exercise physiologist Bertil Sjödin and his colleagues Ira Jacobs and Jan Svedenhag published a paper in 1982 that revealed improvements in running velocity at lactate threshold of about .72 kilometers (.45 mi) per hour in eight well-trained runners over a 14-week period.[8] The average age of these runners was 20, and mean slow-twitch muscle-fiber composition was 62 percent. A key feature of the training was a weekly continuous 20-minute tempo run at the approximated running velocity at lactate threshold; aside from this tempo session, the athletes trained in their usual ways.

$\dot{V}O_2$max failed to move upward during the 14 weeks of training, but average velocity at lactate threshold seemed to improve from 4.69 meters per second (16.88 km/hr [10.49 mi/hr]) to 4.89 meters per second (17.60 km/hr [10.94 mi/hr]), a change described by the Swedes as being statistically significant. However, no control subjects were involved in the study; the athletes' running velocities at lactate thresholds after 14 weeks were simply compared with their own results prior to the 14 weeks of training. (This was a risky thing to do given the naturally wide, individual swings in this variable as illustrated by its nonreproducibility in scientific studies.) Overall, not one of the eight runners in Sjödin's research notched an upgrade to running velocity at lactate threshold as great as 1.6 kilometers per hour (.99 mi/hr); the greatest increase reported was in fact 1.29 kilometers per hour (.80 mi/hr), and this was exceptional. One of the athletes experienced a small dip in running velocity at lactate threshold, and two others nudged this variable upward by only .37 kilometers per hour (.23 mi/hr) or so. In addition, student's t-test for paired observations (a method of statistical analysis) was used to determine the statistical significance of the differences even though such tests provide no indication of random variation between tests.[9]

Despite these many problems, Sjödin's work has become the foundation of much current training directed toward the goal of improving running velocity at lactate threshold. Shortly after the publication of the Swedish investigation, coaches and endurance athletes seized on the study, citing it as validation of the notion that tempo training—exercising for about 20 minutes or so at running velocity at lactate threshold—represents the optimal way to increase running velocity at lactate threshold. As a result, the typical modern runner's training schedule often revolves around a near-weekly tempo run, which is a carryover from Sjödin's 1982 big-bang announcement. Given the shaky statistics and more recent evidence that higher-intensity efforts are more potent than exertions at running velocity at lactate threshold for boosting this variable, such reverence for tempo workouts is likely to be suboptimal.

Effective Ways to Boost Running Velocity at Lactate Threshold

Recent research has disclosed that there are three key ways to upgrade running velocity at lactate threshold: intense training, $v\dot{V}O_2$max training, and sprint training for endurance runners. In addition, several other training modalities, including circuit training, lactate-stacker sessions, super sets, and even running intervals at 5K speed have a positive impact on this variable. All of these training methods are described in the upcoming sections.

Intense Training

Scientific research actually reveals that fairly intense training, not high-volume work at moderate intensities, is the best booster of running velocity at lactate threshold.[10] In a study carried out at the University of North Carolina at Greensboro, runners who suddenly raised their average training intensity by completing two fartlek sessions and one interval workout per week boosted running velocity at lactate threshold significantly in just 8 weeks and as a result shaved more than a minute from their average 10K times. The fartlek work involved 2- to 5-minute bursts at 10K pace, which is about 2 to 3 percent faster than running velocity at lactate threshold; the intervals were completed at about 5K speed, which can be around 5 to 6 percent quicker than running velocity at lactate threshold.[11]

The idea that intense workouts are best for raising running velocity at lactate threshold was reinforced in research carried out at York University by Stephen Keith and Ira Jacobs.[12] In the York investigations, one group of athletes trained exactly at lactate-threshold intensity for 30 minutes per workout. Training *at* lactate threshold (tempo training as noted earlier) is perhaps the most popular modality used by runners in their attempts to advance running velocity at lactate threshold. A second group of exercisers divided their 30-minute workouts into four intervals, each of which lasted for 7.5 minutes. Two of the intervals were completed at an intensity above lactate threshold, while the other two were carried out below threshold. Each group of athletes worked out four times per each of the 8 weeks of the study.

In the second group, the below-threshold exertions, which were used for two of the four 7.5-minute intervals per workout, corresponded with an intensity of about 60 to 73 percent of $\dot{V}O_2$max. The above-threshold intensity, also employed for two 7.5-minute intervals per workout, was set at about 30 percent of the difference between lactate threshold and actual $\dot{V}O_2$max. Thirty percent of the threshold-$\dot{V}O_2$max difference would usually represent an intensity of up to 87 percent of $\dot{V}O_2$max, or about 88 to 93 percent of maximal heart rate. In terms of actual running velocity, it would correspond with a running speed that is almost exactly the same as 10K pace.

After 8 weeks of training, the two sets of athletes had achieved similar increases in $\dot{V}O_2$max and lactate threshold. The gains in threshold were impressive, averaging 14 percent in both groups. Advances in aerobic enzymes were also notable and nearly identical in the two groups of athletes. In an endurance test in which group members exercised for as long as possible at an intensity corresponding to their pretraining lactate threshold, the above-threshold athletes seemed to hold an edge, sustaining their exercise for a total of 71 minutes, while the at-threshold subjects lasted for 64 minutes.

At first glance, these results seem to suggest that there is not a huge advantage to be gained by surging through highly demanding workouts above lactate threshold. Note, however, that the above-threshold athletes really logged only 60 minutes of *quality* work per week (4 × 15 minutes per exertion), while the at-threshold subjects put in 120 weekly minutes of quality effort (4 × 30 minutes). The above-threshold athletes achieved the same gains in lactate threshold and $\dot{V}O_2$max—and perhaps enjoyed a slight advantage in endurance—as the at-threshold individuals, with only half the total quality-training time. It is reasonable to assume that had the above-threshold athletes stepped up their volume of above-threshold work just a little bit, they would have outdistanced the at-threshold subjects.

Why does moving above running velocity at lactate threshold during training seem to be so effective at lifting this variable? Three primary reasons are responsible for the changes: muscles improve their ability to use lactate and pyruvate, aerobic enzyme production increases, and the amount of MCT1 increases.

Teaching Muscles to Use Lactate and Pyruvate

For one thing, work done at faster than running velocity at lactate threshold seems to be particularly important for improving the lactate profiles of fast-twitch muscle fibers. In research carried out at the University of Missouri, several groups of rats hustled along on laboratory treadmills at a variety of different paces ranging from 15 to 37 meters per minute (43-100 min/mi). The faster velocities—by rat standards—that averaged 30 meters per minute and above produced flood tides of lactate in the rodents' bloodstreams, as expected, but the researchers also noticed something very interesting. High lactate levels were linked with glycogen depletion of the rats' fast-twitch muscle fibers, not their slow-twitch cells. In other words, fast-twitch fibers were primarily responsible for the huge upswing in blood lactate.[13]

Of course, fast-twitch fibers are not heavily used during moderately paced exertions but play a larger role as movement speeds increase beyond running velocity at lactate threshold. Compared to slow-twitch cells, fast-twitch fibers are ordinarily somewhat low on mitochondria and aerobic enzymes, and so it is logical that they would release relatively large quantities of lactate into the blood during intense running. If the fast-twitch fibers are poor at oxidizing pyruvate, a closely related chemical precursor to lactate, massive amounts of lactate will be produced, and running velocity at lactate threshold will be reached at a very mediocre pace. As the fast-twitch fibers get better at breaking down pyruvate, less lactate will be produced, and running velocity at lactate threshold will increase. There is only one way to stimulate the fast-twitchers to get better: *Use* them during training, specifically at tough, fast paces. To put it another way, fast-twitch muscle cells can be the culprits underlying a poor running velocity at lactate threshold, and the only way to upgrade their lactate-processing machinery is to engage them and force them to adapt with aerobic enzyme and mitochondrial production.

What if your muscle fibers are primarily slow-twitch? The key problem associated with a low running velocity at lactate threshold is that a low level of this variable is a symptom of a poor lactate-processing capability. From the standpoint of creating energy for faster running, it's suboptimal when lactate is drifting around in the blood, unused, and it's good if the lactate is being broken down at high rates inside muscles and also being pulled into muscles at high rates so that it can be metabolized. Thus, the key problem with a low running velocity at lactate threshold is the inability of muscle cells to create the energy they need by clearing lactate and breaking it down. The only way to teach muscle cells to handle lactate and pyruvate quickly is to expose them to higher concentrations of the two compounds, and that means fast-paced training whether leg-muscle cells are primarily fast-twitch or slow-twitch.

Increasing Aerobic Enzyme Production

Intense running has a dramatic impact on the production of the aerobic enzymes required to break down lactate as illustrated by research completed at the State University of New York at Syracuse.[14] In this study, which was carried out over an 8-week period, the concentration of a key mitochondrial enzyme called cytochrome c increased by about 1 percent per minute of daily training as long as training intensity was set at 85 to 100 percent of $\dot{V}O_2$max, or approximately 92 to 100 percent of maximal heart rate. This means that by carrying out 10 minutes of daily training within this intensity zone, subjects boosted cytochrome c by 10 percent after 8 weeks; with 27 minutes of daily training within the high-intensity zone, cytochrome c increased by 27 percent in 8 weeks. In contrast, working at a lower intensity of only 70 to 75 percent of $\dot{V}O_2$max increased cytochrome c by only 18 percent. Since cytochrome c is a critically important oxidative enzyme found within the mitochondria, upswings in cytochrome c should be linked with improvements in running velocity at lactate threshold.

In this study, the gains associated with faster training were even more impressive from the standpoint of the fast-twitch muscle fibers. Ten minutes of daily training at 100 percent of $\dot{V}O_2$max roughly tripled cytochrome c concentrations within fast-twitch cells, while running 27 minutes per day at 85 percent of $\dot{V}O_2$max increased cytochrome c by just 80 percent, and 90 daily minutes at 70 percent of $\dot{V}O_2$max raised cytochrome c by just 74 percent. In other words, decreases in training intensity were linked with smaller aerobic enzyme adaptations even when the total volume of training was increased ninefold from 10 to 90 minutes per day.

Increasing MCT1

What kind of training is best for studding muscle and mitochondrial membranes with maximal outcroppings of MCT1? In research carried out by lactate expert Arend Bonen and his colleagues at the University of Waterloo in Ontario, Canada, laboratory rats were divided into two different groups, both of which trained for 3 weeks.[15] One group exercised moderately, working at a pace of 21 meters per minute on a treadmill with an incline of 8 percent. The second group of rats trained more intensely at the relatively sizzling speed of 31 meters per minute and with a treadmill angle of 15 percent.

After 3 weeks, the moderately trained rodents had failed to raise their leg-muscle concentrations of MCT1 at all! Not surprisingly, lactate-uptake rate was also no better than before the training began. In contrast, the more intensely trained rats had augmented MCT1 levels in key leg muscles by 70 to 94 percent and had boosted average lactate-uptake rate by around 80 percent!

The more intense training also benefited the *hearts* of the exercising rats. After 3 weeks of moderate training, heart-muscle cells in the medium-intensity rodents did react by firing up MCT1 content by 36 percent; the rate at which the heart swallowed up blood lactate also increased after the moderate training. Once again, however, intense training provided the ticket for considerably stronger MCT1 improvement. Total heart MCT1 expanded by 44 percent in the intensely trained rats, and lactate-uptake rate increased by 173 percent!

Separate research carried out by Carsten Juel and his colleagues at the Copenhagen Muscle Research Centre and the August Krogh Institute in Denmark reveals that intense exercise is a potent MCT1 booster.[16] In this Danish study, six human male subjects performed vigorous one-leg knee-extensor training at a rate of 60 kicks per minute on an ergometer; the other leg served as a control. Each training session consisted of a 5-minute warm-up and then 15 1-minute work intervals at an incredible intensity of 150 percent of thigh $\dot{V}O_2$max with 3-minute recoveries (if you are troubled by the phrase "thigh $\dot{V}O_2$max," remember that just as the whole body has a $\dot{V}O_2$max, each appendage, region, and muscle within the body has its own unique $\dot{V}O_2$max, too). This workout was completed three times a week for 2 weeks, four times a week for 2 more weeks, and then five times a week for 3 to 4 weeks. No other training was completed during the 7- to 8-week period.

At the end of the experimental period, endurance time during a challenging incremental test was 29 percent longer in the trained leg compared with the control, and MCT1 levels in the trained thigh had shot up by 15 percent. Interestingly enough, the amount of lactate *removed* from the blood during the demanding incremental test was 63 millimoles per liter (1.1 gm/dl) for the trained leg versus just 16 millimoles (288 mg/dl) in the untrained leg with poorer MCT1. Only about 29 percent of this difference could be accounted for by the longer time to exhaustion in the trained leg, indicating that a probable reason for the enhanced endurance in the trained leg was its increased ability to use lactate for fuel. Supporting this assumption, the trained thigh had lower levels of *intramuscular* lactate at the exhaustion point even though it had removed much more lactate from the blood compared with the untrained leg.

An earlier investigation, also carried out at the Copenhagen Muscle Research Centre and the August Krogh Institute, revealed that 8 weeks of intense cycling workouts boosted MCT1 concentrations by 76 percent.[17] In this study, the intense training consisted of interval workouts with three to five sets of (2×30 seconds and 3×60 seconds), with top-of-the-line intensities and 2-minute recoveries. No other training was completed during the 8-week period.

Taken together, the available research strongly supports the notion that intense training is best for boosting MCT1 content and the rates of lactate uptake and use—and thus greater resistance to fatigue during hard exercise and a higher running velocity at lactate threshold. It is logical that this would be the case. The most potent stimulus for increasing MCT1 levels may be high blood and muscle lactate levels just as the best stimulus for improving $\dot{V}O_2$max may involve pushing the oxygen envelope by training at high speeds that evoke high rates of oxygen consumption. Of course, you can't have consistently high lactate levels if you carry out the bulk of your training at a speed that is *below* your running velocity at lactate threshold. It is doubtful that carrying out the majority of your training at intensities associated with low lactate levels will stimulate your muscles to suddenly embark on a frenzied MCT1 construction project.

In one study, a runner who trained from 90 to 120 minutes each day at an intensity below lactate threshold developed a decent aerobic capacity (i.e., $\dot{V}O_2$max), but his MCT1 content and lactate-transport capacity were poor, and thus his resistance to fatigue during high-quality running was inferior to that of athletes who trained in higher-quality ways.[3]

In another important study, the highest lactate-transport capacity was found in an Olympic medal winner, who carried out the greatest amount of training at high intensities.[18] The researchers in this investigation concluded that "a large volume of training is not sufficient to improve the ability to transport lactate" and that "regular high-intensity sessions must be included." A corollary research project with laboratory rats revealed that training at about 50 percent of $\dot{V}O_2$max had no effect on lactate-transport capacity; however, working at 90 percent of $\dot{V}O_2$max lifted lactate transport by 58 percent, and training at an intensity of 112 percent of $\dot{V}O_2$max caused lactate-transport ability to soar by 76 percent.[19]

v$\dot{V}O_2$max Training

Science has shown that v$\dot{V}O_2$max training—carrying out work intervals at the intensity of v$\dot{V}O_2$max itself—is great for optimizing running velocity at lactate threshold. This may seem a bit confusing. After all, isn't v$\dot{V}O_2$max training designed to enhance v$\dot{V}O_2$max but not running velocity at lactate threshold? How can one form of training accomplish both things simultaneously?

To answer these questions, one need only look at the research carried out by Veronique Billat and her colleagues at the University of Lille, the Center of Sport Medicine, and the National Center of Health in France. Billat and her co-workers asked a group of experienced runners to take part in 4 weeks of training that included one interval session at v$\dot{V}O_2$max each week. The athletes were specialists in middle- and long-distance running (1,500 meters to half marathon), their mean age was 24, and their average $\dot{V}O_2$max was a very good 71.2 ml • kg^{-1} • min^{-1}.[20]

After just 4 weeks of training with four total v$\dot{V}O_2$max workouts, v$\dot{V}O_2$max was up by 3 percent from 20.5 kilometers (12.7 mi) per hour to 21.1 kilometers (13.1) per hour (i.e., from about 4:43 per mile to 4:34 per mile). In addition, running economy improved by an astounding 6 percent, and heart rates at typical training speeds dipped by 4 percent. Running velocity at lactate threshold also increased by about 3 percent! (See chapters 9 and 26 for additional details.) The reason for this is most likely that the high v$\dot{V}O_2$max training intensity stimulated an increased capacity of lactate oxidation in the muscles and—by promoting high blood lactate levels—forced muscles to maximize their MCT1 concentrations.

Sprint Training

Traditionally, runners have used sprint work to heighten maximal running speed. What many runners don't know is that sprint training can also help optimize running velocity at lactate threshold. Researchers from Imperial College in London, Deakin University, the University of New South Wales, and Queensland University worked with seven endurance-trained runners.[21] This septet was reasonably fit ($\dot{V}O_2$max = 58 ml • kg^{-1} • min^{-1}), and their average age was 27.7 years; the seven athletes had no history of prior sprint training.

The subjects performed three sessions per week of sprint training for 6 weeks. Each workout involved four sets of nearly maximal sprints that were 40 to 100 meters in length. The total number of sprints per session increased from 14 during the first week of training to 30 reps during the sixth week, and the lengths of the reps also expanded from an initial range of 40 to 80 meters during the first week to 80 to 100 meters during the sixth week. To make matters even tougher, recovery times between sprints were gradually tightened: The work-to-rest ratio started at 1:5 during week one but gradually evolved to 1:3 during the final week; recovery between *sets* of sprints held fast at 5 minutes across the 42 days. In addition to the sprint training, the seven athletes also logged about 50K per week of moderate running at below running velocity at lactate threshold.

To get a feeling for how the sprint sessions developed over time, Session 1, the first sprint workout carried out in the first week of the study, included four sets:

1. 4×40 meters

2. 4×50 meters

3. 4×60 meters

4. 2×80 meters

Each rep in the four sets was carried out at 90 percent of maximal effort. For this inaugural sprint session, the work-to-recovery ratio was 1:5; between reps were 5 seconds of recovery for each second of sprinting, and total rest between each *set* was 5 minutes.

In contrast, Session 18, the final sprint workout of the sixth week, included these sets:

1. 8×100 meters

2. 6×100 meters

3. 8×80 meters

4. 6×80 meters

These 28 reps were all struck at 90 to 100 percent of maximal effort with a work-to-recovery ratio of only 1:3, but there were still 5-minute recoveries *between sets*. From sprint session 1 to 18, the number of reps had risen from 14 to 28, and the total sprinting distance had increased from 760 to 2,520 meters (.5-1.6 mi).

The Australian and English researchers involved in this study had asked the seven endurance runners to run as far as possible at an intensity of 110 percent of v$\dot{V}O_2$max before and after the 6 weeks of sprint training. Prior to the 6-week period, the runners were able to hang in there at that intensity for a total of 140 seconds before complete exhaustion set in; they covered 745 meters (.46 mi) during this 140 seconds of red-hot running. In contrast, after the sprint training, even though the longest sprint-training rep was just 100 meters, the runners kept going for 157.7 seconds at 110 percent of v$\dot{V}O_2$max, an 11 percent upgrade, and also covered 838 meters (.52 mi), another 11 percent increase, before falling prostrate on the ground.

In addition to focusing on performance times, the investigators were also quite interested in MCT1. In this study, MCT1 levels in muscles increased by about 50 percent after the 6 weeks of sprint training, an effect that should significantly boost running velocity at lactate threshold.

Other Training Methods

In addition to v$\dot{V}O_2$max and sprint training, other high-quality sessions (defined as being above running velocity at lactate threshold) should also improve running velocity at lactate threshold. Circuit training has been linked with lactate-threshold improvements, probably because of the high oxygen-consumption rates and lactate outputs that can be achieved during such training.[22] Similarly, lactate-stacker sessions, in which a runner alternates 1-minute intervals at faster than $v\dot{V}O_2$max with 2-minute jog recoveries, should be excellent for upgrading both lactate-oxidation rates and MCT1 concentrations—and thus running velocity at lactate threshold. In addition, superset training, in which a runner takes no recovery between high-speed intervals with the first interval being faster than the second, should also bolster running velocity at lactate threshold. In fact, there are an almost infinite number of workouts that would have a positive effect on running velocity at lactate threshold. The key is that sessions to enhance this variable should be conducted at speeds faster than running velocity at lactate threshold. This means that workouts carried out at 10K pace, 5K pace, 3200-meter speed, 3K tempo, mile pace, 1500-meter velocity, and 800-meter should all be productive from the standpoint of increasing running velocity at lactate threshold.

Lactate Monitors

If training is going well, running velocity at lactate threshold should continue to move upward, and performances should also get better, but how can it be determined if running velocity at lactate threshold is really advancing? Some runners are tempted to use lactate monitors. Many fairly inexpensive, portable devices have proven to be remarkably accurate. That is, at any specific point in time, one of these devices will produce a reading for blood lactate that is remarkably close to the true lactate level in the person's blood. This accuracy has excited many coaches and runners. After all, they have reasoned, with just a few finger sticks they can tell very reliably which way running velocity at lactate threshold is heading.

Indeed, validations of certain kinds of training to increase lactate threshold have depended on measured changes in lactate readings. For example, Sjödin's research in the early 1980s (see the Tempo Training section earlier in this chapter) used this sort of lactate reading. However, there is a key element missing in such a conclusion *and* in current beliefs about lactate training and the use of lactate monitors. The missing element is the reproducibility of blood lactate levels. In other words, for lactate monitors to work, blood lactate concentrations need to remain the same at a specific exercise intensity unless an athlete has achieved a real change in fitness. If blood lactate levels vary to a great extent in individual athletes as a result of factors unrelated to fitness, even when exercise intensity remains the same, then it can be very difficult to argue that a change in observed blood lactate is truly the result of altered fitness.

In fact, the lactate levels in an athlete's blood at any specific time during exercise are a function of the intensity of exercise and also the length of time over which the exercise has been conducted. Lactate is also sensitive to a variety of other factors, including the nutritional and psychological status of an athlete. The consumption of a high-carbohydrate meal during the hours leading up to a workout, for example, can drive up blood lactate levels during exercise, while a fattier diet can make blood lactate concentrations more modest. In addition, increased states of tension or anxiety can lead to augmented blood lactate levels, while calmer psychological conditions tend to keep lactate levels at more minimal readings. Mild states of dehydration can make lactate levels appear to be higher than they really are compared with levels in a well-hydrated state. Finally, even time of day can have an effect on lactate concentrations since blood lactate follows a circadian rhythm.

Due to all of these influences, a runner whose running velocity at lactate threshold is measured at 4.47 meters per second (6:00 per mile) does not know if the speed at which lactate begins cresting is determined *completely* by fitness. How much depends on other factors, such as the small measurement errors of the lactate monitor and the potentially big skews associated with nutritional, hydration, and psychological status? And if running velocity at lactate threshold is measured again after 4 weeks or so and is 4.60 meters per second (5:50 per mile), is that a real change in running velocity at lactate threshold? Or does it simply reflect the natural variation that is produced by factors not related to fitness?

For these reasons, lactate monitors cannot be recommended as effective tools for monitoring changes in running velocity at lactate threshold. Because readings can't usually be reproduced for running velocity at lactate threshold, changes in lactate readings picked up by the monitors must be so large to be considered real that an athlete would already know that he or she was in much better or worse shape—thanks to perceived exertion during intense runs—without piercing a digit to take a lactate measurement.

Some studies have suggested that lactate readings are reasonably reproducible,[23, 24] but these investigations have been characterized by deep flaws in their statistical analyses.[25] As a result, we simply don't know by how much a lactate reading has to change in order for us to assume that it represents a real upgrade or downgrade in fitness. If a measured running velocity at lactate threshold changes from 17 kilometers (10.6 mi) per hour to 17.75 kilometers (11.03 mi) per hour, for example, can we trust it? If running velocity at lactate threshold falls from 17 to 16.5 kilometers (10.6-10.3 mi) per hour, should we be perturbed—or should we acknowledge that this drop-off may simply be part of the natural variation in measured running velocity at lactate threshold? These questions are key, and the coach or athlete who ignores them while employing lactate-measuring devices is proceeding in an illogical manner.

Reproducibility of Lactate Levels

To find out how reproducible lactate readings really are, scientists at the Institute of Biomedical and Life Sciences at the University of Glasgow and the National University of Ireland in Galway studied 20 men and 16 women.[26]

All the subjects were physically active, taking part in at least two aerobic dance, cross-country running, volleyball, soccer, or rugby workouts each week. These subjects completed two treadmill lactate-profile tests; almost all the tests were completed 1 week apart and at approximately the same time of day.

Running velocity at lactate threshold was determined for each athlete on those two occasions. The heart rate and perceived effort (using Borg's 6-20 category scale) associated with running velocity at lactate threshold were also measured. To determine whether fitness level has an impact on running velocity at lactate threshold reproducibility, the subjects were divided into two groups: those with a running velocity at lactate threshold equal to or greater than 10.5 kilometers (6.5 mi) per hour (the moderate-fitness group), or a pace of about 9:12 per mile, and those with a running velocity at lactate threshold slower than 10.5 kilometers (6.5 mi) per hour (the lower-fitness group).

As it turned out, fitness and reproducibility were linked: The two running velocity at lactate threshold readings for the moderate-fitness group tended to be closer together than the two separate recordings for the lower-fitness group. This makes sense: As fitness levels increase, fitness should become a stronger factor with respect to running velocity at lactate threshold and should be less likely to be swamped by vicissitudes in other variables.

The sex of the runner did *not* have a significant effect on the reproducibility of running velocity at lactate threshold. However, the Glasgow-Galway research revealed that it is *natural* for running velocity at lactate threshold to vary in an athlete by more than 1 kilometer (.62 mi) per hour in either direction. For example, if true running velocity at lactate threshold was initially measured in the laboratory at 15 kilometers (9.3 mi) per hour, future readings of 14 or 16 kilometers (8.7 or 9.9 mi) per hour would be reasonably interpreted as normal variations around the average running velocity at lactate threshold rather than as significantly different speeds associated with lactate threshold. A conclusion that 16 represented an upswing in fitness or that 14 was associated with a drop-off in capacity would be very tenuous.

Similarly, heart rate at running velocity at lactate threshold exhibited a rather large natural variation. In fact, the research suggested that athletes should expect the heart rate associated with a specific running velocity at lactate threshold to vary by up to 12 to 18 beats per minute from one day to the next! This rather large natural variation in heart rate presents problems for those who believe they have identified a lactate-threshold heart rate and who are carrying out training at that specific heart rate, believing it will be beneficial for enhancing running velocity at lactate threshold. In fact, it would not be unreasonable to expect that the heart rate an athlete had tied to running velocity at lactate threshold might be up to 18 beats off the true rate!

Overall, the Glasgow-Galway investigation revealed that athletes would have to make large improvements in running velocity at lactate threshold before the change could confidently be ascribed to be outside natural variability in measured running velocity at lactate threshold. For example, a member of the moderate-fitness group would have to boost or decrease running velocity at lactate threshold by 1.62 kilometers (1.01 mi) per hour (27 meters per minute) in order to be certain that a change in fitness status had actually been achieved! As an example, an endurance runner with an established running velocity at lactate threshold of 16 kilometers (9.94 mi) per hour would have to achieve a new reading of 17.62 kilometers (10.95 mi) per hour to be confident that his or her running velocity at lactate threshold had really improved. This is in effect a change in tempo at lactate threshold from 6:03 per mile to 5:30 per mile, a 33-second per mile improvement! This is a huge alteration, especially when considering that most cross-country and distance runners do not hope for more than a 16-second per mile improvement in race pace over the course of a three-month season. As the researchers calmly pointed out, "These figures cast doubt on the sensitivity of the blood lactate test to a change of fitness in this population."

One caveat is in order: Although blood-lactate tests do not appear to be sensitive indicators of changes in fitness, the study did find an apparent link between running velocity at lactate threshold reproducibility and high fitness levels. Thus, truly elite athletes may have fairly low natural variations in running velocity at lactate threshold; consequently, their blood lactate tests might have greater power. Further research will have to establish this, however; we cannot assume that this is the case based on one study.

Reproducibility of Rating of Perceived Effort

As mentioned, in the Glasgow-Galway study, *heart rate* at running velocity at lactate threshold was also not highly reproducible. Unfortunately, the story for rating of perceived effort (RPE) was not much better. In the Glasgow research, RPE at running velocity at lactate threshold was found to average 14.1, while RPE at a blood lactate level of 4 mmol/Liter (72 mg/dl), a blood lactate concentration often recommended for training sessions focused on improving lactate threshold, settled at 17.2 out of a maximal score of 20. However, there was again rather wide variability, suggesting that the use of RPE to prescribe workout intensity would be unwise. Overall, an athlete would have to lower RPE at a specific running velocity at lactate threshold by about 3 Borg-scale units (!) in order to assume that a real change in running velocity at lactate threshold had taken place. As the researchers pointed out, "This wide range highlights that the use of RPE to prescribe intensity at [lactate-threshold velocity] has severe limitations."

The RPE story is interesting in its own right. Like lactate, RPE varies according to emotional state and diet. High-carbohydrate diets tend to produce lower RPE scores, for example, while high-fat diets shoot RPE upward. Interestingly, the sex of the athlete appears to have no significant, repeatable effect on RPE, but RPE *is* influenced by the interaction between the sex of the athlete and that of the experimenter. Men and women revise RPE based on the gender of the person they are reporting to. So, in most cases, female scientists or lab assistants take RPEs from female athletes while males jot down the RPEs of male athletes.

In addition, RPE seems to depend to some extent on personality type. Extroverts, for example, generally have lower RPEs during strenuous exercise compared with introverts. The theory underlying this phenomenon is that introverts are bothered to a greater extent by sensory information flowing into their central nervous systems, including the sensations associated with strenuous exercise.

Conclusion

Because running velocity at lactate threshold advancement is a key element of middle-distance and endurance running, a process to maximize improvements should continue throughout the training year. The good news for coaches and runners is that complicated training techniques and sophisticated mesocycles, or periods, of training are not necessary to optimize this variable. Rather, steady use of high-quality workouts throughout the year will keep running velocity at lactate threshold advancing. That being said, an important key is to employ a *variety* of high-quality workouts, alternating sprint, $v\dot{V}O_2max$, superset, lactate-stacker, circuit, and 5K-paced sessions throughout the year; make these workouts more difficult with faster speeds and more reps, for example, as fitness improves.

CHAPTER 28

Increasing Maximal Running Speed

For endurance runners, there is considerable uncertainty about how to improve *maximal running speed*, which is the top velocity that a runner can achieve during an all-out sprint lasting from 20 to 300 meters from a running start. This lack of certainty is partly the result of the traditions of long-distance running that emphasize prolonged submaximal runs as a key element of training while ignoring, or at least deemphasizing, high-speed efforts (chapter 11); these latter efforts are often thought to be anaerobic in nature and thus antithetical to the development of aerobic capacity and the enhancement of endurance. As a result of these traditions, many distance runners and coaches do not take a systematic approach to the development of a higher maximal velocity.

Research reveals that this is a mistake. As described in chapter 11, researcher Kris Berg and his colleagues at the University of Nebraska at Omaha demonstrated that 300-meter sprint time; near-maximal velocity; and plyometric leap distance, also associated with maximal muscular power, were able to explain most of the variation in 10K running performances.[1] Additionally, in an investigation carried out with 17 experienced endurance runners with 5K performance times ranging from about 17:00 to 18:50, Heikki Rusko, Leena Paavolainen, and Ari Nummela of the KIHU Research Institute for Olympic Sports in Finland discovered that 20-meter race speed (i.e., maximal velocity) was an excellent predictor of 5K finishing time, far better than that vaunted variable $\dot{V}O_2$max.[2] This was true even though 20-meter velocity—8.15 meters per second—was 76 percent faster than the runners' mean 5K speed of 4.63 meters per second. If 8.15 meters per second seems unusually fast for an endurance runner, bear in mind that the runners in this study were given a flying 30-meter head start before embarking on the 20-meter efforts.

Training for Maximal Speed

While some long-distance runners do recognize the importance of developing a higher maximal running speed, the training approach taken to improve maximal speed often revolves around carrying out intervals on the track at 5K pace or a similar intensity. While this kind of preparation can certainly upgrade $\dot{V}O_2$max, enhance running economy, and velocity at lactate threshold, there is no evidence to support the idea that such running improves *maximal speed*.

There is an important distinction to be made between speed and maximal speed. As a result of an improvement in overall fitness, a runner might be able to complete a 10K race at a brisk tempo that was previously associated with his or her 5K or 8K (3.1 or 5 mi) competitions. This would of course lead to a 10K personal record, and the runner might pronounce that he or she is faster or has developed more speed. While it is true that this runner is moving at a faster *average* speed during the 10K, what the runner has actually done is to take a familiar pace and extend the distance over which he or she could sustain that tempo. He or she can run at a higher average speed over an extended distance but has not necessarily pushed the envelope and advanced *maximal speed*.

The training path that needs to be taken to increase maximal speed is most likely different from the various strategies that can be used to extend a specific race pace to a longer competitive distance. Because maximal speed is such a strong predictor of finishing time among endurance runners, upgrading maximal speed should lead to additional improvements in distance performances beyond the gains associated with training at below the maximal speed. Training carried out by endurance runners should optimize maximal running speed.

Training Modes Examined by Research

Research investigating the ways in which endurance runners can increase maximal speed has not been very systematic, in part because it is nontraditional to think that upgrades in maximal speed promote improved running in long-distance events completed at submaximal intensities. Research has focused on four possible training modes that have been logically linked with the upgrading of maximal speed; the results have shown that some of these methods far exceed the others.

- High-speed uphill and downhill running
- Running against resistance (e.g., pulling a weighted sled)
- Strength training in conjunction with quality running
- Explosive training

High-Speed Uphill and Downhill Running

Scientific investigations suggest that fast running on slightly inclined uphill and downhill surfaces is a more effective way to improve maximal speed than fast training on a horizontal surface. In a study carried out in the department of physical education and sport science at the University of Athens in Greece, runners who carried out 8 weeks of training that involved running as fast as possible on slight uphill and downhill inclines improved their maximal running speed during 35-meter sprinting by 4.3 percent; those who ran similar distances explosively on a flat surface upgraded maximal speed by just 1.7 percent, and a control group failed to improve maximal speed at all.[3] A key mechanism underlying the augmentation of maximal speed appeared to be a reduction in contact time (i.e., the amount of time spent on the ground by each foot per step) during fast running: Contact time fell by 5.1 percent after the uphill and downhill sprint training. A decrease in contact time increases *stride rate* during fast running and—provided there is no resulting decrement in stride length—thus improves maximal speed.

Research has made a limited attempt to uncover the optimal slope for uphill and downhill training designed to increase maximal speed. A slope of 3 degrees has been proposed by various investigators as the best possible incline for such workouts. In a study carried out at Marquette University, 13 NCAA Division III athletes ran 40-yard (37 m) sprints on downhill slopes of 2.1, 3.3, 4.7, 5.8, and 6.9 degrees in random order.[4] The 5.8-degree slope was best for developing the highest acute speed during the training sprints; it shortened 40-yard (37 m) sprint time by .35 seconds, a 6.5 percent decrease compared with results from flat-ground running. The slope that produced the next fastest times was the 4.7-degree decline, but times on that slope were about 2 percent slower than on the 5.8-degree slope. A presumption is that the advantage of slope running is that it permits higher training speeds compared with flat running and thus fosters special adaptations that enhance maximal running speed. If this assumption is accepted—and it is certainly reasonable to do so—then a logical choice for training would be the decline that allows the fastest possible running.

During downhill running, the foot falls farther with each step compared with running on flat ground. Thus, the collision of the foot with the ground occurs at a higher speed during downhill running because of greater downward acceleration of the foot. This should force a runner's nervous system to adapt in ways that enhance coordination of foot strike at high speeds. This is possibly the direct mechanism that produces the decreased contact times and thus higher stride rates observed after downhill training and could certainly produce a higher maximal speed. Since maximal running speed equals stride rate times stride length, any adaptation that produces a greater stride rate without harming stride length will increase maximal running speed.

Running Against Resistance

Some coaches and exercise scientists have theorized that running as hard as possible against resistance might increase maximal running speed. Theoretically, such training should increase leg strength in a running-specific way and thus lead to natural expansions in stride length, which could heighten maximal running speed as long as there were no counterbalancing decreases in stride rate.

However, research suggests that running against resistance is actually *less* effective from the standpoint of improving maximal speed. In a study carried out in the department of physical education and sport science at Aristotelio University in Thessaloniki, Greece, one group of athletes followed a sprint-training program that involved pulling a 5-kilogram (11 lb) sled during sprint routines while a second group carried out all training without added resistance.[5] For both groups, the training protocol involved 4×20-meter and 4×50-meter maximal speed runs three times a week for 8 weeks.

Although the sled training improved acceleration during the first few meters of all-out 50-meter sprinting, it failed to upgrade stride rate, stride length, or maximal speed between meters 20 and 50. In contrast, training without resistance improved maximal running speed between meters 20 and 50 by the end of the study.

The apparent problem with using resistance is that it slows average training speeds, an effect that would fail to optimize the nervous system's control of high-speed running. It is possible that training using resistance also changes running mechanics in an unspecified way and thus does not spike running speed. Research carried out by Rusko and C. Bosco has shown that running while wearing a weighted vest to provide additional resistance actually has a negative effect on running economy *after the vests are taken off*, suggesting that the use of increased resistance can alter running form in a negative manner.[6]

Strength Training in Conjunction With Quality Running

Research reveals that combining strength training with high-speed running workouts can upgrade maximal running speed. In a study carried out at the department of health and exercise science at the College of New Jersey, 25 male athletes were matched for 30-meter sprint times and assigned for 7 weeks of training to one of three groups: (1) sprint training only, (2) strength training only, or (3) combined sprint and strength training. The sprint training was conducted twice a week and consisted of 8 to 12 sets of maximal 40- to 60-meter sprints with rest intervals of 2 to 3 minutes. The periodized strength training, relying on squats and other related activities, was performed four times per week, with 3 to 4 sets of 6 to 10 repetitions of each exercise per workout. Combined sprint and strength work used both protocols for the 7-week period. All three groups upgraded 1RM (one-repetition maximum) squat strength, but 30-meter sprint times improved significantly only in the group that had combined sprint and strength training.[7]

Explosive Training

Research strongly supports the notion that maximal running speed can be enhanced by explosive training (i.e., work that focuses on fast sprints and extremely quick drills, especially exertions that bear a biomechanical resemblance to some aspect of the gait cycle of running). In an investigation carried out at the University Pablo de Olavide in Seville, Spain, students who performed just one explosive activity—drop jumping—twice a week were able to increase 20-meter sprint time significantly by about 3 percent compared with controls. Drop jumping involves falling from a box and then leaping forward at the instant of contact with the ground. The drop jumps were completed from three different heights (20, 40, and 60 cm [6, 16, and 24 in]), and about 60 drop jumps were performed per workout.[8]

The classic study carried out by Paavolainen, Rusko, and colleagues at the KIHU Research Institute for Olympic Sports in Finland provided the strongest support for the use of explosive drills to improve maximal running speed in endurance runners.[1] Over a 9-week period, a group of experienced 5K runners replaced about 32 percent of their traditional endurance training with explosive work involving high-speed sprints, bounding drills, bilateral countermovement jumps, drop and hurdle jumps, hops, and squats; the drop and hurdle jumps involved dropping from a box or platform to the ground and then leaping, or rebounding, over a hurdle. Despite the loss of 32 percent of their endurance training, which involved running long distances at submaximal paces, these runners improved 20-meter sprint time by nearly 4 percent and 5K performance by almost 3 percent without any uptick in $\dot{V}O_2$max.

Paavolainen and Rusko attributed the improvements in these performances to "improved neuromuscular characteristics" in the runners who received explosive training. They meant that these runners could produce greater amounts of propulsive force in shorter periods of time during the stance phase of running compared with control runners. Thus, in this study, stride rate increased without any decrement in stride length, elevating maximal velocity.

In a follow-up study also completed by Rusko and colleagues at the KIHU Research Institute for Olympic Sports, 13 young distance runners replaced 19 percent of their traditional endurance training with explosive work involving jumps, hops, and sprints. This simple change enhanced 30-meter sprint time by 1.1 percent; the control group failed to improve at all.[9] Tests revealed that the runners using explosive training had improved the force-time characteristics of their muscle actions (i.e., their muscles were producing more force in a shorter time), and that there was more rapid neural activation of their muscles following the explosive training. As Rusko pointed out, most of the improvement in sprint time could be explained by changes in nervous system activity.

While most explosive training takes place without added resistance, there has been considerable speculation about the optimal resistance to use for explosive training. One school of thought suggests that relatively heavy loads (about 80 percent of 1RM, for example) are superior because they automatically induce a rapid, dramatic increase in neural output in order to handle the greater resistance. A contrasting view is that lighter resistances are preferable since they permit quicker movement speeds. Specifically, it has been suggested that loads that *maximize* power output (i.e., permit the attainment of P_{max}, the highest possible level of power) would be best.

Surprising to some runners, such loads are not high percentages of 1RM since heavy resistance slows down movements and thus harms power, which is expressed as force produced per *unit of time*. It is commonly stated that P_{max} for a specific movement occurs at about 30 percent of 1RM, but this may actually be far below or well above P_{max} in individual runners. Since there is considerable variation among runners, this variation in P_{max} probably depends on the movement under consideration.

In a study that examined the effects of strength training with a heavy load versus strength training at P_{max} on maximal running speed, 18 well-trained rugby players were randomly divided into two groups; each group had an equal volume of training for a 7-week period.[10] One of the groups performed squat-jump training with heavy loads at about 80 percent of 1RM; the other carried out squat-jump work at P_{max} at 20 to 43.5 percent of 1RM depending on the athlete. Sprint times for 10 and 30 meters improved by about the same amount *for both groups* after 7 weeks, leaving this question open for further research. It is possible that a combination of heavy load and P_{max} training would be optimal for enhancing maximal speed since heavy-load training might optimize propulsive force during the stance phase of gait and P_{max} training might optimize the *rate* of propulsive-force application during stance. The former would advance stride length, and the latter would increase stride rate.

Explosive Strength Workout

There has been little research concerning the effects of specific explosive drills on improving maximal running speed, but this workout contains a variety of running-specific, explosive movements that should be beneficial. Many of the drills in this session are similar to those used in the Rusko, Paavolainen, and Nummela hallmark study[2] on explosive training, maximal-speed improvement, and 5K performance. (The techniques for many of the drills in this workout are described in detail in chapter 23.)

At least initially, make sure that all activities that enhance explosiveness are completed on a forgiving surface (e.g., soft dirt, grass, cushioned artificial turf, compliant track, or wooden gym floor). The session should be conducted twice a week during periods of training that emphasize maximal-speed development.

1. Warm-up.

    a. Run easily for 12 minutes.

    b. Perform warm-up drills, including toe walking (chapter 23), heel walking (chapter 23), leg swings, skips, jumps, hops, and 60-meter stride-outs (relaxed yet fast running with a high cadence).

    c. Run easily for 2 or 3 additional minutes.

2. Intense running for 1 minute, counting the number of times the foot on one side hits the ground.

    a. Count the number of foot strikes on the other foot, if you prefer, but do not count both feet.

    b. If the number of foot strikes is fewer than 90, rest for a moment and repeat two more times, attempting to increase stride rate to *at least* 90 on each occasion. If your stride rate is 90 or more, move on to step 3. If you don't reach 90, continue to work on this in future sessions.

    c. Enhance this drill by using an electronic metronome. Set the metronome at 90 to 95 and make sure your right or left foot strikes the ground with the beeping. Relax and settle into a rhythm that is fast but smooth. Repeat this drill throughout each training week, making sure your stride rate is at 90 or above even during easy workouts. Use a midfoot strike pattern at all times.

3. Skipping on the balls of the feet for 30 seconds (chapter 23): Rest for a moment, and then repeat.

    a. Use quick leg action.

    b. Keep the feet on the ground for a minimal amount of time.

4. Spring jogging (chapter 23).

    a. Spring jog for 1 minute, then regular jog for 10 seconds.

    b. Spring jog alternating three consecutive contacts with one foot with three contacts with the other foot for 20 meters, then regular jog for 10 seconds.

    c. Spring jog on one foot for 20 meters and then on the other foot for 20 meters.

5. Two-leg hurdle hop (chapter 23): Complete five passes over 8 hurdles.

    a. Set the hurdles 45 inches (1.1 m) apart and set the hurdle height at 6 inches (15 cm); progressively increase the height to 18 inches (46 cm) over time as coordination and leaping ability improve.

      b. Once two-leg hurdle hops are handled successfully, change this drill to one-leg hurdle hops with the reps carried out first on one leg and then on the other. Begin with 6-inch hurdles.

      c. Complete 6 passes of one-leg hurdle hops on each leg.

6. One-leg hop in place (chapter 23): Complete 2 sets of 40 each on each leg.

7. Diagonal hop (chapter 23) for 45 seconds, rest for 15 seconds, and then diagonal hop for 45 more seconds.

8. Greyhound run: Complete 6 on an inclined surface (similar to the greyhound run described in chapter 23).

      a. Use an area that has 100 meters of unobstructed, smooth inclined surface; a slope of about 5 to 6 degrees is best. On the downward slope, accelerate downhill for 20 meters, hold the pace close to maximal speed pace for 60 meters, and then decelerate for 20 meters.

      b. Rest for several seconds by walking around; repeat the high-speed running in the opposite direction back up the slight slope.

      c. Complete 6 reps, 3 down and 3 up. Cautiously increase the number of reps over time.

9. One-leg squat with lateral hops (chapter 23): Perform 2 × 12 on each leg with a 1-minute break between sets.

10. High-knee explosion (chapter 23): Complete 15, rest for a few seconds, and repeat.

      a. Progress with this exercise to eventually perform high-knee explosions on one leg at a time.

11. Shane's In-Place Acceleration (SIPA) (chapter 23): Perform 3 × 20 seconds.

12. Cool-down: about 2 miles (3.2 km) of light running.

Conclusion

As an endurance runner, even a marathon runner, don't enhance your maximal running speed just to improve your finishing kick even though upswings in maximal speed will spike your kick; rather, upgrade your maximal running speed to be a better distance runner. Maximal running speed is a strong predictor of endurance performance and needs to be systematically developed. Maximal speed can't be reached after 6 weeks of training that is faster than usual; thus, work toward maximal speed throughout the year. Explosive training, fast running on slight downhills and uphills, and running-specific strength training combined with quality running should all propel maximal running speed upward.

CHAPTER 29

Promoting Resistance to Fatigue

In order to understand which training techniques are best for promoting improved resistance to fatigue during running, it is first necessary to review some points from chapter 12. As explained in that chapter, athletes often become fatigued while running *before* they reach maximal rates of oxygen consumption, topmost heart rates, or highest levels of blood lactate. Thus, fatigue during running cannot be well explained by oxygen limitation, cardiac limitation, or excessive lactic acid. A more logical explanation is that there are neural-output settings in a runner's brain that do not permit specific intensities, or speeds, of running to be continued beyond fixed durations. Neural output consists of the motor signals sent to the muscles by the brain and spinal cord during running. These signals control the magnitude of muscular force production and the rate at which the force is applied—and thus control running velocity.

A competing view is that loss of *muscle function* during running is the main cause of fatigue, with the nervous system simply toning down neural output as the muscles begin to lose the ability to generate propulsive force. This is an attractive hypothesis, but it fails to explain a key aspect of competitive running: Runners with similar levels of cardiovascular function, $\dot{V}O_2$max, and lactate-threshold speed often *begin* races at different speeds before loss of muscle function can occur. The best explanation for this situation is that neural output has been preset for each runner at the beginning of the race and is then simply maintained or gradually diminished as the race proceeds. Those runners with the highest settings, that is, those who can sustain the highest levels of neural output during the competition, are the top finishers.

The neural-output theory also best explains the surge that takes place during the last work interval in endurance training, or the phenomenon in which endurance runners become fatigued and gradually slow down over the course of an extended interval workout but then magically burn the last work interval at the fastest pace for the entire session. If the fatigue in such sessions were truly the result of a crisis in the muscles as discussed in chapter 12, it would be impossible for the last work interval to be the highest-quality segment of the workout. A better explanation is that neural output is carefully controlled over the course of an intense session in order to minimize potential physiological problems—and then raised to a high level during a safe final work interval. It's safe because of its relatively short duration and the impending end of the workout.

Trainability of Neural Output

If neural output governs competitive and quality workout velocities, then there must be a control center in the nervous system, a center that might aptly be called the *neural governor*. As outlined in chapter 12, there is strong evidence that this neural governor actually creates fatigue during intense or very prolonged running and attempts to limit performances. Fortunately, there is also evidence that the neural governor responds to training. That is, runners can train in certain ways in order to set their governors to allow quicker paces during their races.

The strategy of carrying out long runs at submaximal paces is not a good approach for increasing the neural governor's set point—unless one is preparing for an ultramarathon—since such workouts correspond with submaximal neural outputs. A general rule in exercise physiology is that a well-trained system must be stressed at its limits in order to produce adaptation. Calling on the nervous system to produce minimal levels of neural output is thus unlikely to reset the neural governor to a higher intensity of running although it might somewhat dampen the governor's tendency to create fatigue during very long efforts.

Strength-training research reveals that high-intensity, explosive strength training augments neural output more than other forms of strengthening.[1,2] This is not surprising since explosive training calls for high levels of neural output, and thus the specific, desired result is being rehearsed in training, perhaps teaching the nervous system that high levels of output are safe and manageable.

For runners, it seems certain that intense, high-quality running would enhance neural output to a greater extent than submaximal effort because fast running speeds are closer to the limit of the nervous system's ability to regulate running. Not surprisingly, explosive training—the combination of high-velocity sprints and explosive drills and exercises—has been demonstrated in a number of different scientific studies to enhance endurance performance.[2] It is possible that such training makes high-speed running more permissible and manageable to the neural governor.

Methods for Improving Resistance to Fatigue

Research concerning the promotion of resistance to fatigue is still in its infancy, but scientific explorations suggest that there are several ways for runners to improve their ability to resist fatigue. Conducting workouts at race velocities, modifying recovery durations during interval sessions, enhancing muscle's oxidative capacity and upgrading lactate-threshold velocity, and engaging in running-specific strength training all appear to be viable strategies for optimizing resistance to fatigue. Even nutritional tactics can be beneficial: Avoiding hypoglycemia, maximizing glycogen repletion, and taking specific supplements have all been linked with greater contravention of fatigue.

Extending Training at Race Speed

Extended periods of training at a specific running velocity hike resistance to fatigue at that specified speed. For one thing, such running enhances economy at the chosen velocity (chapter 25). It is clear that confidence in the ability to manage a particular pace will also increase as that tempo is practiced relentlessly. Another effect should be that the neural governor will accept the selected, well-rehearsed speed as one that can be maintained for a more extended period of time. When a runner is preparing for an important 10K, therefore, frequent running at goal 10K pace should promote greater resistance to fatigue at 10K tempo *especially if the 10K work intervals are fairly lengthy*. Intervals of 2,000 meters (1.24 mi) should function more effectively than 800-meter intervals, for example, because the former teach the governor that goal 10K pace can be handled continuously over relatively long periods. Shortening the recovery periods between the 2,000-meter (1.24 mi) intervals should be an effective strategy for promoting resistance to fatigue, too, because doing so begins to simulate actual race conditions more closely.

Adjusting Recovery Times

Resistance to fatigue is important in training as well as racing. High levels of resistance to fatigue during training sessions permit challenging sessions to be completed at target paces, providing an optimal stimulus for physiological adaptation, especially neuromuscular optimization. When high-quality interval workouts are carried out during the initial stages of training, increasing recovery intervals can thwart fatigue and thus upgrade the capacity to hit target speeds during work intervals.[3]

However, expanding recovery intervals simultaneously makes a training session less specific to competitive situations, and there is evidence that *shortening* recoveries is ultimately better for promoting resistance to fatigue. Anecdotally, recovery manipulation is a relatively popular strategy among elite Kenyan runners. When Yobes Ondieki, for example, was preparing to break the world record in the 10K, he completed interval workouts with the work intervals set at exact world-record pace. Over time, he shortened the recoveries between work intervals until recovery time deteriorated to a meager 10 seconds! At that point, Ondieki was running almost world-record 10Ks during his training sessions, and upon breaking the world record, he reported that the record-setting race was actually easier than his preparatory workouts.[4]

Runners who sprint 200 meters (.12 mi) can also improve resistance to fatigue and overall performance by using relatively short recoveries. In research carried out at Aristotle University in Greece, speed sessions were conducted three times a week for 6 weeks. Sprinters who used 10-second recovery intervals during workouts that featured 10-second work intervals at maximal speed were quicker during the second 100 meters of all-out 200-meter efforts than those who employed 60-second recovery intervals. In other words, a 1:1 work-to-recovery ratio produced better performances at 200 meters than a 1:6 work-to-recovery ratio. Concentrations of key anaerobic enzymes—glucose-6-phosphate and fructose-6-phosphate—were also significantly higher in the short-recovery sprinters.[5]

Enhancing Muscle's Oxidative Capacity and Lactate-Threshold Velocity

Elite East African runners have the same $\dot{V}O_2$max values as elite Caucasian runners but have considerably greater resistance to fatigue; the best runners from East Africa can run 21 percent longer at a high-quality velocity (92 percent of maximal speed) compared with topmost Caucasian runners.[6] These same East African runners have greater oxidative enzyme activity in their muscles despite not having higher $\dot{V}O_2$max levels, particularly with regard to a key oxidative compound—citrate synthase—that is 50 percent higher in East African runners than in elite Caucasian runners.[6] The East Africans also accumulate less blood lactate during strenuous running, indicating that lactate-threshold velocity is higher.[6] Thus, it is logical to argue that high skeletal-muscle oxidative capacity and lactate-threshold speed, in concert with heavy neural drive, are factors that promote resistance to fatigue.

Two different types of workouts enhance skeletal-muscle oxidative capacity and lactate-threshold speed. One type includes sessions that incorporate significant segments at 100 percent of $\dot{V}O_2$max and above, including the following:

- $v\dot{V}O_2$max workouts
- Interval workouts at best 1,500-, 1,000-, and 800-meter race paces
- Maximal-speed sessions with relatively short recoveries
- Demanding circuit-training workouts with tough running components
- Hill repeat and fartlek efforts

A second type includes sessions that incorporate a warm-up and then about 45 minutes of intense and primarily sustained running that significantly depletes glycogen. The latter is significant because depleted intramuscular glycogen stores create a strong stimulus for aerobic enzyme synthesis within the muscles. An example of such a session for an elite Kenyan might be 7K (4.35 mi) of steady, hard running followed by a short break lasting 5 or 6 minutes and then 6K (3.73 mi) of intense effort.

Additional Strategies

Other workout strategies for promoting greater resistance to fatigue include consuming a carbohydrate-rich meal a few hours before the session begins to avoid hypoglycemia and eschewing the common tendency to blast through the first repetition of an interval workout at a speed far greater than the runner's goal. The faster the first interval, the more likely fatigue is to appear in later intervals within a workout.[3] Maintaining motivation is a key factor, too, especially since research reveals that fatigue during workouts can result from reduced neural output.[3]

When fatigue is experienced during running, there is often a simultaneous loss of running economy (i.e., an increase in oxygen-consumption rate). Recent research has revealed that runners with excellent muscular-strength endurance, or the ability to maintain muscular-force production by the quads and hamstrings over extended periods during nonrunning tests of strength, suffer smaller decrements in economy during continuous high-intensity running. Thus, it appears that an improvement in muscular-strength endurance preserves running economy during tough efforts and should thereby augment resistance to fatigue.[7] Running-specific strength training is highly recommended for enhancing muscular-strength endurance (chapter 14).

Various nutritional supplements have been marketed as being energizing fatigue fighters. One of the most interesting of such products is a compound rather mysteriously called (-)-epicatechin. In a recent study carried out at the University of California San Diego, (-)-epicatechin supplementation (1 milligram per kilogram [2.21 lb] of body weight twice daily) boosted running performance by 50 percent and enhanced resistance to fatigue by 30 percent.[8] Impressively, oral (-)-epicatechin supplementation had powerful effects on mitochondrial development, muscle capillarity, and muscular oxidative capacity. (-)-Epicatechin is a flavonol naturally found in cacao and tea, but before readers rush to a supplement shop to purchase the product or begin consuming copious amounts of cocoa and green tea, they should be aware that no study has ever linked (-)-epicatechin intake with higher performance in human runners. The San Diego study was carried out with novice athletes—specifically, previously untrained *mice*. The same is true for most other commercial products marketed as energy promoters. (See chapter 46 for the few exceptions to this rule.)

Conclusion

An increased resistance to fatigue enhances endurance performance. Systematic use of intense, high-quality training spikes the amount and duration of neural output, and this boosts resistance to fatigue. Explosive training, extended training at goal race pace, shortened recovery times within interval workouts, and sessions that optimize muscle oxidative capacity and lactate-threshold velocity are all proven fatigue fighters.

PART

VII

Molecular Biological Changes in Running

CHAPTER 30

Training Effects at the Molecular Level

Gaining an understanding of the ways in which workouts turn on genes inside muscle cells and thus produce biochemical and structural adaptations might seem to be an esoteric and overly scientific pursuit to many runners and coaches, but such understanding is actually critical. Approaching training from the molecular perspective takes the guesswork out of running and helps identify the workouts that have the most potent impact on running capacity. The bottom line is that coaches and runners should always be trying to turn on an optimal cascade of biochemical reactions via training. This is not possible without an understanding of what goes on inside muscles at the molecular level.

Effects of Training on Genes

Running training induces an array of significant molecular responses inside muscle cells. Each workout causes a multitude of genes inside muscle cell nuclei to be read, known as transcription. This action initiates an outburst of messenger RNA (mRNA) within muscle fibers; mRNA codes for proteins that will become new, adaptive structures and enzymes inside muscle cells. This activity peaks 3 to 12 hours after a training session is over. Levels of mRNA do not usually return to normal until 24 hours after the end of a training session, indicating that adaptation to the workout is continuing during that time.[1, 2]

Each molecule of mRNA that appears after a workout has been transcribed from a segment of DNA (i.e., a gene) and has a chemical blueprint for a specific protein. A molecule of mRNA carries its gene-derived information to a site of protein synthesis within a muscle cell called a ribosome. At the ribosome, the individual mRNA molecule is translated into a chain of amino acids—a protein. The protein may be structural in nature, increasing the basic strength of the muscle cell in which it is found. It may also act as an enzyme, enhancing the activity of a specific metabolic process inside the muscle. For example, the protein might be a key enzyme called phosphofructokinase, the concentration of which can place an upper limit on the breakdown of carbohydrate for energy during very intense running.

The process just described is the most basic way a workout enables endurance runners to improve their running capacity. A training session produces mechanical and chemical signals inside muscle fibers that cause hundreds of different genes to be read. The reading produces mRNA that is then translated into protein, and the protein functions in ways that can enhance endurance performance. In one sense, when runners train, they are hoping to turn on and transcribe the most advantageous genes so that the best proteins for performance can be produced. Long-term adaptation to training is caused by the additive effects of each workout, leading to alterations in the concentrations of performance-related proteins and new steady-state levels of proteins that promote endurance and speed.[3]

Signals Leading to Adaptation

Molecular biologists have identified a number of different signals that can lead to transcription, protein synthesis, and thus adaptation at the molecular level. The mechanical stretching muscle cells undergo during running is a signaling message. In fact, this mechanical elongation is sometimes referred to as a primary messenger. Molecular biologists know that one specific effect of mechanical stretching is the activation of a chemical called insulin-like growth factor, which is actively involved in muscle growth and repair.[4] The nature of the mechanical stress appears to be very important. For example, axial mechanical stretch, which tugs on a muscle cell in a lengthwise direction, produces completely different molecular, intramuscular responses than transverse mechanical stress, which applies force perpendicular to the long axes of muscle fibers.[5] The use of both kinds of mechanical stretching during training probably produces more complete strengthening of muscle cells.

Calcium

Calcium is a chemical primary messenger that can elicit a cascade of adaptive molecular events. When a neuron stimulates a muscle cell to contract, an internal network of tubular structures within the fiber (i.e., the sarcoplasmic reticulum, or SR) releases calcium ions (Ca^{2+}) into the general subcellular fluid space. The freeing of calcium evokes shortening of the muscle cell. When the fiber relaxes and relengthens, the Ca^{2+} is drawn back into the SR.

Among fairly inexperienced runners, prolonged running at moderate intensity of about 60 to 70 percent of $\dot{V}O_2max$ enhances the calcium reuptake capacity of the SR, probably by increasing the number of active calcium pumps in the walls of the SR. This appears to be a highly adaptive response since it increases the amount of Ca^{2+} available for sustained muscle contractions. Repeated exercise sessions cause the release and reuptake of calcium to become more regular, which enhances resistance to fatigue.[6]

High-intensity running workouts, conducted at intensities above $\dot{V}O_2$max for example, produce a different calcium response. They can promote a short-term, 20 to 50 percent decrease in calcium ion reuptake and thus release, perhaps by shutting down the calcium pumps in some way. This drop-off in calcium transport ability can require at least 60 minutes to correct,[7] which helps explain the extreme muscle fatigue that can occur in response to high-intensity running.

The exact nature of the gene expression and protein synthesis that occur in response to intensity-dependent signals is not yet known, but changes in calcium ion concentrations are believed to represent strong primary messages that produce an array of secondary molecular events and thus create a number of different adaptive pathways for muscle cells.[6] It is clear that the amount and duration of calcium ion flux, and thus the strength of the calcium signal, are determined by the duration, frequency, and intensity of running. The exact way in which these factors interact is not yet understood. Future research will likely examine the ways in which intensity and duration of training influence calcium flux in both experienced and novice runners.

ATP and AMP

Adenosine triphosphate (ATP) is the energy currency of all cells in a runner's body, providing instantly available energy for muscle contractions and an array of other important activities. The relative ratio of ATP and a closely related compound, adenosine monophosphate (AMP), is an important signaling mechanism.[8] Strenuous or prolonged running tends to increase the ratio of AMP to ATP inside muscle fibers. This upswing activates a compound called AMP-activated protein kinase (AMPK), which is a potent second messenger, or additional signal.[8] Activation of AMPK can create a variety of performance-enhancing effects, including improvements in glucose uptake by muscle cells[9] and upgrades in the rate of fatty acid oxidation.[10] Both of these changes make more energy available to muscle cells and thus can prolong endurance and the ability to sustain a desired intensity of effort.

Scientific investigations reveal that faster running speeds and advanced power outputs during cycling invoke heightened AMPK activation when compared with less intense levels of exertion.[11] Long-term aerobic training decreases the acute AMPK response associated with workouts, but this is true only when exercise is conducted at the same pretraining work rate.[12] This is important to note because the pretraining work rate becomes a smaller percentage of maximal work rate as fitness advances over time.

As long as workout intensity is adequately high, AMPK activation will be significantly enhanced: For example, interval training at 90 percent of $\dot{V}O_2$max can increase AMPK activity in well-trained athletes.[12] AMPK activation is also dramatically increased after high-intensity sprint-cycling efforts of short duration.[13] These effects should also be present after similar levels of effort during running. The underlying mechanism is that high levels of effort depress intramuscular ATP concentrations, thus increasing the ratio between AMP and ATP and activating AMPK. The AMP-ATP signaling mechanism suggests that the maintenance of a high average intensity of training is paramount for endurance runners.

Impact of Molecular Adaptations

Many of the molecular adaptations associated with long-term endurance training are well understood. If a previously sedentary individual begins to run three or four times a week, performance-related intramuscular protein content can increase dramatically within a few weeks as appropriate genes are repeatedly transcribed and used to create new proteins. For example, research has shown that endurance training can increase mitochondrial protein content in leg muscles by as much as 100 percent after 6 weeks of workouts, producing a major advance in the leg-muscles' ability to use oxygen and supply the energy (ATP) necessary for sustained running.[14]

Mitochondria are the main subcellular structures in muscle fibers that determine aerobic capacity and resistance to fatigue.[15] A single mitochondrion has about 615 different proteins. Mitochondria carry out the process of oxidative phosphorylation, a series of reactions dependent on oxygen that use the energy found in carbohydrate and fat to synthesize ATP. Without well-developed mitochondria, an endurance runner will lack the ability at the molecular level to run fast over long distances. Increases in mitochondrial protein content are usually associated with improvements in endurance and maximal aerobic capacity, or $\dot{V}O_2$max.[15]

The protein content of muscle cells is quite dynamic, and the half-life of mitochondrial protein can be as short as 1 week.[16] In other words, just half of the mitochondrial protein created on a specific day will be present in the mitochondria 1 week later, and only 25 percent of the original protein will still exist after 2 weeks. This helps explain why a sudden cessation of training can lead to a fairly rapid loss of aerobic capacity. Without the appropriate signals associated with training, the expression of genes related to mitochondrial development and endurance-running capability grinds to a quick halt.

The genes coding for a chemical called PGC-1alpha are crucial for mitochondrial biogenesis, which is an increase in mitochondrial protein content, enzyme activity, and overall density. PGC-1alpha appears to boost mitochondrial biogenesis by co-activating multiple mitochondrial transcription factors. These factors are compounds that cause the reading of numerous genes related to mitochondrial-protein synthesis.[17] Thus, PGC-1alpha is like a master regulator of mitochondrial biogenesis. Studies in which mice were given supplemental genetic material coding for PGC-1alpha showed that such mice significantly improved endurance capacities compared with rodents with normal levels of PGC-1alpha.[18]

PGC-1alpha is also the co-activator of an important compound called PPAR that can enhance fatty acid oxidation, increase mitochondrial DNA content, and convert muscle fibers from fast-twitch to slow-twitch.[19] Slow-twitch muscle cells have higher oxidative capacities and greater resistance to fatigue during submaximal running. One study found that mice that produced unusually large amounts of PPAR improved running performance by as much as 90 percent.[19] So a key goal of training is to optimize the production of PGC-1alpha and thus PPAR. While such effects are well understood, a persistent problem remains: The study of the molecular biology of running has not progressed far enough to know which training sessions and programs produce optimal concentrations of PGC-1alpha and PPAR and thus a maximal rate of mitochondrial biogenesis. This will likely be a subject for future research.

The same can be said for many other key adaptive molecular events within muscles. For example, it is known that endurance training boosts the subcellular production of GLUT4, a chemical that increases the rate at which glucose can be transported into muscle cells.[20] In experimental work, rodents that produce large quantities of GLUT4 can exhibit dramatically improved running performances.[21] However, the form of training that turns on the genetic code for GLUT4 to the greatest extent is not yet known.

The muscles are not the only sites that undergo molecular transformations in response to endurance training. When genes that code for a specific receptor in the heart are highly expressed as a result of training, the heart is capable of a greater total cardiac output, sending more blood and oxygen to the muscles during strenuous workouts and competitions.[22] The best way to signal these genes via training is not yet known.

Conclusion

It is clear that a key goal for the molecular biology of running is to identify the ways in which the intensity, duration, and frequency of training produce unique signaling mechanisms and thus changes in gene expression and protein production within muscle cells and the heart. Such an understanding should upgrade the quality of training programs for runners.

CHAPTER 31

Training Favoring Molecular Enrichment

Molecular biologists who study running may eventually be able to tell runners exactly which genes are expressed in response to different kinds of running workouts, knowledge that will greatly enhance training productiveness. In the meantime, the current understanding of the molecular biology of running (outlined in chapter 30) can help runners and coaches answer key questions about running training.

Specifically, understanding sports molecular biology can assist runners and coaches with their use of strength training for running. Traditionally, strength training has been viewed as an activity that is too anaerobic for distance runners, but molecular research reveals that resistance training can be highly beneficial if conducted in the proper way. Furthermore, molecular research has much to say concerning the best possible frequency of training, the effects of glycogen depletion and repletion on overall fitness, and optimal adaptation to training as will be outlined in this chapter.

Molecular Changes of Strength Training

A historic debate in distance running concerns whether strength training provides significant benefits for the endurance runner. One can begin to resolve that question by thinking about how muscles respond to strength training versus endurance running at the molecular level. If such molecular adaptations are quite different, it is possible that strength training could interfere with the adaptive responses associated with endurance work by forcing muscles to use precious resources to create proteins and structures that do not help—and might even hinder—endurance performance.

Research reveals that when an individual begins to lift weights two or three times a week, the genes associated with the adaptive response to resistance training are expressed, proteins unique to strength-training adaptations are produced, and the overall changes are different from those associated with running training. Usually, muscle cells upgrade their diameter and overall volume in response to resistance training, and as a result, strength may improve rather dramatically. To put it simply, there is a greater amount of muscle tissue available to exert force, and thus strength increases. In contrast, endurance training usually does not produce muscle hypertrophy.

If an athlete *only* pushes weights around in the gym, however, and does not engage in any other form of training, the genes that become active during endurance training will not be well expressed unless the activities are carried out as part of an intense circuit workout; the athlete will struggle during any sustained activity carried out at a significant fraction of $\dot{V}O_2$max in spite of the enhanced muscular strength. The runner's muscles won't respond well in a 10K race, for example, and he or she will finish the competition far behind individuals with considerably less sinuosity and strength. The problem is not that strength training hurts endurance performance; rather, it does not seem to produce—by itself—molecular adaptations that greatly enhance distance running.

The muscles take an entirely different trajectory when an individual avoids the gym and begins a program of regular endurance training, for example running for 45 to 60 minutes five times a week. In this case, the genes for endurance are expressed, the muscle fibers busy themselves with the process of synthesizing increased quantities of aerobic enzymes and higher densities of mitochondria, and muscle cells may signal surrounding capillaries to create bushy new networks of small blood vessels that envelop muscle fibers like tangled spiders' webs. Any fast-twitch cells that are present in the muscles, the kinds of fibers that promote raw strength, undergo at least a partial metamorphosis making them much more like slow-twitch cells. After 8 weeks of this kind of training, moderate-intensity endurance exercise is easy, but a trip to the gym would most likely reveal a surprising lack of strength and coordination. The muscles would be far different—and significantly weaker—compared with the sizable sinews produced by a steady diet of strength training.

It is clear that two different adaptive directions are possible at the molecular level when training consists of resistance or endurance work. With resistance training, muscle cells create new proteins that increase the size of muscle fibers and whole muscles. With endurance training, muscle cells synthesize aerobic enzymes and structures that enhance stamina without increasing muscle bulk. Traditionally, many exercise physiologists and running coaches have said that these two possible adaptive directions are contradictory: If an athlete pushes muscles on a path toward strength, this will retard the development of greater endurance, and vice-versa. The basic idea is that muscles cannot simultaneously involve themselves with the processes of increasing size and augmenting aerobic characteristics. As a result of this kind of thinking, many endurance athletes avoid strength training altogether.

Early Studies on Strength and Endurance Training

This story concerning the potential molecular conflicts associated with synchronous strength and endurance training goes back to the 1970s when Robert Hickson, then a post-doctoral researcher at Washington University in St. Louis, discovered that the running workouts he was completing with his mentor, John Holloszy, seemed to be producing a sharp decrease in his muscle mass. Hickson went on to complete a study in which he demonstrated that endurance training had a negative impact on the gains in strength associated with concurrent resistance training.[1] The lesson from this research was consequently adopted by the running community. Runners began to believe that it made little sense to carry out strength training since endurance-running activities would throttle the possible emergence of greater strength. Furthermore, the two activities seemed to be too disparate—aerobic (running) versus anaerobic (strength training) in the parlance of the day—to be joined together in any serious runner's training log.

What is often forgotten is that Hickson's own follow-up study found that strength training was extremely beneficial to runners. In that inquiry, runners who took part in a 10-week resistance program primarily geared toward upgrading the strength of the quadriceps muscles increased their endurance time while running at an intensity of $\dot{V}O_2$max by a solid 12 percent.[2] In additional research conducted several years later by Hickson and colleagues at the University of Chicago, runners who had reached a "steady-state level of performance" carried out strength training three times a week for 10 weeks, with their regular endurance training remaining constant during this period.[3] This research, far from revealing problems associated with synchronizing strength training with endurance work, revealed that the addition of strength training was linked with a *13 percent enhancement of endurance* during intense running.

Other studies were not able to demonstrate that endurance training harmed the development of strength. In one of the most ingenious of these investigations, some subjects performed endurance training on one leg and a combination of endurance and strength training with the other leg. A second group of athletes carried out strength training on one leg and the combination of endurance and strength training with the other. The endurance training was composed of five 3-minute intervals of cycling per workout at an intensity of 90 to 100 percent of $\dot{V}O_2$max; the strength training centered on six sets of 15 to 22 repetitions of leg presses with challenging resistance.[4]

After 22 weeks, the legs that engaged in both endurance and strength training were just as strong as the legs that performed strength training only, indicating that endurance training did not interfere with the development of force production. An interesting aspect of this research was that the same leg muscles were used for both the endurance and strength training, and the movements involved (pushing on a bike pedal and pressing a leg-press platform) were similar mechanically. This contradicted one common view that endurance-training's depressing effect on strength would be particularly strong if the same muscles were engaged in both types of training.

From the molecular standpoint, it had been thought that individual muscles could never go in two directions at once. It was believed that when asked to do so, muscles would abandon gains in strength and size in favor of endurance-related changes just as Hickson's quads had lost mass when he became a serious runner. In this 22-week study, however, muscles engaged in endurance training had no problem at all with the task of building up strength when they were asked to do so. Since the movements involved in the research (pedaling and pressing) overlapped biomechanically, there was a strong indication that the development of running-specific *strength* would not be retarded at all by using high-quality running workouts.

Why, then, did Hickson's original study detect a negative effect of endurance training on strengthening? It is possible that the strength-endurance subjects in that research simply became overtrained. The strength-endurance subjects were working out at least 70 minutes per day (40 minutes of endurance running and 30 minutes of strengthening) five times per week, whereas the strength-only athletes were training just 30 minutes per day. As strength increased, additional weight was added to maintain maximal resistance for the required numbers of repetitions. In fact, the strength-endurance participants did gain strength, as measured during the parallel squat, at the same rate as the strength-only athletes over the first 6 to 7 weeks of the study before stabilizing and then losing strength over the last 2 weeks. If the study had ended after 6 weeks, the conclusion would have been that endurance training does not hurt the development of strength at all!

An important point to note, too, is that Hickson's strength-endurance athletes did gain strength over the 10 weeks of the study; their gains over 10 weeks were simply not as great as those achieved by the strength-only subjects. From the beginning of the study to the end of the sixth week, the strength-endurance participants upgraded their squat strength by about 35 percent, which is considerable. This makes it unlikely that some powerful molecular mechanism existed that blocked gains in strength as a result of the simultaneous endurance training.

Balancing Strength and Endurance Training

When an athlete engages in resistance exercise, it is clear that hypertrophy occurs when the stimulus originating the adaptation is one of short-duration effort at high intensity (e.g., with increased muscle tension). Research suggests that this kind of strength training produces a cascade of biochemical changes (the signals described in chapter 30) inside muscle cells, alterations that *are* quite different from those occurring in response to endurance training; however, these internal alerts don't necessarily *block* the processes that lead to endurance-related adaptations. Although the possible pathways toward greater strength are quite complex, much of the intramuscular makeover seems to hinge on a critically important protein called mTOR; chemicals that block the actions of mTOR make it impossible for muscles to increase their size in response to resistance exercise.[5]

The protein mTOR is activated when resistance training is performed, probably in response to growth factors released by muscles in response to strength training; to make matters more complicated, it can exist in two different protein complexes. TOR complex 1 is composed of mTor, G-protein beta-like protein, and a unique compound called raptor; this complex is responsible for augmentations of muscle *size*. TOR complex 2, on the other hand, is made up of mTOR, G-protein beta-like protein, and a different chemical called rictor; TOR complex 2 appears to be essential for remodeling the internal *structure*, or cytoskeleton, of muscle fibers. The overall process by which workouts initiate dramatic changes in muscle size and architecture is often referred to as exercise signaling. Once this signaling is completely understood, scientists could check to see which kinds of strength training do the best job of enhancing the two types of mTOR.

If endurance exercise really disrupts gains in muscle strength, it merely needs to interfere with the mTOR complexes, especially TOR complex 1. There is, in fact, a potential mechanism for this. When sustained endurance training is carried out, there is usually an increase in the activity of a chemical called AMP-activated protein kinase (AMPK) that is found inside muscle cells.[6] Heightened AMPK activity leads to a variety of chemical transformations that increase mitochondrial production and augment aerobic enzyme concentrations. However, greater AMPK action also activates a chemical called TSC2, which in turn can at least partially *inactivate* mTOR, leading to a decreased rate of protein synthesis. The AMPK-TSC2 mechanism solves the muscle fibers' potential problem of trying to do too many things at once (i.e., augmenting strength while at the same time improving aerobic characteristics) and pushes adaptation in the direction of endurance development.

Note, though, that AMPK's potential inactivation of mTOR does not mean that muscle growth cannot occur; it suggests rather that it might take place at a slower rate compared with when endurance exercise is not being carried out. It is important to note that athletes in Hickson's study who trained for strength and endurance still managed to boost squatting strength by 35 percent after 6 weeks. Furthermore, there are some kinds of strength training that lead to improvements in strength without hypertrophy; these forms of resistance training would not be harmed by AMPK's blocking effect on mTOR. For example, changes in the way the nervous system recruits and coordinates key collections of muscle cells, or motor units, can greatly improve strength without involving gains in muscle size, and such changes should not be thwarted to any degree by AMPK's inactivation of mTOR.

Although there is debate about whether endurance training slows down gains in strength, there is now a consensus that strength training can boost endurance performances. A variety of studies have shown that appropriately conducted strength training can enhance running economy, decrease foot-contact times, improve leg-muscle stiffness during running, and—the ultimate bottom line—upgrade race performances.

The molecular biology approach has produced interesting insights concerning the merits of concurrent strength and endurance training, and it also suggests that *training balance* is important. If a runner is completing large amounts of weekly running and carrying out small amounts of strength training, for example, this runner is probably covering his or her muscular mTOR with a thick blanket of AMPK and thus will achieve no change, small positive changes, or negative changes in running-specific strength. If training is in balance, however, and moderate-volume, high-quality running training is blended with regular doses of running-relevant strength training, mTOR levels should be adequate and activated, and running-specific strength, speed, and endurance should all improve at the same time. Running-relevant strength training is described in Chapters 14 and 28.

Training Twice Per Day

An understanding of how training produces responses at the molecular level can also help answer questions about *training frequency*. For example, many experienced runners train two times a day, often known as the daily double; the basic argument supporting such training has been that it is a practical way to boost total training volume. The extra volume is then supposed to lead to upswings in aerobic capacity, strength, and endurance. Some physiologists also contend that there is a unique benefit associated with training more frequently; their hypothesis suggests that two 5-mile workouts would be better than a single session of 10 miles because the body has been physiologically jolted by being provided with an adaptation-creating stimulus twice instead of once. From the viewpoint of molecular biology, two instances of cell signaling have been initiated instead of one.

What does molecular biology have to say about this controversy? As it turns out, a recent molecular approach has linked a unique form of the daily double with significant gains in endurance capability. The innovative research suggests that the strategy of conducting two workouts per day can activate special genes in an athlete's muscles that cause the production of protein molecules that fight fatigue and prolong endurance during high-quality exertions. As the investigation reveals, higher performances are the end result.

Training With Low Glycogen Levels

The intriguing story about molecular adaptations to the daily double emerged from the Department of Infectious Diseases and the Copenhagen Muscle Research Centre at the University of Copenhagen in Denmark.[7] There, researchers Anne K. Hansen, Christian Fischer, Peter Plomgard, Jesper Lovind Andersen, Bente Klarlund Pedersen, and Bengt Saltin began exploring the molecular mechanisms responsible for improvements in fitness. They noted that low muscle glycogen levels had been linked with the transcription of a number of genes involved in adaptations to training. (As explained in chapter 30, transcription means that the genes are read; this process leads to the production of proteins, which may have a positive effect on physical capacity.) The scientists began to wonder whether consistent training with low glycogen levels in the muscles might enhance a runner's adaptations to training by stimulating the expression of key genes associated with endurance performance.

At first glance, the idea of training with low glycogen levels might seem bizarre. After all, why would athletes want to train with very little carbohydrate fuel in their legs? Wouldn't that be a sure recipe for fatigue and consistently slow training speeds, plus a heightened probability of injury? However, there *is* a logical underlying principle supporting low-glycogen training. The general principle is that *deficiencies* in a substrate or in a process are what actually lead to major physiological adjustments and thus improvements in performance. From the molecular biology perspective, deficiencies lead to remedial cell signaling, followed by gene expression and the production of proteins that decrease the risk of future deficiencies.

For example, for experienced runners, training at an intensity *above* $\dot{V}O_2$max—a level of effort at which the cardiovascular and muscular system fail to meet the aerobic energy production requirements of the exercise and thus must rely on anaerobic pathways to provide the needed energy—provides a much more potent stimulus for $\dot{V}O_2$max improvement compared with training at piddling intensities below $\dot{V}O_2$max. During the latter efforts, the cardiovascular, nervous, and muscular systems think that everything is in order and may fail to change and adapt because they are able to handle the aerobic energy production requirements of the exercise. Thus, little or no change in $\dot{V}O_2$max is ultimately produced. When intensity soars above $\dot{V}O_2$max, however, the circulatory, nervous, and muscular systems think they are deficient and create adaptations that increase $\dot{V}O_2$max. (The word *think* is employed here to simplify the discussion of the actual triggers that the circulatory, muscular, and nervous systems use to fire up their adaptation processes).

Along similar lines, high-intensity training can create a great problem for muscle cells because the cells often lack the buffering proteins that soak up the excess quantity of fatigue-inducing hydrogen ions produced during such scorching training. This *deficiency* in buffering proteins eventually leads to an expression of buffering-related genes and an increased production of buffers within the muscles; endurance at high intensities can improve considerably as a result. If the training had not exposed the deficiency in the buffer system (e.g., if it had been conducted at moderate intensities with little accumulation of hydrogen ions), there would have been no stimulus for the buffering system to upgrade itself, and performance at high-quality speeds would have been less likely to improve.

Testing the Low-Glycogen Theory

To test the glycogen-deficiency theory, the Danish researchers in the afore-mentioned study recruited seven healthy young men, average age 26. These subjects took part in a rigorous 10-week training program that involved both one- and two-leg exercise. As part of the design of the investigation, the right and left legs of each participant trained quite differently. One leg, chosen at random, carried out two workouts during a day, the second of which was completed under low-glycogen conditions. This two-workout day was then followed by a rest day for that leg during which no training sessions were conducted. In contrast, the other high-glycogen leg trained once per day, every day.

Here's how it worked in actual practice for a sample subject. On the first day of the investigation, the subject exercised both legs *simultaneously* for one hour at an intensity of 75 percent of the maximal possible work rate, or W_{max}. Two hours later on that same day, he exercised his left leg, which had been chosen at random to be the low-glycogen leg, for another hour at 75 percent of W_{max} for that leg. During this left-leg effort, the right leg did absolutely nothing. The left leg was almost out of fuel because its glycogen had been exhausted in the workout that had occurred 2 hours earlier. Furthermore, the continuous hour of effort plunged the left leg into full glycogen despera-tion. No carb loading or eating of any kind was permitted during the 2-hour period between workouts.

Following the second workout of the day, the subject began eating normally and thus began restocking glycogen. On the second day of the study, he exercised his right leg only. The left leg took the day off since it had worked twice on the first day. The right-leg exertion was carried out at 75 percent of the right leg's W_{max}. The right leg was in good glycogen shape on both days. On the first day, it had exercised simultaneously with the left leg; the right leg had an adequate supply of glycogen at that time because the subject had been following a healthy diet. On the second day, the right leg worked by itself for one hour *24 hours* after the two-leg work, which was enough time for glycogen reloading.

On the third day, this basic pattern started over. There was a 1-hour workout with both legs training at the same time. Two hours later, the left leg worked alone on low glycogen. On the fourth day, the right leg worked by itself with plenty of glycogen on board. This regimen was then repeated over and over, which meant that each leg performed exactly the same amount of exercise, at the same intensity, over the course of the study.

Throughout the study, the workouts began in the morning after an overnight fast, making things even tougher for the low-glycogen leg. On the days with two workouts, no food or sports drink was permitted until the second workout was done, but water consumption was *ad libitum*, or at whatever quantity was wanted. Over the course of 10 weeks, the study participants became stronger; workload gradually increased but was exactly the same for the two legs. The subjects consumed a typical athlete's diet during the investigation, with 70 percent of calories coming from carbohydrate, 15 percent from protein, and 15 percent from fat. Two-day rest periods from training were provided approximately every week.

Results of the Low-Glycogen Theory Study

After 10 weeks of this training, one-leg W_{max} had improved considerably in both legs and was absolutely equivalent between the limbs. The W_{max}, or maximal possible work rate, in this case was the topmost intensity that could be reached during a one-leg test that began with a 10-minute warm-up at an intensity of 20 Watts and continued with a step-wise increase in intensity of 10 Watts every 2 minutes until complete exhaustion was reached.

This result suggests that low-glycogen training offers no advantage, but the Danish researchers also gave each leg a test that involved working for as long as possible at a sizzling intensity of 90 percent of the final W_{max}. When this test was carried out, the leg that had trained with low glycogen, now well stocked with glycogen for the actual test, performed much better than the leg that had always trained under high-glycogen conditions. In fact, time to exhaustion *was twice as long for the low-glycogen leg* compared with high-glycogen leg. Naturally, total work performed during this rugged test at 90 percent of W_{max} was also much greater for the leg that had driven glycogen way down during training. The low-glycogen leg was the better one for performance!

The investigators noticed some interesting changes in hormone production associated with the low-glycogen training. Specifically, when the low-glycogen leg worked out for an hour by itself, plasma epinephrine and norepinephrine levels were significantly higher, compared with the case when the high-glycogen leg went solo. Epinephrine and norepinephrine are potent boosters of nervous system activity and can also increase the force which muscles produce when they contract.

Differences were also apparent at the molecular level when two key mitochondrial (i.e., aerobic) enzymes were monitored in each leg. The activity of hydroxyacyl CoA dehydrogenase (HAD), a very important aerobic enzyme, increased significantly only in the low-glycogen leg over the course of the 10-week study. In addition, the relative increase in activity of citrate synthase (CS), another key aerobic enzyme, was significantly more pronounced in the low-glycogen leg compared with the high-glycogen leg. On top of these molecular changes, the percent number and percent area of type II-X (fast-twitch) fibers decreased significantly in the high-glycogen leg but not in the low-glycogen leg. This was possibly because the slow-twitch muscles in the low-glycogen leg became so glycogen depleted during workouts that they *had* to rely on their fast-twitch cells to complete the sessions, creating a stimulus for preserving the II-X fibers.

What is the possible molecular mechanism underlying all these positive changes in the low-glycogen legs? Several transcription factors in muscle cells (i.e., chemicals that cause certain genes to be read) are naturally bound to glycogen molecules within the muscle fibers. When glycogen becomes low (i.e., the signal), these factors are released and trigger the transcription of key genes, including the genetic material that codes for aerobic enzymes such as HAD and CS.[8] As a result, the activities of these enzymes increase, oxygen can be processed at a higher rate, fuel can be provided to muscle cells at greater speed, and endurance at quality intensities may improve significantly—as was the case in the performance test in this study.

In summarizing the Danish results, it is clear that carrying out two workouts every second day, with the end of the first workout separated from the beginning of the second workout by just 2 hours and with no glycogen fill-ups permitted, was superior to training once per day, even though total work performed and actually training intensities were the same in the two cases.

What molecular biology does not tell us is that such training should be approached with caution. For one thing, training schedules that permit muscle glycogen stores to diminish to very low levels have been linked with staleness and the overtrained syndrome.[9] In addition, it is not illogical to think that closely coupled workouts that maximize fatigue in the second session might increase the risk of injury although this has not been meticulously studied in a controlled scientific setting.

Practical Implications for Training Twice Per Day

On a day when quality training and a double are planned, a reasonable approach is to make the *first* workout of the pair the more intense session. Attempting high-quality training with very low muscle glycogen stores might produce muscle damage. In addition, it would be difficult to reach planned high-quality speeds during a low-glycogen workout.

A question that remains from this research is whether it is really necessary to recover for approximately 45 hours after the second of the coupled sessions as the Danish subjects did. Many runners would ask whether it would be possible to train on the following day, too, in most cases with a single session.

Of course, it would be possible for *some* runners—those with good recovery powers—to do this. It can be assumed that the benefits that showed up in the Danish study were present in response to the low-glycogen conditions, not because of the 45-hour rest between the end of the second workout and the start of the next session 2 days later. However, getting right back to the workout grind on the day after double workouts is not ideal for runners with poor running-specific strength because they may damage their leg muscles with such extra running. Most runners are adapted to a certain number of workouts per week, and sudden increases in the number of weekly sessions can create adaptation and recovery problems that lead to injury or the overtraining syndrome.

For the runner who is already carrying out two daily sessions and handling them without problem, it would make sense to couple those workouts, putting them just 2 hours apart, so that the molecular effects of extra-low glycogen concentration can be produced; however, the second exertion should be the easier one. From the standpoint of the glycogen transcription mechanism, this schedule would work better than the usual practice of doubling with a session in the morning and another in the late afternoon or evening, with at least one meal intervening.

What would be the optimal frequency for doubling? The Danes gave their subjects regular rests, so the twice-a-days occurred no more than three times a week and sometimes just twice a week. Bear in mind also that *major* gains occurred in enzyme levels and performance even though the 45-hour furloughs were part of the plan. Such findings suggest that a couple of doubles per week might easily be enough to significantly increase performances, with these doubles separated by rest or light days of training. Overall, the low-glycogen legs in the Danish study hit the lowest glycogen concentrations just five times in each 14-day period, three times during one week and two times during the other.

The following guidelines are important to the strategy of two workouts a day:

• Timing of the second workout matters. The second workout of the day has to be carried out a couple of hours after the first one with no significant glycogen loading of the muscles in between. Stocking up on carbohydrate between workouts would eliminate the boosting effect on fitness and performance of low glycogen detected by the Danish investigators. If a runner had to eat something between workouts, it would have to be very light—and biased toward fat rather than carbohydrate. Protein would not be acceptable between sessions because the human body is actually very good at stripping the nitrogens from proteins and treating them as expensive carbohydrate.

• Second workout is more moderate than the first. There is an element of risk associated with the Danish strategy. Glycogen-depleted muscles are weak muscles, and muscles with subpar force production are more prone to injury. The second workout of the day would ideally be moderate in intensity to temper the stress on fatigued muscles, and any tightness and soreness that developed would need to be closely monitored. It is important to complete a program of running-specific strength training before embarking on a program that emphasizes glycogen-depleting workouts twice a day because such strength training is protective of muscles and connective tissues.

• Glycogen loading needs to occur after the second workout. Following the second workout of the day, quick glycogen loading is optimal. Intramuscular glycogen synthesis is highest during the two hours after an exertion, so ample carbohydrate should be ingested during that time. The use of a high-carbohydrate recovery drink would speed carbs to the muscles. An intake of approximately 1 gram of carbohydrate per pound (.45 kg) of body weight, along with 10 to 20 grams of protein, during the 20- to 30-minute period following the second workout is recommended. Remember that the strategy is *not* to consistently train in the low-glycogen state. The correct strategy is to induce low glycogen levels with the second workout of the day. After that, ample glycogen building should occur to prepare for the next quality workout or Danish double.

• Recovery efforts are essential. The first use of the two-a-day strategy will generally induce a significant amount of unusual fatigue. This will necessitate extra rest and the faithful pursuit of a diet rich in carbohydrates, antioxidants, and healthy fats, and which is adequate in protein. Doubles should not be undertaken during periods when nonrunning life stresses are high.

• Novice runners must work up to a double training load. Because of the likely presence of inherent muscle and connective tissue weaknesses, inexperienced runners should not plunge into the two-a-day strategy. Some novice runners might be able to carry out an hour of easy walking 2 hours after their regular workouts, however, to create a similar low-glycogen effect. They can gradually build up their running-specific strength by using the correct strength training sessions (described in chapter 14), preparing themselves for the possibility of running twice a day on selected occasions as experience and strength are enhanced.

Conclusion

The molecular biology approach to training has already been helpful in resolving the debate over resistance versus endurance training; has pointed to the need for varied, balanced training; and has identified a unique strategy of doubling workouts that produces major gains in endurance performance. In the future, additional advances in the understanding of ways in which specific workouts produce transformations in cell signaling, gene expression, and protein production are certain to enhance the quality and productivity of endurance training for runners.

PART
VIII

Distance-Specific Training

32

Training for 800 Meters

In spite of the brevity of the race, training for 800 meters bears some remarkable similarities to preparing for the longer distances. As is the case with all events, 800-meter training requires a proper periodization of strength training, following the optimal sequence of general, running-specific, hill, and explosive strengthening. Running workouts for 800 meters are similar to those utilized for greater distances, but a special premium is placed on extremely fast training speeds at the expense of submaximal running.

Best Predictors of 800-Meter Performance

Highly informative research concerning 800-meter running has been carried out by Gordon Sleivert and A.K. Reid at the University of Otago in New Zealand.[1] Sleivert and Reid evaluated 17 good-quality middle-distance runners, comparing their 800-meter times with key predictors of performance, including lactate-threshold velocity, running economy, and $\dot{V}O_2$max.

Running experts often preach that maximal aerobic development is critical for achieving one's best 800-meter performances; their argument is partly based on the fact that about half of the energy required to race 800 meters is generated aerobically. However, Sleivert and his colleagues found that $\dot{V}O_2$max was totally unrelated to 800-meter time. In other words, the runners in their study who had high $\dot{V}O_2$max values didn't run 800 meters any faster than individuals with more mediocre $\dot{V}O_2$max data. In this study, the two best predictors of 800-meter performance turned out to be 400-meter time and lactate-threshold speed, the velocity above which lactate begins to accumulate in the blood (Sleivert and colleagues did not measure $v\dot{V}O_2$max).

The Otago findings should not be surprising given that 400-meter time is a measure of muscle contractility, muscle explosiveness, and overall neuromuscular function, three factors that are extremely important for running performance (discussed in chapters 11, 16, and 28). If an athlete can run a fast 400 meters, he or she has the neuromuscular characteristics so highly prized by Heikki Rusko, Tim Noakes, and other groundbreaking exercise scientists and has the potential to run quickly over 800 meters and longer distances, too.

Lactate-threshold speed, which is a great predictor of success not only for 800-meter competitions but also for lengthier races, is a function of the rate at which lactate moves out of the muscles into the blood during running and of the rapidity with which muscles and the heart *remove* lactate from the blood. As explained in chapter 10, lactate is a key fuel for the muscles. It provides a rich store of adenosine triphosphate (ATP), the high-energy compound that triggers muscle contractions, so it is easy to understand why having a high lactate-threshold speed when running would be a good thing. Establishing a lofty lactate-threshold speed means that muscles are unwilling to let energy-rich lactate slip away into the blood and that they are great at clearing lactate from the blood once it gets there. As a result, the muscles have a tremendous source of fuel to use at high rates during powerful 800-meter running.

800-Meter Workouts

It's clear that two key goals of 800-meter training are to optimize both muscular power—a surrogate for 400-meter time—and lactate-threshold velocity. The following workouts, with their emphasis on high-velocity running, develop neuromuscular power steadily over time. Because of their high intensity, they also enhance running economy and generate high blood-lactate levels. Both of these factors lead to advances in lactate-threshold speed.

Lactate Stacker

A workout that accomplishes both goals (upswings in power and lactate-threshold velocity) simultaneously is an exciting session called *the lactate stacker.* To do a lactate-stacker workout, a runner simply warms up thoroughly and then blasts off for 1 minute at a pace faster than $v\dot{V}O_2max$ and almost as fast as maximal running speed. A runner should not strain as he or she does this; it is important to be relaxed and yet produce close to maximal power in the leg muscles.

The distance covered during the 1-minute interval is not of paramount importance: The key to the workout is to run at a pace faster than $v\dot{V}O_2max$ during each 1-minute interval. Since a runner does not have to reckon the distance covered per work interval, it is possible to conduct this workout anywhere. A good choice would be an area where an individual really loves to run—for example, on trails or walkways with good footing in a beautiful park or forest.

Once 1 minute has elapsed, the runner jogs easily for 2 minutes to recover; the actual recovery jogging pace doesn't matter, as long as it is easy. The runner then repeats this pattern of 1 minute of fast running alternating with 2 minutes of easy loping. For the first workout, a runner usually completes six 1-minute surges and then ends the session after a proper cool-down.

Over time, a runner can increase the number of 1-minute accelerations to about 15 to 18.

An interesting aspect of this workout is that the 2-minute recoveries will often *feel* shorter than the 1-minute intervals: During the 1-minute intervals, the runner is trying hard to hold on while during the recoveries he or she is hoping for a slightly longer break. Another interesting facet of the session is that most runners consider it to be fun! Many athletes love to run really fast especially if they have been existing on a diet of inchmeal-paced longer runs. This workout is an excuse to run the way a runner did when he or she was an exuberant child with quick sprints followed by satisfying recoveries.

Lactate stackers work well as preparations for 800-meter competitions because they improve raw running power and upgrade coordination at high speed, which enhances running economy at an 800-meter pace and adds some power to muscle contractility. Anecdotal evidence suggests that 400- and 800-meter race times improve, frequently by a sizable margin, when a runner regularly carries out lactate stackers.

A critical aspect of lactate-stacker work is the effect on lactate dynamics. After each 1-minute surge, blood lactate levels increase because of the powerful running that has occurred. Perhaps surprisingly, blood lactate does not fall during the subsequent 2-minute recoveries, which means that each succeeding 1-minute interval at top speed stacks up even more lactate in the blood. The result is a an extremely potent stimulus for muscles to get better at clearing lactate from the blood and breaking it down for energy within their interiors, which of course heightens lactate-threshold speed, one of the two key predictors of 800-meter success.

Classic 400-Meter Session

Since 400-meter time is a fine predictor of 800-meter performance, a second great workout for 800-meter runners is a classic 400-meter session. A runner simply warms up and begins reeling off 200-meter intervals at a pace that is 1 second per 200 meters faster than his or her best 400-meter tempo. For example, if the best 400-meter time is 60 seconds (30 seconds per 200 meters), the runner could start with 4 × 200 in 29 seconds each and gradually build up to 8 × 200. It is fine to take relatively long recoveries when this workout is performed; the runner is not trying to maintain high oxygen-consumption rates throughout the workout but rather is attempting to ensure that each interval is completed at the appropriate pace, which will create an excellent stimulus for neuromuscular advancement.

If a runner does not know his or her best 400-meter time and thus is not sure about setting the split time for the intervals, the runner can cover 400 meters at all-out speed on the track on a day when he or she is feeling great. If that is not appealing, it is possible to guesstimate 400-meter time from 800-meter personal best, remembering that personal best 400-meter pace will generally be 4 seconds per 400 meters faster than 800-meter speed. If a runner has raced 800 meters in a personal best of 2:20, for example (70 seconds per 400 meters), the estimated 400-meter personal best would be 66 seconds (33 seconds per 200 meters). For the classic 400-meter workout, the runner would then begin with 4 × 200 in 32 seconds each, with 2- to 3-minute recoveries between the 200-meter intervals.

A problem faced by 800-meter runners is a potential inability to hold pace over the last 200 meters of the race when the leg muscles begin to feel as responsive as wood fibers in a pressure-treated post. A way to counter this sinew-collapsing fatigue is to conduct 1,000-meter (.62 mi) intervals in which the first 800 meters are covered at 1,500-meter pace and the last 200 meters are run at goal speed. For example, if the runner's reasonable goal for 800 meters is 2:12 (a pace of 66 seconds per 400 meters and 33 seconds per 200 meters) and the current 1,500-meter personal best is 4:26 (71 seconds per 400 meters), the strategy would be to complete the 1,000-meter interval by cruising through the first 800 meters in 2:22 (2 × 71 seconds) and then striking the last 200 in a crisp 33 seconds. It is reasonable to recover for about 4 minutes between work intervals with this kind of session and start with 1 × 1,000 meters per workout, building gradually to 3 × 1,000 meters over time.

Nixon Kiprotich's 800-Meter Training Regimen

Over the course of my career as a student of running, I have been fortunate enough to visit Kenya on 12 occasions. While there, I frequently discussed 800-meter training with Nixon Kiprotich at his home in Eldoret, and he was kind enough to introduce me to some of the 800-meter workouts he and some of the other successful Kenyan 800-meter runners, including William Tanui and Billy Konchellah, used. Kiprotich is one of the best 800-meter runners of all time. The willowy (6 ft 1 in, 149-pound [1.9 m, 67.6 kg]) athlete won the IAAF/Mobil Grand Prix for 800 meters in both 1990 and 1992, snared a silver medal at the 1992 Olympics in Barcelona (he was beaten by a hair's breadth at the wire by Tanui), garnered gold at both the East African and African Championships, and was rated the top 800-meter runner in the world for 1993 by *Track and Field News*. His 800-meter personal record is 1:43.31.

During a typical training year, Kiprotich liked to take a two-month break during October and November, doing very little training at all during those months. Throughout December and January, he would simply jog 15 kilometers (9 mi) at 10:00 a.m. and 8 kilometers (5 mi) at 5:00 p.m., five days a week—and rest on Saturdays and Sundays. All of the running was easy, and there was no speed work at all. The weekly volume was 115 kilometers (71 mi). Incidentally, running close to 70 miles (113 km) per week is fairly typical for elite Kenyan runners. Although in the Western world Kenyans are rumored to run prodigious training distances, the truth is that many of the elite Kenyans are running about 70 miles (113 km) per week during the cross country season.

In February and March, Kiprotich would carry out the strengthening phase of his overall program, adding hill workouts on Mondays and Saturdays; Tuesday through Friday each week would remain the same as before with easy running each day. The hill workouts were straightforward: On a challenging 200-meter hill, Kiprotich would charge up the slope at close to top speed and then jog to the bottom to recover; he would do this routine for about 20 reps (climbs) per workout. A session like this is excellent for 800-meter running because it greatly enhances muscle contractility—the ability of leg muscles to create propulsive forces each time a foot strikes the ground. Scientific research reveals that this kind of workout is also great for lactate-threshold development because each uphill charge sends blood lactate levels to extraordinarily high levels. Over time, the leg muscles get better at clearing lactate from the blood and breaking it down for energy. Research also indicates that this mode of training should make a runner more economical at 800-meter pace.

Beginning in April, Kiprotich would begin the high-intensity training that fully prepared him for the outdoor season. Here is his actual schedule, containing the workouts that are great for 800-meter performance:

- Monday: 2 sets of 5 × 1,000 meters (.62 mi) with 2 minutes of recovery between reps and 10 minutes of rest between the two sets. The first 800 meters of each interval are run more slowly than 800-meter race pace, but the last 200 meters are covered at race velocity or faster. As mentioned earlier, this workout helps 800-meter runners develop the ability to run at race pace despite significant fatigue. Scientific research strongly suggests that it would also be a great lactate-threshold advancer.

- Tuesday: 8 × 200 meters at very close to goal 800-meter race pace, with just 5 to 10 meters of easy jogging between reps. This workout is incredibly good for developing specific speed endurance—the ability to sustain desired pace for the entire 800 meters. The minimal recovery intervals make the workout almost as tough as the race itself, and Kiprotich believes that the session enhances the ability to overtake other runners over the last 100 meters of the race. The workout is a huge confidence-builder: If one can complete the whole workout at close to goal speed, one can be assured of the ability to finish the 800 at goal velocity. This session provides a stimulus for lactate-threshold advancement as well because of the fast pace and thus large lactate buildup.

- Wednesday: 4 × 600 meters (.37 mi) about two seconds per 200 meters slower than 800-meter race pace, with 2-minute recoveries. Then, 5 × 300 meters (.19 mi), with the first 100 meters at the same speed as the 600s but with the final 200 meters right at 800-meter goal pace; the intervals are followed by 2-minute recoveries again. This workout develops finishing power, or the ability to sustain 800-meter speed in spite of significant fatigue. As with the Monday and Tuesday sessions, this session is a potent stimulus for lactate-threshold augmentation.

- Thursday: 4 × 400 meters with 2-minute recoveries and each 400-meter interval completed about 2 to 3 seconds faster than goal 800-meter speed. This workout develops the ability to run 800-meter competitions more quickly.

- Friday: 4 × 500 meters (.31 mi) with the 500s right at 800-meter race pace. Two-minute recoveries are used. The workout improves economy and confidence at race velocity along with lactate-threshold speed.

When Kiprotich was employing this schedule, he would treat Saturday and Sunday as rest and recovery days with just 40 minutes of light jogging on Saturday and no running at all on Sunday. When the racing season actually began, he would cut back to two quality workouts per week instead of five.

Table 32.1 shows what Kiprotich's workouts would look like for 800-meter competitors with different abilities and goals.

Not everyone can complete five rugged 800-meter workouts per week for a couple of months as Kiprotich did in April and May of each training year. However, the workouts in table 32.1, along with the lactate-stacker and basic 400-meter sessions, are probably the best 800-meter sessions one could ever conduct. Completing two to three of these per week can constitute excellent preparation for 800-meter racing. Note, too, that the hill reps Kiprotich used in the early phase of his 800-meter preparations represent an outstanding way to build running-specific strength and prepare for the intense work needed to reach an 800-meter goal time.

Table 32.1 Workouts Based on Kiprotich's Plan

Day	Workout	Goal = 2:30	Goal = 2:10	Goal = 2:00
Monday	2 sets: 5 × 1,000 m (.62 mi); 2 min between reps and 10 min between sets	Last 200 m (.12 mi) in 37 sec	Last 200 m (.12 mi) in 32 sec	Last 200 m (.12 mi) in 30 sec
Tuesday	8 × 200 m (.12 mi); 10 min between reps	37 sec per 200 m (.12 mi)	32 sec per 200 m (.12 mi)	30 sec per 200 m (.12 mi)
Wednesday	4 × 600 m (.37 mi) and then 5 × 300 m (.19 mi)	600s in 1:57; 300s variable	600s in 1:42; 300s variable	600s in 1:36; 300s variable
Thursday	4 × 400 m (.25 mi)	400s in 72 sec	400s in 62 sec	400s in 57 sec
Friday	4 × 500 (.31 mi)	500s in 93 sec	500s in 81 sec	500s in 75 sec

Additional Training Strategies

Strength training adds a necessary dimension to 800-meter training, promoting the gains in neuromuscular power which are essential for 800-meter improvement. Additional forms of running training, including the use of super sets and greyhound drills, provide the pure power work which bolsters both maximal and 800-meter velocities.

Strength Training

Strength-training sessions are great for 800-meter runners, especially those sessions that emphasize running-specific exercises, including one-leg squats, high-bench step-ups, lunges, bicycle leg swings, runner's poses, and one-leg heel raises (see chapters 13, 14, and 23). True, very few of the Kenyans who dominate 800-meter running have ever bothered to enter a gym. However, almost all of them have grown up in the perfect environment for 800-meter runners: places where there are lots of steep hills. As mentioned, hill running is a specific way to develop lactate dynamics and brute power in the leg muscles, power that can translate into faster 800-meter running.

If a runner is environmentally challenged by living in a pancake-flat part of the world, there is plenty of evidence that strength training can be very helpful. For example, research carried out by Terry Kemp at Ashland University compared high school runners who simply carried out circuit training and others who followed circuit training with power training, including squats, lunges, hamstring curls, pull-downs, and bench presses. The latter group improved 800-meter times by about 3 seconds more than the circuit-only group, a statistically significant effect.[2] (Chapter 14 discusses the benefits of strength training for runners.)

Superset Training

One can also use the superset training philosophy to improve 800-meter performances. Super sets are simply two or more work intervals bound together with no intervening recovery—and with running speed gradually decreasing over the successive work intervals. Adopted from the strength-training community, super sets enhance a runner's ability to sustain desired pace in the face of greatly heightened fatigue. An excellent superset workout for an 800-meter runner could proceed as follows:

1. After a thorough warm-up, run 200 meters at close to all-out speed, followed by 400 meters at current 800-meter race pace with no break between the 200 and 400.

2. Jog or walk easily for 5 minutes to recover, and then repeat this super set (the 200-400 combo) two more times.

As fitness improves, a runner can make this workout more challenging by increasing the number of super sets from three to five or six. This session dramatically improves lactate-threshold velocity, maximal running speed, and the ability to sustain an intense velocity during 800-meter races.

Greyhound Sessions

Greyhound sessions also work perfectly for 800-meter runners. This session consists of running 8×100 meters or yards with short recoveries. A football or soccer field works well, and using a field avoids the problems associated with changing directions on a track and thus colliding with other runners. After a good warm-up, a runner accelerates dramatically over the first 20 yards (18.29 m) of each rep and then holds close-to-top speed for the next 80 yards (73.15 m), decelerating quickly after 100 yards or meters. The runner jogs easily or walks for no more than 10 seconds and then reverses direction and blasts off for 100 yards or meters in the opposite direction, continuing this pattern until eight 100s have been completed. Over time, the number of 100s can be increased to 16. It is important to maintain good form at all times during this workout, moving fluidly and powerfully without tightening up. The greyhound session upgrades maximal running speed, $v\dot{V}O_2max$, lactate threshold, and running economy at high speed—and thus 800-meter performance.

Conclusion

Training for 800 meters can be properly periodized in a manner similar to longer competitions. For full preparation for 800-meter racing, an athlete should complete 3 to 6 weeks of general strength training, 3 to 6 weeks of running-specific strength training, 3 to 6 weeks of hill work, and 3 to 6 weeks of explosive training, dotting each of these four phases with between two and four relevant, high-quality running workouts per week chosen from those noted in this chapter and depending on a runner's ability and overall capacity for training. General strength training is discussed in Chapter 13, running-specific strength training in Chapter 14, hill training in Chapter 15, and explosive training in Chapters 16 and 28.

CHAPTER **33**

Training for 1,500 Meters and the Mile

The 1,500 meters and the mile are exciting racing distances that feature high running velocities. Science nonetheless reveals that it is incorrect *to single these races out* as competitions in which speed is the most important factor since speed is a critical factor for all of the competitive distances discussed in this book, from 100 meters to 100K. Research indicates that the heightening of maximal running velocity is a guiding principle of mile and 1,500-meter training, as are lifting lactate-threshold running speed and $v\dot{V}O_2max$, but the same is true for all other distances of 800 meters and greater.

Research also indicates that the mile and 1,500-meter races are great workouts in their own right—two of the best training sessions that a runner can perform within an overall program. When the fitness benefits of the mile or 1,500 meters are compared with the gains accruing from other competitions, it is certain that runners get a greater bonus per minute of intense running from the mile and the 1,500 meters. Research carried out at the State University of New York at Syracuse demonstrated that running just 5 minutes at about mile race pace increased $\dot{V}O_2max$ approximately as much as running for about 25 minutes at 10K intensity.[1] Thus, it is possible that running two one-mile competitions during a week would have a greater impact on running fitness than a single 10K race, even though the latter event would involve more than triple the total distance!

Anecdotally, competing at a mile or 1,500 meters also makes 5K, 10K, half-marathon, and marathon paces feel considerably easier. Typically, mile race pace is about 40 seconds per mile (1.6 km) faster than 10K tempo and about 72 seconds per mile quicker than marathon-paced running. Practicing mile race velocity makes it mentally easier to handle all longer distances; the perceived effort associated with the longer races decreases appreciably. In addition, rehearsing mile race pace will also have a much stronger positive

---

400-Meter Time—Great Predictor of Mile Time

Scientific research reveals that 400-meter time is a great predictor of mile and 1,500-meter performances.[2] This fits with the overall thesis that improving maximal running speed is critical for middle- and long-distance running success. It also suggests that the use of explosive strength training, along with the employment of running workouts that make use of a runner's best 100-, 200-, and 400-meter velocities, would spike 1,500-meter and mile race abilities.

---

impact on maximal running speed compared with 5K, 10K, or marathon tempos because of the high intensity of a mile effort.

Science suggests that practicing for the mile enhances the ability of the nervous system to coordinate the leg muscles during faster running. The nerves learn to relax the muscles at just the right time to permit longer strides—and also contract them at the precise moment needed to produce maximal power. Mile-pace running also helps runners learn how to use elastic energy stored in their muscles during the gait cycle; this saves energy and permits greater propulsive force to be applied to the ground with each step. Running at mile and 1,500-meter speeds enhances neuromuscular coordination at high velocities, improving economy and generating higher race speeds.

There is also an unparalleled purity to 1,500 meter or mile racing. Competing in these races offers runners a chance to employ the great Herb Elliott's simple, simon-pure racing philosophy: "The only tactics I admire are do-or-die." In these competitions, there is no worry about parceling out energy or sipping sport drinks at just the right time. The entire mental focus is beautifully simple: to run as fast as possible for 1,500 or 1,609 meters.

Training for and running the mile is also great for dynamic flexibility, the ability to achieve greater range of motion at key joints. Because stride lengths for the mile and 1,500 meters are significantly longer than those used during the marathon, the hip joint in particular must pass through a greater range of motion during the gait cycle. In effect, running the mile opens up the hips, causing each leg to swing backward to a greater extent as the glutes and hamstrings work more powerfully. Biomechanists have identified greater average range of motion at the hip as being one of the keys to developing greater speed. The hip-opening effect is transferred directly to longer-distance running, enabling runners to achieve more powerful push-offs and higher speeds when racing distances longer than the mile and 1,500 meters.

Mile and 1,500-Meter Training Regimens From Past Greats

Examining the history of mile and 1,500-meter training is useful to modern runners and coaches because it helps provide an understanding of why mile or 1,500 meter performances have improved so dramatically over the years. Further, it forces us to re-examine our overall philosophy of mile training and also offers some great traditional workouts that still work very well in a current runner's overall training plan.

Walter George

Mile training has an especially interesting history.[3] One of the first great British milers, Walter George, worked in a chemist's shop each day from 7:00 a.m. until 9:00 p.m. and thus had limited time available for training. Rarely able to run outdoors, George developed a system of indoor training in which he ran in place with high knee lifts and a springing action. Despite carrying out most of his workouts in a small room at the chemist's establishment and racing on tracks that resembled plowed fields, George required just 3 minutes and 10 seconds to surge to an impressive victory over archrival Lon Myers in a three-quarter-mile grudge match that was witnessed by 60,000 screaming fans in 1882.

Apparently, the stationary running did not optimize postrace recovery since George lapsed into unconsciousness for 20 minutes following the race; Myers ran a respectable 3:13 and remained even longer in the comatose state—almost 2 hours, according to credible reports. George's best effort came in 1885 when he sizzled through a mile in 4:10.2, a time which was not bettered anywhere in the world for almost 50 years.

Paavo Nurmi

Paavo Nurmi, the incredible Finnish runner of the 1920s, took a slightly different approach to the establishment of a world mark: He trained outdoors, combining both high-volume and high-intensity training. Nurmi was an incredibly strong runner: As a young, impoverished errand boy in Turku, he had pulled heavily loaded carts up and down steep hills. He prepared for his 1,500-meter world record, established in 1924, with a training schedule that each morning included a 12-kilometer (7.46 mi) walk, four or five hard sprints on the track, a high-intensity 400- to 1,000-meter (.62 mi) run for time and then a 3K to 4K run (1.86-2.49 mi) with a very fast last lap.

Each evening, Nurmi bolted 4,000 to 7,000 meters (2.49-4.35 mi) across the hilly countryside, punishing himself at the end of each effort by running at close to maximal speed. His training day ended with four to five lightning-quick sprints. Three weeks before the Paris Olympics in 1924, Nurmi set a

1,500-meter world record of 3:52.6 but was angry at himself for not running at least 2 seconds faster. Forty minutes later on the same evening, Nurmi rolled through 3 miles (4.83 km) in 14:02 and 5K in 14:28.2, both world bests at the time. The amazing Finn had broken three world records in one evening of running!

Gunder Hägg

Swedish runners dominated the world of distance running in the late 1930s and early 1940s, and a Swedish runner named Gunder Hägg became the best competitor in the world at both the mile and 1,500 meters. He employed a new form of training that has retained its popularity even today. Instead of running at a relatively even velocity, Hägg constantly varied his training pace, alternating blasts of speedy running with easy coasting along the forest trails of central Sweden. Coached by the inventor of fartlek training, Gosta Holmer, Hägg also

▶ Paavo Nurmi's (lead runner) intense training schedule prepared him to set 22 official world records.

A Workout From Herb Elliott's Training Plan

A workout employed by the great miler and 1,500-meter runner Herb Elliott can also be productive for middle-distance runners. In this session, high-speed 1-minute bursts at close to top speed are alternated with 3 minutes of steady but moderate pacing for a total of about 44 minutes. This workout will develop greater speed and should also produce a heightened ability to run fast while tired—important for mile and 1,500-meter racing—without overly traumatizing the legs. The session promotes the development of a higher lactate-threshold velocity since sizable quantities of lactate are generated during the 1-minute accelerations and then taken up and used by the leg muscles during the corresponding 3-minute floats. This workout is similar to the lactate-stacker session (chapter 32) except that the slightly longer recoveries (3 minutes instead of 2) permit a faster running pace.

scrambled up hills at full speed, running easily on the descents. During the day, Hägg worked as a tree trimmer, but he usually found time to fartlek his way through two daily 5K rambles, each requiring about 20 total minutes.

The steady diet of fartlek running permitted Hägg to enhance his natural speed and economize his running form, so much so that the Swede blazed his way to 10 new world records over seven distances (the mile, 2 miles, 3 miles, 2K, 3K, 4K, and 5K) during 1942 alone, one of the most amazing competitive-running accomplishments of all time. The world records included a 4:04.6 mile and a 3:45.8 clocking for 1,500 meters. Hägg's success meant that fartlek training had arrived as a performance-enhancing workout for middle-distance competitions.

Roger Bannister

In between the eras of Hägg and Elliott, another form of training arrived: the hard-repeat workouts favored by famed Hungarian runner Emil Zatopek. This kind of speed-building interval training was adopted by the British miler Roger Bannister, who used it to finish fourth in the 1,500-meter competition at the 1952 Olympics in Helsinki in spite of a low-volume training schedule. A typical Bannister workout would not look out of place in any modern miler's log book: Sir Roger liked to run 10 quarter-mile (.4 km) intervals per workout at close to race pace, with about 2 minutes of recovery between each interval.

PA Archive/Press Association Images

▶ Roger Bannister is best known for breaking the 4-minute mile barrier.

Early in 1954, Bannister was running each quarter in about 61 seconds, a pace that left him very disappointed. He knew that he would have to figure out some way to get a little faster if he wanted to break through the coveted 4-minute-mile barrier. Frustrated by his inability to improve, Bannister took a complete 3-day respite from running. When he returned to the track after this furlough, he found that he was suddenly able to run the same 10 quarters in 59 seconds each. Thus, the two cornerstones of Bannister's training had been put in place: (1) 400-meter interval training at close to race speed and (2) periodic total rests to produce freshness, improve speed, and permit the body to adapt and recover. These two principles, race-specific training and enhancement of recovery, remain relevant today.

On May 6, 1954, *after a complete 5-day break from running*, Bannister spent his usual morning working at St. Mary's Hospital, took the train to Oxford, and despite a gusting wind at 15 miles per hour, decided he was ready for the assault on the sub-4-minute mile. With two hares, or rabbit runners, helping him, Bannister passed through the first three quarters in 57.5, 1:58.2, and 3:00.5. Before 1,200 spectators, the outstanding English runner finished the race in 3:59.4 to become the first human to run a mile in under 4 minutes. Later that year, Bannister convincingly trounced Australia's John Landy in what was called a "miracle mile" at Vancouver, British Columbia, a sweet victory since Landy had permitted Bannister's world record to stand for only 6 weeks before running a 3:57.9 in Paavo Nurmi's home town of Turku.

Landy was also interval trained, but he preferred to run 600-yard (.55 km) intervals in about 88 to 89 seconds each, a pace of about 59 seconds per quarter mile (.4 km). The Australian typically carried out 8 to 12 of these 600-yard runs per workout, with 4 minutes of slow jogging between each hard run. Landy was a true midnight rambler, doing most of his training around midnight after a hard day of studying. In addition to five interval workouts per week, Landy found time to hit about three weekly 7-mile (11 km) jaunts.

Bill Bowerman

A sound training scheme for the mile was developed by running coach Bill Bowerman at the University of Oregon. Bowerman experimented with the longer distances advocated by another famous coach, Arthur Lydiard, but eventually became a firm advocate of quality rather than quantity training. "My runners tended to get flat when they ran 90- to 100-mile weeks," said Bowerman in an interview with the author of this book.[4] During his tenure as the dean of collegiate coaches, the Oregon great guided 17 sub-4-minute milers, and a list of his runners reads like a true American Running Hall of Fame, with Steve Prefontaine, Kenny Moore, Jim Grelle, Jim Bailey, Wade Bell, Henry Marsh, Bob Williams, and Dyrol Burleson being just a few of the notable names on the listing.

Bowerman sculpted his athletes' interval-training programs like a master craftsman, gradually increasing the intensity of interval workouts as a training season progressed. The Bowerman interval system revolved around the concepts of "date pace, goal pace, and three-quarters effort." Goal pace was simply the tempo an athlete hoped to run for the mile before the season ended; date pace was the runner's current speed for the mile. For example, if an athlete hoped to run a 4:04 mile but had recently been running 4:20 miles, the goal pace was 61 seconds per quarter mile (.4 km), and the date pace was 65 seconds per quarter.

Of course, date pace tended to change over the course of a training season. In order to properly determine date pace, Bowerman would have his runners participate in time trials every 14 days or so, during which the athletes would course through a mile using three-quarters effort. This worked as follows: If a runner had most recently completed a mile in 4:20, the date pace was 65 seconds per quarter, and Bowerman required the runner to scoot through the first three quarters of the new time trial by running at just 67 to 68 seconds per quarter, 2 to 3 seconds per quarter slower than actual date pace.

For the final 300 yards of the time trial, however, the runner would run as hard as possible (this overall time trial happens to be an excellent workout for the mile in its own right). If this final burst of speed permitted the runner to finish the time trial in less than 4:20, the runner had a new date pace that would be used for subsequent interval training. Bob Williams, who was an All-American steeplechaser under Bowerman's tutelage, explained to the author of this book in a personal communication what he believes to be the key advantage of the time trials: "You learned to run really hard during the last 300 yards of the mile, where a key part of the race takes place. Plus, your emotional perception of the time trial was of racing, even though the trial was actually slower (for the first three quarters) than race pace. As a result, you stayed really sharp mentally, and, since you were running slower than race pace and not overdoing it, you never 'left it on the track'—you stayed fresh."[5]

Bowerman believed that the basic interval distance for any runner should be about one-fourth of actual race distance, so his milers became well acquainted with quarter-mile intervals. Total interval distance per workout was usually 2.5 miles (10 quarters; 4 km). The classic Bowerman interval workout during the training season would be four quarter-mile intervals at date pace, four quarter-mile intervals at goal pace, and then four *200-meter (.12 mi) intervals at 800-meter goal pace.* Closer to the most important competition of the season, the workout would change to only two quarter-mile intervals at date pace, six quarters at goal pace, and four 200s at 800-meter speed (note that the amount of time spent running at goal pace increased over the course of the season). Recovery times between work intervals also tended to diminish later in the season as the runners became more fit.

The Bowerman system has several positive things to offer the mile and 1,500-meter racer. Science indicates that running at date pace, goal pace, and 800-meter velocity all tend to enhance $v\dot{V}O_2max$. In addition, such training increases both lactate-threshold velocity and maximal running speed. Date-pace running improves economy at current race speed, making it easier to move up to higher speeds during competitive situations. Finally, goal-pace effort makes a runner more economical at goal velocity, which makes it easier to step into and sustain goal speed during races. From a practical standpoint, the gradual increase in goal-pace running over the course of a season is a potent progression.

What advice did Bowerman have for the modern miler? "At the end of a workout, you should feel exhilarated, not exhausted," said the man whose knowledge of running was inexhaustible. "Too many individuals simply run themselves into the ground and aren't fresh enough to perform properly on race day. [Recall the experience of Roger Bannister, who optimized freshness in order to break the world record.] If you overwork, you won't be excited about racing, and you may well be worse off than if you had underworked."[4]

Frank Horwill

British coach Frank Horwill, who tutored five sub-4-minute milers, developed a series of excellent workouts for mile and 1,500-meter competitors.[3] Among these are the following:

• Run $2 \times (1 \times 400 + 1 \times 800 + 1 \times 400)$ at current mile pace with 30 seconds of rest after the 400, 60 seconds of recovery after the 800, and then 5 minutes of rest after the second 400 before the start of the second set. After the second set is completed, take another 5-minute rest and then run four 200-meter (.12 mi) intervals full out with adequate recovery in between (adequate recovery is defined as just enough time to allow a runner to produce maximal effort in the ensuing 200). The rest and recovery can consist of either walking or easy jogging. This workout will improve $v\dot{V}O_2$max, lactate threshold, and economy at race pace. With the inclusion of the four 200-meter (.12 mi) intervals at the end, it also works to enhance maximal running speed.

• Complete 1×500 meters (.31 mi) at current-best 800-meter pace and then 1×300 meters at the same speed with 2 minutes of rest between and 5 minutes of recovery following the 300. Immediately after the 5 minutes of recovery, do 2×400 meters at best 800-meter pace, with 1 minute of rest after the first 400 and 5 minutes of recovery after the second. Next, complete 3×200 meters (.12 mi) at 800-meter pace with 45-second recoveries. After yet another 5-minute break, complete 6×80 meters (262 ft) at top speed with enough recovery to permit all-out running during the next 80-meter (262 ft) interval. Science suggests that this session upgrades $v\dot{V}O_2$max and lactate threshold and enhances economy at speeds faster than current mile pace, making it easier to move up to faster velocities in races. It also should improve maximal running speed.

Improving Running Economy

Science indicates that improving running economy at high speeds is crucial for upgrading mile and 1,500-meter performances.[6] As outlined in Chapter 8, if runner A is more economical than runner B, A can move along a road or track with a lower rate of oxygen consumption and thus a reduced perceived effort compared with B when A and B are running at the same speed. Being economical also means that when A and B are using oxygen at the same rate during a race, A will be running faster than B.

The notion that economy is critical for mile and 1,500-meter success may be surprising to those who believe that economy is much more important for longer races like the marathon. The conventional argument is that great economy allows marathon runners to conserve intramuscular glycogen during the 26.2-mile event, giving them a huge advantage over less economical competitors. Such economy is not needed during a 4- to 5-minute mile, it is argued; what's important during such a short exertion is actually the ability to maximize power—not the ability to be parsimonious with oxygen.

Some research *has* suggested that marathon-type runners, not milers, seem to have a stranglehold on running economy. The trouble with this research is that running economy has usually been measured at slow running speeds, sometimes even slower than marathon velocity, not at mile or even at 5K paces.[7] Since an individual runner's economy can vary greatly as a function of running speed (e.g., the runner can be very economical at slow speed and very uneconomical at high speed), it is fairly meaningless to determine a runner's economy at less than race speed and imply that it would be similarly good or bad at faster tempos.

Coach and exercise physiologist Jack Daniels has measured the running economies of hundreds of runners and has unearthed the following fascination information:[7]

- At marathon race pace, there is no difference in running economy between marathoners and 1,500-meter runners. So much for the argument that the marathon attracts the most economical runners!

- At paces slower than marathon race pace, marathon runners are indeed more economical than 1,500-meter runners.

- At 5K race pace and faster, 1,500-meter runners are significantly more economical than competitors specializing in longer distances. Thus, the development of enhanced economy at high speeds would appear to be an important factor for middle-distance success, that is, unless 1,500-meter runners are somehow born with great economy at 1,500-meter pace.

Improving running economy at fast speed is to a large extent a matter of improving running-specific strength and upgrading neuromuscular control and coordination at high velocities. Advancements in running-specific strength can be achieved through running-specific strength training (chapter 14). Augmenting neuromuscular control and coordination at high velocities can be attained through using high-quality training paces and explosive drills (chapters 11, 16, and 28).

Additional Training Strategies

Forms of training that are beneficial for 800-meter racing are also excellent for 1,500-meter and mile preparations. For example, super sets, lactate stackers, and greyhound sessions are valuable components of mile and 1,500-meter programs. Long intervals, hill repetitions, and short races also bolster one-mile and 1,500-meter competitiveness.

Superset Training

The superset training philosophy should be of benefit to mile and 1,500-meter runners. As mentioned in the discussion of 800-meter preparations (chapter 32), super sets are two or more work intervals with no intervening recovery—and with running speed decreasing from interval to interval. Super sets enhance a runner's ability to sustain the desired pace when in a state of nearly insurmountable fatigue. A decent superset workout for a miler could proceed as follows:

After a thorough warm-up, run powerfully for 400 meters at 4 seconds per 400 *faster* than current mile or 1,500-meter race pace. Then, without any rest, settle into current mile race pace for 400 meters, concluding the first super set. Complete about three more of these super sets with 3- to 5-minute breaks in between. Over time, gradually increase the length of the second interval within the super set from 400 meters to 600 meters (.37 mi) and then 800 meters. A session like this will make current mile race pace much more tolerable and will upgrade $v\dot{V}O_2max$, lactate threshold, and economy.

Longer Intervals

Long intervals—even as lengthy as 1,600 meters (.99 mi)—also have a place in preparations for the mile. A good long-interval session would involve covering 1,200 meters (.75 mi) at a pace about 4 to 6 seconds per 400 meters slower than current mile pace and then—without a break—taking off for 400 meters at goal race speed (i.e., about 3 to 4 seconds per 400 meters faster than current 1,500-meter or mile race tempo). Just two of these 1,600-meter intervals are satisfactory for a first workout with the eventual goal of doing three; 4- to 5-minute recoveries between the intervals seem to be optimal. This session should have a positive impact on $v\dot{V}O_2max$, lactate threshold, and economy, and it will improve a middle-distance runner's ability to blaze through the last lap of his or her race.

Hill Training

What about hill training for the mile? A somewhat sarcastic, highly accomplished miler once said, "When they put hills on the track, that's when I will start doing some hill workouts." While this is certainly a clever and humorous comment, it represents a very shortsighted view! The problem with this thinking is that hill training does a great job of improving running-specific strength, which can be the first step in improving running economy. It is also important to note that hill workouts tend to be high-intensity sessions, with lots of lactate produced and high rates of oxygen consumption attained. Thus, it is reasonable to think that hill training is good for $v\dot{V}O_2max$ and lactate-threshold velocity—and thus for 1,500-meter and mile racing.

A variety of hill workouts would be beneficial for the mile runner, including lightning-quick repeats on a 200-meter hill with a modest incline of about 3 to 4 percent; recoveries would be accomplished by jogging back down the hill. The runner would start with 4 to 6 reps and progress to 12 over time. When a runner has access to a 100-meter hill with a steeper incline, say 8 to 10 percent or so, he or she can alternate workouts on separate days on this steeper grade with training on the 200-meter hill. Training on the steeper slope makes the runner work at intensities that are significantly greater than race pace on each climb, with downhill jogs for recoveries and quick turnarounds. The runner could begin with 6 to 8 reps and work up to 15 per session. This hill combo would help to optimize power for 1,500-meter and mile racing.

Shorter Races

Just as 10K runners use 5K races as tune-ups for important 10K competitions, it makes sense for 1,500-meter and mile competitors to compete in a couple of 800-meter races during the 6 to 8 weeks leading up to the most important 1,500-meter or mile competition of the season. The 800-meter racing will make the slower pace of the mile seem much easier to sustain. In addition, milers and 1,500-meter runners often get a big psychological boost out of a decently run 800 meters and begin to think that they are truly capable of running faster in the longer events.

Racing two 800s often puts a miler in a can't-lose situation, too. The first 800 might be a somewhat novel experience, and a runner typically won't do quite as well as expected. In the second 800 competition, the runner will be more familiar with how to run the event and will usually do significantly better. If the second race doesn't go all that well, however, there is still no great loss. A runner can simply say, "These were good experiences for me, but this isn't my best event. Let's get back to what I'm really good at—the mile." Even if the 800s are disappointing, it is good to remember that 800-meter racing helps improve raw running speed, which will pay dividends in the mile.

Lactate Stackers and Greyhound Sessions

Finally, two of the workouts described in chapter 32 on 800-meter training—lactate stackers and greyhound sessions—are also extremely good for 1,500-meter and mile race preparations because of their impacts on maximal running velocity and lactate-threshold speed.

Conclusion

Surprisingly, 1,500-meter and mile training are crafted in a manner similar to the preparation for longer races such as the 10K, half-marathon, and marathon. Intense running is emphasized, but that is also the case for the longer events. As is true for lengthier competitions, optimizing $v\dot{V}O_2max$, running economy, lactate-threshold speed, resistance to fatigue, maximal running speed, and running-specific strength is paramount for the mile and the 1,500 meters. These two races also use the same overall periodization plan, with general-strength training paving the way for running-specific strengthening followed by hill work and then explosive training.

The unique feature of 1,500-meter and mile training is that the intense quality component of the running training has a faster average velocity, with a greater emphasis placed on 100-, 200-, and 400-meter speeds, and a weaker focus on 5K and 10K paced running. For example, a 10K runner would complete 1,600-meter (.99 mi) to 2K (1.24 mi) intervals at goal 10K speed fairly frequently in his or her preparations for an important competition, whereas a 1,500-meter runner would employ such a session much less often. Correspondingly, a 1,500-meter competitor would spend relatively more time running at 200-meter and 400-meter race pace. It is not that such training is bad for the longer-distance runner. Rather, the 10K runner must fit more preparations that are specific to 10K running into the overall pie of available training time, leaving fewer minutes available for the high-speed work.

34

Training for 5Ks

Scientific research indicates that the variables that must be optimized for 5K racing are the same as those needed for competing at shorter distances: It is critically important to boost maximal running speed, $v\dot{V}O_2max$, lactate-threshold velocity, and running economy in order for runners to reach their highest levels of 5K performance. In addition, preparing specifically for the 5K is very important, including workouts at both current and goal 5K velocities.

The use of the specificity of training principle introduces a potential problem since runners may not know their current 5K capability. It may be early in the season before any races have been completed, or a runner may have made a major move in fitness without doing any 5K racing, leading to a suspicion that 5K capacity might be much higher than before. Another possibility is that recent 5Ks have been completed on days when a runner didn't feel good or on occasions when the weather was not conducive to top performance or the courses were unusually hilly and challenging.

Assessing 5K Capacity

There are various ways to estimate current 5K capacity, but one of the simplest methods, which also involves the completion of a great 5K workout, is to perform a 5K test on the track. To perform this test, which was developed by Charles Babineau and Luc Leger of the University of Moncton and the University of Montreal,[1] runners can simply go to the track on a day when they feel great, warm up thoroughly, and then complete three 1,600-meter (.99 mi) work intervals with only 1-minute recoveries between intervals. It is important to run the intervals at the highest possible speed that can be sustained for the duration of the workout. One should not blister the first 1,600 to such an extent that the subsequent two intervals sag badly; the goal is to keep the three work intervals at a relatively uniform pace.

After the third 1,600 is completed, the average pace per 1,600 meters is calculated, and the result will be very close to the 1,600-meter splits in a 5K race. Let's say that a runner completes the intervals in 6:19, 6:20, and 6:24.

Thus, the average time for the three 1600-meter intervals is 6:21—the projected pace for a 5-K race.

Another option is to complete a simulated 5K, which is not a far-fetched idea since the runner is already covering 3 × 1,600 meters in the Babineau-Leger test. But it is simply easier to perform at one's best *during training* when the approximately 5K distance is divided into three segments with two short rests. Thus, the Babineau-Leger test gives a better read on current 5K ability.

The research of Babineau and Leger revealed that two other straightforward workouts also have good predictive power for the 5K. These include 6 × 800 meters with 30-second rest intervals and 12 × 400 meters with 15-second rests. In both of these workouts, the 23 well-trained runners studied by the two Canadian researchers tried to attain the maximal training pace they could sustain for the entire workout. The runners were not always successful in doing so. Pace tended to fall by about 8 percent after approximately eight 400s, for example, only to shoot back up for the final interval; in contrast, 800- and 1,600-meter paces were remarkably steady. The runners' average speeds during the sessions were highly predictive of 5K finishing time.

Generally, the average pace established in the six 800s was about 2.5 percent faster than the speed attainable during a 5K race, and the average tempo of the 400s was 3.7 percent quicker. For example, if a runner completed the 800s in about 3:00 each, the 5K tempo would be approximately 3:04 to 3:05 per 800 meters (or about 6:09 per mile). If a runner completed the 400s in 80 seconds each, the 5K tempo would be around 83 seconds per 400 meters.

5K Workouts

All three of these tests discussed (3 × 1,600 with 1-minute recoveries, 6 × 800 with 30-second recoveries, and 12 × 400 with 15-second recoveries) would actually be great 5K workouts. Runners and coaches may wonder which one will have the most beneficial effect on 5K performance.

One might argue that the 1,600-meter (.99 mi) session would be most specific to the 5K with only two rest periods and an average pace that is extremely close to actual 5K pacing. Total rest on the way to covering 4,800 meters (2.98 mi) is also reduced the most in the 1,600-meter workout: just 2 minutes compared with 2.5 minutes during the six 800s and 2.75 minutes with the dozen 400s. There is not much doubt, too, that the 3 × 1,600 session would be best for building mental toughness. However, one might also make a case in this regard for the 400s since the paltry 15 seconds were closer to the 0-second rests associated with racing. The pace of the 400s at almost 4 percent faster than current 5K tempo would also allow a runner to step more easily into a faster pace for future 5Ks.

In addition, Babineau and Leger found that lactate levels were significantly higher during the 400 workout compared with both the 800 and 1,600 sessions. This is actually a good thing since high lactate levels are a potent stimulus for the improvement of lactate-threshold running velocity, a good predictor of 5K success. Blood lactate concentrations during the 400-meter interval workout were the closest to those in a real 5K race.

The bottom line is that all three workouts would be good for a 5K runner. The 1,600-meter session is fine for predicting what a runner would do in a real race and for building economy at race speed; it would have a positive effect on lactate threshold and $v\dot{V}O_2$max, too. However, the 400-meter interval workout would have a greater impact on lactate threshold and would be superior for upgrading maximal running speed and the ability to run a 5K at goal speed.

A key is to make sure each 400-meter interval is completed as fast as reasonably possible. This pace will probably be about 4 percent faster than the tempo a runner would obtain in a 1,600-meter interval workout. For example, if the 1,600-meter session were completed at a tempo of 90 seconds per 400 meters, the 400-meter workout would probably be struck at 86 seconds per 400, about 4 seconds per 400 faster than current 5K ability. This is in effect a goal-pace session since it is usually reasonable to choose a goal pace for the 5K that is 16 seconds per 1,600 meters faster than current 5K speed.

In addition to these sizzling 1,600-, 800-, and 400-meter interval sessions, other workouts are very productive for 5K runners and help to round out and balance training. Superset training builds fatigue resistance, and circuit training builds ample amounts of whole-body strength and coordination, both of which consequently enhance running economy. Extended runs build stamina at quality speeds, and explosive drills supplement the 400-meter intervals by improving maximal speed and running economy. These sessions are described in detail later in the chapter. In addition, the basic workouts recommended for 800-meter and 1,500-meter training—the $v\dot{V}O_2$max session, greyhound runs, hill training, and lactate stackers—are also excellent for preparing for a best possible 5K.

Superset Training

Superset training is beneficial for 5K runners just as it is for 1,500-meter and 800-meter competitors. A good superset workout for 5K racers involves running 600 meters (.37 mi) at almost maximal intensity followed by 1,000 meters (.62 mi) at current 5K race pace with no recovery between the two. That combination constitutes the first super set. After about a 4-minute jog recovery, which can be abbreviated over time, the runner then repeats that super set of a 600-meter run (.37 mi) followed without recovery by the 1,000-meter run, jogs for four more minutes, and then closes the workout with one final superset combo followed by cool-down jogging. Elite runners and athletes with outstanding running-specific strength as well as individuals who no longer find three super sets to be challenging can perform four sets per workout. It is important to stay relaxed at all times as the sets are completed. Basic running form, including cadence, foot-strike pattern, shank angle, and postural elements, needs to be maintained no matter how tired the runner feels.

Such 5K super sets are great for v$\dot{V}O_2$max, lactate-threshold speed, running economy, and maximal running speed, and they are terrific preparation for 5K competitions. These 5K super sets decrease the perceived effort associated with running at 5K pace, and they help runners handle surges in intensity within 5K races; they are also great tools for surviving overly fast starts in 5K competitions—and for opening up a big gap early in the race on an opponent who has been highly competitive in previous competitions.

Circuit Training

Circuit training also constitutes excellent 5K preparation since it vaults lactate threshold upward, improves coordination and thus economy, and heightens the ability to run at 5K intensity despite significant fatigue. To carry out a 5K preparatory circuit session, a runner warms up with about 12 minutes of light jogging followed by various dynamic mobility routines. The runner then completes 4 × 100 meters at a brisk pace, faster than he or she would usually run during a 5K.

The activities that follow create a 5K performance-enhancing circuit session. Perform the activities in order, moving quickly from exercise to exercise. The exercises themselves should not be performed overly quickly, at least at first. Runners should never sacrifice good form just to get the exertions done in a hurry. The idea is to carry out each activity methodically and efficiently and then almost immediately start on the next drill or exercise. Some of the exercises indicated are presented in detail in chapters 13 and 14. The proper form required for any new exercise is presented after the circuit.

1. Run 400 meters at what feels like 5K race pace: On a scale from 1 to 10, with 1 being the easiest possible exertion and 10 being maximal running, this should feel like 8.5 or 9.
2. Complete 20 six-count squat thrusts with jumps (chapter 13).
3. Do 15 side sit-ups on one side and then 15 on the other side.
4. Perform 20 high lunges with each leg.
5. Run 400 meters at what feels like 5K pace.
6. Do 15 feet-elevated push-ups (chapter 13).
7. Perform 30 low-back extensions with a twisting motion.
8. Complete 15 one-leg squats with one leg and then 15 more with the other leg (chapter 14).
9. Run 400 meters at 5K speed.

10. Carry out 20 bench dips (chapter 13).

11. Complete 15 high-bench step-ups with each leg (chapter 14).

12. Hop on one foot, taking quick steps instead of long, elaborate bounces; rely on the springy action of the supporting ankle to provide most of the required propulsive force and cover 20 meters (66 ft) as fast as possible. Then, do the same on the other foot. Rest for a moment and repeat.

13. Run 1,200 meters (.75 mi) at 5K velocity.

14. Repeat steps 2-13 for two circuits in all; then cool down with about 3K (1.86 mi) of light jogging.

This circuit workout contains 4,400 meters (2.73 mi) of 5K pace running, 400 meters of power running at faster than 5K speed, and a variety of beneficial strengthening activities. The circuits enhance resistance to fatigue, whole-body strength and coordination, running economy, lactate threshold, and probably vVO_2max—not a bad combination of benefits! Many 5K runners report that once they can actually complete the running intervals within the circuits at current 5K pace, moving up to a faster pace during 5K races is a relatively straightforward matter.

Side Sit-up

Lie on one side with the both legs extended and raised slightly off the floor. The side of the upper torso in contact with the floor should lie relaxed on the floor. Place the hand of the bottom arm on the floor to the front so that the arm is perpendicular to the body. Place the hand of the top arm lightly on the back of the head. (Do not pull on the head or neck during the exercise.) Slowly raise the torso, contracting the abdominal muscles on the top side of the trunk and raising the legs at the same time (figure 34.1). Slowly lower the upper torso and the legs back to the starting position on the floor to complete one rep. Don't let the upper body fall to the floor in an uncontrolled manner. Complete 15 reps on one side and then 15 on the other.

▶ **Figure 34.1** Side sit-up.

High Lunge These are similar to the lunge squats in chapter 13. For this version, stand on a 6-inch (15 cm) platform or step so that the forward, lunging foot will undergo an exaggerated downward acceleration. Start with erect posture and feet directly under the shoulders; step down and forward with one foot. After the forward foot makes contact with the ground, move into a squat position so that the thigh of the forward leg becomes almost parallel with the ground (figure 34.2). The upper body may incline forward slightly as this happens. Emphasize action of the gluteal muscles and hamstrings to reverse the squat and return the forward leg onto the platform, under the trunk. Complete one rep by returning to the start position.

▶ **Figure 34.2** High lunge squat position.

Low-Back Extension With a Twist These are a variation on the low-back extensions in chapter 13. Lie on the stomach with arms by the sides, hands extended toward feet, and palms touching the floor. Contract the back muscles to lift and twist the upper body to one side during the first rep (see figure 34.3). Return to the starting position and then lift and twist the torso to the other side during the second rep. Continue alternating sides for the desired number of repetitions. Be sure to fully untwist the upper body each time the trunk moves back toward the ground so that the stomach and chest—not the sides—touch the ground. Perform these movements rhythmically and smoothly while maintaining good control.

▶ **Figure 34.3** Low-back extension with a twist.

Extended Runs

Since 5Ks involve from 12.5 to ~30 minutes of continuous running, depending on ability, carrying out extended quality runs is also a good idea during 5K preparations. Endurance athletes tend to like extended runs a lot, and for good reason: The workouts are simple to carry out, don't take too much time, and are specific to 5K racing. All a runner needs to do is warm up thoroughly and then complete a hard 20-minute run over a favorite training route without any breaks, rests, or recoveries of any kind. The running itself should feel as though it is being conducted at about 10K pace.

This session enhances mental tolerance of the physical duress associated with sustained, intense running, and it elevates confidence and stamina at a quality velocity. It is great from a purely physiological standpoint, too, as the challenging 20-minute effort should have a positive impact on lactate-threshold speed and running economy. Note that it is not necessary to determine the distance run during the 20 minutes; all that is required is to move along at what feels like 10K tempo. This gives runners some freedom; since they are not chained to the watch, for once, the workout becomes much more enjoyable, especially if it is carried out in a very pleasant setting such as on a forest path or at the beach.

The 20-minute extended run is not a traditional tempo run, which by definition would be carried out at lactate-threshold speed, or around 15K (9.32 mi) race pace. The extended run should be completed at a pace that is faster than lactate-threshold speed, which is why the goal is to sustain the perceived effort of a 10K race; 10K running is usually 2 to 3 percent above lactate-threshold velocity. Running at a pace above lactate-threshold speed produces a greater improvement in lactate threshold compared with traditional tempo running, and it is also better for promoting neuromuscular efficiency at race-type speeds.

The 20-minute duration also helps ensure that the runner is not actually putting forth the same effort as for a whole 10K race—it's best to save true competitive fire for real race situations—and most runners recover well and quickly from this overall effort. Another strong feature of the extended run is that it is time efficient. The entire session, including warm-up and cool-down, can usually be completed in about 45 minutes. The quality of a 20-minute extended run can usually be improved when training with an individual who is slightly fitter. This peer will tend to push to a higher intensity during the effort than would be possible if the run were completed solo.

Explosive Drills

As Heikki Rusko and his Finnish colleagues have shown, explosive training is very good for 5K runners,[2] and for that reason it would be wise to include hopping drills such as hurdle hops and sprint hopping in a 5K training program. These two drills can be included in a quality workout after the warm-up and just before the quality running portion. Two-leg hurdle hops can be performed just as described in chapter 23. Be sure to avoid taking a little hop between hurdles. The idea is to land and then explode over the next hurdle, spending as little time as possible on the ground. Sprint hops are described later in this section.

Once the two-leg hurdles hops are mastered, progress to one-leg hurdle hops, performing the hurdle run-throughs on one leg and then the other. Bar height may need to be lowered initially to establish proficiency with one-leg hurdle hopping. Ground-contact time between hurdles should be as minimal as possible, and only a single contact is permitted between hurdles (i.e., no double-clutching). Keep hip and knee flexion moderate on each ground contact, with the most propulsive force coming from ankle action. A runner can progress from four to eight run-throughs on each leg over time.

This series of drills improves coordination as well as the rate and quantity of force production (i.e., power) in each leg. Ultimately, as power improves, it will be possible to run 5K races much more explosively.

Sprint Hop Hop as quickly as possible for 20 meters (66 ft) on one foot, emphasizing extremely quick contacts with the ground and forceful forward explosions each time the foot hits the ground (figure 34.4). Without stopping or resting, hop 20 more meters on the other foot. Without interruption, repeat the exercise on the first foot and then the other foot. Recover by doing 1 minute of light jogging. Repeat this hopping and recovery sequence five more times. A key progression with sprint hopping is to begin performing some of the reps on a hill. Start with a gently sloping incline of about 3 percent and gradually work up to a 10 percent incline if possible and hop both uphill and downhill. Maintain good form and balance at all times and avoid the temptation to look down at the hopping foot.

▶ **Figure 34.4** Sprint hopping.

Additional Training Strategies

Naturally, the basic workouts already recommended for 800-meter and 1,500-meter training—the vVO₂max session, greyhound runs, 400s at mile pace, hill training, and lactate stackers—are also superb for preparing for a best possible 5K. Running a couple of 3K (1.86 mi) or 1,500-meter races during the buildup to the most important 5K would also be a great idea; both events will improve speed, spike lactate threshold, and make 5K pace feel easier to handle. A 3K pace is roughly 2.5 to 3 seconds per 400 meters faster than 5K speed, and 1,500-meter race tempo is approximately 6.5 to 7 seconds per 400 quicker than 5K pace.

If runners feel that they have run these races well, the results can serve as predictors of what can be accomplished in an upcoming 5K. For example, if the 3K race was completed at 85 seconds per 400 meters, the 5K race pace will probably be very close to 88 seconds per 400 meters, or about 3 seconds per 400 slower. If the runner participated in a 1,500-meter or mile race in the best possible way, the 5K race speed should be about 7 seconds per 400 slower.

In addition to running a few races at shorter distances, another great workout for the 5K is Bruce Tulloh's gambler session. Tulloh was a sub-4-minute miler who was Richard Nerurkar's coach (13:23 for 5K, 28:05 in the 10K, and UK cross country champion). The gambler is at first glance nothing more than 3 × 1,200 meters (.75 mi) at planned 5K pace with 3- to 4-minute jog recoveries. However, each 1,200 meters is constructed in a unique way: The first 400 of the 1,200 is completed at planned 5K speed, the second 400 is run at significantly faster than 5K pace, and the third 400 settles back to goal 5K velocity; there is no break between these 400s, of course.

Why the speed upswing on the second lap? "The increased intensity of the middle lap will help you learn to gamble during your 5K competitions," notes Tulloh.[3] "You will learn that you can handle the increases in intensity which occur when you rush past another runner or blast up a hill during a 5K. Once you learn that you can make such surges and still recover pretty nicely, your confidence in yourself as a competitive 5K runner will improve tremendously." It is also possible to perform a standard 5K workout of 3 × 1,600 meters (.99 mi) with the second 400 of each 1,600 at significantly faster than current or planned 5K pace; this session is appreciably more challenging than the 4 × 1,200.

It is important to take it easy with overall training and taper during the week leading up to an important 5K with mileage set at about 15 to 30 percent of usual levels. However, a few days before the 5K, science suggests that it makes sense to complete four or five 200s or else two to three 400s at planned 5K pace to lock the appropriate speed into the neuromuscular system and to stimulate the body to make the last little physiological adjustments that will help with the attainment of a personal record.[4]

Training for 3Ks

The workouts and drills prescribed for 5K training will also work well for individuals preparing for 3K (1.86 mi) competitions. In most cases, a runner can simply substitute 3K pace for the recommended 5K tempo within the training sessions; however, work-interval lengths may need to be adjusted downward in certain situations. For example, a 3K runner might use 400-meter and 800-meter super sets, with the first 400 at close to maximal speed and the follow-up 800 at 3K pace, instead of the combination of 600 meters (.37 mi) and 1,000 meters (.62 mi) recommended for 5K runners. Also, a 3K competitor might employ $3 \times 1,200$ at 3K pace for the interval workout at race pace rather than the $3 \times 1,600$ at 5K tempo used by 5K athletes.

Conclusion

As is the case with training for all distances from 800 meters to 100K, optimal 5K training programs have four phases (general strength, running-specific strength, hill work, and explosive training) and seven variables to optimize (maximal running velocity, $v\dot{V}O_2max$, $t_{lim}v\dot{V}O_2max$, lactate-threshold velocity, running economy, resistance to fatigue, and running-specific strength). Proper periodization of the phases, use of strengthening workouts appropriate to each phase (see chapters 13-16), and inclusion of the high-quality running workouts described in this chapter along with $v\dot{V}O_2max$ training from chapter 26 will provide runners with the greatest opportunities to reach their 5K potentials.

35

Training for 10Ks

Optimal 10K training features an array of challenging workouts and competitions that range in intensity from maximal speed to current 10K velocity. The best 10K preparations always emphasize significant amounts of running time at current 10K speed to improve running economy as well as regular workouts at *goal* 10K speed to heighten lactate-threshold velocity and resistance to fatigue at personal record speed.

Evaluating the Effectiveness of Tempo Training

Traditionally, the staple of 10K training has been the tempo run, defined as a continuous effort with a duration of about 20 to 25 minutes at a pace around 8 to 15 seconds slower per mile (1.6 km) than 10K speed. One supposed advantage of this session is that it teaches runners to sustain and tolerate a quality pace for an extended period of time as is required during racing. In this regard, tempo runs are designed to provide a nice balance to interval training, which often features no more than 5 minutes of continuous hard running. Another presumed advantage is that tempo training significantly boosts lactate threshold.[1]

Science suggests that there are problems with this thinking. It is true that tempo running enhances a runner's ability to sustain a quality running pace, but one difficulty is that the pace that is sustained is more like a 15K (9.32 mi) or half-marathon pace rather than a 10K tempo.[2] Thus, the effort is not really specific to the 10K, nor should it have a major positive impact on running economy at 10K speed. Tempo training is a better workout for 15K and half-marathon runners.

The other problem with tempo training is that a workout conducted at a pace 10 to 15 seconds per mile (1.6 km) *slower* than 10K pace is usually carried out at very close to a typical runner's lactate-threshold speed. This might seem like a good thing, and historically such an intensity level has been viewed as optimal for lactate-threshold improvement, but the truth is that running at lactate-threshold velocity is actually a comparatively *moderate* stimulus for lactate-threshold improvement.

Boosting Lactate-Threshold Speed

To increase lactate-threshold speed the most, it is important to expose the leg muscles to large amounts of lactate so they can become good at picking up lactate from the blood and tissue spaces and using it for energy. By definition, working *at* lactate-threshold intensity produces little lactate. Remember that lactate-threshold velocity is the speed *above* which lactate begins to pile up in the blood. To boost lactate threshold to the greatest possible extent, it is important to work *above* threshold, exposing the muscles to relatively high lactate concentrations so that they get better at the clearing process (see chapter 27).

Training at above lactate threshold also does the best job of stimulating muscles to produce the structures (mitochondria) that prevent lactate from spewing out into the blood in the first place. When the muscles don't release excessive amounts of energy-rich lactate to the blood, and when the muscles are able to effectively clear the lactate that does show up in the blood, a greater lactate-threshold speed is possible. Running at current 10K pace is a good way to achieve this objective and is a beneficial workout for 10K runners. Moving along at 5K, $v\dot{V}O_2$max, mile, 1,500-meter, 800-meter, lactate-stacker, and even maximal pace are also good for lactate-threshold advancement. Hill running will boost lactate threshold because of the high lactate concentrations and elevated overall exercise intensities that usually prevail. Even circuit training is probably better than tempo running for boosting lactate-threshold because of the high exertion rates and blood lactate levels associated with such routines.

Undertaking Intense Workouts

Strong scientific support for the idea of carrying out intense workouts to boost 10K ability—rather than tempo runs or long, moderately paced efforts—comes from research carried out by Peter Snell (gold medalist at 800 meters in the 1960 Olympics in Rome, double gold medalist at 800 and 1,500 meters in the 1964 Olympics in Tokyo). Snell and his colleagues at the University of Texas Southwestern Human Performance Center asked 10 well-trained runners to participate in a scientific study investigating the merits of two differing 10K training plans.[3] The 10 runners, whose $\dot{V}O_2$max averaged a fairly impressive 61.7 milliliters of oxygen per kilogram (2.2 lb) of body weight per minute, began the 16-week study by running 50 miles (81 km) per week at moderate tempos for 6 weeks. All participants were fit at the beginning of the study and had no trouble maintaining this amount of running.

For the subsequent 10 weeks of the research, the runners, whose 10K performance times ranged from 34 to about 42 minutes, were divided into two groups of equal ability. Twice a week, members of one group substituted tempo workouts for their regular daily runs. The tempo sessions involved continuously running for about 29 minutes at a running speed slightly below the pace required to make blood lactate levels begin to skyrocket (i.e., they were exercising at close to lactate-threshold speed and thus conducting traditional tempo workouts). Average intensity during these lactate-threshold sessions was close to 80 percent of $\dot{V}O_2$max.

The runners in the second group carried out no tempo training at all but instead conducted interval workouts twice a week. During the interval sessions, the athletes ran 200-meter intervals in 33 to 38 seconds each and ran their 400-meter intervals in 75 to 85 seconds, carrying out a total of around 4,600 meters (2.86 mi) of interval training per workout. Exercise intensity during the interval running averaged 90 to 100 percent of $\dot{V}O_2$max. Aside from the key difference between interval training in one group and tempo training in the other group, the groups' training schedules were identical and consisted of medium to long, moderately paced runs.

At the end of the 16-week investigation, the runners participated in simulated 800-meter and 10K races. In these appropriate tests, the interval-trained runners fared better than the tempo-trained subjects. For example, the interval-worked athletes decreased 800-meter time by 11.2 seconds and improved 10K performance by a full 2.1 minutes. The tempo-trained runners lowered 800-meter time by 6.6 seconds and bettered previous 10K clockings by an average of just 1.1 minute, about 10 seconds per mile (1.6 km) slower than the interval-trained runners. $\dot{V}O_2$max soared by 12 percent in the interval-trained group compared with the data at the beginning of the 16-week study, but it inched up by only 4 percent among the tempo-trained group.

It's reasonable to think that interval training worked better than tempo training in this study because its intensity better matched the level of work required to run a 10K or 800-meter race. For example, 10K racing is usually carried out at about 90 to 92 percent of $\dot{V}O_2$max, and Snell's intervals were set at 90 to 100 percent of $\dot{V}O_2$max. The faster-paced intervals probably also did a better job of spiking lactate-threshold speed and 10K economy compared with the more slowly paced tempo intervals. In an interview with the author of this book, Snell concluded that "perhaps the best way to train is to spend the maximum-possible amount of training time running at a pace which is closely related to the demands (or actual pace) of the race you are shooting for, without getting overtrained."[4]

Note also the incredible *time economy* of interval training compared with tempo work. The runners studied by Snell and his colleagues spent about 31 minutes per week doing fast interval running or 58 minutes performing tempo runs, and yet the improvements in running performance were larger in the interval group. Each minute of interval running was clearly worth *more than* 2 minutes of tempo exertion in terms of associated fitness gain.

10K Workouts

In addition to Snell's highly productive interval sessions, a number of other workouts provide great benefit for 10K runners. Training at current and goal

10K pace, conducting superset and Kenyan-interval sessions, carrying out intervals at 5K-race speed, competing in 5K races, and using hill workouts—including a treadmill-hill session—are all great 10K preparations.

Training at 10K Pace

As Snell and colleagues learned in their research, carrying out running training at current 10K pace is good for 10K potential; it probably pushes up lactate threshold and makes economy at current 10K velocity better so that it is easier to step up to higher speeds in the race. One great 10K pace workout is to simply warm up and then hit 3 × 8 minutes at *current 10K speed* with 4-minute recoveries. As the ability to handle this workout improves, it is possible to add another work interval and then begin paring down the recovery intervals, first to 3 minutes, then 2:30, then 2:00, and so on.

Some athletes have successfully used workouts in which the entire 10K distance was broken down into work intervals and then covered in a single session. The great Kenyan runner Yobes Ondieki used such a workout as a staple of training during his preparations to establish a new world record in the event; he succeeded, although his 27:08 mark has since been eclipsed. Ondieki divided his 10K training distance into discrete segments, chose world-record pace as his work-interval speed, and started with approximately 2- to 3-minute recoveries, paring these rest periods down over time as his fitness improved. Eventually, he found himself able to trim his recoveries to as little as 10 seconds, making the establishment of the new world record inevitable.[5]

English coach Bruce Tulloh, a former European 5K champion, formalized this kind of workout with the establishment of five work intervals to be completed in the following order:

1. 1,000 meters (.62 mi) at goal 10K pace followed by 2 minutes of rest
2. 3,000 meters (1.86 mi) at goal 10K speed followed by 5 minutes of rest
3. 2,000 meters (1.24 mi) at goal 10K velocity with 4 to 5 minutes of rest
4. 3,000 meters (1.86 mi) at goal 10K pace followed by 5 minutes of rest
5. 1,000 meters (.62 mi) at 10K tempo followed by easy cool-down jogging

The Ondieki-Tulloh workout indoctrinates the neuromuscular system and legs in the art of maintaining goal 10K speed for the full distance of the race, increases the runner's confidence in his or her ability to sustain 10K speed, and upgrades neuromuscular coordination and running economy at 10K velocity. Tulloh recommends using this workout a couple of times during the 6 weeks leading up to a major 10K competition.[6]

The full 6.2 miles (10 km) of work intervals at 10K speed should not be attempted unless the runner is well recovered going into the workout, can allot ample time for recovery following the session (i.e., perhaps 2 to 3 days of easy work or rest), and has established good running-specific strength in advance of the session. Running-specific strength is created by conducting running-specific strength workouts on a regular basis followed by a period of hill training.

Training at 5K pace

Workouts at 5K pace are also terrific for 10K runners for a number of reasons. First, 5K tempo, which is usually about 16 seconds per mile (1.6 km) faster than 10K pace, is often a good *goal* speed for 10K athletes although not necessarily for elite athletes who have already managed to run at close to their top level in the 10K. It represents an improvement of about 100 seconds (1:40) for the race, which is a reasonable improvement. Many 10K runners can improve from 35:00 to 33:20, from 37:00 to 35:20, from 38:40 to 37:00, and from 41:39 to 39:59, for example, with a season or two of appropriate training.

Interestingly enough, this kind of improvement is usually easier to accomplish for relatively slower runners. For example, runners who are currently running 49:00 for the 10K have an easier time getting to 47:20 compared with athletes attempting to move from 35:00 to 33:20. Part of the reason for this is that it is more likely that the 35-minute 10K runner has previously carried out high-quality training and thus may respond less to the insertion of high-intensity exertion into his or her overall training scheme. In addition, a 100-second improvement is just 3 percent of 49:00—but 5 percent of 35:00. At any rate, conducting workouts at 5K speed specifically prepares the way for future 10Ks at that exact pace.

Workouts at 5K pace are simple for 10K runners to carry out. The classic 5K session is simply $3 \times 1,600$ meters (.99 mi) at current 5K pace with 3- to 5-minute recoveries. This workout builds economy at 5K and probably 10K speed, hikes lactate threshold, may have an impact on v$\dot{V}O_2$max, and makes 10K running feel considerably easier.

Many runners wonder why training at 5K pace would enhance running economy at 10K speed while training at 15K (9.32 mi) to half-marathon tempo would not. There is actually no paradox. Economy is to a large extent a function of running-specific strength and coordination; the stronger and more coordinated a runner is during the running gait cycle, the better will be his or her economy.

The coordination part of this should make sense: As a runner becomes more coordinated, less energy is wasted on nonproductive, nonpropulsive actions, and the runner begins to function with less energy cost. A runner's goal is *not* to expend energy stabilizing an uncoordinated body; optimally, all energy usage should be funneled toward creating forward propulsion. The strength part of the equation operates as follows: The stronger a runner becomes, the smaller the number of muscle cells that will need to be recruited to run at a specific speed. For the stronger runner, each muscle cell is stronger than it used to be as well, and a reduced total number of cells will be required to keep a runner jetting along at chosen pace. Since fewer cells are employed, less energy is expended, and economy is improved.

Workout From Herb Elliott's Training Plan

Another great 10K workout can be taken from the strategies of Herb Elliott. True, Elliott was much more of a 1,500-meter and mile racer, rather than a 10K competitor, but many of his workouts can be adapted quite readily for longer-distance preparations, and the workout described here is perfect for 10K competitors. To carry out this workout, a runner needs to warm up thoroughly, run 3 × 800 at 5K pace with 2-minute recoveries, run 2 × 800 at 10K pace with 2-minute recoveries, and then finish up with 3,200 meters (1.99 mi) at current 10K velocity without a halt. This session, which involves running about half of a 5K and half of a 10K at the relevant paces, improves running economy and confidence at 10K speed while also increasing lactate threshold and stamina at high speed.

The other key factor is that gains in strength and coordination *can be very speed specific*. Scientific research reveals that when strength is gained at moderate rates of movement, that gain in strength will usually not translate well to higher speeds. The reason for this is that the nervous system has not learned how to optimally coordinate more difficult, higher-speed movements by controlling the muscular system at slower speeds, and thus it functions suboptimally at higher velocities.

Conversely, science tells us that improving one's strength at high speeds does translate well to slower speeds. If the nervous system can handle a very difficult task at high speed, it should be able to do the same thing when things gear down. This is one reason why training at 5K pace should improve 10K economy. Similarly, the use of running speeds close to maximal will also have a beneficial effect on 10K economy—and even on the running economy of marathon racing.

Superset Training

It would be remiss not to include some superset training for the 10K. To carry out a great 10K superset session, the runner warms up and then strikes 3 × (200-600-1,600 meters), with 3- to 4-minute recoveries between these super sets. The 200 should be an almost all-out run, the 600 (.37 mi) slightly slower, and the 1,600 (.99 mi) at about 10K pace. There are no recoveries between the 200 and 600 or between the 600 and 1,600. This workout strengthens the ability to run at 10K speed despite ample levels of intramuscular hydrogen ions. It also improves running speed, intramuscular buffering capacity (i.e., the ability to temper rises in acidity within the muscles associated with hydrogen ion production), lactate-clearance rate, lactate-threshold speed, running economy, and—most likely—$v\dot{V}O_2$max. It is quite a package! The superset workout can be blended quite nicely with $v\dot{V}O_2$max sessions during the last weeks leading up to a major 10K, and the fact that this workout also improves a runner's ability to survive and even run a personal record race after overly fast 10K starts can also be considered as a positive.

10K Treadmill-Hill Workout

There is one special hill workout that is a knockout 10K training session, and it is carried out on the treadmill. It is a great workout for cold winter days when icy streets make quality outdoor training impossible—or for torrid summer days when heat and humidity make a high-intensity, true hill workout out of the question. This workout is so high quality that it can be inserted profitably into a program at almost any point.

The key to this 10K treadmill-hill workout is to set the treadmill speed at current 10K velocity and set the treadmill incline at exactly 3 percent. After a good warm-up, it is productive to hit 3-minute work intervals at 10K speed with 3-minute recoveries. A runner should continue in this manner until he or she has completed four 3-minute intervals and then stop; over time, he or she can gradually work up to eight of these challenging repetitions per session.

This workout has many strong points. First, because of the treadmill incline, the workout does a terrific job of boosting running-specific strength by teaching a runner to put more force on the ground with each step taken during a race. It also improves economy at 10K pace. Remember that strength and speed are the keys to enhanced economy. In this workout the strength factor is taken care of by working on the inclined treadmill, and the speed is covered by the use of 10K training velocity. In addition, blood lactate and oxygen consumption soar higher with each successive interval, which means that the treadmill-hill training will push $v\dot{V}O_2max$ and lactate-threshold speed upward. Finally, running on these fake hills makes current 10K pace feel considerably easier when it is undertaken on flat ground.

Interval Workout for Staying Power

A runner who has trouble with staying power during 10K racing (i.e., tending to fade in the latter half of the race even when the beginning is not overly fast) will benefit greatly from the sequence of 800-400-200-1,000 in this workout. To carry this out, a runner jogs easily for 15 minutes and then runs 800 meters at current 10K pace. After 2 more minutes of light jogging, the runner completes 400 meters at current 5K speed. Following 60 seconds of light jog recovery, the runner powerfully covers 200 meters at current mile-racing tempo, which will be about 3 seconds per 200 faster than 5K tempo. After a brief 30-second recovery, there are 1,000 meters (.62 mi) of steady running at goal 10K speed to face. Following 4 more minutes of easy jogging, this 800-400-200-1,000 sequence is repeated.

One recommended training approach is to do one of these interval workout sequences for each 15 miles (24.14 km) of running completed per week. For example, runners who complete 30 miles (48.28 km) of training per week are allowed two sequences per workout; at 45 weekly miles (72.42 km), the runner could carry out three 800-400-200-1,000 combinations, and so on. This session heightens stamina at race speed (i.e., improves the ability to run at goal speed while tired), makes 10K races feel easier, enhances economy, and advances lactate-threshold velocity.

Kenyan 10K Session

Another fine 10K workout, and one that can be a lot of fun to complete, is the Kenyan 10K session. Used often by elite Kenyan runners preparing to run in the World Cross Country Championships, the Kenyan 10K session should be completed over a route 10 kilometers long in an area where running is truly enjoyable. Forest paths work well, as do parks and firm-sand beaches. The session is beautifully simple: After an energizing warm-up, the full 10K route is covered while spontaneously alternating 2- to 5-minute bursts at what feels like 10K intensity or slightly faster with 1- to 3-minute periods of easy floating.

Most runners will end up running about 4 of the 6.2 miles (6.43 of the 10 km) of the route at goal 10K speed, which is a fine stimulus for physiological improvement and a superb preparation for a real race. Mentally, the session is not taxing thanks to the breaks and the pleasant surroundings. The workout boosts lactate-threshold speed, economy at 10K pace, confidence, and resistance to fatigue.

Racing 5Ks

As mentioned in previous chapters, running a couple of 800-meter competitions is great race preparation for 1,500-meter runners. Similarly, competing in a few 1,500s is productive for 5,000-meter (3.11 mi) athletes. So it should be no surprise that *contesting a few 5Ks is tremendous for 10K runners*; the 5Ks are in fact as close to the highest-quality workouts a 10K runner can conduct.

Some veteran coaches frown on this idea, claiming that the 5K, at just half the distance of a 10K, fails to teach the mental discipline required to grind out a topflight 10K. But, as mentioned, competing in a 5K race means that the runner will complete half the 10K distance at a pace that is about 16 seconds per mile (1.6 km) faster than current 10K ability. Thus, running a 5K is a great way to develop the capacity to run continuously at a velocity significantly quicker than that of current the 10K pace; as implied earlier, each 5K is a stepping stone to a faster 10K. As a runner's economy at 5K speed improves, it will be possible to run longer distances at current 5K pace and eventually to run 10Ks at present 5K speed.

It doesn't hurt that 5K racing is also great for lactate threshold and probably boosts v$\dot{V}O_2$max a bit. When 5K races are completed with full effort, average intensity comes close to 97 percent of maximal heart rate near the finish and averages 95 percent of the maximal rate of oxygen consumption. It is also nice to know that most runners recover very quickly from 5K races provided they haven't damaged their neuromuscular systems with overly high-volume training leading up to the events. As a result, it can be very productive to compete in two 5Ks before a major 10K, one 4 to 5 weeks before the big day and another 2 weeks in advance of the 10K.

Additional Training Strategies

Many of the sizzling workouts recommended in previous chapters are also sensational for the 10K. The v$\dot{V}O_2$max workouts (chapter 26), of course, as well as greyhound running (chapter 28), lactate stacker exercises (chapters 27 and 32), all of the superset exertions (various chapters), circuit training (chapter 13), mile-pace 400s (chapter 33), and also hill workouts (chapter 15) are outstanding 10K preparations.

Sometimes runners need a specific workout to get them over a hump in their 10K race performances. Many runners, for example, become stuck with performance times around 41 minutes or so—and have considerable trouble reaching their goal of breaking 40 minutes. A sound approach to this problem would be to continue to work toward optimizing maximal running speed, v$\dot{V}O_2$max, lactate threshold, running-specific strength, and running economy, but some specific workouts can also be very helpful.

For example, if a runner has been running 10K races in the range of 40:00 to 41:30 and would like to push his or her time down to 39-something, this runner could simply use *1,000-meter (.62 mi) work intervals* in about 3:55 to 3:56 each with 3 to 4 minutes of jog recovery. A good start would be four such work intervals per session, with a goal of gradually and cautiously building up to eight intervals over time. A sound strategy is to pare down the recovery times as fitness improves.

A more challenging session would involve running 2,000-meter (1.24 mi) intervals. For example, the runner might start with just 2 × 2,000 in 7:50 to 7:55, with 3 to 4 minutes of easy jogging between the intervals. Over time, it is optimal to progress to four intervals and trim the recoveries a bit.

It is productive to use this same approach for other goal 10K times. For example, if a runner would like to break 30 minutes for the 10K and has been running in the 30:30 to 31:15 range, this runner could hit 4 × 1,000 meters (.62 mi) in 2:56 to 2:57 each with 2-minute jog recoveries and gradually progress up the ladder to 8 × 1,000 at 2:56. If a runner wants to break 36 minutes he or she would start with 4 × 1,000 in 3:32 to 3:33. A runner who wants to get under 45 minutes would begin with 4 × 1,000 in 4:25 to 4:26, and so on.

Racing Strategy: Know Your Pace

An interesting feature of 10K racing is that almost everyone goes out too fast. For example, runners who are attempting to break through the 40-minute barrier for the 10K, which represents a 6:25 average pace, will often fly through the first mile (1.6 km) of the race in around 6:10 or so. During the first few minutes of the race, they don't feel much discomfort associated with this overly fast pace; adrenaline and the excitement of racing drown out all possibilities of pain and fatigue.

After 3 minutes or so, basic human physiology begins to take over, however, and even though the first distance marker is passed in a great time, the going gets tough. Intramuscular pH has drifted just a bit too low, and self-talk, instead of revolving around positive statements such as "I'm going to do it," is instead posing confidence-harming queries such as "Did I go out too fast?" The second mile is often covered in 6:40, and so the 2-mile point (3.2 km) is attained in 12:50, right on the desired 6:25 average. Nonetheless, such runners are hardly on schedule for the planned 40-flat 10K.

That's because the first mile of a 10K competition almost always feels too easy at goal pace—and the third mile is usually a mirror image of the second mile. If the runner goes too fast for the first mile, the second mile is

David Davies/PA Wire/Press Association Images

▶ Mo Farah's success in the 10K hinges on his ability to run at a fast but sustainable pace for the duration of the race.

inevitably too slow, and the third mile is too slow as well. There are several reasons for this, but the key factor is that the extra fatigue associated with the too-fast start usually lingers for at least 2 miles (3.2 km) into the race. This makes it very difficult to achieve an overall goal for the race since in the last 3.2 miles (5.2 km) the runner will be struggling to do more than sustain the planned pace—he or she will also have to make up ground lost during the second and third miles.

A 10K runner can avoid this jam by using more patience and restraint during the first mile (1.6 km) of the 10K. It is also good to become an excellent judge of pace so that target pace can be sustained during the crucial first mile. Bob Williams, a former All-American steeplechaser at the University of Oregon, recommends fartlek-style training on the track to improve one's sense of race pace.[7] The idea would be to run 400, 800, or 1,200 meters (.75 mi) on the track at what is believed to be goal race pace while staying relaxed and concentrating on how the pace feels. Once the segment is completed, a quick check of the watch will disclose whether the pace has been faster or slower than goal speed. After a couple of minutes of active recovery, the runner can then try another 400, 800, or 1,200, adjusting pace if necessary. By slowing down or speeding up on subsequent runs, a runner will eventually find race pace and develop a good feeling for the leg-turnover rate and perceived effort associated with it. In the overall program, this pace-judgment session can be substituted for an interval workout.

It is also possible to include race-pace segments within some easy runs. Toward the end of an easy 6-miler (9.7 km), for example, a runner can stride out at what he or she thinks is goal 10K pace over a measured half-mile (800 m) section of the course while timing the effort with a watch. Including a few of these in the program each week does not harm recovery or the ability to perform subsequent high-quality workouts since the amount of quality running is slight, but it does improve a runner's sense of race pace and increases the chances of running a great 10K.

Conclusion

Training for a 10K strongly resembles the preparations for 800-meter, 1,500-meter, mile, and 5K competitions since a high quality of physical work is emphasized and the ultimate goals—optimization of $v\dot{V}O_2max$, $t_{lim}v\dot{V}O_2max$, lactate-threshold velocity, running economy, maximal running velocity, running-specific strength, and resistance to fatigue—are the same. A slight difference is that 10K training ordinarily emphasizes longer work intervals, and thus a slightly lower average training velocity, compared with preparations for shorter distances. For example, staples of training for the 10K are 1,000- to 2,000-meter (.62-1.24 mi) intervals at current or possibly goal 10K pace. These intervals can be productive for runners competing at distances shorter than the 10K, but such competitors will usually be focusing a bit more intently on higher-speed intervals over shorter durations.

CHAPTER 36

Training for Half Marathons

The half marathon is the first race discussed in this book that is actually completed at slower than lactate-threshold velocity. Generally, well-trained athletes run their half marathons at a tempo that is about 2 seconds per 400 meters slower than lactate-threshold speed.[1] As a result, it is the first race that calls for the deliberate use of workouts comprised entirely or partially of running at less than lactate-threshold speed. These sessions do not include a wide array of subthreshold paces, however; they all center around the use of current (or estimated) half-marathon velocity because such running improves economy at current half-marathon tempo and makes it easier to move up to faster paces in the race.

As a race, the half marathon is attractive to distance runners for a number of reasons. Although the half marathon is sometimes looked down upon by incorrigible marathoners, the half marathon can serve as a springboard to improved marathon performances. The half marathon is also a much easier race from which to recover compared with a marathon, and the half marathon is a great race for the 5K and 10K runner who wants to move up to something longer but is not yet ready to tackle a full marathon.

Half Marathon Workouts

When training for a half marathon, a runner does not need to negotiate an 18- to 20-mile (28.97-32.19 km) run during his or her preparations as is the case for a marathon. Nonetheless, preparing for a half marathon is much like premarathon work—and like prepping for the 800, 1,500, 5K, and 10K—in the sense that a runner must attempt to boost maximal running velocity and neuromuscular power characteristics while laying down the key physiological undergirders—$v\dot{V}O_2max$, lactate-threshold speed, running economy, running-specific strength, and overall tolerance of race pace (i.e., resistance to fatigue)—that permit the *sustaining* of high-quality speeds in the race.

Although increasing maximal running speed might appear to be a strange and unneeded goal for the half-marathon runner, it is like adding another room to a house: It gives a runner another place to go. As maximal running velocity increases, the runner is not trapped by the speeds that he or she has always been capable of running. The runner can move up to higher velocities, and as this is accomplished, familiar paces such as current half-marathon capability become much easier to handle. When a specific pace becomes easier to maintain in a race, a runner can usually move up to a speed that is faster than usual and even set a personal record.

A runner who wants to complete a half marathon must have the ability to cover 13.1 miles (21.1 km) in one sustained effort. Gradually building up to a training-run distance of 11 miles (17.71 km) will ensure that a runner is capable of doing that. If a runner can negotiate 11 miles in a training effort, adrenaline and excitement will ensure that he or she can handle 13.1 on race day. A relatively inexperienced runner whose long run is no more than 5 miles (8.1 km) or so can simply add one mile (1.61 km) to this long run each week or every other week, depending on the schedule, until the 11-mile distance is reached.

Lactate-Threshold Workouts

As mentioned, half-marathon speed is related to lactate-threshold speed. Although there is variation among runners, half-marathon pace is about 2 to 3 percent slower than lactate-threshold velocity. This has an interesting consequence that is sometimes ignored by half-marathon competitors: As lactate-threshold speed improves, so will half-marathon tempo. When lactate-threshold velocity is enhanced by 1 percent, half-marathon pace will also move up by about the same amount. When lactate-threshold speed is raised by 5 percent, the result is an almost 5 percent improvement in half-marathon time, which would be about a 4.5 minute gain for the 90-minute half-marathoner.

This means workouts that advance lactate threshold are great for half marathoners. And it also means—somewhat paradoxically for old-school coaches and runners—that some of the same workouts that are terrific for 800-meter and 1,500-meter runners are terrific for half marathoners. Lactate stackers (chapters 27 and 32), for example, are perhaps the best workout in the world for advancing lactate-threshold speed and are wondrously effective for half-marathon athletes. Circuit workouts (chapter 13) are great, too, because of their properties for advancing lactate-threshold speed as are hill workouts (chapter 15), greyhound running (chapters 23 and 28), and all the other quality sessions recommended for the shorter distances. In addition, $v\dot{V}O_2$max efforts (chapter 26) will also pay big dividends in the half marathon.

Training at 10K Pace and Racing 10Ks

Training at 10K pace also works wonderfully well for the half marathon. The reasons for this are simple: The 10-K speed is high quality and above lactate-threshold intensity, yet it is not far above half-marathon velocity at about 4 seconds per 400 meters faster. In fact, unless a runner has already managed to optimize half-marathon performances or is an elite athlete near the top of his or her game, current 10K speed may eventually be the pace used when a half-marathon personal record is set. It is certain that training at 10K pace makes current half-marathon speed feel much easier, and there is little doubt that training at 10-K tempo improves economy at half-marathon pace. Thus, the 10K speed sets the stage for higher-quality half-marathon performances.

Although people automatically tend to connect the half marathon with the marathon as being similar races, the half marathon is actually much closer in terms of distance to the 10K. If a runner has become a skilled 10K runner, he or she needs to add 11 more quality kilometers (6.84 mi) to a single top effort to be a good half-marathon athlete. In contrast, if a runner can handle the half marathon with aplomb, he or she must figure out a way to handle 21 more kilometers (13.05 mi) in a quality way—and in a single effort—before success can be achieved in the marathon. To put it another way, a half marathon is just one-third of the way—not halfway—between a 10K and a full marathon.

Thus, running several 10K races during the 8 weeks leading up to an important half marathon can be part of an excellent overall training plan. These 10K races will improve lactate-threshold speed and half-marathon running economy, and they will make planned half-marathon pace feel much easier to sustain. A 10K race should not be attempted 1 week before an important half marathon, however; a hard 10K requires some recovery time, and 1 week is probably not long enough to restore the neuromuscular system for the stresses of a half-marathon. It is probably best to keep the last preparatory 10K at least 2 to 3 weeks in advance of a significant half marathon.

Some coaches and runners advocate running 10Ks at planned half-marathon pace, but there is little reason to do this. One can run at half-marathon pace quite easily as part of normal training; there is no need to occupy a race with it. In fact, running the 10K to the best of one's ability will do far more for fitness than cutting back the throttle and moving through the 10K at half-marathon speed. Bear in mind that average 10K intensity is about 90 percent of $\dot{V}O_2$max, an excellent level of effort for upgrading economy and lactate-threshold speed.

A training session with 10-minute work intervals at current 10K pace and with 3- to 5-minute jog recoveries works wonders for half-marathon ability. A runner should begin with two 10-minute intervals per workout; once the duo can be handled, add a third *5-minute* work interval at 10K pace to the session.

Training at Half-Marathon Pace

It is important to be totally economical, comfortable, and confident on race day, and so it makes sense to carry out some workouts that are planned at half-marathon pace (PHMP). To determine PHMP, a runner can simply tag on 16 seconds per mile (1.61 km) to current 10K speed. Table 36.1 provides conversions of 10K race times into PHMPs.

Table 36.1 PHMPs for Several Current 10K Times

Current 10K race time	Current 10K speed per mile (1.6 km)	PHMP
32:00	5:10	5:26 per mile
40:00	6:25	6:41 per mile
48:00	7:45	8:01 per mile

Alternatively, a runner can be more aggressive and predict that by the time the half marathon rolls around, he or she will be fitter and 10K speed—and also half-marathon velocity—will be higher. In this case, half-marathon pace can be projected to be just 8 to 10 seconds per mile slower than current 10K speed. However, it is important to be careful in the corresponding workouts. As the distance of PHMP efforts is increased, PHMP should be tempered, that is, reduced in speed, if the workouts are overly difficult.

A good way to start with PHMP sessions is to warm up a bit beforehand, roll through 3 or 4 miles (4.83-6.44 km) at PHMP, and follow with a cooldown. If possible, nearly every week add another mile to the PHMP until a maximum of 8 miles (12.87 km) is reached. If distance feels manageable, success on race day is highly probable.

Of course, most runners would agree that sustaining planned pace is much more difficult over the last 10 kilometers (6.21 mi) of the half-marathon than over the first 11 kilometers (6.84 mi), so it is a good idea to shape PHMP sessions in certain ways. Specifically, once a runner is sure that he or she can run 11 miles (17.71 km) without stopping and is fairly comfortable ticking off 5 miles (8.05 km) at PHMP, a good workout would involve running 4 miles at a very moderate pace; then, with no break in between, 6 miles (9.66 km) at PHMP; and then a 1-mile cool-down. This is also a benchmark workout: If the runner can complete it successfully, the chances of reaching goal time on race day are quite high. To ensure adequate recovery, this workout should be completed at least 2 weeks before the date of a major half marathon.

Superset Training

Superset sessions work well for half-marathon trainees although the sets tend to be significantly longer than those used by runners preparing for shorter distances. A great superset workout for half-marathon runners is the 800-1,600. To do this workout properly, a runner simply warms up thoroughly and then completes 800 meters at current 10K speed; without stopping, he or she then covers 1,600 meters (.99 mi) at PHMP to complete the first super set. A 5-minute recovery can be employed between super sets, and a runner can profitably begin with three of these supersets per workout; this provides roughly 1.5 miles (2.41 km) at 10K speed and 3 miles (4.83 km) at PHMP for the session.

A considerably more challenging superset session is the 400-1,200-3,200. After a very thorough warm-up, a runner hits $2 \times$ (400-800-2,000) with the 400 *at 5K intensity*, the 800 at about current 10K speed, and the 2,000 meters (1.24 mi) at goal half-marathon pace. There is no recovery at all between the 400, 800, and 2,000 within each set. The recovery between sets is 5 minutes of jogging, and the cool-down after the second set consists of 2 miles (3.22 km) of very relaxed running. The 400-800-2,000 superset boosts lactate-threshold running speed and enhances economy and confidence at goal half-marathon pace. It is terrific for increasing the ability to sustain tempo at planned half-marathon pace even when the neuromuscular system appears to be in a rather pronounced state of rebellion.

Hill Training

Hill sessions improve running-specific strength and resistance to fatigue for half-marathon runners, so they are also recommended. A particularly ideal slope for half-marathon athletes would be a gently rising hill, with an incline of about 3 percent, that continues its upward slope for a mile (1.61 km) or so. The planned workout would involve climbing the hill at half-marathon speed, which will feel harder than usual because of the upslope. Due to the length of the hill and the possibility for jarring, eccentric damage to the leg muscles, it makes little sense to jog back down the hill for recovery. Instead, a friend may drive the runner to the base of the slope, if possible, and a bit of jogging at the bottom can keep the runner loose; total recovery can last 4 or 5 minutes. The number of climbs per workout can begin with two and progress to four or more over time.

PHMP Circuit Training

Naturally, PHMP circuits can also have an extremely positive effect on half-marathon capacity. To carry these out, warm up with about 10 minutes of light jogging followed by light stretching activities and dynamic-mobility exercises. Next, run (4 to 6) $\times$ 100 at what feels like 5K speed, with short recoveries, and then perform the following activities in order. Move quickly from exercise to exercise but don't perform the exertions overly quickly. Don't sacrifice good form just to get them done in a hurry. The idea is to carry out each activity methodically and efficiently—and then almost immediately start on the next exercise.

1. Run 1 mile (1.61 km) at planned half-marathon pace (PHMP).
2. Complete 20 six-count squat thrusts with jumps (chapter 13).
3. Do 50 abdominal crunches (chapter 13).
4. Perform 20 high lunges with each leg (chapter 34); keep the nonlunging foot on a step or platform that is about 6 inches (15 cm) off the ground.
5. Carry out 50 low-back extensions (chapter 13).
6. Do 10 push-ups (chapter 13).
7. Complete 15 one-leg squats (chapter 14) with one leg and then 15 more with the other leg.
8. Run one-half mile (.8 km) at PHMP.
9. Carry out 30 bench dips (chapter 13).
10. Complete 15 high-bench step-ups with each leg (chapter 14).
11. Jump 100 times in place with propulsive force coming from ankles not the knees. Carry out the last 30 jumps at an especially quick tempo. For all 100 jumps, don't try for great height; the feet should only come off the ground a few inches or centimeters. Minimize ground-contact times.
12. Carry out 30 cross-body leg swings with each leg.
13. Run 1 more mile at PHMP.
14. Repeat steps 2-13 for two circuits in all; then cool down with 2 miles (3.22 km) of light jogging.

This is a fairly tough workout, with 4 miles (6.44 km) of PHMP running and a variety of somewhat exhausting exercises. Once the half-way point of the first circuit is reached, blood-lactate levels will be rather high, so this turns out to be an excellent session for lactate-threshold improvement. The PHMP circuits also enhance whole-body strength and coordination, making a runner more economical at PHMP. In addition, the PHMP circuits fortify general resistance to fatigue and give a runner the ability and confidence to run at half-marathon pace no matter how rugged it feels. As a runner completes the last 3 or 4 miles (4.83-6.44 km) of the goal half-marathon, he or she will be thankful to have completed these PHMP circuits a couple of times during preparatory training.

Cross-Body Leg Swings Lean slightly forward with one hand on a wall or other support. Place full body weight on leg on the same side as the hand on the wall. Then, swing the nonsupporting leg across the front of the body (figure 36.1a), pointing the toes upward as the foot reaches its farthest point of motion. After this, swing the nonsupporting leg back to the other side as far as comfortably possible (figure 36.1b); point the toes up as the foot reaches its final point of movement. Repeat this overall motion 30 times and then performing 30 reps with the other leg.

▶ **Figure 36.1** Swings *(a)* across the body and *(b)* out to the side.

Quality Over Quantity

Runners often inquire about the optimal weekly distance for half-marathon training, but it is important to remember that there is no such thing. Runners complete their best half-marathons when they have reached their highest fitness levels, not necessarily when they have racked up the most distance or attained a magical total volume of distance run. Achieving the greatest fitness level means maximizing $v\dot{V}O_2max$ and lactate-threshold speed, enhancing economy to the greatest possible degree, boosting maximal running velocity, increasing running-specific strength and resistance to fatigue, and preparing the body to flawlessly handle the specific demands of half-marathon race pace. Quality training and PHMP efforts do that far better than the simple accumulation of large numbers of miles or kilometers.

Conclusion

Half-marathon training proceeds in a fashion similar to 10K training with the exception that workouts geared specifically to running at planned half-marathon paces are included. These sessions include the super sets, PHMP circuits, hill workouts at PHMP, and long runs with inner PHMP segments, all of which are described in this chapter. The overall progression of half-marathon training follows the usual pattern: General strength comes first, followed by running-specific strength, hill work, and then explosive training.

CHAPTER 37

Training for Marathons

The marathon is often called the toughest of all popular road races and with good reason. Participation in the event can produce dehydration, overhydration with consequent hyponatremia, severe muscle cramping, gastrointestinal distress, hypothermia, and hyperthermia. Research also reveals that running a marathon increases a runner's risk of respiratory infection. Of all the popular races, the marathon is also associated with the highest death rate per competition. It is an event in which the 3-hour finisher needs more than 32,000 impacts with the ground to complete the race, and thus it is a competition that requires extended postrace recovery.

More Training Is Not Better

There is wide disagreement about how to prepare properly for the marathon, but it is reasonable to say that the philosophy of more is better is currently holding sway. According to many marathon experts, increased workout frequency and volume are the keys to success, and moving above 50 miles (81 km) of training per week is thought to be far better than completing just 30 to 40 weekly miles (48-64 km). The idea seems to be this: It's a long race, so training should be geared toward a high volume of total weekly work.

Scientific research has provided little support for such conceptions. In a study carried out at the University of Northern Iowa, for example, surplus miles and augmented workout frequencies had little positive effect on marathon performances.[1] In this research, 18 college-age males and 33 college-age females took part in an 18-week marathon training program. All 51 subjects were active, healthy, and fairly fit at the beginning of the study, and almost all of the individuals were running fewer than 10 miles (16 km) per week when the research began.

The Northern Iowa participants were divided into two groups. The longer-distance group increased training volume from 23 to 48 miles (37-77 km) per week over the course of the 18-week inquiry, averaging six workouts per week. The shorter-distance group hiked training volume from 18 to 39 miles (29-63 km) per week by the end of the study while training just 4 days per week.

A typical schedule for the longer-distance runners near the end of the 18-week training program was as follows:

- Monday—45 minutes of running
- Tuesday—90 minutes
- Wednesday—45 minutes
- Thursday—90 minutes
- Friday—45 minutes
- Saturday—long run
- Sunday—complete rest

The shorter-distance group simply omitted the Monday and Wednesday 45-minute efforts to arrive at their four times per week schedule. Actual exercise intensity during all workouts was the same for both groups: about 75 percent of maximal heart rate. Both groups tapered for two weeks prior to the actual marathon.

The duration of the Saturday long run for both groups was 60 minutes at the beginning of the study but eventually advanced for both groups to 2.5 hours after 14 weeks of training. Each group completed three of these 2.5-hour runs over the course of the training program. Thus, even though the shorter-distance runners ran 20 percent fewer miles during the overall training period, both groups carried out the same long runs on Saturdays.

At the end of the 18-week period, both groups had improved body composition and running capacity. Each group trimmed percent body fat by about 10 percent and increased muscle mass by 3 to 5 percent. In addition, the groups raised maximal aerobic capacity ($\dot{V}O_2$max) by 3 to 12 percent, improved running economy by 10 percent, lowered lactate levels while running by 25 percent or more, and reduced the heart rates associated with submaximal paces by up to 15 percent. These improvements *were absolutely equivalent* between the groups even though the shorter-distance runners had logged 20 percent fewer miles.

Marathon times were exactly the same, too, averaging about 4:17 for males in both groups (the range was from 3:36 to 4:53) and approximately 4:51 for females in both groups (the range was 3:51 to 6:32). In other words, the extra workouts and extra miles completed by the longer-distance athletes had not sheared even a tenth of a second from marathon performance times. Running 39 miles (63 km) per week, parceled into four workouts, was as effective a marathon preparation as covering 48 weekly miles (77 km) with six weekly workouts. As this book has noted in previous chapters, science suggests that the mere addition of distance to training schedules that already feature around 35 to 40 miles (56-64 km) of weekly running rarely upgrades performance times for most runners, and this appears to be true even in a long race like the marathon.

A take-home message is that if a runner is covering about 35 to 40 miles (56-64 km) per week in training and wants to become a better marathoner, he or she should not simply add on more distance to the schedule in the belief that it will improve marathon prospects. The best predictor of marathon finishing time is average workout speed, not weekly distance run.[2] This suggests that if an athlete is running about 35 to 40 miles per week, it is important to upgrade the intensity of training sessions before thinking about tacking on additional distance. This could be accomplished by progressively increasing the number of intervals in interval workouts and gradually adding length to other high-quality sessions before adding more moderate-speed workouts. Research suggests that small increases in intense work will do far more for marathon fitness than sizable upswings in the amount of distance run.

Traditional Weekly Long Run Is Unnecessary

During marathon preparations, it is important to avoid the common tendency to carry out a long run each weekend. There is little value in such repeated efforts, and in fact such incessant hammering at the door of prolonged running usually heightens injury risk and lowers the quality of the training carried out during the week between the long runs. The general belief is that such long running is needed to prepare for the rigors of the marathon, but the truth is that there is nothing about the marathon per se that requires a *weekly* leg-pounding run. Implicit in the philosophy of the long run is the suggestion that the human body will somehow forget how to go long, will not remember how to have enough endurance to run a marathon, unless a weekly battering is administered to the leg muscles. Nothing could be further from the truth!

While it is important to gradually work up to a 20- to 22-mile (32-35 km) training run in preparation for a marathon, it is not necessary to conduct such a workout on a weekly basis. As is the case with all the distances studied so far in this book, increased fitness and not expanded training volume or a high frequency of long runs is the factor that will produce the best possible marathon performances. Fitness is improved more effectively by a scorching $v\dot{V}O_2max$ workout, a lactate-stacker session, 2,000-meter (1.24 mi) intervals at 10K pace, or a sizzling fartlek effort on wooded trails than by inching along for 13 to 20 miles (21-32 km) at medium paces.

It is far better to reserve the long run for every other weekend, or even every third weekend, and to carry out high-quality efforts on days that were formerly designated for the long slogs. A runner who has completed a 20- to 22-mile training run as part of his or her marathon preparations, with a good chunk of this effort completed at goal pace, and who has also optimized $v\dot{V}O_2max$, lactate-threshold speed, running economy, running-specific strength, and maximal running speed during the premarathon buildup, will be totally prepared for the big race.

The Marathon Is a Power Race

It is clear that the marathon should be treated *as a power race* by competitive runners, not merely as a test of endurance. Unfortunately, most marathon trainees don't concentrate on bolstering their speed during their premarathon preparations, preferring instead—by focusing on long, slow runs—to teach their muscles to contract meekly for long periods of time. That can be a bigger mistake in the marathon than it is in a high-power event like the 5K. If a runner's stride rate is 180 steps per minute, and it takes him or her about 3.5 hours to complete a marathon, the race requires a grand total of 37,800 steps. Greater leg-muscle power can do two basic things: (1) It allows a runner to spend less time on the ground with each foot strike since the leg muscles are contracting more explosively, or quickly, and (2) it increases stride length. More ground is covered between steps because muscle contractions are more forceful.

If the improved power decreases the time spent on the ground per foot strike by just .02 seconds, an almost infinitesimal change and therefore one that most runners can easily make, the gain in performance time would be 37,800 steps × .02 seconds, or a 756-second improvement. The marathoner would upgrade finishing time from 3:30 down to a nifty 3:17:24! Similarly, a 3:10 runner would improve performance by 34,200 × .02 = 684 seconds, slipping neatly under the 3-hour mark and finishing in just 2:58:36.

If the improved power also increases the distance between foot strikes by one-half inch (1.3 cm), again a change most runners can manage by making modest improvements in leg-muscle power, another positive change in performance would ensue: 37,800 steps × .5 inches equals almost 500 meters (1,640 ft). In other words, the runner would be able to beat every runner who currently finishes up to 500 meters ahead of him or her in the marathon. The runner would shave more than 2 additional minutes from total marathon time.

▶ Improving maximal speed has a positive impact on overall marathon performance.

It is clear that no marathon runner is too explosive or too powerful. Any marathon runner can profit from a decrease in foot-strike time and appropriate expansion of stride length. To become more powerful, it is wise to first become stronger by relying on hill running and running-specific strengthening movements. After upgrading strength, a runner can then learn to apply that strength more quickly by running explosively up hills, carrying out plyometric drills (e.g., hops, bounds, one-leg hops in place), and practicing running fast using the quality workouts outlined in this book. By doing so, a runner will become faster, and as sports medicine expert Tim Noakes has pointed out, "The fastest runners at the shorter distances are the best marathon runners."[3]

Marathon Workouts

Many different types of workouts will boost marathon performances. Goal-pace training, circuit workouts, "Tegla sessions," super-set routines, lactate-threshold-advancing efforts, and half-marathon competitions all provide significant benefits for the marathon runner.

Training at Goal Pace

Many marathon trainees believe that 18- to 20-mile (29-32 km) long runs prepare their bodies to handle the rigors of a full marathon, forgetting that such runs simply reinforce the ability to run a partial marathon at a pace slower than goal velocity. To make long training runs (i.e., the ones carried out every other week or every third week during training) relevant to the race, it is important to make such efforts race specific. This means including a significant chunk of miles at goal marathon pace within the overall run. Runners can be very progressive in this regard: If the current long run is 6 miles (9.66 km), for example, a runner can include 3 miles (4.83 km) at goal marathon tempo by warming up with 2 easy miles (3.22 km), pacing along for 3 miles at goal speed, and then cooling down with 1 light mile (1.61 km). Over time, a runner can increase the length of the long run by 1 or 2 miles per workout until 20 to 21 miles (32-34 km) are reached—with about 10 of those miles (16 km) at goal marathon speed.

It makes sense, in fact, to complete one race simulator about 4 to 5 weeks before the actual marathon date. To complete the simulator, a runner can cover 9 miles (14.48 km) fairly easily at a pace about 45 seconds per mile slower than goal marathon tempo. Then, without stopping, the runner can click off 10 more miles at goal marathon speed before cooling down with 2 miles at 45 to 60 seconds off marathon pace. This great workout, which involves running close to half a marathon at goal race velocity while already tired, is a diagnostic one; it will reveal whether the chosen goal is either too lofty or too humble. It is also great preparation for the marathon itself since it forces a runner to reel off 10 goal-speed miles when the neuromuscular system is already in a fatigued state. Finally, the simulator improves confidence and running economy at hoped-for marathon intensity.

Ample recovery will be required after the simulator with only light training during the following week and a steady and progressive tapering of training between the date of the simulator and the marathon. As mentioned, the simulator should be completed 4 to 5 weeks before the marathon. If the two runs—the simulator and marathon—are squeezed together with a shorter interim period, a runner will not be fully recovered on race day and thus will not be able to achieve his or her best possible performance.

Circuit Training

Since the marathon involves a prolonged fight against fatigue, challenging circuit sessions are also great marathon preparations. As the circuits are completed, a runner should move steadily from drill to drill without rushing and yet without resting. All of the running segments and exercises should be completed in a relaxed manner with good form. The following is an example of a marathon circuit workout. A runner should warm up with 1.5 to 2 miles (2.41 km-3.22 km) of light running. Descriptions of the exercises can be found in chapters 13 and 14.

1. Run 800 meters at current 10K pace, or about 16 seconds per 800 faster than planned marathon tempo. If the runner is in a setting in which it is difficult to judge pace accurately, he or she should simply make sure that the chosen pace is significantly faster than marathon tempo without running at full-bore speed.
2. Complete 20 squat thrusts with jumps (chapter 13).
3. Perform 12 push-ups (chapter 13).
4. Do 15 one-leg squats with each leg (chapter 14).
5. Run 800 meters at planned marathon speed.
6. Do 50 abdominal crunches (chapter 13).
7. Complete 15 lunge squats (chapter 13) with each leg.
8. Perform 50 low-back extensions (chapter 13).
9. Run 800 meters at projected marathon velocity.
10. Hit 12 feet-elevated push-ups (chapter 13).
11. Do 20 bench dips (chapter 13).
12. Complete 15 high-bench step-ups (chapter 14).
13. Run 1,600 meters (.99 mi) at goal marathon pace.
14. Repeat steps 2-13 for two circuits in all; then cool down by jogging 2 easy miles. This circuit provides 8.5 miles (13.7 km) of total running and 4.5 miles (7.24 km) at marathon speed along with a great deal of whole-body strengthening.

A runner in an early stage of marathon training can cut back on the number of exercise reps and the lengths of the running intervals starting with 400s, for example; it is also okay to begin with just one circuit instead of two. Otherwise, when conducted every 10 to 14 days or so, the full-blown session just outlined is ideal for the last 2 to 3 months before a marathon. The circuits build a tremendous foundation of whole-body strength and resistance to fatigue, both critically important for marathon running. The circuits also improve economy while running at marathon intensity and help to raise lactate threshold (more on this later in this chapter). Finally, the marathon circuits enhance a runner's ability to settle into goal marathon tempo even when he or she is feeling wiped out with fatigue. The marathon circuit workout is a tremendous confidence builder.

Tegla Workout

A Tegla workout produces a series of fantastic physiological effects while simultaneously advancing a runner's optimism about his or her impending marathon performance. This workout is simple in conception but extremely challenging to complete. To carry it out, a runner simply finds a trail or road that slowly but steadily increases in elevation for about 12 kilometers (7.46 mi), warms up, and runs from the bottom to the top without stopping, using an intensity that feels tougher than goal marathon speed. The workout is named for Kenyan runner Tegla Loroupe, holder of four world records, who trained on such a route on the Menengei Crater near Nakuru, Kenya, in advance of all of her major long-distance races.

Such running routes are easy to find in Kenya, but environmentally challenged runners may have to complete this workout on a treadmill, varying the incline from 2 to 5 percent during the overall effort. At first, a runner would use the slighter incline for most of the run and then progress to greater amounts of time at 4 to 5 percent. The session improves running-specific strength and upgrades the ability to sustain a submaximal yet very tough pace for a prolonged period of time (i.e., run a marathon).

A runner who actually has a 10- to 12- kilometer (6.21-7.46 mi) hill available for training should not hesitate to take walking breaks the first few times the slope is attacked. Treadmill-bound runners should start with 30 minutes as a workout duration and gradually progress to 60 steady minutes of climbing. This workout can be made as challenging as necessary, too. Great Kenyan marathon runners such as Sammy Lelei have used mountain trails in their marathon preparations that require *85 minutes* of absolutely relentless, steady climbing.[4]

Superset Training

Marathon super sets can also have a profound impact on marathon performance. As mentioned earlier in this book, super sets enhance the runner's ability to run at goal speed in the face of overwhelming fatigue. Super sets are also certainly high enough in intensity to produce upswings in lactate-threshold speed and enhancements in running economy at race-type paces. To carry out marathon super sets, a runner warms up and then runs $3 \times (400\text{-}400\text{-}2{,}400)$, completing the first 400 meters at 5K pace, the second 400 meters at current 10K pace, and the closing 2,400 meters (1.49 mi) at goal marathon speed. No recovery should be taken between the two 400s within each super set or between the second 400 and the 2,400. Four minutes of recovery are permitted between super sets. This outstanding workout makes marathon pace feel easier, increases a runner's confidence that marathon speed can be handled quite effectively, and improves lactate threshold and running economy at three race speeds: 5K, 10K, and marathon.

Lactate-Threshold Speed Training

Why is lactate threshold so important for marathon running? Lactate-threshold, which can vary tremendously between runners, is just the running intensity above which large amounts of lactate begin to accumulate in the blood. It can be expressed as a specific running speed—say 268 meters (.17 mi) per minute (6-minute mile pace)—or it can be represented as a fraction of $\dot{V}O_2max$. For example, if a runner reached $\dot{V}O_2max$ (i.e., the maximal rate for using oxygen) at a running speed of 300 meters (.19 mi) per minute, his or her lactate threshold might occur at 80 percent of $\dot{V}O_2max$ pace, in this case, 240 meters (.15 mi) per minute.

Scientific research reveals that lifting one's lactate-threshold speed can have a big impact on marathon performance. In a benchmark study, Swedish researchers Bertil Sjödin and Jan Svedenhag found that lactate-threshold velocity did a very good job of predicting the pace that marathon runners would be able to sustain during the race.[5]

Lactate threshold, of course, can respond rather dramatically to training. For instance, an untrained individual might reach lactate threshold at a paltry intensity of only 55 percent of $\dot{V}O_2max$, while the elite runner who has trained diligently to elevate lactate threshold might not experience large upswings in blood lactate until he or she is running at a pace corresponding to almost 90 percent of $\dot{V}O_2max$. Such improvements would have a big impact on marathon time because marathoners tend to run the marathon at a speed just *under* lactate-threshold pace. If lactate threshold rests at 65 percent of $\dot{V}O_2max$, a runner would have to complete the marathon at just 60 percent of $\dot{V}O_2max$ or so. If lactate threshold is lifted to 90 percent of $\dot{V}O_2max$, the runner could cruise along at least 33 percent faster in the big race at about 85 to 86 percent of $\dot{V}O_2max$.

Scientific studies show that elite marathoners commonly run the marathon at an intensity of 85 to 86 percent of $\dot{V}O_2max$ while runners who complete the marathon in the 2:46 to 3:12 range are usually running at about 75 to 76 percent of $\dot{V}O_2max$.[6] The superior runners are faster than the good marathoners (2:46 to 3:12) in part because they have higher lactate thresholds and can run comfortably at a higher percentage of $\dot{V}O_2max$.

This means that the circuit workout outlined earlier would be particularly good for marathon preparations (recall from chapter 13 that circuit training upgrades lactate threshold). It also means that the workouts prescribed earlier in this book for lactate-threshold improvement, including the scorching lactate-stacker session that alternates 1 minute at almost all-out intensity with 2 minutes of recovery jogging, would be great for marathon runners. Marathon competitors, of course, can't live on lactate stackers alone; they will still have to carry out their marathon-specific runs every other or every third week and blend a variety of other sessions into their overall training, including the necessary vV̇O₂max sessions.

The lactate-stacker routine, as a big lactate-threshold booster, will have a sizably positive effect on marathon time. It is a great workout to do on Sunday instead of the usual humdrum, leg-numbing long run; a runner could alternate back and forth between lactate stackers and longish runs on consecutive weekends. An important point to note is that most marathon runners *love* lactate stackers partly because they are such a contrast with long, slow running. It is great to be able to go out and simply open up the jets instead of plodding along for two hours.

Importantly, too, lactate stackers can be quite diagnostic: Runners whose hamstrings become quite sore after lactate stackers are the ones who often end up with hamstring cramps toward the end of the marathon. These runners should systematically incorporate strength training for their hamstrings as part of their overall training by using routines such as high-bench step-ups and bicycle leg swings (see chapter 14).

Evaluating Half-Marathon Racing as Training for Marathons

In previous chapters, 800-meter races have been recommended as great preparatory workouts for 1,500-meter runners, 1,500-meter competitions as super sessions for 5K runners, 5K races as terrific warm-ups for 10K athletes, and 10K races as fine preparations for half-marathoners. That being true, is a competitive half-marathon a great set-up for a marathon personal record?

In one sense, a strong half-marathon race would indeed be a good marathon workout. Half-marathon pace is ordinarily about 16 seconds per 1,600 meters (.99 mi) faster than marathon tempo, and thus the completion of a half-marathon at full effort would improve tolerance of marathon velocity and make marathon tempo feel comparatively easier to sustain. In addition, 13 miles (20.92 km) of running at half-marathon pace might help improve running economy at marathon speed because strength and coordination gained at specific speeds should be transferable to slower speeds.

However, half-marathon pace is slower than lactate-threshold speed, so it would be hard to argue that it is actually a great lactate-threshold lifter. In addition, after a runner has done his or her best in a half marathon, that runner will usually need at least a 2-week recovery period before systematic, high-quality training can resume again. This means that it may be tough to fit both the half-marathon race and a marathon simulator into an overall program; recall that a simulator involves about 9 miles (14.48 km) at an easy pace, followed by 10 miles (16 km) at planned marathon speed and a 2-mile (3.22 km) cool-down. For many runners, it would be imprudent to run a half-marathon at maximal effort and then a simulator 2 to 3 weeks later. Anecdotal evidence indicates that such a pairing combines too much long, race-relevant running in too short a period of time.

If a runner had to choose between the two races, the simulator would appear to be far better for marathon preparation since its length—21 miles (34.80 km)—more nearly matches the marathon duration. In addition, running 10 miles on fatigued legs at marathon pace during the simulator more closely matches what happens on marathon race day than does streaking 13.1 miles of the half marathon after a fresh start and at a tempo that is faster than that of the marathon.

Why not just run a half-marathon at goal marathon speed? This is possible, but there are two problems: (1) As mentioned, the simulator does a better job of mimicking what will occur on marathon race day. Race-specific preparations are almost always better than less-specific prepping. True, a runner could warm up with 7 miles (11.27 km) of easy running before the start of the half marathon and then cruise through the race at goal marathon tempo, taking advantage of a well-measured course and the regular provisioning of sport drinks. While that sounds appropriate, it leads to the second problem. (2) Anecdotal evidence suggests that running 13 miles at marathon pace within the context of a 20- to 22-mile (32-35 km) workout is simply too much for most marathon trainees; 10 miles seems to be the upper limit. When runners complete 13 miles at marathon goal speed within a 22-mile (35.41 km) session, they really tend to struggle during the ensuing weeks; it becomes difficult to carry out the additional needed quality training and to show up on race day completely recovered and ready to perform in an optimal manner.

Conclusion

Although the marathon is the longest of popular race distances, there is no reason for a runner to abandon the principles of endurance training and embark on a program of prolonged submaximal running. As is the case with shorter competitions, marathon success hinges on optimizing $v\dot{V}O_2$max, lactate-threshold velocity, running economy, running-specific strength, resistance to fatigue, and maximal running velocity. For the marathon, training designed to optimize these variables needs to be combined with long runs that progressively approach 20 to 21 miles (32-34 km) in length and incorporate sizable sections at goal marathon velocity.

Training
for Ultramarathons

Science favors a high-quality approach to training for running events like the 100K rather than a high-volume approach. There are a variety of reasons for this. One key is simply that high-quality training is the best way to optimize fitness, and fitness is the best performance predictor for any racing distance. Compared with weekly poundings of 150 kilometers (93 mi) or more, quality work also produces less damage to muscles, tendons, ligaments, and bones.

Another factor to consider is that increasing maximal running speed and ability to run fast in shorter races like 5Ks and 10Ks will increase average pace in a race like the 100K because it will make better speeds easier to carry out. As is the case for any of the other races, doing one's best in an ultramarathon competition depends on optimizing power, $v\dot{V}O_2max$, lactate threshold, running economy, running-specific strength, and resistance to fatigue.

Greater Distances Are Not Better

Both anecdotal and scientific support exist for the contention that piling on more distance does not equal success. First, analyses of great ultramarathon runners such as Jackie Mekler—five-time winner of the Comrades Marathon, an 88K (55 mi) ultra, not a standard marathon—reveal that the highest-volume training years are not associated with the best ultramarathon performances.[1] Similarly, nine-time Comrades winner Bruce Fordyce began to succeed in his ultramarathons when he "resolved not to follow the usual pattern exhibited by most runners who, tasting success for the first time at a marathon or ultramarathon, conclude that they would do even better next time by training with much higher mileage."[1] In the five months leading up to his nine successful Comrades races, Fordyce averaged about 134 kilometers (83 mi) of training per week, comparatively light by ultramarathon standards. In 1982, one of his Comrades-winning years, the South African runner averaged just 42 miles (68 km) per week of running during February, a key buildup period for the ultra. His training for Comrades revolved around high-quality hill sessions and speed workouts on the track rather than the accumulation of distance.

When Fordyce completed the Comrades and London-to-Brighton ultramarathons within 14 weeks of each other in 1983, he also discovered that a high frequency of long runs is not essential for successful ultramarathon running.[1] Fordyce recovered for 6 weeks from Comrades and devoted 2 weeks to tapering for the London-to-Brighton event, leaving him just 6 weeks for actual training. During that 6-week period, he finished just two long runs of 50K or greater compared with the popular practice of completing a long run almost every weekend, yet he ran one of the world's fastest times for 50 miles (81 km) in the London-to-Brighton competition.

The lesson here is the same lesson referred to in chapter 37 on marathon training: Once the human body has developed the ability to run for a long distance, it does not lose that capability by the following weekend; therefore, it does not require a repeat of the prolonged run after a mere 7 days to maintain the appropriate amount of endurance.

Even more important, repeating the long run on a weekly basis is unlikely to produce sizable upswings in the key physiological variables of performance (i.e., $v\dot{V}O_2max$, $t_{lim}v\dot{V}O_2max$, lactate-threshold velocity, running economy, running-specific strength, race-relevant resistance to fatigue, and maximal running speed, or power), whereas using a much-shorter, high-intensity workout would be very likely to boost physiological fitness. Finally, the weekly long run is certain to heighten the risk of overuse injuries. It is interesting to note that Bruce Fordyce never bothered to finish his club's prerace 70K (44 mi) training run, believing it to be too long!

Ultramarathon Workouts

The workouts that are optimal for the marathon (see chapter 37) are also highly productive for ultramarathon runners. These include prolonged, race-specific runs, "Teglas," circuit training, and all forms of lactate-threshold advancing work (as lactate-threshold velocity advances, ultramarathon pace will also increase). In addition, the quality sessions, including $v\dot{V}O_2max$ workouts, hill running, fartlek efforts, and interval sessions at 5K and 10K paces, will be extremely beneficial for ultramarathon runners. Furthermore, running-specific strength training with proper progressions will enhance running economy and fatigue resistance among ultramarathon runners and will also help to protect against injury.

Speed Work

As part of his base period for ultra racing, Fordyce would carry out a weekly speed session on the track; during the 2-month buildup to each Comrades race, he conducted two high-quality sessions each week, choosing from an 8K (5 mi) time trial, intervals on the track (usually 800s, 1,200s, and 1,600s), and hills, along with a *third* intense effort: a cross country race on Saturday.[1] During the summer off-season after the Comrades in May, Fordyce would focus on 1,500-meter and 10K competitions. As Fordyce expressed it, such fast training and racing upgraded his peak cruising speed for the ultramarathons. He felt that if he could average 3 minutes per kilometer (.62 mi) in a 10K race, cruising at a pace of 3:30 per kilometer in an ultramarathon would feel easy for him. As pointed out previously, improving maximal speed pulls all race speeds up with it.

Another great quality workout for ultramarathon preparations involves continuous super-set running, where 1,600-meter intervals at 10K pace are alternated with 4,800 meters at goal ultramarathon pace until five or six intervals have been completed.

Long Runs and Training Volume

Fordyce did occasionally move beyond 80 miles (129 km) per week of training, but one of his rules was that such volume should never be sustained for more than 8 weeks. There is scientific support for the idea that high-volume training should be limited in its scope. Some research has detected a dramatic *decline* in performances and maximal aerobic capacity after 6 weeks of high-volume work in experienced, competitive runners.

True, long runs need to be included in 100K training as specific preparation for the challenges of the race. The longest run necessary would be approximately 60 to 70K (37-43 mi) completed just one time; in addition, an ultramarathoner could also complete several 45K (28 mi) efforts along with a number of 30K to 36K (19-22 mi) workouts. These long runs should be separated by periods of at least 2 weeks; 3 weeks may be even better from recovery and quality training standpoints. Long runs should be blended with the high-quality workouts described for the marathon and 10K, along with consistent v$\dot{V}O_2$max sessions, in order to produce the highest possible fitness for the race.

About 6 to 8 weeks before the ultramarathon competition, the long run should consist of 15K of warm-up, 30 to 40K at goal ultramarathon pace, and then 10 to 15K of easy jogging.

Evaluating the Practice of Fueling With Fat

An interesting aspect of 100K training and racing is that intakes of *fat* are often recommended during such running. The reasoning behind such recommendations does not at first glance appear to be farfetched. In a 100K race, for example, a runner can be expected to burn well over 6,000 calories. To supply that amount of energy from carbohydrate, a runner would have to eat at a rather prodigious rate during the race. It would require more than

60 bananas to supply all those calories, or around 1 banana every 8 minutes during an 8-hour race. Since fatty foods are more calorie dense, they would give an ultramarathoner's jaws and digestive system a bit of a breather.

Many ultra runners don't have difficulties with the theory of fat feasting and are willing to ingest cakes, cookies, and chocolate bars as they cruise along. Unfortunately, there are a couple of problems with the fat-favoring hypothesis: One is that to burn fat a runner does not really need to *eat fat* during the ultra or prolonged workout; a runner can actually energize his or her efforts simply by relying on the tallow parked in the tummy and thighs even if the body fat in those areas appears to be minimal. Fat is so energy rich that a 120-pound runner with 8 percent body fat could theoretically race for over 150 miles (240 km) using just half of his or her own fat stores for fuel.

Another problem is that when a runner focuses primarily on fat consumption, he or she may not take in enough carbohydrate to keep the leg muscles functioning at a high level. Leg muscles require more oxygen and are less able to support fast running when glycogen levels are low even if there is an abundance of available fat. If the leg muscles become too low in carbohydrate, race pace automatically slows even when rich lodes of fat are moving toward the muscles via the bloodstream.

Many ultra runners like to ingest a 6 to 8 percent carbohydrate, 4 percent medium-chain triglyceride sport drink throughout an ultramarathon, taking in five to six regular swallows every 15 minutes or so. Medium-chain triglycerides are absorbed more quickly and metabolized more efficiently than normal fats, and some research has suggested that their use can improve endurance during races lasting longer than 3.5 hours; unfortunately, studies have indicated that ingesting medium-chain triglycerides during an ultramarathon is also associated with a heightened risk of gastrointestinal problems.[2]

During the race itself, it is also important to ingest some solid foods that are easy to digest and contain rich lodes of carbohydrate: Jelly sandwiches and fruit are good examples. Ultra runners should experiment with various kinds of food before the race to make sure the chosen foods are easily tolerated by the digestive system.

Conclusion

Training for an ultramarathon is much like preparing for a 42-kilometer marathon. The exception is that long-run duration is expanded from about 13 to 20 miles (21-32 km) to 20 to 40 miles (32-64 km); such long running should be carried out every 2 to 3 weeks, not every week. As is the case with shorter distances, optimal fitness should be the goal of training, and thus every effort should be made to maximize the major performance variables. The intense workouts required are blended with long running to produce full readiness for ultramarathon competition. This approach—blending quality training with a long run about every 20 days—will produce superior ultramarathon running capacity and will feature a lower risk of overuse injury than the common pattern of grinding out high volumes of training week after week.

Sports Medicine
for Runners

CHAPTER 39

Running Injuries and Health Risks

Endurance runners are injured at an alarming rate. Scientific studies reveal that about 60 to 65 percent of all endurance runners become injured during an average year. By definition, an injury is a running-related physical problem that is severe enough to force a reduction in training.[1] Research suggests that the injury rate may be even higher—about 90 percent—in runners who are training for a marathon.[2]

Runners miss more workouts because of injury than other types of endurance athletes. Scientific investigations disclose that endurance runners are forced to cancel about 5 to 10 percent of their training sessions due to injury.[3] Injuries are an important cause of training disruption and thus an obstacle to the attainment of optimal running fitness.

Common Types of Injury

Injury to the core—the abdominal area and lower back—is relatively rare in endurance running; most problems occur in the leg or foot, both of which must deal with 85 to 95 repetitive-impact stresses per minute during running. Research suggests that functionally weak parts of the foot and leg can be damaged by the impacts associated with a training session; the damage can accumulate over time as training continues unless adequate recovery is provided. Recovery is defined as the rebuilding of damaged structures between workouts and the replenishment of energy stores within muscles.[4] It is clear that muscular weakness or, more specifically, muscular weakness during the movement patterns associated with running and lack of recovery are risk factors for injury. Most running injuries are thus overuse problems in which a weak area of the leg or foot is subjected to an amount of training that exceeds recovery capacity and thus incurs injury.

There are five anatomical hot spots for overuse running injuries:[1, 5]

1. The knee area (25 to 30 percent of all running injuries)
2. The calf and shin (20 percent of running injuries)

3. The iliotibial band, the sheath of muscle and connective tissue that runs down the outside of the leg from the hip to just below the knee (about 10 percent of injuries)

4. The Achilles tendon (approximately 10 percent of overuse problems)

5. The foot, including the plantar fascia that runs along the bottom of the foot (another 10 percent)

Iliotibial band problems appear to require the longest recovery period following the occurrence of injury compared with the other four areas. In this case, recovery is defined as the adaptive and healing processes that eventually produce a return to normal training. The good news is that approximately 65 percent of runners report that they are running pain free 8 weeks after the initial occurrence of an injury.[6] The bad news is that this finding means that 35 percent of runners are on the shelf for longer than 2 months when an injury occurs, which is an extended recovery process.

Another sobering fact is that the occurrence of an injury is associated with an increased risk of future overuse injury; runners who have previously been injured are more likely to get hurt again over any relevant period compared with runners who have been injury free.[5,7,8] In fact, science reveals that the *absolute best predictor* of running injury is a prior history of injury. About 50 percent of injuries occur in the exact spot where a prior injury had occurred, suggesting that weakness of the injured area is a root cause of running malady.[9]

Despite increased knowledge about training and sports medicine and the advent of sophisticated, allegedly injury-preventing running shoes, rates of overuse running injuries have not lessened over the past 30 years. There is some evidence that the frequency of *knee* injuries among runners has actually increased over the past three decades. This suggests that the fundamental causes of running injury have not been understood or properly addressed by runners and coaches.

Risk Factors for Injuries

The risk factors associated with running injury have been explored in various research studies. Many coaches and runners believe that males have higher injury rates than females, but research indicates that male and female runners have very similar frequencies of injury per hour of training. This is not true among high school cross country runners, however. Research reveals that high school girls running cross country have an injury rate of about 19.6 injuries per 1,000 athletic exposures (AEs), where athletic exposure is defined as a workout or race.[10] This equates to one injury per 51 sessions or races, which would mean that nearly every young woman on a typical team would be likely to suffer injury over the course of a 12-week season that would usually include 60 to 72 workouts or races. Male high school cross country runners have an injury rate of approximately 15 injuries per 1,000 AEs, or one injury per 67 workouts or races. Compared to the general population of runners, high school girls also have significantly higher rates of types of injuries from which recovery takes longer than 15 days.

Training speed, racing speed, running surface (e.g., running on concrete instead of trail or track), and body weight (i.e., having a greater body mass) are often cited as risk factors for running injury, but scientific research indicates that they are not linked with a heightened frequency of problems. There is controversy about whether foot-strike pattern—landing on the heel versus striking the ground with the forefoot or the middle of the foot—has an effect on the risk of running injury.[11]

Newcomers to the sport of endurance running are significantly more likely to be injured compared with experienced runners who have been in training for 3 or more years.[11, 12] This suggests again that running-specific weakness is a risk factor for injury and further implies that many runners would profit from undertaking a systematic program of running-specific strengthening prior to embarking on an actual running program.

The part of the body at risk of injury depends to some extent on preferred race distance. Marathon runners are more likely to develop foot problems such as plantar fasciitis than runners favoring shorter competitions, and middle-distance competitors have higher risks of back and hip difficulties. Sprinters injure their hamstrings much more frequently compared with endurance runners, and sprinters have about double the rate of injury per hour of actual training.[1] For endurance runners, an extremely good injury predictor is simply the distance run during the previous month of training. For example, a runner who engages in high-volume training in November is at significantly increased risk of injury in December.[13]

Among the general running population, the actual rate of injury is about 1 injury per 150 to 200 hours of training; this does not conflict with the high school runner data because high school runners tend to be more inexperienced and lacking in running-specific strength. This means that total training distance is generally a solid predictor of injury: The more miles or kilometers a runner accrues per week, the higher the risk of injury in any relevant time period.[5, 8] The increased risk may be an exponential rather than a linear function of distance: Scientific investigations have found a marked upswing in injury risk when runners logged over 40 miles (64 km) of training per week.[2, 12]

As mentioned, the best predictor of injury is a prior history of injury. Scientific investigations suggest that the second-best predictor may be the number of consecutive days of training without a recovery day.[14] This finding reinforces the idea that recovery days can stop cumulative stress on muscles and connective tissues and promote the kind of rebuilding processes that can keep injuries at bay. A runner who runs 6 miles (9.6 km) per day Monday through Friday and rests on Saturday and Sunday is posting 5 consecutive days of training per week and could probably reduce his or her risk of injury by running just 4 times a week (e.g., Monday, Wednesday, Friday, and Saturday) for 7.5 miles (12.1 km) per session. In the latter case, weekly distance run would be the same as for the 5-day plan, but the number of consecutive days of training would fall from 5 to 2, and injury risk would be reduced because of the extra recovery time. In a similar vein, the serious or elite runner who runs every day could probably reduce the risk of injury—with no negative impact on fitness and quite possibly a positive one—by taking one complete day of recovery each week.

Psychological factors can play a role in producing running injury.[15, 16] Research suggests that individuals who score high on inventories measuring exercise dependency and Type A behavior patterns tend to have higher rates of injury, especially stress fractures of the tibia. The scientific work suggests that runners who depend on regular running to manage stress-related mood states are at greater risk, perhaps because they are more apt to conduct higher-volume training and are more willing to train through pain than runners who do not depend on running for psychological relief.

Marathon training and racing are particularly risky as they are usually performed without appropriate running-specific strength training. About 16 percent of marathon entrants suffer a significant new injury *during the month* preceding their marathons, and approximately 18 percent become injured during the race itself.[17]

Although the information about injury rates among endurance runners is somewhat bleak, there is good news: Research suggests that running injury rates can be cut by at least 25 percent—and probably more.[18] Two effective strategies for cutting the risk of injury are to optimize recovery between workouts and to upgrade running-specific strength. These practices are discussed thoroughly in chapters 14 and 21.

Acute Health Risks Associated With Endurance Running

Although running reduces the risk of heart attack, runners are not immune to cardiac problems. The act of running actually increases the likelihood of a heart-related difficulty *during* the exertion (compared with resting), especially if there are any underlying disorders in the cardiovascular center. Running beyond one's usual limits can also produce an occasionally life-threatening disorder called rhabdomyolysis, in which muscle and kidney function can be drastically disrupted. Running strenuously or for very long periods can also increase the risk of developing an infectious disease, and exercising in a cold or hot environment is associated with various risks.

Risks to the Cardiovascular System

According to legend, one of the first endurance runners in recorded history—Pheidippides—dropped dead shortly after a 21-mile, 1,470-yard run from the plain of Marathon to the agora of Athens in 490 B.C. No autopsy was performed on the Greek messenger, and it is possible that his death could have been caused by dehydration, heat stress, or an unsettling encounter with the god Pan in the mountains north of Athens as described in some early accounts of this first marathon. A more likely cause of death would have been myocardial infarction, or heart attack.

Such exertion-related sudden deaths are not as uncommon as many runners believe. One scientific study suggested that the death rate during marathon running is about one fatality per 50,000 participants,[19] which would make marathon running far less safe than traveling in a commercial airliner. This investigation followed a total of 215,413 runners who competed either in the Marine Corps Marathon from 1976 to 1994 or in the Twin Cities Marathon from 1982 to 1994. Three of these runners died during their races, in all cases after the 15-mile (24 km) point of the competition, and one succumbed shortly after completion of the event. All four deaths were attributed to heart attacks.

Other research suggests that the death rate associated with running might be somewhat lower. One study found that in male runners between the ages of 30 and 64 who have not been diagnosed with heart disease, there is approximately one death per each 800,000 person hours of running or jogging.[20] This finding essentially means that if 800,000 apparently healthy middle-aged males began running the London Marathon, one of them would die during the first hour, another during the second, a third within the third hour, and so on.

There have been eight cardiac deaths at the London Marathon during its 27-year history, a rate of one death per 3.4 years, or one death per 80,000 completed marathons;[21] this is somewhat lower than the 50,000 calculated from the Marine Corps–Twin Cities inquiry. Overall, a male marathon runner is about seven times more likely to die during or shortly after a marathon compared with engaging in nonrunning activities over the same period.[22] Female marathon runners have a significantly lower risk than males, but their actual mortality rate has not been determined.

While such numbers are troubling to some runners, it is important to note that the rate of one death per 800,000 hours means that an individual runner's risk is quite low. A healthy, middle-aged male who runs for 1 hour each day can expect to die while running once every 2,192 years (800,000 hours/365 hours of running per year = 2,192 years). Individuals who run 2 hours per day have a risk of dying while running about once every 1,096 years. Viewed in this light, many endurance runners believe that the risks of cardiac death are acceptably low especially since the *overall* risks of heart disease and myocardial infarction are *diminished* by endurance training.

When cardiac deaths occur during running, they are usually not random events caused by fleeting disturbances in heart function. Postmortem analyses characteristically reveal that something was wrong with the dead runner's heart prior to the fatal run. In the Marine Corps–Twin Cities study, three of the four runners who passed away had atherosclerotic coronary artery

Exercise Stress Tests: Effective Screening?

Findings concerning cardiac problems and death during running suggest that screening marathon entrants for heart troubles prior to the race would be a good idea. For middle-aged and senior male runners, it has been suggested that *exercise stress tests* might detect existing heart disease and thereby decrease the number of deaths on race day. About 34 percent of physicians who run the Boston Marathon believe that individuals should undergo an exercise stress test before beginning a marathon training program.[23]

While this appears to be a reasonable concept, exercise stress tests have their own set of problems. Up to 63 percent of those who fail such exams have completely normal cardiovascular systems.[24] The rate of such false positives can be even higher among endurance runners because of the natural thickening of the heart walls in response to endurance training; this thickening produces changes in EKG signals which can be interpreted as being abnormal.

Stress tests themselves are by no means risk free. The death rate associated with taking a stress test has been estimated to be as high as one per 20,000 tests[25] and as low as one per 500,000 tests.[26] If the true rate is greater than one per 80,000, undergoing a stress test would be more risky than running a marathon, the event for which the stress test is supposed to reduce risk.

Finally, the majority of individuals who die during running because of heart troubles would have completely *normal* stress tests even if the tests were administered the day before death occurred.[27] Some experts believe that stress testing can detect only 20 to 25 percent of the likely victims of sudden, running-related death. The one London Marathon fatality who had undergone a stress test prior to the race had received a negative test result—an all-clear indication to run the competition.[21]

disease (i.e., narrowing of two or three key coronary vessels) even though they had been symptom free prior to their races. The fourth individual had an anatomical defect related to the origin of his left main coronary artery; this runner was also symptom free going into his race.[19] Out of the eight deaths at the London Marathon, five individuals were found during autopsies to have coronary artery disease, and the other three suffered from hypertrophic cardiomyopathy or idiopathic left-ventricular hypertrophy, enlargements of the heart wall.[21] Only one of the eight runners had reported symptoms of heart disease to his physician or family before the race.

Perhaps up to 50 percent of individuals who have heart attacks while running do experience some warning signals during the weeks leading up to the attacks even though they do not necessarily report these symptoms to friends and family,[22] so it is important for endurance runners to monitor themselves closely during training. Premonitory symptoms of heart trouble, for both men and women, include chest discomfort, squeezing sensations in the chest, throat tightness, pain that radiates into the left jaw or left shoulder and arm, unusual fatigue, a sudden unexplained decrease in performance capability, and heart palpitations. Discomfort that appears during running and then disappears afterward is of particular concern.[22]

Rhabdomyolysis

Long training runs, marathon competitions, and ultramarathon running can produce significant damage to leg-muscle cells as the exercise is being conducted. This process of muscle destruction can produce a condition called exertional rhabdomyolysis. In many cases, the damage is moderate and is resolved gradually during the days following the workout or race even when there is considerable harm to the muscle fibers as in a 246K (153 mi) race like the Spartathlon.[28]

When the damage is quite significant, however, potassium can pour out of muscle cells into the blood and surrounding tissues and interfere with normal heart function. Muscle proteins, including a unique protein called myoglobin, are also released into the blood through ruptured muscle membranes. Inside muscle cells, myoglobin acts as a storage depot for oxygen. When it is dropped into the blood in extra quantities as a result of rhabdomyolysis and reaches the kidneys, myoglobin can break down into a toxic chemical called ferrihaemate that injures kidney cells. The damaged renal cells may then fail to eliminate the rising tide of potassium ions.[29]

Myoglobin's accelerated appearance in the kidneys can also lead to myoglobinuria, the presence of excess amounts of myoglobin in the urine. Runners can identify this condition without medical testing; in myoglobinuria, the urine is dark purple, resembling the color of Coca-Cola. Excessive quantities of myoglobin in the kidneys can produce acute renal failure.[30] The risk of kidney failure appears to be increased if the runner is dehydrated or taking analgesic medications, including nonsteroidal antiinflammatory drugs such as ibuprofen.[30]

The risk of serious rhabdomyolysis increases as a function of the distance run. The Comrades Marathon, a 90K (56 mi) race, averages about one case of significant kidney damage per year.[31, 32] The regular marathon distance is not immune to the problem, and deaths from rhabdomyolysis have been reported in association with marathon running.[29]

Risk factors for developing serious rhabdomyolysis during running include having a recent viral illness, experiencing dehydration, using analgesics and nonsteroidal antiinflammatory medications, and engaging in running that is significantly longer than usual. Running in hot weather also appears to increase the risk. The best strategy for avoiding rhabdomyolysis is to stay within usual limits of intensity of volume and to avoid runs that are far more extended than usual. The runner who ordinarily runs 5 miles (8 km) per day and suddenly decides to run a half marathon, especially if it is in the heat, would be a prime candidate for significant rhabdomyolysis.

Running and Infections

Scientific research suggests that strenuous running can worsen the effects of a bacterial or viral infection. Although it has been nearly wiped out through vaccination, the polio virus provides an example of how strenuous exercise worsened an infection. A series of papers published in the *British Medical Journal* in the late 1940s linked intense physical activity with the severity and extent of paralysis suffered by individuals with polio. The research suggested that heavy exertion weakened the resistance of motor neurons in the spinal cord and offered polio viruses increased opportunities to occupy and destroy these muscle-controlling cells.[33]

Many researchers believe that there are risks of extremely serious complications, including death, when a runner trains during an acute viral infection particularly if the infection is produced by a Coxsackie virus.[34] This virus, when unchecked, has a tendency to invade the heart muscle where it can potentially produce arrhythmias. Some reports suggest that athletes who engage in prolonged physical exercise during an upper respiratory system infection have a significantly increased risk of irreversible heart muscle damage.[35]

Given such evidence, Randy Eichner, MD, team physician for the University of Oklahoma, believes that infected runners should perform a "neck check" before deciding to perform a workout.[36] Eichner's neck check works in this way: If symptoms of illness are primarily above the neck (e.g., runny nose, scratchy throat, sneezing), it is reasonable to train at a moderate intensity and increase the level of effort if symptoms ease during the session. If symptoms are below the neck (e.g., fever, aching muscles, mucous-producing cough, vomiting, or diarrhea), resting, not running, is the prudent thing to do.

There is evidence that prolonged running can impair immune system function and increase the risk of illness in *healthy* runners. Marathon-type running produces negative changes in various components of the immune system, including the lungs, skin, upper respiratory tract, mucous linings of the digestive and respiratory systems, peritoneal cavity, blood, and muscles.[37] The numbers and functioning of special immune system cells—natural killer (NK) cells, T lymphocytes, neutrophils, and macrophages—are also altered in response to marathon running or extended training sessions. An open window of immune dysfunction may last from 3 to 72 hours after a marathon or prolonged workout, thereby increasing the risk of infection.[37]

Various strategies have been proposed to thwart the negative changes in the immune system that can occur as a result of prolonged running. The ingestion of carbohydrate-containing beverages (i.e., sport drinks) during extended running may be the most effective strategy.[37] Intake of such drinks seems to control the production of stress hormones that are linked to increased susceptibility to illness. Unfortunately, consumption of sport drinks is unable to control the suppression of antibody production and inhibition of NK cell and T lymphocyte activity that is common after challenging exertion. Marketers of sport supplements have promoted the use of glutamine, vitamin C, and bovine colostrum as immune-system boosters, but there is no scientific evidence that the use of such agents actually decreases the risk of illness in runners.[38]

Researchers have looked for other ways to preserve immune function during prolonged running. Workouts lasting less than 60 minutes have a smaller negative effect on the immune system than longer sessions,[39] so it would appear that higher quality training, with an emphasis on recovery days, would be better for immune system function than repeated days of prolonged workouts. Mental stress, inadequate intake of calories, quick weight loss, and poor hygiene also impair the immune system, so they should be avoided, as much as possible, during periods of challenging training.[39]

Running in Hot Environments

In a hot or warm, humid environment, running capacity can be dramatically reduced,[40] and the risk of hyperthermia induced by heat stress can increase. Hyperthermia is defined as an abnormally large—and potentially damaging—increase in core body temperature. Hyperthermia, and quite possibly even a too-rapid rate of increase in core temperature, can cause the central nervous system to reduce neural drive (i.e., neural output to muscles), thus lowering running velocity and overall intensity of effort.[41] Nausea, dizziness, a loss of rational thinking ability, and a reduction in sweat rate can occur once core temperature surpasses 40 to 41 degrees Centigrade (104-105.8°F; cellular damage, especially to the nervous system, can take place at core temperatures above 43 to 44 degrees Centigrade (109.4-111.2°F). There is little evidence to suggest that older runners are at greater risk of hyperthermia compared with younger athletes.[42, 43]

The key strategy for preventing hyperthermia is to avoid running for any extended period of time in an environment to which one has not become physiologically adapted. Physiological adaptations to exercising in the heat include advanced rates of sweating, more-efficient sweating with sweat emitted more prominently from sweat glands all over the body rather than from smaller areas such as the arm pits, a quicker onset of sweating during exercise, and re-distribution of blood flow to augment blood flow to the skin. These adaptations promote the maintenance of a sub-40-degree core body temperature during hot-weather running, but the magnitude of the responses depend on the environment in which training is conducted and take time to be produced. For example, it takes 7 to 14 days to be acclimatized to 85-degree weather, and that acclimatization process must include daily, slowly progressing training at 85 degrees. Working out regularly at 75 degrees, even though such conditions might be warmer than usual, does not provide adequate acclimatization for hotter conditions.

Running in Cold Environments

Running in a cold environment for an extended period of time can increase a runner's risk of hypothermia, a physiologically significant decrease in core body temperature. In such a situation, a runner's rate of heat production during running simply cannot keep up with the rate of heat loss to the environment, and body temperature steadily falls. Unfortunately, a drop in core temperature can impair judgment, leading to an especially heightened risk of cold injury.

Heightened levels of body fat do not enhance running performance, but they do decrease the risk of cold injury during running.[44] For this reason, female runners usually tolerate cold temperatures better than males and have a lower risk of hypothermia during cold weather running.[45]

Loren Holmes/Accent Alaska.com

▶ Women tolerate cold-weather running more effectively than men and have a lower risk of hypothermia.

Risk factors for hypothermia include reduced air temperature, wetness of clothing and skin, wind, exhaustion, sudden slowing of running pace, and the appearance of clouds on a previously sunny day. Many runners are surprised to learn that hypothermia can occur under relatively warm conditions. For example, even on a relatively warm spring day a sudden chilling rain can produce hypothermia relatively quickly, especially if one stops running.

The best ways to reduce the risk of hypothermia are to wear adequate clothing with wicking properties that minimize skin moisture, carry a waterproof jacket on days when there is a risk of rain, and avoid longer than usual runs under cold conditions. Longer runs that may require a slowing in pace or even stopping because of fatigue can heighten the risk of hypothermia. On windy cold days, it is better to go out against the wind and come back with the wind. This will help prevent slowing down during the second half of the run.

Conclusion

Running improves fitness and overall health, but it also carries with it certain risks. A key problem is the currently high likelihood of overuse injury. The risk of getting hurt as a result of running training can be lowered by upgrading running-specific strength training and enhancing recovery processes. Chapter 40 explores some techniques used for lowering the likelihood of running injuries.

The adoption of running as a long-term, almost daily form of physical activity lowers the risk of heart attack, but the specific act of running, either during a workout or race, is linked with a momentarily increased risk of cardiovascular mortality; thus, runners should be acutely aware of symptoms and signals of cardiac disorder and work closely with their primary care physicians when such warning signs appear. Periods of extended or intense running may also increase the chances of rhabdomyolysis and infection, but these potential consequences of exercise can be minimized when a runner trains prudently, increasing volume and intensity of exertion only moderately from session to session. The many positive health effects of running will be outlined in chapter 41.

Finally, running in hot and cold environments increases the risk of hyperthermia and hypothermia, respectively, but the risks of such disorders can be lowered through the use of special training techniques and strategic adjustments of clothing. Acclimatization to warmer weather requires progressively prolonged training sessions carried out under the warmer temperature or increased humidity conditions. To avoid hypothermia when exercising in cold weather, do not expose wet skin to suddenly cooler air, do not slow down in cold weather, and do not get exposed to sudden bursts of wind during an extended run.

CHAPTER 40

Prevention of Running Injuries

Training is the primary producer of running injury. For any individual runner, there is a level of training beyond which injury will occur. This injury threshold varies dramatically between runners:[1] An elite Kenyan runner might surpass his or her ability to stay healthy with a weekly load of 25 quality miles (40 km) and 100 total miles (161 km) while a novice runner could cross over the injury threshold with just 10 total miles (16 km) and 1 quality mile (1.6 km) per week. The limit undoubtedly rises for each runner as strength and fitness improve. To avoid injury during a progressive training program in which volume or intensity are increasing, every runner must find ways to lift the limit as high as possible and avoid crossing over the threshold. Runners should use mechanisms that prevent training stresses from outpacing adaptive processes in muscles, tendons, ligaments, cartilage, and bones.

Evaluating the Effectiveness of Flexibility

Despite the popular perception that enhanced flexibility helps to limit the risk of running-related injury, scientific research does not support this connection. One inquiry found that both high and low levels of flexibility were associated with a greater likelihood of injury in individuals undergoing strenuous training.[2] A key problem in this area of research is that there are many ways to measure flexibility. It can be

- static (depending on the end of range of motion [ROM] at joint),
- dynamic passive (a measure of stiffness or compliance of the muscles and connective tissues when they are at rest),
- dynamic active (stiffness or compliance of the muscles when they are attempting to contract),[3] or
- running specific (the extent of range of motion of the ankle, knee, and hip joints during the act of running).

Running-specific flexibility is seldom measured even though it would appear to be the key flexibility variable associated with running injury, and the links between the other forms of flexibility and running-specific flexibility are unknown. It would be possible, for example, for a runner to have high static flexibility (the most commonly measured variable) and yet run quite stiffly. Overall, there is no scientifically based prescription for flexibility training for running, and no convincing assertions can be made about the link between flexibility and running injury.[3]

Stretching is often touted as an injury reducer, and research reveals that it can expand static flexibility.[3] Given the uncertain relationship between flexibility and injury, however, it is not surprising that research concerning the effects of stretching on injury has produced mixed results. Two studies have linked stretching with a reduced risk of lower-limb injury. In one of these studies, preworkout stretching correlated with a higher chance of injury while postworkout stretching was associated with a lower risk.[4] In the second investigation, the performance of three stretching sessions per week for the hamstrings cut the hamstring injury rate by about 42 percent over a 13-week period during the basic training of army recruits.[5]

Four other inquiries have found that stretching has no impact on injury rate;[6-9] in three of these studies, stretching was conducted immediately before training sessions. It is possible that stretching, especially when it is performed postworkout, might have a small effect on reducing injury rates among runners, but this effect is often swamped by training excesses that overcome stretching's protective action. Stretching might raise the injury threshold a little way but not enough to prevent injury from occurring in the majority of runners who stretch. If this is true, it would explain why stretching is seldom linked with protection against injury in scientific studies.

In one study, 159 Dutch runners were taught how to warm up, cool down, and stretch effectively while a second group of 167 similar runners received no instruction in these activities at all.[9] The warm-up and cool-down consisted of 6 minutes of very light running and 3 minutes of muscle-relaxing exercises; the stretching was carried out twice a day for 10 minutes at a time, with an emphasis on increasing the flexibility of the hamstrings, quadriceps, and calf muscles. Over a 4-month period, injury rates were identical in the two groups, averaging about one injury per 200 hours of running.

A subsequent study actually found that preworkout stretching was linked with a *higher* rate of injury compared with no presession stretching while postworkout stretching was associated with lower injury rates.[10] The mechanisms responsible for these findings are uncertain although it is certainly possible that stretching after training optimally prepares muscles and tendons for the quiescent, or rest, period that generally follows workouts. There is also some evidence from research conducted with chickens that postworkout stretching increases amino acid uptake by muscles and consequent protein synthesis, effects that should promote better recovery.[11]

Stretching after workouts is still a good idea, however. It relaxes muscles for the quiescent activities that follow training sessions, and there is evidence that stretching may improve carbohydrate uptake and glycogen synthesis in muscles.

Eccentric Strengthening Versus Flexibility Training

Hypothetically, flexibility training could be excellent for reducing the risk of muscle damage. It could extend the point at which muscles stop elongating in response to strain and thus delay reaching the point at which muscles begin to be torn apart in response to the forces being placed on them.[12] To find out whether flexibility training or eccentric strengthening could do a better job of preventing training-related injury, researchers from the Norwegian School of Sport Science in Oslo and the University of Iceland in Reykjavik worked with a large group of athletes.[13] For the research, male soccer teams were recruited from the highest-level Icelandic and Norwegian leagues. About 14 teams from Iceland participated in the study over a 4-year period, and 14 Norwegian teams took part during a 3-year research period; the number of players varied from 18 to 24 athletes per team.

The flexibility training includes a variety of traditional and partner-assisted stretches. The eccentric strength-training program involved one simple exercise: the Nordic hamstring drill. This exercise is performed as follows: Two partners kneel one behind the other and facing the same way. The front partner keeps the torso straight, staying extended at the back and hips. The back partner leans over just enough to hold onto the feet of the front partner. The front partner leans forward with a smooth movement, keeping the back and hips extended and working to resist forward falling for as long as possible by activating the hamstring muscles. While the front partner descends, the back partner maintains pressure on the front partner's lower legs or ankles to keep the front partner from falling over. When the front partner's hands and chest reach the ground, he or she forcefully pushes up and back with the hands to return to the kneeling position with the torso upright.

A key progression in the study with this exercise was to withstand the forward fall for a longer period of time; another was to increase the speed of the starting phase of forward motion. In addition, the partner in back added difficulty to the exercise over time by pushing on the backs of the front partner's shoulders during the forward movement while the front partner resisted this additional pressure. Three sets of 12, 10, and 8 repetitions, respectively, were used per training session, and the Nordic hamstring training was carried out about three times per week.

During the subsequent season, flexibility training did not reduce the risk of hamstring injury at all while the eccentric strength training significantly cut the rate of hamstring malady. Overall, the rate of hamstring injury was 65 percent lower among the teams that employed the eccentric strength program compared with teams not using eccentric strength training. Hamstring injuries that did occur were also less severe when eccentric strength training had been used. This study suggests that the regular performance of challenging eccentric exercises can be protective against injury.

Such a finding is not overly surprising since eccentric actions appear to be the most stressful types of actions on the hamstrings during running. Electromyographic (EMG) analyses during high-speed running have shown that hamstring muscle activity is highest during the late swing phase of gait when the hamstrings are working *eccentrically* to decelerate the forward movement of the leg.[14] Unfortunately, few endurance runners conduct systematic eccentric strengthening for their leg muscles, perhaps explaining why injury rates are so high during endurance training. As outlined in chapter 39, about 65 percent of endurance runners sustain a significant injury during a year of training, and as many as 93 percent of *marathon* runners are hurt over the course of a year.

In a related study, Roald Bahr and four colleagues from the Oslo Sports Trauma Research Center at the Norwegian University of Sport and Physical Education and the Stabaek Clinic in Bekkestua, Norway, researched the question of whether eccentric strengthening would be better than concentric strengthening for purposes of reducing the risk of injury. In contrast with eccentric actions, concentric activities involve force production and simultaneous shortening by muscles; eccentric actions involve force creation and synchronous elongation. Bahr and colleagues worked with 22 competitive soccer players, 10 of whom were from the first-division national club Stabaek Fotball and 12 of whom were from second- through fourth-division teams. At the beginning of the study, all athletes underwent basic tests of hamstring flexibility and strength as well as quadriceps muscle forcefulness. None of the 22 players were suffering from prior hamstring strains at the start of the study.[15]

The 22 athletes were divided into two equal groups: a traditional hamstring curl (HC) group and a Nordic hamstring (NH) group. Both groups then began a 10-week training program. The HC athletes performed their hamstring curls on a traditional hamstring curl machine. During the eccentric phase (i.e., the lowering of the weight), the athletes used as little effort as possible, providing minimal resistance to the dropping of the weight.

The Nordic hamstring exercise was the same one used in the Norwegian School of Sport Science study described earlier. Each group completed about 23 hamstring workouts during the 10-week training period, and there was no difference in the total amount of other training carried out, including soccer training, strength training, and endurance running. Postworkout soreness remained fairly minimal with no real difference between groups—a plus for the NH athletes since eccentric exercise is often linked with the invocation of muscle pain—and there were no changes in hamstring flexibility in either the NH or HC subjects.

Over the course of the 10 weeks, the HC athletes did achieve significant gains in strength *while performing concentric hamstring curl exercises*, boosting their 10-rep maximal resistance to 45 kilograms (99 lb). However, when the two groups were compared for maximal torque during eccentric actions—the ones believed to cause most hamstring injuries—the NH athletes were absolutely dominant. In fact, there were no improvements at all in eccentric strength for the HC players while the Nordic hamstring subjects exhibited a major increase in eccentric strength. The NH athletes boosted maximal *eccentric* hamstring torque by 11 percent while HC participants failed to get any better.

This is an example of mode specificity, which means that if athletes train their muscles using eccentric activities, their eccentric strength will improve, but they should not expect gains in concentric strength. Likewise, focusing on concentric actions tends not to lead to much improvement in eccentric strength. Overall, the gain in strength is specific to the mode of muscle activity. That is probably why a separate study carried out with college students produced results similar to those found by Bahr and his colleagues. In the college research, 12 workouts that revolved around eccentric hamstring strengthening (two training sessions per week for 6 weeks) produced significantly greater gains in peak eccentric hamstring torque compared with the same number of workouts stressing concentric work for the hamstrings.[16]

Improving Eccentric Muscle Strength

There is a general consensus in the scientific community that a lack of muscular strength increases the risk of running injury,[17-19] and research suggests that increasing the *eccentric* strength of key muscles in the legs is one of the best ways to raise the injury threshold.[20] Eccentric activities, in which muscles are forced to elongate while they are simultaneously attempting to shorten, tend to be more damaging to muscles than concentric and isometric actions, and eccentric muscular activity is quite pronounced during running. For example, the hamstring muscles in each leg are exposed to eccentric strain approximately 90 times per minute as they attempt to control forward swing of the leg. The hamstrings become active and pull back on the leg as it moves forward during swing, but the leg moves ahead nonetheless, producing significant eccentric strain; the hams are literally pulled apart as they attempt to shorten.

Eccentric strengthening of the hamstrings should help them handle these tearing actions by enhancing neural control of hamstring eccentric activity and by fortifying individual muscle cells within the hamstrings, thus boosting their resistance to damage. A lack of eccentric strength should heighten the risk of injury. To upgrade eccentric strength of the hamstrings, runners should carry out the bicycle leg swings exercises first discussed in chapter 14 and addressed further in this chapter.

The other key muscle groups in the legs are also exposed to eccentric forces. The calf muscles (gastrocnemius and soleus) work eccentrically when their associated ankle goes through dorsiflexion during the stance phase of gait, and the quadriceps muscles in the front of the thigh work eccentrically during stance as the knee flexes naturally. The muscles on the bottom of the foot also work eccentrically during stance as the arch flattens after impact with the ground. Eccentric strengthening should thus have a wide-ranging impact on injury reduction, providing protection against many or all of the common running-related leg injuries.

To be most effective at preventing injury, exercises that feature eccentric actions for key muscle groups should be running specific. They should replicate the actions those muscles undergo during the gait cycle of running. Such exercises are not very difficult to design. The running-specific strengthening exercises described in chapter 14 all emphasize eccentric actions of the leg muscles during running-relevant movements. The bicycle leg swing (see chapter 14) is simple in conception but incorporates the exact kind of eccentric stress that is placed on the hamstrings during running; this exercise intensifies and expands that stress to produce a significant upswing in eccentric strength of the hamstrings.

Science and the 10 Percent Rule

One of the most popular strategies in the running community for preventing injury is the use of the 10 percent rule, which states that running volume should never increase by more than 10 percent from one week to the next. There is a certain logic to this dogma since it recognizes that an injury threshold exists and that runners should be wary about soaring above the threshold with their training plans. Ten percent would appear to be a reasonable governor of training-volume expansion since it permits training progressions to occur in seemingly reasonable increments.

Unfortunately, no scientific research has documented the benefits of the 10 percent dictum. The rule also has obvious problems. First, it focuses only on the distance run without taking training intensity, including running speed or percent $\dot{V}O_2$max into account. Increasing volume by 10 percent from one week to the next while reducing intensity or holding it constant should place a different total stress on the leg muscles and connective tissues compared with augmenting volume by 10 percent and boosting intensity by 5 percent. It is possible that intensity should be temporarily decreased whenever volume increases although there has been little research in this area.

The 10 percent rule also fails to take into account workout types and may be overly conservative in some cases. An athlete who runs 5 miles (8 km) per workout three times a week without a hint of injury could probably boost volume by 20 percent (i.e., from 15 to 18 miles [24-29 km] per week) without significantly increasing injury risk by adding in a fourth workout of 3 miles (5 km) on another day of the week. In this case, the 10 percent rule is too conservative. The same athlete might run into trouble if he or she changed the schedule to two workouts of 9 miles (14 km) each per week even though the percent expansion of training volume would be the same. The 9-mile runs might have a more damaging effect on the legs because of the number of miles run in a state of significant fatigue than the combination of 5- and 3-mile sessions.

Another factor that should be considered is that expanding from 10 to 11 miles (16-18 km) per week probably is much easier to do without raising injury risk than increasing training from 50 to 55 miles (81-89 km) per week even though both moves involve a 10-percent change. The latter would add 5 miles per week—and thus more than 5,000 additional impacts with the ground per week—to legs already fairly heavily stressed by training. However, it could also be argued that the legs accustomed to running 50 miles (81 km) per week would be stronger and would thus be more prepared for the advancement compared with legs that can handle only 10 weekly miles (16 km).

Anecdotal evidence suggests that a too-rapid advance in training can increase the risk of injury dramatically. Nevertheless, the 10 percent rule appears to be too general and unscientific to be used successfully by the majority of runners. The rate at which a runner can increase his or her level of training is highly individualized, and it is up to each runner to recognize personal limits. Listening to one's body and reducing volume or intensity at the first sign of lower-limb discomfort is an unscientific yet sound principle to follow.

Massage and Other Options for Injury Prevention

Studies of running injuries imply that other practices in addition to eccentric strength training should also decrease the likelihood of running-related injury. As pointed out in chapter 21, improved recovery—including more sleep, better restoration of muscle glycogen between workouts, more rest days per week, and fewer consecutive days of training—is associated with a significantly lower risk of injury. Avoiding high-volume training, especially programs that soar above 40 miles (64 km) of running per week, is connected with less injury. No specific style or technique of running (e.g., the pose method or chi running) has been linked with a reduction in injury rate.

Massage is another practice that receives a lot of attention. Many runners and coaches believe that regular massage therapy reduces muscular soreness and tightness and thus helps to limit or prevent overuse injuries. Elite Kenyan runners in particular make massage a nearly mandatory component of their recovery regimes, which also include ample sleep, postworkout glycogen replenishment, and a high-carbohydrate diet; most top Kenyan runners believe that massage keeps the injury bug at bay.

What does science say about massage and injury? There is strong evidence that massage reduces muscle pain after intense or prolonged workouts, and recent research indicates that the therapeutic intervention can produce a number of positive effects on muscle cell functioning. In a study carried

---

Icing for Pain Relief?

Although no one believes that icing can prevent injuries, many coaches and runners have faith in the notion that icing, or cryotherapy, *is* an effective method of treatment for muscles and connective tissues that have already been damaged, and that the intervention not only reduces pain but can also speed recovery. Research in this area is far from comprehensive and varies significantly in methodology and overall quality, but it appears that cryotherapy can be a fairly effective pain reducer for a variety of injuries.

However, there is very little evidence to suggest that icing leads to enhancement of range of motion or to improvement in muscular function following injury.[21] In addition, excessive use of cryotherapy can occasionally produce nerve damage to iced areas of the body.[22] Overall, icing seems to have little impact on the duration or quality of recovery following an overuse running injury.

---

out at McMaster University, massage decreased inflammation and reduced the concentration of heat shock protein that is synthesized in muscles under stress in exercise-damaged muscles of young male subjects.[23] Furthermore, massage was able to stimulate mitochondrial biogenesis, the enhanced production of the key energy-producing structures inside muscle fibers.

A separate inquiry carried out in China with animals has demonstrated that massage following muscle damage can increase the production of key proteins that are part of a muscle fiber's cytoskeleton, which is the arrangement of force-producing structures and proteins inside the cell. The increase in these key proteins should help muscle cells restore themselves following damage.[24]

Despite popular perceptions, massage does not diminish lactate concentrations in muscles nor should it: Lactate is actually an important source of muscular energy. It appears that elite Kenyans are on the right track: Massage produces a number of effects that should help limit muscle trauma and promote recovery.

Conclusion

Running-specific strength training, with an emphasis on movements that mimic the mechanics of running and thus have large eccentric components, is a key way to progress more quickly—and farther—with training without getting hurt; it thus represents an important mechanism for injury prevention. Optimal recovery is also crucial for injury avoidance, and postworkout stretching may also help prevent injuries. Gradual progressions in training probably temper the likelihood of injury compared with more aggressive increases in the volume and intensity of workouts. Other traditional injury-fighting strategies, including preworkout stretching and flexibility training, appear to have little impact on the risk of injury while running.

CHAPTER 41

Health Benefits
of Running

Runners can expect to live about 5 years longer than couch potatoes.[1] As epidemiologist Ralph Paffenbarger once said, "Each hour of running adds about two hours to a runner's life." A key reason for running's salutary effect on longevity is that involvement in the sport reduces the risk of dying from the two major causes of mortality in developed countries: cardiovascular disease and cancer. In addition, running decreases the risks of developing lifespan-limiting disorders such as type 2 diabetes and high blood pressure; running also has positive effects on mental health and rates of obesity, and it limits the likelihood of becoming disabled.

Lowering the Risk
of Coronary Heart Disease

The Health Professionals' Follow-Up Study, carried out with 44,452 men between 1986 and 1998, found that there was an inverse relationship between running and the risk of coronary heart disease (CHD).[2] In this research, there were 1,700 new cases of CHD over the course of 475,755 person years. Men who ran for just an hour or more per week, an average of only 8.6 minutes per day, had a 42 percent reduction in the risk of developing CHD compared with individuals who did not run at all. Strength training and rowing also produced reductions in CHD risk, but they tended to be smaller than the benefits associated with running.

A separate investigation, the Harvard Alumni Health Study, also found an inverse link between running and cardiovascular disease.[3] The Harvard Study followed 12,516 middle-aged and older men (mean age 57.7 years, range 39-88 years) from 1977 through 1993; 2,135 cases of CHD occurred during this time period. Men who ran just 10 to 20 miles (16-32 km) per week enjoyed a 10 percent reduction in CHD risk; running more than 20 miles (32 km) weekly cut the likelihood of CHD by 20 percent.

Research indicates that running is also protective against CHD in women. In research carried out with 39,372 healthy female health professionals aged

45 years and older between 1992 and 1999, jogging or walking from 6 to 15 miles per week (10-24 km) trimmed the risk of CHD by about 45 percent.[4]

Importance of Total Energy Expenditure

The Harvard research revealed that workout duration was not an independent factor associated with CHD risk: Men who carried out longer workouts were not at lower risk of CHD than individuals whose training sessions were shorter as long as total energy expended during exercise was similar between the groups.[5] To express this in another way, accumulated shorter sessions were just as valuable as longer sessions from the standpoint of preventing CHD as long as *total* distance was comparable.

The total amount of energy expended during running and other activities appears to be a key factor that protects against CHD: The more energy expended, the lower the risk even when the diet is somewhat atherogenic (i.e., high in saturated fat or low in antioxidants). This conclusion is supported by analyses of members of the Maasai tribe in Tanzania who follow a diet high in saturated fat and low in carbohydrates and antioxidants and yet have normal blood lipids and little evidence of cardiovascular disease.[6] Maasai expend about 2,565 calories per day *above* their basal caloric requirements compared with an excess of just 1,500 calories in rural Bantu people who live near the Maasai and consume a nonatherogenic, high-carbohydrate, low-fat diet. Both groups have similar blood lipid profiles despite the Maasai's preference for saturated fat.

It is important to note, however, that while running reduces the risk of CHD, it does not provide complete protection from the disease. Some marathon runners mistakenly believe that their protracted training programs make the probability of CHD infinitesimal.[7] In a study carried out with 36 marathon runners who had suffered heart attacks, Timothy Noakes of the University of Cape Town found the average age of the stricken athletes to be 43.8 (range of 18-70) and mean marathon performance to be 3:28 (range of 2:33-4:28). Average training distance was 50 miles (81 km) per week, but several of the heart attack victims compiled 95 to 100 miles (153-161 km) of training weekly, and 16 of the 36 had finished at least one 90K (56 mi) ultramarathon.[8] Nineteen of the 36 marathoners had received warnings of heart trouble prior to the actual attacks but had basically ignored them. The stricken runners tended to have a family history of heart disease, high LDL cholesterol levels, and high blood pressure although some of the individuals had none of these factors. It is clear that running effectively reduces the risk of CHD but is not an absolute barrier to the development of the disease.

Scientific investigations indicate that running may be helpful for those individuals *already suffering* from CHD. In an inquiry carried out with 2,137 men and 1,367 women with preexisting CHD, jogging just once a week was connected with a 20 percent reduction in the risk of death for men and a 32 percent drop for women compared with no exercise at all.[9] Exercising more frequently further diminished the chances of dying from CHD.

Impact on Cholesterol Levels

One of the mechanisms by which running reduces the risk of CHD is the elevation of HDL, or good, cholesterol that is usually produced by regular training; other mechanisms include a reduction in blood pressure, drop in weight, and reduction in the blood's tendency to form clots. Runners naturally wonder if there is an optimal level of running that heightens HDL cholesterol to the greatest possible extent.

Research suggests that there is no clear link between running volume and HDL. In one study, 56 distance runners between the ages of 20 and 56 whose average HDL cholesterol level was 63 mg/dl (3.19 mmol/L) were divided into two groups: those whose mean HDL cholesterol concentration was 73 (HIGH) and those whose average level was just 53 (LOW).[10] Running volume was absolutely equivalent between these two groups. Members of both groups had also been running for about the same amount of time (6 years). Therefore, total distance and time spent running could not have accounted for the HDL cholesterol disparities.

Paul Thompson, one of the principal investigators in this study, believes that it is very difficult to predict the effect training distance will have on HDL cholesterol.[11] One investigation found that jogging just 11 miles (18 km) per week produced dramatic increases in HDL cholesterol in some individuals, but running 40 miles (64 km) per week had little effect on cholesterol in other athletes.[12] Genetic factors may account for some of the differences in HDL cholesterol concentrations observed in runners.[13]

Role of Training Intensity

Scientific research has been somewhat unclear whether the intensity of running training has a specific role to play in protecting against CHD. If two runners cover 25 miles (40 km) of running per week but one runs at an average intensity of 85 percent of $\dot{V}O_2$max and the other completes his or her workouts at 65 percent of $\dot{V}O_2$max, the higher-intensity runner should be fitter and therefore would expect to have greater protection against heart disease. The higher-intensity runner should also expend somewhat more calories per week during training partly because of greater postexercise caloric burns associated with the faster training. As mentioned, total calories expended on a weekly basis is an inverse predictor of CHD risk.

Definitive work in this area is lacking especially among well-trained runners, but there is evidence to support the idea that intense exercise provides more protection from CHD risk compared with low-intensity work. In the Harvard Alumni Health Study,[3] individuals who expended more than 400 calories per week during vigorous activity, including running and lap swimming, had a lower risk of death; individuals who burned more than 400 weekly calories during nonvigorous activities (e.g., slow walking, yard work, gardening) did not enjoy increased protection. The Harvard Study only compared vigorous with nonvigorous activities, however; it did not look at the effects of changes in intensity within specific vigorous pursuits such as running.

A Swiss study did suggest that higher-intensity running might produce greater protection against CHD than slower-paced exertion. In the Swiss research, one group of men ran three times a week for about 30 minutes per workout at an average intensity of 75 percent of $\dot{V}O_2$max while a second group trained four times a week for 30 minutes per session at a work level of just 50 percent of $\dot{V}O_2$max.[1] The lower-intensity group ran for 30 minutes more each week than the higher-intensity runners; energy expenditures were not actually measured. After 6 months, only the members of the higher-intensity group displayed a relationship between amount of exercise and HDL cholesterol concentrations: The more running the higher-intensity individuals completed, the higher their HDL cholesterol levels. No one experienced a cardiovascular event during this research, but loftier HDL cholesterol concentrations should protect against CHD over the long run.

Decreasing the Risk of Cancer

In addition to its strong protective effect against coronary heart disease, there is also compelling evidence that regular running lowers the likelihood of certain types of cancer, including malignancies of the blood, bladder, eye, mouth, esophagus, stomach, colon, rectum, pancreas, thyroid gland, lungs, breasts, ovaries, uterus, cervix, and vagina.

The Harvard Alumni Study already mentioned in this chapter uncovered a link between exercise and the overall risk of various forms of cancer.[14] In the Harvard Study, individuals who burned more than 2,000 calories per week while running, the equivalent of running about 20 weekly miles (32 km), or engaging in other vigorous activities, had a lower death rate from cancer compared with those who expended fewer than 500 calories in weekly activity. This result was not an artifact of lower rates of smoking in the more active population.

Female Runners and Cancer

Research indicates that *premenopausal* women who run for about 3.25 hours per week (approximately 28 minutes per day) experience a 23 percent lower risk of breast cancer compared with women whose activity levels are lower.[15] Scientific studies suggest that the protective effect of running and other forms of physical activity against breast cancer are even stronger among *postmenopausal* women, with the drop in risk probably greater than 30 percent.[16] Even women who *wait* until they are in their 50s to take up running or other endurance sports enjoy a 27 percent reduction in breast cancer incidence as a result of their activity as long as they exercise fairly vigorously.[17]

Research suggests that there are several mechanisms by which regular running could decrease the risk of breast cancer. A key factor appears to be that running maintains a beneficial level of body leanness. Leaner women tend to produce a form of estrogen that is less potent and less likely to stimulate uterine and breast cells to divide actively. Since cell division is decreased, there is less chance that a group of cells will become malignant and begin spreading through surrounding breast tissue.[18]

To learn more about exercise and cancer in women, Rose Frisch and her colleagues at the Harvard School of Public Health monitored 5,398 living alumnae from 10 colleges and universities whose graduating classes spanned the time period from 1925 to 1981. Active alumnae had participated in track, cross country, basketball, crew, fencing, swimming, or tennis while in college and tended to exercise regularly after college. The runners within this active group averaged about 10 miles of running (16 km) per week. In contrast, approximately half of the 5,398 females had not participated in athletics during their college days and were significantly less likely to exercise regularly after college.[19]

Frisch and co-workers found that the nonactive women had about twice the risk of breast cancer and 2.5 times the likelihood of cancer of the reproductive system, including cancer of the ovaries, uterus, cervix, and vagina, than the active women. Family histories of cancer were similar between the groups, so the disparate rates of cancer were quite probably the result of activity levels not genetic factors.

Frisch and her fellow scientists found that the active women had a reduced risk of cancers unrelated to the reproductive system, too. Nonactive women experienced twice the frequency of lymphoma, leukemia, myeloma, Hodgkin's disease, and thyroid cancer than runners and other active women. One out of every 550 nonactive women suffered from cancer of the bladder, lung, eye, or mouth while very few of the active women developed such cancers. One out of 550 nonactive women contracted cancer of the digestive system (i.e., esophagus, stomach, colon, or rectum), the frequency of which was zero in the active women. Among all cancers, only the rates of melanoma and skin cancer were similar in the two groups; in no case did runners have a higher incidence of malignancy.[20]

Other research supports Frisch's findings. An inquiry that monitored the health of 25,000 women workers in the state of Washington between 1972 and 1979 discovered that physically active women, including runners, had significantly lower rates of both breast and colon cancer compared with nonactive females.[21]

Male Runners and Prostate Cancer

Strenuous running programs tend to reduce androgen levels in male runners, and thus the maintenance of a challenging training plan over extended periods of time should decrease the risk of prostate cancer. Cancerous prostate cells tend to grow and divide more quickly when testosterone levels are high.

Research concerning the effects of running on the risk of prostate cancer has produced mixed results, however. One investigation that followed 430,000 men in the state of Washington from 1950 to 1979 found no reduction at all in the rate of prostatic cancer with increased activity.[21] An analysis of 56,683 former Harvard and University of Pennsylvania students discovered that higher levels of physical activity were associated with a reduced risk of colon cancer but were linked with *higher* rates of prostate cancer.[22]

The most recent evidence suggests that running and other forms of activity are connected with a lower rate of serious prostate cancer. In a prospective study carried out in Norway over a 17-year period with a cohort of 29,110 Norwegian men, the frequency and duration of exercise were inversely associated with the risk of *advanced* prostatic cancer. Those men who engaged in the highest category of physical exercise, including running, had a 36 percent reduction in the risk of advanced prostate cancer and a 33 percent drop in the likelihood of dying from the disease. Interestingly, there was no association between physical activity and the overall risk of prostate cancer, suggesting that running and other endurance sports do not block the initiation of prostate cancer but are associated with preventing it from becoming invasive and deadly.[23]

Colon Cancer

The link between running and a reduced risk of colon cancer is extremely strong; numerous studies have documented this relationship.[18] Research carried out with 488,720 participants in the NIH-AARP (National Institutes of Health and the American Association of Retired Persons) Diet and Health Study who were 50 to 71 years at baseline were monitored for more than 7 years. The study found that running or engaging in other sustained exercise five times per week lowered the risk of colon cancer by about 21 percent in men and the likelihood of rectal cancer by 26 percent in men; there was a trend for exercise to decrease colon cancer risk in women as well, but it was not statistically significant.[24] Low-, moderate-, and vigorous-intensity exercise provided protection for the men as long as the running or other form of exertion was carried out five or more times per week with a weekly total duration of 7 hours or greater, which is fairly high; just 8.6 minutes per day of running has been linked with a reduction in CHD risk.

Exciting recent research with laboratory rats indicates that participation in a regular running program actually changes gene expression in the mucosal inner lining of the colon, decreasing the expression of an array of genes and increasing the transcription of several others.[25, 26] The betain-homocysteine methyltransferase 2 (BHMT2) gene is one of the key bits of genetic code suppressed by running. Repression of this gene is thought to contribute to a decreased risk of developing colon cancer.

Science also suggests that prolonged running may protect the colon when it is exposed to carcinogens. In a study carried out with rats that had consumed 1,2-dimethylhydrazine (DMH), a known colon cancer inducer, the animals that ran at low intensities for 120 minutes per day, 5 days per week, had significantly fewer aberrant crypt foci (i.e., clusters of cells that are the precursors to colon malignancies) after 4 weeks compared with the rats that did not run.[27]

The mechanisms in addition to alterations in gene expression by which running reduces the risk of colon cancer are uncertain. Bile acids are thought to be carcinogenic, and research carried out in New Zealand found that runners had lower levels of bile acids in their colons than sedentary individuals. This decrease in bile acid concentration was found to be the result of greater fiber intake by the runners: Fiber tends to dilute colon contents. Without the added fiber, bile acid concentrations would have been the same in the two groups. After adjustment for differences in fiber intake, frequency of defecation was higher in the running group.[28] More frequent defecations should permit noxious chemicals, including bile acids, to pass out of the colon more quickly, thus decreasing cancer risk.

Preventing Obesity

As one would expect, running and other forms of physical activity decrease the risk of obesity, defined as Body Mass Index (BMI) >30 kg/m^2.[29] This effect on obesity is one mechanism by which running lowers the risk of cardiovascular disease and cancer since these conditions are strongly linked with heightened body mass. Running and other modes of sustained exercise also prevent the weight gain associated with aging to a dramatic extent compared with inactivity.[30]

In a recent study carried out in Thailand with nearly 75,000 adults, running and other types of physical activity were linked with a substantially reduced risk of obesity, defined by the Asian criterion of BMI >25.[31] In this research, the number of weekly sessions of running and other physical exertion was inversely related to the chance of obesity, and there was about an 18 percent increase in the likelihood of obesity with every 2 hours of daily screen time, or television watching. Both men and women who ran or engaged in other exercise daily enjoyed a 33 percent reduction in the risk of obesity.

Preventing Diabetes

Controlled trial evidence also indicates that running or other moderate physical activity combined with weight loss and a balanced diet can reduce the risk of developing diabetes by 50 to 60 percent in individuals who are at risk of developing the disease.[32] Several other studies have suggested that running and walking can reduce the incidence of diabetes in men and women.[33-35]

Research carried out by Paul Williams as part of the National Runners' Health Study indicates that running *intensity* may play a particularly important role in reducing the risk of developing diabetes.[36] In this inquiry, which

How Much Running?

The amount of running necessary to achieve some health benefit is believed to be quite small. In the United States, national physical activity recommendations call for at least 30 minutes of moderate activity (e.g., walking) on most days of the week or a minimum of 20 minutes of vigorous exertion (e.g., running) three times per week. To see if such guidelines are appropriate, researchers from the Nutritional Epidemiology Branch of the Division of Cancer Epidemiology and Genetics at the National Cancer Institute recently prospectively examined physical activity and mortality among 252,925 men and women who were participating in the NIH-AARP Diet and Health Study.[37]

During 1,265,347 person years of follow-up, 7,900 individuals in the research died. The results indicated that exercising 30 minutes at a moderate intensity most days of the week reduced the risk of mortality by about 27 percent; exercising vigorously for 20 minutes three times per week diminished mortality by approximately 32 percent. *Meeting both of these criteria* (i.e., including 3 × 20 minutes of vigorous exercise within the overall framework of moderate exertion) dropped the risk of death by 46 percent. An interesting aspect of this study was the finding that engaging in exercise for less than *either* recommended level also conferred a smaller benefit, lowering the risk of dying by about 19 percent. It is clear that even modest amounts of running are protective against serious health problems.

included 25,552 male and 29,148 female participants, the men were carrying out running training at an average intensity of 3.3 meters per second (8.3 minutes per mile) and the women were running at a mean of 3.0 meters per second (9.2 minutes per mile). Williams found that each meter-per-second upgrade in training speed for men and women reduced the probability of antidiabetic medication usage by 50 percent and 75 percent, respectively.

In Williams' work, men who trained at faster than 7 minutes per mile (1.6 km) were 67 percent less likely to use diabetic medication compared with males who trained more slowly than 10 minutes per mile. Women who trained more quickly than 8 minutes per mile were 87 percent less likely to take antidiabetes medicine compared with women who ran at 11 minutes per mile or slower during training. Williams also showed that higher running intensities were linked with lower frequencies of high blood pressure and high LDL cholesterol levels. Although Williams' findings do not prove causality, they do suggest that antidiabetic benefits are greater in association with faster training. This linkage was present independent of training volume: Runners could not make up for the weaker protective effect of slower training paces by running for greater total distance.

Prolonging Health During Aging

Running represents an outstanding strategy for preventing long-term disability associated with aging. Contrary to popular opinion, running does not increase the risk of osteoarthritis in knee joints; in fact, running may have a protective effect against joint degeneration in both the knees and hips.[38] One study tracked 45 serious long-distance runners and 53 nonrunning controls over nearly two decades of life. All the individuals in the research were middle-aged or older; mean age was 58, and the range was 50 to 72 years at the beginning of the investigation.[39] Despite the 20 years of hard pounding experienced by these older runners, there was no increased risk of either routine or severe osteoarthritis in the running group. In another study, 28 runners who were members of a running club and 27 nonrunner controls, initial age 51 to 68 years, were monitored for 9 years. The results indicated that runners were not at higher risk for osteoarthritis and had greater bone mineral density in their lumbar vertebrae than the nonrunners.[40]

A study initiated by researchers from Stanford University in 1984 tracked 538 runners for 21 years; these runners were initially 50 years of age or older, and key goals of the research were to assess how running influenced the risks of *disability* and mortality;[41] the study also included 423 healthy, nonrunning controls. Disability was assessed by means of the Health Assessment Questionnaire Disability Index (HAQ-DI), which is scored from 0 (no difficulties at all) to 3 (unable to perform).

Zuma Press/Icon SMI

▶ Running can prolong life and lower the risk of disabling conditions and diseases.

The average HAQ-DI score increased in both runners and sedentary controls with aging, as one would expect, but it advanced to a lesser degree in runners. Runners had a 38 percent lower risk of developing a HAQ-DI score of 0.5, which represents a beginning point for disability, compared with nonrunners. After 19 years, 34 percent of the controls had died compared with only 15 percent of the runners; overall, runners enjoyed a 39 percent lower chance of dying during the study period. Even as the participants in the research approached their ninth decade of life, individuals who kept running had survival and disability curves on graphical plots of either variable versus time that continued to veer away from the curves of the sedentary controls. It is clear from this Stanford research that running does not increase the risks of joint deterioration and disablement; rather, it lowers those risks while prolonging life.

Running is beneficial to the brain. In laboratory animals, running has been linked with elevated levels of brain-derived neurotrophic factor, a compound that stimulates the healthy growth of nerve cells;[42] running also promotes increased synaptic plasticity, or the ability of nerve cells to form new links with each other.[43] In addition, running improves performance on spatial navigation learning tasks.[44] There is also considerable evidence—at least in lab animals—that running leads to the creation of *new* nerve cells in the brain in defiance of the long-standing principle that the brain's maximal nerve cell count is fixed at an early age.[45] Thus, it is not surprising that running has been linked with upgraded cognitive performance.[46]

Furthermore, there is evidence that running reduces the risk of depression and has pronounced antianxiety effects.[47] A positive effect of running on psychological health has been uncovered in cross-sectional studies and randomized clinical trials that have looked at the effectiveness of exercise as a treatment intervention. In such studies, running has been shown to reduce symptoms of depression and frequency of clinical depression especially among older adults.[48] There is also evidence that running and other forms of exercise can facilitate the restoration of normal function following serious brain injury.[49]

Conclusion

Running upgrades physiological variables associated with fitness, but it also has profound overall effects on health. As discussed in this chapter, running has a profoundly positive effect on lowering the risk of coronary heart disease and can dramatically lower the chances of developing a plethora of cancers. Running fights obesity and disability, and it has strong antidepressant and antianxiety effects that are great for mental health. Running prevents hypertension and lowers the chances of developing diabetes. As such a simple activity that requires little technical skill and is easy to learn, running provides an amazing array of health benefits.

CHAPTER 42

Health Considerations for Special Running Populations

Running has unique effects on young athletes—and especially on young female athletes who engage in strenuous training. Concerns have been raised regarding the safety of long-distance running for children from the standpoints of musculoskeletal safety and thermal adaptation, and young female runners are at increased risk of the female athlete triad. Running during pregnancy has also stirred much debate with some studies linking running with poor health outcomes for the fetus. Older runners recover less quickly from strenuous training, compared with their younger counterparts, and thus may be at greater risk of running-related injury.

Younger Runners

Exercise scientists have debated whether long-distance running is a healthful activity for children. Some experts suggest that prolonged running harms developing joints and active growth plates in bones. However, the Kenyan experience suggests that endurance running is not harmful to children and in fact promotes better health during young adulthood. Childhood running is a natural activity in Kenya, free from adult pressures and considered an essential aspect of life. Young Kenyan kids probably run greater distances than youngsters from any other part of the world and begin doing so at a very early age—often when they are just 5 years old or even younger.

Instead of experiencing bone, joint, and other problems, a high percentage of these children become extremely advanced—and healthy—distance runners, and many go on to become national- and international-level competitors. Compared to runners from Europe and the United States, young Kenyan runners appear to have lower rates of musculoskeletal injuries, including the shin splints, stress fractures, and bouts of plantar fasciitis that plague Western runners.[1]

When cast in Kenyan light, running appears to be a health-promoting rather than damaging activity for children. One reason for this may be that children's running in Kenya is free from adult expectations; another is that the total training load is increased gradually as Kenyan children get older. It certainly cannot hurt that most childhood running in Kenya is carried out barefooted, which should build tremendous foot, ankle, and leg strength. Furthermore, barefoot running is almost always carried out with a midfoot-striking pattern, which diminishes the impact forces the legs must absorb on every foot strike.

The scientific research shows that young runners can engage in strenuous running training without endangering their long-term health as long as the running training is varied and gradually progressive in nature, includes precautions about heat stress, is associated with healthy eating practices, does not restrict calories, and is carried out without parental pressure. The desire to run long distances should originate with the child and not be the result of a parent's desire for vicarious athletic experiences. Parents are strongly advised to provide emotional and practical support for their children's running endeavors and to avoid pressuring young runners to meet high expectations.

Heating and Cooling

Science reveals that there are several problems associated with endurance training in young runners, however. The ratio of body surface area to mass (S/M) is higher in children than adults; with their smaller corporeal volumes, children have considerably more skin area per unit weight. This would seem to be advantageous for children since a higher S/M provides greater convective cooling. In effect, a child has relatively more skin from which he or she can transport heat to air flowing over the outside of the body compared with an average adult. Under very hot conditions, however, a high S/M can be a problem: The rate of heat transfer from the external world into the body can be increased. When the weather is cold, a high S/M also hikes the rate at which heat is lost to the outside world. A child engaged in a long run on a cold, windy day would have a significantly higher risk of hypothermia than an adult carrying out the same workout.[5]

Running's Impact on Autism

Science reveals that running training can be quite beneficial for young people suffering from various health disorders, including those who have been diagnosed with autism. Research indicates that compared with engaging in mild physical activity, just 15 minutes of steady running by autistic children reduces the frequency of stereotypic behaviors that can interfere with on-task responsiveness.[2] Running and other forms of aerobic exercise are believed to be productive tools for the management of autism in children.[3] Positive changes in behavior in response to participation in aerobic running have also been observed in autistic adults.[4]

Although they have relatively more skin area than adults, children have relatively less blood volume even when the total quantity of blood is expressed in relation to body weight. This effect could make exercise in the heat more demanding for children than adults since relatively reduced amounts of blood would be sent to the skin for cooling during exertion.

Children's sweat glands also show diminished sensitivity to situations involving thermal stress, a condition that persists until about the age of 14. During approximately the first 13 years of life, the onset of sweating is delayed during strenuous exercise in the heat, and actual sweating rates are lower in children compared with adults. Children also do a poorer job of acclimatizing themselves to the heat: The extent of acclimatization achieved during 6 days of hot-weather exertion by adults might require 12 days for 8- to 10-year-old children.[6] It is not surprising that what is commonly called heat stroke is believed to be the third leading cause of exercise-related death in young people after head injuries and cardiac disorders.[5]

Positive Training Effects

Despite the thermal disadvantages associated with being a young distance runner, there are actually many positives associated with endurance training in children. Young people who run on a regular basis usually enter adulthood with lower levels of body fat compared to their more sedentary counterparts, which appears to lower the risk of high blood pressure and type 2 diabetes during later life.[5] Research also suggests that adult females who exercised regularly at a young age have a 60 percent lower risk of cancers of the uterus, ovaries, cervix, and vagina compared with nonexercisers and about a 50 percent reduction in breast cancer risk.[5]

Concerns About Injury

While endurance running, conducted in a safe manner with special attention to the risks of heat illness, would appear to be a health-promoting activity for young people, special concerns have been expressed regarding the participation of youngsters in long-distance events such as the marathon. Since a child is not structured proportionally to an adult, a major worry is the possibility of serious injury. Research reveals that the legs account for about 50 percent of an adult's height but make up less than half of a child's stature.[7] This creates a situation in which a child has relatively less leg to absorb the ground-impact forces associated with running. More impact force can theoretically be transferred to the hips and upper portions of the body.

Scientific investigations also indicate that the ratios of contractile muscle strength and static tendon strength to bone length are lower in children than in adults because bone growth tends to precede the development of corresponding muscular and tendon strength. In children, each unit length of leg bone is surrounded and protected by weaker muscles and tendons. This mismatch leaves bones and joints less shielded from injury in children compared with adults, possibly increasing the risk of stress fractures and joint and cartilage maladies in young distance runners.[8]

A close examination of the possible connection between heavy-duty training and injury in young athletes was completed at the Sports Clinic of the Deaconess Institute of Oulu in Finland. Researchers monitored 48 young track and field athletes over a 3-year period. At the start of the study, 7 were age 10, 3 were 11, 6 were 12, 9 were 13, and 23 others were either 14 or 15; the mean age was 13. Twenty-two of the athletes were girls, and 26 were boys.[9]

Twenty of the 48 young athletes trained at least six times a week for about 10 hours per week, 23 worked out four or five times weekly for 6 to 10 hours, and 5 trained three times per week for 3 to 6 hours. The training was quite rigorous and produced 39 Finnish Championship medals. Three of the young athletes garnered medals at European Championships.

▶ Young runners can engage in varied training programs with a low risk of injury.

During the 3-year period of track and field training, there were 41 exercise-related injuries severe enough to curtail training, an unusually low rate of physical difficulty. Expressed in another way, 28 percent of the young athletes were injured during a typical year. Studies of injury rates among adult runners engaged in similar durations of training have detected injury rates of 40 to 65 percent—and as high as 93 percent—per year. Although the exact nature of training is not identical in these inquiries, the research at least suggests that running training is no more harmful in children than it is in adults.

Although a concern remains that children's injuries might be more damaging in the long term, most of the physical problems that occurred in the Finnish study were slight. In spite of the relatively heavy training loads—over 40 percent of the Finnish youngsters trained more than 10 hours per week—no surgical interventions were necessary, and one-third of the ailments required no special therapies at all. Sixty percent of the training-related injuries healed completely within 2 months, and no lasting injuries were sustained.

One lesson to be learned from the Finnish study may be that variation is an essential part of training for both younger and older runners. The young Finnish athletes did not specialize but instead participated in a number of different track and field events during the 3-year period. Employing a variety of different training techniques involving the development of speed, coordination, technique, strength, and endurance, the young Finns avoided the repetitive pounding of running for long distances. This was much to their advantage since a strong predictor of running-related injury is simply the volume of miles run per week.

A concern has been that endurance running might harm growth plates in children's bones, but research reveals that long-distance running is not a risk factor for growth-plate problems.[10] The American Academy of Pediatrics has concluded that there is no solid reason to preclude marathon running for prepubertal kids as long as their lesser tolerance for heat stress is heeded.[11]

Female Runners

Despite this generally positive news about running for the younger population, it is nonetheless true that running can sometimes be associated with serious problems when it is carried out in strenuous fashion by young female athletes. Such training can lead to problems with sexual maturation and menstrual cycling as well as difficulties with bone health and disorders related to eating patterns.

Female Athlete Triad

It appears that participation in a rigorous running program at an early age delays sexual maturation in female runners in Great Britain and the United States—and that such late maturers might be more likely to experience amenorrhea in later life. Females who take part in an aggressive running program that delays sexual maturity may increase their risk of stress fractures and osteoporosis especially if their nutritional practices are suboptimal. Science also discloses that young female runners are at a heightened risk for anorexia nervosa.[5] Up to 25 percent of female collegiate runners in the United States exhibit significant symptoms of disordered eating.[12]

It is important to point out that it is not running per se that produces anorexia; rather, the combination of excessive running and inadequate eating is the result of underlying psychological difficulties. The triad of problems encountered in many young female runners—anorexia, osteoporosis, and amenorrhea—is not common in young Kenyan female athletes even though the Kenyan females appear to train more strenuously than their counterparts in the Western world; for example, young Kenyan females ranging in age from 13 to 16 often run about 60 to 70 miles (97-113 km) per week during the cross country season.[12] In my observations, the reasons for this may be that young Kenyan females are stronger, in part because of their barefoot, hill-top running at an early age, and that young Kenyans are less likely to attempt to restrict calories intentionally. "Our bodies need a lot of fuel so that we can run well," young Kenyan female runners often say.

In spite of the prevalence of the athlete triad among female runners, research conducted by Kathleen Pantano revealed that less than half of U.S. Division I collegiate distance-running coaches in the United States are able to identify the three components of the disorder.[13] It goes without saying, then, that the majority of college coaches are unable to identify the triad in their female athletes or recommend proper treatment.

Myths about female runners' responses to strenuous training may make identification of the triad more difficult. Pantano found that 24 percent of coaches believe that absent or irregular menstruation is a normal consequence of training even though dysfunctional menstruation is one of the key aspects of the triad. Triad intervention strategies are most likely to be successful when they include a multidisciplinary team approach.[13] Coordination between the coach, a nutritionist, an athletic trainer, and a mental health professional is believed to be the optimal way to help a female athlete avoid the perils of the triad.[13]

One way to counter the osteoporotic effects of disordered eating and amenorrhea would be to encourage strength training in female runners, particularly those at risk for the athlete triad. Research reveals that regular strength training involving the lower limbs significantly improves mineral density in bones.[14] Naturally, such resistance training would not produce optimal effects unless it was undertaken with an appropriate nutritional program that includes increased calories and calcium to support the energy and mineral intake demands of the training.

Pregnancy

Many female runners wonder whether it is all right to continue with running training during pregnancy. Current guidelines in the United States and Europe suggest that pregnant female runners can continue training at a moderate level throughout much of their pregnancy. Running during pregnancy has beneficial effects on many maternal health outcomes, including reduced risks of preeclampsia[15] and gestational diabetes.[16] However, the impact of running during pregnancy on the health of the fetus is less clear.[17] Running during pregnancy can potentially reduce placental blood flow because of redistribution of blood to the leg muscles and may make the fetus hyperthermic, release hormones that stimulate uterine contractility, and promote fetal hypoglycemia because the leg muscles rob the fetus of glucose during intense or prolonged runs.

Research in this area has been inconclusive. Three studies have found no link at all between exercise during pregnancy and miscarriage,[18-20] and one inquiry actually found that regular exercise protected against miscarriage.[21] However, a recent Danish investigation carried out with 92,671 pregnant women detected a stepwise, increasing relationship between exercise and the risk of miscarriage.[22] For example, according to this study, women who exercised more than 7 hours per week had an almost fourfold increase in the risk of miscarriage. However, running and other exercise was not connected with an increased chance of miscarriage beyond 18 weeks of gestation. It is clear that female runners who are pregnant should consult closely with their physicians.

Older Runners

Older runners experience declines in muscle mass, muscle contractility, muscle elasticity, and bone density, along with drops in overall immune-system functioning. Such concerns are particularly relevant, given that masters and grand-masters participation in long-distance running events like the marathon has increased significantly in the last 10 years. Some studies have indeed shown that older runners have increased risks of leg injuries, compared with younger runners, especially including problems with the Achilles tendon, hamstrings, and calf muscles.

However, running also provides many benefits for the older athlete, including decreased risks of heart disease, diabetes, high blood pressure, cancer, anxiety, depression, excess weight gain, and loss of mobility and coordination. If carried out properly, without the risk of overtraining, regular running can actually increase bone density in the feet, ankles, and legs, compared with a sedentary lifestyle. The use of running-specific strength training should further augment bone density and decrease the risk of injury in older runners.

Older female runners are at higher risk for osteoporosis compared with their male peers and should be particularly conscious of maintaining sound nutritional practices, recovering well between workouts, and conducting running-specific strength training at least twice a week.

Despite recent reports that running might in effect run a high-volume runner right into the grave, there is actually little evidence to suggest that a normal running program is damaging to the heart. There is a slight increase in risk for a cardiovascular event during running with aging, but a master runner's heart responds to and recovers from training in a manner very similar to a younger runner's.

Conclusion

Reasonable and progressive amounts of running appear to do no harm to children and can promote healthy levels of fitness and strength. Injury risk is actually lower in younger runners compared with older athletes, particularly if training is *varied* and does not focus entirely on running. Young female athletes are at increased risk of the female athlete triad, a condition requiring a multidisciplinary approach for proper intervention. The osteoporotic effects of the triad can be partially countered with a resistance-training regime supported by sound nutritional practices. Moderate levels of running appear to be safe during pregnancy especially after 18 weeks of gestation. Older runners can protect themselves from injury by enhancing recovery between workouts and conducting running-specific strength training on a regular basis.

Running Nutrition

CHAPTER 43

Energy Sources and Fuel Use for Runners

According to the popular dictum, "You are what you eat." This maxim is particularly appropriate for endurance runners, who depend on intakes of the appropriate amounts and types of nutrients to maintain their running performances. Failure to ingest adequate quantities of certain nutriments can lead to dramatic falloffs in performance times. Like all humans, runners rely on the carbohydrate, fat, and protein found in ingested foods to provide the energy and structural components necessary to maintain normal cellular activities.

During actual running, the main nutrients used for energy are the carbohydrate and fat stored within a runner's body. Protein contributes a very small portion of the energy that is needed.[1] Carbohydrate, fat, and protein cannot directly provide the energy required for muscular contractions, however. During a workout or race, chemical pathways convert carbohydrate, fat, and a tiny amount of protein into a form of energy that muscles can use directly to shorten and thus create propulsive forces. The process by which the energy in carbohydrate and fat is converted into usable energy is called bioenergetics.

Converting Carbohydrate to Energy

Ingested carbohydrate stored in a runner's body provides a quickly available form of energy. A single gram of carbohydrate (about .035 ounces) provides four kilocalories of energy—enough to run approximately 1/25th of a mile (1.6 km).[2] As a point of reference, a banana furnishes 25 grams (.88 oz) of carbohydrate that—when stored in the muscles—would supply enough energy to run one mile.

Carbohydrates exist in three forms: monosaccharides, disaccharides, and polysaccharides.[3] Monosaccharides are simple sugars with just six or fewer carbon atoms. There are dozens of monosaccharides, including fructose, galactose, mannose, ribose, and xylose, but the most important monosaccharide for runners is glucose, aka blood sugar. The term *blood sugar* is a bit misleading from a functional standpoint because glucose plays its most critical role inside muscle cells where it can be broken down to produce adenosine triphosphate (ATP), which is the actual and immediate source of usable energy for muscle contraction.

Disaccharides are formed by combining two monosaccharides and are also important for runners. Table sugar, or sucrose, is the most common disaccharide found in runners' diets. Table sugar is formed from two monosaccharides: glucose and fructose, which is sometimes called fruit sugar because of its ubiquitous presence in fruits. Sucrose can supply runners with large fractions of their daily energy needs. For example, research has shown that about 10 to 20 percent of the daily caloric intake of elite Kenyan runners comes from table sugar.[4]

Polysaccharides, complex carbohydrates that contain three or more monosaccharides, are enormously important in endurance running. The two most common forms of polysaccharides found in plants are starch and cellulose; the starch found in vegetables, grains, and beans is an essential source of carbohydrate in a runner's daily eating plan. After they are eaten, polysaccharides are broken down by a runner's digestive system to form monosaccharides such as glucose that can be used immediately for energy (i.e., ATP production). If the glucose is not needed right away for energy, it can be linked together in long chains to form glycogen, which is the key polysaccharide found in runners' and all animals' muscle fibers.

Glycogen provides most of the energy required for runners to run at their best-possible speeds in competitions lasting from 2 to 180 minutes. Glycogen depletion, or the reduction of glycogen concentrations within muscle cells to low levels, is linked with strong sensations of fatigue; it has also been found to be an important signal that stimulates muscles to adapt to the training being conducted. Glycogen molecules are stored inside muscles and are usually quite large, consisting of hundreds to thousands of glucose molecules.[5]

When runners conduct workouts or participate in 5Ks, 10Ks, or marathons, their muscle cells break down stored glycogen to release glucose molecules in a process called glycogenolysis. The glucose can then be used to produce ATP, providing the energy needed for muscle contractions. This process of splitting off glucose molecules from glycogen and then using glucose to generate ATP is the main source of energy for endurance runners in events lasting up to three hours. The liver joins the muscles in glycogenolysis by producing glucose and releasing it into the bloodstream where it can be picked up by muscle cells to provide an additional source of energy.[5]

Despite its importance, glycogen is stored inside a runner's body in rather small amounts, and glycogen can be nearly totally depleted from the muscles and liver after just a couple of hours of steady running. Furthermore, intramuscular glycogen concentrations can fall far enough in just one hour of running to reduce the quality of performance because the process of breaking glucose off from glycogen to generate ATP is hindered. For that reason, glycogen synthesis and storage are processes that should be optimized by competitive endurance runners. The greater the amount of glycogen stored in muscles and the liver, the longer an endurance runner can sustain a quality running pace. Not surprisingly, high-carbohydrate diets tend to enhance glycogen storage while low-carbohydrate diets reduce muscle glycogen. Guidelines for carbohydrate ingestion are provided in chapter 44.

▶ Consuming carbohydrate boosts intramuscular glycogen synthesis.

McPHOTO/BLE/Insandco/age fotostock

Converting Fat to Energy

Fat molecules contain the same three elements found in carbohydrate—carbon, oxygen, and hydrogen—but the ratio of carbon to oxygen is much greater in fats.[5] This has an important consequence that will be explained later in the chapter. A gram of fat also provides more than two times as much energy as an equivalent amount of carbohydrate: Each gram of fat yields nine kilocalories, enough energy to run about 1/11th of a mile (.15 km).[6] (Recall that a gram of carbohydrate provides adequate energy to run just 1/25th of a mile [.06 km].) An interesting comparison is that a whole banana, which is all carbohydrate, is needed to provide adequate fuel to run a mile (1.6 km), whereas a single tablespoon of olive oil, which is all fat, can supply the energy needed to complete that same mile.

Fatty acids represent the primary type of fat used by muscle cells to create the energy necessary for running. Fatty acids are stored in the muscles, fat cells, and other tissues as triglycerides. Each triglyceride consists of three molecules of fatty acids and one molecule of glycerol linked together. During running, triglycerides can be broken down into their component fatty acids and glycerol, and the fatty acids can be used to create ATP; this overall process is called lipolysis. Muscle fibers cannot use glycerol directly for energy, but the liver can convert glycerol to glucose, the key ATP-generating monosaccharide.

While the storage of glycogen is rather tightly capped inside a runner's body, fat can be stored to an almost unlimited degree. In this sense, fat represents a productive and reliable source of fuel for endurance runners. Even the skinniest runner ordinarily has enough body fat to run for extraordinarily long distances. For example, a slender, 120-pound (54 kg) male runner with just 4 percent body fat and thus 4.8 pounds (2.2 kg) of fat mass, could run for nearly 170 miles (274 km) using fat as the source of energy assuming that all his body fat could be broken down to create ATP. In contrast, the same athlete could ordinarily run no farther than 18 to 20 miles (29-32 km) when relying solely on carbohydrate.

This might suggest that endurance runners should eat or train in ways that would ultimately produce less reliance on carbohydrate for energy and promote greater fat usage during running. However, because fat has a higher ration of carbon to oxygen compared with carbohydrate, the use of fat rather than carbohydrate as the primary fuel source during running raises the oxygen consumption rate associated with a particular speed. This means that the chosen velocity is carried out at a higher percentage of $\dot{V}O_2$max. Since perceived effort and percentage of $\dot{V}O_2$max are fairly tightly linked, the selected speed will feel much more difficult to sustain when fat is the primary source of energy even though total fuel availability with fat is greater than with carbohydrate.

Converting Protein to Energy

Proteins are composed of carbon, oxygen, hydrogen, and an additional element: nitrogen. All proteins are composed of subunits called amino acids. At least 20 types of amino acids are needed by a runner's body for normal functioning. As is the case with carbohydrate, a gram of protein provides four kilocalories of energy. Protein can provide energy for running in two ways.[5] First, an amino acid called alanine can be converted in the liver to glucose, which can then move through the blood to the muscles where it can be used for immediate energy or to create glycogen. Second, many amino acids can be converted inside muscle cells into compounds called metabolic intermediates, which can then be broken down directly to create ATP.[7]

If a running workout or competition lasts less than an hour, protein generally provides less than 2 percent of the energy required to complete the exertion. When exercise is more prolonged, protein can contribute from 5 to 15 percent of the needed energy during the final minutes of the effort.[8] It is clear that carbohydrate and fat furnish the largest share of energy during running even when a run is quite extended.

Which Fuel the Body Prefers and When

The relative balance between carbohydrate and fat breakdown during running is influenced by a number of factors, including diet, running intensity (i.e., speed), and the duration of the effort. Science tells us that high-fat, low-carbohydrate diets tend to increase the rate of fat breakdown during running while high-carbohydrate, low-fat diets tends to heighten the use of carbohydrate for fuel during workouts and races. Fats are the primary source of fuel for muscles during low-intensity running carried out at less than 30 percent of $\dot{V}O_2$max (i.e., less than 55 percent of maximal heart rate) while carbohydrates are the preferred fuel during running carried out at intensities higher than 70 percent of $\dot{V}O_2$max (i.e., greater than 80 percent of maximal heart rate).[9, 10]

A general rule is that carbohydrate increases its relative contribution to the needed energy as running speed increases. The result is that carbohydrate furnishes *all* of the energy required for running at intensities of 100 percent of $\dot{V}O_2$max and greater. There appear to be two mechanisms underlying the increased role of carbohydrate as a fuel for muscles at higher running speeds. One is that higher speeds increase the recruitment of fast-twitch muscle fibers within the leg muscles.[1] These fast-twitch cells generally have a poor ability to oxidize fat and can be considered carbohydrate specialists.

A second factor is that higher running velocities are linked with the greater production and release of a key hormone called epinephrine. Higher levels of epinephrine, aka adrenaline, in the blood increase breakdown rates of glycogen in the muscles and spur carbohydrate metabolism in general. During high-intensity running, epinephrine may also indirectly block the availability of fat as a substrate for energy production.[11] As a result, the maintenance of high running speeds (i.e., at 10K speed and faster) is almost entirely dependent on carbohydrate as the fuel source.

Exercise duration also influences the relative rates at which carbohydrate and fat are used as fuel. As the length of a running workout or competition gradually increases beyond 30 minutes, there is a progressive shift in energy creation from carbohydrate metabolism to the breakdown of greater and greater amounts of fat.[12] This pattern is related to running intensity since longer runs tend to be carried out at slower speeds. In addition, the shift to fat as duration expands can be partly offset by the ingestion of carbohydrate-containing sport drinks.

ATP as the Body's Primary Energy Currency

As mentioned, the energy contained in the food that a runner eats, whether it is carbohydrate, protein, or fat, must first be converted to energy within ATP molecules before it can be used by muscle cells to provide propulsive forces. ATP is always present in muscle cells and indeed in all the living cells in a runner's body; without ATP, cells would quickly stop working and die. ATP is often called the universal energy donor because it provides energy to all cells, not just a select few, but perhaps a better name would be the body's primary energy currency. Carbohydrate, fat, and protein are not directly usable by cells for energy, but ATP is immediately available; it is the only energy molecule that is *directly* serviceable for muscle contraction and other cellular activities.

Since ATP is so important, runners and coaches sometimes think that it might be possible and beneficial to increase intrinsic ATP concentrations inside muscle cells. However, science reveals that human cells refuse to stockpile the precious high-energy phosphate; they are much more interested in storing carbohydrate and fat. Since ATP is stored to a very limited degree, and since running depends on a steady, often expansive supply of ATP to provide the energy needed for muscular contractions, there is a strong need for muscles to have dependable metabolic pathways that can provide ATP at a rapid, reliable rate. If there is not going to be much ATP at the ready, then there has to be some way for runners to manufacture it in a quick, predictable manner. As it turns out, runners have three such ATP-creating pathways—that is, three unique and distinct series of chemical reactions whose sole purpose is creating ATP. These three pathways are discussed in turn in the following sections.

ATP-PC System

The simplest and most rapid pathway involves a chemical found inside muscle cells called phosphocreatine. Phosphocreatine cannot provide energy for muscle contractions directly—only ATP can do that—but it is very willing to donate a high-energy phosphate group to a chemical called ADP to form ATP. This critically important reaction is catalyzed by an enzyme called creatine kinase, which is consequently found in significant concentrations inside muscle cells. The ubiquity of creatine kinase in muscle tissue explains why high levels of creatine kinase in the blood are associated with muscle breakdown, including the kinds of catastrophes that can occur in cardiac muscle tissue after a heart attack.

One special feature of phosphocreatine is that its intramuscular levels are not as tightly capped as ATP concentrations. This means the muscles can allow phosphocreatine concentrations to soar quite dramatically, which helps explain why *creatine supplementation* has been so successful from a performance standpoint in high-power athletics. Creatine added to the diet is absorbed readily and makes it way to the muscles where it combines with the phosphates that are always present to make phosphocreatine. Runners who have a substantial amount of phosphocreatine in their muscle cells can generate a lot of ATP in a very short period of time. These runners will have the potential to improve sprinting ability, which depends on a readily available source of large amounts of ATP.

All physiological systems have their limits, however. The system just described, which is sometimes called the ATP-PC system or even the phosphagen system, has definite limitations. A key factor is that the phosphagen system, even in athletes who have creatine-loaded their muscles, can probably provide energy for no more than about 8 to 10 seconds of intense muscular exertion, at which point phosphocreatine becomes depleted. This means that the system can work effectively for high jumpers, power weightlifters, 50-meter sprinters, elite 100-meter sprinters, pole vaulters, cricket bowlers, soccer players racing across the pitch during the opening moments of play, and other athletes whose sports call for short bursts of high-intensity exertion.

The phosphagen system becomes less important in running events that last longer than 10 seconds. For the runner who wants to run as fast as possible for 200 meters, the phosphagen system would ordinarily get him or her less than halfway to the finish line. Without another ATP-generating pathway to use, the runner would fall, fatigued, in a miserable heap well short of the target. Incidentally, this limitation of the phosphagen system explains why creatine supplementation has often been linked with better performances in athletes engaged in high-power, short-duration sports—and why creatine has *not* been strongly tied to better times in endurance athletes.[13]

The fact that the phosphagen system works for only 8 to 10 seconds or so is puzzling to many serious runners. After all, if creatine is still present inside muscle fibers after it donates its phosphate to ADP, why can't creatine simply pick up some of the phosphate that is a natural constituent of cells and thus form phosphocreatine again, rejuvenating the ATP-creation process? The problem is that phosphocreatine reformation actually *requires* ATP and thus generally occurs only during recovery from exercise when the ATP that is present is not being used to help muscles contract.

Glycolysis

Fortunately, there is a second ATP-producing pathway that allows running to be sustained for a longer period of time. This second system takes a little longer to get started since it does not depend on ATP that is already present in muscle cells or on a simple reaction between phosphocreatine and ADP. This second system can get going fairly quickly; it can really get rolling after

8 to 10 seconds, making it a nice complement to the phosphagen system. This second pathway is called glycolysis, and it involves the breakdown of carbohydrate (either an existing glucose molecule or a glucose molecule cleaved from glycogen) within muscle cells to form two molecules of pyruvic acid or lactic acid.

As was the case with the phosphagen system, not a single molecule of oxygen is required for this to happen. A further advantage is that glycolysis does not depend on phosphocreatine; rather, the energy locked up in a glucose molecule is used in a way that allows a phosphate group to link up with ADP, forming ATP in the process. For every molecule of glucose split during glycolysis, two robust molecules of usable ATP are formed. Glycolysis is the *dominant* ATP-production system for strenuous activities requiring longer than 10 seconds but less than about 120 seconds, or two minutes, for completion. The ability to generate energy via glycolysis without the use of oxygen is sometimes referred to as a runner's anaerobic capacity since no oxygen is required to make glycolysis proceed at the necessary rate.

Aerobic Pathway

In activities lasting longer than two minutes, the well-known aerobic pathway for ATP production holds sway. During aerobic ATP production, which occurs inside special cellular structures called mitochondria, hydrogen atoms are stripped away from segments of carbohydrates, proteins, and fats and passed on to special hydrogen-accepting molecules. These hydrogen atoms actually contain the potential energy found in the original food molecules, and this energy can be used to combine phosphate with ADP to make ATP!

The pathway is termed aerobic because oxygen is the final hydrogen acceptor in the overall process, and without oxygen the entire series of energy releasing reactions would grind to a halt. If the rate of oxygen provisioning to muscle cells cannot be increased, then the rate at which ATP is generated aerobically cannot be increased either. If runners understand the aerobic ATP-generating pathway, then they can also comprehend why increases in $\dot{V}O_2$max, or maximal aerobic capacity, often lead to improvements in endurance performance. If the muscles can use oxygen at a higher rate to accept hydrogens, then ATP can be generated at a greater rate, too, and runners thus have the potential to exercise more intensely during endurance competitions.

Training Implications

The three ATP pathways are generally associated with three speeds of movement. Athletic events lasting 10 seconds or less are usually linked with incredibly intense (i.e., maximal) exertion, and thus the phosphagen system is depended on most heavily for movement at high speeds. Competitions lasting from 10 to 120 seconds are also carried out at fast speeds, although not as fast as the shorter-duration exertions. Finally, competitions engaged in for more than 120 seconds are conducted at fairly moderate speeds compared with the torrid movements linked with shorter efforts. As a result, the phosphagen system has been wedded in runners' and coaches' minds to the performance of maximal speeds, the glycolytic (i.e., anaerobic) system to fast speeds, and the aerobic process to more modest velocities.

Modes of training have consequently fallen into three general types. Athletes whose events last no more than 10 seconds tend to train by emphasizing short intervals of work lasting 10 seconds or less. If such runners have some physiological knowledge, they might proclaim that they are working on their phosphagen systems during training. Athletes who compete for 10 to 120 seconds tend to run a bit slower during training; their work intervals generally last from 10 to 120 seconds, as one might expect. Such athletes may talk about building anaerobic capacity since the glycolytic system provides most of the energy for their efforts or—less commonly—about maximizing their glycolytic potential.

Finally, athletes who compete for longer than 120 seconds tend to abhor training intervals shorter than 2 minutes; these athletes work at slower speeds over intervals lasting from 2 to 10 minutes and at continuous efforts that may last for considerably longer. These endurance athletes are extremely attracted to the process of maximizing their aerobic systems, and they may even speak about improvements in heart function, upswings in breathing capacity, vine-like growths of capillaries around their muscle fibers, and the increased ability of their muscles to use oxygen.

Is this traditional thinking about training correct? Should the 100-meter, phosphagen-based sprinter, for example, completely eschew longer glycolytic or aerobic running? Should the 50-second, glycolysis-using athlete avoid phosphagen-enhancing efforts or exertions lasting more than 2 minutes since such activities would seemingly tax the wrong energy producing systems? And should the aerobic endurance athlete stay away from phosphagenic and glycolytic efforts?

Science suggests that it is best to start with the easiest answer: The phosphagen athlete does not need to worry about conducting training efforts that use the glycolytic or aerobic systems. It is not possible to construct a compelling argument for such training especially since scientific evidence suggests that longer-duration work intervals might convert fast-twitch muscle cells into slow-twitch fibers!

Of course, upgrading the phosphagen system is not the whole story for such athletes. Simple manipulations of phosphocreatine and creatine kinase may well help an athlete sprint faster, but by themselves they will not produce an athlete's best-possible performances. Performance, after all, is not just a chemical story. Short-distance sprinters will also want to upgrade leg-muscle size in order to produce more propulsive force and also improve nervous system control of muscles so that higher amounts of force can be produced in shorter periods. These changes can occur independently of upswings in phosphagen use in muscle cells. Furthermore, it is possible that advancements in the phosphagen system might not produce any improvements in running performance at all unless nervous system function and leg-muscle size are enhanced.

Should the endurance athlete engage in the type of training that is the ordinary providence of the phosphagen or glycolysis athlete? To answer that question completely, it is necessary to picture a real-life situation. Consider the case of a well-trained runner competing in a half-marathon competition. The runner might notice an athlete about 15 meters ahead who needs to be picked off. The runner knows that it's going to be tough, but he or she shifts into a higher gear and begins to accelerate. In 10 seconds or so, this runner is ahead of the other competitor, but there is fatigue from the sprint and the troubling awareness that the competitor might end up coming back. So, this runner keeps up his or her sudden surging for a full 60 seconds before falling back to normal velocity. When the runner looks back, he or she is satisfied that the competitor has been left in the dust.

What ATP systems did this athlete rely on for the sudden sprint? Did he or she use the phosphagen system to catch up with the competitor in 10 seconds and then the glycolytic system to power past the competitor over the next 50 seconds? Such thoughts are certainly reasonable, but the truth is that most of the energy for the sprint, both the high-speed 10-second component and the follow-up 50-second surge, would have to be produced via the aerobic pathway.

To understand this, it is important to remember that the rules established so far apply when the exercise begins from a relatively quiescent physiological state. In other words, the phosphagen system controls exercise lasting 10 seconds or less, glycolysis dominates exertion requiring 10 to 120 seconds, and the aerobic pathway swamps everything else. When an athlete begins from physiological ground zero, the phosphagen system is ready to go, but it takes about 10 seconds for glycolysis to come up to speed and as long as 2 minutes for oxygen to really penetrate muscle cells in truly significant amounts, thus permitting aerobic pathways to take precedence.

However, everything changes when a runner has already been in motion for awhile; in fact, everything is altered when an athlete has been running for just 2 minutes. In the example just mentioned, when the runner was cruising along during the half-marathon race, he or she was probably working at about 85 percent of maximal aerobic capacity, or $\dot{V}O_2$max. During the sudden 1-minute sprint, the runner probably soared to 95 percent of $\dot{V}O_2$max or so. In other words, the aerobic ATP-generating system had enough room to handle the upswing in running intensity; the runner simply stepped up the rate at which he or she was using oxygen to catch hydrogen and increase energy supply inside the muscle cells. The runner was going fast, but the aerobic system was functioning well enough to handle the speed.

Yes, glycolysis would have perked up as running speed increased. However, for each molecule of glucose broken down, the aerobic pathway generates about 19 times as much usable energy compared to glycolysis alone. Thus, it's hard to argue that glycolysis, or anaerobic capacity, provided the lion's share of the energy for the sprint; the glycolytic-system's contribution was in fact pretty puny. The phosphagen system, too, was nonproductive because it was exhausted just 10 seconds into the race.

That makes it seem as though the endurance runner does not need to worry about glycolysis, the phosphagen system, or even about the fast training speeds associated with improving those systems. If we change the event slightly, however, the analysis comes into a different focus. For example, the 1,500-meter runner competing to the best of his or her ability is an endurance athlete whose performance depends primarily on the aerobic pathway for ATP generation since the event requires at least 3:26—the current male world record—to complete.

Two minutes into the event, however, the athlete has already reached $\dot{V}O_2$max, and thus the kick, or increased speed, that occurs during the last lap cannot be propelled by advanced use of the aerobic pathway; glycolysis must fill the bill. It's clear that endurance athletes who reach $\dot{V}O_2$max during their competitions must train like glycolytic competitors, too, in addition to carrying out their aerobic training. In general, athletes who compete in events lasting 12 minutes or less will hit $\dot{V}O_2$max as they compete, and thus their fate in competition might depend strongly on glycolytic capacity.

What about the plus-12-minute crowd? Perhaps surprisingly, they also need to train like the glycolytic competitors. Even a marathon runner, who might get less than 1 percent of total ATP during competition from glycolysis, should spend significant amounts of time training fast, using work intervals as short as 15 to 30 seconds. From an ATP-generation standpoint, this would not seem to be the case, but it is important not to get too trapped by the ATP-creating paradigm. There are other factors besides ATP-pathway development that are important for athletic success. Maximal speed is one: As an athlete's maximal rate of movement increases, usual race paces feel easier and more sustainable. One way to enhance maximal running velocity is to carry out the short-interval, high-intensity efforts from the realm of glycolytic training (see chapters 16 and 28).

In addition, economy of movement is critically important to the endurance athlete. Economy is simply the oxygen cost of moving at a specific speed (i.e., the rate of oxygen consumption associated with that speed). As economy improves, along with a parallel drop in cost or rate, specific speeds are sustained at a lower percentage of $\dot{V}O_2$max and feel appreciably easier, allowing the athlete to graduate to higher speeds in competitions. As it turns out, scientific research indicates that high-speed training, using very intense work intervals that often last from 10 to 120 seconds, is one of the most potent ways to upgrade economy (see chapters 25 and 28).

A continuity rule is also important. When an endurance athlete begins a workout by blasting along very quickly for 30 seconds, a significant amount of the energy will come from the phosphagen system; an even greater amount will be produced via glycolysis, with the aerobic pathway chipping in comparatively little energy. However, as the workout continues—assuming, for example, that the athlete uses typical recovery intervals of 30 seconds or so—the rate of oxygen consumption will rise dramatically over the course of the workout. In fact, after the seventh or eighth interval, the athlete may find himself or herself exercising right at $\dot{V}O_2$max and will probably stay at $\dot{V}O_2$max for the remainder of the exertion. Exercise scientists believe that training at $\dot{V}O_2$max is one of the best ways to enhance the aerobic ATP pathway. So a workout seemingly designed to enhance glycolysis can actually be very good for aerobic ATP production.

What about the athlete who competes in events lasting from 10 to 120 seconds? How should he or she train? Fast starts are essential in such competitions, so the runner will have to do some training that bears a resemblance to the work of the phosphagenic athlete who competes in events that are over in about 10 seconds. Ten-second maximal efforts, with long recovery intervals to allow the phosphagen system to restore itself, will do the trick. This athlete will also have to do some traditional aerobic work using intervals or efforts lasting longer than 2 minutes. The reason for this is that even if the competition lasts only 30 seconds, the aerobic pathway chips in 20 percent of the needed energy; if the event lasts 60 seconds, aerobics add 30 percent of the kilocalories. Thus this athlete, even though he or she may never hit $\dot{V}O_2$max during competitions, will still need to develop the aerobic system to a certain extent to make sure it is there, waiting, to chip in its piece of the energy pie during races.

Conclusion

Intramuscular, stored carbohydrate provides most of the fuel for running that lasts for 3 hours or less. In general, competitive runners at all distances ranging from 100 meters to the marathon should avoid eating and training strategies designed to enhance fat metabolism since carbohydrate will actually be the key fuel for such endeavors. At first glance, an understanding of the bioenergetics of running suggests that endurance runners should never carry out short, high-speed intervals. The truth, however, is far different. While it is true that sprinters should never run long, endurance runners should often run fast. This is because endurance athletes require high-velocity work to upgrade their neuromuscular systems, boost maximal running speed, and enhance running economy. Plus, such anaerobic training is actually highly aerobic in nature, with $\dot{V}O_2$max being attained as fast intervals are repeated over the course of a session.

CHAPTER 44

Eating for Enhanced Endurance and Speed

Runners can eat in ways that either promote or limit their endurance capacities and overall performances. Fortunately, optimal eating is straightforward and relatively easy to accomplish with a diet that revolves around heavy carbohydrate consumption, moderate protein ingestion, and the intake of reasonable levels of health-promoting omega-3 and monounsaturated fat. Elite Kenyan runners follow the best eating plan in the world for endurance running and yet routinely ingest no more than 12 food items, most of which are rich in carbohydrate and low in fat.

Carbohydrate Loading

Since the early 1970s, exercise scientists have known that high-carbohydrate diets foster enhanced endurance performances. In a classic study carried out in Sweden, 10 fit physical education students ran a 30K (18.6 mi) race, trained normally for 3 weeks, and then repeated the 30K competition.[1] Four of the 10 runners consumed a mixed diet with moderate amounts of carbohydrate during the week leading up to the first 30K race. The other 6 participants ran the first race after a special program of carbohydrate loading (i.e., manipulating dietary intake in order to maximize glycogen storage in the muscles).

Approximately 1 week before the first race, these six runners exercised heavily for at least 2 hours to deplete muscle glycogen stores. After the race, the individuals followed a carbohydrate-free diet for 3 days while carrying out moderate training. Following this carbohydrate fast, the athletes consumed about 2,500 calories (625 grams) of carbohydrate each day for 3 days in association with light training. This pattern represents a depletion-repletion method of carbohydrate loading that was once quite popular among endurance athletes.

Prior to the second 30K competition, the two groups switched dietary plans so that each participant in the study ran a 30K with and without carbohydrate-loaded leg muscles. Muscle biopsies were taken from the leg muscles of each runner before and after each race to assess actual glycogen levels. The depletion-repletion carbohydrate-intake strategy had a major impact on average muscle glycogen concentrations. The average was 35 grams per kilogram of muscle with the special loading regimen and just 17 grams per kilogram with the mixed, moderate-carbohydrate diet.

When the mixed diet preceded the race, glycogen stores in the leg muscles were almost completely wiped out at the end of the competition for 6 of the 10 athletes. After the carbohydrate-loading regimen, glycogen levels at the end of the race were still fairly high (above 11 grams per kilogram) for 9 of the 10 runners. All 10 participants achieved better times in the 30K with the carbohydrate-loading diet than with the lower-carbohydrate, mixed diet. The average improvement in running time with carbohydrate loading was 8 minutes—from 143 to 135 minutes. This represents an improvement in race pace of almost 26 seconds per mile (1.6 km).

The idea that the difference in running time between races was directly related to muscle glycogen levels was supported by the finding that if an individual's glycogen levels were already reasonably high after the mixed diet, the improvement in time with the carbohydrate diet would be small. The biggest improvements in 30K running time were observed in runners who had low glycogen levels after the mixed diet but were able to dramatically increase muscle glycogen with the special carbohydrate-loading regimen.

The mechanism for the improved running time with the high-carbohydrate diet was that increased glycogen concentrations permitted a quality running pace to be sustained longer during the race. Identical paces were maintained by all runners for the low- and high-carbohydrate runs during the first 3.75 kilometers (2.33 mi) of the 30K race. By the 11.25-kilometer (6.99 mi) mark, however, three of the mixed-diet runners had slowed their speeds, and by the end of the 30K all mixed-diet runners had slowed down. In the two races, the first individuals to slow down were those with the lowest muscle glycogen levels, and these tended to be the athletes whose leg-muscle glycogen depots had not been loaded.

This classic study was one of the first scientific investigations to show a direct link between muscle glycogen levels and endurance performance. It demonstrated that the problem associated with limited glycogen concentrations was an inability to maintain pace during prolonged running (i.e., during running lasting longer than one hour).

Carbohydrate Requirements for Runners

Scientific research has addressed the question of how much carbohydrate runners need to ingest in order to maximize muscle glycogen concentrations. An early study found that 150-pound (68 kg) males who consumed 280 grams of carbohydrate during the 24 hours following an exhaustive workout doubled the glycogen content of their leg muscles compared to eating just

100 grams of carbohydrate during the 24-hour period. However, ingesting 500 grams of carbohydrate *quadrupled* intramuscular glycogen concentration.[2]

In subsequent research, 10 experienced runners with an average $\dot{V}O_2$max of 58 ml • kg^{-1} • min^{-1} completed a highly demanding, glycogen-depleting workout consisting of 16 kilometers (9.94 mi) of running at an intensity of 80 percent of $\dot{V}O_2$max followed by five 1-minute sprints at the lofty power output of 130 percent of $\dot{V}O_2$max.[3] This session was completed on four occasions and was followed by the ingestion of 188, 375, 525, or 648 grams of carbohydrate during the 24-hour period after the workout. The greatest extent of glycogen synthesis occurred when the runners consumed 648 grams of carbohydrate. It made no difference whether the carbohydrate was consumed in two big meals or seven smaller snacks—glycogen restoration was the same.

Glycogen storage in a runner's muscles increases in direct proportion to the amount of carbohydrate consumed up to a high threshold intake beyond which intramuscular glycogen depots are full and no further storage is possible.[4] The amount of dietary carbohydrate required to refill glycogen storage areas in the muscles depends on a runner's body size. The runners in the 648-gram study weighed about 165 pounds (75 kg); less-massive runners would usually need less carbohydrate to fill glycogen depots while heavier competitors would need more.

Follow-up research indicated that about 4 grams of carbohydrate per pound (.45 kg) of body weight are required to restore muscle glycogen maximally following a strenuous, glycogen-depleting workout.[5] Thus, a 120-pound (54 kg) runner would need approximately 480 grams of carbohydrate (1,920 calories of carbohydrate) during the 24 hours after a demanding workout, but a 175-pound (79 kg) runner would require 700 grams (2,800 calories). Anecdotal evidence suggests that many runners take in far less than the ideal 4 grams per pound;[6] it is likely that their training and race performances suffer as a result.

Simple and Complex Carbohydrates

Runners often wonder whether simple or complex carbohydrates are better for maximizing muscle glycogen concentrations on a day-to-day basis. By definition, simple carbohydrates are sugars while complex carbohydrates are starches (i.e., sugars linked end to end in long molecules). It is tempting to believe that simple carbohydrates might be processed more quickly by the digestive system and reach the muscles more rapidly after meals. Scientific research, however, tells us that while the terms *simple* and *complex* do have specified chemical definitions, the two types of carbohydrate can be processed fairly similarly inside a runner's body. The digestive system quickly breaks down the complex carbohydrates in foods such as white bread, potatoes, and white rice into glucose and speeds the passage of glucose into the bloodstream almost as quickly as it would permit entry for a dose of pure glucose.[7]

To determine whether simple or complex carbohydrates are more effective in promoting glycogen storage, researchers from the Loughborough University of Technology in the United Kingdom studied 6 female and 9 male runners.[8] To deplete their muscle glycogen stores, the 15 athletes ran to exhaustion on treadmills at an intensity of 70 percent of $\dot{V}O_2$max. The athletes were then randomly assigned to either a control, pasta (i.e., complex carbohydrate), or confectionery (i.e., simple carbohydrate) group.

The pasta-group runners doubled their normal carbohydrate intake for the 3 days following the 70 percent workout by eating extra pasta. The confectionery-group athletes also doubled carbohydrate intake but focused on sugary foods such as cake, cookies, candy, and pie. Both groups took in about 540 grams (2,160 calories) of total carbohydrate per day while control subjects consumed just 322 grams (1,288 calories) of carbohydrate daily.

After the 3 days of special eating, the athletes once again ran until exhaustion at 70 percent of $\dot{V}O_2$max. The pasta and confectionery groups upgraded the total distance completed by 26 percent after their carbohydrate loading, but the control group increased distance covered by only 6 percent. The logical conclusions were that an ample intake of carbohydrate (~540 grams per day) enhances recovery from exhausting exercise and improves performance during strenuous, follow-up exercise, and that simple and complex carbohydrates were equally effective from the standpoints of glycogen loading and endurance enhancement. Of course, the nutritional value of cakes and cookies is lower than that of whole-grain foods and fruits and vegetables, so the latter would be preferable from a health standpoint.

Research has also addressed the question of whether the original Swedish depletion-repletion strategy of carbohydrate loading produces higher muscle glycogen concentrations than more conventional eating plans. As mentioned at the beginning of the chapter, the depletion-repletion technique called for runners to exercise to exhaustion, consume a low-carbohydrate diet for 3 days (depletion), exercise to exhaustion again, and then follow a high-carbohydrate diet with as much as 95 percent of total daily calories coming from carbohydrate for 3 more days in order to maximize glycogen storage in the muscles.

While the depletion-repletion approach did produce higher muscle glycogen levels, it was not without problems. The low-carbohydrate component of the strategy tended to make runners irritable—and also reduced their capacity to carry out high-quality training.[9] The two exhaustive running sessions also made it more difficult for runners to peak for important races. Fortunately, a study carried out at Ohio State University disclosed that the same level of glycogen supercompensation achieved with the Swedish depletion-repletion plan could be attained with a less counterproductive combination of exercise and diet.[9]

In this study, eight fit runners tapered by running 90, 40, 40, 20, and then 20 minutes per day over a 5-day period and rested on the sixth day. During this 6-day period, the runners' food-consumption pattern included 3 days of a 50 percent carbohydrate diet (353 grams of carbohydrate and 3,000 total calories per day) followed by 3 days on a 70 percent carbohydrate diet (542 grams of carbohydrate and 3,000 total calories each day). With this plan, muscle glycogen levels were as high as those achieved with the difficult depletion-repletion strategy.

A separate study verified that the depletion-repletion pattern is not necessary for achieving extra-high muscle glycogen concentrations but suggested that intake of simple carbohydrate might provide an advantage from the standpoint of glycogen synthesis. In research carried out at the University of Western Ontario in London, Ontario, 20 experienced runners who trained about 50 miles (81 km) per week and had completed an average of five marathons were divided into four groups of five subjects.

One group consumed a high-protein, high-fat, low-carbohydrate diet (i.e., the Swedish depletion approach) for 3 days in which only 15 percent of total calories came from carbohydrate, and then ingested a high-carbohydrate diet dominated by simple carbohydrates (e.g., sugared cereal, ripe fruit, candy, sweet breads, pastries) for the subsequent 3 days. A second group also followed the depletion approach for 3 days with the 15 percent carbohydrate diet but then ate lots of complex carbohydrates (e.g., nonripe fruits and vegetables; whole-grain breads, cereals, and pasta) for the final 3 days. The third and fourth groups ingested a more normal diet for the first 3 days, with 50 percent of calories coming from carbohydrate, and then switched to either simple or complex carbohydrate for the last 3 days.

Over the final high-carbohydrate days, all 20 runners took in 70 percent of total calories in the form of carbohydrate. During the 6 days of dietary manipulation, the runners carried out their normal training but ran only 3 miles (4.8 km) on the sixth day to enhance glycogen storage.[10]

The three days of depletion were not helpful. Those runners who had not used depletion stored just as much glycogen over the 6-day period as those who had used the depletion plan. Interestingly, the greatest upswing in glycogen storage occurred in the group whose members ate fairly normally for 3 days, with 50 percent of calories coming from carbohydrate, and then consumed simple carbohydrate for three days. This pattern roughly doubled the rate of glycogen storage in muscles achieved by the other three plans. This research suggests that the ingestion of simple carbohydrates might boost glycogen storage during periods when either the rapid restoration of glycogen or the maximal stockpiling of glycogen is necessary. It is interesting to note that the ultimate simple carbohydrate, table sugar, often makes up 10 to 15 percent of an elite Kenyan runner's daily caloric intake.

Protein Requirements for Runners

Scientific research has addressed the question of whether endurance runners have heightened dietary protein requirements. Among endurance competitors, protein demands might be increased because of training-related needs in order to synthesize increased quantities of aerobic enzymes, build new capillaries around the muscles, amplify mitochondrial biogenesis, strengthen connective tissues, and fortify the heart. Protein also furnishes a small but relevant portion of the energy required to perform prolonged running; increased protein synthesis is also required to repair subcellular damage to muscles, tendons, and ligaments incurred during prolonged or intense training.[11]

The evidence suggests that the recommended daily allowance (U.S. RDA) of protein of about 0.8 grams of protein per kilogram (2.2 lb) of body weight is inadequate for runners engaged in regular endurance training. In one study, well-trained endurance runners who ran from 7 to 9 miles (11-14 km) daily consumed either 0.86 grams of protein per kilogram of body mass per day (i.e., close to the recommended amount) or a high-protein diet of 1.49 grams per kilogram of body mass while their sweat and urine were collected to determine losses of body nitrogen.[12] Since nitrogen is contained in protein, nitrogen losses in sweat and urine can be used to estimate the amount of protein metabolized within the body each day.

The endurance runners consuming approximately the recommended daily allowance of protein actually experienced a net loss of nitrogen (i.e., they lost more protein than they took in) on about 50 percent of their training days while the runners consuming a greater amount of protein never sustained a nitrogen deficit. This suggests that recommended levels of protein intake are inadequate for runners engaged in vigorous endurance training and that about 1.5 grams of protein per kilogram of body mass would be adequate.

Follow-up research has indicated that an intake of just 1.0 gram per kilogram of body mass is adequate for runners engaged in very light training; accomplished runners engaged in high-volume or high-quality training may need 1.5-1.6 grams per kilogram of body weight per day.[13] One and one-half grams of protein per kilogram are the same as 0.7 grams per pound of body weight. Most North American and European endurance runners routinely ingest an adequate amount of protein to satisfy their daily needs without supplementation.

Fat Requirements for Runners

Most runners have no problem satisfying their daily fat-intake requirements. With carbohydrate making up about 70 percent of the total energy pie, 15 percent of calories can come from fat and 15 percent from protein. From an energy standpoint, the source of fat makes little difference: Each gram of ingested fat can provide 9 calories of potentially energy for running. From a health standpoint, the story changes. Runners should bias their fat intake toward lipid sources which are rich in omega-3 and monounsaturated fats, including dark-fleshed fish and olive oil. These fats have beneficial effects on cardiovascular and immune-system functioning while simultaneously providing needed energy.

Some runners attempt to restrict fat intake nearly completely, which is a huge mistake. Fat plays a vital role in human and exercise physiology, not only supplying energy but also supporting cell functioning, including the establishment of healthy cell membranes. It promotes the absorption of certain vitamins, protects vital organs, and preserves body temperature.

Proper Diet for Sprinters

Throughout the history of running competitions, athletes have believed that the intake of certain foods could optimize high-speed sprinting. As long ago as the fifth century BC, Charmis, a sprinter from Sparta, thought that eating nothing except figs during training would boost his performances while Dromeus of Stymphalos became highly successful in high-velocity competition while consuming only meat.[14]

The modern sprinter tends to align himself with Dromeus rather than Charmis, believing that high-protein diets are essential for sprint success.[15] However, science reveals that the high-intensity interval training favored by sprinters can deplete glycogen reserves in the muscles to a significant extent, suggesting that high-carbohydrate diets would be preferable to high-protein intakes. One study found that just 30 seconds of all-out sprinting reduced muscle glycogen concentrations by up to 25 percent.[16] Another investigation detected a 14 percent drop-off in glycogen after only 6 seconds of sprinting.[17]

Carbohydrate Needs

Given the impact of high-speed running on muscle glycogen levels, it is not surprising that high-protein, low-carbohydrate diets tend to reduce an athlete's ability to perform the kind of high-intensity training favored by sprinters.[18] Such diets may lower muscle glycogen concentrations to such an extent during periods of vigorous training that it is impossible for leg muscles to sustain high levels of force production. Research reveals that sprint performance declines by 10 to 15 percent when leg-muscle glycogen concentration drops below about 25 millimoles per kilogram wet weight of muscle.[19]

Individual workout quality can drop precipitously when a low-carbohydrate diet is followed. In one inquiry, just 2 days of low-carbohydrate eating reduced leg-muscle glycogen concentrations by approximately 50 percent compared with a high-carbohydrate diet. This approach significantly reduced the average intensity of training during both 10- and 30-minute interval workouts.[20]

In a separate study, athletes who followed either a high- or low-carbohydrate eating pattern for 36 hours undertook a rigorous interval workout involving repeated 60-second sprints with 3-minute recovery intervals.[21] The high-carbohydrate athletes were able to complete an average of 14.3 sprint intervals compared to just 10.4 intervals for the low-carbohydrate runners, and total exercise time increased by 37 percent (from 42 to 57.5 minutes) in the high-carbohydrate group. The first few sprint intervals were similar in power output for the two groups, but intensity fell dramatically for the low-carbohydrate subjects as the workout proceeded. This suggests that low-carbohydrate eating can lead to situations in which performance-hampering levels of muscle glycogen are reached earlier in high-intensity training sessions, decreasing the quality of the subsequent work performed.

A greater intake of carbohydrate may stimulate recovery between high-speed interval sessions on the track. In one study, athletes carried out an interval workout consisting of five sets of 5 maximal sprints with 30 seconds of recovery between sprints and 5 minutes of active recovery between the sets.[22] This was followed by one last set of 10 6-second sprints with 30 seconds of recovery. The overall workout was repeated 2 days later. During the 2 days of recovery between the workouts, some of the athletes followed a normal daily carbohydrate intake of 450 grams per day while a second group followed a high-protein, low-carbohydrate plan providing under 100 grams of carbohydrate each day. During the second workout, the normal-carbohydrate athletes were able to increase power during the first 5 sets of sprints compared with results from the first training session, an improvement that the low-carbohydrate athletes were unable to achieve.

In another study, athletes repeated a challenging interval workout involving 6-second sprints on successive days.[23] The athletes who followed a high-carbohydrate diet during the 24-hour recovery period were able to perform with greater power during the first 20 minutes of the second-day's session than those who consumed a low-carbohydrate diet. Performance was not significantly greater for the high-carbohydrate athletes during the final 40 minutes of the workout. This suggests that an ample carbohydrate intake is necessary for recovery between workouts that occur on consecutive days, but that the glycogen-depleting nature of sprint sessions may nonetheless deplete the glycogen stores of athletes following a high-carbohydrate diet and slow performance during the latter stages of workouts. Prior to extended sprint workouts, it appears to be very important to load leg muscles maximally with glycogen.

Overall, scientific evidence suggests that sprinters should avoid the high-protein, carbohydrate-restricted diets that are fairly popular today and should include an ample amount of carbohydrate in their daily eating.[24] For sprinters and endurance runners engaged in high-quality training sessions, adequate carbohydrate intake appears to help performance during extended sprint workouts and enhance recovery between demanding sprint sessions.[24]

Protein Needs

Considerable research has focused on how much protein sprinters actually need in their diets in order to improve training adaptations and maximize performances. A popular theory is that sprinters require more daily protein than endurance athletes in order to optimize gains in strength and power. Many sprinters engage in strength training along with their high-intensity running training and attempt to increase muscle mass in their legs and upper bodies, believing this will enhance maximal speed. Thus, it is logical to think that added protein might be beneficial for sprinters.

Scientists and coaches from Eastern Europe have recommended that sprinters and other power athletes who are engaged in weight training should ingest as much as 3 grams of protein per kilogram (2.2 lb) of body weight per day. This is a huge intake given that normal, recommended protein intake rates are often set at 0.8 grams per kilogram of body weight per day.[25] There is little published research that supports such recommendations.

Current recommendations call for sprinters to consume from 1.2 to 1.7 grams of protein per kilogram of body weight per day especially during early phases of training when increases in muscle mass and muscle-repair processes may be operating at their highest levels.[26] Such provisos have emerged from nitrogen-balance studies seeming to show that protein requirements increase during periods of chronic, intense exercise. A key flaw in this research is the fact that athletes become more efficient with their protein usage over extended periods of time, and most nitrogen-balance studies have rather short durations. Another problem is that a high protein intake by itself tends to increase protein use.[27] Thus, nitrogen-balance studies might overestimate protein requirements in sprinters.

Research regarding the effects of elevated protein intakes on performance, strength, and power has generally been carried out with strength trainers rather than sprinters and has produced contradictory results. One inquiry found that a daily protein intake of 2.1 grams per kilogram of body weight per day produced a significant gain in muscle mass over a 6-week period, but a normal intake of 1.2 grams of protein per kilogram of body weight failed to do so.[28] In contrast, a broad survey of high-quality, published studies concerning the effects of high protein intake on muscle strength suggested that supplemental protein ingestion has little impact on strength and body mass.[29]

The debate over whether sprinters should ingest 1.2 grams, 1.7 grams, or some higher number of grams of protein per day is softened by studies that reveal that most power athletes, including sprinters, take in well over 2 grams of protein each day during training. The exception to this rule is the case of female sprinters who are reducing their daily energy intake in hopes of controlling weight and body fat. Such athletes may indeed be consuming too little protein and could usually benefit from an increase in overall daily energy intake, which almost automatically increases protein consumption.

Conclusion

During periods of strenuous or prolonged training, a high-carbohydrate diet that focuses on the consumption of 4 grams of carbohydrate per pound (0.45 kg) of body weight per day is optimal for glycogen storage and therefore endurance performance. The classic repletion stage of carbohydrate loading is not necessary and in many cases is counterproductive from a psychological standpoint. The protein requirement for endurance runners is about 1.5 grams per kilogram of body weight per day, which is easily met with a standard Western diet. Even sprinters should follow a high-carbohydrate eating plan in order to optimize tough training sessions. The best endurance athletes in the world—the Kenyan runners—follow a diet that is extremely rich in carbohydrate, moderate in protein, and low in fat.

CHAPTER 45

Fueling Strategies During a Run

Many runners are still stuck in the dark ages when it comes to sport drink use. Ingesting a sport drink during workouts and competitions lasting longer than an hour, and during some very intense running sessions, can enhance carbohydrate oxidation in the muscles and thus advance both endurance and speed. Research has established not only the overall effectiveness of sport drinks but has also shown runners how much to consume, how to time their sport drink intakes, and how to combine carbs within a sport drink in order to maximize carbohydrate absorption.

Usefulness of Sport Drinks

Ingesting a carbohydrate-containing sport drink *just before and during* running sessions lasting longer than an hour can increase average running speed and delay exhaustion. This simple fact has been known for over 30 years, and yet many endurance runners today fail to use sport drinks properly during their long runs.

Interest in using a sport drink to enhance performance originated in the early 1970s after exercise physiologist David L. Costill of Ball State University traveled to Sweden to study the highly successful Swedish National Ski Team. The main purpose of Costill's Scandinavian journey was to measure the sky-high $\dot{V}O_2$max readings of the amazing Swedish cross-country skiers, but what startled Costill the most was the Swedes' strange drinking habits. Prior to their 180-minute training sessions, the skiers prepared prodigious quantities of tea and then completely saturated the tea with honey. The athletes were mixing up 36 percent carbohydrate solutions with 360 grams (13 oz) of carbohydrate (from honey) in each liter (1.06 qt) of tea.[1] At the time, 2.5 percent sport drinks were considered to be highly concentrated, and the majority of exercise physiologists were advocating the ingestion of plain water during prolonged running rather than a carbohydrate-containing beverage. There was a belief that carb ingestion during running could disturb blood insulin levels or upset the digestive system.

During their workouts, the Swedish skiers drank about one liter (1.06 qt) per hour of their hyperconcentrated brew, an intake rate of approximately 8 ounces (.2 L) every 15 minutes. When Costill pumped out the Swedes' stomachs after their workouts (a remarkably inhospitable act by a foreign guest), he found them to be almost empty! Nearly all of the ingested tea had moved into the skiers' small intestines during their training sessions, presumably supplying rich lodes of easily absorbed carbohydrate to sustain their activities.

Costill was shocked by such findings because one of his early sport drink inquiries had revealed that water drained from the stomach into the small intestine more quickly than a 2.5 percent sport drink, which in turned emptied more rapidly than a 5 percent sport beverage. Because of such slow emptying rates, it had appeared doubtful that the carbohydrate contained in sport drinks could ever be absorbed quickly enough to make a significant energy contribution during sustained running.

But those first investigations by Costill were carried out with individuals at rest, and as the exercise physiologist soon learned, running changed everything. The mechanical jostling associated with running helps to force fluids of varying carbohydrate concentrations down and out of the stomach and into the small intestine (where actual absorption occurs) *at similar rates*. As a result, most carbohydrate-containing sport drinks can exit the stomach during running as quickly as pure water.

In follow-up research, Costill demonstrated that taking in carbohydrate during sustained exercise could boost performance significantly.[2] In the subsequent inquiry, 10 subjects consumed either an artificially sweetened beverage or a combination of 43 grams (1.5 oz) of table sugar (sucrose) and 400 milliliters (13.5 oz) of water. The latter created a 10.75 percent sport drink once the sugar and water mixed together. The subjects swallowed one of these two alternatives immediately before and after 1, 2, and 3 hours of continuous exercise at a mild intensity of 50 percent of $\dot{V}O_2$max (i.e., about 65 percent of maximal heart rate). During the prolonged effort, exercisers who ingested the sucrose-water combination depleted glycogen stores in their quadriceps muscles at a slower rate and had higher blood glucose concentrations than participants who ingested the artificially sweetened drink.

After 4 hours of exercise, each of the 10 individuals exercised at 100 percent of $\dot{V}O_2$max and 100 percent of maximal heart rate until unable to continue. The exercisers who had consumed the sucrose and water kept going for 45 percent longer at $\dot{V}O_2$max. Costill concluded that the ingested sucrose was used effectively by the leg muscles for energy during exercise, saving intramuscular glycogen. The increased glycogen levels present in the leg muscles for the final, intensive exercise period then boosted performance during the highly demanding effort.

Fueling High-Intensity Workouts

Although sport drink consumption has classically been linked with exertions lasting longer than an hour, there is increasing evidence that it can be beneficial in shorter *high-intensity efforts* as well. Several studies have connected sport drink ingestion with improved performance in high-quality interval workouts lasting 60 minutes or less.[10-13] Carbohydrate intake seems to upgrade carbohydrate oxidation during such efforts, promoting faster running. The simple rule of ingesting some sport drink 10 minutes before an intense workout begins (see the following section) and then downing six regular swallows of sport drink every 15 minutes or so should help promote superior-quality training sessions.

Since Costill's groundbreaking research was published in 1984, follow-up scientific investigations have indicated that imbibing a carbohydrate-containing sport drink during prolonged running has four positive effects:

1. It raises blood glucose levels and increases the rate at which carbohydrate supplies the energy needed for running, especially during late stages of a workout or competition.[3, 4]

2. It preserves glycogen stores in the liver; this is beneficial because the liver can then release more glucose into the blood during a prolonged exertion.[5]

3. It increases glucose uptake by the muscles.[6]

4. It slows the rate at which muscle glycogen is broken down, leaving greater supplies of glycogen available to sustain desired paces over long distances.[7, 8]

It is also possible that the heightened carbohydrate availability associated with sport drink ingestion may upgrade the functioning of the central nervous system during extended running.[9] This may be especially important since current theories concerning the cause of fatigue during running pinpoint the nervous system as the originating source of tiredness.

For some runners, consuming a sport drink can be a problem when they attempt to swallow fluid on the run. If this is a problem, runners may tuck a straw into the waistband of their running shorts and use it to suck 1-ounce (29.6 mL) portions of the sport drink out of a cup or container without risk of aspiration or slowing of pace.

When and How Much to Drink

Research suggests that sport drink use is especially beneficial during a glycogen-depleting running event like the marathon. In a study carried out by Robert Cade, the inventor of Gatorade, and his colleagues at the University of Florida, 21 experienced marathon runners (18 men and three women) from the Florida Track Club were divided into three groups of roughly equivalent running ability.[14] Members of one group drank plain water while running a marathon; those in a second group consumed a glucose-electrolyte solution of 5 percent glucose with sodium, chloride, and phosphate; and subjects in a third group ingested a mixture that was half water and half glucose-electrolyte solution, yielding a 2.5 percent concoction. To ensure maximal muscle glycogen levels at the start of the race, all 21 runners carb loaded during the days prior to the marathon, relying on diets that were rich in carbohydrate.

Ten of the runners experienced difficulties during the last third of the race that caused them to drastically reduce pace from 6 to 9 or 10 minutes per mile (1.6 km) or to adopt a walk-run strategy for finishing. This drop-off in speed took place in 67 percent of the runners who drank only water during the competition. Fifty percent of the athletes who consumed the half-strength beverage hit the wall in this way. Only 29 percent of the glucose-electrolyte drinkers suffered from such precipitous falls in pacing. Overall, use of the sport drink reduced the risk of bonking.

Science has also addressed the important question of exactly *how much* carbohydrate should be ingested during prolonged running. If a runner takes in too little carbohydrate during prolonged running, the effect on muscle glycogen use will be minimal. If too much carbohydrate is ingested, significant amounts of water will be pulled osmotically into the stomach from surrounding tissues to dilute the carbs, and gastric upset and diarrhea will follow.

Traditionally, the highest rate at which ingested carbohydrate can be broken down for energy during running has been thought to be about 1 gram per minute in the average runner.[15]

It is easy for runners to adjust their drinking on the run in order to take

Richard Wareham/age fotostock

▶ Ingesting a sport drink during a run lasting longer than an hour can preserve speed and promote endurance.

in 1 gram of carbohydrate per minute (60 grams per hour). By definition, an 8 percent sport drink is a beverage with 8 grams of carbohydrate per 100 milliliters (3.4 oz). To hit the 60-gram mark, a runner needs to swallow 750 milliliters (25.4 oz) per hour (or 60/8 = 7.5 100-mL portions of the drink). A regular swallow of fluid approximates 1 ounce, so the desired intake amount could be achieved with a 6- to 7-ounce intake every 15 minutes, producing an ingestion rate of 24 to 28 ounces per hour. Thus, a simple rule is established: During running workouts or competitions that last longer than an hour, a runner should ingest six or seven regular swallows of an 8 percent sport drink every 15 minutes. A slightly smaller intake rate would be needed with a stronger sport drink, and a higher rate would be required with a weaker sport drink.

When using sport drinks in this way, it is important to avoid the intake of plain water throughout the prolonged effort; ingested water dilutes the sport drink in the stomach and thus decreases the rate of carbohydrate absorption. It is important and reassuring to know that sport drinks are just as effective as water for the prevention of dehydration during running.

Training Effect on Rate of Carbohydrate Oxidation

Exercise scientists have wondered whether it is possible to increase the rate of carbohydrate oxidation during running by employing specific kinds of training; such an upgrade would provide muscles with fuel at a more rapid rate and thus foster faster running. The leg muscles of well-trained runners normally do a remarkable job of removing carbohydrate from the blood and oxidizing it during exercise, especially when blood glucose and insulin concentrations are high.[16, 17]

Training-induced changes provide mechanisms for this upgraded carbohydrate oxidation capacity. Capillary densities expand in response to endurance training, and higher capillary densities promote a faster delivery rate of glucose to muscle fibers. GLUT4, a glucose transporter protein that facilitates the passage of glucose into muscle cells, also responds to endurance workouts. Finally, the enzymes responsible for breaking down glucose inside muscle cells increase their activity in response to running workouts.

The exact form of training that is best for optimizing these three factors is not precisely known; it would seem, though, that high-intensity training would have a larger impact on carbohydrate oxidation rate than would lower-intensity, higher-volume work. The reason for this is that higher-intensity running would seem to be a more powerful promoter of capillary growth and would rely more heavily on carbohydrate use than would more moderate running. Moderate running depends on fat oxidation to a greater extent, and this would be unlikely to optimize GLUT4 activity.

Carbohydrate Concentration

Research indicates that the optimal carbohydrate concentration for sport drinks is about 6 to 10 percent.[18] Drinks with less than a 6 percent carbohydrate content probably do not provide enough exogenous energy to make a significant difference during endurance running. Some runners are tempted to follow the strategy of Costill's Swedish skiers and ingest drinks with a carbohydrate concentration greater than 10 percent, but there are risks involved.

Highly concentrated drinks tend to drag water into the stomach via osmosis, creating sensations of bloating and feeling overfull. More concentrated sport drinks also increase the risk of nausea during prolonged runs. In one study, 70 percent of the athletes who ingested 12 percent sport beverages became nauseated during 2 hours of exercise while just 20 percent felt unwell when using 6 percent sport drinks.[18] Table 45.1 provides a list of popular sport drinks and their nutrient composition, including carbohydrate concentrations. Note that Shaklee Performance Pure Hydration provides the greatest amount of carbohydrate to the muscles per minute.

Table 45.1 Composition of Sport Drinks and Water

Sport drink	Grams of carbohydrate per liter	% Carbohydrate	Grams of carbohydrate delivered to the muscles per minute*
Accelerade	60	6	0.7
Dasani Water	0	0	0
Gatorade	60	6	0.7
Mizone Formulated Sports Water	37	3.7	0.4
Powerade XION4	59	5.9	0.7
Powerbar Endurance Formula	70	7	0.83
Propel Zero Sport	0	0	0
Shaklee Performance Pure Hydration	105	10.5	1.24
Staminade	72	7.2	0.84

*The number of grams of carbohydrate delivered to the muscles per minute is based on the consumption of six ounces of sport drink every 15 minutes while running.

Energy Gels

The issue of carbohydrate concentration makes the use of energy gels problematic during sustained endurance running. Although the gels are attractive from a weight standpoint, and it's much easier to carry them during a run than lugging heavy bottles of sport drinks, their use can easily create hyperconcentrated stomach solutions that can increase the risks of gastric distress and diarrhea. A typical small pack of energy gel contains 25 grams of carbohydrate. If this were ingested with a 6-ounce portion of water on a relatively empty stomach, the result would be a 14 percent gastric solution that would increase the risk of gastrointestinal discomfort.

Topping off a steady stream of sport drink intake with gel could be worse yet, as the carbs in the gel would mix with those from the sport drink in the stomach to make a molasses-like mixture. Runners who insist on using gels should calculate appropriate amounts of gel and water before running. One half of a gel pack, with 12.5 grams of carbohydrate, could be consumed with 175 ml (6 oz) of plain water to create a 7 percent sport drink–like solution in the stomach. To be effective, this exact intake would have to be repeated approximately every 15 minutes. Individuals who are attracted to gels should be aware that such products do *not* provide an energy boost at mile 20 of the marathon as many runners believe. The gel carbohydrate taken into the stomach at that late stage of a marathon will usually not even reach the muscles to be oxidized until the runner is wrapped in a heat sheet after finishing the race.

Calculating Carbohydrate Concentration

Given the potential negative effects of too high a concentration of carbohydrate, runners need to know how to determine the concentration of a sport drink. This is an important consideration: Some races feature sport drinks with carb concentrations outside the optimal range; runners should be aware of this and plan accordingly by bringing their own sport beverage. Sometimes, an attractive new sport drink looks appealing but does not clearly state its carbohydrate potency in percentage fashion; a runner then may wonder if the drink is actually worth buying.

Fortunately, it is easy to figure the carbohydrate concentration in any sport drink. Carbohydrate concentration in a sport beverage is always reckoned as grams of carbohydrate per 100 milliliters (3.38 oz) of fluid. For example, if a sport drink declares that it has 7 grams of carbohydrate in each 100 milliliters, it is a 7 percent sport drink. But sometimes it takes a little bit of reckoning to figure things out. For example, a liter (1.06 qt) of sport drink found on a store shelf might state its carbohydrate content at 80 grams (320 calories). A liter has 10 100-milliliter components, and thus by dividing 80 grams by the number of components, a runner can determine that the sport drink has 8 grams per 100 ml. The carb content of this drink is 8 grams per 100 ml, and so the beverage has an acceptable 8 percent carbohydrate concentration.

At other times, the math can get a bit trickier. As an example, a sport drink product might state its carb concentration at 27 grams per 12 ounces. In this case, the ounces need to be converted to liters. One liter is 33.9 ounces so the following equation converts the ounces to liters:

12 ounces/33.9 ounces = .35 liters or 350 mL

Thus the sport drink contains 27 grams of carbohydrate per 350 milliliters. There are 3.5 100-milliliter units within 350 milliliters, so the following equation can be used to reach grams per 100 milliliters:

$$27/3.5 = 7.7 \text{ grams per 100 mL}$$

Thus, the drink in question is a 7.7 percent sport beverage. It is within the optimal range of 6 to 10 percent and can be used successfully during prolonged runs lasting an hour or more and during very intense sessions as well.

Carbohydrate Type

Exercise scientists have carried out research to determine the best *type* of carbohydrate for sport drinks. Asker Jeukendrup and his colleagues in the Human Performance Laboratory at the School of Sport and Exercise Sciences at the University of Birmingham in the United Kingdom have discovered that the presence of varied *intestinal transport mechanisms* in the small intestine means that a mix of carbohydrates is preferable over a single carb source. Mixing carbohydrates together can actually raise carbohydrate oxidation during exercise above the gold standard of 1 gram (.04 oz) per minute.

Transport mechanisms come into play because glucose, fructose, sucrose, and other carbohydrates cannot move freely across the wall of the small intestine. Their movement from inside the hollow small intestine into the small blood capillaries that will carry the carbs into general circulation and thus to the muscles depends on transport proteins embedded in the walls of the small intestine. These proteins help give carbohydrate molecules an inward-directed ride through the wall of the gut and thus into the circulatory system, one example of how a transport mechanism works.

Glucose absorption depends on a sodium-dependent glucose transporter called SGLT1. Sodium-dependent means that sodium must be present for SGLT1 to do its job, which is a key reason why sport drinks contain sodium. Fructose, another simple, six-carbon sugar, seems to depend entirely for its absorption on a transporter called GLUT5 that is quite different from SGLT1. The mechanism underlying the absorption of sucrose, aka table sugar, which is a disaccharide composed of one part glucose and one part fructose, is controversial. Some scientists argue that sucrose is simply hydrolyzed to glucose and fructose at the small intestine's inner membrane, followed by absorption of the two constituents using the SGLT1 and GLUT5 transporters. However, there is some evidence that disaccharides like sucrose are actually absorbed by specific disaccharidase-related transporters that are independent of SGLT1 and GLUT5.[19]

There are not an infinite number of SGLT1 transporters in the inner walls of the small intestine, nor is there an overwhelming quantity of GLUT5 carriers. The densities of these carriers appear to be rather moderate—good enough for a sedentary person but not ample enough for the endurance athlete who wants to maximize the carbohydrate exit rate from the small intestine and subsequent carbohydrate entry into the circulatory system during exercise. What may happen if a runner's sport drink contains only glucose is that all of the SGLT1 carriers may become busy (i.e., attached to glucose molecules) as the runner moves along during his or her half marathon or marathon. Other glucose molecules wait impatiently in the small intestine, looking forward to their speedy passage to the muscles, but they can't move into the blood because all of the transport vans, or carriers, in the intestinal wall are fully booked.

If this is the case, a drink that contains glucose plus an additional carbohydrate, thus relying on both SGLT1 and a second type of transporter, should provide a speedier passage of carbs into the blood. In theory, a beverage with three types of carbohydrate would be better still as long as there were three separate transporter mechanisms.

To see if combinations of carbs were really absorbed and oxidized more quickly than single carbs during exercise and to get a feeling for which specific carbs might be optimal, Jeukendrup and his colleagues carried out a definitive study.[20] Eight well-trained male cyclists or triathletes carried out three exercise trials consisting of 150 minutes of sustained cycling at an intensity of about 62 percent of $\dot{V}O_2$max (~75 percent of maximal heart rate). During one of the tests, the athletes ingested plain water, during a second trial they took in a drink that contained only glucose, and during a third trial they drank a beverage with glucose, sucrose, and fructose in a 2:1:1 ratio. The average rate of glucose intake with the pure-glucose drink was 2.4 grams per minute during the trial. For the mixed-source beverage, the mean intake rate of glucose was 1.2 grams per minute while sucrose and fructose each checked in with .6 grams per minute. Thus, the total carb intake rates were equivalent in those two trials (2.4 grams per minute).

Although carb intake rates were identical in the trials using the glucose beverage and the mixture of glucose, sucrose, and fructose, the rate of actual oxidation of exogenous carbohydrate peaked at 1.70 grams per minute for the mixed-source concoction versus just 1.18 grams per minute for pure glucose, about a 44 percent difference. Total exogenous carbohydrate oxidation for the entire trial was 50 percent higher for the mixed-source drink compared with the glucose beverage—and was 70 percent higher than the traditional standard of 1 gram per minute.

This innovative research indicates that muscles can break down exogenous carbohydrate for energy at extremely high rates: 1.70 grams of carbohydrate per minute when 2.4 grams per minute are ingested if sport drinks contain a mix of carbohydrates. Previous work in Jeukendrup's laboratory had revealed that an intake of 1.8 grams per minute of mixed carbs led to an exogenous carbohydrate oxidation rate of 1.3 grams per minute, also well above the benchmark of 1 gram per minute.

It should be noted that this research was carried out with cyclists, however, and the benefits for runners may not be as attainable because of the large fluid intakes required. A runner using an 8 percent sport drink in hopes of taking in 2.4 grams of carbohydrate per minute would have to consume 1.8 liters (1.9 qt) of beverage per hour, an enormous amount of fluid. For an intake of 1.8 grams per minute, the runner would have to take in 1.35 liters (1.43 qt) per hour, also a very heavy load. Such large intakes are much easier for cyclists to handle during exertion. This is a key reason why a sport drink with a higher carb concentration like Shaklee Performance Pure Hydration would be preferred for runners. At 10 percent, Shaklee Performance would provide 83 grams of carbohydrate per hour with a seven-swallow per 15-minute ingestion rate, 1.4 grams per minute. That's not as much as cyclists are getting, but it is 25 percent more carbohydrate per hour than one gets with an 8 percent sport drink.

Runners who are interested in trying mixed-carbohydrate sport drinks can make their own. The recipe in figure 45.1 is for a 10 percent drink. Powdered glucose and fructose can be purchased from various online sources, and sucrose is readily available.

Figure 45.1 Recipe for Mixed-Carbohydrate Sport Drink

1 liter (4.2 c) water
50 g (1.8 oz) powdered glucose (or powdered glucose polymer)
25 g (.9 oz) sucrose (table sugar)
25 g (.9 oz) powdered fructose
1/3 tsp salt
Artificially sweetened drink mix (optional)

To the water, add the powdered glucose, the table sugar, and the powdered fructose. Stir well to dissolve the sugars and then add the salt while continuing to stir. Since this concoction will taste somewhat like trough water, it is acceptable to flavor it with *artificially sweetened* Kool-Aid or some other artificially sweetened commercial drink. Make sure that added flavoring contains no sugar, which would throw off the concentration of carbs.

The result will be a 10 percent sport drink with the exact relative composition of sugars used by Jeukendrup in his study, the combo that boosted exogenous carbohydrate oxidation to 1.7 grams per minute. To achieve a carbohydrate-intake rate of 1.8 grams per minute, a runner would have to ingest about 1.1 liters (1.16 qt) of this beverage per hour—or .26 liter (9 oz) every 15 minutes.

Runners who are concerned about the increasingly high cost of commercial sport beverages or who do not want to go to the trouble of mixing types of powders can make their own, perfectly workable 7.6 percent sport drink with the recipe in figure 45.2.

Figure 45.2   Recipe for Simple Sport Drink

1 quart (.95 L) water
6 tbl sugar
1/3 tsp salt
Artificially sweetened drink mix (optional)

To the water, add the sugar and mix well. Then add the salt while continuing to stir. If desired for better taste, add the artificially sweetened drink powder and stir well.

This mixture is not quite as sophisticated or effective as Jeukendrup's triad of glucose, sucrose, and fructose, but it will support 1 gram per minute of carbohydrate oxidation when six swallows are ingested every 15 minutes and thus will enhance performance during races and workouts lasting longer than an hour.

Absorption Rate

A final obstacle to overcome with the use of sport drinks is their relatively slow passage from the stomach into the small intestine, where absorption actually occurs; the stomach is a kind of holding pouch with nonabsorptive walls. Since a typical stomach-emptying rate for fluid is about 10 milliliters (.34 oz) per minute, approximately 600 milliliters (20 oz) of water or sport drink can move into the intestine from the stomach each hour under average conditions. A runner ingesting about 25 ounces (.74 L) of sport drink per hour would thus accumulate 5 ounces (.15 L) of water in his or her gullet each hour unless emptying rate could be advanced.

The good news is that water movement from the stomach to the small intestine can be optimized with a minor intervention. Research carried out by Nancy Rehrer and her colleagues has determined that the rate at which water moves from the stomach into the intestine depends on how much water is actually in the stomach, with larger volumes of stomach water permitting greater emptying rates.

In her investigations, Rehrer asked nine endurance athletes to ingest about 584 milliliters (20 oz) of sport drink and then run at the moderate pace of 70 percent of V̇O₂max, 7:34 per mile (1.6 km), for 80 minutes while swallowing an additional 146 milliliters (5 oz) of sport drink every 20 minutes during the run. Two sport drinks were used: (a) Isostar, an 8.1 percent carbohydrate concoction containing sucrose, maltose, maltodextrin, glucose, and fructose as well as electrolytes, and (b) Perform, a 19.1 percent carbohydrate drink that also contained electrolytes. On another occasion, the nine athletes consumed the sport drinks without exercising, and then they drank an artificially sweetened drink containing no carbohydrate while exercising to see whether the carbohydrate in Isostar and Perform tended to slow the stomach-emptying process.[21]

Over 90 percent of the Isostar ingested by the runners moved from stomach to intestine during the 80 minutes of exercise. The key to such fast movement was the large, 584-milliliter (20 oz) bolus of fluid consumed by the athletes just before they began running. This large quantity of water forced about 400 milliliters (13.5 oz) of water to pass into the small intestine within only 20 minutes, a remarkable emptying rate of about 20 milliliters (.67 oz) per minute—twice the average.

This pattern—filling the stomach well before a long race or training run and then taking in more sport drink at regular intervals—keeps the stomach full enough to maximize gastric emptying without significantly heightening the risk of gastric distress. As a result, runners can optimize water and carbohydrate absorption during endurance running; carbohydrate absorption increases because more carbohydrate is carried into the small intestine along with the water.

Many runners avoid Rehrer's bolus prior to running out of ignorance or because they dislike running with a relatively full stomach. The latter effect is counteracted by repeated use of the prerunning bolus technique during training, which makes the presence of fluid in the gut increasingly more comfortable over time. Anecdotally, a 10-ounce (295 mL) prerun bolus, taken 10 minutes before the onset of a long run, also seems to enhance gastric-emptying rate and carbohydrate absorption and is much more comfortable than the 20-ounce (584 mL) sample originally tested by Rehrer.

Conclusion

Carbohydrate ingestion during intense interval workouts and sustained runs lasting longer than an hour enhances endurance and upgrades average running speed. The use of sport drinks provides an ideal way to ingest readily available, performance-enhancing carbohydrate. The optimal sport drink composition is from 6 to 10 percent, and runners should attempt to take in at least 60 grams of carbohydrate per hour, somewhat less for small runners, or more if a mixed-carbohydrate sport drink is employed since more carb can be absorbed with such a beverage. A 10-ounce bolus (295 mL) of sport drink, taken 10 minutes before running begins, speeds gastric emptying and thus stops the stomach from limiting the rate of carbohydrate absorption.

CHAPTER 46

Weight Control and Body Composition

For endurance runners, nonessential body fat can be a distinct disadvantage. Scientific research reveals that there is an inverse relationship between endurance-running performance and percent body fat. Runners who carry more body fat tend to run more slowly in competitive events for a variety of reasons.[1] In general, female runners naturally have more body fat than male runners, and this is a key reason why women's world records are roughly 8 to 10 percent slower than men's marks. Gradual losses of body fat can have a positive effect on performance, but such drop-offs must be undertaken carefully and are not without health risks. A cautiously created training plan involving small but steady increases in volume and intensity in combination with an eating program that eliminates a moderate number of unnecessary calories without harming overall nutritional quality provides the best and safest path to improved body composition.

Fat has four key negative effects on running capacity:

1. Increases energy costs. Fat adds mass to a runner's body without providing any propulsive force. Surplus fat thus increases the energy cost of running at a specific speed because there is more weight to be dragged along.

2. Hampers running economy. As percent body fat increases, the oxygen-consumption rate associated with a particular running velocity also rises because a greater mass must be moved at a specific speed. This hurts running economy, a key predictor of endurance performance.

3. Lessens ability to accelerate. Excess fat also makes it difficult for runners to accelerate and surge within races. During running, the ability to accelerate is inversely proportional to nonpropulsive body mass. As a result, extra fat mandates slower changes in running velocity for a given level of force production.[1] For runners locked in a hard-fought competition, the outcome of the final sprint to the finish line can depend on which runner has the lowest percent body fat. Other factors being equal, the runner with the leanest body composition will often have the most suddenly initiated and most powerful kick at the end of the race.

4. Diminishes $\dot{V}O_2$max. Upswings in body fat also reduce maximal aerobic capacity ($\dot{V}O_2$max). A 70 kilogram (154 lb) male endurance runner with a $\dot{V}O_2$max of 60 ml • kg^{-1} • min^{-1} uses 4,200 milliliters (142 oz) of oxygen each minute ($70 \times 60 = 4,200$) when he is running at $\dot{V}O_2$max intensity. If he adds just 1 kilogram (2.2 lb) of fat to his frame, increasing his mass to 71 kilograms (157 lb), his new $\dot{V}O_2$max will be 59.15 ml • kg^{-1} • min^{-1} ($4,200/71 = 59.15$), a 1.4 percent fall-off that could hurt performance by a similar amount. (For these calculations, the logical and reasonable assumption is that the gain in body fat has no significant, positive effect on $\dot{V}O_2$max. In other words, the extra fatty tissue has minimal metabolic demands and does not hike the oxygen burn rate significantly during running.)

The performance-thwarting effects of unit gains in body fat are inversely proportional to initial body weight. A 50 kilogram (110 lb) female runner with a $\dot{V}O_2$max of 60 ml • kg^{-1} • min^{-1} who augments body mass with one kilogram of fat would have a new $\dot{V}O_2$max of 58.8 ml • kg^{-1} • min^{-1} ($3,000/51 = 58.8$), a 2 percent diminishment. Since female runners are generally smaller than males, unit increases in fat mass tend to have a more detrimental effect on aerobic capacity in females than with males. Percent body fat is usually higher in competitive female runners compared with competitive male runners, and this is one reason why top female athletes have lower values of $\dot{V}O_2$max than males.

Range of Body Composition Among Runners

Given the four negative effects of fat, it is not surprising that the best endurance runners in the world are very trim. Studies have revealed that male Olympic marathon runners have just 3 to 4 percent body fat (i.e., fat accounts for only 3 to 4 percent of total body mass).

The running community at large displays a broad range of body compositions, however. Scientific research suggests that genes can account for 25 to 40 percent of such differences in amount of fat between endurance runners.[2] This information has emerged from studies of monozygotic twins in which individuals experienced an energy surplus or deficit over an extended period of time.

In one investigation, identical twin pairs were underfed to produce a negative energy balance of 1,000 calories per day over a 93-day period.[3] Since the negative caloric balance was the same for all individuals, everyone should have lost about the same amount of weight, but actual weight loss ranged from 2 to 18 pounds per person! Within each twin pair, however, body mass changes were extremely similar, illustrating the significant role played by genes in weight change. Such research reveals that because of genetic differences, endurance runners will not lose weight at the same rate even when their diets have exactly the same negative energy balance. At least 250 genes are known to have an impact on body fat.[4]

Since genes account for 25 to 40 percent of the variation in body fat between endurance runners, the other 60 to 75 percent must be due to environmental factors: disparities in energy (food) intake and energy expenditure. The latter includes the energy expended during routine metabolism, daily activity, and endurance training and competition. The large role played by environmental factors suggests that endurance runners can put major dents in their levels of body fat by manipulating diet or training.

Pitfalls Associated With Trimming Fat and Weight

Endurance running is considered to be a lean-body sport, and many endurance runners make a concerted effort to trim body fat. The effects of body fat on performance are relatively well known in the running community, and runners also pursue fat loss for aesthetic and cultural reasons. Such efforts can limit the four negative effects of excess fat and thus lead to considerably improved performances, but they can sometimes have disastrous effects on health and competitive ability.

One pitfall associated with weight loss is that a sizable amount of body fat is essential: The human body cannot function optimally without it. Essential body fat is present throughout the nervous system, in the bone marrow, and around all organs in the body, where it provides a form of protective cushioning. Loss of this essential fat disturbs physiological functioning and harms overall health. In male endurance runners, essential body fat is believed to be approximately 3 percent of total body weight; for female runners, the percentage is believed to be about 12 percent, although this may vary from woman to woman.[1]

The remainder of an endurance-runner's body fat is storage fat, an energy depot composed primarily of triglyceride-containing adipose cells that gets bigger when energy intake, or calories consumed, is consistently greater than energy expenditure and shrinks when energy expenditure crests above intake. In the United States, total body fat—essential plus storage—averages about 12 to 15 percent for young men and 25 to 28 percent for young women.[5]

Although from a performance standpoint it might appear that an appropriate goal would be to eliminate almost all storage fat and leave essential fat untouched, many endurance athletes engaged in weight-loss processes encounter performance and health problems when their *storage-fat* levels are still considerable. An inescapable truth is that there is no accepted percentage body fat standard for endurance runners. A 6 percent level of body fat might be optimal for one male endurance runner—associated with the highest-possible levels of performance and excellent overall health—but the same percentage of body fat, once achieved, could actually be linked with increased fatigue and poorer running in another male athlete. Endurance runners should approach weight loss cautiously. The attempt to achieve an ideal, leaner body composition is a trial-and-error process during which an athlete gradually develops an understanding of what levels of body fat and overall mass are best for his or her performances *and* health.

Losing the Fat

Endurance runners can lose body fat by increasing daily energy expenditure through increasing running volume or upgrading the intensity of training sessions; by trimming total food consumption; by changing the quality of the diet and moving from high-calorie foods to those that are less calorie dense such as fruits, vegetables, and grains; or by employing a combination of these strategies.

Experienced runners with significant training volumes often find it impractical to lose weight by expanding training. A realistic, relatively safe rate of weight loss is believed to be about 1 pound (0.45 kg) per week,[1] which would require an increase in energy expenditure through additional running or cross-training of about 500 calories a day. If eating habits remain the same, 4 to 5 miles (6.4-8.1 km) of additional daily running would be required to induce this energy shortfall, or about 28 to 35 extra miles (45-56 km) per week. Such an increase in training might represent a reasonable goal for low-volume runners, but it would be a near impossibility for busy runners who are already logging about 35 miles (56 km) of running per week.

This means that a change in dietary intake will be the key factor in weight loss for many runners who train on a regular basis. Such runners have already come close to optimizing their rates of energy expenditure and thus need to explore ways to reduce energy intake. Reducing the percentage of fat in the diet can be an effective way to enhance leanness.[6] Compared with carbohydrate and protein, dietary fat has an increased potential for preserving weight or stimulating weight gain in runners for the following reasons:[7]

- Each gram of fat in the diet has more than twice as many calories as a gram of carbohydrate or protein.
- Fat is digested and assimilated quite efficiently compared with carbohydrate and protein. Thus, little energy is expended to process fat. Almost all of fat's energy can be used for metabolic requirements, training, or for *the storage of new fat within the body.*
- Unlike carbohydrate intake, which leads to heightened carbohydrate metabolism, the ingestion of fat does not stimulate increased fat oxidation.

Determining Weight Goals

Determining a body weight goal can be a relatively straightforward process. After body fat is estimated by a competent professional, current lean body weight can be calculated. For example, a male runner with a weight of 180 pounds (82 kg) and a determined body-fat percent of 15 percent has a lean mass of 153 pounds (69 kg) (.85 × 180 = 153). In consultation with a health professional, he may decide that he wants to lower his percent body fat to 10 percent. To determine his body weight goal, he would then divide his current lean body weight (153) by the desired percent lean body weight (90) and multiply the resulting value by 100. In this case 153/90 × 100 = 170 pounds (7 kg), which is the goal weight.

There are potential pitfalls involved in this process, however. Body weight history should be considered: If a runner has never weighed less than goal mass in his or her adult life, the desired weight may be very difficult to achieve.[7] Furthermore, the changes in diet that are undertaken to achieve reductions in percent body fat, especially if they produce very rapid weight loss, can lead to a number of problems, including an inadequate intake of vitamins and minerals, a lack of energy, negative changes in mood, a loss of muscle mass, reduced endurance, and even depressed immune function.[9]

Research suggests that weight loss should proceed slowly at no more than 1 pound (0.45 kg) per week. Runners should monitor themselves closely for negative health or performance effects associated with reduced weight. As mentioned, it is impossible to prescribe in advance an ideal percent body fat for an individual runner.

Science suggests that a reduction in dietary fat is not a magical way to improve body composition, however. It promotes weight loss only when it diminishes average daily energy intake.[8] In most cases, a runner consuming 1,500 calories per day and 25 grams (225 calories) of daily fat will not necessarily lose more weight than another runner who takes in 1,500 calories with 50 grams (450 calories) of lipids, provided that genetic factors do not play a significant role. Fortunately, for runners desiring to lose weight, the removal of fat-rich foods from the diet often leads to a reduced daily caloric intake and thus a higher probability of weight loss because the lower-fat foods that replace the high-fat products have lower energy densities (i.e., fewer calories per unit mass).

This does not mean that fat should be eliminated from a runner's diet. Extremely low-fat diets can lead to vitamin and mineral deficiencies and are unnecessary for weight loss.[7] A reasonable recommendation is for fat to make up 15 to 20 percent of daily energy intake, with omega-3 and mono-unsaturated fats making up the bulk of this lipid consumption.

In an effort to lose body fat, some endurance runners are tempted to follow extremely low-calorie diets, in some cases ingesting as few as 800 to 1,000 calories per day while still maintaining a regular training program. Such dietary plans can lead to fairly rapid weight loss, but the initial decline in mass is almost entirely accounted for by decreases in internal glycogen concentrations and water levels.[1] Since total carbohydrate intake is low because of the modest intake of total calories, muscle glycogen stores become depleted, and blood glucose levels are maintained by a process called gluconeogenesis, in which glycerol from triglycerides and an amino acid called alanine are used to create blood sugar. Because of the glycogen drain from the muscles, endurance runners engaged in low-calorie dieting experience an inability to conduct high-quality workouts, greater fatigue, and a loss of competitive ability. Disturbing potential consequences of such diets also include the loss of body protein, electrolyte imbalances, and dehydration.

Strategies for Losing Weight While Training

Popular dietary plans such as the Zone Diet, the Atkins Diet, the Sugar-Busters Diet, and various high-protein plans present particular problems for endurance runners engaged in regular training. One of the key difficulties is that these eating strategies are simply too low in carbohydrate. In the Zone Diet, for example, carbohydrate accounts for only 40 percent of daily caloric intake, and relative carbohydrate input can be even lower in the Atkins, Sugar-Buster, and high-protein plans. Such eating patterns can lead to the exhaustion of glycogen stores in the muscles and liver and thus a reduced ability to perform during prolonged or intense workouts.[10] The plans can produce rather quick initial weight loss, but the consequent reductions in training volume and intensity can make the maintenance of weight loss difficult.

Best Intensity for Burning Body Fat

Endurance runners are sometimes told that specific running intensities are optimal for burning body fat and thus producing the greatest improvement in body composition. Such recommendations are based on an inescapable fact about fat metabolism: The rate at which fat is metabolized for energy during running does depend heavily on the intensity of the running being conducted. During high-intensity efforts—a 400-meter sprint or a 5K race, for example—almost no fat is broken down to provide the needed energy.

However, a jog carried out at a very easy pace will rely to a larger extent on stored fat to furnish the necessary energy, especially if the exertion continues for longer than 30 to 60 minutes. The slower the pace, the greater the contribution made by fat to the required energy pie.

At a running intensity of 50 percent of $\dot{V}O_2$max, which often corresponds with about 65 percent of maximal heart rate, fat can provide about half of the energy, or calories required to keep moving. If this kind of easy exertion is sustained for a long time, fat's share of the energy pie increases. After two hours of jogging at 50 percent of $\dot{V}O_2$max, fat will be contributing 70 percent or more of the total required energy.[11]

Such findings suggest that the use of easy running paces might be best for getting rid of unwanted body fat. Indeed, for purposes of upgrading body composition, some trainers, aerobics instructors, health professionals, and coaches recommend exercising within what is often called the fat-burning zone, generally thought to be the range of intensities between 50 and 60 percent of $\dot{V}O_2$max (i.e., 65 to 73 percent of maximal heart rate). For many endurance runners, this would mean running at speeds ranging from 1.5 to 3 minutes per mile (1.6 km) slower than marathon pace.[11]

Scientific research reveals that such advice is misguided. While it is true that fat provides only 33 percent of the required calories when an endurance runner moves along at 75 percent of $\dot{V}O_2$max (i.e., 84 percent of maximal heart rate), the total calories expended per minute are greater with the higher-intensity running and thus the potential for weight loss is greater. A moderately fit runner exercising at 50 percent of $\dot{V}O_2$max burns about 220 calories during a 30-minute workout; the same runner, when working at 75 percent of $\dot{V}O_2$max, would expend roughly 330 calories in the same time. Since 50 percent of 220 and 33 percent of 330 yield the identical number—110 calories—it is easy to see that total fat burning is identical in the two kinds of sessions, and that energy expenditure is greater in the latter. Training in the so-called fat-burning zone often provides no special increase in fat burning, and such training would certainly have a less potent effect on overall weight loss and fitness compared with higher training intensities. Greater fitness is an excellent stimulus for fat loss since it is generally associated with longer and higher-quality workouts.

Some endurance runners worry that high-intensity training will burn little fat *during* workouts and thus will not be conducive to chipping away at unwanted storage fat. Such concerns are ill-founded. High-quality training can induce a substantial caloric deficit and a significant decline in internal glycogen stores. During the 24 hours following a high-quality session, as glycogen depots are gradually being refilled, a runner's body must turn to other internal stores of energy to keep metabolism going and stimulate recovery. The source of this energy will often be stored fat, and the greater energy deficits associated with high-quality training will lead to a dramatically increased draw on stored fat. Anecdotally, the leanest endurance runners in the world are the elite Kenyans, and they seldom train at low intensities or in the fat-burning zone.[12]

Impact of Strength Training

The overall training program that produces optimal changes in body composition for endurance runners has not yet been identified. However, it is clear that engaging in regular strength training can be beneficial.[13, 14] Strength training can increase the amount of metabolically active tissue (i.e., muscle) in a runner's body and therefore enhance daily energy expenditure, making it easier for a runner working toward leanness to keep his or her daily energy budget in the red on a frequent basis. Weight loss can lower resting metabolic rate (RMR) and thus make it difficult to preserve decreases in weight, but resistance training can counteract this effect by transforming the body into a more metabolically active collection of tissues.[1]

Effects of Resting Metabolic Rate on Weight Loss

A problem for runners who want to reduce weight is that losses in body mass become increasingly difficult to make as the number on the scale drops. One difficulty is that RMR diminishes as weight is lost.[15] This lowers daily energy expenditure and thus potentially pushes a runner's energy budget up into the black (i.e., out of deficit territory), and caloric intake exceeds the newly decreased expenditure. In humans and other animals, a kind of autoregulatory feedback mechanism appears to operate during periods of sustained weight loss and causes the body to become more efficient with energy expenditure. This mechanism can block further weight loss even though an apparent net energy deficit is being maintained[1] and can even lead to weight gain in situations in which caloric intakes appear to be quite low and strenuous training is being maintained.[16]

This accounts for the discovery that some endurance runners, particularly females, have unusually low energy intakes that would not appear to be able to satisfy the combined demands of resting metabolism, normal daily activity, and training. Research has shown that some highly trained female runners have energy intakes comparable in magnitude to sedentary women of the same age despite the fact that the athletes are running from 30 to 90 kilometers (19-56 mi) each week![17, 18]

Female runners with high-volume training programs and modest intakes of calories are more likely to have significantly depressed resting metabolic rates and to experience amenorrhea.[19] To avoid amenorrhea—and thus protect bone mass—and to perform at a higher level by refilling depressed glycogen stores in the muscles, such female runners would have to increase food intake; however, increased eating would very likely lead to unwanted gains in body weight since the runners' metabolic processes have become more efficient. The optimal strategy for emerging from this energy efficiency trap has yet to be determined. It would seem, however, that a gradual, inchmeal increase in food intake might be the best way to restore menstrual status, improve performance, and move away from energy superefficiency without piling on undesired mass.

Tracking Caloric and Carbohydrate Intake

Endurance runners are often unaware of how many calories they ingest on a daily basis. This lack of awareness can have significant consequences for weight loss, glycogen replenishment, and performance. Runners who are attempting to lose weight are at even more risk of consuming too few calories even when they think they are following a healthy diet.

When caloric and carbohydrate intakes are too low, performance problems can occur, and a form of energy overefficiency may be induced. Athletes should record what they eat for a several-day period and then calculate their intakes using a tool such as the USDA National Nutrient Database for Standard Reference, which can be found at the USDA website and provides nutrition information for a wide variety of foods. If carbohydrate or caloric intakes are low, optimal adaptation to training cannot occur.

Consider the case of a 26-year-old male runner who was preparing to be competitive in 5K and 10K races and considering competing at the National Cross Country Championships. He had been a runner in college, posting a 4:16 personal record for the mile. In a 6-minute, $v\dot{V}O_2max$ test in an early stage of his training, he covered nearly 2,000 meters (1.24 mi) for an average pace of 72 seconds per 400 meters and an estimated $v\dot{V}O_2max$ of 5.56 meters (18.24 ft) per second. This would predict a 5K pace of about 74 seconds per 400 for a 5K time of 15:25, which would be reasonable for the preliminary phase of his overall progression. As he resumed serious training, his speed workouts went well. He clipped off 28- to 29-second 200s and hit 400s in 60 seconds each on the track. Predicting 5K times in the 14s did not appear to be too much of a stretch.

As part of his effort to carry out high-quality, sustained running, he entered some 5K and 10K races, and here a problem revealed itself. He crashed badly in the last mile (1.6 km) of every 5K and over the last 2 to 3 miles (3.22-2.83 km) of the 10Ks. His interval workouts, too, had a similar pattern. The first halves of the sessions were great, but the intervals in the second halves were performed at significantly slower paces. In a $v\dot{V}O_2max$ session, for example, he could perform the first three 800s at 2:24, but the last two might drop to 2:37 or even 2:43. In a 4 × 1,600 session, the fall-off over the last two intervals was even more dramatic, and with a 5 × 1,600, he often had to stop when attempting to carry out the closing interval.

The runner was training faithfully, getting plenty of sleep, and avoiding stress, but the pattern of decreased running velocity persisted during workouts and competitions. The problem turned out to be that his daily intake of calories and carbohydrate were too low. This athlete's food choices tended to be low in fat, moderate in protein, and fairly rich in carbohydrate. His weight was stable, and so he assumed that he was taking in sufficient calories and carbohydrate. However, his dietary log revealed that this was not the case. Table 46.1 shows his total food intake for a typical day.

Although calorie burning varies widely for individuals, estimate daily caloric needs by multiplying body weight in pounds by 15 and then adding about 100 calories per mile of training. As discussed in chapter 44, during challenging training, endurance runners should ingest a minimum of 4 grams (0.14 oz) of carbohydrate per pound of body weight on a daily basis. Top-quality Kenyan runners ingest almost 5 grams of carbohydrate per pound of weight.[20] Protein intake for endurance athletes engaged in strenuous training could be as high as 1.5 to 1.6 grams per kilogram of body weight.

The runner weighed 140 pounds (64 kg) and ran about 9 miles (15 km) per day, so his caloric intake should have been 3,000 calories per day:

$$(140 \text{ pounds} \times 15) + 900 \text{ calories for the miles} = 3,000 \text{ calories}$$

On the day represented in table 46.1, a typical day, he took in less than 1,900 calories, about 62 percent of the estimated caloric need. Additionally, he was ingesting just 381/140 = 2.7 grams of carbohydrate per pound, less than 70 percent of the recommended amount and barely over half of what the Kenyans would be eating. Protein intake was also somewhat low, suggesting that the muscle-repair processes that occur during recovery might be hampered. A runner should take in about 95 grams of protein; instead, he ingested a little over 58 grams on this particular day.

The runner was counseled to *gradually* increase the amount of food he was eating. Gradual changes are necessary in this case because of the potential mitigating factor of energy efficiency. Since the runner had been seriously

Table 46.1 Example Runner's Typical Daily Food Intake

Food	Calories	Carbs (grams)	Protein (grams)
1 cup cooked dhal (pigeon peas)	203	39	11.4
4 bagels	728	144	28
1 cup Wheaties cereal	106	24	3
1 cup 2 percent milk	122	11	8
2 cups cooked rice	410	88	8
2 apples	200	50	0
1 banana	100	25	0
Grand Totals	**1,869**	**381**	**58.4**

undereating, there was a good chance that his body was quite conservative in burning calories. A sudden jump to 4 grams of carbohydrate per pound of body weight might be treated by his body as a major surplus, leading to storing large quantities of body fat. An increase of just 25 grams of carbs (100 calories) per day, with this new total sustained for several days, then another similar increase appeared to be the optimal way to proceed.

During this period of gradual change, the athlete discovered one morning that his weight had jumped to 144 pounds (65 kg). He was reassured that he was simply storing more carbohydrate (i.e., glycogen) in his muscles and liver, that carbohydrate weighs more than twice as much as fat for the equivalent amount of calories, that glycogen storage includes water storage as well, and that the higher-quality and longer-duration training he could now perform as a result of the carbohydrate storage would ultimately keep his weight stable. He was also extremely happy when his ability to sustain quality paces during challenging workouts and races took a dramatic upswing.

The runner also found that muscle soreness between workouts decreased. Muscle glycogen is not only a fuel during exercise, but it also provides energy for recovery processes. In addition, glycogen-poor muscles probably produce less protective joint stabilizing forces during strenuous running than glycogen-rich muscles. Thus, the amount of damage may be greater when glycogen is low, inducing soreness and necessitating longer recoveries.

Conclusion

Runners with low to moderate training volumes can lose weight effectively via a combination of increased training and reduced caloric intake that produces an average daily energy deficit of about 500 calories. Higher-volume runners often have difficulty increasing volume and thus must rely on changes in energy intake to achieve goal weight. A reduction in the percentage of dietary fat consumed can be an effective weight-loss strategy as long as it is not extreme, healthy fats (e.g., omega-3) are retained in the diet, and the effect is a drop in total caloric intake. Dietary plans that restrict carbohydrate should be avoided since they deplete muscle glycogen and lead to a reduction in training quality.

Keeping an accurate dietary log can help endurance runners understand how many calories they are consuming per day. This is especially important for runners who are experiencing significant fatigue during intense or prolonged workouts or who are underperforming during competitions; such athletes' intakes of carbohydrate and total calories may be too low. For those runners with excess body fat, knowledge of calorie consumptions permits a gradual reduction in caloric intake or a revision in dietary habits that can promote desired weight loss.

CHAPTER 47

Ergogenic Aids for Running

More than $90 billion worth of sport supplements are sold to athletes each year around the world by an industry that is growing at a 24 percent annual rate.[1] Runners and other athletes find themselves tempted by an amazing array of allegedly performance-enhancing products ranging from Andro Xtreme to Xenadrine RFA-1 and zeranol.

Given the growth of the sport supplement business, many runners are surprised to learn that scientific research has linked only three relatively inexpensive supplements—caffeine, sodium bicarbonate, and creatine monohydrate—with improved running performances. Two of these supplements—caffeine and sodium bicarbonate—are readily available to runners without the purchase of high-priced commercial products.

Caffeine Boost for Endurance Running

Of the trio, caffeine has the strongest scientific support as an ergogenic aid *for distance runners*. Ergogenic aids are substances with the potential to improve performance, especially resistance to fatigue. In one well-designed (i.e., randomized, double-blind, crossover) study carried out in Australia, 15 well-trained and 15 recreational runners completed two randomized 5K time trials after ingesting either 5 milligrams of caffeine per kilogram (2.2 lb) of body weight or a placebo.[2] The intake of caffeine significantly upgraded the 5K performances of both the well-trained and recreational runners by approximately 1 percent compared with placebo ingestion.

In a second investigation completed at Edge Hill College in the United Kingdom, eight trained male distance runners participated in an 8K race (4.97 mi) 1 hour after ingesting 3 milligrams of caffeine per kilogram (2.2 lb) of body weight, a placebo, or no supplement at all.[3] This inquiry attempted to detect the mechanism underlying caffeine's ergogenic activity by analyzing heart rate, blood lactate concentration, and rating of perceived effort

(RPE) during the competition. The use of caffeine resulted in a 1.2 percent, 23-second enhancement of performance for the 8K runners compared with placebo use and no supplementation. Caffeine had no significant effect on heart rate or RPE, but it was linked with elevated blood lactate levels. Two interpretations for the higher lactate concentrations are possible: (1) The faster running associated with caffeine supplementation might have generated more lactate, or (2) the caffeine may have stimulated lactate production, increasing fuel availability during the race and thus enhancing performance.

A third piece of research undertaken at the College of St. Scholastica in Minnesota linked caffeine use with benefits for cross country runners.[4] Ten college-age cross country runners (five women and five men) completed a $\dot{V}O_2$max test and then ran for 30 minutes on a treadmill at an intensity of 70 percent of $\dot{V}O_2$max. In one case, the athletes ingested 7 milligrams of caffeine per kilogram of body weight prior to the submaximal run; in another, they consumed a placebo (7 mg/kg using vitamin C). The crossover treatments were randomized, and the study was completed in a double-blind manner. The results revealed that the intake of caffeine reduced perceived effort during the 30-minute runs and also augmented respiratory function, including tidal volume (i.e., the amount of air taken in per breath) and alveolar ventilation (i.e., the degree to which the lung's small sacs filled with air during running).

There is also evidence that acute ingestion of caffeine may be helpful in shorter-duration, higher-intensity running events such as the mile and 1,500 meters. In an exploration conducted at Christ Church College in Canterbury, United Kingdom, well-trained club-, county-, and national-level runners ran 1,500 meters on a treadmill as fast as possible and also engaged in a 1-minute finishing burst following a high-intensity run after ingesting either caffeinated or decaffeinated coffee. Drinking the caffeinated coffee reduced the amount of time needed to run 1,500 meters, heightened the velocity of the finishing burst, and also augmented the oxygen consumption rate during the 1,500-meter run compared with ingestion of decaffeinated coffee.[5]

Finally, caffeine seems to boost performance during supramaximal effort, that is, during running carried out at speeds considerably faster than $v\dot{V}O_2$max and thus much quicker than 1,500-meter or mile velocities. In work carried out at the University of Luton in the United Kingdom, nine well-trained male runners were able to run significantly longer at an intensity of 125 percent of $v\dot{V}O_2$max after ingesting 5 milligrams of caffeine per kilogram (2.2 lb) of body weight compared with the ingestion of a placebo.[6]

Caffeine is available to runners in four forms:

1. As a natural constituent of regular, not decaffeinated coffee
2. As a compound found in so-called energy drinks (e.g., Red Bull, Jolt, Mountain Dew Red Alert, Surge)

3. In caffeinated gels (e.g., Torq Gel, Octane Energy Gel, Power Gel, Hammer Gel)

4. In pill form in popular supplements (e.g., Alert, No Doz, Vivarin, Stay Awake) that are sold without prescription in many drug stores

The pill supplements commonly provide from 50 to 200 milligrams of caffeine per tablet. The actual amount of caffeine in coffee depends on a number of factors, including the type of bean, the soil and overall environment in which the coffee was grown, the grind with which the coffee was prepared, and the method and length of brewing. A 6-ounce (177 mL) cup of coffee may have as few as 50 milligrams or as many as 200 milligrams of caffeine.

This imprecision of caffeine content tells endurance runners interested in caffeine's ergogenic effects that the use of caffeine tablets, gels, or caffeinated energy drinks might be preferable from a performance-enhancing standpoint compared with sipping mugs of java before competitions. Also making the use of coffee even more problematic for the endurance athlete is the evidence that coffee contains compounds that may at least partially suppress some of the physiological actions of caffeine.[7] When athletes exercise at an intensity of 85 percent of $\dot{V}O_2$max, they derive much more benefit, or increased endurance, from caffeine provided in pill form than from an equivalent amount of caffeine in coffee.

A majority of endurance athletes are aware that caffeine intake prior to exercise is ergogenic but are unaware of how much caffeine must actually be ingested to produce performance enhancement.[8] Exercise scientists generally agree that an ergogenic dose of caffeine is about 3 to 9 milligrams per kilogram of body weight taken one hour before running begins.[9] There are few adverse side effects associated with caffeine use just before and during exercise,[8] and caffeine consumption prior to performance is no longer banned by the International Olympic Committee, the IAAF, or the NCAA. Caffeine is considered to be a diuretic, but its ability to induce diuresis is blunted by exertion.

Some exercise scientists have speculated that the *chronic* ingestion of coffee or caffeine-containing products might block the acute, positive effects of caffeine on performance on a specific day. Regular users of caffeine do have significantly different metabolic responses to the intake of the compound compared with nonusers.[10] Nonetheless, no research has shown that caffeine-related enhancements in performance are different in caffeine users and nonusers. In one study, complete withdrawal from caffeine for 2 to 4 days had no impact on the effect of caffeine on performance; the ergogenic dose of caffeine in this investigation was 6 milligrams per kilogram of body weight.[11]

There is evidence that the use of caffeine combined with another compound called ephedrine may boost running performances to a greater extent for events ranging in duration from 10 to 20 minutes compared with the ingestion of caffeine alone.[12, 13] However, ephedrine supplementation has been linked with a number of deaths and adverse cardiovascular side effects, and its use is generally discouraged by sports medicine physicians. Ephedrine is also on the prohibited list published by the World Anti-Doping Agency (WADA): An athlete violates this prohibition when his or her urine level of ephedrine exceeds 10 micrograms per milliliter.[14]

Sodium Bicarbonate and Middle-Distance Running

Like caffeine ingestion, sodium bicarbonate (i.e., baking soda) supplementation is legal, and some exercise physiologists contend that bicarbonate intake may be particularly helpful to middle-distance runners. Sodium bicarbonate is a strong buffer, a chemical that can prevent the blood from becoming unusually acidic during intense running. This makes bicarbonate attractive as a supplement because upswings in blood acidity have been correlated with fatigue in some research.

In a study carried out at Ball State University by exercise physiologist David L. Costill and his colleagues, eight healthy male athletes pedaled bicycle ergometers at the high intensity of 125 percent of $\dot{V}O_2$max until they became exhausted.[15] One hour prior to exertion, the individuals ingested a solution of either sodium bicarbonate or sodium chloride (table salt). All of the athletes were eventually tested with each type of solution. Ingestion of the baking soda slightly increased endurance time at 125 percent of $\dot{V}O_2$max from 98.6 to 100.6 seconds, but this difference was not statistically significant. A related study revealed that ingesting bicarbonate did not upgrade performance in a 400-meter run.[16]

The Ball State researchers found that the blood of the cyclists who consumed bicarbonate recovered more quickly following the intense effort (i.e., returned to a normal level of acidity more rapidly). This heightened recovery suggested to the scientists that the *muscles* of the exercisers might also have recovered more quickly, and they hypothesized that bicarbonate could enhance performance during workouts that involved *repeated* high-intensity intervals.

In their follow-up study, 11 athletes (10 males and 1 female) completed an interval session consisting of five high-intensity intervals; this workout was completed 1 hour after ingesting either sodium bicarbonate or sodium chloride.[17] The workload during the intervals was again set at 125 percent of $\dot{V}O_2$max, and a 1-minute recovery interval separated each minute of exercise. The first four work intervals lasted 1 minute, but the fifth interval was sustained for as long as possible.

The athletes taking bicarbonate performed much better during the fifth interval than the sodium chloride control group. For the fifth interval, bicarbonate users exercised 160.8 seconds prior to exhaustion while control individuals managed to keep going for only 113.5 seconds. The fittest individuals benefited the most from sodium bicarbonate ingestion: The athletes who had the longest performance times with sodium chloride achieved the biggest improvements with sodium bicarbonate, perhaps because their sustained power outputs advanced blood acidity to the greatest extent and therefore needed buffering the most.

A separate study carried out at the University of Western Australia supported the idea that ingesting sodium-bicarbonate could heighten the quality of high-intensity interval workouts.[18] In this study, seven female team-sport athletes ingested sodium bicarbonate on day and a placebo on another day, both shortly before performing an intermittent-sprint workout consisting of two 36-minute halves during which high-intensity work intervals alternated with easy recovery periods. During the second halves of these training sessions, total work output was significantly greater during 7 of the 18 intervals after ingesting sodium bicarbonate rather than a placebo.

Costill's research team contended that bicarbonate ingestion is useless in running events lasting less than 1 minute but can enhance performance during repeated intervals of high-intensity running. The Costill group suggested that bicarbonate might also be beneficial during single runs lasting longer than a minute, a hypothesis that was supported by subsequent work with 800-meter runners.[19] In this follow-up inquiry, athletes who ingested 0.3 grams of sodium bicarbonate per kilogram (2.2 lb) of body weight improved 800-meter race times by 2.9 seconds.

Other research suggests that bicarbonate ingestion might aid performance during 3K (1.86 mi) competitions. In a study carried out at the University of South Carolina, 10 highly trained runners ($\dot{V}O_2max$ = 69.4 ml • kg^{-1} • min^{-1}) ran for as long as possible on a treadmill at an intensity of 100 percent of $\dot{V}O_2max$ after ingesting either a placebo or 0.3 grams of sodium bicarbonate per kilogram of body weight.[20] Sodium bicarbonate ingestion significantly increased running time to exhaustion at 100 percent of $\dot{V}O_2max$ from 564 to 578 seconds, a 2.5 percent improvement.

Sodium bicarbonate as baking soda is easily and cheaply obtained, and it appears to improve performance in high-intensity competitions lasting longer than 1 minute but requiring less than 10 minutes to complete. Research suggests that the ergogenic dose is about 0.3 grams of sodium bicarbonate per kilogram of body weight ingested approximately an hour prior to intense exertion. The appropriate amount of sodium bicarbonate is dissolved in a glass of water, using just enough water to put the bicarbonate into solution, and then drunk. In addition to bolstering race performances in events lasting from 1 to 10 minutes, acute baking soda supplementation appears to boost the quality of interval workouts carried out over longer periods of time.

Unlike caffeine supplementation, sodium bicarbonate ingestion is linked with a variety of unpleasant side effects, including diarrhea, cramping, and general gastric discomfort.[21] Runners intending to ingest sodium bicarbonate prior to a major race would be well advised to practice consuming it several times in less-important races in advance of the big day.

Supplements Without Scientific Backing

The list of supplements marketed to runners and other athletes is a long one, including those in the list that follow. There is no convincing scientific evidence that any of these can enhance running performance. A variety of antioxidant formulas are also sold to runners, including products containing omega-3 fatty acids. Such products may be beneficial for overall health, but their use has not been linked with increased running capacity.

acetylcholine	glucosamine
androstenedione	glutamine
arginine	MCT
bee pollen	phosphatidylserine
branched-chain amino acids	octacosanol
carnitine	royal jelly
choline	sodium citrate
chondroitin	sodium phosphate
chromium	spirulina
coenzyme Q10	vanadium
conjugated linoleic acids	wheat germ oil
ginseng	

Effects of Creatine on Running

A third supplement—creatine monohydrate—can boost sprinting capacity and enhance body composition and muscle mass when it is taken over an extended period of time. Creatine monohydrate is probably the most widely used supplement taken by athletes in an attempt to improve athletic success.[22]

There is a logical scientific rationale for creatine's ability to improve high-power performances. Research has revealed that supplementary creatine intake can raise muscle creatine concentrations by 20 percent or more, with a significant portion of this added creatine stored as a compound called phosphocreatine within muscles. Muscle phosphocreatine is a source of energy during sprint events; it acts by donating its phosphate group to a chemical called ADP in order to create ATP (adenosine triphosphate) within muscle fibers. ATP is the energy for muscle contractions (see chapter 43).

Just 6 seconds of all-out sprinting can deplete normal muscle phosphocreatine levels in an athlete who has not loaded creatine, explaining the fall-offs in velocity that occur near the end of a 100-meter sprint.[23] Four to six daily portions of 5 grams of creatine monohydrate over a five-day period—called a loading dose—can cause phosphocreatine concentrations to reach maximal levels inside muscles.[24] Comparable advances can be attained with a lower intake of 3 grams of creatine per day sustained for a month. Three grams per day is considered to be a maintenance dose of creatine.[25]

One meta-analysis of peer-reviewed scientific studies, published in 2003, uncovered 18 investigations in which creatine supplementation was linked with improvements in strength, body composition, or performance;[26] since then, many additional studies have documented creatine's benefits. The creatine studies reviewed in the meta-analysis were usually 8 weeks in duration, the average loading dose was 19 grams of creatine per day for 5 days, and the mean maintenance dose was 7 grams each day.

Scientific evidence suggests that creatine supplementation can enhance sprint performances and upgrade the overall quality of high-intensity interval workouts. In a study carried out in Spain with trained male handball players, 5 days of creatine supplementation involving a loading dose of 20 grams of creatine per day improved running velocity during the initial 5 meters of 15-meter sprint (initial 16.40 ft of 49.21 ft) intervals by about 3 percent.[27] Creatine loading was also linked with upgrades in lower-body maximal strength and repetitive power and heightened resistance to fatigue during repeated jumping activity. In another study, a creatine intake of 20 grams per day for 5 days augmented muscular phosphocreatine concentrations and advanced the quality of high-intensity repetitions performed during interval workouts lasting for 80 minutes; the work intervals used in this research were extremely short, taking just 4 seconds to complete.[28]

Creatine and Endurance Runners

Can creatine supplementation benefit endurance runners? The previously mentioned meta-analysis revealed that creatine supplementation is linked with a net weekly gain in strength of about 1.1 percent in athletes carrying out resistance work compared with carrying out strength training without any supplementation at all. While that might seem like a small effect, it could lead to substantial differences in strength over time. Although there is no scientific evidence to support the idea that creatine supplementation directly boosts endurance-running performance, distance-running success hinges on running speed. Running speed is a function of the amount of force applied to the ground by the legs, and creatine supplementation—combined with effective running-specific strength training—could magnify that propulsive force. Creatine's ability to improve the quality of interval workouts might also aid endurance-running performance after an extended period during which interval work was emphasized.

One study carried out with middle-distance runners demonstrated the dramatic effect that creatine supplementation can have on interval training.[29]

Five runners at Tartu University in Estonia supplemented their diets with 30 grams of creatine monohydrate per day over a 6-day period; the creatine was taken in six 5-gram doses parceled out over the course of a day. During the 6 days, five other Estonian middle-distance runners of comparable ability supplemented their diets daily with 30 grams of a glucose placebo. The runners were unaware of the actual compositions of their supplements.

Prior to and following the 6 days of supplementation, the athletes ran four 300-meter (.19 mi) intervals and—on a separate day—four 1,000-meter (.62 mi) intervals with 3 minutes of rest between the 300-meter intervals and 4 minutes of recovery between the 1,000-meter repetitions. Compared with the placebo group, improvement in the final 300-meter interval from pre- to postsupplementation was more than twice as great for creatine users; the upgrade was more than three times as large for the runners using creatine in the final 1,000-meter interval. Total time required to run all four 1,000-meter intervals improved from 770 to 757 seconds after creatine supplementation, a statistically significant result. The placebo group slowed by 1 second after the 6 days of glucose ingestion from 774 to 775 seconds. This meant that the performance gap between the two groups over 4,000 meters (2.49 mi) of interval running had increased from 4 to 18 seconds.

A weakness in this Estonian study was that the researchers, including the highly respected Eric Hultman, who has been called the father of the strategy of carb loading for endurance runners, did not use a crossover design. In such a design, the runners who supplemented with creatine would have crossed over and tried glucose, while those who had used glucose would have loaded with creatine. Crossing over wasn't possible because once leg muscles are fully loaded with creatine, it can take 6 to 9 months without creatine supplementation to clear the surplus creatine from muscle fibers and return to baseline creatine concentrations.[29]

Weight Gain

In the meta-analysis, creatine supplementation resulted in a *net* gain in lean mass of 0.36 percent per week compared with placebo use. This meant that those supplementing with creatine were adding about three-fourths of a pound (340 g) of new lean tissue to their bodies every 7 days. With creatine supplementation, the average net gain in muscular strength was about 1.1 percent per week compared with placebo use.

The issue of weight gain is a primary caveat in creatine supplementation. Muscle storage of creatine is associated with storage, which would make a creatine-loaded endurance runner a bit heavier. Creatine's anabolic action also adds body mass. In one study carried out at the Karolinska Institutet in Stockholm, Sweden, nine well-trained runners ingested 5 grams of creatine monohydrate four times per day for 6 days, while nine other experienced runners consumed a placebo.[30] After the 6 days, they all competed in a 6K

(3.73 mi) race over rolling terrain. The endurance runners who supplemented their diets with creatine increased body weight by 1 percent; their 6K race times slowed by the same percentage.

More research needs to be conducted before informed advice can be given to endurance runners regarding creatine supplementation. It is possible that the weight gain and interval-training improvements resulting from creatine intake tend to balance each other out over extended training periods and that creatine therefore does not enhance endurance running. This possibility has not been examined carefully by exercise scientists.

Dosage and Contamination Concerns

Creatine is sold to the runner in various formats, including such exotic preparations as Createk, Freakit, Cell-Tech Hard Core, CellMass, but there is absolutely no evidence that special preparations of creatine monohydrate are more effective than the basic compound itself. The scientifically accepted loading dose for creatine is 20 grams per day for 5 to 7 days; the maintenance dose is considered to be 3 to 5 grams per day for 2 weeks to 6 months depending on the training being conducted.[22] Although no studies have examined the effects of long-term supplementation with creatine, there is no compelling evidence that creatine supplementation is associated with adverse side effects.

Runners interested in supplementing their diets with creatine should be aware that current legislation does very little to protect them from creatine products and other supplements that might be contaminated or even contain unsafe ingredients.[31] Poorly manufactured creatine may be contaminated with the by-products creatinine and dicyandiamide.[32] Purity is especially important for creatine supplementation because doses taken by athletes are so large. Runners wishing to learn more about the quality of a specific creatine product may check reports published by independent testing laboratories such as ConsumerLab.com.

Conclusion

Elite Kenyan endurance runners don't take nutritional supplements, and for good reason. Supplements are expensive, and in most cases there is little evidence that they promote higher performances. Only three compounds—caffeine, sodium bicarbonate, and creatine—have been documented as performance enhancers. Caffeine is legal and inexpensive. Sodium bicarbonate is legal and even less costly, but it can cause gastrointestinal distress and diarrhea. Creatine supplementation works well for enhancing sprint performances, but its effect on endurance running capacity is unclear. It may boost endurance running in some runners by upgrading the quality of interval workouts.

XI

Psychology
of Running

CHAPTER 48

The Brain and the Experience of Fatigue

The traditional view in running is that fatigue, or the inability to continue a desired running velocity, is caused by the accumulation of metabolites in the muscles, the depletion of intramuscular energy stores, or increased body temperature. In this well-accepted conception, the muscles are believed to be the center of fatigue. One theory is that muscle fibers allow calcium to leak from them as strenuous running proceeds, lessening the force of muscle contraction. This occurs because the flow of calcium into muscle cells is a key stimulus for muscle-fiber shortening. Another frequently cited hypothesis—that science has proved to be incorrect—is that a buildup of lactic acid inside muscle cells is the dominant cause of fatigue during intense running.

A fundamental problem with the lactic acid and calcium concentrations theories is that neither corresponds to the real world. An often-forgotten implication of these conventional conceptions is that runners would slow down continuously during challenging runs as the leakiness of muscle fibers gradually increased or as lactic acid continued to pile up. If lactic acid is the true cause of fatigue, running pace should slow rather steadily over the course of a 5K or 10K race as intramuscular lactic acid concentrations increased.

The actual performances of well-trained runners reveal that race velocities vary widely over the course of a competition and are not tightly linked with calcium leaking from muscles or lactic acid level. When Haile Gebrselassie set his 10K world record, for example, his calcium leakiness and lactate level surely advanced steadily over the course of 10,000 meters of hard running, but his fastest pace was actually achieved over the last kilometer (.62 mi), which he covered in 2:31.3; most of the prior 1,000-meter segments of the race were completed in 2:37 to 2:38.[1] He was running fastest when lactic acid levels and calcium leakiness had reached their apices.

The theory that fatigue during running is caused by biochemical, intramuscular factors is clearly inadequate.[1] If muscle biochemistry were the true source of fatigue, there would be a clear link between muscle metabolite concentrations and actual running velocity. Some other system must be at work to explain why runners slow down during workouts and races.

Brain Regulates Pace and Fatigue

A key point to remember is that running velocity during a workout or competition is always a direct function of the rate of work performed by the muscles, but the instructions the muscles receive to work at various rates are always provided by the brain. The brain must take into account a variety of factors in order to choose the velocity at which an athlete will run. The brain might monitor body temperature, muscle metabolites, distance left to run, and other variables in order to reach a decision about running pace. The brain might even create a sensation of fatigue in order to enforce its decision—to prevent a runner from exceeding certain physiological thresholds. The brain could regulate running pace by generating strong feelings of fatigue in order to prevent physiological failure.

Anecdotal evidence that the brain acts as a regulator of fatigue and running pace is abundant although usually ignored. A classic example of the brain's anticipatory role in running performance, presented by sports scientist Ross Tucker,[2] is the case of a 40-minute 10K runner who is transported to either high altitude or a venue with hot, humid conditions and then asked to run a 10K race. In both situations, the runner's 10K pace is much slower than usual from the very beginning of the 10K, not at some point within the race when inadequate oxygen delivery to the muscles or high internal temperatures become physiologically limiting.

Traditional theory would indicate that the slowdown in these situations was the result of oxygen depletion or high body temperature, but this is clearly wrong since the slowing occurred before either of these events. The brain must be able to anticipate physiological failure and thus slows pace and creates fatigue in certain situations in order to prevent too great a disturbance in physiological equilibrium. Since the brain anticipates and regulates, the overall process is thus called *anticipatory regulation* of running velocity.

A clear example of the shift in thinking that has occurred from the old model of fatigue to the new anticipatory regulation schema can be found in research carried out on the role played by overheating in causing fatigue. Traditional investigations suggest that athletes run in the heat until core body temperature reaches a certain limit, usually thought to be approximately 40 degrees Celsius (104°F), at which point the brain stimulates the muscles to a lesser degree and heat-related fatigue occurs.[3-5] Fatigue (i.e., the slowdown) is thus believed to be caused by a failure to maintain adequate coolness of the body during running.

However, such studies have been carried out in the unnatural situation in which athletes are required to continue exercising at a fixed rate until they are unable to continue. This is rarely the case during running workouts or races where pace varies considerably as the exertion proceeds. In fact, research carried out with athletes running in the heat when they are *not* forced to run at a single pace verifies the anticipatory regulation model by demonstrating that runners don't slow down *because* they are overheated;

rather, they decrease their pace in order to *prevent* themselves from getting too hot.[6,7] The failure to run as quickly in the heat as would be the case under cool conditions is thus the result of anticipatory regulation by the brain, not an overheating phenomenon within the muscles or brain itself.

If the anticipatory regulation theory of fatigue is sound, there should be studies that show that the nervous system gradually reduces its stimulation of muscles during fatiguing exercise and that this reduction parallels the actual increases in fatigue. Such a finding would be in contrast with the traditional view of fatigue, which would suggest that the nervous system continues a high level of stimulation while the muscles simply fail to continue functioning. Such investigations do exist. In one inquiry, cyclists completed a 100K ride sprinkled with all-out 1-kilometer (.62 mi) sprints.[8] The quality of the sprints declined over the duration of this 100K effort. In parallel with this drop-off in sprint power, integrated EMG (IEMG) activity also fell, which indicated that the central nervous systems of the athletes were recruiting fewer and fewer motor units as the ride progressed. This was true even though less than 20 percent of the available motor units in the cyclists' leg muscles were being recruited at any one time even though there was an opportunity for the athletes' nervous systems to bring more motor units into play—if they so desired.

In a separate study, experienced cyclists completed a 60-minute time trial that included six maximal sprints.[9] As predicted by the anticipatory regulation hypothesis, there was a reduction in power output and IEMG activity from the second through the fifth sprint as the nervous system cautiously tempered intensity in order to avoid physiological failure. However, both power and IEMG magically revived—and increased significantly—during the sixth sprint, which took place during the last minute of the overall ride. There was no real magic in the revival, however. Rather, the nervous system simply took the brakes off and allowed nonfatigued muscles to operate at high levels. The muscles were not fatigued during the second through fifth intervals—they were simply reined in by the nervous system.

Nervous system control of training intensity is a familiar phenomenon to many runners even though the dominant role is often not clearly grasped. Faced with an interval workout consisting of 6 × 800 meters, runners find the first interval to be fast and the second through fifth intervals to be progressively slower. The sixth interval, however, is often the quickest of the entire workout even though peripheral (i.e., muscular) fatigue should be the greatest and body temperature the highest. As the last work interval is reached, the brain is anticipating the ending of the workout and recognizing that physiological limits will not be exceeded even if a high running intensity is maintained. Thus the running pace over that last interval is fastest even though peripheral fatigue should be at its highest point.

The anticipatory regulation model of fatigue may help explain the dominance of Kenyan endurance runners. Various studies have shown that elite

Kenyan athletes can sustain a higher percentage of $\dot{V}O_2$max in their races than runners from the rest of the world.[10] While most highly competitive runners toil away at about 90 to 92 percent of $\dot{V}O_2$max during their 10K races, elite Kenyans have the ability to complete the distance at an intensity of 94 to 95 percent of $\dot{V}O_2$max. Traditionally, this difference has been explained as being due to greater resistance to fatigue, but the actual, physiological nature of this heightened resistance has never been detected or adequately explained.

Swiss researcher Bengt Kayser suggests that in elite competition, the difference between the winner and loser may not be the result of differences in $\dot{V}O_2$max but "rather in how big a safety margin the CNS (central nervous system) imposes in order for the organism to stay clear of serious damage (to the heart and muscles)." Kayser postulates that one reason Kenyans do so well is that "they are able to push the limits imposed by the CNS closer to the danger zone . . ."[11] To put it another way, the Kenyans' governor of exercise intensity is more permissive.

Training the Brain for Racing

If the central nervous system regulates performance, it begs this question: "Can you train your brain to allow you to go faster?" To answer this question, first note that anticipatory regulation is of more than esoteric interest to the serious endurance runner: It should also shape racing strategies and training-program creation. It is clear that fatigue and thus distance-running performance are influenced not just by factors related to oxygen consumption, body temperature increases, and muscle metabolite accumulation but also by muscle recruitment by the nervous system and the consequent production of propulsive force—and in which the nervous system anticipates unwanted disturbances in overall physiological equilibrium.

It is also certain that when runners move up to higher speeds, their nervous systems are recruiting more motor units in their leg muscles and recruiting those motor units more quickly. When runners slow down, they are using fewer motor units and recruiting those units less quickly. Electromyographic studies reveal that EMG values go up during 5Ks as runners speed up and drop as runners decelerate. Since EMG recordings reflect neural input to the muscles, it is clear that pace changes during the race are not the result of fatigue within the muscles but rather are the outcome of changes in stimulation of the muscles by the nervous system. Thus, training that teaches the nervous system to sustain higher outputs, and thus greater inputs to the muscles, should help improve race performances. It is doubtful that this teaching can be best accomplished by long, slow distance training, which features and rehearses low neural inputs.

Runners who can keep their muscle recruitment by the nervous system at the highest-possible levels fare the best in endurance competition.[12] Based on *past experience of running*, a runner develops the capacity to set the optimal velocity for a competitive effort.[13, 14] This again points to the importance of high-quality training, as well as to *specific training*. That is, those runners who have religiously practiced goal race paces over suitable interval distances during training will have nervous systems that are most ready and willing to lock in those paces during actual race situations.

High-speed training improves motor-unit recruitment and also advances the synchronization of motor units;[15] it is best for promoting neuromuscular attributes and for enhancing nervous system tolerance of high-quality running. High-intensity strength training with challenging resistance also enhances neural output to the muscles during activity. Contrary to popular belief, high-quality training is also optimal for advancing aerobic attributes since high training speeds are generally closer to $\dot{V}O_2max$ than long-run pacings. The constant proximity to $\dot{V}O_2max$ forces the heart to become a better oxygen pump and

▶ High-quality and high-intensity training not only prepare the muscles but also prepare the nervous system to sustain a faster pace over time.

the leg muscles to become better oxygen users, raising aerobic capacity and even $v\dot{V}O_2max$ since fast-pace training also enhances economy.

Conclusion

These findings should lead to changes in the overall planning of workouts. The time-honored routine of the weekly Sunday long run should be replaced with a long run every third Sunday and explosive routines on the other two Sundays. These Sunday explosive days, featuring plyometric drills, high-speed and running-specific strength training, and high-velocity running intervals, would force the runner's anticipatory regulation system to reset and would create a nervous system that would be much more permissive to high running intensities, allowing greater speeds to be maintained for longer periods. Such training recognizes the dominating impact of the brain in anticipating the velocity that is manageable for each quality workout and race and then regulating that speed throughout the overall exertion.

CHAPTER 49

Psychological Strategies for Improved Performance

Arunner's psychological state has a profound effect on his or her physiological response to running. This basic truth has been known for more than 30 years. Initial research carried out by exercise scientists in the 1970s and 1980s revealed that individuals using meditation and relaxation techniques were able to walk significantly longer on a treadmill at an intensity of 80 percent of $\dot{V}O_2$max compared with exercisers who did not use such techniques.[1] Several other studies demonstrated that the use of simple stress management strategies significantly decreased oxygen consumption rates during exercise.

The major role played by the mind in determining the physiological reaction to exercise was illustrated by a study in which individuals who were actually lifting 10- to 16-kilogram (22-35 lb) weights were told that they were either lifting 0.3- or 30-kilogram (0.66 or 66 lb) weights. When they were informed of the purported light loads, the lifters' ventilation and oxygen consumption rates plunged by 20 to 30 percent; the deception that 30-kilogram weights were being used caused increases of about 50 percent in ventilation rate and oxygen usage.[1]

The conclusions reached from such research were that emotions and thoughts can influence a runner's physiological state rather dramatically during workouts and competitions—and that runners should develop mental strategies that decrease the energy cost of running at specific velocities as well as coping strategies for dealing with the fatigue and discomfort of strenuous effort. A fundamental concept is that a runner in the same physical condition as another athlete will hold a competitive advantage over that individual at any race pace by having more positive perceptions of his or her ability to continue and fewer negative and pessimistic thoughts concerning the feelings of pain and fatigue coming from the legs and other parts of the body.

Mental Coping Strategies

Early research suggested that there are three basic kinds of mental coping strategies that runners can use in an attempt to enhance performance:[2]

1. **Association** occurs when runners constantly monitor body sensations (e.g., respiration rate, respiratory comfort, body temperature, muscle pain, muscle tightness), remind themselves to relax, and modify stride and pace in order to produce greater comfort and economy.

2. **Dissociation** is when runners block out bodily feelings instead of focusing on them and ignore pain, fatigue, or boredom by concentrating on a favorite or pleasant subject or repeating a mantra.

3. **Positive self-talk** involves repeating phrases such as "I can do it," "I'm not really tired," or "I'm going to make it" at key points during a hard workout or competition.

A classic study suggested that elite runners tend to use association during intense running while less-experienced runners prefer to engage in dissociation.[3] Research concerning the effectiveness of these strategies has produced conflicting results. In one study, treadmill runners listening to a tape recording of street sounds (an example of dissociation) experienced reduced fatigue and a lower frequency of sore muscles compared with runners who were running at the same pace but concentrating on the sounds and feelings associated with their breathing (an example of association).[4] Dissociation has also proved to be better at delaying feelings of strong discomfort during exercise.[4] However, such investigations have seldom looked at the effects of coping strategy on *actual performance*.

In an investigation in which running performance was monitored, 60 runners who ordinarily ran about 15 miles (24 km) per week were divided into four equal groups and asked to run as far as possible on a track in 30 minutes.[2] One group attempted to ignore feelings of exertion and imagined themselves engaged in a pleasant activity unrelated to running during the 30-minute effort (dissociation). A second group constantly monitored body sensations while running and paid close attention to feelings related to breathing, fatigue, and the conditions of the stomach and leg muscles, altering running velocity according to how they were feeling (association). Members of the third group gave themselves pep talks during the 30-minute exertion (positive self-talk) while the runners in the fourth group received no instruction about mental strategy.

The four groups performed equally well on the track, covering about the same distance with similar heart rates and feelings of fatigue, challenging the principle that coping strategy plays a large role in performance. However, for a psychological strategy to alter performance, a runner would probably have to not only use the strategy but also *believe* that it would be effective. Such belief would probably only be acquired after adequate training while using the strategy—and as a result of successful racing with the strategy in play. In the 30-minute, four-group study, instruction in the use of the various strategies was quite brief in nature.

Attention Control

Association and dissociation are examples of attention control, a topic of great interest to sport psychologists. Despite the rather unconvincing research concerning the effectiveness of association and dissociation, the optimization of attention control may produce significant gains in running performance.[5] Feelings of fatigue, day-to-day concerns, anxieties about family and business affairs, and thoughts of past poor performances or unsatisfactory training sessions tend to intrude into runners' thoughts, making it hard to relax and focus on the coordination of running gait. It is possible that negative thinking might also decrease neural output to the muscles during strenuous efforts, thus diminishing running pace. In theory, once distracting thoughts are minimized through the development of proper attention control, a runner's nervous system can focus completely and freely on the act of running at a best-possible pace.

Famed men's basketball coach John Wooden of UCLA was a noted proponent of proper attention control development. The Westwood legend permitted large numbers of boisterous spectators to attend UCLA practices and instructed the UCLA pep band to play the upcoming-opponent's fight song during important practices before road games even though the raucous sounds drowned out coaching instructions and communications between teammates. Wooden believed that regular exposures to distracting circumstances enhanced the ability of his athletes to concentrate during games, and his Bruin players were noted for their unflappability and mistake-free play.

The use of attention control appears to be beneficial to endurance runners. In one attention-control study, 18 collegiate distance runners were divided into three equal groups.[6] Over a 6-week period, six of the runners were given psychological skills training (PST), which included guidance in the use of attention control, relaxation techniques, and self-instructional tutoring. Six other runners were told about the potential value of psychological skills training and were given a description of what it entailed—but did not practice attention control or any of the PST techniques. Six other runners served as controls: They received no instruction or practice in PST and were not informed of its possible value.

Running training was identical in the three groups; not surprisingly, $\dot{V}O_2$max and percent body fat did not change in any of the groups during the 6-week study. At the beginning and end of the study, all 18 runners participated in a continuous exercise test that contained the following elements:

1. Six minutes of treadmill running at a moderate intensity of 50 percent of $\dot{V}O_2$max
2. Six minutes of treadmill running at an intensity of 60 percent of $\dot{V}O_2$max
3. Six minutes at an intensity of 70 percent of $\dot{V}O_2$max

4. Four minutes at 80 percent of $\dot{V}O_2$max

5. Four minutes at 90 percent of $\dot{V}O_2$max

6. One minute at the lofty intensity of 98 percent of $\dot{V}O_2$max

After the challenging minute at 98 percent of $\dot{V}O_2$max, the 27th minute of continuous running, the treadmill grade was changed from level to 2 percent, and the athletes ran for as long as they could, simulating a final drive to the finish line in the closing minutes of a 10K race. Once the treadmill incline was lifted to 2 percent, the runners were actually exercising at an intensity of 100 percent of $\dot{V}O_2$max.

At the beginning of the research, all 18 athletes were able to run for about 60 seconds after the treadmill grade was raised. After the 6 weeks of psychological skills and attention-control training, PST participants were able to run for 115 seconds during this rugged final stage of the test, a 55-second improvement. The other 12 runners were not able to improve their performances.

Running economy also improved significantly for the six runners who had taken part in PST, with oxygen demand dropping by 4 percent at moderate intensities of 50 to 70 percent of $\dot{V}O_2$max. This allowed runners engaged in PST to run about 15 seconds per mile faster after the 6 weeks of training—without any significant increase in effort. At higher intensities (80 to 98 percent of $\dot{V}O_2$max), there was a tendency for the PST runners to be more economical. None of the non-PST athletes managed to improve running economy.

Body Checking

The attention-control skills developed by the PST runners included body checking, a practice in which a runner systematically checks in with his or her head, neck, shoulders, chest, stomach, back, hips, thighs, knees, lower legs, ankles, and feet to see if they are complaining about tension, fatigue, or pain. Each body region is relaxed as it is checked. During body checking, family disputes, checkbook balances, a troublesome week at work, and all other intruding thoughts are not permitted: A runner's entire focus is on checking, relaxing, and regulating the body.

According to principal researcher Jeffery P. Simons, body checking prevents runners from dwelling on their worst nemesis: fatigue.[7] During a body check, the part of the body that is feeling the most fatigued is quickly identified and remedial action is immediately taken. If the legs feel uncomfortable, unresponsive, and fatigued, for example, a runner can concentrate totally on relaxing the lower limbs and on changing or quickening strides slightly. This seems to immediately relieve discomfort and would cause the leg muscles to be used in slightly different ways, potentially recruiting less-fatigued motor units. The focus on the legs might also increase neural output to the leg muscles.

Many of the PST trainees who performed well during the maximal exercise test reported that they ran at such a high level because they "had something to think about" as they attempted to deal with the rugged intensity and its associated discomfort. They were thinking about their bodies and about ways to relax and change their strides, at the same time refusing to get carried away by performance-crippling sensations of pain and fatigue.

Attention control, used in this manner, is a clear example of association rather than dissociation. "The trouble with dissociation," says Simons, "is that it causes a loss of concentration and a decrease in self-monitoring, leading to a diminishment of self-control and thus poorer running performances. If you want to run well, it's much better to stay on top of what's happening in your body. Eventually, PST runners get so good at self-awareness that a coach can yell 'body check' and see an immediate response from the standpoints of more-relaxed, more-economical running."

Positive Imagery and Relaxation

It's possible that the doubling of high-intensity endurance was not solely the result of attention-control training, however. The six PST runners also received *self-instructional training*, in which they learned to form positive images of themselves while running. These images combined confidence, power, and relaxation with the feeling of moving smoothly and quickly. One runner visualized himself as a cheetah during fast running, another formed an image of a high-speed antelope, a third felt as though he were running "like the wind," and a fourth visualized rapidly flowing water. The runners gradually eliminated negative images and begin to visualize themselves as powerful figures capable of graceful, high-quality running.

The six PST athletes also employed relaxation training, in which they relaxed their diaphragms and used deep gut breathing during hard running. Simons encouraged PST runners to "drop their stomachs" and let their diaphragms move freely as they ran. The runners also routinely engaged in Jacobson's Progressive Muscular Relaxation (PMR), a technique in which muscle groups in one part of the body are ferociously tightened for a moment and then slackened completely—usually not while running but during other parts of the day—in an attempt to release as much tension as possible. Anecdotally, athletes report that the use of PMR makes their muscles feel much looser and more responsive, and the technique has also become a somewhat-popular method of easing tension in individuals suffering from insomnia. PST individuals also focused on relaxing while running; they avoided the tendency to slow down as part of the relaxation process by linking the process of speeding *up* with each increase in the relaxed state.

Science suggests that relaxation and body checking can be a powerful combination for endurance runners. At the University of Oregon, exercise scientists assessed running economy in 36 accomplished, experienced runners (27 males and 9 females). These runners ranged in age from 18 to 40, averaged 47 miles (75.64 km) per week of running, and were accomplished competitors; the mean 10K time for the males was 35:18 while females clocked in at 41:36. Economy was determined at decent speeds—6:30 per mile (1.61 km) for the men and 7:30 for the women—and the runners were ranked according to how economically they ran. The 12 least economical runners (10 males and 2 females) were then compared with the 12 most economical athletes with regard to their attention-control strategies while running.[8]

The least and most economical runners used associative (i.e., body-checking) strategies with about the same frequency. The big difference was that the most economical group spent most of the rest of their time focused on relaxing while the least economical athletes were dissociating by letting their minds focus on things unrelated to running: music, passing scenery, relationships, concerns about work, and so on. The combination of body checking plus relaxing thus appears to be quite economy enhancing and should thus have a positive impact on performance.

Centering

Research carried out with eight competitive male and female endurance runners at the University of Otago in New Zealand suggested that PMR training and a special attention-control technique called centering can be quite beneficial.[9] Centering is a relaxation and concentration exercise that emphasizes abdominal breathing and the use of specific key words. While centering, a runner focuses on a point just behind his or her navel and attempts to feel the relationship of the entire body to this point. Centering also involves being aware of the motions of the abdominal area as it expands and contracts during breathing, and it is associated with abdominal—rather than chest-focused—breathing. As he or she breathes in, a centered runner repeats a key cue word to remember to center, usually either *center* or *focus*. As he or she exhales, the centered runner utters another word that enhances relaxation such as *relax*, *smooth*, or *fluid*. Over the course of the 6-week Otago study, runners practiced PMR and centering for a total of about 15 minutes per day.

At the end of the 6-week period, the athletes carried out a relaxation and centering session and then began running on treadmills at their predetermined lactate-threshold velocities. After five minutes of such running, the athletes attempted to lower ventilatory, oxygen-consumption, and heart rates by employing centering and relaxation techniques. While still at lactate-threshold speed, the runners were able to reduce ventilatory rate by over 9 percent, oxygen consumption by more than 7 percent (thus running economy improved by 7 percent), and heart rate by almost 3 percent. In effect, this positive change would improve lactate-threshold velocity, a key predictor of performance, because lactate output would be lessened at the previous lactate-threshold speed. This could lead to an improvement in performance without any underlying physical change in fitness. The key factor in the upgrade would be the neural changes (i.e., the focus on centering and relaxation), not any structural or biochemical changes to the heart or muscles.

Preventing Burnout

Sports psychologists have also begun to explore the overall background psychological characteristics that permit some runners to excel while others fail. This research reveals that the very factors that help some endurance athletes persevere through challenging workouts, rugged training, and competitive conditions may also increase the risk of burnout. Researchers from the Norwegian School of Sport Science in Oslo and the University of Bedfordshire in the United Kingdom have been able to show, in a study carried out with 141 high-performing athletes, that specific motivational profiles may produce early successes in athletic endeavors but may ultimately raise the likelihood of frustration, poor competitive performances, and even withdrawal from sport.[10] In effect, the desire to achieve great things may eventually lead to very poor training responses and competitions that are less than optimal if the underlying psychological mechanisms and motivational constructs are faulty.

Exercise scientists have defined burnout as a state of mental, emotional, and physical fatigue produced during the pursuit of challenging goals.[11] Burn-out is usually characterized by disillusionment with one's sporting activity and by the appearance of psychological and physical symptoms associated with reduced self-esteem.[12] True burnout is thought to be accompanied by three key indicators:

1. Lack of emotional and physical energy
2. Reduced sense of accomplishment and a feeling that desired goals are very unlikely to be attained
3. Devaluation of one's sport and a decreased interest in performing at a high level[13]

The possible mechanisms by which burnout appears in athletes have been hotly debated. In a benchmark study of burnout, researchers proposed that athletes with high initial levels of motivation tend to make significant investments in training; these investments then lead to early competitive success and thus intense enjoyment, which in turn produce further commitments in training. A key factor involved in this process for many athletes appears to be that successes enhance feelings of self-worth. While this would appear to be a healthy response, it can lead to a situation in which self-esteem gradually becomes more and more dependent on athletic success. Consequently, the inevitable athletic disappointments and failures that occur as competition becomes more rigorous produce threats to self-worth, which can lead to a motivational shift in which an intense desire to train hard and to succeed begins to wane and is replaced by a kind of protective physical and psychological disengagement from the sport.[14]

This groundbreaking research suggests that when an athlete takes a view of athletic achievement that fails to protect him or her from the psychological stresses associated with sustained difficulties and unavoidable failures to reach important goals, it is almost inevitable that some degree of burnout will occur. The resulting psychological, emotional, and behavioral withdrawals make the ultimate attainment of goals more unlikely.

Task Goals Versus Ego Goals

To prevent burnout and maximize the opportunity for goal attainment, an athlete needs to create proper goals and develop an optimal motivational climate. Scientific research has identified two types of goals that are present to greater or lesser degrees in athletic-achievement contexts: task goals and ego goals.[15] When a task goal is adopted by an athlete, achievement is assessed in self-referent terms, rather than in relation to how others have fared in comparison, and success and failure are determined according to whether one has mastered an activity, improved a performance time, or reached a self-imposed marker. For example, when a runner says, "I want to run a 2:59 at Boston," he or she is setting a task goal. Similarly, when a runner proclaims, "I want to train in a way that will keep me injury free this year," he or she is also setting a task goal.

In contrast, the adoption of an ego goal means that achievement will be evaluated in comparative rather than self-referent terms, and a runner will strive to demonstrate performance prowess—or to avoid displaying a lack of performance capability—in comparison with other runners. For example, a runner adopting an ego goal might decide that "The key thing is to beat Paul in the upcoming race" or "I have to finish in the top three in this competition" or "I have to show everyone that I am the best runner in my age group." The adoption of an ego goal might also mean attempting to win the approval or change the mind of a significant other—perhaps a coach or another athlete. A runner who has received a negative comment from an another person in the running community might decide that he or she must win a race to prove the person wrong, for example.

Scientific research has supported the idea that runners fare better when they adopt task rather than ego goals. For example, some studies have shown that athletes using task goals tend to seek out challenges, put forth high levels of effort, display persistence, sustain interest in training, and maintain mammoth motivational levels, trends that are inconsistent with burnout and consistent with the development of a high degree of fitness.[16]

In contrast, using ego goals seems to leave athletes more vulnerable to burnout,[17] perhaps in part because it is impossible to control the performances and opinions of others, which makes the attainment of ego goals more uncertain. A runner might achieve an excellent performance time, perhaps even a personal record, but could still view overall performance as a failure if certain competitors finished with even-faster times. Furthermore, achieving a very creditable time might nonetheless produce a disparaging comment from a hypercritical coach or fellow athlete (e.g., "You went out too fast," "You finished too slowly," "You seemed to struggle on the hills"), producing frustration and disappointment in an athlete oriented toward the achievement of an ego goal, in this case, the winning over of another person.

Research suggests that when athletes become dominated by ego goals, they tend to feel that they must repeatedly display their superior competitive ability with respect to others, and their sense of self-worth may become tightly connected with their capacity to do so. Rather than inching their way forward with gradually better times and feeling satisfied with doing so, ego-goal runners constantly need to out-do others, an impossible task for all but the Paul Tergats and Catherine Nderebas of the world. The failures that inevitably occur, which are typically viewed as inadequacies, are then remedied with the application of more training effort; however, physical and emotional stresses tend to increase as competitive situations are increasingly viewed as being personally threatening and potentially damaging to self-esteem. In theory, burnout can then occur much more easily compared with a situation in which a runner is merely trying to gain greater mastery of an event without his or her worth being tied to the time on the clock, relative finishing position in a race, or the opinion of another person.

Performance Climate Versus Mastery Climate

In addition to goal characteristics (task vs. ego), *motivational climate* may have a strong impact on the possibility of burnout. Two key motivational climates have been identified by sport psychologists: a performance climate and a mastery climate. When a runner's day-to-day life is characterized by a significant focus on interrunner competitions, comparisons with other runners, the presence of a coach who emphasizes winning at all costs, and public recognition of comparative ability, then a performance climate is said to prevail. Performance climates are believed to foster ego involvement and the setting of ego goals rather than the establishment of task goals perhaps because the underlying schema is "I can only be good if I am better than you," rather than "I'm good if I make steady progress with my performance times." A significant number of sport psychologists believe that performance climates can increase the risk of burnout compared with mastery climates.

A mastery climate prevails in a runner's life when an emphasis is placed on the learning and mastery of skills (e.g., when a runner learns to carry out running-specific strength training, when a runner develops the ability to maintain stride rate on tough hills), effort is valued as an end in itself rather than as a way of establishing self-worth, and there is a private, personal recognition of effort rather than a public comparison with other runners. The presence of a mastery climate increases the likelihood that a runner will be task-involved rather than ego-involved in his or her training and competitions because the pursuits and practices of other runners are irrelevant to whether the runner can master a specific running task.[18]

Perfectionism

One last motivational factor—in addition to goal orientation and motivational climate—that can have a large impact on running performance is the character trait of perfectionism. Some studies have suggested that perfectionism is a key characteristic displayed by high-achieving athletes.[19] This seems reasonable enough since perfectionism is often linked with an intense pursuit of extremely high performance standards, a pursuit that can lead to outstanding competitive outcomes.

However, a key problem is that perfection is unattainable. The perfect race is unachievable, and in fact a perfect race may be especially unachievable to a perfectionist runner, who is likely to be predisposed to picking apart his or her performance even when it is outstanding. Thus, perfectionism may in fact leave an athlete constantly vulnerable to failure, which can then lead to psychological distress and—ultimately—to an impairment of athletic ability.[20] Various lines of research suggest that when perfectionist athletes inevitably fail to live up to their extremely lofty performance expectations, shame, anger, and anxiety may result, and the risk of burnout can be increased.[21] In addition, there is evidence that perfectionist runners tend to set very lofty task *and* ego goals simultaneously, in effect giving themselves too much to do and achieve. They eventually become overburdened with all of the goals that must be met—after all, they have to be perfect.

Research on Burnout

The hypotheses in the Norwegian research were that (a) athletes with an ego orientation, a performance climate, and elements of perfectionism would be at increased risk of burn-out while (b) athletes setting task goals, adopting a mastery climate, and having modest amounts of perfectionism would have a reduced risk of burning out. The Norwegian and UK scientists worked with 141 athletes, 45 of whom were current Olympic team members; the other 96 were junior elite athletes who were attending national sports academies in Norway. Over half of the research participants had previous World Cup or World Championship experience. There were 81 males and 60 females (age range from 17 to 32), and the athletes competed in Nordic skiing, alpine skiing, the biathlon, speed skating, and Nordic combined. All of the athletes were given standardized tests to assess their achievement goals, motivational climates, perceived abilities, degrees of perfectionism, and levels of burnout (yes, there is a test called the Athlete Burnout Questionnaire, which appears to do a decent job of measuring this phenomenon).[10]

The results confirmed the scientists' basic hypotheses. Specifically, the two motivational profiles of (1) ego orientation, performance climate, and perfectionism and (2) task orientation, mastery climate, and lack of perfectionism yielded significantly different burnout scores; the former profile (ego, performance, perfection) fared more poorly and produced more burnouts. Thus, this research suggests that the use of a maladaptive motivational profile (i.e., perfectionism, ego goal setting, and engagement in a performance rather than mastery climate) increases the risk of performance-thwarting burnout.

One of the take-home lessons for runners appears to be that cognitive, emotional, and psychological approaches to running can have a profound impact on performances and risk of burnout. When competitions become threats to self-worth, the risks of excessive stress and burnout increase. When races are viewed as exciting challenges and opportunities for time improvements and mastery, the risk of burnout is reduced, and the chance of performing at a higher level is increased.

When runners believe that their actions such as training sessions will lead to desired outcomes such as reasonable and specific performance times, their motivation increases, and they have the best chance of performing at a top level. In contrast, striving constantly to achieve perfection and belittling small improvements increases the likelihood of developing debilitating burnout.

The ultimate bottom line is that motivational profile matters a great deal, and in some cases it may matter more than the training carried out, the recovery between workouts, and the manner in which a runner eats. Poor motivational profiles can make a fit runner feel unfit and can wrap a runner in a coat of lethargy and withdrawal that makes quality training and the attainment of goals impossible. A bad motivational setup makes decently conducted workouts seem like failures and lets self-worth depend on every vagary of training and performance. Runners seem to operate best when they use a motivational profile that includes task-goal orientation, a mastery climate, and a break from perfectionism. This profile is forward seeking and lets runners take satisfaction in even small gains in workout quality and competitive performance. It also gives an individual runner a break, letting him or her have enough pressure-free time to achieve long-term goals. It never, ever links self-worth with the time on the race clock or relative finishing position in a competition.

Conclusion

Scientific research reveals that psychological skills training, which includes components of relaxation, attention control, and body checking, can enhance running economy and bolster running performances. Positive imagery and centering also seem to upgrade running capacity. Finally, the establishment of a motivation profile that includes task orientation, a mastery climate, and relatively little focus on perfectionism appears to be best for avoiding burnout during training and consequently creating the best-possible running performances.

CHAPTER 50

Addictive Aspects of Running

Some runners are involved in their running training for reasons other than, or in addition to, improving fitness or running a fast 5K: They rely on running to maintain a normal mood state. When this happens, running can become a kind of addiction, with classic symptoms of withdrawal occurring when running is taken away because of injury, schedule conflicts, or family commitments; in contrast, at other times running can produce a sense of contentment or near euphoria when workouts are undertaken and completed.[1, 2]

Research reveals that individuals addicted to running often display significant forms of psychological distress such as nervousness, depression, and anger whenever a running workout is missed or curtailed. In this sense, running can become somewhat like other traditional addictive behaviors such as drug taking and gambling, with the classic trio of dependency, withdrawal, and tolerance (i.e., the need for more and more running as training proceeds) being displayed.[3] For some runners, training becomes a compulsive activity because of its mood-regulating properties.[3] Of course, when running becomes addictive, it usually does not feature the same extreme negative behaviors associated with other addictions, such as breaking the law to obtain drugs or destroying financial stability to engage in gambling. However the negative effects of a running addiction can still be debilitating.

The presence of exercise dependence and addiction among runners was addressed in a study involving 60 members (30 males and 30 females) of a running club who were preparing for a major competition.[4] From this group, 15 men and 15 women were randomly selected to miss their next scheduled training session (the exercise-deprived group) while the remaining 30 runners continued their training uninterrupted (the controls). The exercise-deprived runners reported significant withdrawal-like symptoms of depressed mood; reduced energy levels; and increased tension, anger, fatigue and confusion within 24 hours after the missed workout. Exercise-deprived runners even displayed elevated heart rates. Control-group runners showed no changes in mood or resting heart rate.

Runner's High

Running can become addictive in part because substantial levels of endogenous opiates, opium-like compounds that can be synthesized and released by nerve cells within the brain, are produced during intense or prolonged running workouts. This process stimulates reward pathways within the brain and provides a sort of runner's high that can be psychologically satisfying to many runners.

Running can also trigger the release of catecholamines (adrenaline and noradrenaline) that have a stimulating and pleasantly arousing effect on the nervous system and various physiological functions. Finally, a strenuous running workout can also stimulate dopaminergic brain areas (i.e., parts of the brain that produce dopamine, a chemical that helps regulate mood) and can thus have a significantly positive impact on emotional state.[5]

Research reveals that the endorphin response to running, which is the presumed basis for the runner's high phenomenon, varies greatly among runners. In some runners, endorphins are released after about 30 minutes of intense running; such runners tend to favor shorter, high-quality workouts and 5K to 10-K competitions. Among other runners, endorphins are not released in significant quantities until 90 to 120 minutes of submaximal running have been completed; these individuals tend to favor high-volume training and often are confirmed marathoners. Finally, some individuals produce very little endorphin in response to running training; such individuals are often relatively uncommitted to regular running. Some observers of the running scene have proposed that a runner's best event is the one that produces the greatest endorphin release—and thus is practiced for the most.

Running Dependency

Running dependence has often been called a "positive addiction" because of running's numerous beneficial effects on overall health (see chapter 41). In one sense, a dependency on running may lie on the healthy end of the addiction spectrum, perhaps with compulsive buying and Internet addiction in the middle and drug addiction and gambling on the unhealthy side.[6] In many cases, running addiction is probably relatively harmless aside from injuries caused by overtraining, and the health benefits associated with running (e.g., a decreased risk of cancer, heart disease, type 2 diabetes) would certainly seem to outweigh the negative effects of exercise dependence. Science indicates, however, that exercise addiction is often linked with bulimia or some other form of eating disorder,[7,8] conditions which—especially in female runners—can lead to reduced bone density, an increased risk of stress fractures, and amenorrhea (in females).

Running can certainly be a very healthy habit, and it is very natural and normal for runners to be temporarily disappointed and frustrated when a workout cannot be completed and to be happy and satisfied when a training session or competition goes well. But some runners do cross the line from a psychologically productive engagement with running to an unhealthy addiction. The physiological mechanisms for endorphin release discussed in the previous section provide positive benefits but can also help to explain the occurrence of such running dependencies. Psychological state also has an effect on the risk of exercise dependence, with some research suggesting that those runners who exhibit perfectionist personality traits tend to be more likely to develop an exercise addiction.[9] A correlation has also been found between general anxiety level and exercise dependency: The greater the general anxiety, the stronger the dependence on running.[10] Depression also heightens the likelihood of running addiction as do disordered eating habits and anorexia; 40 to 50 percent of individuals with eating disorders exhibit a corresponding exercise addiction. Ultra runners tend to have a higher risk of running addiction compared with marathoners and 5K and 10K specialists,[11] and individuals who are work addicted also tend to have an exercise addiction.

Defining a Running Addiction

The presence of a running addiction is based on the following criteria:[9]

- Tolerance. A runner must gradually increase the amount of running in order to achieve the desired effect, whether it is a kind of psychological buzz or a sense of accomplishment.
- Withdrawal. In the absence of a running workout, a runner experiences negative effects such as anxiety, irritability, restlessness, or sleep problems.
- Lack of control. Attempts at reducing one's amount of running or even ceasing running for a certain period of time are unsuccessful.
- Intention effect. A runner is unable to stick to his or her routine and consistently exceeds the intended or planned amount of running.
- Time. An unusually great amount of time is spent preparing for, engaging in, and recovering from running.
- Reduction in other activities. As a direct result of the commitment to running, healthy occupational, social, or recreational activities occur less often or are stopped.
- Continuance. A runner continues to engage in running training despite knowing that the training is creating or exacerbating physical, psychological, or interpersonal problems.

One study of running addiction and eating disorders featuring 265 female runners and nonrunners ages 20 to 35 included 66 nonrunners, 69 low-intensity runners, 67 medium-intensity runners, and 63 high-intensity runners.[12] The higher-intensity runners in this research were the leanest and lowest in body fat—and scored highest on eating disorder measures and exercise addiction. Twenty-five percent of the women who ran more than 30 miles (48 km) per week had Eating Attitude Test (EAT) scores that indicated a high risk for anorexia. It is not clear whether the desire to be a high-level runner increases the risk of running addiction and eating disorder or whether a fundamental psychological problem pushes some female runners into becoming high-intensity, addicted, and unhealthy from a food-intake standpoint. However, it is clear that a running addiction may be a marker of psychological problems that need to be addressed.

A practical danger for the exercise-dependent runner is that he or she may be at higher risk for overtraining (i.e., performing an amount or intensity of training for which the body cannot adapt satisfactorily and indeed which might harm rather than help overall fitness). A relatively straightforward test—the Exercise Addiction Inventory—has been developed which is a valid and reliable way to identify runners affected by, or at risk of, exercise addiction.[13]

Overcoming a Running Addiction

The remedies for running dependence are varied and would appear to be highly individual.[14] There is some evidence that the analysis of one's reasons for running and a search for the meaning of running (i.e., what it signifies or symbolizes to the individual) appears to lessen the severity of exercise dependence.[15] Therapies associated with the treatment of other addictions, including efforts leading to the gaining of greater self-esteem and self-understanding, appear to be beneficial for the treatment of exercise dependency.[12] When running is used to overcome anxiety or depression, the development of other ways of combating anxiousness and depressive symptoms will decrease the risk of running addiction.[15]

An intriguing aspect of running addiction is that few addicted runners seek professional advice or rehab for their dependencies. When they do appear in a doctor's office, it is usually in a sports medicine—rather than psychiatric—setting, and the presenting problem is often a case of severe plantar fasciitis, a stress fracture, or a serious bout of Achilles tendonitis rather than an abusive relationship with running. Running addicts often have trouble recovering from such injuries because they are quite reluctant to stop—or even temporarily reduce—their training. In one study on exercise addiction, a researcher could not get a subset of his subjects to stop training no matter how much money he offered them.[16] Clearly, treatment in such cases involves identifying and dealing with the family, occupational, or internal stressors that are creating the addiction.

Conclusion

Although a running addiction can produce seemingly great physical health, it can also thwart the development of a rewarding and productive social and professional life, and it can be a way of avoiding issues that are producing unhappiness and depression. Treatment of a running addiction first involves the acknowledgment that the dependency exists; then, the focus can be on the addicted-runner's conception that running is always good even if it is carried out in an obsessive or driven manner. The ultimate goal is to enjoy the innumerable positive aspects of running without letting running dominate life to such an extent that negative consequences can occur. Running is just one of the many ways in which happiness can be achieved and self-esteem advanced.

Epilogue

The Future of Running

The science of running has an exciting future, partly because the causes of that basic performance-limiting factor called fatigue are not yet completely understood. Research will continue to trim away at fatigue's clouded veil, and those inquiries will lead to breakthroughs in training and preparations for all races ranging from 100 meters to the ultramarathon.

Many of the investigations will continue to explore various aspects of the anticipatory regulation of training, and other research will focus on specific forms of strength training for running, examining which strength routines and drills provide the biggest performance bonus for runners. Likewise, lactate—and the best training methods for improving lactate-threshold velocity—will remain in the spotlight, as will nutritional supplements for running and optimal psychological strategies for reaching a performance peak.

A reasonable prediction is that the top endurance runners of the future will spend much less time logging miles at submaximal paces and much more time focusing on high-quality running training plus the kinds of workouts that boost explosiveness, maximal running speed, resistance to fatigue, running-specific strength, and coordination as defined in this book.

Running itself is poised for several decades of exhilarating performances. For example, elite men have set their sights on completing a marathon in under 2 hours, and elite women are ready to attack 2:12 for that race. To run a 2-hour marathon, an elite male runner would have to average 68 seconds per 400 meters during the competition. That means he would have to be capable of 65 seconds per 400 for a half-marathon and 62 seconds per 400 for the 10K, which would be a world record (based on current times) of 25:48!

On the women's side, an elite female runner would have to average 75 seconds per 400 meters to hit 2:12 for the race—about 26 consecutive miles at a tempo of 5 minutes per mile! She would have to be able to run at 72 seconds per 400 in the half marathon and 69 seconds per 400 for the 10K, which would produce a world record of 28:45, currently a reasonably good elite male's time. These exciting breakthroughs in performance—and others like them—will be guided by the science of running.

References

Chapter 1 Running's Nature-Versus-Nurture Debate

1. Burfoot, A. White men can't run. *Runner's World*, pp. 89-95, Aug. 1992.

2. Andersen, J. et al. Muscle, genes and athletic performance. *Scientific American*, Vol. 283, pp. 31-37, 2000.

3. Dennis, C. Rugby team converts to give genes test a try. *Nature*, Vol. 434, p. 260, 2005.

4. Rankinen, T. et al. The human gene map for performance and health-related fitness phenotypes: The 2005 update. *Medicine & Science in Sports & Exercise*, Vol. 38 (11), pp. 1863-1888, 2006.

5. Bouchard, C. Genetics of human obesity: Recent results from linkage studies. *Journal of Nutrition*, Vol. 127, pp. 1887S-1890S, 1997.

6. Rupert, J.L. The search for genotypes that underlie human performance phenotypes. *Comparative Biochemistry and Physiology Part A*, Vol. 136, pp. 191-203, 2003.

7. Scott, R.A. et al. Genotypes and distance running: Clues from Africa. *Sports Medicine*, Vol. 37 (4-5), pp. 424-427, 2007.

8. Matthews, P. World and continental records. In Athletics '87. *International Track and Field Annual*. London: International Publishers, pp. 249-266, 1987.

9. IAAF all-time outdoor lists, June 2003. http://iaaf.org.

10. Larsen, H.B. Kenyan dominance in distance running. *Comparative Biochemistry and Physiology Part A*, Vol. 136, pp. 161-170, 2003.

11. Onywera, V.O. et al. Demographic characteristics of elite Kenyan endurance runners. *Journal of Sports Sciences*, Vol. 24 (4), pp. 415-422, 2006.

12. Scott, R.A. et al. Demographic characteristics of elite Ethiopian endurance runners. *Medicine & Science in Sports & Exercise*, Vol. 35 (10), pp. 1727-1732, 2003.

13. Sonna, L.A. et al. Angiotensin-converting enzyme genotype and physical performance during US Army basic training. *Journal of Applied Physiology*, Vol. 91, pp. 1355-1363, 2001.

14. Tanser, T. Train hard, win easy: *The Kenyan way*. Tafnews Press, 2001.

15. Familial aggregation of submaximal aerobic performance in the HERITAGE Family Study. *Medicine & Science in Sports & Exercise*, Vol. 33, pp. 597-604, 2001.

16. Klissouras, V. Heritability of adaptive variation: An old problem revisited. *Journal of Sports Medicine & Physical Fitness*, Vol. 37, pp. 1-6, 1997.

17. Bouchard, C. et al. Familial aggregation of V·O$_2$max response to exercise training: Results from the HERITAGE Family Study. *Journal of Applied Physiology*, Vol. 87, pp. 1003-1008, 1999.

18. Bouchard, C. et al. Familial resemblance for V·O$_2$max in the sedentary state: The HERITAGE Family Study. *Medicine & Science in Sports & Exercise*, Vol. 30, pp. 252-258, 1998.

Chapter 2 Genes That Influence Performance

1. Hamel, P. et al. Heredity and muscle adaptation to endurance training. *Medicine & Science in Sports & Exercise*, Vol. 18, pp. 690-696, 1986.

2. Bouchard, C. et al. Familial aggregation of V·O$_2$max response to exercise training: Results from the HERITAGE Family Study. *Journal of Applied Physiology*, Vol. 87, pp. 1003-1008, 1999.

3. Tsianos, G. et al. The ACE gene ion/deletion polymorphism and elite endurance swimming. *European Journal of Applied Physiology*, Vol.92 (3), pp. 360-362, 2004.

4. Montgomery, H. et al. Angiotensin-converting enzyme gene ion/deletion polymorphism and response to physical training. *Lancet*, Vol. 353 (9152), pp. 541-545, February 13, 1999.

5. Williams, A.G. et al. The ACE gene and muscle performance. *Nature*, Vol. 403, p. 614, Feb.10, 2000.

6. Hugh Montgomery, personal communication.

7. Myerson, S. et al. Human angiotensin I-converting enzyme gene and endurance performance. *Journal of Applied Physiology*, Vol. 87, pp. 1313-1316, 1999.

8. Saltin, B. et al. Aerobic exercise capacity at sea level and at altitude in Kenyan boys, junior and senior runners compared with Scandinavian runners. *Scandinavian Journal of Medicine & Science in Sports*, Vol. 5, pp. 209-221, 1995.

9. Larsen, H.B. et al. Training response of adolescent Kenyan town and village boys to endurance running. *Scandinavian Journal of Medicine & Science in Sports*, Vol. 15 (1), pp. 48-57, Feb. 2005.

10. Saltin, B. Response to exercise after bed rest and after training. *Circulation*, Vol. 38 (5), Suppl. VII, pp. 1-78, 1968.

11. Wenger, H.A. et al. Endurance training: The effects of intensity, total work, duration, and initial fitness. *Journal of Sports Medicine*, Vol. 15, pp. 199-211, 1975.

12. Fournier, M. et al. Skeletal muscle adaptation in adolescent boys: Sprint and endurance training and detraining. *Medicine & Science in Sports & Exercise*, Vol. 14, pp. 453-456, 1982.

13. Barton-Davis, E. et al. Viral mediated expression of insulin-like growth factor I blocks the aging-related loss of skeletal muscle function. *Proceedings of the National Academy of Sciences USA*, Vol. 95 (26), pp. 15603-15607, Dec. 22, 1998.

14. Lee, S. et al. Viral expression of insulin-like growth factor-I enhances muscle hypertrophy in resistance-trained rats. *Journal of Applied Physiology*, Vol. 96 (3), pp. 1097-1104, Mar. 2004.

15. de la Chapelle, A. et al. Truncated erythropoietin receptor causes dominantly inherited benign human erythrocytosis. *Proc Natl Acad Sci USA*, Vol. 90 (10), pp. 4495-4499, 1993.

16. Yang, N. et al. ACTN3 genotype is associated with human elite athletic performance. *American Journal of Human Genetics*, Vol. 73 (3), pp. 627-631, 2003.

17. Sweeney, H.L. Gene doping. *Scientific American*, pp. 63-69, July 2004.

18. Gao, G. Erythropoietin gene therapy leads to autoimmune anemia in macaques. *Blood*, Vol. 103 (May 1), pp. 3300-3302, 2004.

19. Brownlee, C. Gene doping: Will athletes go for the ultimate high? *Science News Online*, Vol. 166 (18), Oct. 30, 2004.

20. Barré, L. et al. A genetic model for the chronic activation of skeletal muscle AMP-activated protein kinase leads to glycogen accumulation. *American Journal of Physiology, Endocrinology, & Metabolism*, Vol. 292 (3), pp. E802-11, Mar. 2007.

21. Dartmouth researchers identify a gene that enhances muscle performance. 2006. *Dartmouth News Release*, www.dartmouth.edu/~news/releases/2006/11/14.html.

22. Ash, G.I. et al. No association between ACE gene variation and endurance athlete status in Ethiopians. *Sci Sports Exerc*. Vol. 43(4), pp. 590-597, 2011.

Chapter 3 Genetic Differences Between Elite and Nonelite Runners

1. Ruiz, J.R. et al. Is there an optimum endurance polygenic profile? *Journal of Physiology*, Vol. 587 (Part 7), pp. 1527-1534, 2009.

2. Cieszczyk, P. The angiotensin converting enzyme gene I/D polymorphism in polish rowers. *International Journal of Sports Medicine*, Vol. 30 (8), pp. 624-627, 2009.

3. Niemi, A.K. et al. Mitochondrial DNA and ACTN3 genotypes in Finnish elite endurance and sprint athletes. *European Journal of Human Genetics*, Vol. 13, pp. 965-969, 2005.

4. Papadimitriou, I.D. The ACTN3 gene in elite Greek track and field athletes. *International Journal of Sports Medicine*, Vol. 29, pp. 352-355, 2008.

5. Lucia, A. et al. ACTN3 genotype in professional endurance cyclists. *International Journal of Sports Medicine*, Vol. 27 (11), pp. 880-884, 2006.

6. Ruiz, J.R., et al. GNB3 C825T polymorphism and elite athletic status: A replication study with two ethnic groups. *International Journal of Sports Medicine*, Vol. 32 (2), pp. 151-3, Feb. 2011.

7. Ash, G.I. et al. No association between ACE gene variation and endurance athlete status in Ethiopians. *Medicine in Science and Sports & Exercise*, Vol. 43 (4), pp. 590-7, Apr. 2011.

8. How to Become an Olympic Athlete—Hint: Choose Your Parents Wisely! 2008. www.sportsscientists.com/search?q=genetics+of+running.

9. Onywera, V.O. et al. Demographic characteristics of elite Kenyan endurance runners. *Journal of Sports Sciences*, Vol. 24 (4), pp. 415-422, 2006.

10. Scott, R.A. et al. Demographic characteristics of elite Ethiopian endurance runners. *Medicine & Science in Sports & Exercise*, Vol. 35 (10), pp. 1727-1732, 2003.

11. Scott, R.A. et al. Genotypes and distance running: Clues from Africa. *Sports Medicine*, Vol. 37, pp. 424-427, 2007.

12. Saltin, B. et al. Aerobic exercise capacity at sea level and at altitude in Kenyan boys, junior, and senior runners compared with Scandinavian runners. *Scandinavian Journal of Medicine & Science in Sports*, Vol. 5 (4), pp. 209-221, 1995.

13. Eynon, W. et al. Genes and elite athletes: a road map for future research. Journal of Physiology, Vol. (589), pp. 3063-3070, 2011.

14. Michael Phelps Bio. http://www.2008.nbcolympics.com/athletes/athlete=2/bio/index.html.

15. Woods, D.R. et al. Endurance enhancement related to the human angiotensin I-converting enzyme I-D polymorphism is not due to differences in the cardiorespiratory response to training. *European Journal of Applied Physiology*, Vol. 86 (3), pp. 240-244, 2002.

16. Gayagay, G. et al. Elite endurance athletes and the ACE I allele: The role of genes in athletic performance. *Human Genetics*, Vol. 103, pp. 48-50, 1998.

17. Montgomery, H.E. et al. Human gene for physical performance. *Nature*, Vol. 393, pp. 221-222, 1998.

18. Myerson, S. et al. Human angiotensin I-converting enzyme gene and endurance performance. *Journal of Applied Physiology*, Vol. 87 (4), pp. 1313-1316, 1999.

19. Alvarez, R. et al. Genetic variation in the renin-angiotensin system and athletic performance. *European Journal of Applied Physiology*, Vol. 82 (1-2), pp. 117-120, 2000.

20. Rankinen, T. et al. Angiotensin-converting enzyme ID polymorphism and fitness phenotype in the HERITAGE Family Study. *Journal of Applied Physiology*, Vol. 88, pp. 1029-1035, 2000.

21. Nazarov, I.B. et al. The angiotensin converting enzyme I/D polymorphism in russian athletes. *European Journal of Human Genetics*, Vol. 9 (10), pp. 797-801, 2001.

22. Cam, S. et al. ACE I/D gene polymorphism and aerobic endurance development in response to training in a non-elite female cohort. *Journal of Sports Medicine and Physical Fitness*, Vol. 47 (2), pp. 234-8, June 2007.

23. Woods, D. et al. Elite swimmers and the D allele of the ACE I/D polymorphism. *Human Genetics*, Vol. 108, pp. 230-232, 2001.

24. Scott, R.A. et al. No association between angiotensin converting enzyme (ACE) gene variation and endurance athlete status in Kenyans. *Comparative Biochemistry and Physiology Part A Molecular and Integrative Physiology*, Vol. 141 (2), pp. 169-175, 2005.

25. Rankinen, T. et al. No association between angiotensin-converting enzyme ID polymorphism and elite endurance athlete status. *Journal of Applied Physiology*, Vol. 88 (5), pp. 1571-1575, 2000.

26. Scott, R.A. et al. Mitochondrial DNA lineages of elite Ethiopian athletes. *Comparative Biochemistry and Physiology Part B Biochemistry and Molecular Biology*, Vol. 140 (3), pp. 497-503, 2005

27. Colin, N.M et al. Y Chromosome haplogroups of elite Ethiopian endurance runners. *Human Genetics*, Vol. 115 (6), pp. 492-497, 2004.

Chapter 4 The Body While Running

1. Williams, K.R. Biomechanics of distance running. In *Current issues in biomechanics*, Mark D. Grabiner, ed. Champaign, IL: Human Kinetics, 1993, p. 4.

2. Cavanagh, P.R. *Biomechanics of distance running*. Champaign, IL: Human Kinetics, 1990.

3. Powers, S.K. and Howley, E.T. *Exercise physiology: Theory and application to fitness and performance.* New York: McGraw-Hill, 2001, p.146.

4. Nicol, C. et al. The stretch-shortening cycle: A model to study naturally occurring neuromuscular fatigue. *Sports Medicine*, Vol. 36 (11), pp. 977-999, 2006.

5. Behm, D.G. and Sale, D.G. Velocity specificity of resistance training. *Sports Medicine*, Vol. 15 (6), pp. 374-388, 1993.

6. Martin, D.E. and Coe, S. Developing total fitness: Strength, flexibility, and health. In *Better training for distance runners.* Champaign, IL: Human Kinetics, 1997, p. 293.

7. Jones, M. Technique of lifting. In *Strength training.* Birmingham: British Amateur Athletic Board, 1990, p.56.

Chapter 5   Refinement in Running Form

1. Messier, S. and Cirillo, K. Effects of a verbal and visual feedback system on running technique, perceived exertion, and running economy in female novice runners. *Journal of Sport Sciences*, Vol. 7, pp. 113-126, 1989.

2. Anderson, O. Running economy remains elusive to even the most earnest experts. *Running Research News*, Vol. 5 (5), pp. 1, 3-5, Sept.-Oct. 1989.

3. Heinert, L.D. et al. Effect of stride length variation on oxygen uptake during level and positive grade treadmill running. *Research Quarterly for Exercise and Sport (RQES)*, Vol. 59 (2), pp. 127-130, 1988.

4. Cavanagh, P.R. and Williams K.R. The effect of stride length variation on oxygen uptake during distance running. *Medicine & Science in Sports & Exercise*, Vol. 14, pp. 30-35, 1982.

5. Morgan, D.W. and Martin, P.E. Effects of stride length alteration on racewalking economy. *Canadian Journal of Applied Sport Science*, Vol. 11 (4), pp. 211-217, 1986.

6. Anderson, O. Be a better runner without higher fitness—with the right form. *Running Research News*, Vol. 13 (1), pp. 1, 6-8, 1997.

7. Nancy Hamilton, interview with author, Jan.1997.

8. McMahon, T.A. et al. Groucho running. *Journal of Applied Physiology*, Vol. 62, pp. 2326-2337, 1987.

9. Williams, K.R and Cavanagh, P.R., Relationship between distance running mechanics, running economy, and performance. *Journal of Applied Physiology*, Vol. 63 (3), pp. 1236-1245, 1987.

10. Williams, K.R. and Cavanagh, P.R. Biomechanical correlates with running economy in elite distance runners. *Proceedings of the North American Congress on Biomechanics*, pp. 287-288, 1986.

11. Andersen, T. et al. Running economy, anthropometric dimensions, and kinematic variables. *Medicine & Science in Sports & Exercise*, Vol. 26 (5), p. S170, 1994.

12. Anderson, O. Form II: What you have to do. *Running Research News*, Vol. 13 (5), pp. 6-8, June-July 1997.

13. Hasegawa, H. et al. Foot strike patterns of runners at the 15-km point during an elite-level half marathon. *Journal of Strength & Conditioning Research*, Vol. 21 (3), pp. 888-893, 2007.

14. Paavolainen, L. et al. Explosive-strength training improves 5-km running time by improving running economy and muscle power. *Journal of Applied Physiology*, Vol. 86 (5), pp. 1527-1533, 1999.

15. Walt Reynolds, CSCS, interview with author, Aug. 16, 2011.

16. Anderson, O. Making headway on improving economy: Can freeloading African women help? *Running Research News*, Vol. 17 (5), pp. 1-5, June-July 2001.

17. Arendse, R.E. et al. Reduced eccentric loading of the knee with the pose running method. *Medicine & Science in Sports & Exercise*, Vol. 36 (2), pp. 272-277, 2004.

18. Dallam, G. et al. Effect of a global alteration of running technique on kinematics and economy. *Journal of Sports Sciences*, Vol. 23 (7), pp. 757-764, 2005.

Chapter 6   Running Surfaces, Shoes, and Orthotics

1. Williams, K.R. Biomechanics of distance running. In *Current issues in biomechanics*, Mark D. Grabiner, ed. Champaign, IL: Human Kinetics, 1993, p. 23.

2. Anderson, O. Impact forces—and the heavy impacts of the myths they create. *Running Research News*, Vol. 17 (3), pp. 1, 5-9, April 2001.

3. Radin, E.L et al. Effect of prolonged walking on concrete on the knees of sheep. *Journal of Biomechanics*, Vol. 15 (7), pp. 487-492, 1982.

4. Feehery, R.V. Jr. The biomechanics of running on different surfaces. *Clinics in Podiatric Medicine and Surgery*, Vol. 3 (4), pp. 649-659, 1986.

5. Ferris, D.P. et al. Running in the real world: Adjusting leg stiffness for different surfaces. *Proceedings of the Royal Society of London B Biological Science*, Vol. 265 (1400), pp. 989-994, 1998.

6. Ferris, D.P. and Farley, C. Interaction of leg stiffness and surface stiffness during human hopping. *Journal of Applied Physiology*, Vol. 82 (1), pp. 15-22, 1997.

7. Ferris, D.P. et al. Runners adjust leg stiffness for their first step on a new running surface. *Journal of Biomechanics*, Vol. 32 (8), pp. 787-794, 1999.

8. The influence of surface characteristics on the impulse characteristics of drop landings. *Proceedings of the 15th Annual Meeting of the American Society of Biomechanics*, Aug. 23-25, Burlington, VT, pp. 92-93, 1989.

9. Robbins, S.E. and Gouw, G.J. Athletic footwear: Unsafe due to perceptual illusions. *Medicine & Science in Sports & Exercise*, Vol. 23 (2), pp. 217-224, 1991.

10. Clarke, T.E. et al. Biomechanical measurement of running shoe cushioning properties. In *Biomechanical aspects of sport shoes and playing surfaces*, B.M. Nigg and B.A. Kerr, eds. Calgary: University of Calgary, pp. 25-33, 1983.

11. Nigg, B.M. and Bahlsen, A. Influence of heel flare and mid-sole construction on pronation, supination, and impact forces for heel-toe running. *International Journal of Sport Biomechanics*, Vol. 4, pp. 205-219, 1988.

12. Nigg, B.M. et al. The influence of running velocity and midsole hardness on external impact forces in heel-toe running. *Journal of Biomechanics*, Vol. 20, pp. 951-959, 1987.

13. Fredericson, M. and Misra, A.K. Epidemiology and aetiology of marathon running injuries, *Sports Medicine*, Vol. 37 (4-5), pp. 437-439, 2007.

14. Relationship between running injuries and running shoes. In *The shoe in sport*. W. Pforringer and B. Segesser, eds. Chicago: Year Book Medical, 1989, pp. 256-265.

15. Klinghan, R.T. et al. Do you get value for money when you buy an expensive pair of running shoes? *British Journal of Sports Medicine*, Vol. 42 (2), pp. 189-193, 2007.

16. Anderson, O. Should running shoes be changed? Marti, Nigg, and Ellis provide clues. *Running Research News*, Vol. 8 (1), pp. 1-5, Jan.-Feb.1992.

17. Robbins, S. and Waked, E. Hazard of deceptive advertising of athletic footwear. *British Journal of Sports Medicine*, Vol. 31, pp. 299-303, 1997.

18. Hamill, J. and Bates, B.T. A kinetic evaluation of the effects of in vivo loading on running shoes. *Journal of Orthopaedic and Sports Physical Therapy*, Vol. 10 (2), pp. 47-53, 1988.

19. Robbins, S.E. and Gouw, G.J. Athletic footwear: Unsafe due to perceptual illusions. *Medicine & Science in Sports & Exercise*, Vol. 23 (2), pp. 217-224, 1991.

20. Robbins, S. et al. Athletic footwear affects balance in men. *British Journal of Sports Medicine*, Vol. 28 (2), pp. 117-123, 1994.

21. Cook, S.D. et al. Running shoes: Their relationship to running injuries. *Sports Medicine*, Vol. 10 (1), pp. 1-8, 1990.

22. Cheung, R. et al. Association of footwear with patellofemoral pain syndrome in runners. *Sports Medicine*, Vol. 36 (3), pp. 199-205, 2006.

23. MacDougall, C. *Born to run*. New York: Knopf, 2009.

24. Lieberman, D. et al. Foot strike patterns and collision forces in habitually barefoot versus shod runners. *Nature*, Vol. 463, pp. 531-535, Jan. 28, 2010.

25. Barefoot running—New evidence, same debate. Jan. 29, 2010. www.sportsscientists.com/2010/01/running-barefoot-vs-shoes.html.

26. Donatelli, R.A. et al. Biomechanical foot orthotics: A retrospective study. *Journal of Orthopaedic & Sports Physical Therapy*, Vol. 10 (6), pp. 205-212, 1988.

27. Sperryn, P.N. and Restan, L. Podiatry and the sports physician: An evaluation of orthoses. *British Journal of Sports Medicine*, Vol. 7, pp. 129-134, 1983.

28. Razeghi M. and Batt, M.E. Biomechanical analysis of the effect of orthotic shoe inserts. *Sports Medicine*, Vol. 29 (6), pp. 425-438, 2000.

29. D'Ambrosia, R.D. Orthotic devices in running injuries. *Clinics in Sports Medicine*, Vol. 4, pp. 611-618, 1985.

30. Brody, D.M. Techniques in the evaluation and treatment of the injured runner. *Orthopedic Clinics of North America*, Vol. 13, pp. 541-558, 1982.

31. Gross, M.L. et al. Effectiveness of orthotic shoe inserts in the long-distance runner. *American Journal of Sports Medicine*, Vol. 19 (4), pp. 409-412, 1991.

32. Hamill, J. et al. Relationship between selected static and dynamic lower extremity measures. *Clinical Biomechanics*, Vol. 4, pp. 217-225, 1989.

33. Knutzen, K.M. and Price, A. Lower extremity static and dynamic relationship with rearfoot motion in gait. *Journal of the American Podiatric Medical Association*, Vol. 84 (4), pp. 171-180, 1994.

34. McPoil, T.G. and Hunt, G.C. Evaluation and management of foot and ankle disorders: Present problems and future directions. *Journal of Orthopaedic & Sports Physical Therapy*, Vol. 21 (6), pp. 381-388, 1995.

35. Aström, M. and Arvidson, T. Alignment and joint motion in the normal foot. *Journal of Orthopaedic & Sports Physical Therapy*, Vol. 22 (5), pp. 216-222, 1995

36. Stacoff, A. et al. Effects of foot orthoses on skeletal motion during running. *Clinical Biomechanics*, Vol. 15 (1), pp. 54-64, 2000.

37. Donoghue O.A, Orthotic control of rear foot and lower limb motion during running in participants with chronic Achilles tendon injury. *Sports Biomechanics*, Vol. 7 (2), pp. 194-205, 2008.

Chapter 7   Maximal Aerobic Capacity ($\dot{V}O_2$max)

1. Hill, A.V. and Lupton, H. Muscular exercise, lactic acid, and the supply and utilization of oxygen. *Quarterly Medical Journal*, Vol. 16, pp. 135-171, 1923.

2. Saltin, B. and Åstrand, P. Maximal oxygen uptake in athletes. *Journal of Applied Physiology*, Vol. 23, pp. 353-358, 1967.

3. Åstrand, P. et al. *Textbook of work physiology.* 3rd ed. New York: McGraw Hill, 1986.

4. Howley, E. et al. *Health fitness instructor's handbook.* 3rd ed. Champaign, IL: Human Kinetics, 1997.

5. Noakes, T. Physiological capacity of the elite runner. In *Running & science—in an interdisciplinary perspective*, J. Bangsbo and H. Larsen, eds. Copenhagen: Munksgaard, 2000.

6. Pollock, M.L. Submaximal and maximal working capacity of elite distance runners, part 1: Cardiorespiratory aspects. *Annals of the New York Academy of Sciences*, Vol. 301, pp. 310-321, 1977.

7. Dempsey, J. et al. Limitations to exercise capacity and endurance: Pulmonary system. *Canadian Journal of Applied Sport Science*, Vol. 7, pp. 4-13, 1982.

8. Noakes, T. High V·O₂max with no history of training is due to high blood volume: An alternative explanation. *British Journal of Sports Medicine*, Vol. 39, p. 578, 2005.

9. St. Clair Gibson, A. and Noakes, T. Evidence for complex system integration and dynamic neural regulation of skeletal muscle recruitment during exercise in humans. *British Journal of Sports Medicine*, Vol. 38, pp. 797-806, 2004.

10. Noakes, T. and St. Claire Gibson, A. Logical limitations to the "catastrophe" models of fatigue during exercise in humans. *British Journal of Sports Medicine*, Vol. 38, pp. 648-649, 2004.

11. Ekblom, B. Effect of physical training on oxygen transport system in man. *Acta Physiologica Scandinavica*, Vol. 328 (Suppl.), pp. 1-45, 1969.

12. Hickson, R.C. et al. Potential for strength and endurance training to amplify endurance performance. *Journal of Applied Physiology*, Vol. 65, pp. 2285-2290, 1988.

13. Rowell, L.B. *Human circulation: Regulation during physical stress.* New York: Oxford University Press, 1986.

14. Saltin, B. Physiological effects of physical conditioning. *Medicine & Science in Sports*, Vol. 1, pp. 50-56, 1969.

15. Coyle, E.F. et al. Effects of detraining on cardiovascular responses to exercise: Role of blood volume. *Journal of Applied Physiology*, Vol. 60, pp. 95-99, 1986.

16. Coyle, E.F. et al. Maximal oxygen uptake relative to plasma volume expansion. *International Journal of Sports Medicine*, Vol. 11, pp. 116-119, 1990.

17. Blomqvist, C.G. and Saltin, B. Cardiovascular adaptations to physical training. *Annual Review of Physiology*, Vol. 45, pp. 169-189, 1983.

18. Holloszy, J.O. and Coyle, E.F. Adaptations of skeletal muscle to endurance exercise and their metabolic consequences. *Journal of Applied Physiology*: Respiratory, Environmental, and Exercise Physiology, Vol. 56, pp. 831-838, 1984.

19. Owen Anderson, personal observation.

20. Bassett D.R. Jr and Howley E. Maximal oxygen uptake: "Classical" versus "contemporary" viewpoints. *Medicine & Science in Sports & Exercise*, Vol. 29, pp. 591-603, 1997.

21. Costill, D. et al. Fractional utilization of the aerobic capacity during distance running. *Medicine & Science in Sports & Exercise*, Vol. 5, pp. 248-252, 1973.

22. Costill, D. The relationship between selected physiological variables and distance running performance. *Journal of Sports Medicine & Physical Fitness*, Vol. 7, pp. 61-66, 1967.

23. Davies, C.T. and Thompson, M.W. Aerobic performance of female marathon and male ultramarathon athletes. *European Journal of Applied Physiology*, Vol. 61, pp. 611-617, 1979.

24. Foster, C. $V \cdot O_2$max and training indices as determinants of competitive running performance. *Journal of Sports Sciences*, Vol. 1, pp. 13-22, 1983.

25. Foster, C. et al. Skeletal muscle enzyme activity, fiber composition, and $V \cdot O_2$max in relation to distance running performance. *European Journal of Applied Physiology*, Vol. 39, pp. 73-80, 1978.

26. Matsui, H. et al. Maximum oxygen intake and its relationship to body weight of Japanese adolescents. *Medicine & Science in Sports*, Vol. 3, pp. 170-175, 1972.

27. Running performance from the viewpoint of aerobic power. In *Environmental stress: Individual human adaptations*. L.J. Folinsbee, J.A. Wagner, J.F. Borgia, B.L. Drinkwater, J.A. Gliner, and J.F. Bedi, eds. New York: Academic Press, 1978, pp. 183-194.

28. Wyndham, C.H. et al. Physiological requirements for world-class performances in endurance running. *South African Medical Journal*, Vol. 43, pp. 996-1002, 1969.

29. Noakes, T. Time to move beyond a brainless exercise physiology: The evidence for complex regulation of human exercise performance. *Applied Physiology, Nutrition, and Metabolism*, Vol. 36, pp. 23-35, 2011.

30. Noakes, T. et al. Peak treadmill running velocity during the $V \cdot O_2$max test predicts running performance. *Journal of Sports Sciences*, Vol. 8, pp. 35-45, 1990.

31. Scott, B.K. and Houmard, J.A. Peak running velocity is highly related to distance running performance. *International Journal of Sports Medicine*, Vol. 15, pp. 504-507, 1994.

32. Cairns, S.P. Lactic acid and exercise performance: culprit or friend? *Sports Medicine* Vol. 36(4), pp. 279-291, 2006.

33. de Paoli, F.V., Ørtenblad, N., Pedersen, T.H., Jørgensen, R., Nielsen, O.B. Lactate per se improves the excitability of depolarized rat skeletal muscle by reducing the Cl-conductance. *Journal of Physiology* Vol. 588(23), pp. 4785-4794.

34. Smith, T.P. et al. Effects of 4-wk training using vmax/tmax on $V \cdot O_2$max and performance in athletes. *Medicine & Science in Sports & Exercise*, Vol. 31 (6), pp. 892-896, 1999.

35. Paton, C. and Hopkins, W. Effects of high-intensity training on performance and physiology of endurance athletes. *Sports Science*, Vol. 8, pp. 25-40, 2004.

36. Wenger, H. and Macnab, R. Endurance training: The effects of intensity, total work, duration, and initial fitness. *Journal of Sports Medicine*, Vol. 15, pp. 199-211, 1975.

37. Anderson, O. Plodding won't produce peak aerobic capacity: Using the right running speed seems to be the key. *Running Research News*, Vol. 4 (6), pp. 1-5, 1988.

38. Wenger, H. et al. The interactions of intensity, frequency, and duration of exercise training in altering cardiorespiratory fitness. *Sports Medicine*, Vol. 3, pp. 346-356, 1986.

39. The effect of distance training and interval training on aerobic and anaerobic capacity, muscle fiber characteristics, and performance in endurance-trained runners. *Twelfth European Track Coaches' Congress*, Acoteias, Portugal, pp. 10-16.

40. Anderson, O. Sweating out those last little gains in $V \cdot O_2$max: How "anaerobic" running produces large aerobic gains. *Running Research News*, Vol. 7 (1), pp. 1, 3-4, 1991.

Chapter 8   Running Economy

1. Morgan, D.W. et al. Factors affecting running economy. *Sports Medicine*, Vol. 7 (5), pp. 310-330, 1989.

2. Conley, D.L. and Krahenbuhl, G.S. Running economy and distance running performance of highly trained athletes. *Medicine & Science of Sports & Exercise*, Vol. 12 (5), pp. 357-360, 1980.

3. Spurrs, R. et al. The effect of plyometric training on distance running performance. *European Journal of Applied Physiology*, Vol. 89, pp. 1-7, 2003.

4. Davies, C.T. and Thompson, M.W. Aerobic performance of female marathon and male ultra-marathon athletes. *European Journal of Applied Physiology*, Vol. 41, pp. 233-245, 1979.

5. Economy of movement and endurance performance. In *Endurance in sport*. R.J. Shephard and P.O. Astrand, eds. Oxford: Blackwell Scientific, 1992, pp. 179-185.

6. Bailey, S. and Pate, R. Feasibility of improving running economy. *Sports Medicine*, Vol. 12, pp. 228-236, 1991.

7. Pugh, L. The influence of wind resistance in running and walking and the mechanical efficiency of work against gravity. *Journal of Physiology*, Vol. 213, pp. 255-276, 1971.

8. Liefeldt, G. et al. Oxygen delivery does not limit peak running speed during incremental downhill running to exhaustion. *European Journal of Applied Physiology*, Vol. 64, pp. 493-496, 1992.

9. Robergs, R. et al. Oxygen consumption and energy expenditure of level versus downhill running. *Journal of Sports Medicine & Physical Fitness*, Vol. 37, pp. 168-174, 1997.

10. Burkett, L. et al. Effects of shoes and foot orthotics on $V \cdot O_2$ and selected frontal plane knee kinematics. *Medicine & Science in Sports & Exercise*, Vol. 17 (1), pp. 158-163, 1985.

11. Kerdok, A. et al. Energetics and mechanisms of human running on surfaces of different stiffnesses. *Journal of Applied Physiology*, Vol. 92 (2), pp. 469-478, 2002.

12. Daniels, J. A physiologist's view of running economy. *Medicine & Science in Sports & Exercise*, Vol. 17, pp. 332-338, 1985.

13. Morgan, D.W. and Craib, M. Physiological aspects of running economy. *Medicine & Science in Sports & Exercise*, Vol. 24, pp. 456-461, 1992.

14. Lucia, A. et al. Physiological characteristics of the best Eritrean runners: Exceptional running economy. *Applied Physiology, Nutrition, & Metabolism*, Vol. 31 (5), pp. 530-540, 2006.

15. Kram, R. and Taylor, R. Energetics of running: A new perspective, *Nature*, Vol. 346, pp. 265-267, 1990.

16. Heise, G.D. and Martin, P.E. Are variations in running economy in humans associated with ground reaction force characteristics? *European Journal of Applied Physiology*, Vol. 84, pp. 438-442, 2001.

17. Heise, G.D. and Martin, P.E. Neuromuscular characteristics and muscle power as determinants of 5-km running performance. *Medicine & Science in Sports & Exercise*, Vol. 31, pp. 124-130, 1999.

18. Nummela, A. et al. Factors related to top running speed and economy. *International Journal of Sports Medicine*, Vol. 28, pp. 655-661, 2007.

19. Blum, Y., Lipfert, S.W., and Seyfarth, A. Effective leg stiffness in running. *Journal of Biomechanics*, Vol. 42 (14), pp. 2400-2405, 2009.

20. Gleim, G. et al. The influence of flexibility on the economy of walking and jogging. *Journal of Orthopaedic Research*, Vol. 8, pp. 814-823, 1990.

21. Craib, M. et al. The association between flexibility and running economy in sub-elite male distance runners. *Medicine & Science in Sports & Exercise*, Vol. 28, pp. 737-743, 1996.

22. Anderson, T. Biomechanics and running economy. *Sports Medicine*, Vol. 22, pp. 76-89, 1996.

23. Cavanagh, P.R. and Williams, K.R. The effect of stride length variation on oxygen uptake during distance running. *Medicine & Science in Sports & Exercise*, Vol.14 (1), pp. 30-35, 1982.

24. Morgan, D. et al. Effect of step length optimization on the aerobic demand of running. *Journal of Applied Physiology*, Vol. 77 (1), pp. 245-251, 1994.

25. Svedenhag, J. and Sjödin, B. Maximal and submaximal oxygen uptakes and blood lactate levels in elite male middle- and long-distance runners. *International Journal of Sports Medicine*, Vol. 5, pp. 255-261, 1984.

26. Houmard, J. et al. The effects of taper on performance in distance runners. *Medicine & Science in Sports & Exercise*, Vol. 26, pp. 624-631, 1994.

27. Endurance conditioning. In *Endurance in sport*, R.J. Shephard and P.O. Astrand, eds. Oxford: Blackwell Scientific, 1992, pp. 294-295.

28. Johnston, R. et al. Strength training in female distance runners: Impact on running economy. *Journal of Strength & Conditioning Research*, Vol. 11 (4), pp. 224-229, 1997.

29. Paavolainen, L. et al. Explosive-strength training improves 5-km running time by improving running economy and muscle power. *Journal of Applied Physiology*, Vol. 86 (5), pp. 1527-1533, 1999.

30. Daniels, J., and Daniels, N. Running economy of elite male and elite female runners. *Medicine & Science in Sports & Exercise*, Vol. 24, pp. 483-489, 1992.

31. Beneke, R. and Hütler, M. The effect of training on running economy and performance in recreational athletes. *Medicine & Science in Sports & Exercise*, Vol. 37 (10), pp. 1794-1799, 2005.

Chapter 9   Minimum Velocity for Maximal Aerobic Capacity (v$\dot{V}O_2$max)

1. Anderson, O. $\dot{V}O_2$max is a poor predictor of performance, but computing your velocity at $\dot{V}O_2$max can pay big benefits. *Running Research News*, Vol. 10 (5), pp. 1-3, Sept.-Oct.1994.

2. McLaughlin, J. et al. Test of the classic model for predicting endurance running performance. *Medicine & Science in Sports & Exercise*, Vol. 42 (5), pp. 991-997, 2010.

3. Cunningham, L. Relationship of running economy, ventilatory threshold, and maximal oxygen consumption to running performance in high school females. *Research Quarterly for Exercise and Sport*, Vol. 61 (4), pp. 369-374, 1990.

4. Morgan, D. et al. 10 kilometer performance and predicted velocity at $\dot{V}O_2$max among well-trained male runners. *Medicine & Science in Sports & Exercise*, Vol. 21 (1), pp. 78-83, 1989.

5. Billat, L.V. and Koralsztein, J.P. Significance of the velocity at $\dot{V}O_2$max and time to exhaustion at this velocity. *Sports Medicine*, Vol. 22 (2), pp. 90-108, 1996.

6. Billat, V. et al. Interval training at $\dot{V}O_2$max: Effects on aerobic performance and overtraining markers. *Medicine & Science in Sports & Exercise*, Vol. 31 (1), pp. 156-163, 1999.

7. Anderson, O. Things were so easy, until v$\dot{V}O_2$max and then tlimv$\dot{V}O_2$max had to come along. *Running Research News*, Vol. 15 (2), pp. 1-5, 1999.

Chapter 10   Velocity at Lactate Threshold

1. Bassett D.R. Jr and Howley, E.T. Limiting factors for maximum oxygen uptake and determinants of endurance performance. *Medicine & Science in Sports & Exercise*, Vol. 32 (1), pp. 70-84, 2000.

2. Noakes, T.D. and St. Clair Gibson, A. Logical limitations to the "catastrophe" models of fatigue during exercise in humans. *British Journal of Sports Medicine*, Vol. 38(5), p. 648-649.

3. Noakes, T.D. Time to move beyond a brainless exercise physiology: The evidence for complex regulation of human exercise performance. *Applied Physiology, Nutrition, and Metabolism*, Vol. 36(1), p. 23-35.

4. Miles, M.P. and Clarkson, P.M. Exercise-induced muscle pain, soreness, and cramps. *Journal of Sports Medicine and Physical Fitness*, Vol. 34(3), p. 203-216.

5. Tenan, M.S., McMurray, R.G., Blackburn, B.T., McGarth, M., Leppert, K. The relationship between blood potassium, blood lactate, and electromyography signals related to fatigue in a progressive cycling exercise test. *Journal of Electromyography and Kinesiology*, Vol. 21(1), p. 25-32.

6. Astrand, P. et al. Disposal of lactate during and after strenuous exercise in humans. *Journal of Applied Physiology*, Vol. 61 (1), pp. 338-343, 1986.

7. Jacobs, I. Blood lactate: Implications for training and sports performance. *Sports Medicine*, Vol. 3, pp. 10-25, 1986.

8. Tanaka, K. et al. A longitudinal assessment of anaerobic threshold and distance-running performance. *Medicine & Science in Sports & Exercise*, Vol. 16 (3), pp. 278-282, 1984.

9. Martin, D. et al. Physiological changes in elite male distance runners training for Olympic competition. *The Physician and Sports Medicine*, Vol. 14 (1), pp. 152-171, 1986.

10. Marc Rogers, personal communication.

11. Orlander, J. and Aniansson, A. Effects of physical training on skeletal muscle metabolism and ultrastructure in 70- to 75-year-old men. *Acta Physiologica Scandinavica*, Vol. 109, pp. 149-156, 1980.

12. Young, J.C. et al. Maintenance of the adaptations of skeletal muscle mitochondria to exercise in old rats. *Medicine & Science in Sports & Exercise*, Vol. 15, pp. 243-251, 1983.

13. Grimby, G. and Saltin, B. The ageing muscle. *Clinical Physiology*, Vol. 3, pp. 209-218, 1983.

14. Allen, W. et al. Lactate threshold and distance-running performance in young and older endurance athletes. *Journal of Applied Physiology*, Vol. 58 (4), pp. 1281-1284, 1985.

Chapter 11 Maximal Running Speed

1. Noakes, T. et al. Peak treadmill running velocity during the V·O₂max test predicts running performance. *Journal of Sports Sciences*, Vol. 8 (1), pp. 35-45, 1990.

2. Slattery, K. et al. Physiological determinants of three-kilometer running performance in experienced triathletes. *Journal of Strength & Conditioning Research*, Vol. 20 (1), pp. 47-52, 2006.

3. Sinnett, A. et al. The relationship between field tests of anaerobic power and 10-km run performance. *Journal of Strength & Conditioning Research*, Vol. 15 (4), pp. 405-412 2001.

4. Paavolainen, L. et al. Explosive strength training improves 5-km running time by improving running economy and muscle power. *Journal of Applied Physiology*, Vol. 86 (5) pp. 1527-1533, 1999.

5. Weyand, P. et al. Faster top running speeds are achieved with greater ground forces, not more rapid leg movements. *Journal of Applied Physiology*, Vol. 89 (5), pp. 1991-1999, 2000.

Chapter 12 Resistance to Fatigue

1. Coetzer, P. et al. Superior fatigue resistance of elite black South African distance runners. *Journal of Applied Physiology*, Vol. 75, pp. 1822-1827, 1993.

2. Noakes, T. et al. Peak treadmill velocity during the V·O₂max test predicts running performance. *Journal of Sports Sciences*, Vol. 8 (1), pp. 35-45, 1990.

3. Weston, A. et al. African runners exhibit greater fatigue resistance, lower lactate accumulation, and higher oxidative enzyme activity. *Journal of Applied Physiology*, Vol. 86 (3), pp. 915-923, 1999.

4. Bergström, J. et al. Diet, muscle glycogen, and physical performance. *Acta Physiologica Scandinavica*, Vol. 71, pp. 140-150, 1967.

5. Coyle, E. et al. Muscle glycogen utilization during prolonged strenuous exercise when fed carbohydrate. *Journal of Applied Physiology*, Vol. 61, pp. 165-172, 1986.

6. Noakes, T. Physiological models to understand exercise fatigue and the adaptations that predict or enhance athletic performance. *Scandinavian Journal of Medicine & Science in Sports*, Vol. 10, pp. 123-145, 2000.

7. Noakes, T. D. *Lore of running*. 3rd ed. Cape Town: Oxford University Press, 1992.

8. McCann, D. and Adams, W. Wet bulb globe temperature index and performance in competitive distance runners. *Medicine & Science in Sports & Exercise*, Vol. 29, pp. 955-961, 1997.

9. González-Alonso, J. Influence of body temperature on the development of fatigue during prolonged exercise in the heat. *Journal of Applied Physiology*, Vol. 86, pp. 1032-1039, 1999.

10. Dennis, S. and Noakes, T. Advantages of smaller body mass for distance running performances in warm, humid conditions. *European Journal of Applied Physiology*, Vol. 79, pp. 280-284, 1999.

11. Owen Anderson, personal observation.

12. Komi, P. Stretch-shortening cycle fatigue. In *Biomechanics and biology of movement*, B. Nigg et al., ed. Champaign, IL: Human Kinetics, 2000.

13. Lieberman, D.E. et al. Foot strike patterns and collision forces in habitually barefoot versus shod runners. *Nature,* Vol. 463 (7280), pp. 531-5, Jan. 2010.

14. Brooks, J.H. et al. Incidence, risk, and prevention of hamstring muscle injuries in professional rugby union. *American Journal of Sports Medicine*, Vol. 34 (8), pp. 1297-306, Aug. 2006.

15. Billat, V. Training and bioenergetic characteristics in elite male and female Kenyan runners. *Medicine & Science in Sports & Exercise*, Vol. 35, pp. 297-304, 2003.

16. Kayser, B. Exercise starts and ends in the brain. *European Journal of Applied Physiology*, Vol. 90, pp. 411-419, 2003.

17. St. Clair Gibson, A. et al. Reduced neuromuscular activity and force generation during prolonged cycling. *American Journal of Physiology–Regulatory, Integrative Comparative Physiology*, Vol. 281, pp. R187-R196, 2001.

18. Kay, D. et al. Evidence for neuromuscular fatigue during high-intensity cycling in warm, humid conditions. *European Journal of Applied Physiology*, Vol. 84, pp. 115-121, 2001.

19. Nummela, A. et al. Neuromuscular factors determining 5 km running performance and running economy in well-trained athletes. *European Journal of Applied Physiology*, Vol. 97(1), pp. 1-8, 2006.

20. Aagaard, P. et al. Increased rate of force development and neural drive of human skeletal muscle following resistance training. *Journal of Applied Physiology*, Vol. 93 (4), pp. 1318-26, Oct. 2002.

Chapter 13   General Strength Training

1. Wilmore, J.H. et al. Energy cost of circuit weight training. *Medicine & Science in Sports*, Vol. 10 (2), pp. 75-78, 1978.

2. Wilmore, J.H. et al. Physiological alterations consequent to circuit weight training. *Medicine & Science in Sports*, Vol. 10 (2), pp. 79-84, 1978.

3. Anderson, O. Training technique from 70s returns with vengeance, but don't expect disco to follow. *Running Research News*, Vol. 14 (5), pp. 1, 6-10, June-July 1998.

Chapter 14   Running-Specific Strength Training

1. Anderson, O. Things mom forgot to tell you about strength training. *Running Research News*, Vol. 15 (3), pp. 1, 3-5, Apr. 1999.

2. Paavolainen, L. et al. Explosive strength training improves 5-km running time by improving running economy and muscle power. *Journal of Applied Physiology*, Vol. 86 (5), pp. 1527-1533, 1999.

Chapter 15   Hill Training

1. Gabaldón, A. et al. Mechanical function of two ankle extensors in wild turkeys: Shifts from energy production to energy absorption during incline versus decline running. *Journal of Experimental Biology*, Vol. 207 (Part 13), pp. 2277-2288, June 2004

2. Gascon, S.S. and Gottschall, J.S. The optimal method of hill interval training: Continuous versus random. *Medicine & Science in Sports & Exercise*, Vol. 42 (5), p. 140, 2010.

3. Anderson, O. What Heikki taught me. *Running Research News*, Vol. 17 (1), pp. 1, 5-7, 2001.

4. Owen Anderson, personal observation.

5. Escamilla, R.F. et al. Effects of throwing overweight and underweight baseballs on throwing velocity and accuracy. *Sports Medicine*, Vol. 29 (4), pp. 259-272, 2000 .

6. Byrnes, W.C. and Clarkson, P.M. Delayed onset muscle soreness and training. *Clinics in Sports Medicine*, Vol. 5 (3), pp. 605-614, 1986.

7. Braun, W.A. and Dutto, D.J. The effects of a single bout of downhill running and ensuing delayed onset of muscle soreness on running economy performed 48 h later. *European Journal of Applied Physiology*, Vol. 90 (1-2), pp. 29-34, 2003.

8. Endurance conditioning. In *Endurance in sport*, R.J. Shephard and P.O. Astrand, eds. Oxford: Blackwell Scientific, 1992, pp. 294-295.

9. Larsen, H.B. Kenyan dominance in distance running. *Comparative Biochemistry and Physiology Part A: Molecular & Integrative Physiology*, Vol. 136 (1), pp. 161-170, 2003.

10. Owen Anderson, personal observation

Chapter 16   Speed Training

1. Horwill, F. *An Obsession for running*. Carnforth: Colin Davies, 1994.

2. Daniels, J. *Daniels' running formula*. 2nd ed. Champaign, IL: Human Kinetics, 2005.

3. Schatzle, J., Jr. Finding fartlek: The history and how-to of speed play. *Running Times*, www.runnersworld.com/workouts/finding-fartlek, nov. 2002.

Chapter 17   Cross-Training

1. Anderson, O. Do running and cycling provide reciprocal benefits, or is there a one-way street? *Running Research News*, Vol. 10 (1), pp. 10-11, Jan.-Feb.1994.

2. Anderson, O. More evidence that runners can pedal their way to faster running race times. *Running Research News*, Vol. 10 (5), pp. 10-11, Sept.-Oct. 1994.

3. Miller, T. Racing responses of trained runners to performance programming instruction during standing bike-interval training. PhD Thesis, University of Utah, 1993.

4. Anderson, O. Recover during hard training and race faster with the "Miller method." *Running Research News*, Vol. 9 (5), pp. 1-4, Sept.-Oct. 1993.

5. Moroz, D. and Houston, M. The effects of replacing endurance running training with cycling in female runners. *Canadian Journal of Applied Sports Science*, Vol. 12, pp. 131-135, 1987.

6. Anderson, O. Can stair machines help your running? *Running Research News*, Vol. 10 (1), pp. 11-12, Jan.-Feb.1994.

7. Eyestone, E. et al. Effect of water running and cycling on maximum oxygen consumption and 2-mile run performance. *American Journal of Sports Medicine*, Vol. 21 (1), pp. 41-44, 1993.

8. Bushman, B. et al. Effects of four weeks of deep-water run training on running performance. *Medicine & Science in Sports & Exercise*, Vol. 29 (5), pp. 694-699, 1997.

9. Svedenhag, J. and Seger, J. Running on land and in water: Comparative exercise physiology. *Medicine & Science in Sports & Exercise*, Vol. 24 (10), pp. 1155-1160, 1992.

10. DeMaere, J.M. and Ruby, B.C. Effects of deep water and treadmill running on oxygen uptake and energy expenditure in seasonally trained cross-country runners. *Journal of Sports Medicine and Physical Fitness*, Vol. 37 (3), pp. 175-181, 1997.

11. Anderson, O. Things your mother forgot to tell you about cross training. *Running Research News*, Vol. 11 (6), pp. 1, 5-7, 1995.

Chapter 18   Altitude Training

1. Prommer, N. et al. Total hemoglobin mass and blood volume of elite Kenyan runners. *Medicine & Science in Sports & Exercise*, Vol. 42 (4), pp. 791-797, 2010.

2. Saunders, P. et al. Improved running economy and increased hemoglobin mass in elite runners after extended moderate altitude exposure. *Journal of Science & Medicine in Sport*, Vol. 12 (1), pp. 67-72, 2009.

3. Neya, M. et al. The effects of nightly normobaric hypoxia and high intensity training under intermittent normobaric hypoxia on running economy and hemoglobin mass. *Journal of Applied Physiology*, Vol. 103 (3), pp. 828-834, 2007.

4. Vogt, M. and Hoppeler, H. Is hypoxia training good for muscles and exercise performance? *Prog Cardiovascular Disease*, Vol. 52 (6), pp. 525-533, 2010.

5. Bärtsch, P. et al. Intermittent hypoxia at rest for improvement of athletic performance. *Scandinavian Journal of Medicine & Science in Sports*, Vol. 18 (Suppl.1), pp. 50-56, 2008.

6. Buskirk, E. et al. Maximal performance at altitude and on return from altitude in conditioned runners. *Journal of Applied Physiology*, Vol. 23, pp. 259-266, 1967.

7. Wilber, R. Application of altitude/hypoxic training by elite athletes. *Medicine & Science in Sports & Exercise*, Vol. 39 (9), pp. 1610-1624, 2007.

8. Lydiard, A. *Running to the top.* 2nd ed. G. Gilmour, ed. Aachen, Germany: Meyer & Meyer Sport, 1997.

9. Roels, B. et al. Is it more effective for highly trained swimmers to live and train at 1200 m than at 1850 m in terms of performance and haematological benefits? *British Journal of Sports Medicine*, Vol. 40 (2), p. e4, 2006.

10. Bailey, D. et al. Implications of moderate altitude training for sea-level endurance in elite distance runners. *European Journal of Applied Physiology and Occupational Physiology*, Vol. 78 (4), pp. 360-368, 1998.

11. Richalet, J.P. and Gore, C.J. Live and/or sleep high: Train low, using normobaric hypoxia. *Scandinavian Journal of Medicine & Science in Sports*, Vol. 18, Suppl. 1, pp. 29-37, Aug. 2008.

12. Stray-Gundersen, J. and Levine, B.D. Live high, train low at natural altitude. *Scandinavian Journal of Medicine & Science in Sports*, Vol. 18, Suppl. 1, pp. 21-28, Aug. 2008.

13. Robertson, E. et al. Reproducibility of performance changes to simulated live high/train low altitude. *Medicine & Science in Sports & Exercise*, Vol. 42 (2), pp. 394-401, 2010.

14. Millet, G. et al. Combining hypoxic methods for peak performance. *Sports Medicine*, Vol. 40 (1), pp. 1-25, 2010.

Chapter 19 Frequency and Volume

1. Larsen, H.B. Training principles in distance running. In *Running & science: In an interdisciplinary perspective*, J. Bangsbo and H.B. Larsen, eds. Copenhagen: Munksgaard, 2000, pp. 123-147.

2. Pollock, M.L. et al. Frequency of training as a determinant for improvement in cardiovascular function and body composition of middle-aged men. *Archives of Physical Medicine & Rehabilitation*, Vol. 56 (4), pp. 141-145, 1975.

3. Wenger, H.A. and Bell, G.J. The interactions of intensity, frequency, and duration of exercise training in altering cardiorespiratory fitness. *Sports Medicine*, Vol. 3 (5), pp. 346-356, 1986.

4. Hagan, R. et al. Marathon performance in relation to maximal aerobic power and training indices. *Medicine & Science in Sports & Exercise*, Vol. 13 (3), pp. 185-189, 1981.

5. Hagan, R. et al. Marathon performance in relation to maximal aerobic power and training indices in female distance runners. *British Journal of Sports Medicine*, Vol. 21 (1), pp. 3-7, 1987.

6. Marti, B. et al. Relationship of training and life-style to 16-km running time of 4000 joggers: The '84 Bern "Grand-Prix" study. *International Journal of Sports Medicine*, Vol. 9 (2), pp. 85-91, 1988.

7. DeBusk, R. et al. Training effects of long versus short bouts of exercise in healthy subjects. *American Journal of Cardiology*, Vol. 65 (15), pp. 1010-1013, 1990.

8. Murphy, M.H. and Hardman, A.E. Training effects of short and long bouts of brisk walking in sedentary women. *Medicine & Science in Sports & Exercise*, Vol. 30 (1), pp. 152-157, 1998.

9. Anderson, O. Best training methods to improve aerobic capacity. *Running Research News*, Vol. 2 (6), pp. 1-2 & 5-6, 1986.

10. Dotan, R. et al. Relationships of marathon running to physiological, anthropometric, and training indices. *European Journal of Applied Physiology*, Vol. 51, pp. 281-293, 1983.

11. Sjödin, B. and Jacobs, I. Onset of blood lactate accumulation and marathon running performance. *International Journal of Sports Medicine*, Vol. 2 (1), pp. 23-26, 1981.

12. Grant, S. et al. First-time marathoners and distance training. *British Journal of Sports Medicine*, Vol. 18, pp. 241-243, 1984.

13. Foster, C. et al. Physiological and training correlates of marathon running performance. *Australian Journal of Sports Medicine*, Vol. 9, pp. 58-61, 1977.

14. Anderson, O. Extra miles and workouts don't help novice marathoners. *Running Research News*, Vol. 11 (2), pp. 1, 5-6, 1995.

15. Costill, D. *Inside running: Basics of sports physiology.* Indianapolis, Indiana: Benchmark Press, 1986, pp. 85-121.

16. Sjödin, B. and Svedenhag, J. Applied physiology of marathon running. *Sports Medicine*, Vol. 2 (2), pp. 83-99, 1985.

17. Costill, D. et al. Adaptations to swimming training: Influence of training volume. *Medicine & Science in Sports & Exercise*, Vol. 23, pp. 371-377, 1991.

Chapter 20 Intensity

1. Burke, E. and Franks, D. Changes in $\dot{V}O_2$max resulting from bicycle training at different intensities holding total mechanical work constant. *Research Quarterly*, Vol. 46 (1), pp. 31-37, 1975.

2. Smith, D. and Wenger, H. The 10 day aerobic mini-cycle: The effects of interval or continuous training at two different intensities. *Journal of Sports Medicine*, Vol. 21, pp. 390-394, 1981.

3. Helgerud, J. et al. Aerobic high-intensity intervals improve $\dot{V}O_2$max more than moderate running. *Medicine & Science in Sports & Exercise*, Vol. 39 (4), pp. 665-671, 2007.

4. Snell, P. et al. High intensity training programs for well-conditioned runners. *Medicine & Science in Sports & Exercise*, Vol. 21 (2), # 448, 1989.

5. Paavolainen, L. et al. Explosive strength training improves 5-km running time by improving running economy and muscle power. *Journal of Applied Physiology*, Vol. 86, pp. 1527-1533, 1999 .

6. Acevedo, E.O. and Goldfarb, A.H. Increased training intensity effects on plasma lactate, ventilatory threshold, and endurance. *Medicine & Science in Sports & Exercise*, Vol. 21 (5), pp. 563-568, 1989.

7. Mikesell, K.A. and Dudley, G.A. Influence of intense endurance training on aerobic power of competitive distance runners. *Medicine & Science in Sports & Exercise*, Vol. 16 (4), pp. 371-375, 1984.

8. Davies, C.T. and Knibbs, A.V. The training stimulus: The effects of intensity, duration and frequency of effort on maximum aerobic power output. *Internationale Zeitschrift für Angewandte Physiologie, Einschliesslich Arbeitsphysiologie*, Vol. 29, pp. 299-305, 1971.

9. Karvonen, R. et al. The effects of training on heart rate: A "longitudinal study." *Ann Med Exper Biol Fenn*, Vol. 35, pp. 307-315, 1957.

10. Faria, I. Cardiovascular response to exercise as influenced by training of various intensities. *Research Quarterly*, 41 (1), pp. 44-50, 1970.

11. Nordesjo, L.O. The effect of quantified training on the capacity for short and prolonged work. *Acta Physiologica Scandinavica*, Vol. 90, Suppl. 405, 1974.

12. Gaesser, G.A. and Rich, R.G. Effects of high- and low-intensity exercise training on aerobic capacity and blood lipids. *Medicine & Science in Sports & Exercise*, Vol. 16 (3), pp. 269-274, 1984.

13. Henritze, J. et al. Effects of training at and above the lactate threshold on the lactate threshold and maximum oxygen uptake. *European Journal of Applied Physiology*, Vol. 54, pp. 84-88, 1985.

14. Shephard, R. Intensity, duration and frequency of exercise as the determinants of the response to a training regime. *Internationale Zeitschrift für Angewandte Physiologie, Einschliesslich Arbeitsphysiologie*, Vol. 26, pp. 272-278, 1968.

15. Schantz, P. et al. Adaptation of human skeletal muscle to endurance training of long duration. *Clinical Physiology*, Vol. 3, pp. 141-151, 1983.

16. Saltin, B. et al. Response to exercise after bed rest and after training. *Circulation*, Vol. 38 (5 Suppl.), VII, pp. 1-78, 1968.

17. Wenger, H.A. and Macnab, R.B. Endurance training: The effects of intensity, total work, duration and initial fitness. *Journal of Sports Medicine*, Vol. 15, pp. 199-211, 1975.

18. Midgley, A. et al. Is there an optimal training intensity for enhancing the maximal oxygen uptake of distance runners? *Sports Medicine*, Vol. 36 (2), pp. 117-132, 2006.

19. Anderson, O. Things were so easy until $vV \cdot O_2max$ and then $tlimvV \cdot O_2max$ had to come along. *Running Research News*, Vol. 15 (2), pp. 1-5, 1999.

20. Paton, C. and Hopkins, W. Effects of high-intensity training on performance and physiology of endurance athletes. *Sportscience*, Vol. 8, pp. 25-40, 2004.

21. Anderson, O. Best training methods to improve aerobic capacity. *Running Research News*, Vol. 2 (6), pp. 1-2, 5-6, 1986.

Chapter 21 Recovery

1. Cosca, D. and Navazio, F. Common problems in endurance athletes. *American Family Physician*, Vol. 76(2), pp. 237-244, 2007.

2. Reilly, T. and Brooks, G. Exercise and the circadian variation in body temperature measures. *International Journal of Sports Medicine*, Vol. 7, pp. 358-362, 1986.

3. Sleep deprivation and the athlete. In *Sleep deprivation*, C. Kushida, ed. New York: Marcel Decker, 2004, pp. 313-314.

4. Effect of an active warm-down following competitive soccer. In *Science and football IV*, W. Spinks, T. Reilly, and A. Murphy, eds. London: Routledge, 2002, pp. 226-229.

5. Bonen, A. and Belcastro, A.N. Comparison of self-selected recovery methods on lactic acid removal rates. *Medicine & Science in Sports & Exercise*, Vol. 8, pp. 176-178, 1976.

6. Lactate removal at rest and during exercise. In *Metabolic adaptations to prolonged physical exercise*, H. Howald and J.R. Poortmans, eds. Basel: Birkhauser Verlag, 1975, pp. 101-105.

7. Fox, E.L. *Sports physiology*. Philadelphia: Saunders, 1984, p. 81.

8. Costill, D. *Inside running: Basics of sports physiology*. Indianapolis, Indiana: Benchmark Press, 1986, pp. 107-108.

9. Muscle glycogen and electrolytes following exercise and thermal dehydration. In *Metabolic adaptations to prolonged physical exercise*, H. Howald and J. R. Poortmans, eds. Basel: Birkhauser Verlag, 1975, pp. 352-360.

10. Dimsdale, J. et al. Post-exercise peril: Plasma catecholamines and exercise. *Journal of the American Medical Association*, Vol. 251, pp. 630-632, 1984.

11. The efficacy of deep-water running. In *Contemporary ergonomics*, P. McCabe, ed. London: Taylor & Francis, 2002, pp. 162-166.

12. Maughan, R. Fluid and electrolyte loss and replacement in exercise. *Journal of Sports Sciences*, Vol. 9 (special issue), pp. 117-142, 1991.

13. Reilly, T. et al. Long-haul travel and jet lag: Behavioural and pharmacological approaches. *Medicina Sportiva*, Vol. 7, pp. E115-E122, 2003.

14. Burke, E. and Ekblom, B. Influence of fluid ingestion and dehydration on precision and endurance in tennis. *Athletic Training*, pp. 275-277, 1982.

15. Cleak, M. and Eston, R. Delayed onset muscle soreness: Mechanisms and management. *Journal of Sports Sciences*, Vol. 10, pp. 325-341, 1992.

16. Newham, D. The consequences of eccentric contractions and their relationship to delayed-onset muscle pain. *Journal of Applied Physiology*, Vol. 57, pp. 353-359, 1988.

17. Clarkson, P. et al. Muscle soreness and serum creatine kinase activity following isometric, eccentric, and concentric exercise. *International Journal of Sports Medicine*, Vol. 7, pp. 152-155, 1986.

18. Schwane, J.A. and Armstrong, R.B. Effect of training on skeletal muscle injury from downhill running in rats. *Journal of Applied Physiology*, Vol. 55, pp. 969-975, 1983.

19. Ebbeling, C. and Clarkson, P. Exercise-induced muscle damage and adaptation. *Sports Medicine*, Vol. 7, pp. 207-234, 1989.

20. Pierrynowski, M.R. et al. Effects of downhill or uphill training prior to a downhill run. *European Journal of Applied Physiology*, Vol. 56, pp. 668-672, 1987.

21. Overtraining, Immunosuppression, exercise-induced muscle damage, and anti-inflammatory drugs. In *The clinical pharmacology of sport and exercise*, M. Gleeson, A. K. Blannin, and N. P. Walsh, eds. Amsterdam: Excerpta Medica, 1997, pp. 47-57.

22. Howatson, G. and Van Someren, K.A. Ice massage: Effects on exercise-induced muscle damage. *Journal of Sports Medicine and Physical Fitness*, Vol. 43, pp. 500-505, 2003.

23. Dawson, B. et al. Effects of immediate post-game recovery procedures on muscle soreness, power, and flexibility levels over the next 48 hours. *Communication to the Annual Meeting of the Australian Society for Sports Medicine*, 2002.

24. Eston, R. and Peters, D. Effects of cold water immersion on the symptoms of exercise-induced muscle damage. *Journal of Sports Sciences*, Vol. 17, pp. 231-238, 1999.

25. Sellwood, K. et al. Ice-water immersion and delayed-onset muscle soreness: A randomised controlled trial. *British Journal of Sports Medicine*, Vol. 41 (6), pp. 392-397, 2007.

26. Experts pour cold water on athletes' ice-bath remedy. Nov. 4, 2010. Fox Boston. www.myfoxny.com/story/17449882/experts-pour-cold-water-on-athletes-ice-bath-remedy?clienttype=printable.

27. Reilly, T. and Piercy, M. The effect of partial sleep deprivation on weight-lifting performance. *Ergonomics*, Vol. 37, pp. 107-115, 1994.

28. Owen Anderson, personal observation.

29. Wilson, P.B. et al. Dietary tendencies as predictors of marathon time in novice marathoners. Int J Sport Nutr Exerc Metab, Vol. 23 (2), pp. 170-177, 2013.

30. Tarnopolsky, M. et al. Postexercise protein-carbohydrate and carbohydrate supplements increase muscle glycogen in men and women. *Journal of Applied Physiology*, Vol. 83(6), pp. 1877-1883, 1997

31. Roy, B. and Tarnopolsky, M. Influence of differing macronutrient intakes on muscle glycogen resynthesis after resistance exercise. *Journal of Applied Physiology*, Vol. 84, pp. 890-896, 1998.

32. Roy, B. and Tarnopolsky, M. Effect of glucose supplement timing on protein metabolism after resistance training. *Journal of Applied Physiology*, Vol. 82, pp. 1882-1888, 1997.

33. Roy, B. et al. Macronutrient intake and whole body protein metabolism following resistance exercise. *Medicine and Science in Sports and Exercise*, Vol. 32, pp. 1412-1418, 2000.

Chapter 22   Periodization and Block Systems

1. Verkhoshansky, Y. *Programming and organization of training*. Moscow: Fizkultura i Sport, 1985.

2. Verkhoshansky, Y. *Supertraining*. 3rd ed. Painesville, Ohio: Vision Press, 1997.

3. Owen Anderson, personal observation.

4. Ryan, A. Anabolic steroids are fool's gold. *Federation Proceedings*, Vol. 40, pp. 2682-2688, 1981.

5. Anderson, O. Things your mom forgot to tell you about the periodization of your training. *Running Research News*, Vol. 13 (6), pp. 1-9, 1997.

6. Vorobyev, A.N. *Periodization of sports training*. Moscow: Fiscultura I Sport, 1966.

7. Lydiard, A. *Running with Lydiard*. 2nd ed. G. Gilmour, ed. Aachen, Germany: Meyer & Meyer Sport, 2000.

8. Horwill, F. An *Obsession for Running*. Carnforth: Colin Davies, 1994.

9. Daniels, J. *Daniels' running formula*. 2nd ed. Champaign, IL: Human Kinetics, 2005.

Chapter 23   Integrated Strength and Endurance Training Programs

1. Mikkola, J. et al. Concurrent endurance and explosive type strength training improves neuromuscular and anaerobic characteristics in young distance runners. *International Journal of Sports Medicine*, Vol. 28 (7), pp. 602-611, 2007.

2. Spurrs, R. et al. The effect of plyometric training on distance running performance. *European Journal of Applied Physiology*, Vol. 89 (1), pp. 1-7, 2003.

3. Taipale, R. et al. Strength training in endurance runners. *International Journal of Sports Medicine*, Vol. 31 (7), pp. 468-476, 2010.

4. Gettman, L. et al. A comparison of combined running and weight training with circuit weight training. *Medicine & Science in Sports & Exercise*, Vol. 14 (3), pp. 229-234, 1982.

5. Taşkin H. Effect of circuit training on the sprint-agility and anaerobic endurance. *Journal of Strength & Conditioning Research*, Vol. 23 (6), pp. 1803-1810, 2009.

6. Marcinik, E. et al. Effects of strength training on lactate threshold and endurance performance. *Medicine & Science in Sports & Exercise*, Vol. 23 (6), pp. 739-743, 1991.

7. Chtara, M. et al. Effects of intra-session concurrent endurance and strength training sequence on aerobic performance and capacity. *British Journal of Sports Medicine*, Vol. 39 (8), pp. 555-560, 2005.

8. Esteve-Lanao, J. et al. Running-specific, periodized strength training attenuates loss of stride length during intense endurance running. *Journal of Strength & Conditioning Research*, Vol. 22 (4), pp. 1176-1183, 2008.

9. Endurance conditioning. In *Endurance in sport*, R.J. Shepherd and P.O. Astrand, eds. Oxford: Blackwell Scientific, 1992, pp. 294-295.

10. Ebben, W. The optimal downhill slope for acute over-speed running. *International Journal of Sports & Physiological Performance*, Vol. 3 (1), pp. 88-93, 2008.

11. Berryman, N. et al. Effect of plyometric vs dynamic weight training on the energy cost of running. *Journal of Strength & Conditioning Research*, Vol. 24 (7), pp. 1818-1825, 2010.

12. Hamilton, R. et al. Effect of high-intensity resistance training on performance of competitive distance runners. *International Journal of Sports Physiological Performance*, Vol. 1 (1), pp. 40-49, 2006.

Chapter 24　Increasing V̇O₂max

1. Anderson, O. What should you do when you "build a base"? Do your capillaries count? *Running Research News*, Vol. 16 (9), pp. 1, 4-7, 2000.

2. Martin, D. and Coe, P. Developing running with periodization of training. In *Better training for distance runners*. Champaign, IL: Human Kinetics, 1997, p. 193.

3. Daniels, J. *Daniels' running formula*. Champaign, IL: Human Kinetics, 1998, p. 149.

4. Lydiard, A. *Running to the top*. 2nd ed. G. Gilmour, ed. Aachen, Germany: Meyer and Meyer Sport, 1997.

5. Hermansen, L. and Wachtlova, M. Capillary density of skeletal muscle in well-trained and untrained men. *Journal of Applied Physiology*, Vol. 30, pp. 860-863, 1971.

6. Laughlin, M.H. and Ripperger, J. Vascular transport capacity of hind-limb muscles of exercise-trained rats. *Journal of Applied Physiology*, Vol. 62, pp. 438-444, 1987.

7. The parallelism of changes in oxidative metabolism and capillary supply of skeletal-muscle fibers. In *Modern neurology*, S. Locke, ed. Boston: Little, Brown, 1969, pp. 203-217.

8. Jurimae, T. et al. Running training, physical working capacity, and lipid and lipoprotein relationships in man. *Finnish Sports Exercise Medicine*, Vol. 3, pp. 104-112, 1984.

9. Gaesser, G. and Rich, R. Effects of high- and low-intensity exercise training on aerobic capacity and blood lipids. *Medicine & Science in Sports & Exercise*, Vol. 16 (3), pp. 269-274, 1984.

10. Dudley, G. et al. Influence of exercise intensity and duration on biochemical adaptations in skeletal muscle. *Journal of Applied Physiology*, Vol. 53, pp. 844-850, 1982.

11. Behm, D.G. and Sale, D.G. Velocity specificity of resistance training. *Sports Medicine*, Vol. 15 (6), pp. 374-388, 1993.

12. Gibala, M. et al. Short-term sprint interval versus traditional endurance training: Similar initial adaptations in human skeletal muscle and exercise performance. *Journal of Physiology*, Vol. 575 (3), pp. 901-911, 2006.

13. Henriksson, J. and Reitman, J.S. Quantitative measures of enzyme activities in type i and type ii muscle fibres of man after training. *Acta Physiologica Scandinavica*, Vol. 97, pp. 392-397, 1976.

14. Saltin, B. et al. The nature of the training response; peripheral and central adaptations of one-legged exercise. *Acta Physiologica Scandinavica*, Vol. 96, pp. 289-305, 1976.

15. Burgomaster, K. et al. Six sessions of sprint interval training increases muscle oxidative potential and cycle endurance capacity in humans. *Journal of Applied Physiology*, Vol. 98, pp. 1985-1990, 2005.

16. Burgomaster, K. et al. Effect of short-term sprint interval training on human skeletal muscle carbohydrate metabolism during exercise and time-trial performance. *Journal of Applied Physiology*, Vol. 100, pp. 2041-2047, 2006.

17. Eddy, D. et al. The effects of continuous and interval training in women and men. *European Journal of Applied Physiology and Occupational Physiology*, Vol. 37, pp. 83-92, 1977.

18. Edge, J. et al. The effects of training intensity on muscle buffer capacity in females. *European Journal of Applied Physiology*, Vol. 96, pp. 97-105, 2006.

19. Weston, A. et al. Skeletal muscle buffering capacity and endurance performance after high-intensity interval training by well-trained cyclists. *European Journal of Applied Physiology and Occupational Physiology*, Vol. 75, pp. 7-13, 1997.

Chapter 25　Enhancing Economy

1. Dumke, C.L. Two-hour marathon and running economy. *Journal of Applied Physiology*, Vol. 110 (1), p. 287, 2011.

2. Messier, S.P. and Cirillo, K.J. Effects of a verbal and visual feedback system on running technique, perceived exertion and running economy in female novice runners. *Journal of Sports Sciences*, Vol. 7 (2), pp. 113-126, 1989.

3. Hasegawa H., Yamauchi T., and Kraemer W.J. Foot strike patterns of runners at the 15-km point during an elite-level half marathon. *Journal of Strength & Conditioning Research*, Vol. 21 (3), pp. 888-893, 2007.

4. Lieberman, D.E., Venkadesan, M., Werbel, W.A., Daoud, A.I., D'Andrea, S., Davis, I.S., Mang'eni, R.O., and Pitsiladis, Y. Foot strike patterns and collision forces in habitually barefoot versus shod runners. *Nature*, Vol. 463 (7280), pp. 531-535, 2010.

5. Saunders, P.U., Pyne, D.B., Telford, R.D., and Hawley, J.A. Factors affecting running economy in trained distance runners. *Sports Medicine*, Vol. 34 (7), pp. 465-485, 2004.

6. Daniels, J. and Daniels, N. Running economy of elite male and elite female runners. *Medicine & Science in Sports & Exercise*, Vol. 24 (4), pp. 483-489, 1992.

7. Spurrs, R.W., Murphy, A.J., and Watsford, M.L. The effect of plyometric training on distance running performance. *European Journal of Applied Physiology*, Vol. 89 (1), pp. 1-7, 2003.

8. Paavolainen, L., Hakkinen, K., Hamalainen, I., Nummela, A., and Rusko, H. Explosive strength training improves 5-km running time by improving running economy and muscle power. *Journal of Applied Physiology*, Vol. 86 (5), pp. 1527-1533, 1999.

9. Billat, V.L., Flechet, B., Petit, B., Muriaux, G., and Koralsztein, J.P. Interval training at V̇O₂max: Effects on aerobic performance and overtraining markers. *Medicine & Science in Sports & Exercise*, Vol. 31 (1), pp. 156-163, 1999.

10. Yamamoto, L.M., Lopez, R.M., Klau, J.F., Casa, D.J., Kraemer, W.J., and Maresh, C.M. The effects of resistance training on endurance distance running performance among highly trained runners: A systematic review. *Journal of Strength & Conditioning Research*, Vol. 22 (6), pp. 2036-2044, 2008.

11. Taipale, R.S., Mikkola, J., Nummela, A., Vesterinen, V., Capostagno, B., Walker, S., Gitonga, D., Kraemer, W.J., and Hakkinen, K. Strength training in endurance runners. *International Journal of Sports Medicine*, Vol. 31 (7), pp. 468-476, 2010.

12. Guglielmo, L.G., Greco, C.C., and Denadai, B.S. Effects of strength training on running economy. *International Journal of Sports Medicine*, Vol. 30 (1), pp. 27-32, 2009.

13. Jung, A.P. The impact of resistance training on distance running performance. *Sports Medicine*, Vol. 33 (7), pp. 539-552, 2003.

14. Behm, D.G. and Sale, D.G. Velocity specificity of resistance training. *Sports Medicine*, Vol. 15 (6), pp. 374-388, 1993.

15. Sale, D.G. Neural adaptation to resistance training. *Medicine & Science in Sports & Exercise*, Vol. 20 (5) (Suppl.), pp. S135-S145, 1988.

16. Divert, C., Mornieux, G., Freychat, P., Baly, L., Mayer, F., and Belli, A. Barefoot-shod running differences: Shoe or mass effect? *International Journal of Sports Medicine*, Vol. 29 (6), pp. 512-518, 2008.

17. Squadrone, R. and Gallozzi, C. Biomechanical and physiological comparison of barefoot and two shod conditions in experienced barefoot runners. *Journal of Sports Medicine & Physical Fitness*, Vol. 49 (1), pp. 6-13, 2009.

18. Smith, A.L., Gill, D.L., Crews, D.J., Hopewell, R., and Morgan, D.W. Attentional strategy use by experienced distance runners: Physiological and psychological effects. *Research Quarterly for Exercise and Sport*, Vol. 66 (2), pp. 142-150, 1995.

19. Birrer, D. and Morgan, G. Psychological skills training as a way to enhance an athlete's performance in high-intensity sports. *Scandinavian Journal of Medicine & Science in Sports*, Suppl. 2, pp. 78-87, 2010.

20. Houmard, J.A., Scott, B.K., Justice, C.L., and Chenier, T.C. The effects of taper on performance in distance runners. *Medicine & Science in Sports & Exercise*, Vol. 26, pp. 624-631, 1994.

21. Houmard, J.A., Costill, D.L., Mitchell, J.B., Park, S.H., Hickner, R.C., and Roemmich, J.N. Reduced training maintains performance in distance runners. *International Journal of Sports Medicine*, Vol. 11, pp. 46-52, 1990.

22. Endurance conditioning. In *Endurance in sport*, R.J. Shephard and P.O. Astrand, eds. Oxford: Blackwell Scientific. 1992, pp. 294-295.

23. Anderson, O. Things were so easy, until $vV\cdot O_2max$ and then $tlimvV\cdot O_2max$ had to come along. *Running Research News*, Vol. 15 (2), pp. 1-5, 1999.

24. Hausswirth, C. and Brisswalter J. Strategies for improving performance in long duration events: Olympic distance triathlon. *Sports Medicine*, Vol. 38 (11), pp. 881-891, 2008

25. Anderson, O., personal observation.

26. Larson, H.B. Kenyan dominance in distance running. Comp Biochem Physiol A Mol Integr Physiol, Vol. 136 (1), pp.161-170, 2003.

27. Wilber, R.L. and Pitsiladis, Y.P. Kenyan and Ehtiopian distance runners: what makes them so good? Int J Sports Physiol Perform, Vol. 7 (2), pp, 92-102, 2012.

28. Raichlen, D.A., Armstrong, H., and Lieberman, D.E. Calcaneus length determines running economy: Implications for endurance running performance in modern humans and neandertals. *Journal of Human Evolution*, Vol. 60 (3), pp. 299-308, 2011.

29. Rusko, H. and Bosco, C.C. Metabolic response of endurance athletes to training with added load. *European Journal of Applied Physiology and Occupational Physiology*, Vol. 56 (4), pp. 412-418, 1987.

Chapter 26 Gaining $v\dot{V}O_2max$

1. Anderson, O. Things were so easy, until $v\dot{V}O_2max$ and then $tlimv\dot{V}O_2max$ had to come along. *Running Research News*, Vol. 15 (2), pp. 1-5, 1999.

2. Billat, V. et al. Interval training at $\dot{V}O_2max$: Effects on aerobic performance and overtraining markers. *Medicine & Science in Sports & Exercise*, Vol. 31 (1), pp. 156-163, 1999.

3. Billat, V. et al. Intermittent runs at the velocity associated with maximal oxygen uptake enables subjects to remain at maximal oxygen uptake for a longer time than intense but submaximal runs. *European Journal of Applied Physiology*, Vol. 81 (3), pp. 188-196, 2000.

4. Anderson, O. Torrid new $v\dot{V}O_2max$ sessions keep you at $\dot{V}O_2max$—and are easier to carry out. *Running Research News*, Vol. 16 (7), pp. 1-4, 2000.

5. Smith, T. et al. Optimising high-intensity treadmill training using the running speed at maximal O(2) uptake and the time for which this can be maintained. *European Journal of Applied Physiology*, Vol. 89 (3-4), pp. 337-343, 2003.

Chapter 27 Upgrading Lactate Threshold

1. McDermott, J. and Bonen, A. Endurance training increases skeletal muscle lactate transport. *Acta Physiologica Scandinavica*, Vol. 147 (3), pp. 323-327, 1993.

2. McCullagh, K. et al. Role of lactate transporter (MCT1) in skeletal muscles. *American Journal of Physiology*, Vol. 271, (Endocrinology and Metabolism 34), pp. E143-150, 1996.

3. Thomas, C. et al. Monocarboxylate transporters, blood lactate removal after supramaximal exercise, and fatigue indexes in humans. *Journal of Applied Physiology*, Vol. 98 (3), pp. 804-809, 2005.

4. Thomas, C. Monocarboxylate transporters, blood lactate removal after supramaximal exercise, and fatigue indexes in humans. *Journal of Applied Physiology*, Vol. 98 (3), pp. 804-809, 2005.

5. Billat, V. et al. The concept of maximal lactate steady state: A bridge between biochemistry, physiology, and sport science. *Sports Medicine*, Vol. 33 (6), pp. 407-426, 2003.

6. Jack Daniels, personal communication.

7. O'Brien, M.J., et al. Carbohydrate dependence during marathon running. *Medicine and Science in Sports and Exercise*, Vol. 25 (9), pp. 1009-17, Sept. 1993..

8. Sjödin, B. et al. Changes in onset of blood lactate accumulation (OBLA) and muscle enzymes after training at OBLA. *European Journal of Applied Physiology and Occupational Physiology*, Vol. 49 (1), pp. 45-57, 1982.

9. Anderson, Owen, Lactate lift-off, Lansing: SSS, 1998.

10. Evertsen, F. et al. Effect of training intensity on muscle lactate transporters and lactate threshold of cross-country skiers. *Acta Physiologica Scandinavica*, Vol. 173 (2), pp. 195-205, 2001.

11. Acevedo, E.O. and Goldfarb, A.H. Increased training intensity effects on plasma lactate, ventilatory threshold, and endurance. *Medicine & Science in Sports & Exercise*, Vol. 21 (5), pp. 563-568, 1989.

12. Keith, S.P. et al. Adaptations to training at the individual anaerobic threshold. *Medicine & Science in Sports & Exercise*, Vol. 23 (4), Suppl. # 197, 1991.

13. Special workout helps lift lactate threshold toward $\dot{V}O_2$max. *Running Research News*, Vol. 7 (4), pp. 1, 4-5, 1991.

14. Dudley, G. et al. Influence of exercise intensity and duration on biochemical adaptations in skeletal muscle. *Journal of Applied Physiology*, Vol. 53 (4), pp. 844-850, 1982.

15. Baker, S. et al. Training-intensity-dependent and tissue-specific increases in lactate uptake and MCT-1 in heart and muscle. *Journal of Applied Physiology*, Vol. 84 (3), pp. 987-994, 1998.

16. Juel, C. et al. Effect of high-intensity intermittent training on lactate and H+ release from human skeletal muscle. *American Journal of Physiology, Endocrinology & Metabolism*, Vol. 286, pp. E245-E251, 2004.

17. Pilegaard, H. et al. Effect of high-intensity exercise training on lactate/H+ transport capacity in human skeletal muscle. *American Journal of Physiology, Endocrinology & Metabolism*, Vol. 276, pp. E255-E261, 1999.

18. Pilegaard, H. et al. Lactate transport studied in sarcolemmal giant vesicles from human muscle biopsies: Relation to training status. *Journal of Applied Physiology*, Vol. 77 (4), pp. 1858-1862, 1994.

19. Pilegaard, H. et al. Lactate transport studied in sarcolemmal giant vesicles from rats: Effect of training. *American Journal of Physiology*, Vol. 264, pp. E156-E160, 1993.

20. Billat, V. et al. interval training at V·O_2max: Effects on aerobic performance and overtraining markers. *Medicine and Science in Sports and Exercise*, Vol. 31(1), pp. 156-163, 1999.

21. Bickham, D. et al. The effects of short-term sprint training on MCT expression in moderately endurance-trained runners. *European Journal of Applied Physiology*, Vol. 96 (6), pp. 636-643, 2006.

22. Petersen, S. et al. The influence of high-velocity circuit resistance training on V·O_2max and cardiac output. *Canadian Journal of Sport Sciences*, Vol. 14 (3), pp. 158-63, Sept. 1989. .

23. Weltman, A. et al. Reliability and validity of a continuous incremental treadmill protocol for the determination of lactate threshold, fixed blood lactate concentrations, and $\dot{V}O_2$ max. *International Journal of Sports Medicine*, Vol. 11, pp. 26-32, 1990.

24. Heitkamp, H.-Ch. et al. The reproducibility of the 4 mmol/l lactate threshold in trained and untrained women. *International Journal of Sports Medicine*, Vol. 12, pp. 363-368, 1991.

25. Atkinson, G. and Nevill, A. Statistical methods for assessing measurement error (reliability) in variables relevant to Sports Medicine. *Sports Medicine*, Vol. 26, pp. 217-238, 1998.

26. Grant, S., et al. (2002). Reproducibility of the blood lactate threshold, 4 mmol marker, heart rate and ratings of perceived exertion during incremental treadmill exercise in humans. *European Journal of Applied Physiology*, Vol. 87, pp. 159-166, 2002.

Chapter 28 Increasing Maximal Running Speed

1. Sinnett, A., et al. The relationship between field tests of anaerobic power and 10-km run performance. *Journal of Strength and Conditioning Research*, Vol. 15 (4), pp. 405-12, Nov. 2001.

2. Paavolainen, L. et al. Explosive-strength training improves 5-km running time by improving running economy and muscle power. *Journal of Applied Physiology*, Vol. 86 (5), pp. 1527-33, May 1999.

3. Paradisis, G. et al. Combined uphill and downhill sprint running training is more efficacious than horizontal. *International Journal of Sports Physiology and Performance*, Vol. 4 (2), pp. 229-43, June 2009.

4. Ebben, W. et al. Effect of the degree of hill slope on acute downhill running velocity and acceleration. *Journal of Strength and Conditioning Research*, Vol. 22 (3), pp. 898-902, May 2008.

5. Zafeiridis, A. et al. The effects of resisted sled-pulling sprint training on acceleration and maximum speed performance. *Journal of Sports Medicine and Physical Fitness*, Vol. 45 (3), pp. 284-90, Spet. 2005.

6. Rukso, H. and Bosco, C. Metabolic response of endurance athletes to training with added load. *European Journal of Applied Physiology and Occupational Physiology*, Vol. 56 (4), pp. 412-8, 1987.

7. Ross, R. et al. The effects of treadmill sprint training and resistance training on maximal running velocity and power. *Journal of Strength and Conditioning Research*, Vol. 23 (2), pp. 385-94, Mar. 2009.

8. de Villarreal, E. et al. Low and moderate plyometric training frequency produces greater jumping and sprinting gains compared with high frequency. *Journal of Strength and Conditioning Research*, Vol. 22 (3), pp. 715-25, May 2008.

9. Nummela, A. et al. Neuromuscular factors determining 5 km running performance and running economy in well-trained athletes. *European Journal of Applied Physiology*, Vol. 97 (1), pp. 1-8, May 2006.

10. Harris, N. et al. Squat jump training at maximal power loads vs. heavy loads: Effect on sprint ability. *J Strength Cond Res*, Vol. 22 (6), pp. 1742-9, Nov. 2008.

Chapter 29 Promoting Resistance to Fatigue

1. Fimland, M. et al. enhanced neural drive after maximal strength training in multiple sclerosis patients. *European Journal of Applied Physiology*, Vol. 110 (2), pp. 435-443, 2010.

2. Markovic, G. and Mikulic, P. Neuro-musculoskeletal and performance adaptations to lower-extremity plyometric training. *Sports Medicine*, Vol. 40 (10), pp. 859-895, 2010.

3. Girard, O. et al. Repeated-sprint ability part 1: Factors contributing to fatigue. *Sports Medicine*, Vol. 41 (8), pp. 673-694, 2011.

4. Yobes Ondieki, conversation with the author, Eldoret, Kenya, February 7, 1995.

5. Saraslanidis, P. et al. Muscle metabolism and performance improvement after two programmes of sprint running differing in rest interval duration. *Journal of Sports Sciences*, Vol. 29 (11), pp. 1167-74, 2011.

6. Weston, A. et al. African runners exhibit greater fatigue resistance, lower lactate accumulation, and higher oxidative enzyme activity. *Journal of Applied Physiology*, Vol. 86 (3), pp. 915-923, 1999.

7. Hayes, P. et al. The effect of muscular endurance on running economy, *Journal of Strength & Conditioning Research*, 25(9), pp. 2464-2469, 2011.

8. Nogueira, L. et al. (-)-Epicatechin enhances fatigue resistance and oxidative capacity in mouse muscle. *Journal of Physiology*, 589 (18), pp 4615-4631, 2011.

Chapter 30 Training Effects at the Molecular Level

1. Laye, M. et al. Increased shelter in mRNA expression in peripheral blood mononuclear cells and skeletal muscle following an ultra-long-distance running event. *Journal of Applied Physiology*, Vol. 112 (5), pp. 773-81, Mar. 2012.

2. Groves-Chapman, J. et al. Changes in mRNA levels for brain-derived neurotrophic factor after wheel running in rats selectively bred for high- and low-aerobic capacity. *Brain Research*, Vol. 1425, pp. 90-7, Nov. 2011.

3. Keller, P. et al. A transcriptional map of the impact of endurance exercise training on skeletal muscle phenotype. *Journal of Applied Physiology*, Vol. 110 (1), pp. 46-59, Jan. 2011.

4. Iwanuma, O. et al. Effects of mechanical stretching on caspase and IGF-1 expression during the proliferation process of myoblasts. *Zoological Science*, Vol. 25 (3), pp. 242-7, Mar. 2008.

5. Haghighipour, N. et al. Differential effects of cyclic uniaxial stretch on human mesenchymal stem cell into skeletal muscle cell. *Cell Biology International*, Vol. 36 (7), pp. 669-75, July 2012.

6. Inashima, S. et al. Effect of endurance training and acute exercise on sarcoplasmic reticulum function in rat fast- and slow-twitch skeletal muscles. *European Journal of Applied Physiology*, Vol. 89 (2), pp. 142-9, Apr. 2003. Epublished Jan. 31, 2003.

7. Matsunaga, S. et al. Oxidation of sarcoplasmic reticulum Ca(2+)-ATPase induced by high-intensity exercise. *Pflugers Archives*, Vol. 446 (3), pp. 394-9, June 2003. Epublished April 9, 2003.

8. Richter, E.A. and Ruderman, N.B. AMPK and the biochemistry of exercise: Implications for human health and disease. *Biochemical Journal*, Vol. 418 (2), pp. 261-75, Mar. 2009.

9. Magnoni, L. et al. AMP-activated protein kinase plays an important evolutionary conserved role in the regulation of glucose metabolism in fish skeletal muscle cells. *PLoS One*, Vol. 7 (2), p. e31219, 2012.

10. Liu, T. et al. Fueling the flame: Bioenergy couples metabolism and inflammation. *Journal of Leukocyte Biology*, May 9, 2012 [Epublished ahead of print].

11. Chen, Z. et al. Effect of exercise intensity on skeletal muscle AMPK signaling in humans. *Diabetes*, Vol. 52 (9), pp. 2205-12, Sept. 2003.

12. Krook, A. et al. Sending the signal: Molecular mechanisms regulating glucose uptake. *Medicine and Science in Sports and Exercise*, Vol. 36 (7), pp. 1212-7, July 2004.

13. Little, J.P. et al. An acute bout of high-intensity interval training increases the nuclear abundance of PGC-1α and activates mitochondrial biogenesis in human skeletal muscle. *American Journal of Physiology–Regulatory, Integrative Comparative Physiology*, Vol. 300 (6), pp. R1303-10, June 2011.

14. Holloszy, J. Regulation by exercise of skeletal muscle content of mitochondria and GLUT4. *Journal of Physiological Pharmacology*, Vol. 59 Suppl. 7. , pp. 5-18, Dec. 2008.

15. Eynon, N. et al. The champions' mitochondria: Is it genetically determined? A review on mitochondrial DNA and elite athletic performance. *Physiological Genomics*. Vol. 43 (13), pp. 789-98, July 2011.

16. Yang, Y. et al. Murine Sirt3 protein isoforms have variable half-lives. *Gene*, Vol. 488c(1-2), pp. 46-51, Nov. 2011.

17. Carter, H. and D. Hood. Contractile activity-induced mitochondrial biogenesis and mTORC1. *American Journal of Physiology–Cell Physiology*, June 13, 2012 [Epublished ahead of print].

18. Ikeda, S. et al. Muscle type-specific response of PGC-1 alpha and oxidative enzymes during voluntary wheel running in mouse skeletal muscle. *Acta Physiologica* (Oxford), Vol. 188 (3-4), pp. 217-23, Nov.-Dec. 2006.

19. Lira, V. et al. PGC-1alpha regulation by exercise training and its influences on muscle function and insulin sensitivity. *American Journal of Physiology–Endocrinology and Metabolism*, Vol. 299 (2), pp. E145-61, Aug. 2010.

20. Little, J. et al. A practical model of low-volume high-intensity interval training induces mitochondrial biogenesis in human skeletal muscle: Potential mechanisms. *Journal of Physiology*, Vol. 588(Pt 6), pp. 1011-22, Mar. 2010.

21. Gulve, E. et al. Effects of wheel running on glucose transporter (GLUT4) concentration in skeletal muscle of young adult and old rats. *Mechanisms of Ageing Development*, Vol. 67 (1-2), pp. 187-200, Feb. 1993.

22. Ellison, G. et al. Physiological cardiac remodelling in response to endurance exercise training: Cellular and molecular mechanisms. *Heart*, Vol. 98 (1), pp. 5-10, Jan. 2012.

Chapter 31 Training Favoring Molecular Enrichment

1. Hickson, R. Interference of strength development by simultaneously training for strength and endurance. *European Journal of Applied Physiology and Occupational Physiology*, Vol. 45 (2-3), pp. 255-63, 1980.

2. Hickson, R. et al. Strength training effects on aerobic power and short-term endurance. *Medicine and Science in Sports and Exercise*, Vol. 12 (5), pp. 336-9, 1980.

3. Hickson, R. et al. Potential for strength and endurance training to amplify endurance performance. *Journal of Applied Physiology*, Vol. 65 (5), pp. 2285-90, Nov. 1988.

4. Sale, D. et al. Interaction between concurrent strength and endurance training. *Journal of Applied Physiology*, Vol. 68 (1), pp. 260-70, Jan. 1990.

5. Farnfield, M. et al. Activation of mTOR signalling in young and old human skeletal muscle in response to combined resistance exercise and whey protein ingestion. *Applied Physiology, Nutrition, and Metabolism.* Vol. 37 (1), pp. 21-30, Feb. 2012 [Epublished Dec. 13, 2011].

6. Calegari, V. et al. Endurance training activates AMP-activated protein kinase, increases expression of uncoupling protein 2 and reduces insulin secretion from rat pancreatic islets. *Journal of Endocrinology*, Vol. 208 (3), pp. 257-64, Mar. 2011.

7. Hansen, A. et al. Skeletal muscle adaptation: Training twice every second day vs. training once daily. *Journal of Applied Physiology*, Vol. 98 (1), pp. 93-9, Jan. 2005.

8. Yeo, W. et al. Skeletal muscle adaptation and performance responses to once a day versus twice every second day endurance training regimens. *Journal of Applied Physiology*, Vol. 105 (5), pp. 1462-70, Nov. 2008.

9. Snyder, A. Overtraining and glycogen depletion hypothesis. *Medicine and Science in Sports and Exercise*, Vol. 30 (7), pp. 1146-50, July 1998.

Chapter 32   Training for 800 Meters

1. Lactate threshold running speed. www.pponline.co.uk/encyc/0079.htm.

2. 800 metres. www.pponline.co.uk/encyc/0287.htm.

Chapter 33   Training for 1,500 Meters and the Mile

1. Anderson, O. Plodding won't produce peak aerobic capacity: Using the right running speed seems to be the key. *Running Research News*, Vol. 4 (6), pp. 1-5, 1988.

2. Anderson, O. 12 reasons to run the mile. *Running Research News*, Vol. 13 (3), pp. 1-4, 1997.

3. Anderson, O. Mammoth mileage not mandatory for magnificent miles: Masterful milers have used diverse training plans. *Running Research News*, Vol. 6 (3), pp. 1-10, 1990.

4. Bowerman, Bill, interview with the author, April 1992.

5. Williams, Bob, interview with the author, July 1992.

6. Ingham, S. et al. Determinants of 800-m and 1500-m running performance using allometric models. *Medicine and Science in Sports and Exercise*, Vol. 40 (2), pp. 345-50, Feb. 2008.

7. Daniels, J. and Daniels, N. Running economy of elite male and elite female runners. *Medicine and Science in Sports and Exercise*, Vol. 24(4), pp. 483-9, Apr. 1992.

Chapter 34   Training for 5Ks

1. Babineau, C. and Léger, L. Physiological response of 5/1 intermittent aerobic exercise and its relationship to 5 km endurance performance. Ecole d'Education Physique et de Loisir, Université de Moncton, New Brunswick. *International Journal of Sports Medicine*, Vol. 18 (1), pp. 13-9, Jan. 1997.

2. Paavolainen, L. et al. Explosive-strength training improves 5-km running time by improving running economy and muscle power. *Journal of Applied Physiology*, Vol. 86 (5), pp. 1527-33, May 1999.

3. Bruce Tulloh, conversation with the author.

4. Houmard, J.A. et al. The effects of taper on performance in distance runners. Medicine & Science in Sports & Exercise, Vol. 26 (5), pp. 624-631, 1994.

Chapter 35   Training for 10Ks

1. Beneke, R. et al. Blood lactate diagnostics in exercise testing and training. *International Journal of Sports Physiology and Performance*, Vol. 6 (1), pp. 8-24, Mar. 2011.

2. Jack Daniels, personal communication.

3. Anderson, O. What Does Science Have to Say about the 10K? *Running Research News*, Vol. 12 (2), pp. 1-3, 1996.

4. Peter Snell, personal communication.

5. Yobes Ondieki, interview with author, Eldoret, Kenya, February 1995.

6. Bruce Tulloh, interview with author, London, England, March, 1995.

7. Bob Williams, personal communication.

Chapter 36   Training for Half Marathons

1. Jack Daniels, personal communication.

Chapter 37   Training for Marathons

1. Dolgener, F. et al. Long slow distance training in novice marathoners. *Research Quarterly for Exercise and Sport*, Vol. 65 (4), pp. 339-46, Dec. 1994.

2. Grant, S. et al. First-time marathoners and distance training. *British Journal of Sports Medicine*, Vol. 18, pp. 241-243, 1984.

3. Tim Noakes, personal communication.

4. Sammy Lelei, personal communication.

5. Sjödin, B. and Svedenhag, J. *Applied physiology of marathon running. Sports Medicine*, Vol. 2 (2), pp. 83-99, Mar-Apr. 1985.

6. Anderson, O. Training for the marathon part II: Learning to run at close to your lactate threshold pace. *Running Research News*, Vol. 5 (3), pp. 1-5, 1989.

Chapter 38   Training for Ultramarathons

1. Noakes, T., *Lore of Running*. 4th ed. Champaign, IL: Human Kinetics, 2002.

2. Jeukendrup, A. et al. Effect of medium-chain triacylglycerol and carbohydrate ingestion during exercise on substrate utilization and subsequent cycling performance. *American Journal of Clinical Nutrition*, Vol. 67 (3), pp. 397-404, Mar. 1998.

Chapter 39   Running Injuries and Health Risks

1. Anderson, O. What you don't know about running injuries can hurt you. *Running Research News*, Vol. 9 (5), pp. 8-9, 1993.

2. Fredericson, M. and Misra, A.K. Epidemiology and aetiology of marathon running injuries. *Sports Medicine*, Vol. 37 (4-5), pp. 437-439, 2007.

3. Byrnes, W. et al. Incidence and severity of injury following aerobic training programs emphasizing running, racewalking, or step aerobics. *Medicine & Science in Sports & Exercise*, Vol. 25 (5), p. S81, 1993.

4. Hreljac, A. Impact and overuse injuries in runners. *Medicine & Science in Sports & Exercise*, Vol. 36 (5), pp. 845-849, 2004.

5. van Gent, R. et al. Incidence and determinants of lower extremity running injuries in long distance runners: A systematic review. *British Journal of Sports Medicine*, Vol. 41 (8), pp. 469-480, 2007.

6. Pinshaw, R., Atlas, V., and Noakes, T. The nature and response to therapy of 196 consecutive injuries seen at a runners' clinic. *South African Medical Journal*, Vol. 65 (8), pp. 291-298, 1984.

7. Paluska, S. An overview of hip injuries in running. *Sports Medicine*, Vol. 35 (11), pp. 991-1014, 2005.

8. Wen, D. Risk factors for overuse injuries in runners. *Current Sports Medicine Reports*, Vol. 6 (5), pp. 307-313, 2007.

9. Walter, S. et al. The Ontario cohort study of running-related injuries. *Archives of Internal Medicine*, Vol. 149 (11), pp. 2561-2564, 1989.

10. Rauh, M. et al. Epidemiology of musculoskeletal injuries among high-school cross-country runners. *American Journal of Epidemiology*, Vol. 163 (2), pp. 151-159, 2006.

11. Marti, B. et al. On the epidemiology of running injuries: The 1984 Bern Grand-Prix study *American Journal of Sports Medicine*, Vol. 16 (3), pp. 285-294, 1988.

12. Macera, C. et al. Predicting lower-extremity injuries among habitual runners. *Archives of Internal Medicine*, Vol. 149 (11), pp. 2565-2568, 1989.

13. Lysholm, J. and Wiklander, J. Injuries in runners. *American Journal of Sports Medicine*, Vol. 15 (2), pp. 168-171, 1987.

14. Anderson, O. Best predictors of running injury. *Running Research News*, Vol. 8 (4), p. 10, 1992.

15. Fields, K. et al. A prospective study of Type A behavior and running injuries. *Journal of Family Practice*, Vol. 30 (4), pp. 425-429, 1990.

16. Ekenman, I. et al. Stress fractures of the tibia: Can personality traits help us detect the injury-prone athlete? *Scandinavian Journal of Medicine & Science in Sports*, Vol. 11 (2), pp. 87-95, 2001.

17. Van Middelkoop, M. et al. Prevalence and incidence of lower extremity injuries in male marathon runners. *Scandinavian Journal of Medicine & Science in Sports*, Vol. 18 (2), pp. 140-144, 2008.

18. van Vulpen, A. *Sport for all: Sport injuries and their prevention*. Oosterbeek: Council of Europe, Netherlands Institute of Sports Health Care, 1989.

19. Maron, B. et al. Risk of sudden cardiac death associated with marathon running. *Journal of the American College of Cardiology*, Vol. 28, pp. 428-431, 1996.

20. Thompson, P. et al. Incidence of death during jogging in Rhode Island from 1975 through 1980. *Journal of the American Medical Association*, Vol. 247 (18), pp. 2535-2538, 1982.

21. Tunstall, P. and Dan, S. Marathon cardiac deaths: The London experience, *Sports Medicine*, Vol. 37 (4-5), pp. 448-450, 2007.

22. Paul Thompson, MD, personal communication.

23. Rynearson, R.R., et al. Do physician athletes believe in pre-exercise examinations and stress tests? *New England Journal of Medicine*, Vol. 301, pp. 792-793, 1979.

24. Borer, J. et al. Limitations of the electrocardiographic response to exercise in predicting coronary-artery disease. *New England Journal of Medicine*, Vol. 293, pp. 367-371, 1975.

25. Stuart, R. and Ellestad, M. National survey of exercise stress testing facilities. *Chest*, Vol. 77, pp. 94-97, 1980.

26. Anderson, O. Sudden deaths during running: How preventable are they? Should you have an exercise stress test? *Running Research News*, Vol. 5 (6), pp. 1, 6-10, 1989.

27. Epstein, S. et al. Sudden cardiac death without warning: Possible mechanisms and implications for screening asymptomatic populations. *New England Journal of Medicine*, Vol. 32, pp. 320-324, 1989.

28. Skenderi, K, et al. Exertional rhabdomyolysis during a 246-km continuous running race. *Medicine & Science in Sports & Exercise*, Vol. 38 (6), pp. 1054-1057, 2006.

29. Anderson, O. Rhabdomyolysis claims life of Houston marathon runner. *Running Research News*, Vol. 8 (2), pp. 9-12, 1992.

30. Clarkson, P. Exertional rhabdomyolysis and acute renal failure in marathon runners. *Sports Medicine*, Vol. 37 (4-5), pp. 361-363, 2007.

31. MacSearraigh, E. et al. Acute renal failure in marathon runners. *Nephron*, Vol. 24 (5), pp. 236-240, 1979.

32. Seedat, Y. et al. Acute renal failure in the "Comrades Marathon" runners. *Renal Failure*, Vol. 11 (4), pp. 209-212, 1989-1990.

33. Weinstein, L. Poliomyelitis: A persistent problem. *New England Journal of Medicine*, Vol. 288, pp. 370-372, 1973.

34. Roberts, J. Viral illnesses and sports performance. *Sports Medicine*, Vol. 3, pp. 296-303, 1986.

35. Burch, G. Viral diseases of the heart. *Acta Cardiologica*, Vol. 1, pp. 5-9, 1979.

36. Anderson, O. Can running prolong a cold? *Running Research News*, Vol. 14 (10), p. 9, 1998.

37. Nieman, D. Marathon training and immune function. *Sports Medicine*, Vol. 37 (4-5), pp. 412-415, 2007.

38. Akerström, T. and Pedersen, B. Strategies to enhance immune function for marathon runners: What can be done? *Sports Medicine*, Vol. 37 (4-5), pp. 416-419, 2007.

39. Nieman, D. Exercise immunology: Practical applications. *International Journal of Sports Medicine*, Vol. 18, Suppl. 1, pp. S91-100, 1997.

40. Morris, J. et al. Effect of a hot environment on performance during prolonged, intermittent, high-intensity shuttle running. *Journal of Sports Sciences*, Vol. 16, pp. 677-686, 1998.

41. Sawka, M. Physiological consequences of hypohydration: Exercise performance and thermoregulation. *Medicine & Science in Sports & Exercise*, Vol. 24, pp. 657-670, 1992.

42. Pandolf, K. et al. Thermoregulatory responses of middle-aged men and young men during dry-heat acclimatization. *Journal of Applied Physiology*, Vol. 65, pp. 65-70, 1988.

43. Thomas, C. et al. Aerobic training and cutaneous vasodilation in young and older men. *Journal of Applied Physiology*, Vol. 86, pp. 1676-1686, 1999.

44. Horvath, S. Exercise in a cold environment. *Exercise and Sport Science Reviews*, Vol. 9, pp. 221-263, 1981.

45. Nunneley, S. Physiological responses of women to thermal stress: A review. *Medicine & Science in Sports & Exercise*, Vol. 10, pp. 250-255, 1978.

Chapter 40   Prevention of Running Injuries

1. Expanding on Running Injuries. June 19, 2008. www.sportsscientists.com/search/label/injuries.

2. Jones, B. and Knapik, J. Physical training and exercise-related injuries: Surveillance, research and injury prevention in military populations. *Sports Medicine*, Vol. 27 (2), pp. 111-125, 1999.

3. Glein, G. and McHugh, M. Flexibility and its effects on sports injury and performance. *Sports Medicine*, Vol. 24 (5), pp. 289-299, 1997.

4. Anderson, O. New study links stretching with higher injury rates. *Running Research News*, Vol. 10 (3), pp. 5-6, 1994.

5. Hartig, D. and Henderson, J. Increasing hamstring flexibility decreases lower extremity overuse injuries in military basic trainees. *American Journal of Sports Medicine*, Vol. 27, pp. 173-176, 1999.

6. Andrish, J. et al. A prospective study on the management of shin splints. *Journal of Bone and Joint Surgery*, Vol. 56, pp. 1697-1700, 1974.

7. Pope, R. et al. Effects of ankle dorsiflexion range and pre-exercise calf muscle on injury risk in army recruits. *Australian Journal of Physiotherapy*, Vol. 44, pp. 165-172, 1998.

8. Pope, R. et al. A randomized trial of preexercise stretching for prevention of lower limb injury. *Medicine & Science in Sports & Exercise*, Vol. 32, pp. 271-277, 2000.

9. van Mechelen, W. et al. Prevention of running injuries by warm-up, cool-down, and stretching exercises. *American Journal of Sports Medicine*, Vol. 21, pp. 711-719, 1993.

10. Anderson, O. New study links stretching with higher injury rates. *Running Research News*, Vol. 10 (3), pp. 5-6, 1994.

11. Holly, R. et al. Stretch-induced growth in chicken wing muscles: A new model of stretch hypertrophy. *American Journal of Physiology*, Vol. 7, pp. C62-C71, 1980.

12. Witvrouw, E. et al. Muscle flexibility as a risk factor for developing muscle injuries in male professional soccer players: A prospective study. *American Journal of Sports Medicine*, Vol. 31, pp. 41-46, 2003.

13. Arnason, A. et al. Prevention of hamstring strains in elite soccer: An intervention study. *Scandinavian Journal of Medicine & Science in Sports*, Vol. 18 (1), pp. 40-48, 2008.

14. Jönhagen, S. et al. Amplitude and timing of electromyographic activity during sprinting. *Scandinavian Journal of Medicine & Science in Sports*, Vol. 6, pp. 15-21, 1996.

15. Mjølsnes, R. et al. A 10-week randomized trial comparing eccentric vs. concentric hamstring strength training in well-trained soccer players. *Scandinavian Journal of Medicine & Science in Sports*, Vol. 14, pp. 311-3177, 2004.

16. Kaminski, T. et al. Concentric versus enhanced eccentric hamstring strength training: Clinical implications. *Journal of Athletic Training*, Vol. 33, pp. 216-221, 1998.

17. Yamamato, T. Relationship between hamstring strains and leg muscle strength: A follow-up study of collegiate track and field athletes. *Journal of Sports Medicine and Physical Fitness*, Vol. 33, pp. 194-199, 1993.

18. Jönhagen, S. et al. Hamstring injuries in sprinters. *American Journal of Sports Medicine*, Vol. 22, pp. 262-266, 1994.

19. Orchard, J. et al. Preseason hamstring muscle weakness associated with hamstring muscle injury in Australian footballers. *American Journal of Sports Medicine*, Vol. 25, pp. 81-85, 1997.

20. Verrall, G. et al. The effect of sports specific training on reducing the incidence of hamstring injuries in professional Australian Rules football players. *British Journal of Sports Medicine*, Vol. 39, pp. 363-368, 2005.

21. Hubbard, T. and Denegar, C. Does cryotherapy improve outcomes with soft tissue injury? *Journal of Athletic Training*, Vol. 39 (3), pp. 278-279, Sept. 2004.

22. Moeller, J. et al. Cryotherapy-induced common peroneal nerve palsy. *Clinical Journal of Sport Medicine*, Vol. 7 (3), pp. 212-6, July 1997.

23. Crane, J. et al. Massage therapy attenuates inflammatory signaling after exercise-induced muscle damage. *Science Translational Medicine*. Vol. 4, p. 119ra13, 2012.

24. Hou, Y. et al. Zhongguo Xiu Fu Chong Jian Wai Ke Za Zhi. [Promoting effect of massage on quadriceps femoris repair of rabbit in vivo.][Article in Chinese.] Vol. 26 (3), pp. 346-51, Mar. 2012.

Chapter 41   Health Benefits of Running

1. Anderson, O. Exercise helps you live longer, but does intensity matter? *Running Research News*, Vol. 12 (2), pp. 1, 3-5, 1996.

2. Tanasescu, M. et al. Exercise type and intensity in relation to coronary heart disease in men. *JAMA*, Vol. 288 (16), pp. 1994-2000, 2002.

3. Sesso, H. et al. Physical activity and coronary heart disease in men: The Harvard Alumni Health Study. *Circulation*, Vol. 102 (9), pp. 975-980, 2000.

4. Lee, I. et al. Physical activity and coronary heart disease in women: Is "no pain, no gain" passé? *JAMA*, Vol. 285 (11), pp. 1447-1454, 2001.

5. Lee, I. et al. Physical activity and coronary heart disease risk in men: Does the duration of exercise episodes predict risk? *Circulation*, Vol. 102 (9), pp. 981-986, 2000.

6. Mbalilaki, J. et al. Daily energy expenditure and cardiovascular risk in Masai, rural, and urban Bantu Tanzanians. *British Journal of Sports Medicine*, 2010, 44 (2): 121-126.

7. Anderson, O. Heart disease in marathon runners. *Running Research News*, Vol. 3 (6), pp. 3-4, 1987.

8. Noakes, T. Heart disease in marathon runners: A review. *Medicine & Science in Sports & Exercise*, Vol. 19 (3), pp. 187-194, 1987.

9. Moholdt, T. et al. Physical activity and mortality in men and women with coronary heart disease: A prospective population-based cohort study in Norway (the HUNT Study). *European Journal of Cardiovascular Prevention & Rehabilitation*, Vol. 15 (6), pp. 639-45, Dec. 2008.

10. Sady, S. et al. Training, diet, and physical characteristics of distance runners with low or high concentrations of high density lipoprotein cholesterol. *Atherosclerosis*, Vol. 53, pp. 273-281, 1984.

11. Paul Thompson, MD, personal communication.

12. Thompson, P. Exercise and HDL cholesterol in middle-aged men. *Physician and Sportsmedicine*, Vol. 8, pp. 74-79, 1980.

13. Anderson, O. Is there a best amount of running to maximize HDL-cholesterol? *Running Research News*, Vol. 5 (2), pp. 1, 5-6, 1989.

14. Paffenbarger, R. et al. Physical activity, all-cause mortality, and longevity of college alumni. *New England Journal of Medicine*, Vol. 314, pp. 605-613, 1986.

15. Maruti, S. et al. A Prospective study of age-specific physical activity and pre-menopausal breast cancer. *Journal of the National Cancer Institute*, vol. 100 (10), pp. 728-737, 2008.

16. Friedenreich, C. and Cust, A. Physical activity and breast cancer risk: Impact of timing, type and dose of activity and population subgroup effects. *British Journal of Sports Medicine*, Vol. 42 (8), pp. 636-647, 2008.

17. Peplonska, B. et al. Adult lifetime physical activity and breast cancer. *Epidemiology*, Vol. 19 (2), pp. 226-236, 2008.

18. Anderson, O. Can Running reduce the risk of cancer? Recent research sounds optimistic note, but puzzles remain. *Running Research News*, Vol. 6 (4), pp. 8-10, 1990.

19. Frisch, R. et al. Lower prevalence of breast cancer and cancers of the reproductive system among former college athletes compared to non-athletes. *British Journal of Cancer*, Vol. 32, pp. 885-891, 1985.

20. Frisch, R. et al. Lower prevalence of non-reproductive system cancers among female former college athletes. *Medicine & Science in Sports & Exercise*, Vol. 21 (3), pp. 250-253, 1989.

21. Vena, J. et al. Occupation exercise and risk of cancer. *American Journal of Clinical Nutrition*, Vol. 45, pp. 318-327, 1987.

22. Paffenbarger, R. et al. Physical activity and incidence of cancer in diverse populations: A preliminary report. *American Journal of Clinical Nutrition*, Vol. 45, pp. 312-317, 1987.

23. Nilsen, T. et al. Recreational physical activity and risk of prostate cancer: A prospective population-based study in Norway (the HUNT Study). *International Journal of Cancer*, Vol. 119 (12), pp. 2943-2947, 2006.

24. Howard, R. et al. Physical activity, sedentary behavior, and the risk of colon and rectal cancer in the NIH-AARP Diet and Health Study. *Cancer Causes Control*, Vol. 19 (9), pp. 939-953, 2008.

25. Buehlmeyer, K. et al. Alteration of gene expression in rat colon mucosa after exercise. *Annals of Anatomy*, Vol. 190 (1), pp. 71-80, 2008.

26. Buehlmeyer, K. et al. Exercise associated genes in rat colon mucosa: Upregulation of ornithin decarboxylase-1. *International Journal of Sports Medicine*, Vol. 28 (5), pp. 361-377, 2007.

27. Fuku, N. et al. Effect of running training on DMH-induced aberrant crypt foci in rat colon. *Medicine & Science in Sports & Exercise*, Vol. 39 (1), pp. 70-74, 2007.

28. Sutherland, W. et al. Fecal bile acid concentration in distance runners. *International Journal of Sports Medicine*, Vol. 12 (6), pp. 533-536, 1991.

29. Pan, L. et al. Incidences of obesity and extreme obesity among US adults: Findings from the 2009 Behavioral Risk Factor Surveillance System. *Population Health Metrics*, Vol. 9, p. 56, 2011.

30. Kruk, J. Physical activity in the prevention of the most frequent chronic diseases: An analysis of the recent evidence. *Asian Pacific Journal of Cancer Prevention*, Vol. 8 (3), pp. 325-338, 2007.

31. Banks, E. et al. Relationship of obesity to physical activity, domestic activities, and sedentary behaviours: Cross-sectional findings from a national cohort of over 70,000 Thai adults. *BMC Public Health*, Vol. 11, p. 762, 2011.

32. Bauman, A. Updating the evidence that physical activity is good for health: An epidemiological review 2000-2003. *Journal of Science & Medicine in Sport*, Vol. 7 (1 Suppl.), pp. 6-19, 2004.

33. Hu, F. et al. Physical activity and television watching in relation to risk for type 2 diabetes mellitus in men. *Archives of Internal Medicine*, Vol. 161, pp. 1542-1548, 2001.

34. Hu, F. et al. Walking compared with vigorous physical activity and risk of type 2 diabetes in women. *JAMA*, Vol. 282, pp. 1433-1439, 1999.

35. Williams, P. Reduced diabetic, hypertensive, and cholesterol medication use with walking. *Medicine & Science in Sports & Exercise*, Vol. 40 (3), pp. 433-443, 2008.

36. Williams, P. Relationship of running intensity to hypertension, hypercholesterolemia, and diabetes. *Medicine & Science in Sports & Exercise*, Vol. 40 (10), pp. 1740-1748, 2008.

37. Leitzmann, M. et al. Physical activity recommendations and decreased risk of mortality. *Archives of Internal Medicine*, Vol. 167 (22), pp. 2453-2460, 2007.

38. Cymet, T. and Sinkov, V. Does long-distance running cause osteoarthritis? *Journal of the American Osteopathic Association*, Vol. 106 (6), pp. 342-345, 2006.

39. Chakravarty, E. et al. Long distance running and knee osteoarthritis: A prospective study. *American Journal of Preventative Medicine*, Vol. 35 (2), pp. 133-138, 2008.

40. Lane, N. et al. The relationship of running to osteoarthritis of the knee and hip and bone mineral density of the lumbar spine: A 9-year longitudinal study. *Journal of Rheumatology*, Vol. 25 (2), pp. 334-341, 1998.

41. Chakravarty, E. et al. Reduced disability and mortality among aging runners: A 21-year longitudinal study. *Archives of Internal Medicine*, Vol. 168 (15), pp. 1638-1646, 2008.

42. Neeper, S. et al. Physical activity increases mRNA for brain-derived neurotrophic factor and nerve growth factor in rat brain. *Brain Research*, Vol. 726, pp. 49–56, 1996.

43. Farmer, J. et al. Effects of voluntary exercise on synaptic plasticity and gene expression in the dentate gyrus of adult male Sprague-Dawley rats in vivo. *Neuroscience*, Vol. 124, pp. 71–79, 2004.

44. van Praag, H. et al. Running enhances neurogenesis, learning, and long-term potentiation in mice. *Proceedings of the National Academy of Sciences USA*, Vol. 96, pp. 13427-13431, 1999.

45. van Praag, H. et al. Running increases cell proliferation and neurogenesis in the adult mouse dentate gyrus. *Nature Neuroscience*, Vol. 2, pp. 266–270, 1999.

46. Stranahan, A. et al. Running induces widespread structural alterations in the hippocampus and the entorhinal cortex. *Hippocampus*, Vol. 17, pp. 1017–1022, 2007.

47. Duman, C. et al. Voluntary exercise produces antidepressant and anxiolytic behavioral effects in mice. *Brain Research*, Vol. 1199, pp. 148–158, 2008.

48. Churchill, J. et al. Exercise, experience and the aging brain. *Neurobiology of Aging*, Vol. 23, pp. 941–955, 2002.

49. Griesbach, G. et al. Voluntary exercise following traumatic brain injury: Brain-derived neurotrophic factor upregulation and recovery of function. *Neuroscience*, Vol. 125 (1), pp. 129–139, 2004.

Chapter 42   Health Considerations for Special Running Populations

1. Author, personal observation.

2. Kern, L. et al. The influence of vigorous versus mild exercise on autistic stereotyped behaviors. *Journal of Autism and Developmental Disorders*, Vol. 14 (1), pp. 57-67, 1984.

3. Jones, A. et al. Autistic spectrum disorders 2: Diagnosis and management. *Community Practice*, Vol. 79 (4), pp. 128-130, 2006.

4. Elliott, R. et al. Vigorous, aerobic exercise versus general motor training activities: Effects on maladaptive and stereotypic behaviors of adults with both autism and mental retardation. *Journal of Autism and Developmental Disorders*, Vol. 24 (5), pp. 565-576, 1994.

5. Anderson, O. Should children run marathons? *Running Research News*, Vol. 17 (1), pp. 1- 5, Jan.-Feb. 2001.

6. Sullivan, J. and Anderson, S. eds. Care of the young athlete. *Rosemont: American Academy of Pediatrics and American Academy of Orthopaedic Surgeons*, 2000, p. 69.

7. Physical growth and maturation. In *Motor development issues and applications*, M.V. Ridenour, ed. East Windsor: Princeton Book, pp. 3-27, 1978.

8. The child runner. *JOPERD*, Vol. 53 (4), pp. 78-81, 1982.

9. Orava, S. and Saarela, J. Exertion injuries to young athletes. *American Journal of Sports Medicine*, Vol. 6 (2), pp. 68-74, 1978.

10. Caine, D. and Lindner, K. Growth plate injury: A threat to young distance runners? *Physician and Sportsmedicine*, Vol.12 (4), pp. 118-124, 1984.

11. American Academy of Pediatrics. Risks in distance running for children. *Pediatrics*, Vol. 86 (5), pp. 799-800, 1990.

12. Reinking, M. and Alexander, L. Prevalence of disordered-eating behaviors in undergraduate female collegiate athletes and nonathletes. *Journal of Athletic Training*, Vol. 40 (1), pp. 47-51, 2005.

13. Pantano, K. Current knowledge, perceptions, and interventions used by collegiate coaches in the U.S. regarding the prevention and treatment of the female athlete triad. *North American Journal of Sports & Physical Therapy*, Vol. 1 (4), 195-207, 2006.

14. Nikander, R. et al. Targeted exercise against osteoporosis: A systematic review and meta-analysis for optimising bone strength throughout life, *BMC Medicine*, Vol. 8, p. 47, 2010.

15. Sorensen, T. et al. Recreational physical activity during pregnancy and risk of preeclampsia. *Hypertension*, Vol. 41, pp. 1273–80, 2003.

16. Dye, T. et al. Physical activity, obesity, and diabetes in pregnancy. *American Journal of Epidemiology*, Vol. 146, pp. 961–965, 1997.

17. Kramer, M. and McDonald, D. Aerobic exercise for women during pregnancy. *Cochrane Database Systematic Reviews*, July 19, 2006, Issue 3.

18. Magann, E. et al. Antepartum, intrapartum, and neonatal significance of exercise on healthy low-risk pregnant working women. *Obstetrics & Gynecology*, Vol. 99, pp. 466–472, 2002.

19. Rose, N. et al. Self-rated physical activity level during the second trimester and pregnancy outcome. *Obstetrics & Gynecology*, Vol. 78, pp. 1078–1080, 1991.

20. Clapp, J. The effects of maternal exercise on early pregnancy outcome. *American Journal of Obstetrics & Gynecology*, Vol. 161, pp. 1453–1457, 1989.

21. Latka, M. et al. Exercise and spontaneous abortion of known karyotype. *Epidemiology*, Vol. 10, pp. 73–75, 1999.

22. Madsen, M. et al. Leisure time physical activity during pregnancy and the risk of miscarriage: A study within the Danish national birth cohort. BJOG, Vol. 114 (11), pp. 1419-1426, 2007.

Chapter 43   Energy Sources and Fuel Use for Runners

1. Gollnick, P. Metabolism of substrates: Energy substrate metabolism during exercise and as modified by training. *Federation Proceedings*, Vol. 44, pp. 353-356, 1985.

2. McMurray, W. *Essentials of human metabolism.* New York: Harper & Row, 1977.

3. McArdle, W. et al. *Exercise physiology: Energy, nutrition, and human performance.* Baltimore: Williams & Wilkins, 1996.

4. Onywera, V.O., Kiplamai, F.K., Tuitoek, P.J., Boit, M.K., and Pitsiladis, Y.P. Food and macronutrient intake of elite Kenyan distance runners. Int J Sport Nutr Exerc Metab. Vol. 14 (6), pp. 709-719, 2004.

5. Powers, S. and Howley, E. *Exercise physiology: Theory and application to fitness and performance*. 4th ed. Boston: McGraw Hill, 2001.

6. Stanley, W. and Connett, R. Regulation of muscle carbohydrate metabolism during exercise. *FASEB Journal*, Vol. 5, pp. 2155-2159, 1991.

7. Voet, D. and Voet, J. *Biochemistry*. Menlo Park: Benjamin-Cummings, 1996.

8. Hood, D. and Terjung, R. Amino acid metabolism during exercise and following endurance training. *Sports Medicine*, Vol. 9, pp. 23-35, 1990.

9. Brooks, G. and Mercier, J. Balance of carbohydrate and lipid utilization during exercise: The "crossover" concept. *Journal of Applied Physiology*, Vol. 76, pp. 2253-2261, 1994.

10. Coyle, E. Substrate utilization during exercise in active people. *American Journal of Clinical Nutrition*, Vol. 61 (Suppl.), pp. 968s-979s, 1995.

11. Lipid metabolism during exercise. In *Exercise Metabolism*, M. Hargreaves and L. Spriet, eds. Champaign, IL: Human Kinetics, 1995, pp. 99-130.

12. Powers, S. et al. A comparison of fat metabolism in trained men and women during prolonged aerobic work. *Research Quarterly for Exercise and Sport*, Vol. 52, pp.427-431, 1980.

13. Williams, M. and Branch, J. Creatine supplementation and exercise performance: An update. *Journal of the American College of Nutrition*, Vol. 17, pp. 216-234, 1998.

Chapter 44   Eating for Enhanced Endurance and Speed

1. Karlsson, J. and Saltin, B. Diet, muscle glycogen, and endurance performance. *Journal of Applied Physiology*, Vol. 31, pp. 203-206, 1971.

2. Bergström, J. et al. Diet, muscle glycogen and physical performance. *Acta Physiologica Scandinavica*, Vol. 71, pp. 140-150, 1967.

3. Costill, D. et al. The role of dietary carbohydrates in muscle glycogen resynthesis after strenuous running. *American Journal of Clinical Nutrition*, Vol. 34, pp. 1831-1836, 1981.

4. Sherman, W. and Costill, D. The marathon: Dietary manipulation to optimize performance. *American Journal of Sports Medicine*, Vol. 12 (1), pp. 44-51, 1984.

5. Diet and recovery processes. In *Physiological Chemistry of Training and Detraining*, P. Marconnet et al., eds., Basel: Karger Books, 1984, pp. 148-160.

6. Anderson, Owen, personal observation.

7. Willett, T. *Eat, drink, and be healthy*. Free Press: New York, 2001, pp. 18-19.

8. Influence of diet on recovery from prolonged exercise. *Proceedings of the Nutrition Society*, Vol. 44 (1), p. 28A, 1985.

9. Anderson, O. Pasta or cakes, pies, and cookies. *Running Research News*, Vol. 2 (3), pp. 5-6, 1986.

10. Roberts, K. et al. Simple and complex carbohydrate-rich diets and muscle glycogen content of marathon runners. *European Journal of Applied Physiology*, Vol. 57, pp. 70-74, 1988.

11. Lemon, P. et al. The importance of protein for athletes. *Sports Medicine*, Vol. 1 (6), pp. 474-484, 1984.

12. Effect of protein intake and endurance exercise on daily protein requirements. *Medicine & Science in Sports & Exercise*, Vol. 17 (2), 1985.

13. Tarnopolsky, M. Protein requirements for endurance athletes. *Nutrition*, Vol. 20 (7-8), pp. 662-668, 2004.

14. Perrottet, T. *The naked olympics*. New York: Random House, 2004.

15. Mullins, V. et al. Nutritional status of US elite female heptathletes during training. *International Journal of Sport Nutrition and Exercise Metabolism*, Vol. 11, pp. 299-314, 2001.

16. Greenhaff, P. et al. The metabolic responses of human type I and II muscle fibres during maximal treadmill sprinting. *Journal of Physiology*, Vol. 478, pp. 149-155, 1994.

17. Gaitanos, G. et al. Human muscle metabolism during intermittent maximal exercise. *Journal of Applied Physiology*, Vol. 75, pp. 712-719, 1993.

18. Maughan, R. et al. Diet composition and the performance of high-intensity exercise. *Journal of Sports Sciences*, Vol. 15, pp. 265-275, 1997.

19. The effects of glycogen exhaustion on maximal short-term performance. In *Exercise and Sports Performance*, P.V. Komi, ed. Champaign, IL: Human Kinetics, 1982, pp. 103-108.

20. Balsom, P. et al. High-intensity exercise and muscle glycogen availability in humans. *Acta Physiologica Scandinavica*, Vol. 165, pp. 337-345, 1999.

21. Rockwell, M. et al. Effects of muscle glycogen on performance of repeated sprints and mechanisms of fatigue. *International Journal of Sport Nutrition and Exercise Metabolism*, Vol. 13, pp. 1-14, 2003.

22. Fulcher, K. and Williams, C. The effect of diet on high-intensity intermittent exercise performance. *Journal of Sports Sciences*, Vol. 10, pp. 550-551A, 1992.

23. Nevill, M. et al. Effect of diet on performance during recovery from intermittent sprint exercise. *Journal of Sports Sciences*, Vol. 11, pp. 119-126, 1993.

24. Burke, L. *Practical sports nutrition*. Champaign, IL: Human Kinetics, 2007, p. 178.

25. Lemon, P. Protein and amino acid needs of the strength athlete. *International Journal of Sport Nutrition*, Vol. 1, pp. 127-145, 1991.

26. Lemon, P. Effect of exercise on protein requirements. *Journal of Sports Sciences*, Vol. 9, pp. 53-70, 1991.

27. Millward, D. et al. Physical activity, protein metabolism and protein requirements. *Proceedings of the Nutrition Society*, Vol. 53, pp. 223-240, 1994.

28. Burke, D. et al. The effect of whey protein supplementation with and without creatine monohydrate combined with resistance training on lean tissue mass and muscle strength. *International Journal of Sport Nutrition and Exercise Metabolism*, Vol. 11, pp. 349-364, 2001.

29. Nissen, S. and Sharp, L. Effect of dietary supplements on lean mass and strength gains with resistance exercise: A meta-analysis. *Journal of Applied Physiology*, Vol. 94, pp. 651-659, 2003.

Chapter 45   Fueling Strategies During a Run

1. David L. Costill, personal communication.

2. Hargreaves, M. et al. Effect of carbohydrate feedings on muscle glycogen utilization and exercise performance. *Medicine & Science in Sports & Exercise*, Vol. 16 (3), pp. 219-222, 1984.

3. Coyle, E. et al. Muscle glycogen utilization during prolonged strenuous exercise when fed carbohydrate. *Journal of Applied Physiology*, Vol. 61, pp. 165-172, 1986.

4. Coggan, A. and Coyle, E. Reversal of fatigue during prolonged exercise by carbohydrate infusion or ingestion. *Journal of Applied Physiology*, Vol. 63, pp. 2388-2395, 1987.

5. Bosch, A. et al. Influence of carbohydrate ingestion on fuel substrate turnover and oxidation during prolonged exercise. *Journal of Applied Physiology*, Vol. 76, pp. 2364-2372, 1994.

6. McConell, G. et al. Effect of carbohydrate ingestion on glucose kinetics during exercise. *Journal of Applied Physiology*, Vol. 77, pp. 1537-1541, 1994.

7. Tsintzas, O. et al. Carbohydrate ingestion and single muscle fibre glycogen metabolism during prolonged running in men. *Journal of Applied Physiology*, Vol. 81, pp. 801-809, 1996.

8. Tsintzas, O. et al. Influence of carbohydrate supplementation early in exercise on endurance running capacity. *Medicine & Science in Sports & Exercise*, Vol. 28, pp. 1373-1379, 1996.

9. Davis, J. et al. Effects of carbohydrate feedings on plasma free tryptophan and branched-chain amino acids during prolonged cycling. *European Journal of Applied Physiology*, Vol. 65, pp. 513-519, 1992.

10. Below, P. et al. Fluid and carbohydrate ingestion independently improve performance during 1 h of intense exercise. *Medicine & Science in Sports & Exercise*, Vol. 27, pp. 200-210, 1995.

11. Davis, J. et al. Carbohydrate drinks delay fatigue during intermittent, high-intensity cycling in active men and women. *International Journal of Sport Nutrition*, Vol. 7, pp. 261-273, 1997.

12. Jeukendrup, A. et al. Carbohydrate-electrolyte feedings improve 1h time trial cycling performance. *International Journal of Sports Medicine*, Vol. 18, pp. 125-129, 1997.

13. Nicholas, C. et al. Influence of ingesting a carbohydrate-electrolyte solution on endurance capacity during intermittent, high intensity shuttle running. *Journal of Sports Sciences*, Vol. 13, pp. 283-290, 1995.

14. Anderson, O. Glucose electrolyte solutions and the marathon. *Running Research News* Vol. 2 (2), pp. 4-5, 1986.

15. Wagenmakers, A. et al. Oxidation rates of orally ingested carbohydrates during prolonged exercise in men. *Journal of Applied Physiology*, Vol. 75, pp. 2774-2780, 1993.

16. Coyle, E. et al. Carbohydrate metabolism during intense exercise when hyperglycemic. *Journal of Applied Physiology*, Vol. 70, pp. 834-840, 1991.

17. Hawley, J. et al. Glucose kinetics during prolonged exercise in euglycemic and hyperglycemic subjects. *Pflugers Archives*, Vol. 426, pp. 378-386, 1994.

18. Anderson, O. Water is no longer the drink of champions. *Running Research News*, Vol. 4 (4), pp. 1-3, 1988.

19. Malathi, P. et al. Studies on the transport of glucose from disaccharides by hamster small intestine in vitro. I. Evidence for a disaccharidase-related transport system. *Biochimica et Biophysica Acta*, Vol. 307, pp. 613-626, 1973.

20. Jentjens, R. et al. High oxidation rates from combined carbohydrates ingested during exercise. *Medicine & Science in Sports & Exercise*, Vol. 36(9), pp. 1551-1558, 2004.

21. Rehrer, N. et al. Gastric emptying with repeated drinking during running and bicycling. *International Journal of Sports Medicine*, Vol. 11 (3), pp. 238-243, 1990.

Chapter 46   Weight Control and Body Composition

1. Jeukendrup, A. and Gleeson, M. *Sport nutrition: An introduction to energy production and performance.* Champaign, IL: Human Kinetics, 2004, p. 268.

2. Bouchard, C. *The genetics of obesity.* Boca Raton: CRC Press, 1994, pp. 223-233.

3. Bouchard, C. et al. The response to exercise with constant energy intake in identical twins. *Obesity Research*, Vol. 2, pp. 400-410, 1994.

4. Rankinen, T. et al. The human obesity gene map: The 2001 update. *Obesity Research*, Vol. 10 (3), pp. 196-243, 2002.

5. Lohman, T. and Going, S. Multi-component models in body composition research: Opportunities and pitfalls. *Basic Life Sciences*, Vol. 60, pp. 53-58, 1993.

6. Sheppard, L. et al. Weight loss in women participating in a randomized trial of low-fat diets. *American Journal of Clinical Nutrition*, Vol. 54 (5), pp. 821-828, 1991.

7. Walberg-Rankin, J. Forfeit the fat, leave the lean: Optimizing weight loss for athletes. *Sports Science Exchange*, Vol. 13 (1), pp. 1-4, 2000.

8. Golay, A. et al. Similar weight loss with low- or high-carbohydrate diets. *American Journal of Clinical Nutrition*, Vol. 63, pp. 174-178, 1996.

9. Lose body fat safely. *Sports Science Exchange*, Suppl. Vol. 13 (1), 2000.

10. Walberg-Rankin, J. Dietary carbohydrate as an ergogenic aid for prolonged and brief competition in sport. *International Journal of Sport Nutrition*, Vol. 5, pp. S13-S28, 1995.

11. The myth of the "fat-burning zone": You can exercise there, but don't assume that you are breaking down more fat. *Running Research News*, Vol. 9 (2), pp. 10-11, Mar.-Apr. 1993.

12. Anderson, O. How the Kenyan cross-country system really works. *Running Research News*, Vol. 10 (4), pp. 1-4, July-Aug. 1994.

13. Broeder, C. et al. Assessing body composition before and after resistance or endurance training. *Medicine & Science in Sports & Exercise*, Vol. 29 (5), pp. 705-712, 1997.

14. Ballor, D. and Keesey, R. A meta-analysis of the factors affecting exercise-induced changes in body mass, fat mass, and fat-free mass in males and females. *International Journal of Obesity*, Vol. 15 (11), pp. 717-726, 1991.

15. Dulloo, A. and Jacquet, J. Adaptive reduction in basal metabolic rate in response to food deprivation in humans: A role for feedback signals from fat stores. *American Journal of Clinical Nutrition*, Vol. 68 (3), pp. 599-606, 1998.

16. Owen Anderson, personal observation.

17. Drinkwater, B. et al. Bone mineral content of amenorrheic and eumenorrheic athletes. *New England Journal of Medicine*, Vol. 311 (5), pp. 277-281, 1984.

18. Myerson, M. et al. Resting metabolic rate and energy balance in amenorrheic and eumenorrheic runners. *Medicine & Science in Sports & Exercise*, Vol. 23 (1), pp. 15-22, 1991.

19. Lebenstedt, M. Reduced resting metabolic rate in athletes with menstrual disorders. *Medicine & Science in Sports & Exercise*, Vol. 31 (9), pp. 1250-1256, 1999.

20. Anderson, O. The Science of Kenyan eating. *Running Research News*, Vol. 21 (1), pp. 1, 5-8, Jan.-Feb. 2005.

Chapter 47 Ergogenic Aids for Running

1. Supplements, Part 1: Bitter Pills Swallow Sports. July 15, 2001. www.privatelabelnutra.com/supplement-manufacturer-blog/sports-performance-supplements-2013-gowth-and-market-tends/

2. O'Rourke, M. et al. Caffeine has a small effect on 5-km running performance of well-trained and recreational runners. *Journal of Science & Medicine in Sport*, Vol. 11 (2), pp. 231-233, 2008.

3. Bridge, C. and Jones, M. The effect of caffeine ingestion on 8 km run performance in a field setting. *Journal of Sports Sciences*, Vol. 24 (4), pp. 433-439, 2006.

4. Birnbaum, L. and Herbst, J. Physiologic effects of caffeine use on cross-country runners. *Journal of Strength & Conditioning Research*, Vol. 18 (3), pp. 463-465, 2004.

5. Wiles, J. et al. Effect of caffeinated coffee on running speed, respiratory factors, blood lactate, and perceived exertion during 1500-m treadmill running. *British Journal of Sports Medicine*, Vol. 26 (2), pp. 116-120, 1992.

6. Doherty, M. The effects of caffeine on the maximal accumulated oxygen deficit and short-term running performance. *International Journal of Sport Nutrition*, Vol. 8 (2), pp. 95-104, 1998.

7. Anderson, O. More buzz about joe. *Running Research News*, Vol. 11 (1), pp. 10-11, Jan.-Feb.1995.

8. Desbrow, B. and Leveritt, M. Well-trained endurance athletes' knowledge, insight, and experience of caffeine use. *International Journal of Sport Nutrition and Exercise Metabolism*, Vol. 17 (4), pp. 328-339, 2007.

9. Spriet, L. Caffeine and performance. *International Journal of Sport Nutrition*, Vol. 5 (Suppl.), pp. S84-S99, 1995.

10. Van Soeren, M. et al. Caffeine metabolism and epinephrine responses during exercise in users and non-users. *Journal of Applied Physiology*, Vol. 75 (2), pp. 805-812, 1993.

11. Van Soeren, M. and Graham, T. Effect of caffeine on metabolism, exercise endurance, and catecholamine responses after withdrawal. *Journal of Applied Physiology*, Vol. 85 (4), pp. 1493-1501, 1998.

12. Bell, D. et al. Effect of ingesting caffeine and ephedrine on 10-km run performance. *Medicine & Science in Sports & Exercise*, Vol. 34 (2), pp. 344-349, 2002.

13. Bell, D. et al. Effects of caffeine, ephedrine, and their combination on time to exhaustion during high-intensity exercise. *European Journal of Applied Physiology and Occupational Physiology*, Vol. 77 (5), pp. 427-433, 1998.

14. The 2008 prohibited list, international standard. www.wada-ama.org/rtecontent/document/2008_List_En.pdf.

15. Katz, A. et al. Maximal exercise tolerance after induced alkalosis. *International Journal of Sports Medicine*, Vol. 5 (2), pp. 107-110, 1984.

16. Anderson, O. Baking soda: An ergogenic aid? *Running Research News*, Vol. 1 (3), pp. 3-4, 1986.

17. Costill, D. et al. Acid-base balance during repeated bouts of exercise: Influence of HCO3. *International Journal of Sports Medicine*, Vol. 5 (5), pp. 228-231, 1984.

18. Bishop, D. and Claudius, B. Effects of induced metabolic alkalosis on prolonged intermittent-sprint performance. *Medicine & Science in Sports & Exercise*, Vol. 37 (5), pp. 759-767, 2005.

19. Wilkes, D. et al. Effect of acute induced metabolic alkalosis on 800-m racing time. *Medicine & Science in Sports & Exercise*, Vol. 15, pp. 277-280, 1983.

20. Effect of orally administered sodium bicarbonate on performance of high intensity exercise. Presented at the *Annual Meeting of the American College of Sports Medicine*, May 26-29, 1985.

21. Spriet, L. et al. Legal pre-event nutritional supplements to assist energy metabolism. *Essays in Biochemistry*, Vol. 44, pp. 27-43, 2008.

22. Bemben, M. and Lamont, H. Creatine supplementation and exercise performance: Recent findings. *Sports Medicine*, Vol. 35 (2), pp. 107-125, 2005.

23. Hirvonen, J. et al. Breakdown of high-energy phosphate compounds and lactate accumulation during short supramaximal exercise. *European Journal of Applied Physiology*, Vol. 56, pp. 253-259, 1987.

24. Harris, R. et al. Elevation of creatine in resting and exercised muscle of normal subjects by creatine supplementation. *Clinical Science*, Vol. 83, pp. 367-374, 1992.

25. Hultman, E. et al. Muscle creatine loading in men. *Journal of Applied Physiology*, Vol. 81, pp. 232-237, 1996.

26. Nissen, S. and Sharp, R. Effect of dietary supplements on lean mass and strength gains with resistance exercise: A meta-analysis. *Journal of Applied Physiology*, Vol. 94, pp. 651-659, 2003.

27. Izquierdo, M. et al. Effects of creatine supplementation on muscle power, endurance, and sprint performance. *Medicine & Science in Sports & Exercise*, Vol. 34 (2), pp. 332-343, 2002.

28. Preen, D. et al. Effect of creatine loading on long-term sprint exercise performance and metabolism. *Medicine & Science in Sports & Exercise*, Vol. 33 (5), pp. 814-821, 2001.

29. Anderson, O. Creatine propels british athletes to olympic gold medals: Is creatine the one true ergogenic aid? *Running Research News*, Vol. 9 (1), pp. 1-5, Jan.-Feb. 1993.

30. Anderson, O. Creatine supplements linked with slower 6-k performances. *Running Research News*, Vol. 10 (3), pp. 12-13, May-June 1994.

31. Jeukendrup, A. and Gleeson, M. *Sport Nutrition: An Introduction to Energy Production and Performance*. Champaign, IL: Human Kinetics, 2004, p. 263.

32. ConsumerLab.com finds that not all creatine supplements meet label claims. August 7, 2000. http://www.consumerlab.com/news/Creatine_Tests/8_7_2000/.

Chapter 48   The Brain and the Experience of Fatigue

1. Fatigue and exercise part I A: The pacing strategy—why the "obvious" is crucially important. Dec. 21, 2008. www.sportsscientists.com/2008/05/fatigue-and-exercise-part-i.htmlhttp://www.sportsscientists.com/2008/05/fatigue-and-exercise-part-i.html.

2. The mystery of fatigue and the limits of performance. Dec. 21, 2008. www.sportsscientists.com/search/label/fatigue.

3. Nybo, L. and Nielsen, B. Hyperthermia and central fatigue during prolonged exercise in humans. *Journal of Applied Physiology*, Vol. 91, pp. 1055-1060, 2001.

4. Nybo, L. and Nielsen, B. Perceived exertion is associated with an latered brain activity during exercise with progressive hyperthermia. *Journal of Applied Physiology*, Vol. 91, pp. 2017-2023, 2001.

5. Nybo, L. et al. Inadequate heat release from the human brain during prolonged exercise with hyperthermia. *Journal of Physiology*, Vol. 545, pp. 697-704, 2002.

6. Marino, F. et al. Superior performance of African runners in warm, humid but not in cool environmental conditions. *Journal of Applied Physiology*, Vol. 96, pp.124-130, 2004.

7. Marino, F. Anticipatory regulation and avoidance of catastrophe during exercise-induced hyperthermia. *Comparative Biochemistry and Physiology Part B*–Biochemistry and Molecular Biology, Vol. 139, pp. 561-569, 2004.

8. St. Claire Gibson, A. et al. Reduced neuromuscular activity and force generation during prolonged cycling. *American Journal of Physiology*–Regulatory, Integrative and Comparative Physiology, Vol. 281, pp. R187-R196, 2001.

9. Kay, D. et al. Evidence for neuromuscular fatigue during high-intensity cycling in warm, humid conditions. *European Journal of Applied Physiology*, Vol. 84, pp. 115-121, 2001.

10. Billat, V. et al. Training and bioenergetic characteristics in elite male and female Kenyan runners. *Medicine & Science in Sports & Exercise*, Vol. 35, pp. 297-304, 2003.

11. Kayser, B. Exercise starts and ends in the brain. *European Journal of Applied Physiology*, Vol. 90, pp. 411-419, 2003.

12. Nummela, A. et al. Neuromuscular factors determining 5 km running performance and running economy in well-trained athletes. *European Journal of Applied Physiology*, Vol. 97, pp. 1-8, 2006.

13. Ansley, L. et al. Anticipatory pacing strategies during supramaximal exercise lasting longer than 30 seconds. *Medicine & Science in Sports & Exercise*, Vol. 36, pp. 309-314, 2004.

14. Ansley, L. et al. Regulation of pacing strategies during successive 4-km time trials. *Medicine & Science in Sports & Exercise*, Vol. 36, pp. 1819-1825, 2004.

15. Creer, A. et al. Neural, metabolic and performance adaptations to four weeks of high intensity sprint-interval training in trained cyclists. *International Journal of Sports Medicine*, Vol. 25, pp. 92-98, 2004.

Chapter 49   Psychological Strategies for Improved Performance

1. Morgan, W. Psychogenic factors and exercise metabolism: A review. *Medicine & Science in Sports & Exercise*, Vol. 17 (3), pp. 309-316, 1985.

2. Weinberg, R. et al. Effects of association, dissociation, and positive self-talk strategies on endurance performance. *Canadian Journal of Applied Sport Science*, Vol. 9 (1), pp. 25-32, 1984.

3. Morgan, W. and Pollack, M. Psychogenic characterization of the elite distance runner. *Annals of the New York Academy of Sciences*, Vol. 301, pp. 382-403, 1977.

4. Anderson, O. Mental strategies for runners. *Running Research News*, Vol. 1 (2), pp. 1-2, Sept.-Oct. 1985.

5. Anderson, O. Psychological skills training boosts running performance. *Running Research News*, Vol. 7 (6), pp. 1, 4-6, Nov.-Dec.1991.

6. Psychological skills training. *Second IOC World Congress on Sport Sciences*, Barcelona, Spain, Oct. 26-31, 1991.

7. Jeffery P. Simons, interview with author, *Second IOC World Congress on Sport Sciences*, Barcelona, Spain, Oct. 26-31, 1991.

8. Smith, A. et al. Attention strategy use by experienced distance runners: Physiological and psychological effects. *Research Quarterly for Exercise and Sport*, Vol. 66 (2), pp. 142-150, 1995.

9. Anderson, O. Let your mind control your heart—and make you a better runner. *Running Research News*, Vol. 12 (10), pp. 1-4, Dec. 1996.

10. Lemyre, P. et al. A social cognitive approach to burnout in elite athletes. *Scandinavian Journal of Medicine & Science in Sports*, Vol. 18 (2), pp. 221-234, 2008.

11. Freudenberger, H.J. *Burnout*. New York: Doubleday Press, 1980.

12. Gold, Y. and Roth, R. *Teachers managing stress and preventing burnout: The professional health solution*. London: Falmer Press, 1993.

13. Raedeke, T. Is athlete burnout more than just stress? A sport commitment perspective. *Journal of Sport & Exercise Psychology*, Vol. 19, pp. 396-417, 1997.

14. Gould, D. et al. Burnout in competitive junior tennis players. I. A quantitative psychological assessment. *Sport Psychology*, Vol. 10, pp. 322-340, 1996.

15. Understanding the dynamics of motivation in physical activity: The influence of achievement goals on motivational processes. In *Advances in motivation in sport and exercise*, G.C. Roberts, ed. Champaign, IL: Human Kinetics, 2001, pp. 1-50.

16. Understanding the dynamics of motivation in sport and physical activity: An achievement goal interpretation. In *Handbook of sport psychology*, R. Ecklund and G. Tenenbaum, G. eds. New York: McMillan, 2007, pp. 3-21.

17. Lemyre, P. *Determinants of burnout in elite athletes: A multi-dimensional perspective*. Oslo, Norway: Norwegian School of Sport and Physical Education, 2005.

18. Treasure, D. and Roberts, G. Applications of achievement goal theory to physical education: Implications for enhancing motivation. *Quest*, Vol. 47, pp. 475-489, 1995.

19. Anshel, M. and HanJoo, E. Exploring the dimensions of perfectionism in sport. *International Journal of Sport Psychology*, Vol. 34, pp. 255-271, 2003.

20. Perfectionism: A hallmark quality of world-class performers, or a psychological impediment to athletic development? In Perspectives in sport and exercise psychology: *Essential processes for attaining peak performance*, Vol. 1, D. Hackfort and G. Tenenbaum, eds. Oxford: Meyer & Meyer, 2005, pp. 179-211.

21. Gould, D. Personal motivation gone awry: Burnout in competitive athletes. *Quest*, Vol. 48, pp. 275-289, 1996.

Chapter 50   Addictive Aspects of Running

1. Fisher, L. and Wrisberg, C. Sport psychology & counseling: Recognizing and dealing with exercise addiction [Editorial]. *Athletic Therapy Today*, Vol. 9 (1), pp. 36-37, 2003.

2. Griffiths, M. Exercise addiction: A case study. *Addiction Research*, Vol. 5 (2), pp. 161-168, 1997.

3. Davis, C. Exercise abuse. *International Journal of Sport Psychology*, Vol. 31 (2), pp. 278-289, 2000.

4. Aidman, E. and Woollard, S. The influence of self-reported exercise addiction on acute emotional and physiological responses to brief exercise deprivation. *Psychology of Sport and Exercise*, Vol. 4 (3), pp. 225-236, 2003.

5. Adams, J. and Kirkby, R. Excessive exercise as an addiction: A review. *Addiction Research & Theory*, Vol. 10 (5), pp. 415-437, 2002.

6. Lejoyeux, M. et al. Prevalence of exercise dependence and other behavioral addictions among clients of a Parisian fitness room. *Comprehensive Psychiatry*, Vol. 49 (4), pp. 353-358, 2008.

7. Bamber, D. et al. The pathological status of exercise dependence. *British Journal of Sports Medicine*, Vol. 34 (2), pp. 125-132, 2000.

8. Estok, P. and Rudy, E. The relationship between eating disorders and running in women. *Research in Nursing and Health*, Vol. 19 (5), pp. 377-387, 1996.

9. Hausenblas, H. and Downs, D. How much is too much? The development and validation of the Exercise Dependence Scale. *Psychology & Health*, Vol. 17 (4), pp. 387-404, 2002.

10. Klein, D. et al. Exercise "addiction" in anorexia nervosa: Model development and pilot data. *CNS Spectrums*, Vol. 9 (7), pp. 531-537, 2004.

11. Allegre, B. et al. Individual factors and the context of physical activity in exercise dependence: A prospective study of "ultra-marathoners." *International Journal of Mental Health and Addiction*, Vol. 5, pp. 233–243, 2007.

12. Draeger, J. et al. The obligatory exerciser: Assessing an over-commitment to exercise [Review]. *Physician and Sportsmedicine*, Vol. 33 (6), pp. 13-23, 2005.

13. Griffiths, M. et al. The Exercise Addiction Inventory: A quick and easy screening tool for health practitioners. *British Journal of Sports Medicine*, Vol. 39 (6), p. e30, 2005.

14. Cox, R. and Orford, J. A qualitative study of the meaning of exercise for people who could be labeled as "addicted" to exercise: Can "addiction" be applied to high-frequency exercising?" *Addiction Research & Theory*, Vol. 12 (2), pp. 167-188, 2004.

15. Freimuth, M. *Addicted? Recognizing destructive behavior before it's too late.* Lanham: Rowman & Littlefield, 2008.

16. Mellion, M.B., Putukian, M., and Madden C.C., eds. *Sports medicine secrets.* 3rd ed. Philadelphia: Hanley & Belfus, 2002, pp. 181-183.

Index

Note: The italicized *f* and *t* following page numbers refer to figures and tables, respectively.

About the Author

Owen Anderson, PhD, has been a regular contributor to *Runner's World*, *Shape*, *Men's Health*, *Peak Performance*, *National Geographic Adventure*, and *Sports Injury Bulletin*. He has written extensively on the topics of running training, strength training for running, sports nutrition, and injury prevention, and he developed the neural system of training, which diminishes the emphasis on mileage and promotes the use of high-quality running and the progression of running-specific strength training to achieve optimal running fitness.

Anderson is the founder of Lansing Sports Management, which coaches elite athletes from Kenya and manages their international competitions. He has enjoyed a successful career coaching runners of all levels, including notables such as Benjamin Simatei, the winner of the Park Forest 10-mile race in Chicago, Illinois, and Chemtai Rionotukei, who in 2012 and 2013 has six victories, two course records, and 14 top-four finishes in U.S. road races, including a win at the 2013 Fifth Third River Bank 25K.

Anderson is the race director of the annual Lansing Marathon, Lansing Half Marathon, and Ekiden Relay. In addition, he hosts running camps throughout the U.S., including the Lansing Marathon Running Camp in Thetford Center, Vermont. Anderson is also the CEO of Lansing Moves the World, a nonprofit foundation that coordinates three projects, including an after school program for Lansing children age 9 to 14, a tree planting program in east Africa, and a program for families and children victimized by the recent violence in the Tana River Delta district of Kenya.

Anderson was awarded a National Science Foundation fellowship and completed his PhD at Michigan State University.